Suspended
IN LANGUAGE

Other books about scientists from G.T. Labs

Safecracker: A Two-Fisted Science Comic
Two-Fisted Science: Stories About Scientists
Wild Person in the Woods
Dignifying Science: Stories About Women Scientists
"Talking" Orangutans in Borneo (for The Orangutan Foundation International)
Fallout: J. Robert Oppenheimer, Leo Szilard, and the Political Science of the Atomic Bomb

Suspended in Language

Niels Bohr's life, discoveries, and the century he shaped

Written by Jim Ottaviani
Illustrated and lettered by Leland Purvis

Additional art by Jay Hosler, Roger Langridge, Steve Leialoha,
Linda Medley, and Jeff Parker

G.T. LABS

Suspended in Language:
Niels Bohr's life, discoveries, and the century he shaped

First Edition: June, 2004

ISBN 0-9660106-5-5
Library of Congress Control Number: 2003091535

A General Tektronics Labs production.

G.T. Labs
P.O. Box 8145
Ann Arbor, MI 48107

info@gt-labs.com
www.gt-labs.com

5 4 3 2 1

Contents

Chapter 1

WHEN **NIELS BOHR** DISAGREED WITH YOU—AND NOT JUST MILDLY, BUT WHEN HE REALLY THOUGHT YOU WERE NUTS—HE WOULD EXPRESS IT IN THE STRONGEST POSSIBLE TERMS:

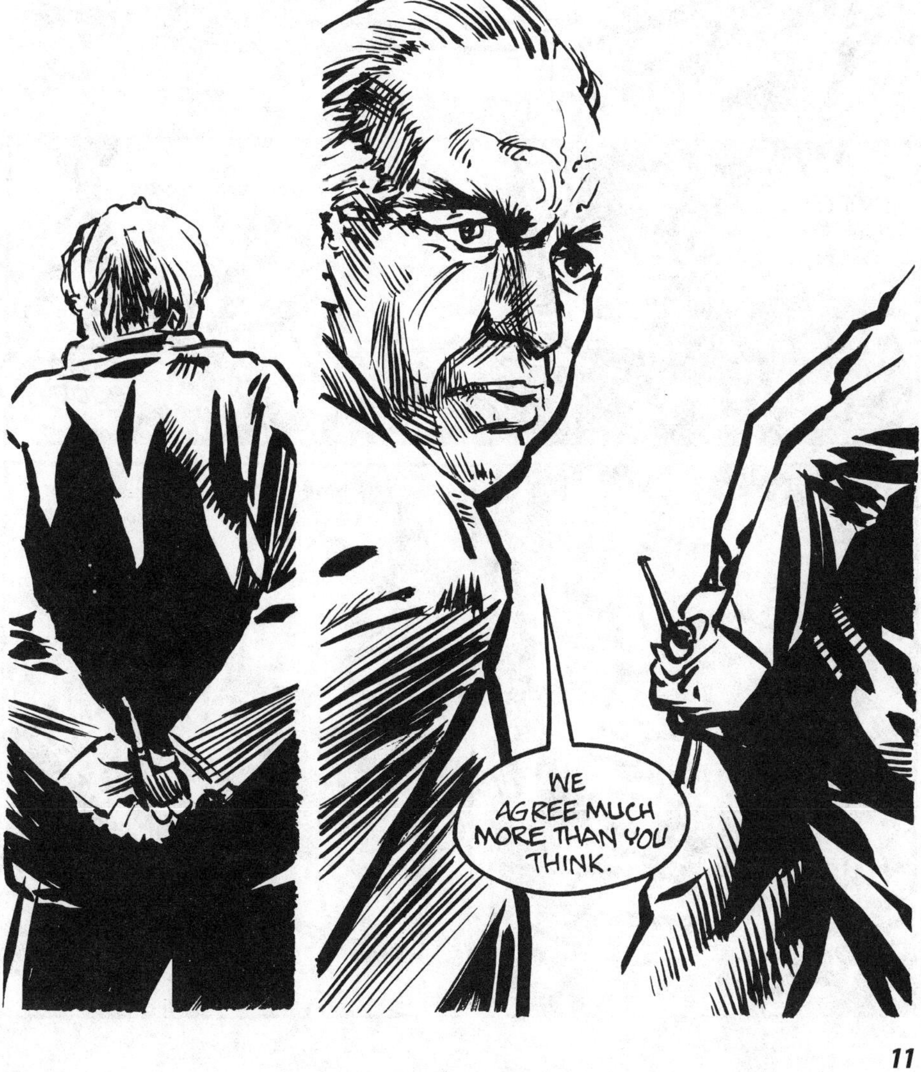
WE AGREE MUCH MORE THAN YOU THINK.

HARSH? YES, BUT HE WAS A TOUGH CUSTOMER FROM THE BEGINNING—EVEN WITH HIS CLOSEST AND LIFELONG FRIEND **HARALD** (HIS YOUNGER BROTHER). AS BOYS THEY SOMETIMES PLAYED A GAME WHERE THEY WOULD TAKE TURNS TEASING EACH OTHER.

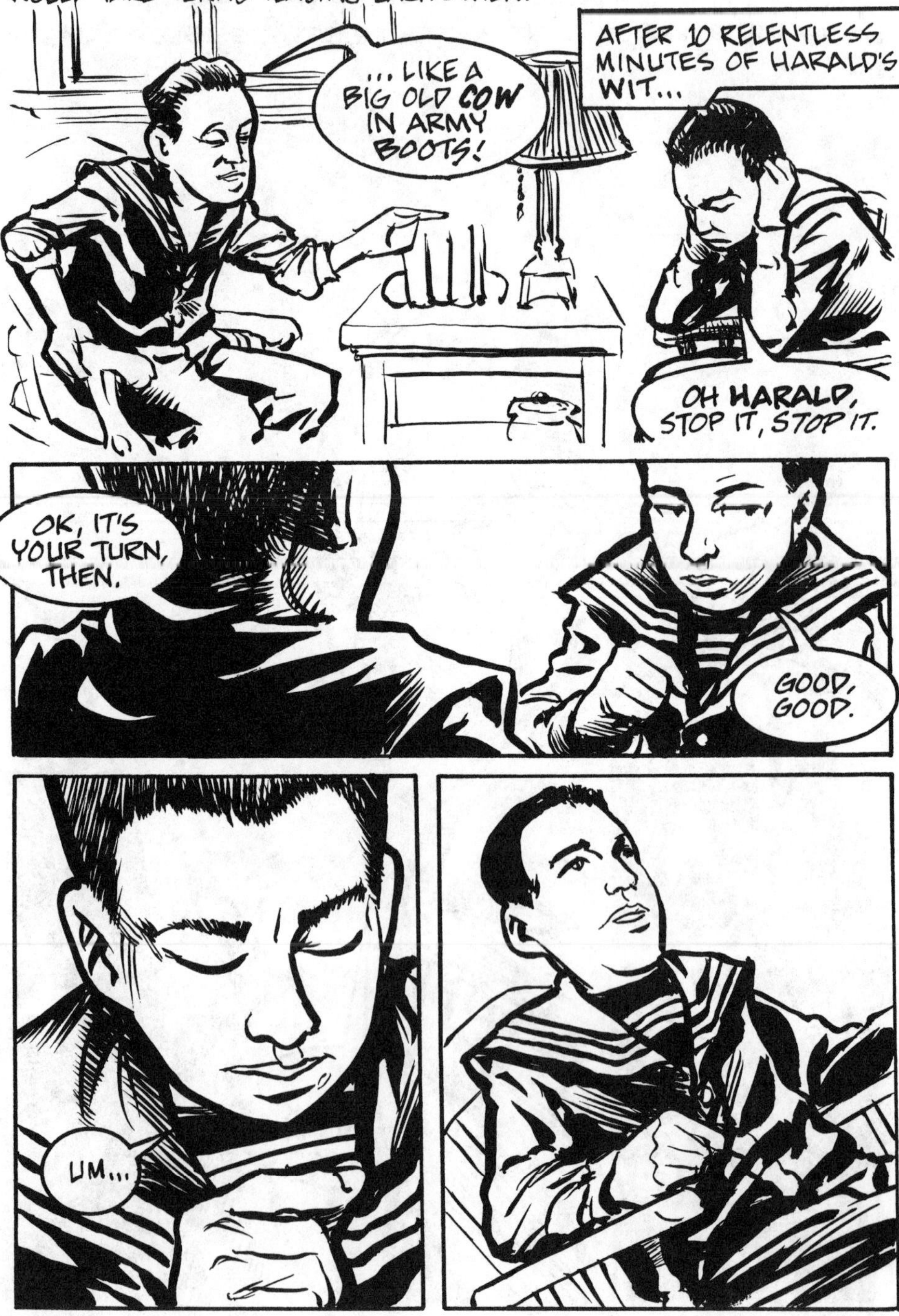
AFTER 10 RELENTLESS MINUTES OF HARALD'S WIT...
...LIKE A BIG OLD COW IN ARMY BOOTS!
OH HARALD, STOP IT, STOP IT.
OK, IT'S YOUR TURN, THEN.
GOOD, GOOD.
UM...

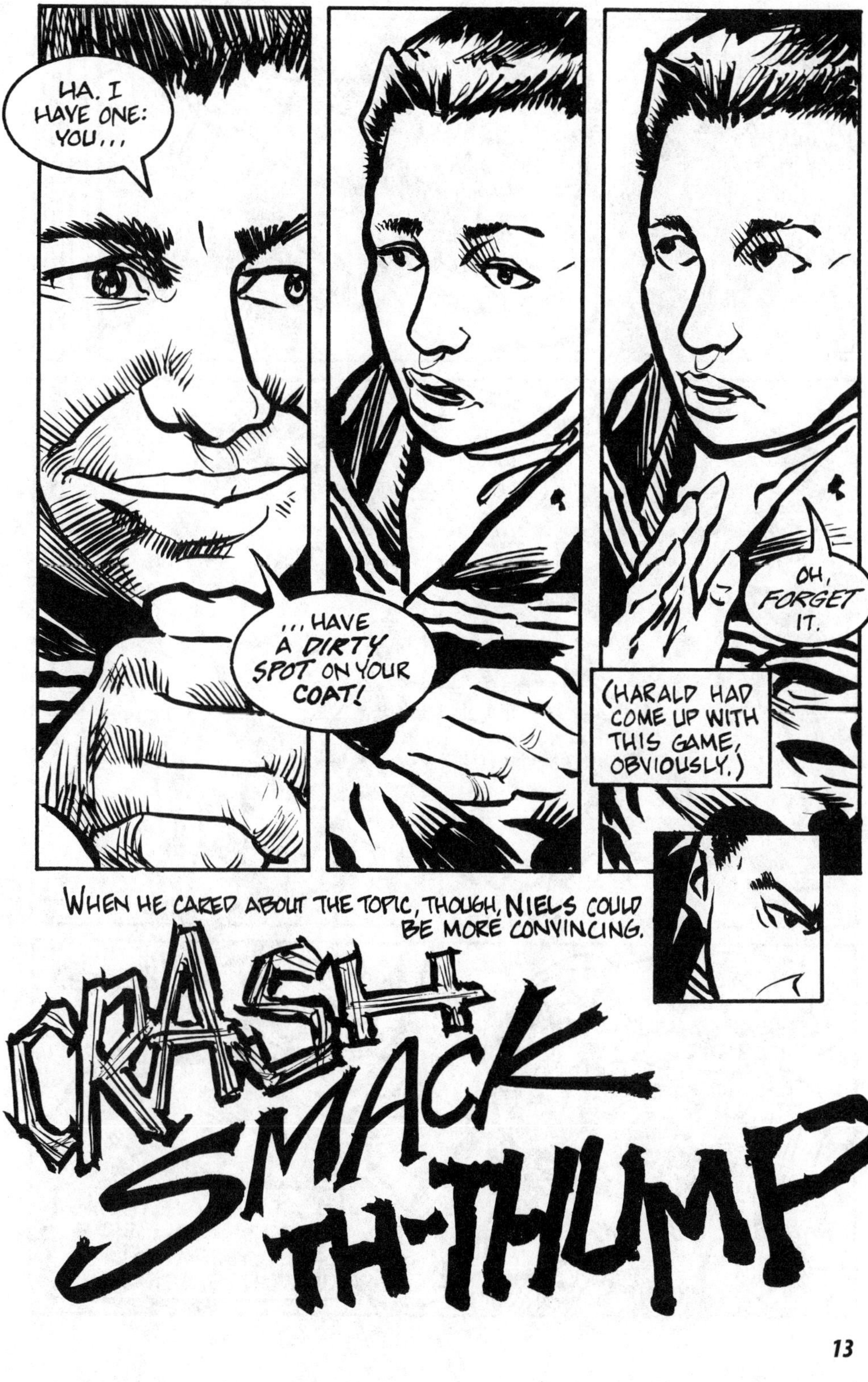
HA. I HAVE ONE: YOU...
...HAVE A DIRTY SPOT ON YOUR COAT!
OH, FORGET IT.
(HARALD HAD COME UP WITH THIS GAME, OBVIOUSLY.)
WHEN HE CARED ABOUT THE TOPIC, THOUGH, NIELS COULD BE MORE CONVINCING.
CRASH
SMACK
TH-THUMP

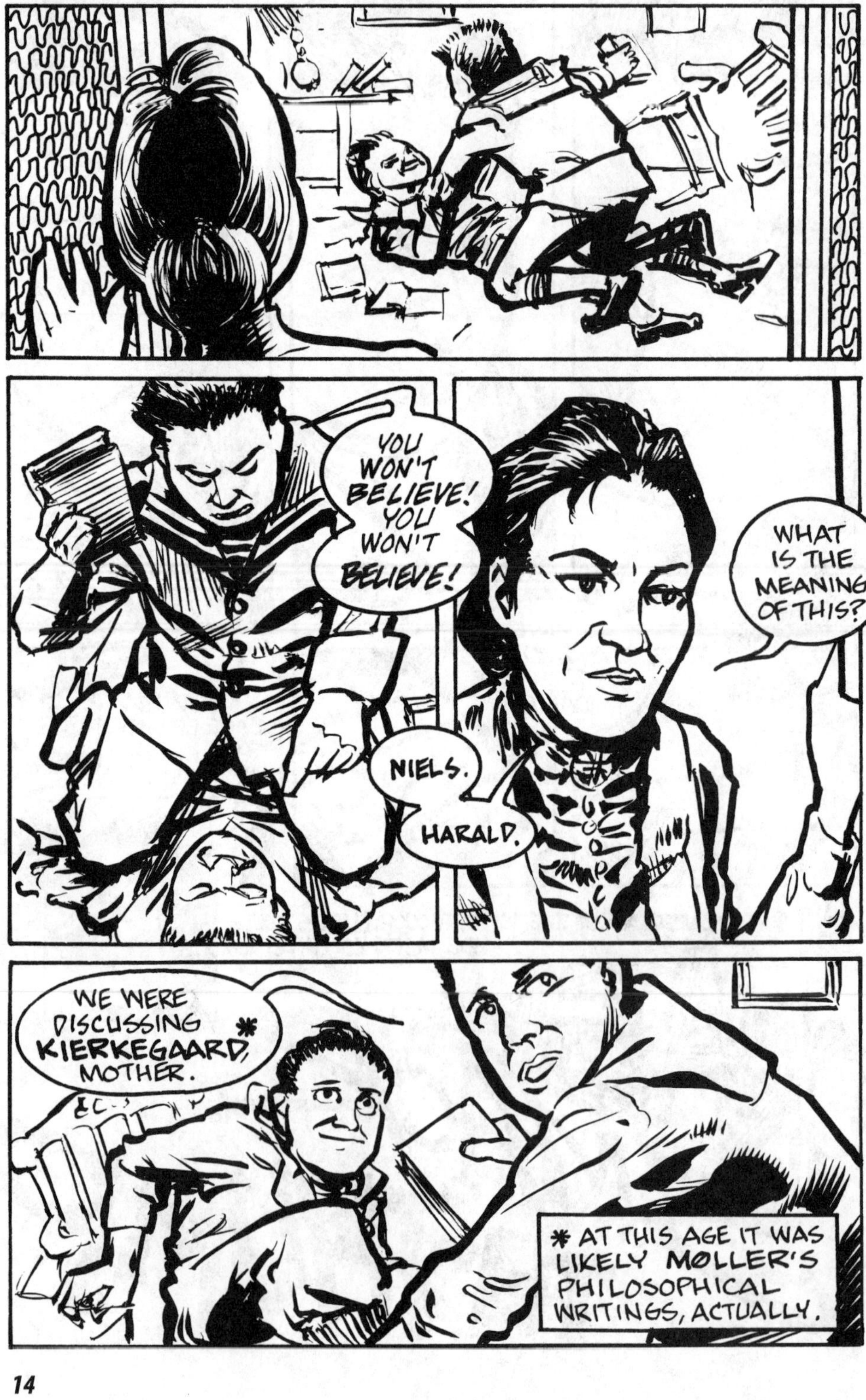
YOU WON'T BELIEVE! YOU WON'T BELIEVE!
WHAT IS THE MEANING OF THIS?
NIELS.
HARALD.
WE WERE DISCUSSING KIERKEGAARD,* MOTHER.
* AT THIS AGE IT WAS LIKELY MØLLER'S PHILOSOPHICAL WRITINGS, ACTUALLY.

BOHR POSSESSED GREAT PHYSICAL STRENGTH ALL HIS LIFE, BUT DIDN'T USE IT TO SETTLE PHILOSOPHICAL DIFFERENCES AFTER HIS GRADE SCHOOL YEARS.

HE CAME, AFTER ALL, FROM A FAMILY THAT WAS "HIGH TO THE CEILING."

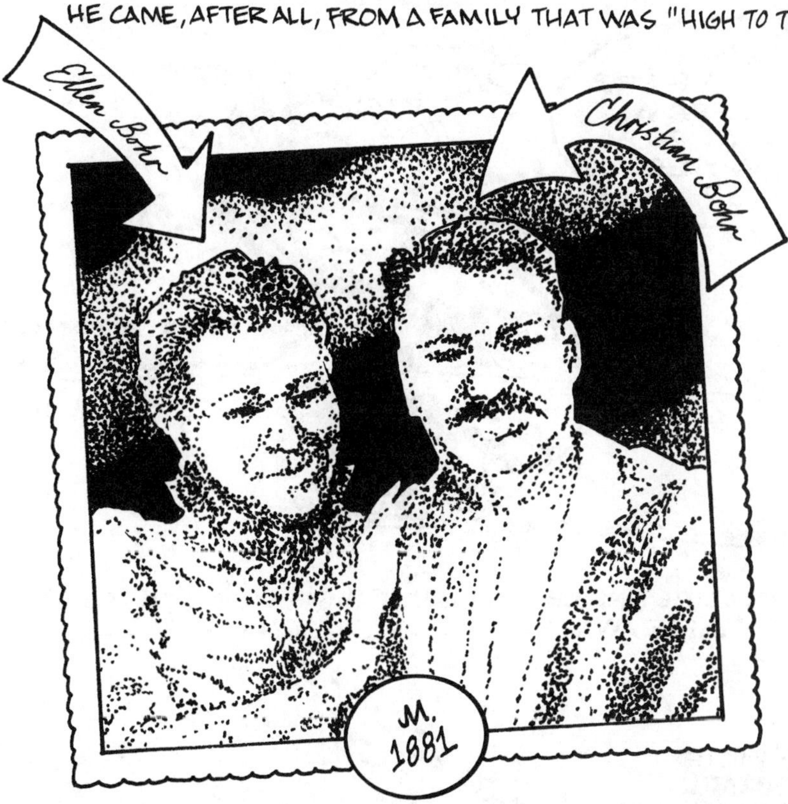

Ellen Bohr
Christian Bohr
M. 1881

THIS TERM, RESERVED BY **DANES** FOR THOSE OF HIGH SOCIAL AND INTELLECTUAL STANDING, FIT ***CHRISTIAN HARALD LAURITZ PETER EMIL BOHR*** AND **ELLEN BOHR** (NEE ADLER) PERFECTLY.

ELLEN IMPRESSED GOODNESS AND AN INTEREST IN ALL PEOPLE UPON HER CHILDREN, AND **CHRISTIAN** – A UNIVERSITY PROFESSOR AND PHYSICIAN– BROUGHT THEM UP WITH AN INTEREST IN SCIENCE AND IN A HOME WHERE DISCUSSING AND DEBATING ***IDEAS*** WAS AN IMPORTANT PART OF EVERYDAY LIFE.

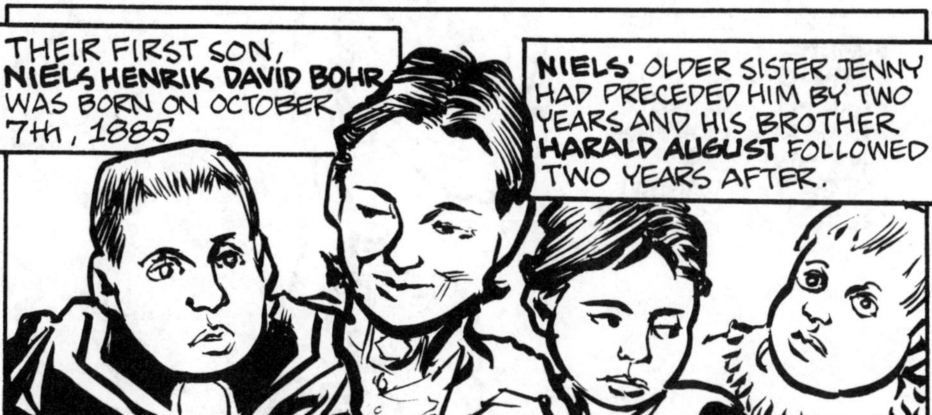

THEIR FIRST SON, **NIELS HENRIK DAVID BOHR** WAS BORN ON OCTOBER 7th, 1885
NIELS' OLDER SISTER JENNY HAD PRECEDED HIM BY TWO YEARS AND HIS BROTHER **HARALD AUGUST** FOLLOWED TWO YEARS AFTER.

NIELS LIVED AND WORKED IN **DENMARK** HIS WHOLE LIFE, SO LIKE FELLOW **DANE** HANS CHRISTIAN ANDERSEN, HE COULD SAY:

" IN DENMARK I WAS BORN, 'TIS THERE MY HOME IS, FROM THERE MY ROOTS, FROM THERE MY WORLD EXTENDS."

Wolfgang, George Gamow

...uli, Robert Oppenheimer, Max Born, Paul Dirac   Max Debrück, Lev Landau, Szilard

...e Meitner, Otto Frisch, Henrik Kramers, Marie Curie, E...   Schrödinger, Hans Bethe, Leo

...nest Rutherford, Albert Einstein, Enrico Fermi

vibe

THIS MAKES **BOHR** QUITE UNLIKE SO MANY OF HIS FELLOW SCIENTISTS, WHO ENDED UP LIVING FAR AWAY FROM THEIR ORIGINAL HOMES.

AT **NIELS'** BIRTH IN 1885 **DENMARK** WAS EUROPE'S OLDEST KINGDOM.

BUT IT HAD GROWN PROGRESSIVELY *SMALLER* SINCE THE DAYS OF THE **KALMAR UNION** OF 1397, WHICH COMBINED **DENMARK, NORWAY** AND **SWEDEN** UNDER THE DANISH QUEEN MARGRETE I.

NORWAY

SWEDEN

DENMARK

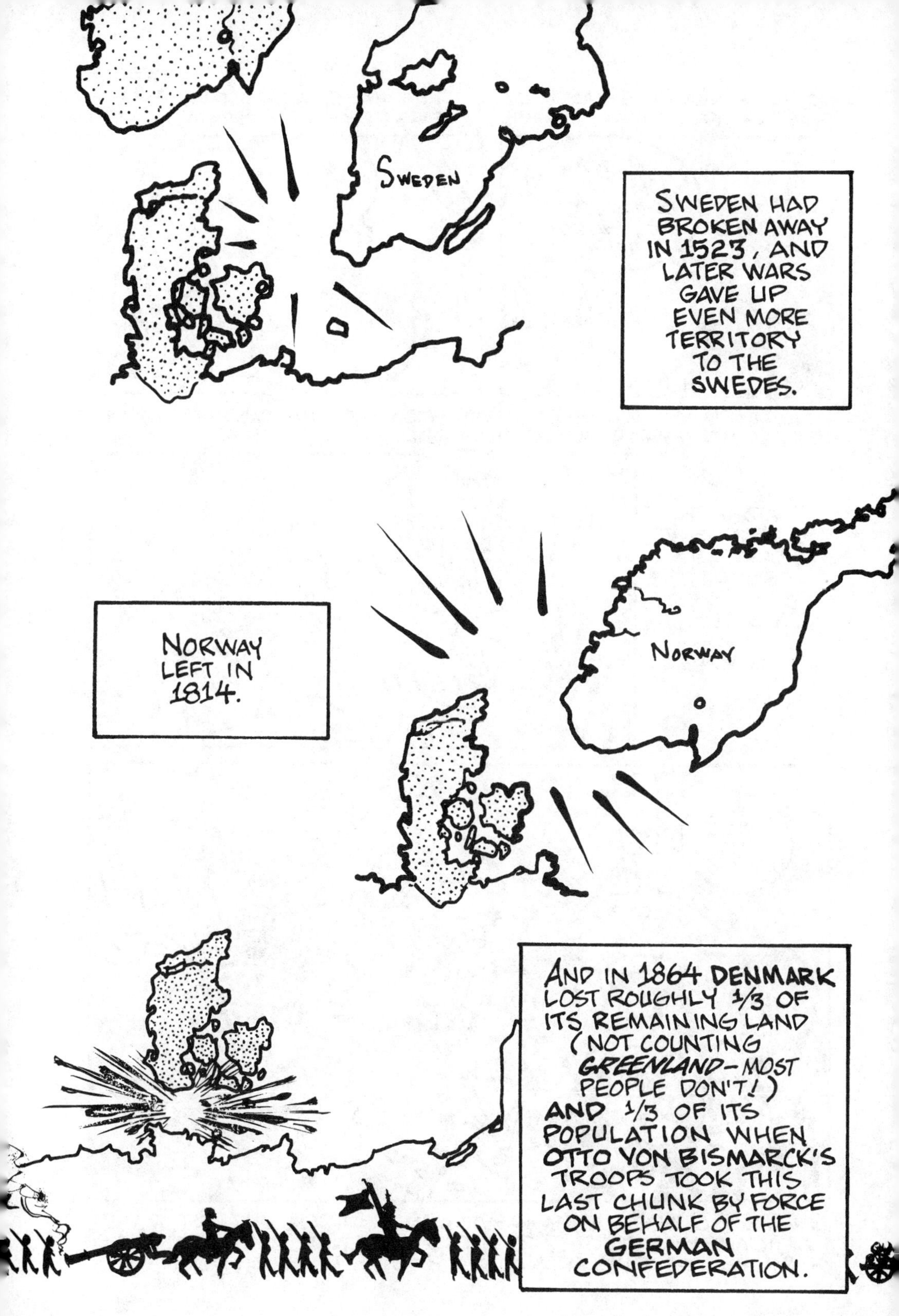
SWEDEN
SWEDEN HAD BROKEN AWAY IN 1523, AND LATER WARS GAVE UP EVEN MORE TERRITORY TO THE SWEDES.
NORWAY LEFT IN 1814.
NORWAY
AND IN 1864 DENMARK LOST ROUGHLY 1/3 OF ITS REMAINING LAND (NOT COUNTING GREENLAND—MOST PEOPLE DON'T!) AND 1/3 OF ITS POPULATION WHEN OTTO VON BISMARCK'S TROOPS TOOK THIS LAST CHUNK BY FORCE ON BEHALF OF THE GERMAN CONFEDERATION.

SO, YOUNG NIELS WAS BORN INTO A SMALL COUNTRY, STILL HUMILIATED BY A CRUSHING DEFEAT JUST OVER TWENTY YEARS BEFORE. THE OFFICIAL REACTION?

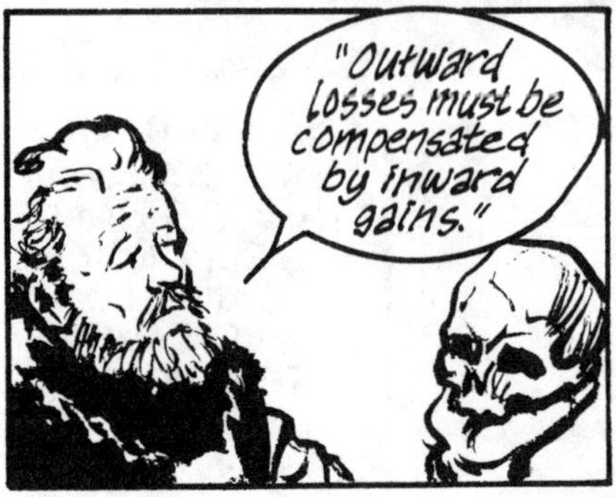
"Outward losses must be compensated by inward gains."

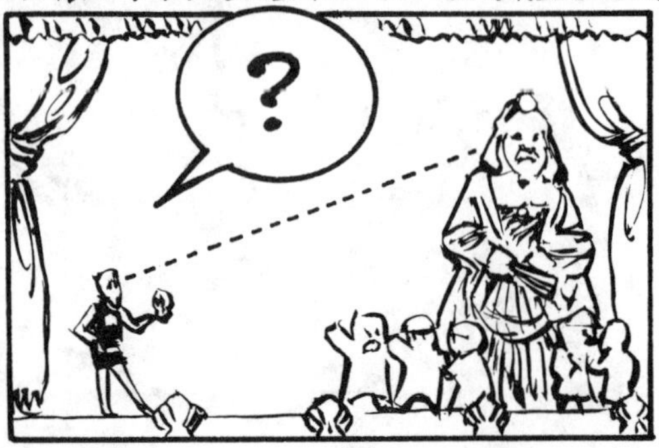
?

A PHILOSOPHICAL POLICY STATEMENT WORTHY OF **DENMARK'S** MOST FAMOUS PRINCE, BUT VERY MUCH *NOT* FICTIONAL.

WITH IT, THE DANISH GOVERNMENT STEPPED OFF CENTER STAGE IN WORLD POLITICS, BECOMING...

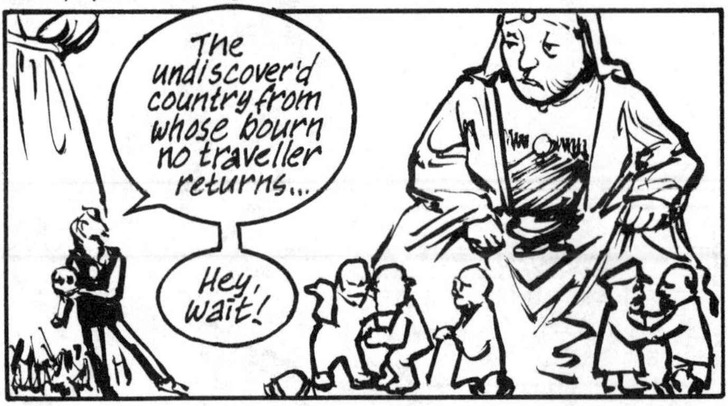
The undiscover'd country from whose bourn no traveller returns...
Hey, wait!

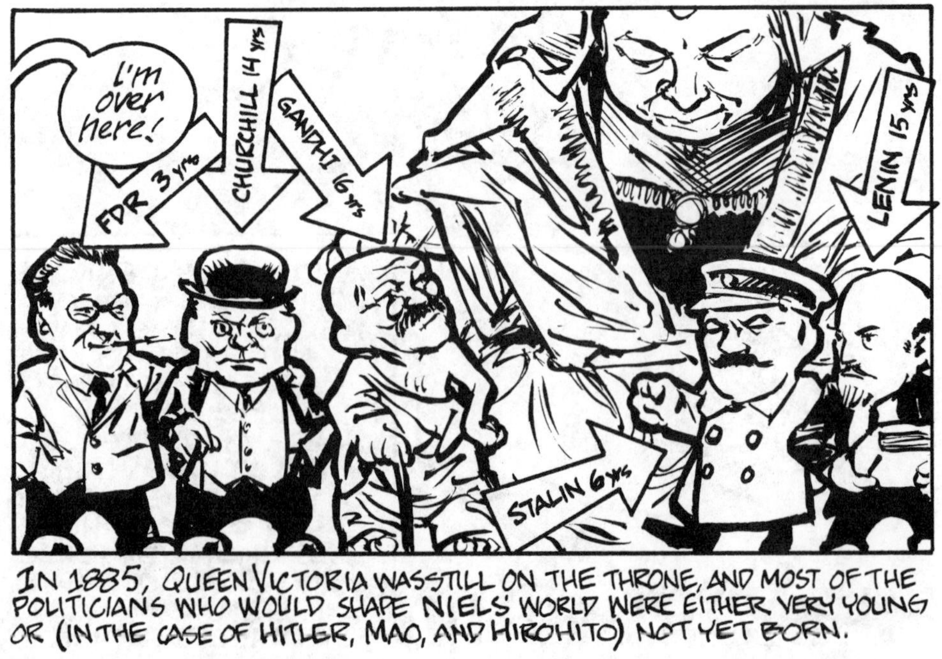
I'm over here!
FDR 3 yrs
CHURCHILL 14 yrs
GANDHI 16 yrs
LENIN 15 yrs
STALIN 6 yrs

IN 1885, QUEEN VICTORIA WAS STILL ON THE THRONE, AND MOST OF THE POLITICIANS WHO WOULD SHAPE NIELS' WORLD WERE EITHER VERY YOUNG OR (IN THE CASE OF HITLER, MAO, AND HIROHITO) NOT YET BORN.

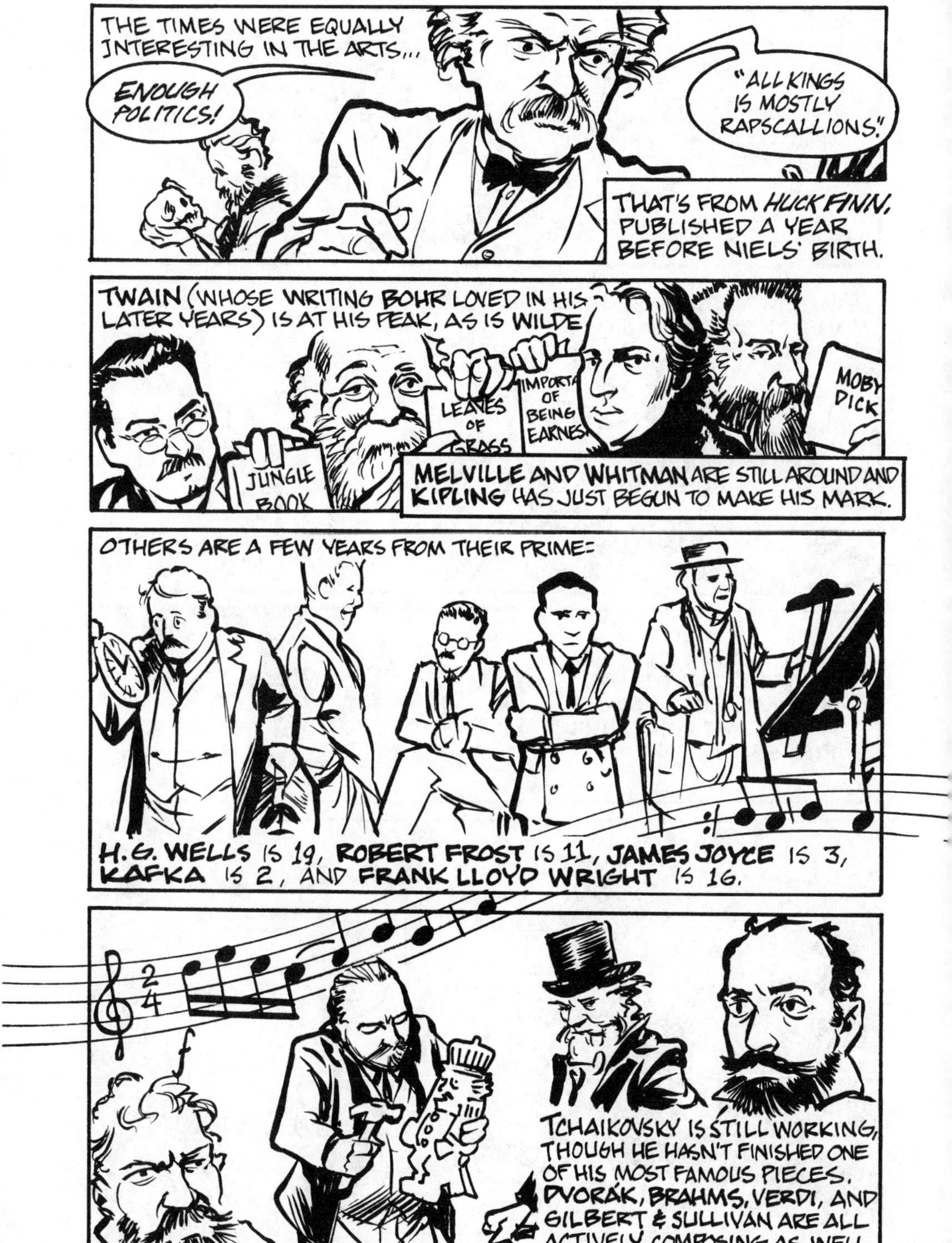
THE TIMES WERE EQUALLY INTERESTING IN THE ARTS...
ENOUGH POLITICS!
"ALL KINGS IS MOSTLY RAPSCALLIONS."
THAT'S FROM *HUCK FINN*, PUBLISHED A YEAR BEFORE NIELS' BIRTH.
TWAIN (WHOSE WRITING BOHR LOVED IN HIS LATER YEARS) IS AT HIS PEAK, AS IS WILDE
LEAVES OF GRASS
IMPORTA OF BEING EARNES
MOBY DICK
JUNGLE BOOK
MELVILLE AND WHITMAN ARE STILL AROUND AND KIPLING HAS JUST BEGUN TO MAKE HIS MARK.
OTHERS ARE A FEW YEARS FROM THEIR PRIME:
H.G. WELLS IS 19, ROBERT FROST IS 11, JAMES JOYCE IS 3, KAFKA IS 2, AND FRANK LLOYD WRIGHT IS 16.
TCHAIKOVSKY IS STILL WORKING, THOUGH HE HASN'T FINISHED ONE OF HIS MOST FAMOUS PIECES. DVORÁK, BRAHMS, VERDI, AND GILBERT & SULLIVAN ARE ALL ACTIVELY COMPOSING AS WELL.

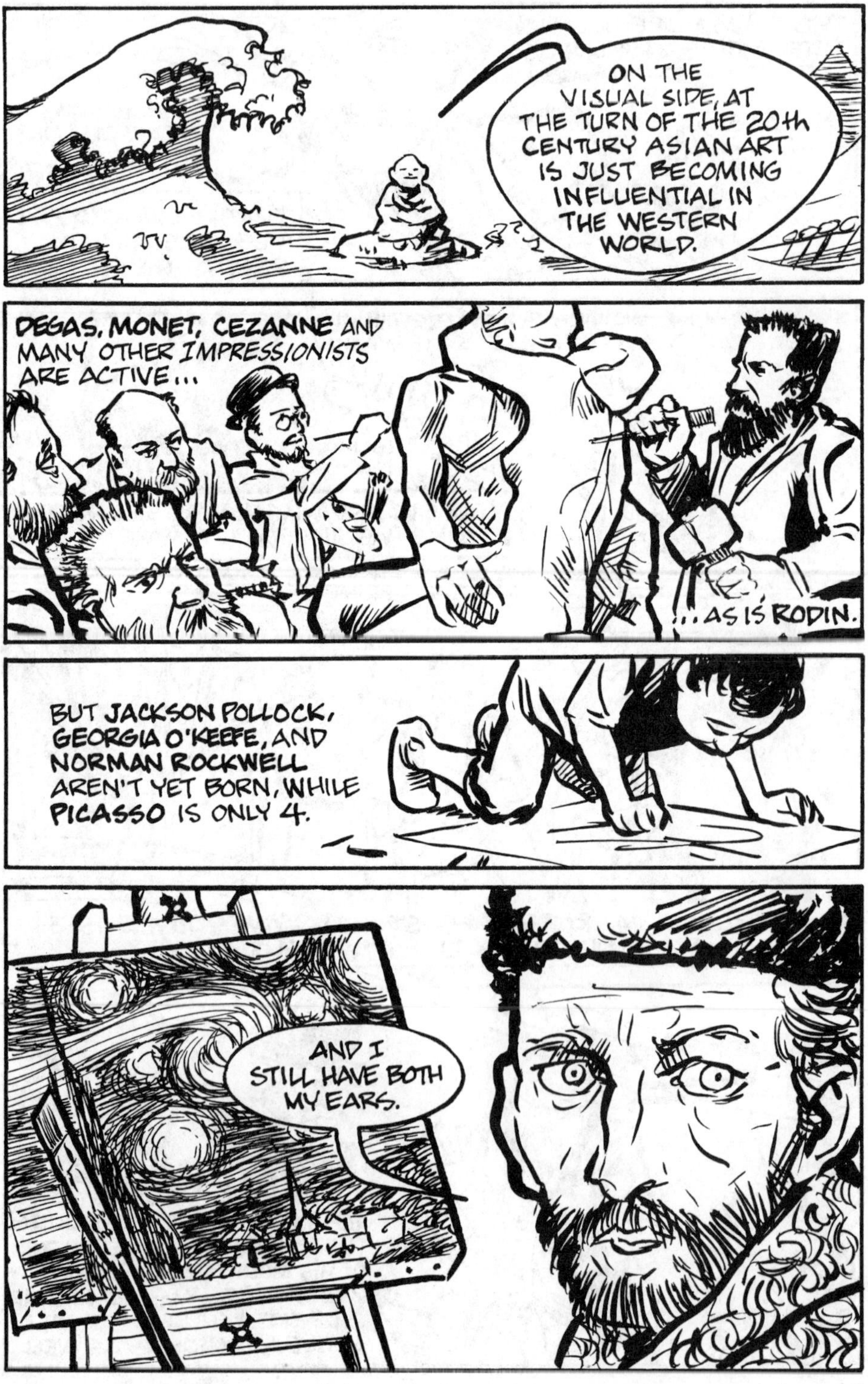
ON THE VISUAL SIDE, AT THE TURN OF THE 20th CENTURY ASIAN ART IS JUST BECOMING INFLUENTIAL IN THE WESTERN WORLD.
DEGAS, MONET, CEZANNE AND MANY OTHER IMPRESSIONISTS ARE ACTIVE...
...AS IS RODIN.
BUT JACKSON POLLOCK, GEORGIA O'KEEFE, AND NORMAN ROCKWELL AREN'T YET BORN, WHILE PICASSO IS ONLY 4.
AND I STILL HAVE BOTH MY EARS.

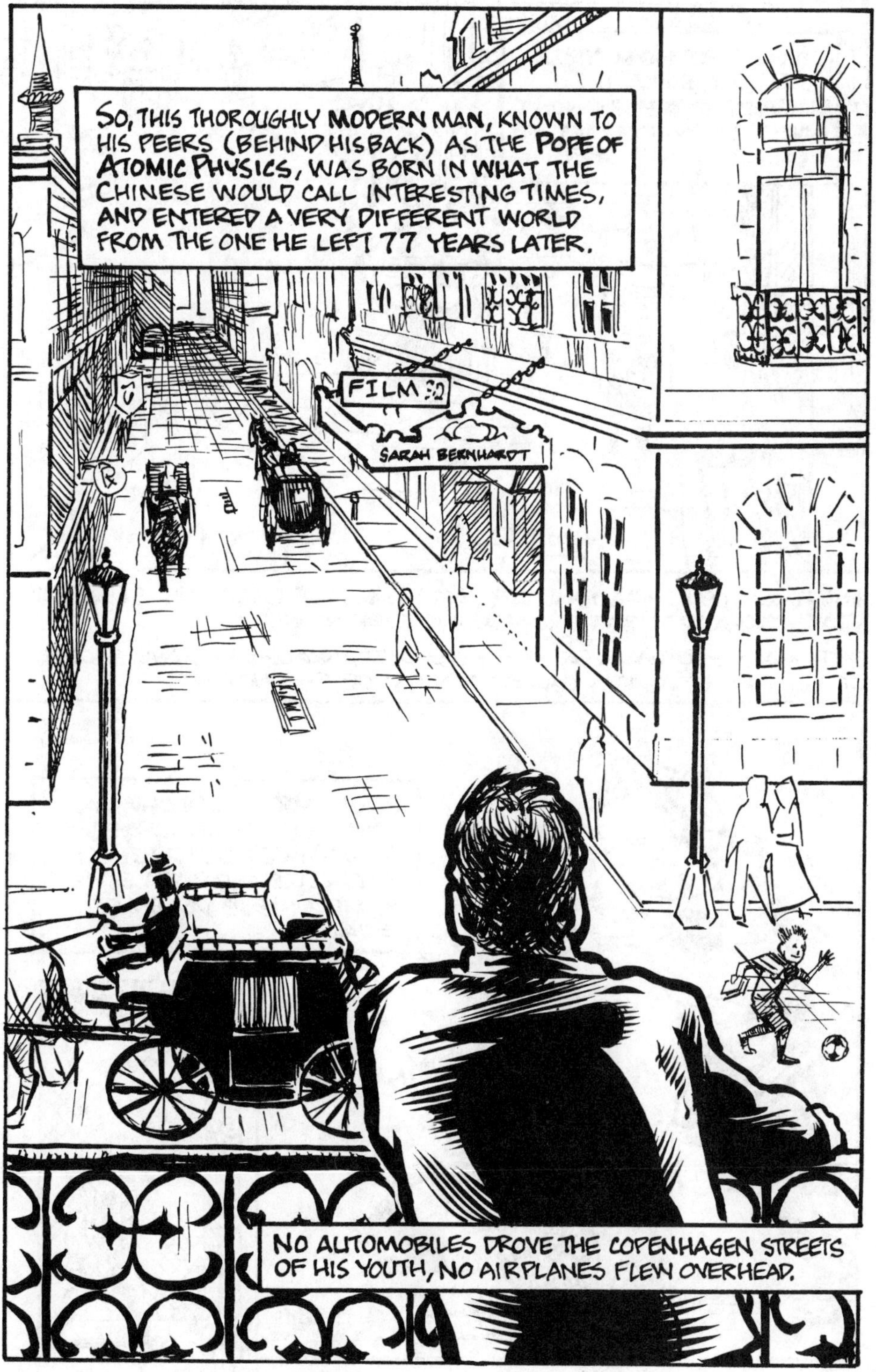
SO, THIS THOROUGHLY MODERN MAN, KNOWN TO HIS PEERS (BEHIND HIS BACK) AS THE POPE OF ATOMIC PHYSICS, WAS BORN IN WHAT THE CHINESE WOULD CALL INTERESTING TIMES, AND ENTERED A VERY DIFFERENT WORLD FROM THE ONE HE LEFT 77 YEARS LATER.
FILM
SARAH BERNHARDT
NO AUTOMOBILES DROVE THE COPENHAGEN STREETS OF HIS YOUTH, NO AIRPLANES FLEW OVERHEAD.

THERE WERE NO MOVIES EITHER, SINCE THE **LUMIERE BROTHERS** WON'T INVENT THE MOTION PICTURE CAMERA UNTIL *1895*.

AND FORGET CELL PHONES AND CD'S: AFTER ALL, THE TELEPHONE IS ONLY NINE YEARS OLD AND THE PHONOGRAPH IS EVEN NEWER.

BUT THANKS TO THEIR FATHER, NIELS AND HARALD DID HAVE SOCCER! OR FOOTBALL, AS IT'S CALLED IN MOST OF THE WORLD.

PROF. CHRISTIAN BOHR HAD FOUNDED THE UNIVERSITY OF COPENHAGEN'S *AKADEMISK BOLDKLUB* AND BOTH BOYS PLAYED. **NIELS** DEFENDED GOAL...

22

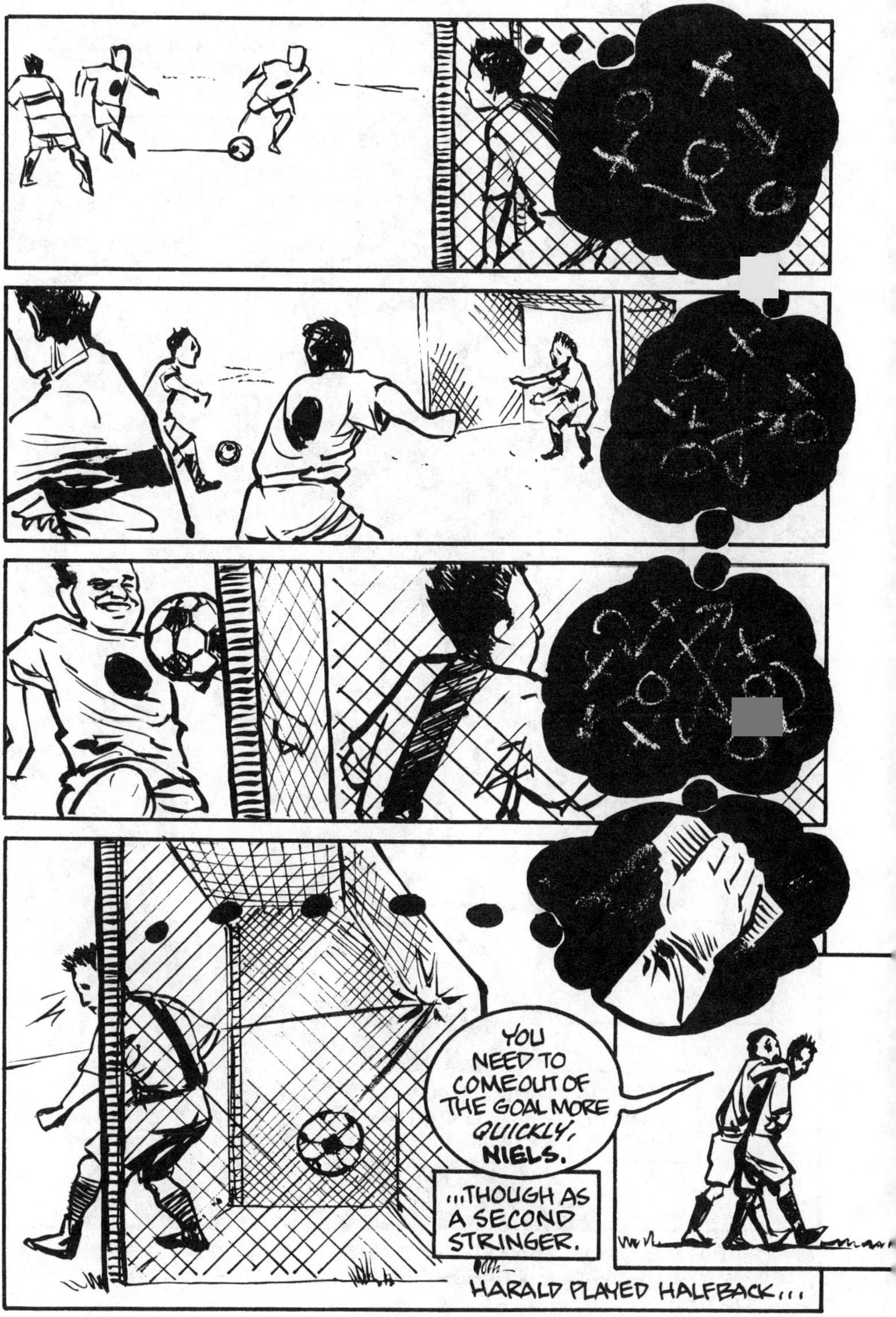
YOU NEED TO COME OUT OF THE GOAL MORE *QUICKLY,* **NIELS.**
HARALD PLAYED HALFBACK...
...THOUGH AS A SECOND STRINGER.

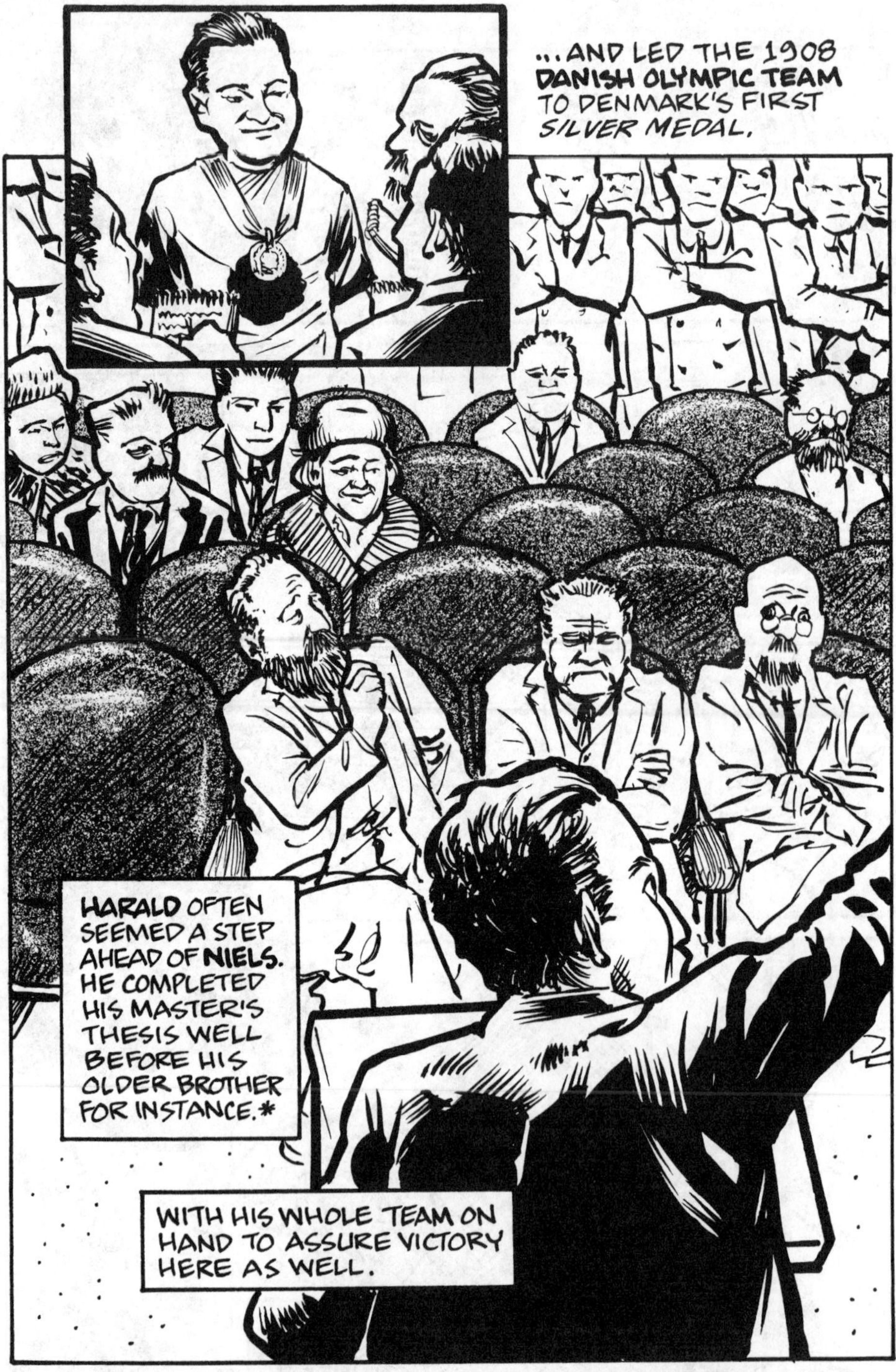
...AND LED THE 1908 **DANISH OLYMPIC TEAM** TO DENMARK'S FIRST *SILVER MEDAL*.
HARALD OFTEN SEEMED A STEP AHEAD OF **NIELS**. HE COMPLETED HIS MASTER'S THESIS WELL BEFORE HIS OLDER BROTHER FOR INSTANCE.*
WITH HIS WHOLE TEAM ON HAND TO ASSURE VICTORY HERE AS WELL.

* NOT THAT NIELS WAS A BAD STUDENT, *PER SE*. SEE "APOCRYPHA" ON PAGE 277 FOR ONE POSSIBLE REASON WHY IT TOOK NIELS SO LONG TO GRADUATE.

Chapter 2

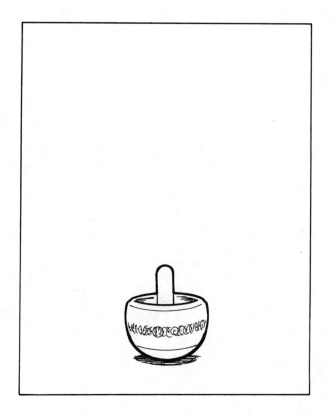

THROUGHOUT HIS LIFE, **NIELS** WAS NOT KNOWN AS A PARTICULARLY QUICK THINKER, HENCE HIS YOUNGER BROTHER BEATING HIM TO HIS MASTER'S THESIS.

BUT HIS POWERS OF CONCENTRATION WERE LEGENDARY, AND STARTED YOUNG.

" 'BUT THE EMPEROR HASN'T GOT ANYTHING ON,' A LITTLE CHILD SAID."

PEOPLE WOULD SAY, "THAT POOR MOTHER..."

BUT IT'S ALL RIGHT, THEY WEREN'T **ALWAYS** SO INTENSE

...THEY RELAXED A LITTLE WHEN THEY **SLEPT,** FOR INSTANCE.

TO SOME, THIS SLACK-JAWED CONCENTRATION MADE HIM LOOK SOMETHING OF A FOOL, BUT LOOKS DECEIVE.

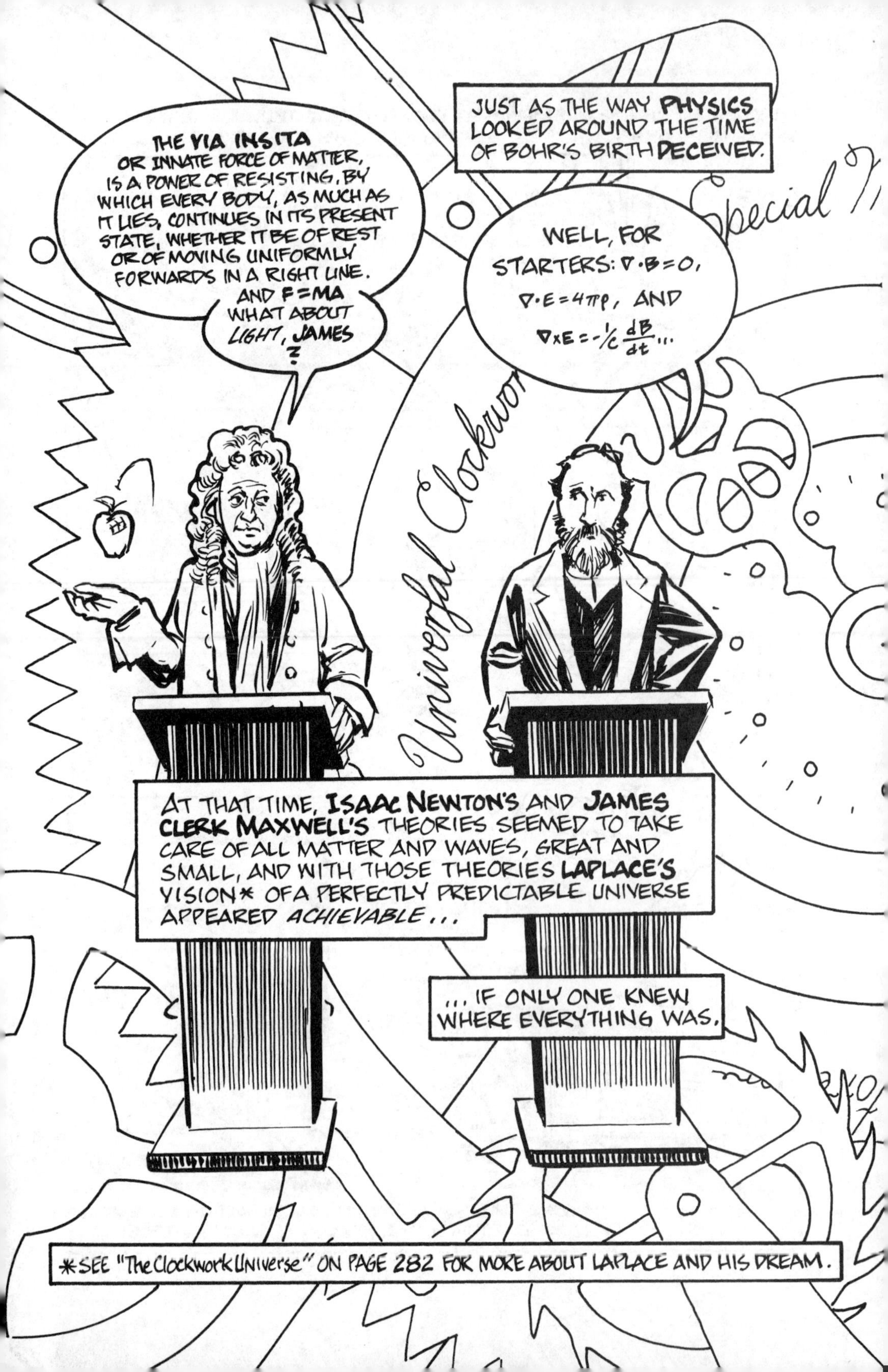
JUST AS THE WAY PHYSICS LOOKED AROUND THE TIME OF BOHR'S BIRTH DECEIVED.
THE VIA INSITA OR INNATE FORCE OF MATTER, IS A POWER OF RESISTING, BY WHICH EVERY BODY, AS MUCH AS IT LIES, CONTINUES IN ITS PRESENT STATE, WHETHER IT BE OF REST OR OF MOVING UNIFORMLY FORWARDS IN A RIGHT LINE. AND F=MA
WHAT ABOUT LIGHT, JAMES?
WELL, FOR STARTERS: $\nabla \cdot B = 0$, $\nabla \cdot E = 4\pi\rho$, AND $\nabla \times E = -\frac{1}{c}\frac{dB}{dt}$...
AT THAT TIME, ISAAC NEWTON'S AND JAMES CLERK MAXWELL'S THEORIES SEEMED TO TAKE CARE OF ALL MATTER AND WAVES, GREAT AND SMALL, AND WITH THOSE THEORIES LAPLACE'S VISION* OF A PERFECTLY PREDICTABLE UNIVERSE APPEARED ACHIEVABLE...
... IF ONLY ONE KNEW WHERE EVERYTHING WAS.
*SEE "The Clockwork Universe" ON PAGE 282 FOR MORE ABOUT LAPLACE AND HIS DREAM.

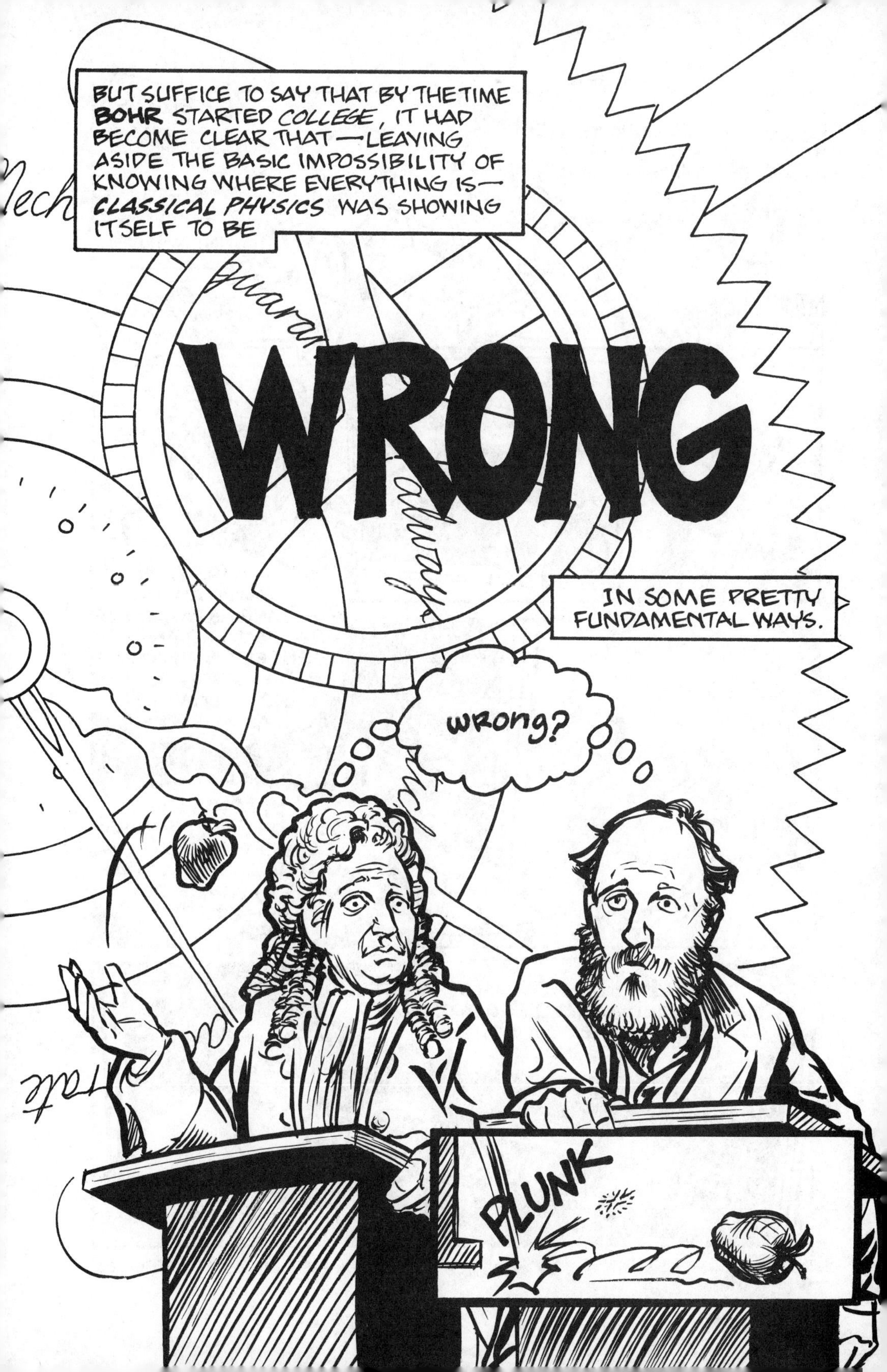
BUT SUFFICE TO SAY THAT BY THE TIME BOHR STARTED COLLEGE, IT HAD BECOME CLEAR THAT—LEAVING ASIDE THE BASIC IMPOSSIBILITY OF KNOWING WHERE EVERYTHING IS—CLASSICAL PHYSICS WAS SHOWING ITSELF TO BE
WRONG
IN SOME PRETTY FUNDAMENTAL WAYS.
wrong?
PLUNK

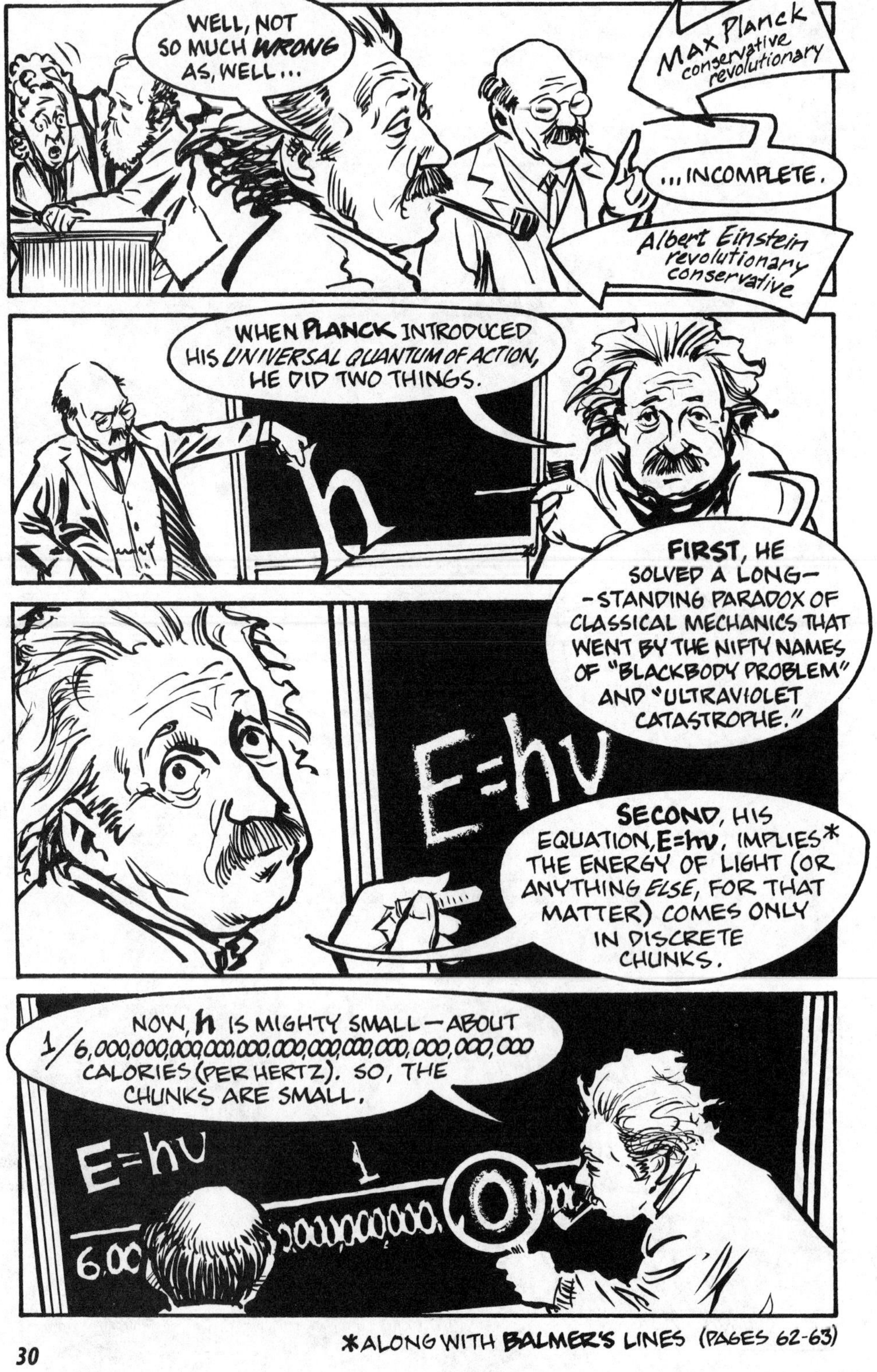

WELL, NOT SO MUCH **WRONG** AS, WELL...
Max Planck conservative revolutionary
...INCOMPLETE.
Albert Einstein revolutionary conservative
WHEN **PLANCK** INTRODUCED HIS *UNIVERSAL QUANTUM OF ACTION*, HE DID TWO THINGS.
h
FIRST, HE SOLVED A LONG--STANDING PARADOX OF CLASSICAL MECHANICS THAT WENT BY THE NIFTY NAMES OF "BLACKBODY PROBLEM" AND "ULTRAVIOLET CATASTROPHE."
E=hν
SECOND, HIS EQUATION, **E=hν**, IMPLIES* THE ENERGY OF LIGHT (OR ANYTHING *ELSE*, FOR THAT MATTER) COMES ONLY IN DISCRETE CHUNKS.
NOW, **h** IS MIGHTY SMALL—ABOUT 1/6,000,000,000,000,000,000,000,000,000,000,000,000 CALORIES (PER HERTZ). SO, THE CHUNKS ARE SMALL.
E=hν

*ALONG WITH **BALMER'S** LINES (PAGES 62-63)

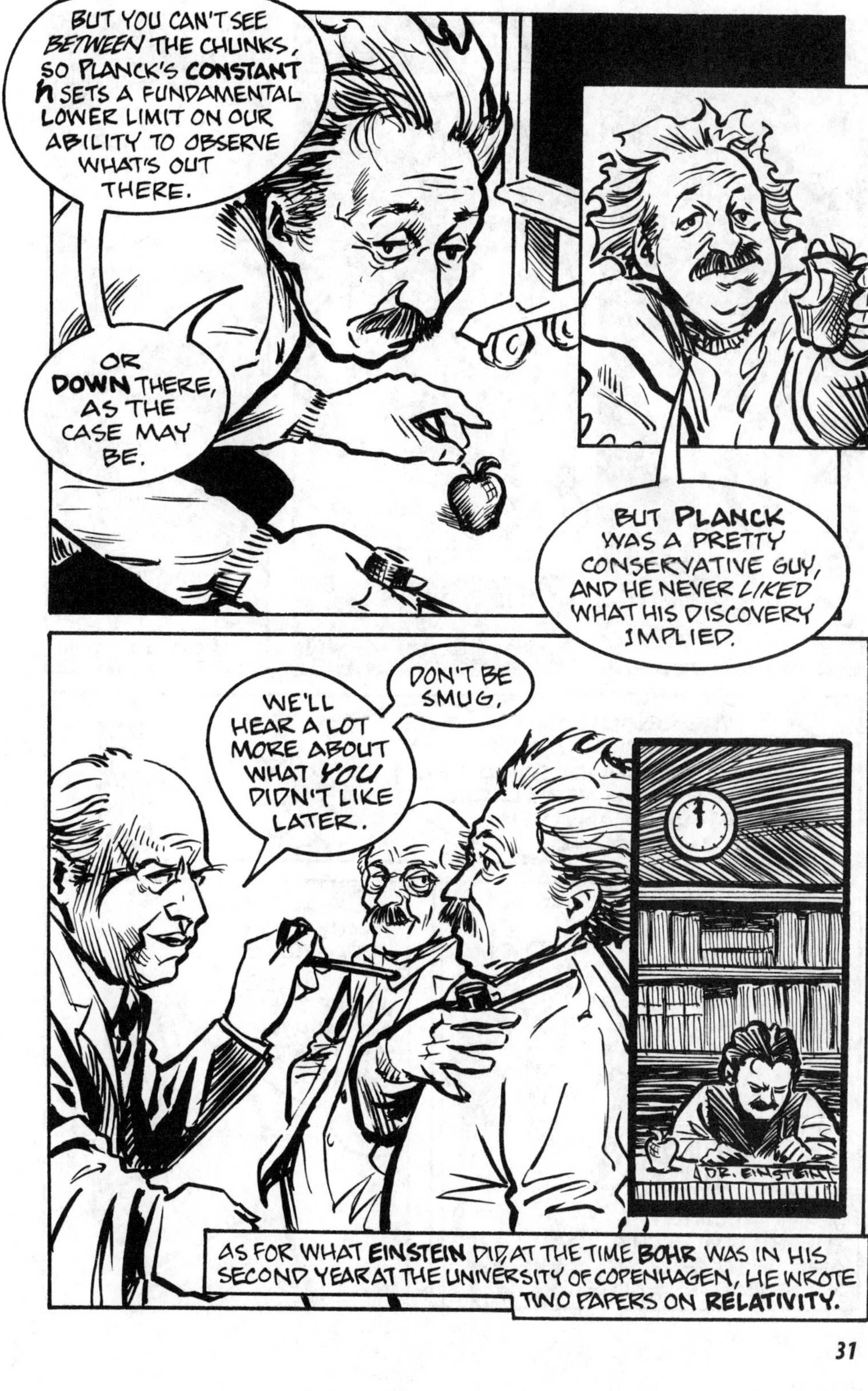
BUT YOU CAN'T SEE *BETWEEN* THE CHUNKS, SO PLANCK'S **CONSTANT** *h* SETS A FUNDAMENTAL LOWER LIMIT ON OUR ABILITY TO OBSERVE WHAT'S OUT THERE.
OR **DOWN** THERE, AS THE CASE MAY BE.
BUT **PLANCK** WAS A PRETTY CONSERVATIVE GUY, AND HE NEVER *LIKED* WHAT HIS DISCOVERY IMPLIED.
DON'T BE SMUG.
WE'LL HEAR A LOT MORE ABOUT WHAT *YOU* DIDN'T LIKE LATER.
DR. EINSTEIN
AS FOR WHAT **EINSTEIN** DID, AT THE TIME **BOHR** WAS IN HIS SECOND YEAR AT THE UNIVERSITY OF COPENHAGEN, HE WROTE TWO PAPERS ON **RELATIVITY**.

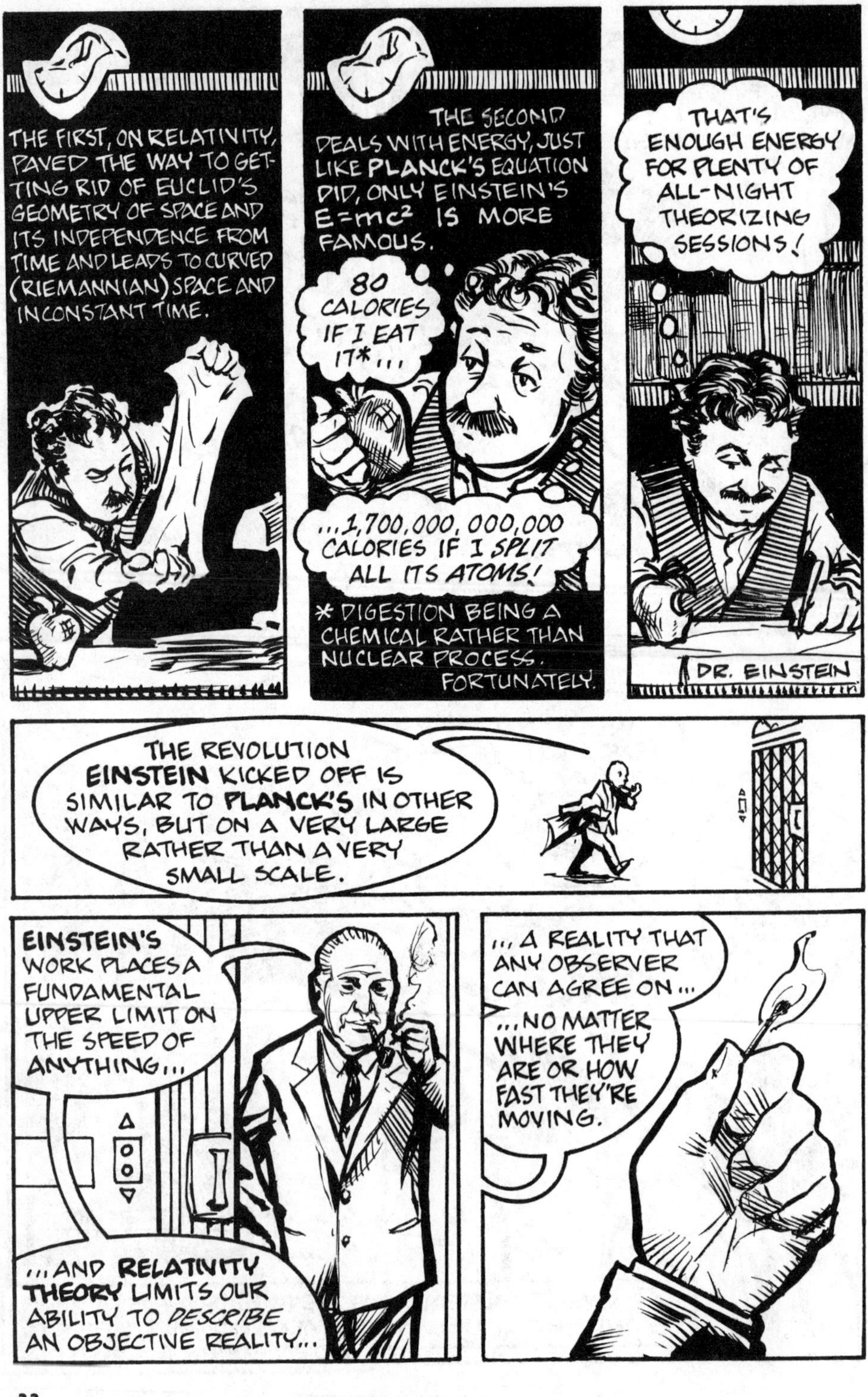
THE FIRST, ON RELATIVITY, PAVED THE WAY TO GETTING RID OF EUCLID'S GEOMETRY OF SPACE AND ITS INDEPENDENCE FROM TIME AND LEADS TO CURVED (RIEMANNIAN) SPACE AND INCONSTANT TIME.
THE SECOND DEALS WITH ENERGY, JUST LIKE PLANCK'S EQUATION DID, ONLY EINSTEIN'S E=mc² IS MORE FAMOUS.
80 CALORIES IF I EAT IT*...
...1,700,000,000,000 CALORIES IF I SPLIT ALL ITS ATOMS!
* DIGESTION BEING A CHEMICAL RATHER THAN NUCLEAR PROCESS. FORTUNATELY.
THAT'S ENOUGH ENERGY FOR PLENTY OF ALL-NIGHT THEORIZING SESSIONS!
DR. EINSTEIN
THE REVOLUTION EINSTEIN KICKED OFF IS SIMILAR TO PLANCK'S IN OTHER WAYS, BUT ON A VERY LARGE RATHER THAN A VERY SMALL SCALE.
EINSTEIN'S WORK PLACES A FUNDAMENTAL UPPER LIMIT ON THE SPEED OF ANYTHING...
...AND RELATIVITY THEORY LIMITS OUR ABILITY TO DESCRIBE AN OBJECTIVE REALITY...
...A REALITY THAT ANY OBSERVER CAN AGREE ON...
...NO MATTER WHERE THEY ARE OR HOW FAST THEY'RE MOVING.

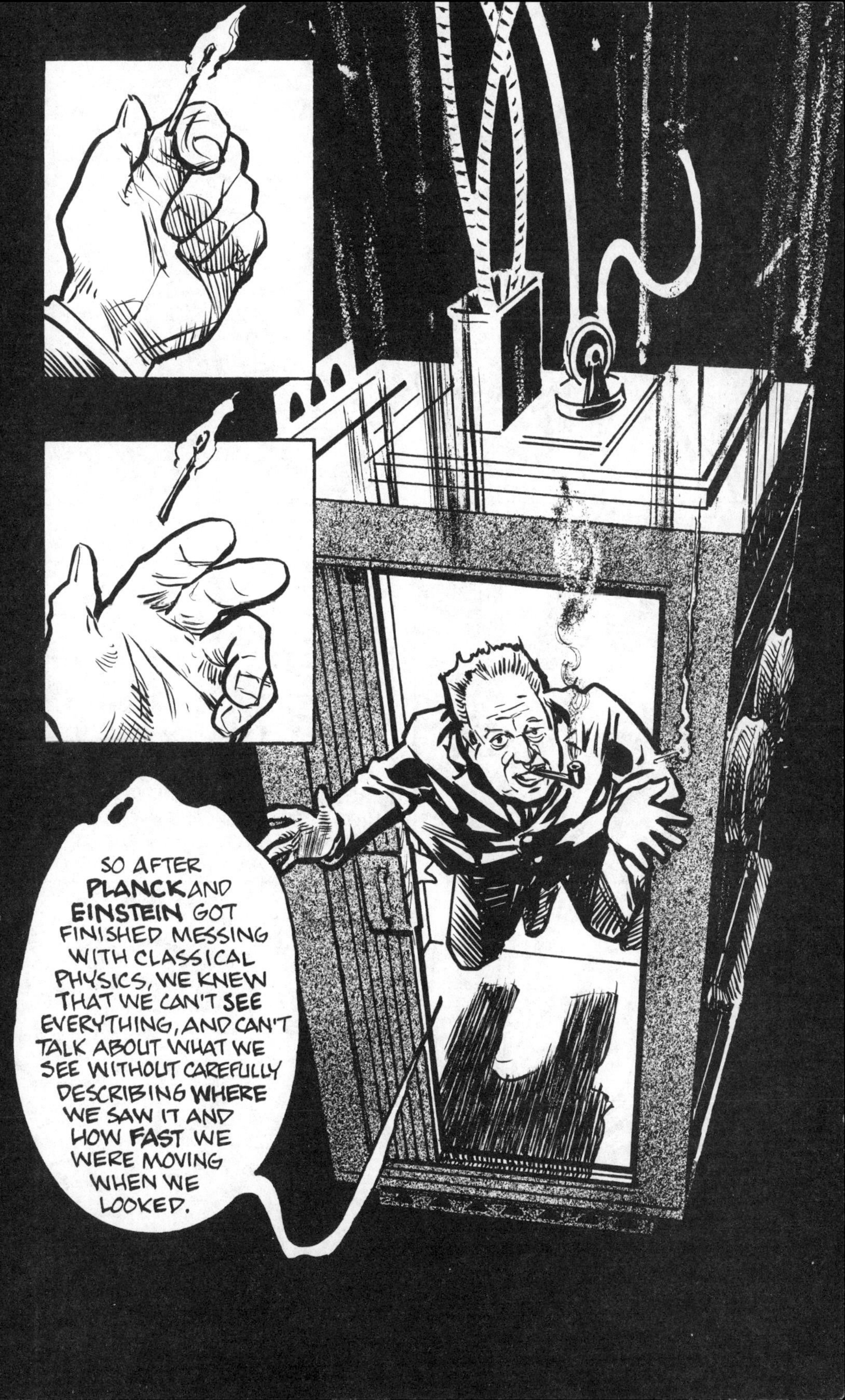
SO AFTER PLANCK AND EINSTEIN GOT FINISHED MESSING WITH CLASSICAL PHYSICS, WE KNEW THAT WE CAN'T SEE EVERYTHING, AND CAN'T TALK ABOUT WHAT WE SEE WITHOUT CAREFULLY DESCRIBING WHERE WE SAW IT AND HOW FAST WE WERE MOVING WHEN WE LOOKED.

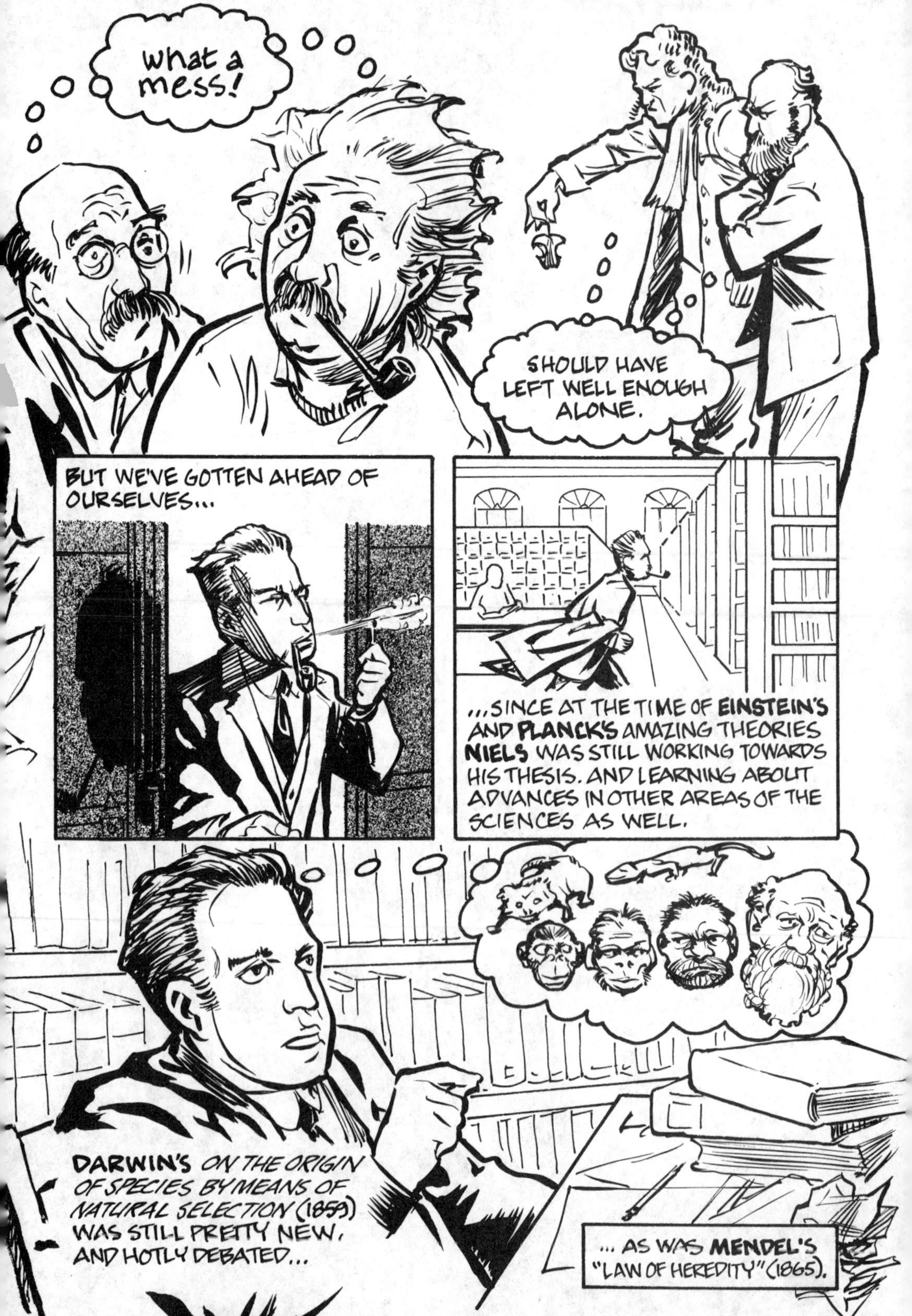

what a mess!
SHOULD HAVE LEFT WELL ENOUGH ALONE.
BUT WE'VE GOTTEN AHEAD OF OURSELVES...
...SINCE AT THE TIME OF **EINSTEIN'S** AND **PLANCK'S** AMAZING THEORIES **NIELS** WAS STILL WORKING TOWARDS HIS THESIS. AND LEARNING ABOUT ADVANCES IN OTHER AREAS OF THE SCIENCES AS WELL.
DARWIN'S *ON THE ORIGIN OF SPECIES BY MEANS OF NATURAL SELECTION* (1859) WAS STILL PRETTY NEW, AND HOTLY DEBATED...
... AS WAS **MENDEL'S** "LAW OF HEREDITY" (1865).

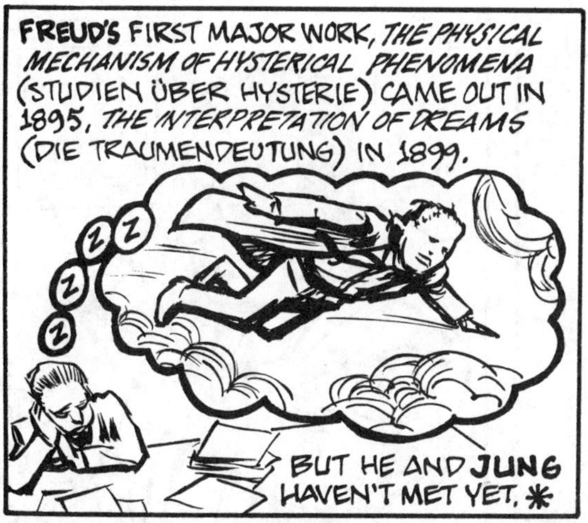
FREUD'S FIRST MAJOR WORK, THE PHYSICAL MECHANISM OF HYSTERICAL PHENOMENA (STUDIEN ÜBER HYSTERIE) CAME OUT IN 1895, THE INTERPRETATION OF DREAMS (DIE TRAUMENDEUTUNG) IN 1899.
Z Z Z Z
BUT HE AND JUNG HAVEN'T MET YET. *

* THIS SEEMS A GOOD PLACE TO MENTION JENNY, NIELS' OLDER SISTER. SHE WON'T APPEAR AGAIN, SINCE LITTLE IS WRITTEN ABOUT HER. SHE SUFFERED FROM MENTAL ILLNESS THROUGH MUCH OF HER LIFE, AND THE CAUSE OF HER DEATH (IN 1933) WAS LISTED AS MANIC DEPRESSION, IN THE MANIC PHASE.

HARALD'S EULOGY NOTED HOW THEIR MOTHER'S DEATH THREE YEARS BEFORE HAD PUSHED HER OVER THE BRINK, AND YET HER BROTHERS' THOUGHT, "SHE WAS STRONG IN SPITE OF HER WEAKNESS, AND HEALTHY IN SPITE OF HER ILLNESS."

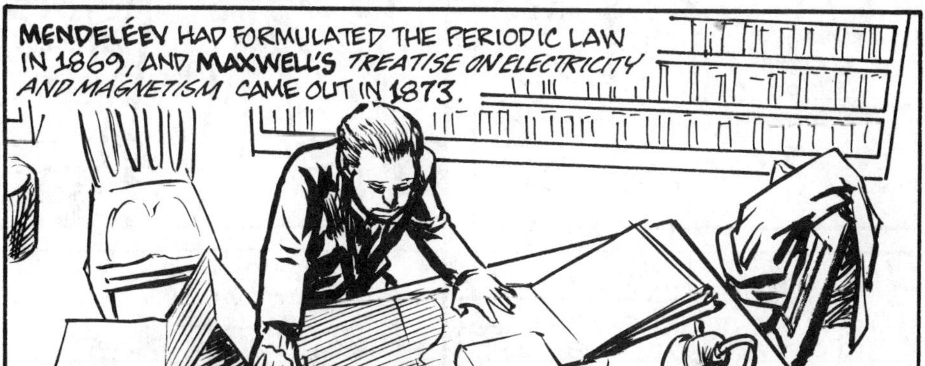
MENDELÉEV HAD FORMULATED THE PERIODIC LAW IN 1869, AND MAXWELL'S TREATISE ON ELECTRICITY AND MAGNETISM CAME OUT IN 1873.

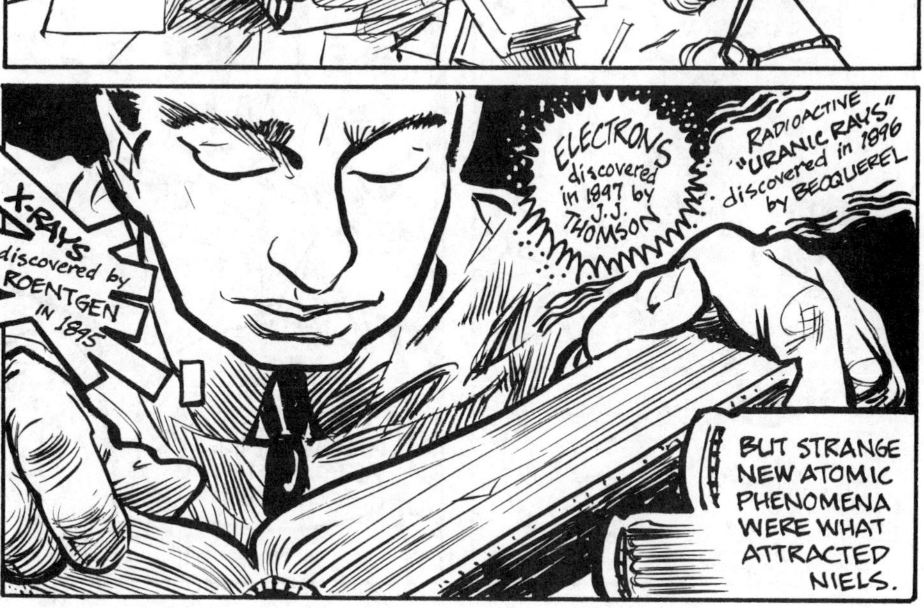
X-RAYS discovered by ROENTGEN in 1895
ELECTRONS discovered in 1897 by J.J. THOMSON
RADIOACTIVE "URANIC RAYS" discovered in 1896 by BECQUEREL
BUT STRANGE NEW ATOMIC PHENOMENA WERE WHAT ATTRACTED NIELS.

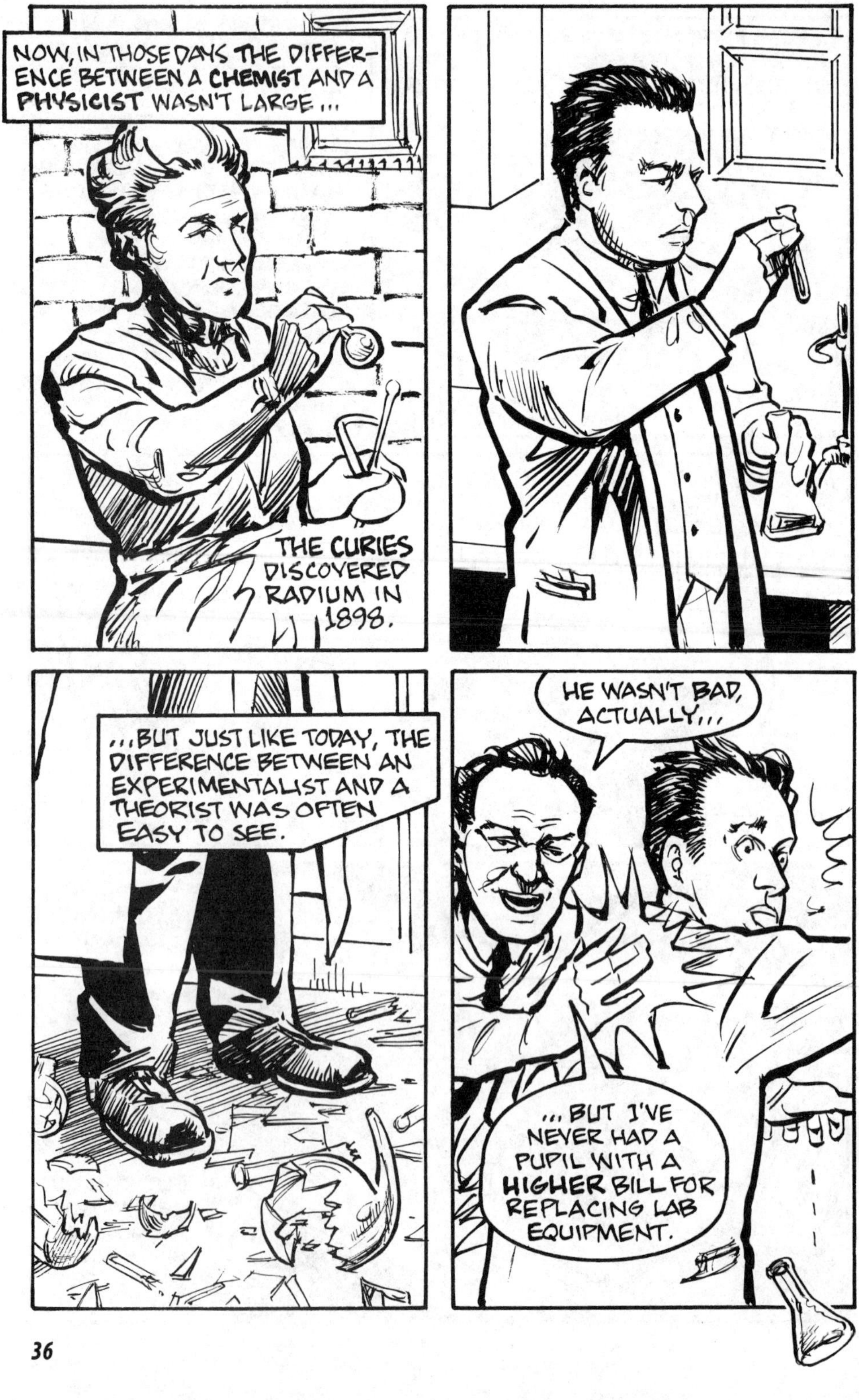
NOW, IN THOSE DAYS THE DIFFERENCE BETWEEN A CHEMIST AND A PHYSICIST WASN'T LARGE...
THE CURIES DISCOVERED RADIUM IN 1898.
...BUT JUST LIKE TODAY, THE DIFFERENCE BETWEEN AN EXPERIMENTALIST AND A THEORIST WAS OFTEN EASY TO SEE.
HE WASN'T BAD, ACTUALLY...
...BUT I'VE NEVER HAD A PUPIL WITH A HIGHER BILL FOR REPLACING LAB EQUIPMENT.

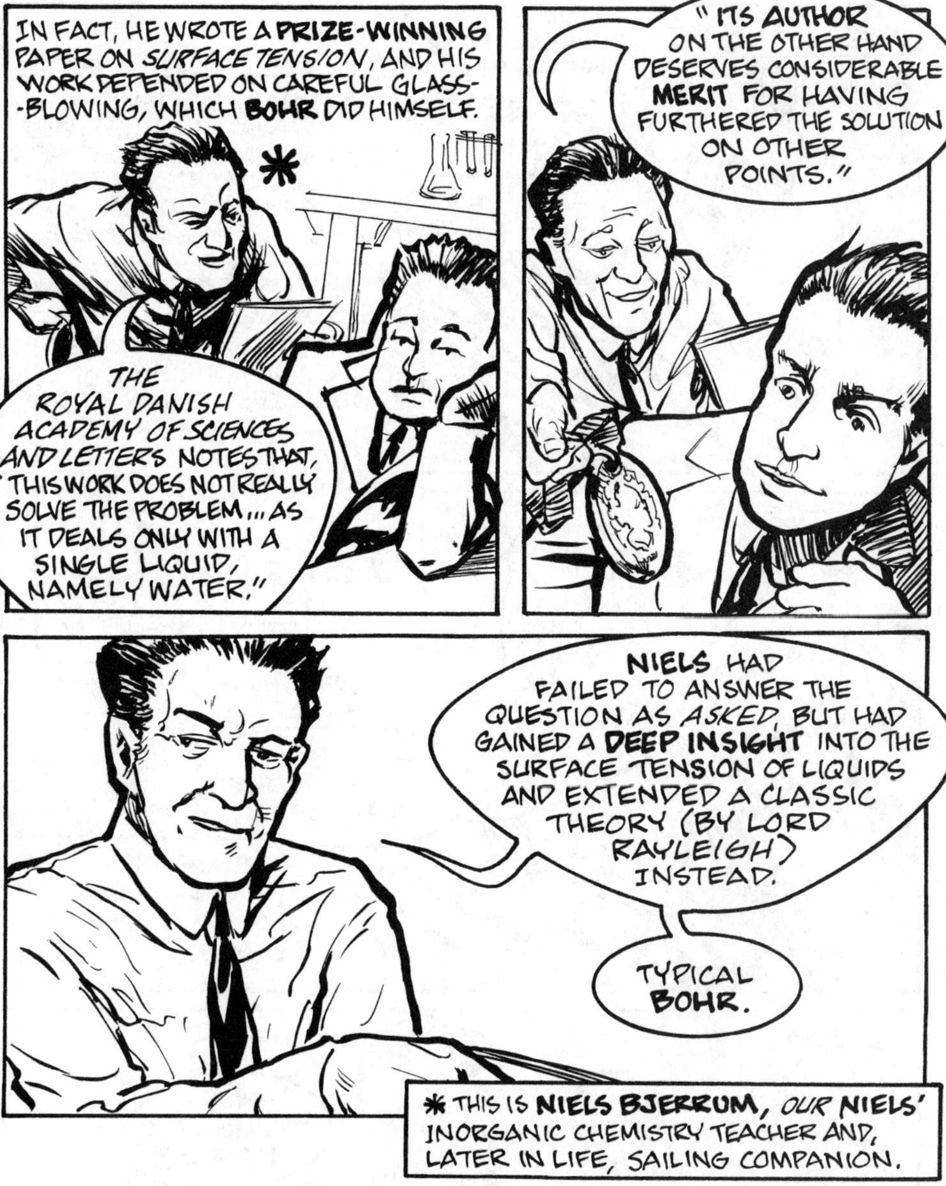
IN FACT, HE WROTE A PRIZE-WINNING PAPER ON SURFACE TENSION, AND HIS WORK DEPENDED ON CAREFUL GLASS-BLOWING, WHICH BOHR DID HIMSELF.
*
THE ROYAL DANISH ACADEMY OF SCIENCES AND LETTERS NOTES THAT, "THIS WORK DOES NOT REALLY SOLVE THE PROBLEM... AS IT DEALS ONLY WITH A SINGLE LIQUID, NAMELY WATER."
"ITS AUTHOR ON THE OTHER HAND DESERVES CONSIDERABLE MERIT FOR HAVING FURTHERED THE SOLUTION ON OTHER POINTS."
NIELS HAD FAILED TO ANSWER THE QUESTION AS ASKED, BUT HAD GAINED A DEEP INSIGHT INTO THE SURFACE TENSION OF LIQUIDS AND EXTENDED A CLASSIC THEORY (BY LORD RAYLEIGH) INSTEAD.
TYPICAL BOHR.
* THIS IS NIELS BJERRUM, OUR NIELS' INORGANIC CHEMISTRY TEACHER AND, LATER IN LIFE, SAILING COMPANION.

SO, AS **DARWIN** EXPLAINED THE DIVERSITY OF LIFE, THE PHYSICISTS HAD BEGUN TO DISCOVER A DIVERSITY OF **PARTICLES AND RAYS**. AND AS **FREUD** DUG INTO THE MIND, PHYSICISTS WERE DIGGING INTO THE ATOM.

IN ADDITION TO X-RAYS AND ELECTRONS, AND THAT WEIRD **RADIUM** STUFF THE **CURIES** WERE WORKING WITH, NEW ZEALANDER **ERNEST RUTHERFORD** (WHO HAD WORKED WITH **J.J. THOMSON** FOR A WHILE) HAD DISCOVERED BOTH ALPHA PARTICLES AND BETA RAYS IN 1899.

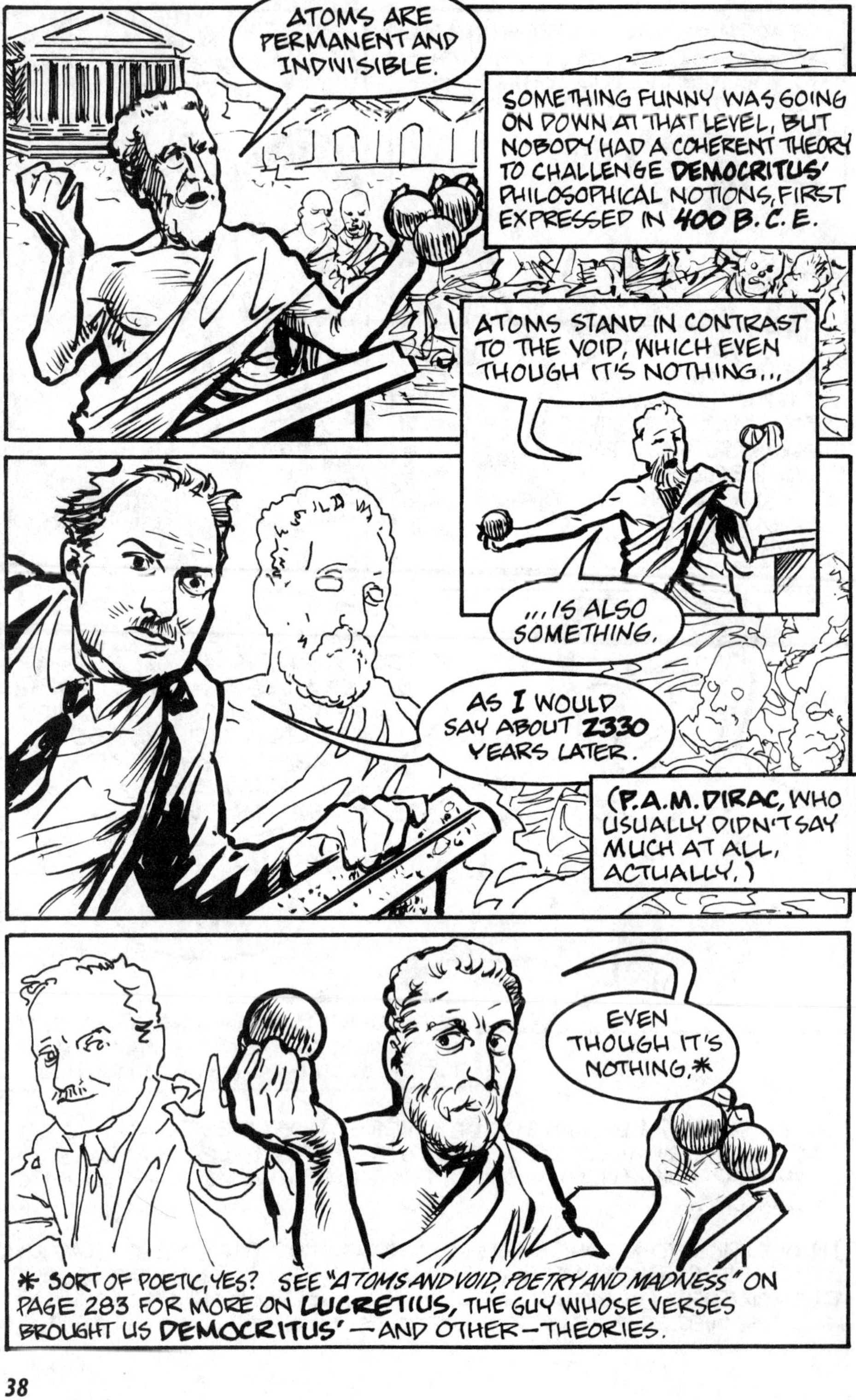
ATOMS ARE PERMANENT AND INDIVISIBLE.
SOMETHING FUNNY WAS GOING ON DOWN AT THAT LEVEL, BUT NOBODY HAD A COHERENT THEORY TO CHALLENGE DEMOCRITUS' PHILOSOPHICAL NOTIONS, FIRST EXPRESSED IN 400 B.C.E.
ATOMS STAND IN CONTRAST TO THE VOID, WHICH EVEN THOUGH IT'S NOTHING...
...IS ALSO SOMETHING.
AS I WOULD SAY ABOUT 2330 YEARS LATER.
(P.A.M. DIRAC, WHO USUALLY DIDN'T SAY MUCH AT ALL, ACTUALLY.)
EVEN THOUGH IT'S NOTHING.*
* SORT OF POETIC, YES? SEE "ATOMS AND VOID, POETRY AND MADNESS" ON PAGE 283 FOR MORE ON LUCRETIUS, THE GUY WHOSE VERSES BROUGHT US DEMOCRITUS' — AND OTHER — THEORIES.

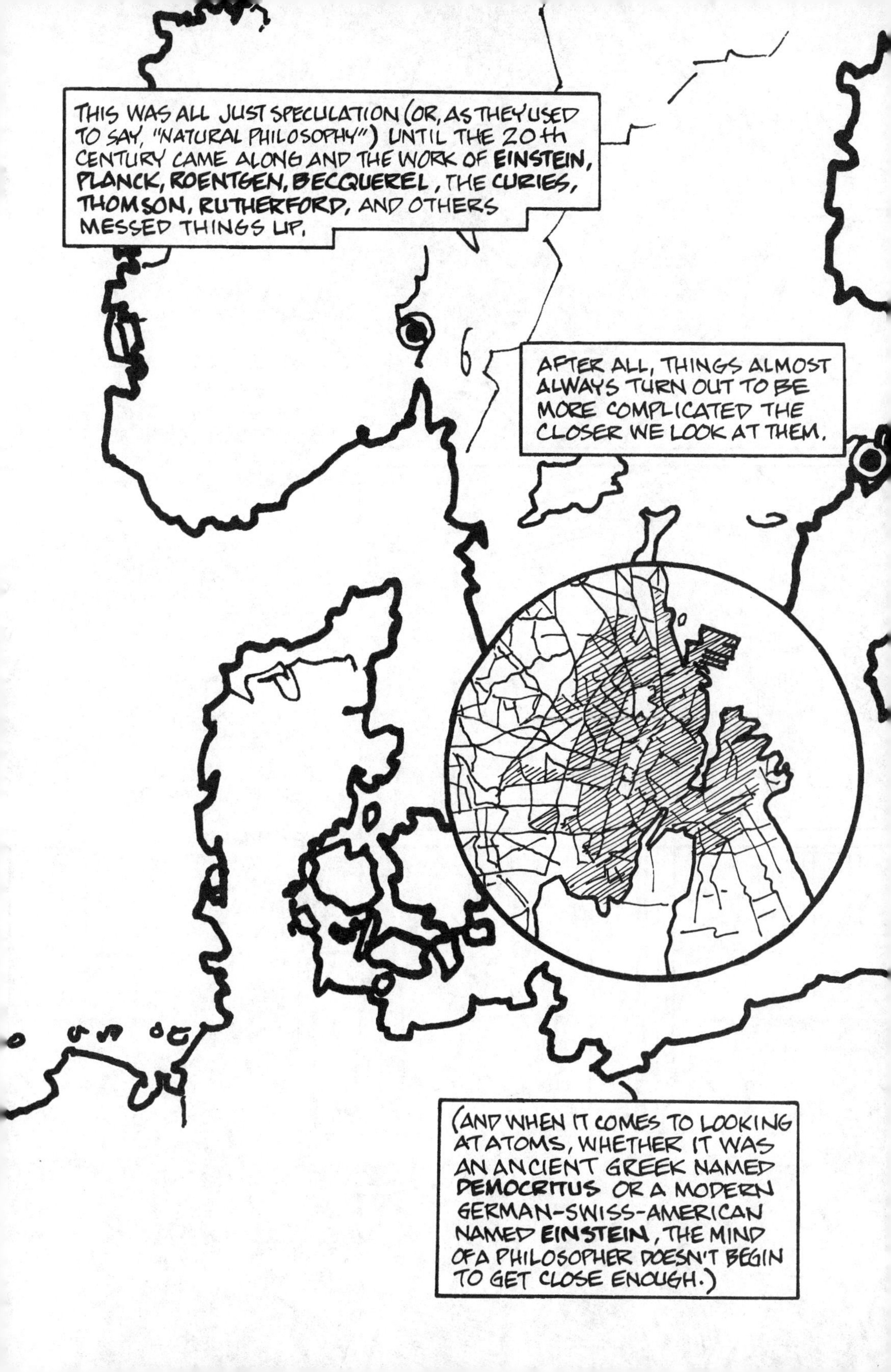
THIS WAS ALL JUST SPECULATION (OR, AS THEY USED TO SAY, "NATURAL PHILOSOPHY") UNTIL THE 20th CENTURY CAME ALONG AND THE WORK OF **EINSTEIN, PLANCK, ROENTGEN, BECQUEREL**, THE **CURIES, THOMSON, RUTHERFORD**, AND OTHERS MESSED THINGS UP.
AFTER ALL, THINGS ALMOST ALWAYS TURN OUT TO BE MORE COMPLICATED THE CLOSER WE LOOK AT THEM.
(AND WHEN IT COMES TO LOOKING AT ATOMS, WHETHER IT WAS AN ANCIENT GREEK NAMED **DEMOCRITUS** OR A MODERN GERMAN-SWISS-AMERICAN NAMED **EINSTEIN**, THE MIND OF A PHILOSOPHER DOESN'T BEGIN TO GET CLOSE ENOUGH.)

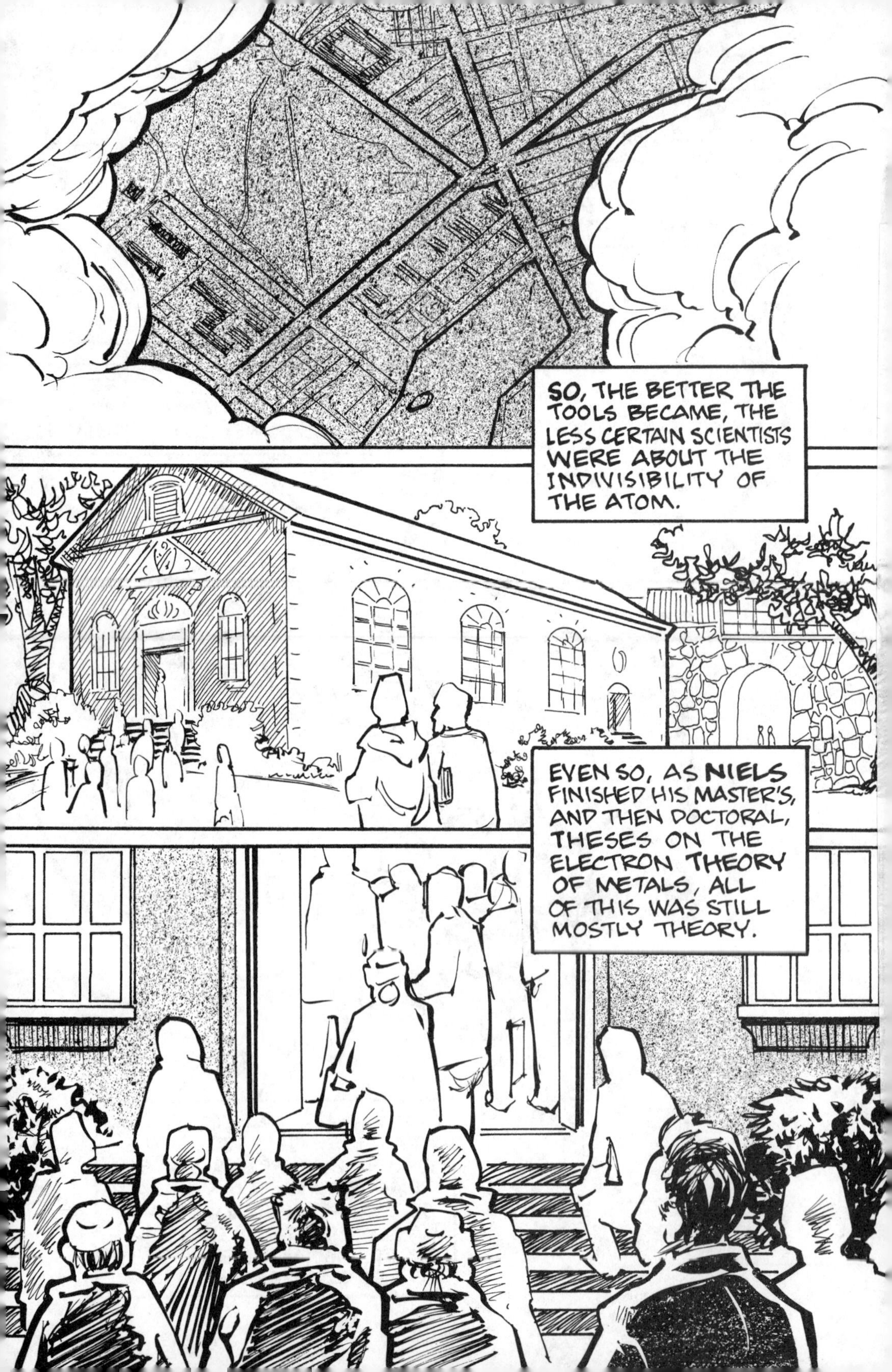
SO, THE BETTER THE TOOLS BECAME, THE LESS CERTAIN SCIENTISTS WERE ABOUT THE INDIVISIBILITY OF THE ATOM.
EVEN SO, AS NIELS FINISHED HIS MASTER'S, AND THEN DOCTORAL, THESES ON THE ELECTRON THEORY OF METALS, ALL OF THIS WAS STILL MOSTLY THEORY.

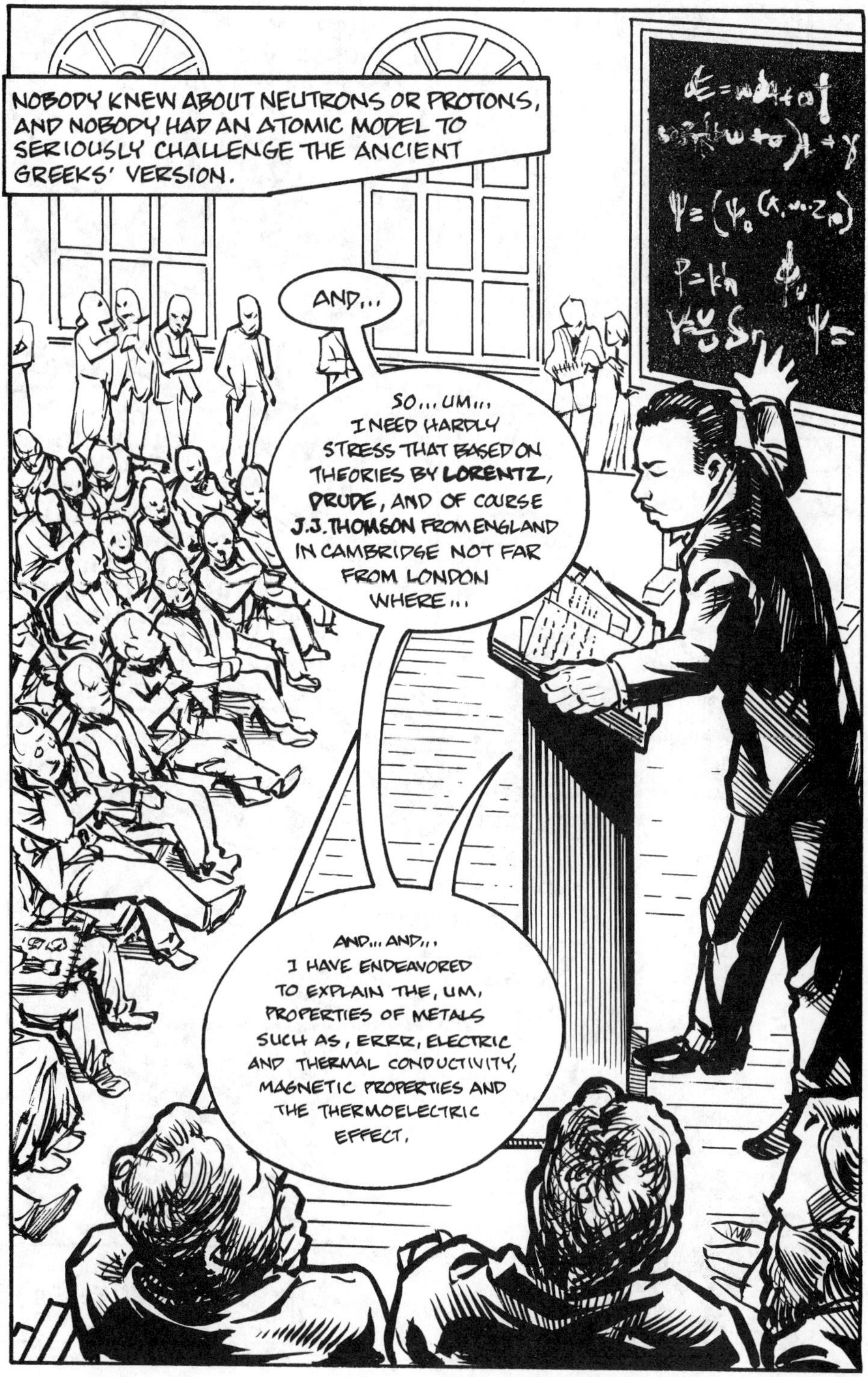
NOBODY KNEW ABOUT NEUTRONS OR PROTONS, AND NOBODY HAD AN ATOMIC MODEL TO SERIOUSLY CHALLENGE THE ANCIENT GREEKS' VERSION.
AND...
SO... UM... I NEED HARDLY STRESS THAT BASED ON THEORIES BY **LORENTZ**, **DRUDE**, AND OF COURSE **J.J. THOMSON** FROM ENGLAND IN CAMBRIDGE NOT FAR FROM LONDON WHERE...
AND... AND... I HAVE ENDEAVORED TO EXPLAIN THE, UM, PROPERTIES OF METALS SUCH AS, ERRR, ELECTRIC AND THERMAL CONDUCTIVITY, MAGNETIC PROPERTIES AND THE THERMOELECTRIC EFFECT.

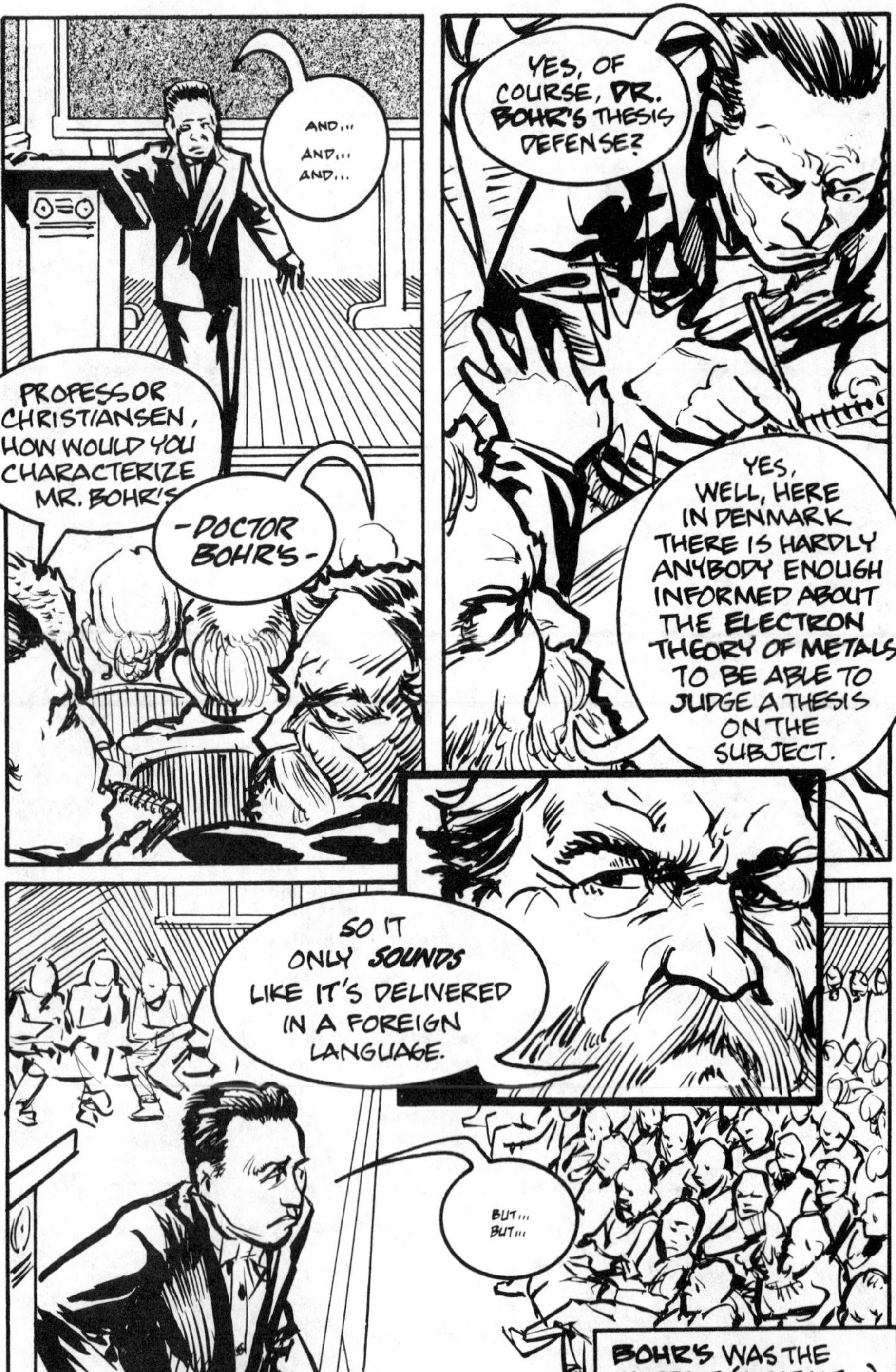
AND... AND... AND...
YES, OF COURSE, DR. BOHR'S THESIS DEFENSE?
PROFESSOR CHRISTIANSEN, HOW WOULD YOU CHARACTERIZE MR. BOHR'S
-DOCTOR BOHR'S-
YES, WELL, HERE IN DENMARK THERE IS HARDLY ANYBODY ENOUGH INFORMED ABOUT THE ELECTRON THEORY OF METALS TO BE ABLE TO JUDGE A THESIS ON THE SUBJECT.
SO IT ONLY SOUNDS LIKE IT'S DELIVERED IN A FOREIGN LANGUAGE.
BUT... BUT...
BOHR'S WAS THE SHORTEST (SUCCESSFUL) DEFENSE ON RECORD.

Chapter 3

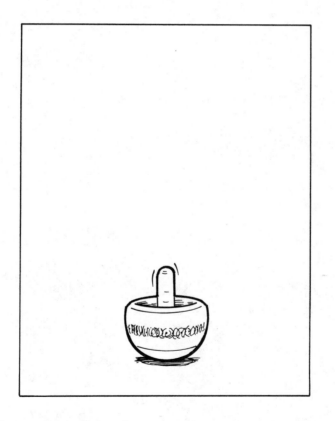

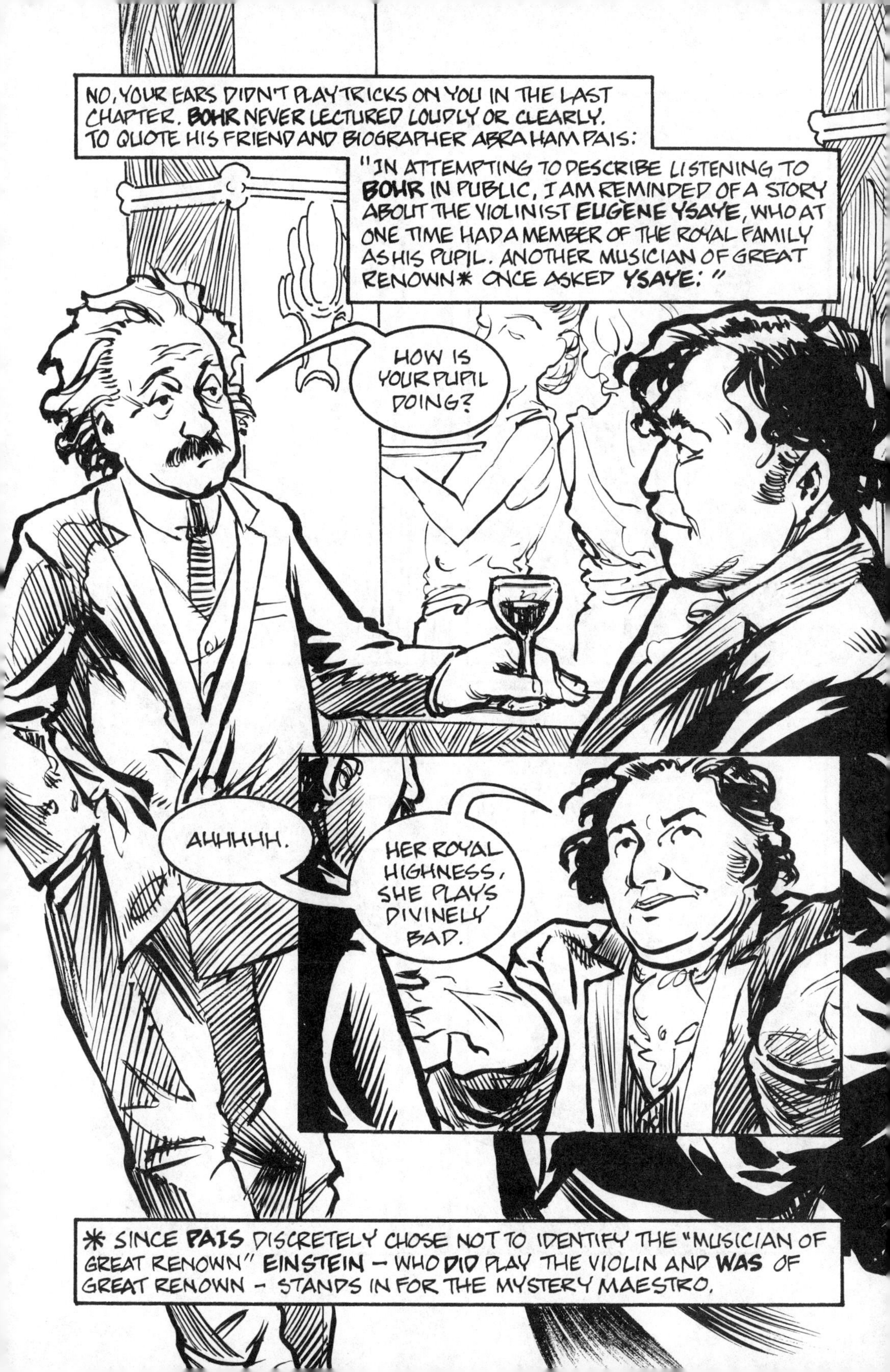
NO, YOUR EARS DIDN'T PLAY TRICKS ON YOU IN THE LAST CHAPTER. BOHR NEVER LECTURED LOUDLY OR CLEARLY. TO QUOTE HIS FRIEND AND BIOGRAPHER ABRAHAM PAIS:
"IN ATTEMPTING TO DESCRIBE LISTENING TO BOHR IN PUBLIC, I AM REMINDED OF A STORY ABOUT THE VIOLINIST EUGÈNE YSAYE, WHO AT ONE TIME HAD A MEMBER OF THE ROYAL FAMILY AS HIS PUPIL. ANOTHER MUSICIAN OF GREAT RENOWN* ONCE ASKED YSAYE:"
HOW IS YOUR PUPIL DOING?
AHHHHH.
HER ROYAL HIGHNESS, SHE PLAYS DIVINELY BAD.
* SINCE PAIS DISCRETELY CHOSE NOT TO IDENTIFY THE "MUSICIAN OF GREAT RENOWN" EINSTEIN – WHO DID PLAY THE VIOLIN AND WAS OF GREAT RENOWN – STANDS IN FOR THE MYSTERY MAESTRO.

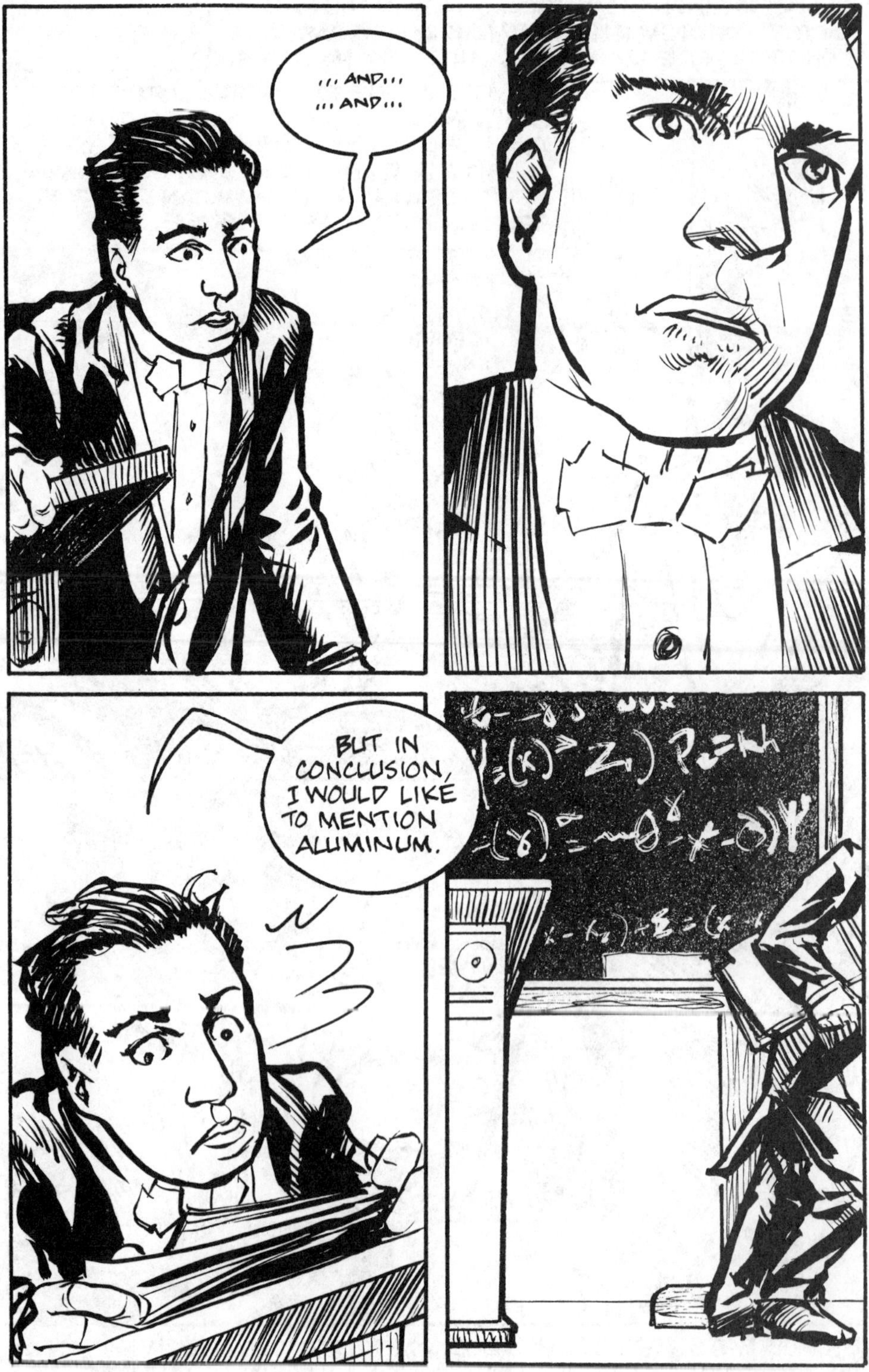
...AND...
...AND...
BUT IN CONCLUSION, I WOULD LIKE TO MENTION ALUMINUM.

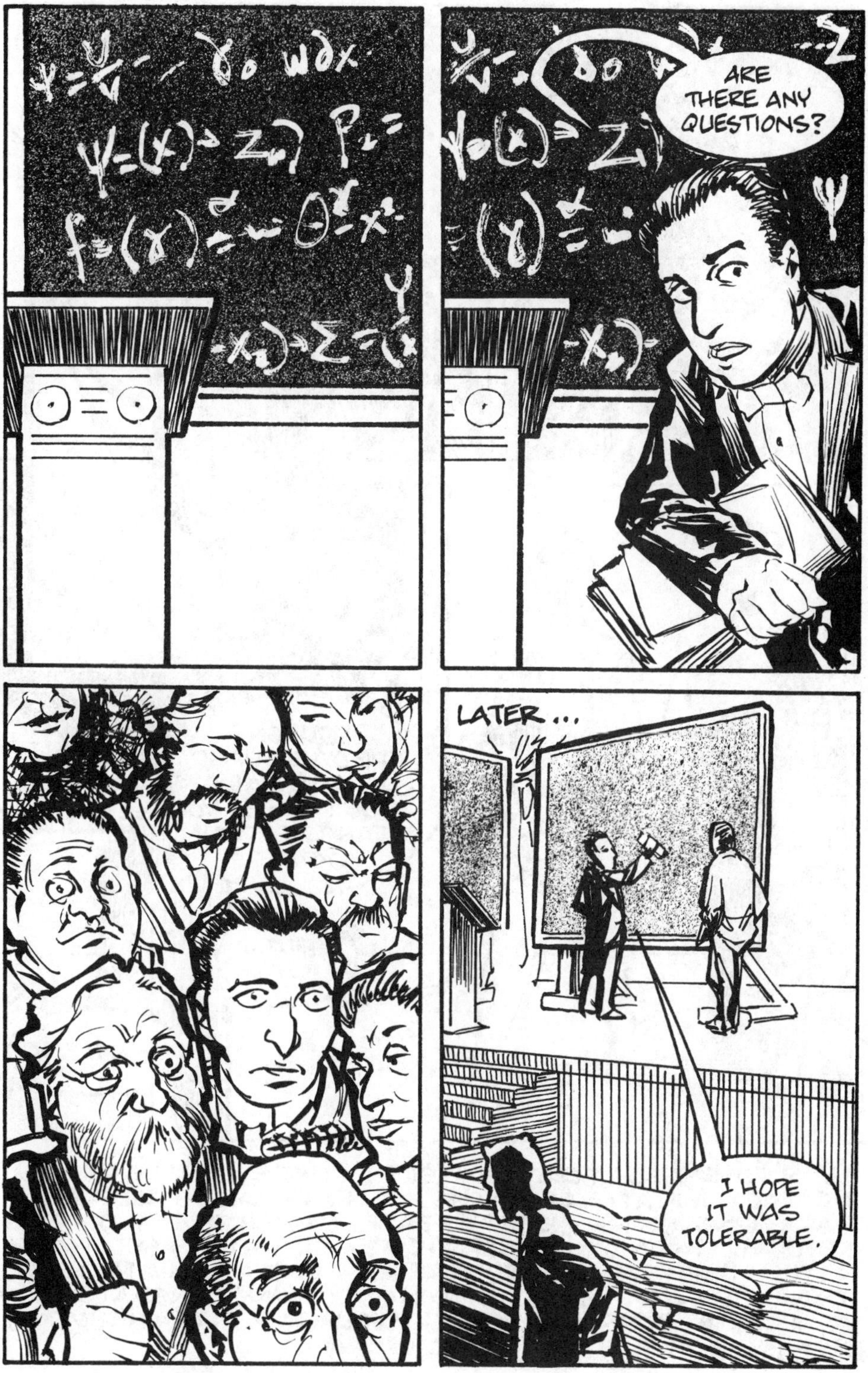
ARE THERE ANY QUESTIONS?
LATER...
I HOPE IT WAS TOLERABLE.

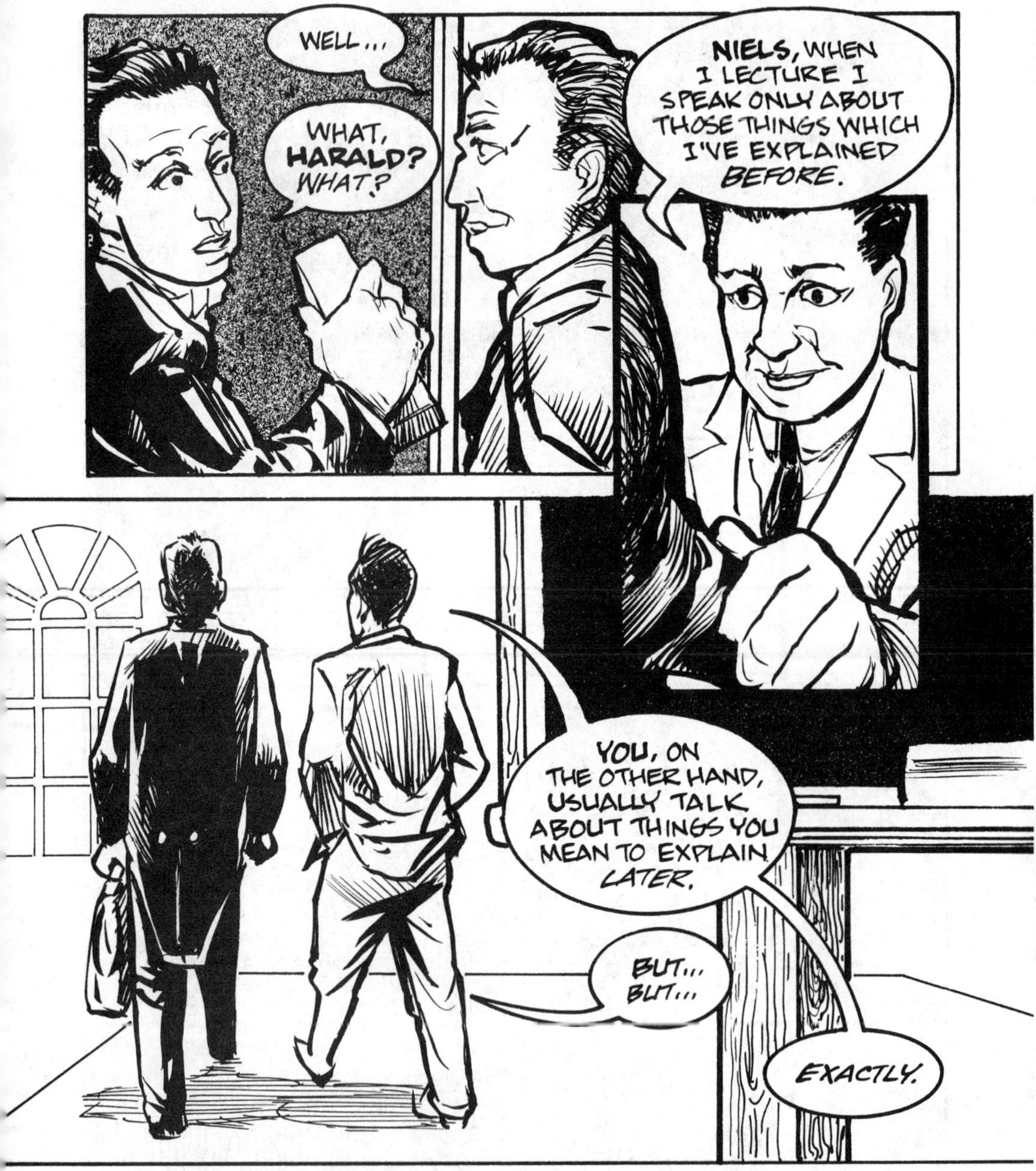
WELL...
WHAT, HARALD? WHAT?
NIELS, WHEN I LECTURE I SPEAK ONLY ABOUT THOSE THINGS WHICH I'VE EXPLAINED BEFORE.
YOU, ON THE OTHER HAND, USUALLY TALK ABOUT THINGS YOU MEAN TO EXPLAIN LATER.
BUT... BUT...
EXACTLY.

LÉON ROSENFELD RELATES THIS STORY, HOWEVER: WHILE SITTING NEXT TO **BOHR** AT CELEBRATIONS HONORING **JAMES CLERK MAXWELL** IN CAMBRIDGE, ONE OF THE SPEAKERS COMMENTED ON **MAXWELL'S** REPUTATION AS A POOR LECTURER. THE SPEAKER THEN TEASED **BOHR** A LITTLE ("SO PERHAPS WITH OUR FRIEND **BOHR**: HE MIGHT WANT TO INSTRUCT US ABOUT THE CORRELATION OF TOO MANY THINGS AT ONCE.") AT WHICH POINT **BOHR** WHISPERED TO **ROSENFELD**, IN ASTONISHMENT, "IMAGINE, HE THINKS ***I'M*** A POOR LECTURER!"

THE PROBLEM WASN'T **BOHR'S** GOAL OF NEVER SPEAKING MORE CLEARLY THAN HE THOUGHT, SINCE HE *THOUGHT* VERY CLEARLY. IT WAS MORE THAT HE SOMETIMES FORGOT TO ARTICULATE THE THOUGHTS THAT CAME IN THE PAUSE *BETWEEN* THE "AND...AND..." AND THE "BUT..."

THE **MAXWELL** CELEBRATION IN CAMBRIDGE HAPPENED IN 1931, BY THE WAY, BUT HIS FIRST VISIT TO CAMBRIDGE WAS MUCH EARLIER— SOON AFTER HIS Ph.D., IN FACT WHEN HE ACCEPTED A POST-DOCTORAL POSITION WITH...

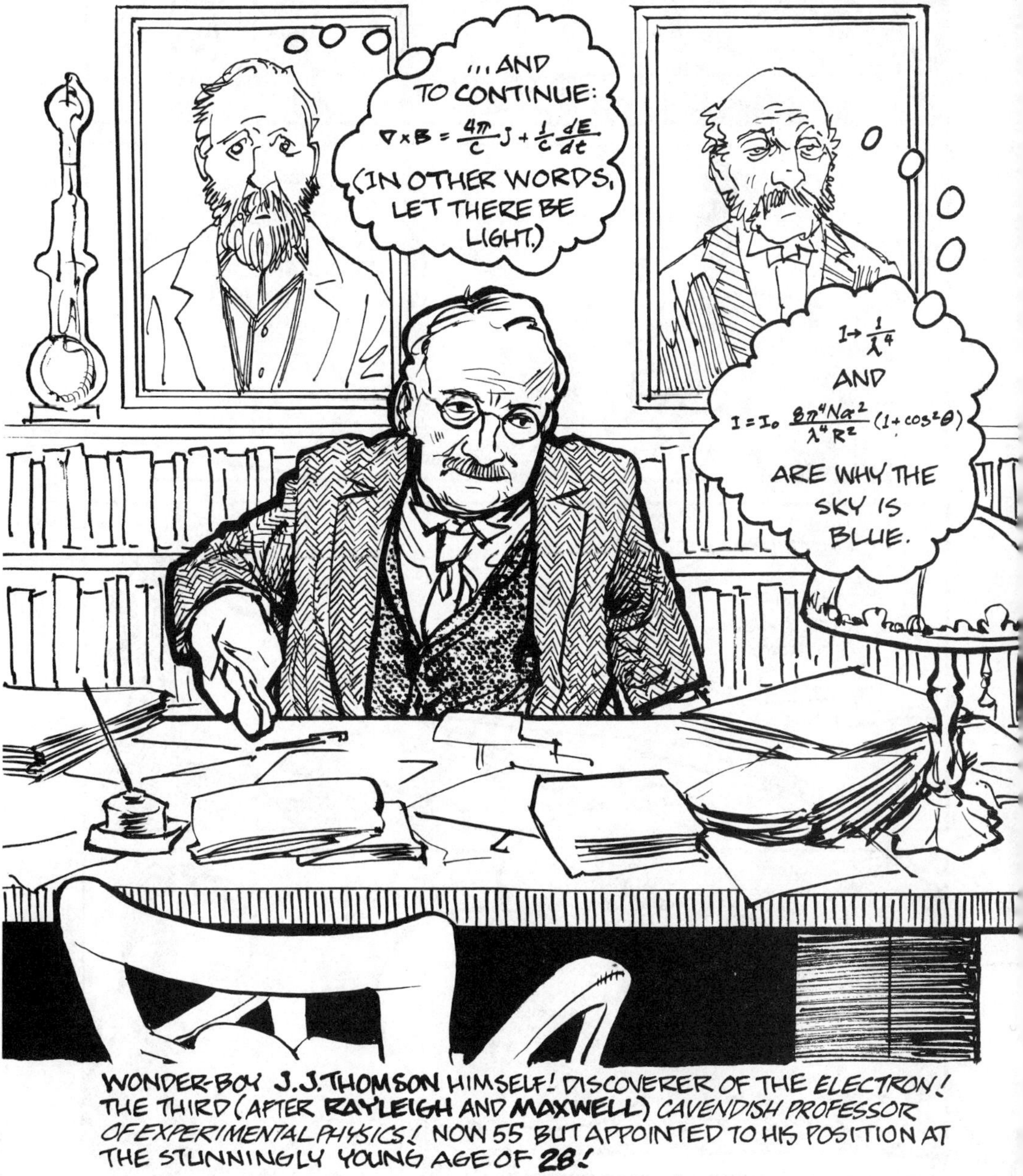

...AND TO CONTINUE:
$\nabla \times B = \frac{4\pi}{c} J + \frac{1}{c}\frac{dE}{dt}$
(IN OTHER WORDS, LET THERE BE LIGHT.)
$I \rightarrow \frac{1}{\lambda^4}$
AND
$I = I_0 \frac{8\pi^4 N\alpha^2}{\lambda^4 R^2}(1+\cos^2\theta)$
ARE WHY THE SKY IS BLUE.

WONDER-BOY **J.J. THOMSON** HIMSELF! DISCOVERER OF THE *ELECTRON*! THE THIRD (AFTER **RAYLEIGH** AND **MAXWELL**) *CAVENDISH PROFESSOR OF EXPERIMENTAL PHYSICS*! NOW 55 BUT APPOINTED TO HIS POSITION AT THE STUNNINGLY YOUNG AGE OF **28**!

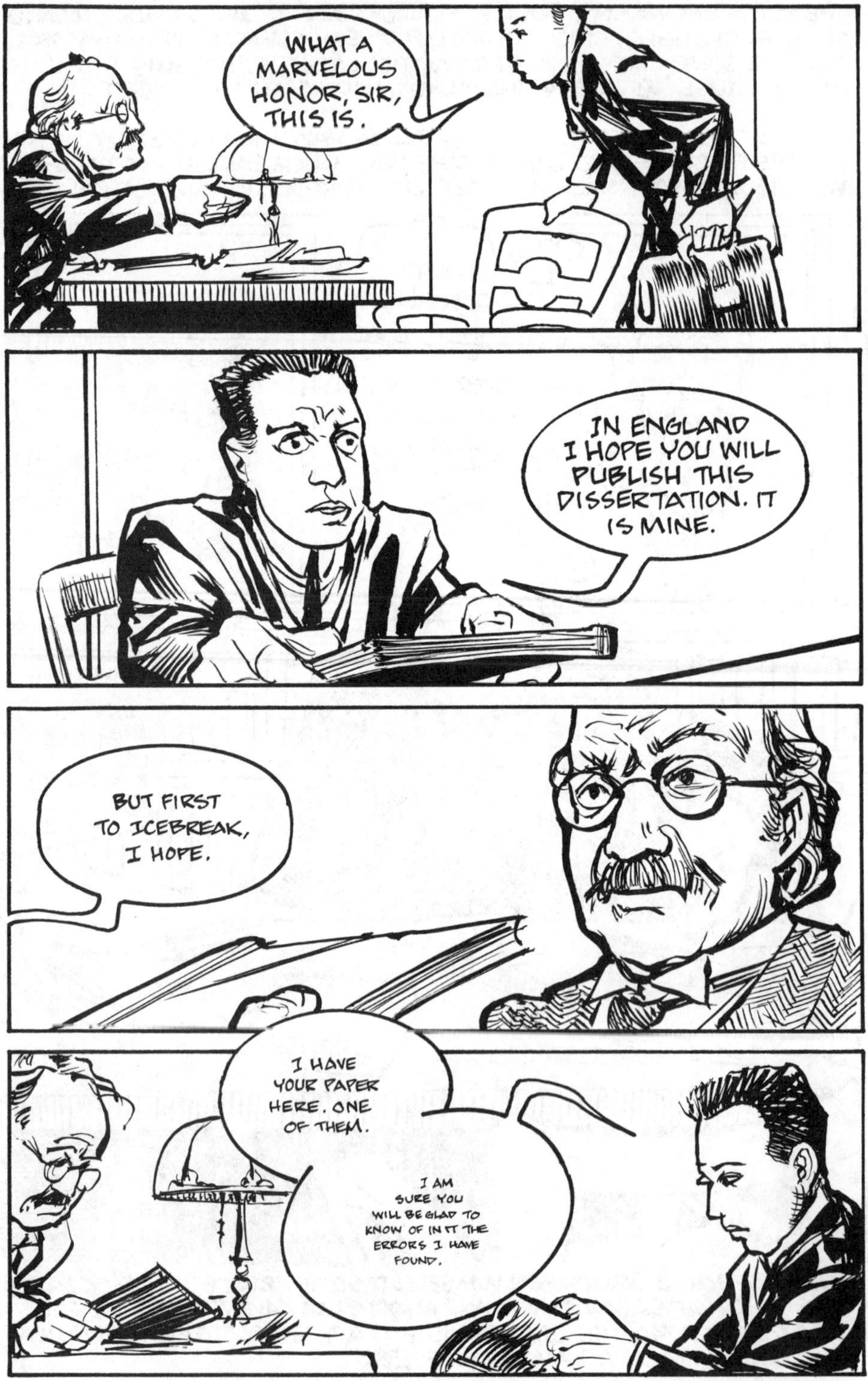
WHAT A MARVELOUS HONOR, SIR, THIS IS.
IN ENGLAND I HOPE YOU WILL PUBLISH THIS DISSERTATION. IT IS MINE.
BUT FIRST TO ICEBREAK, I HOPE.
I HAVE YOUR PAPER HERE. ONE OF THEM.
I AM SURE YOU WILL BE GLAD TO KNOW OF IN IT THE ERRORS I HAVE FOUND.

* BOHR'S ENGLISH IMPROVED QUICKLY.

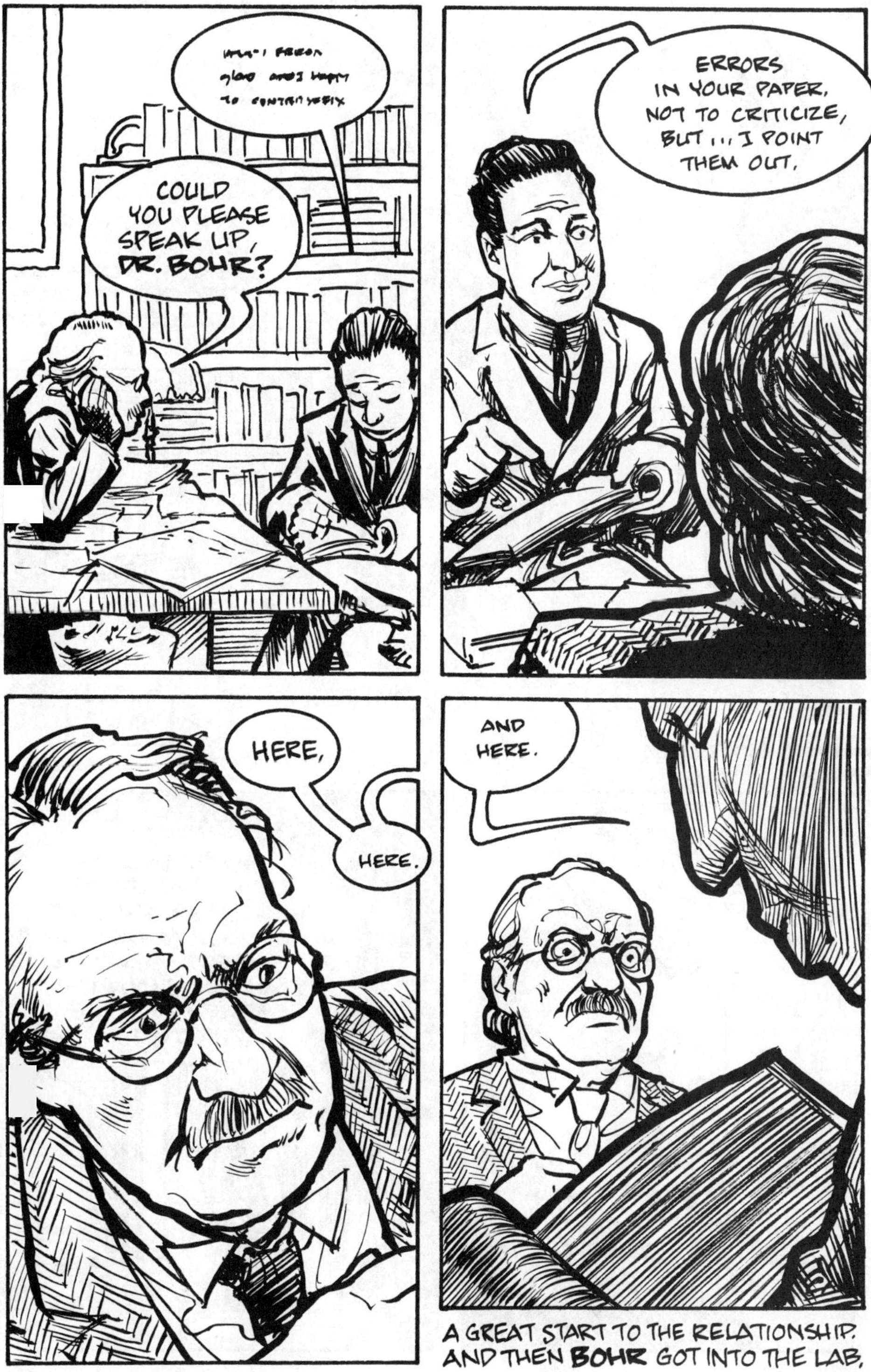
COULD YOU PLEASE SPEAK UP, DR. BOHR?
ERRORS IN YOUR PAPER, NOT TO CRITICIZE, BUT ... I POINT THEM OUT.
HERE,
HERE.
AND HERE.

A GREAT START TO THE RELATIONSHIP. AND THEN **BOHR** GOT INTO THE LAB.

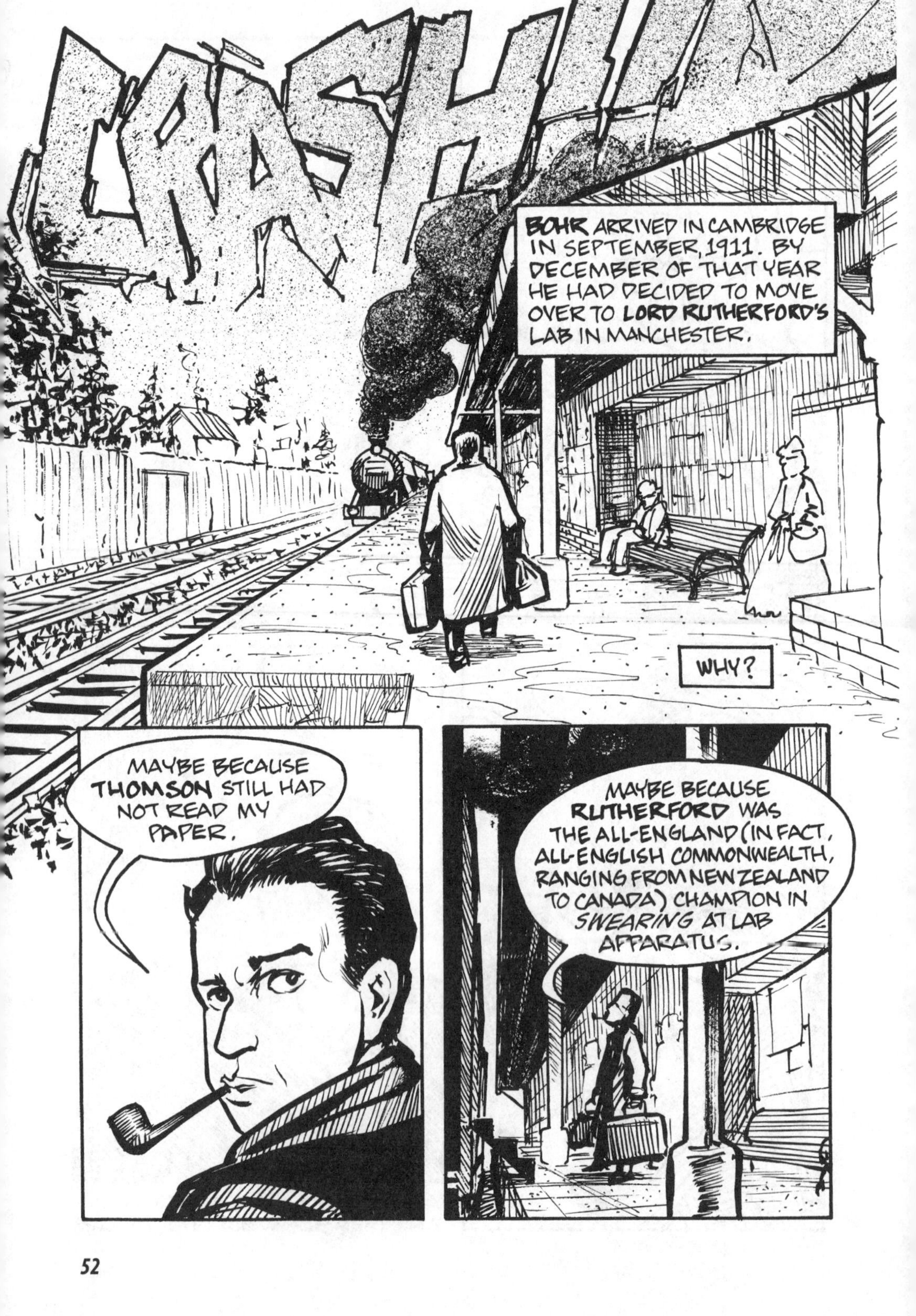
CRASH!!!
BOHR ARRIVED IN CAMBRIDGE IN SEPTEMBER, 1911. BY DECEMBER OF THAT YEAR HE HAD DECIDED TO MOVE OVER TO LORD RUTHERFORD'S LAB IN MANCHESTER.
WHY?
MAYBE BECAUSE THOMSON STILL HAD NOT READ MY PAPER.
MAYBE BECAUSE RUTHERFORD WAS THE ALL-ENGLAND (IN FACT, ALL-ENGLISH COMMONWEALTH, RANGING FROM NEW ZEALAND TO CANADA) CHAMPION IN SWEARING AT LAB APPARATUS.

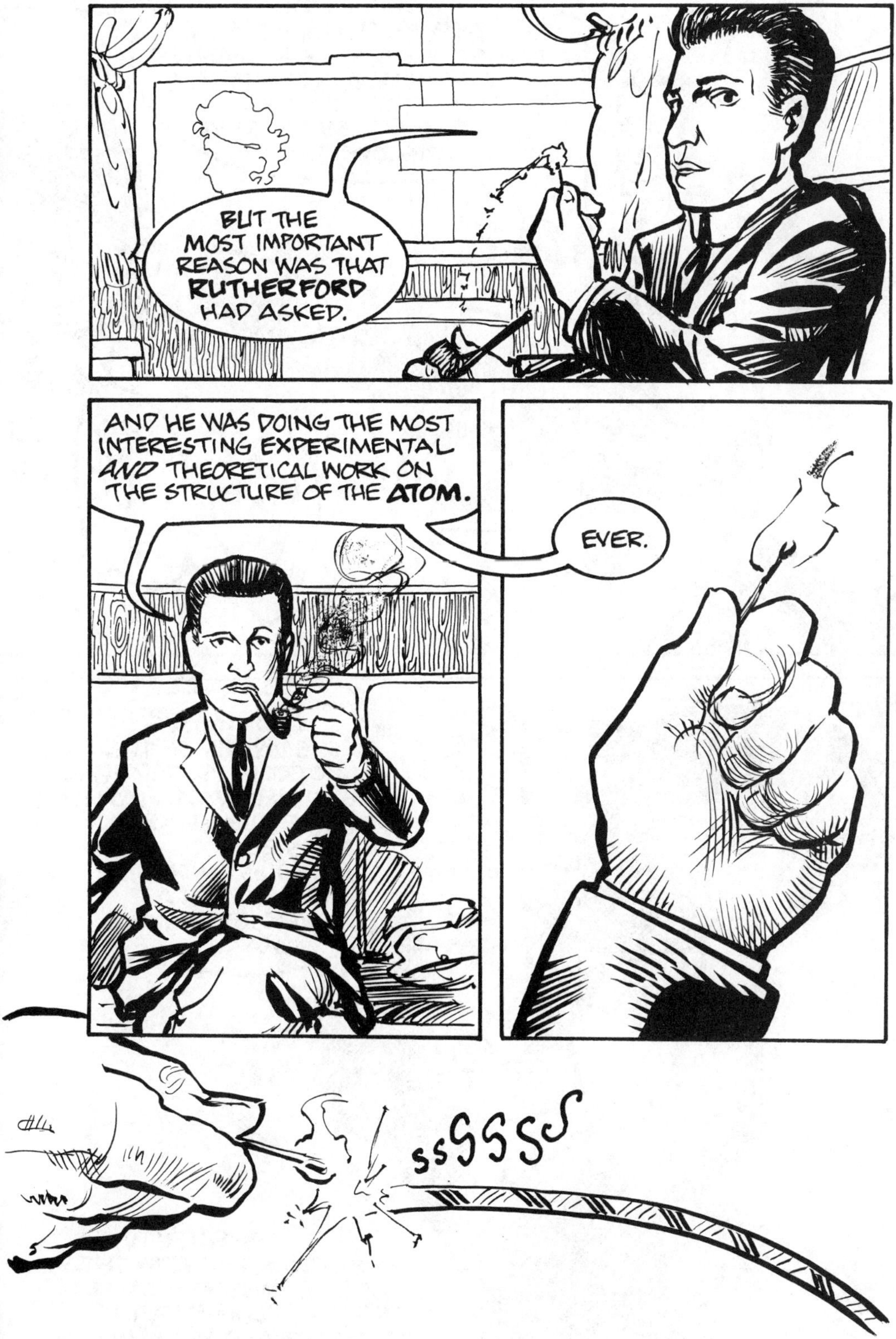

BUT THE MOST IMPORTANT REASON WAS THAT **RUTHERFORD** HAD ASKED.
AND HE WAS DOING THE MOST INTERESTING EXPERIMENTAL *AND* THEORETICAL WORK ON THE STRUCTURE OF THE **ATOM**.
EVER.
ssSSSS

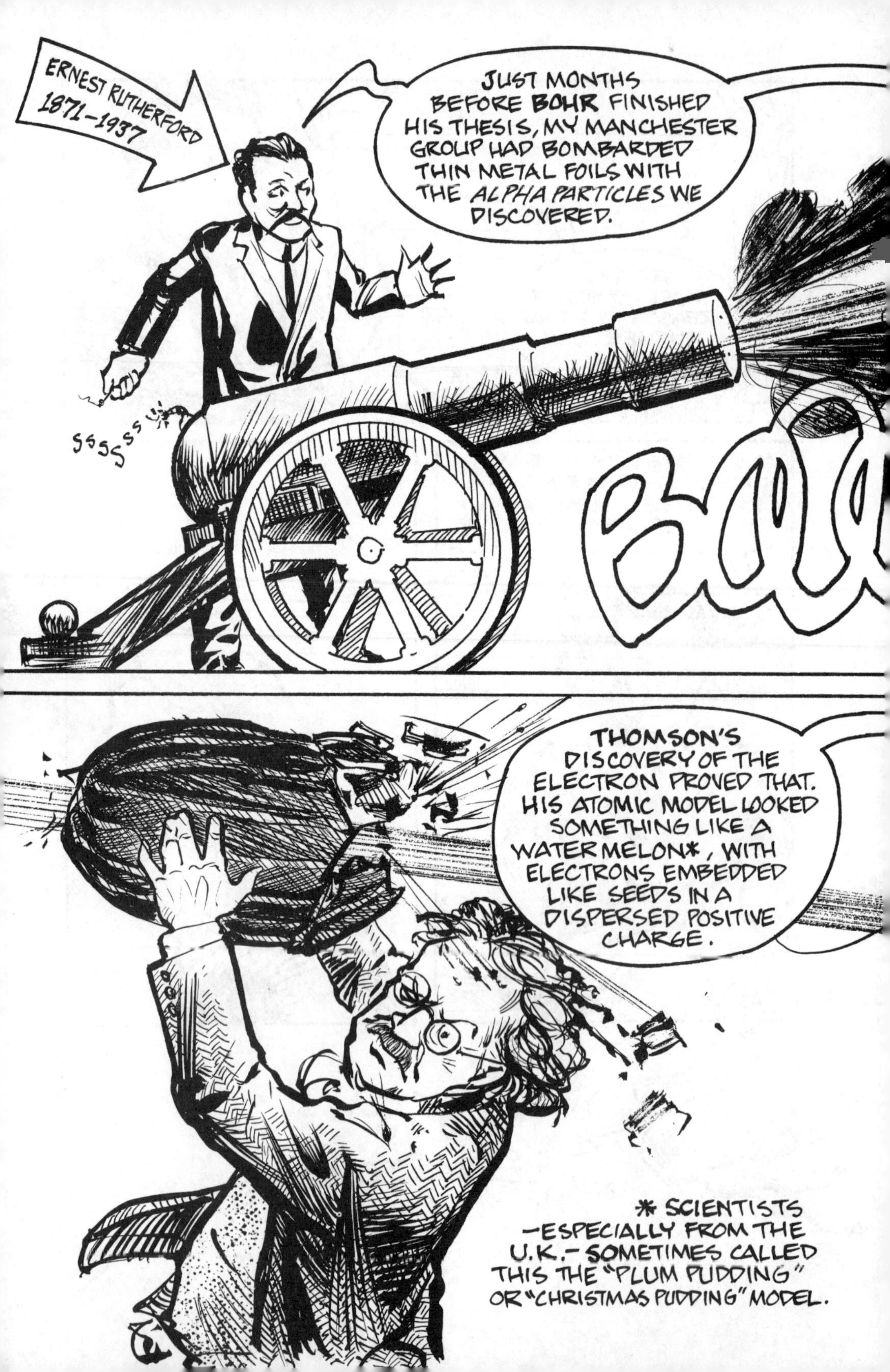
ERNEST RUTHERFORD 1871–1937
JUST MONTHS BEFORE BOHR FINISHED HIS THESIS, MY MANCHESTER GROUP HAD BOMBARDED THIN METAL FOILS WITH THE *ALPHA PARTICLES* WE DISCOVERED.
SSSSSSS
THOMSON'S DISCOVERY OF THE ELECTRON PROVED THAT. HIS ATOMIC MODEL LOOKED SOMETHING LIKE A WATERMELON*, WITH ELECTRONS EMBEDDED LIKE SEEDS IN A DISPERSED POSITIVE CHARGE.
* SCIENTISTS –ESPECIALLY FROM THE U.K.– SOMETIMES CALLED THIS THE "PLUM PUDDING" OR "CHRISTMAS PUDDING" MODEL.

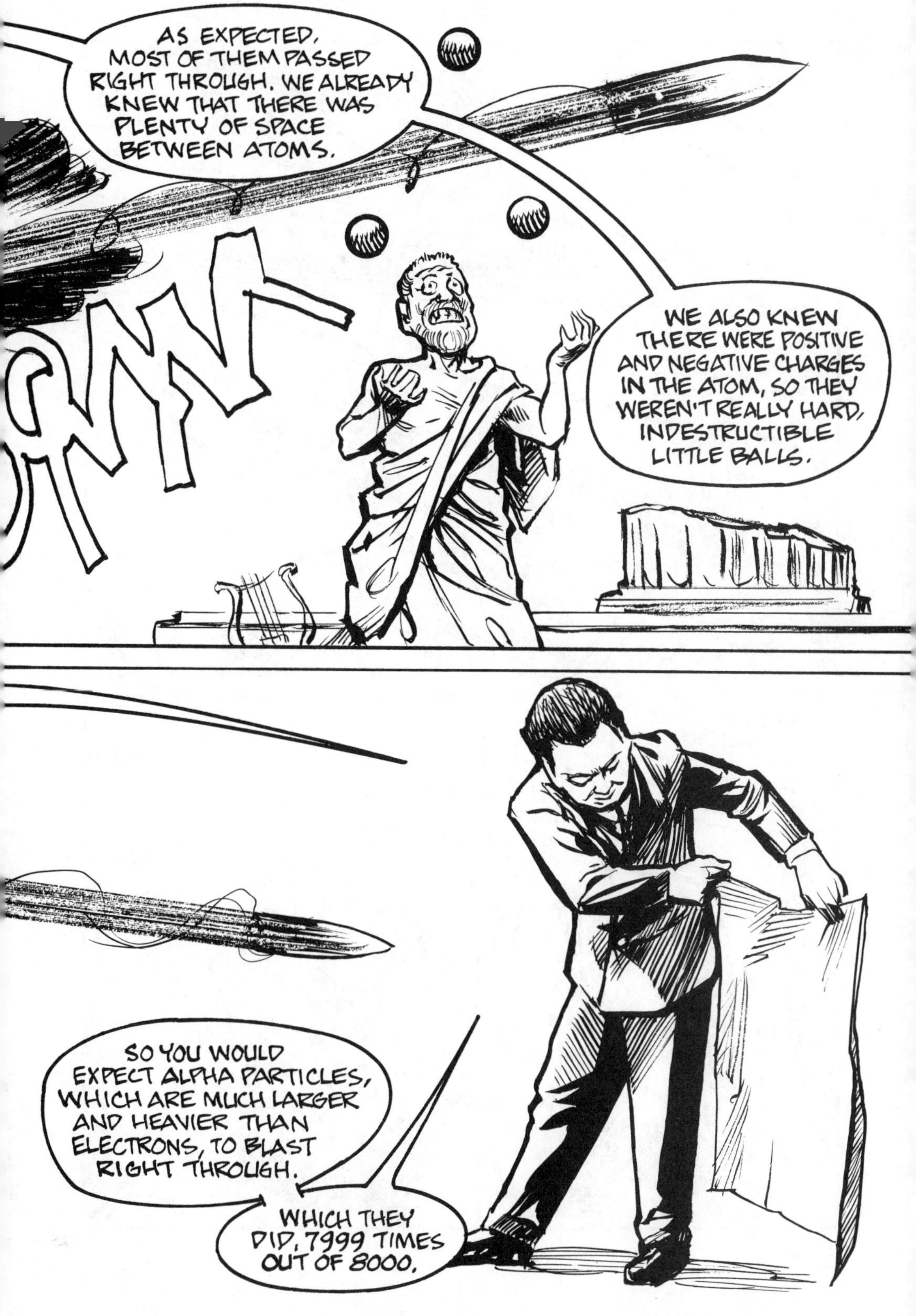
AS EXPECTED, MOST OF THEM PASSED RIGHT THROUGH. WE ALREADY KNEW THAT THERE WAS PLENTY OF SPACE BETWEEN ATOMS.
WE ALSO KNEW THERE WERE POSITIVE AND NEGATIVE CHARGES IN THE ATOM, SO THEY WEREN'T REALLY HARD, INDESTRUCTIBLE LITTLE BALLS.
SO YOU WOULD EXPECT ALPHA PARTICLES, WHICH ARE MUCH LARGER AND HEAVIER THAN ELECTRONS, TO BLAST RIGHT THROUGH.
WHICH THEY DID, 7999 TIMES OUT OF 8000.

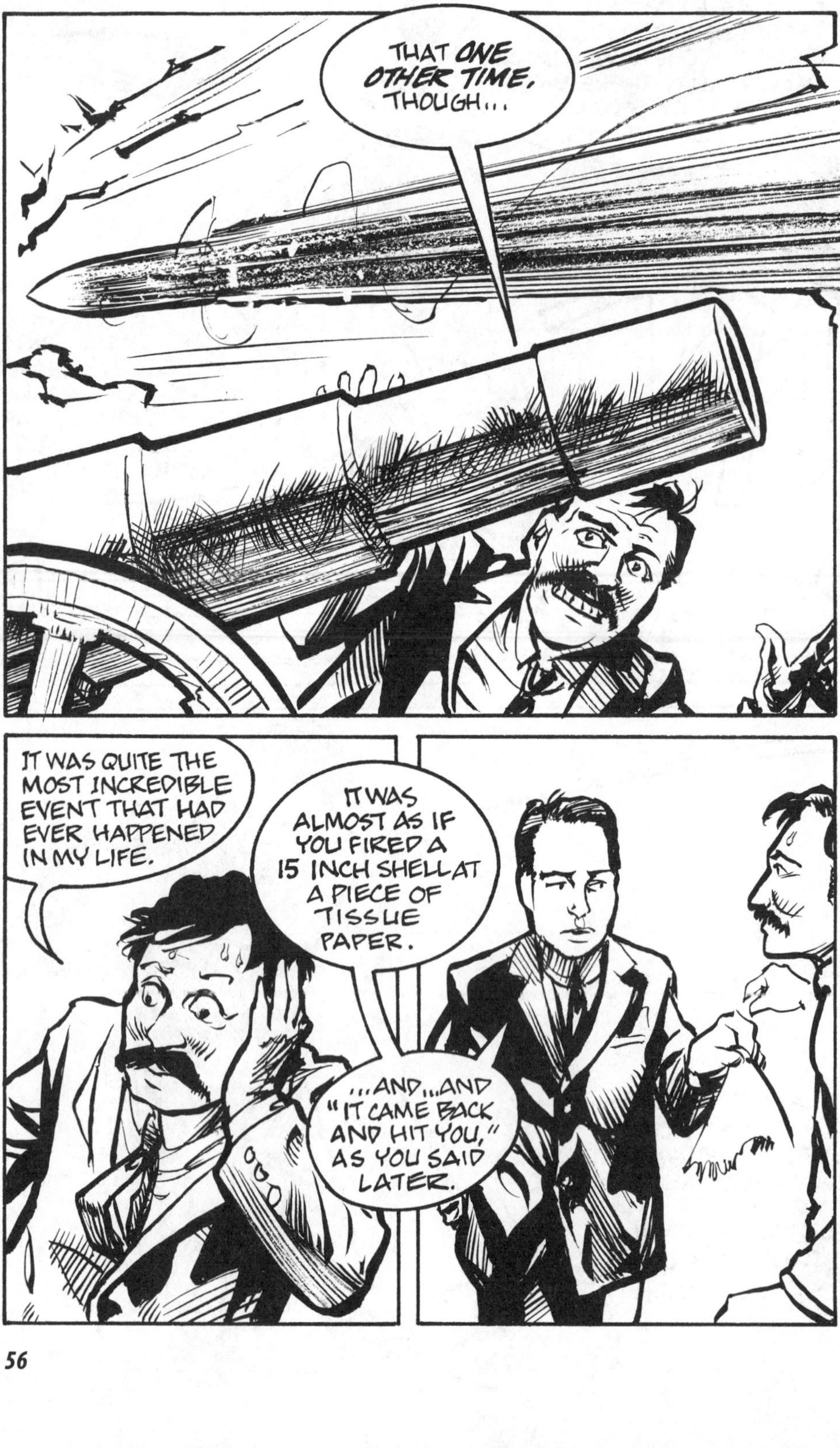
THAT ONE OTHER TIME, THOUGH...
IT WAS QUITE THE MOST INCREDIBLE EVENT THAT HAD EVER HAPPENED IN MY LIFE.
IT WAS ALMOST AS IF YOU FIRED A 15 INCH SHELL AT A PIECE OF TISSUE PAPER.
...AND...AND "IT CAME BACK AND HIT YOU," AS YOU SAID LATER.

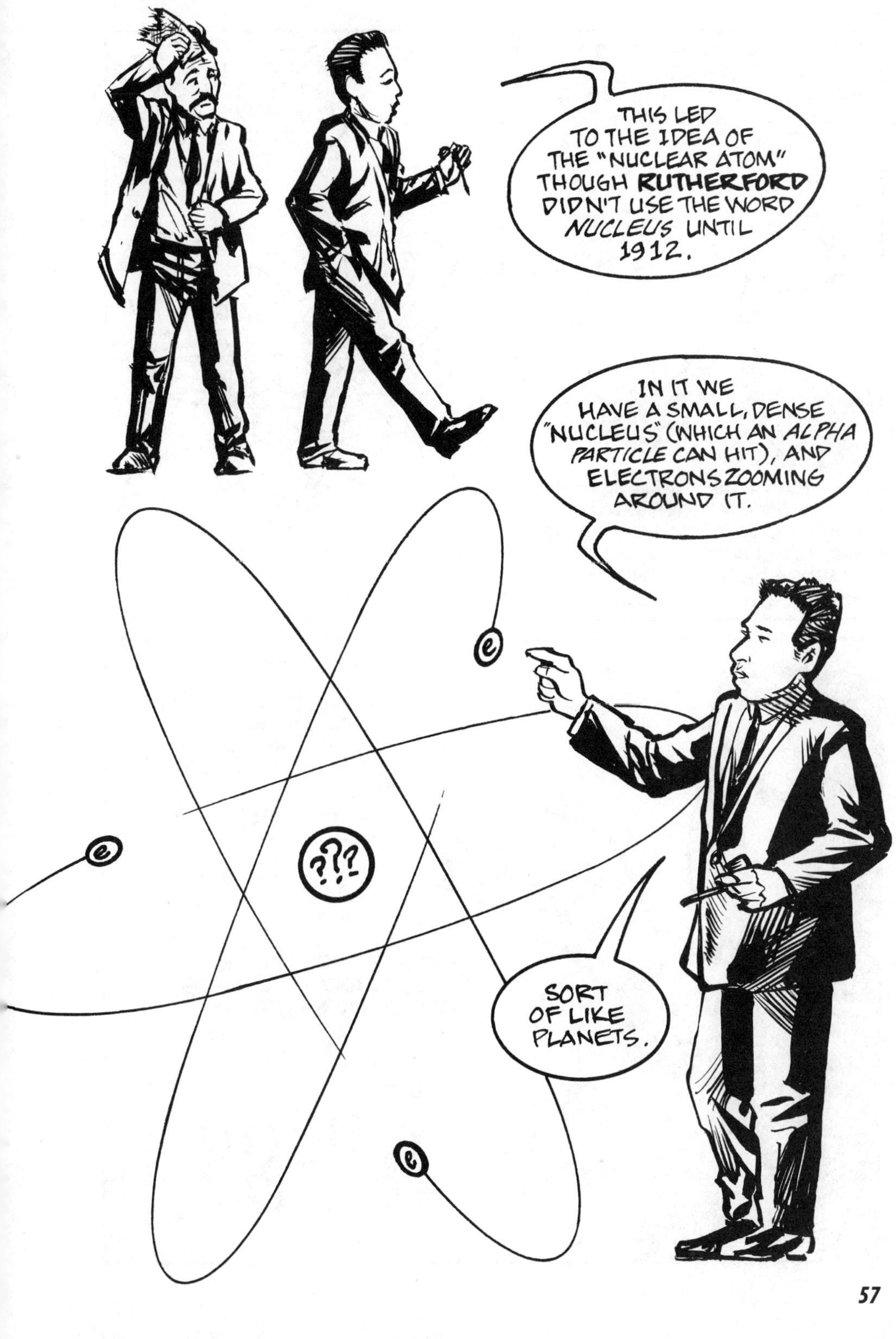
THIS LED TO THE IDEA OF THE "NUCLEAR ATOM" THOUGH **RUTHERFORD** DIDN'T USE THE WORD *NUCLEUS* UNTIL 1912.
IN IT WE HAVE A SMALL, DENSE "NUCLEUS" (WHICH AN *ALPHA PARTICLE* CAN HIT), AND ELECTRONS ZOOMING AROUND IT.
SORT OF LIKE PLANETS.
e
e
e
???

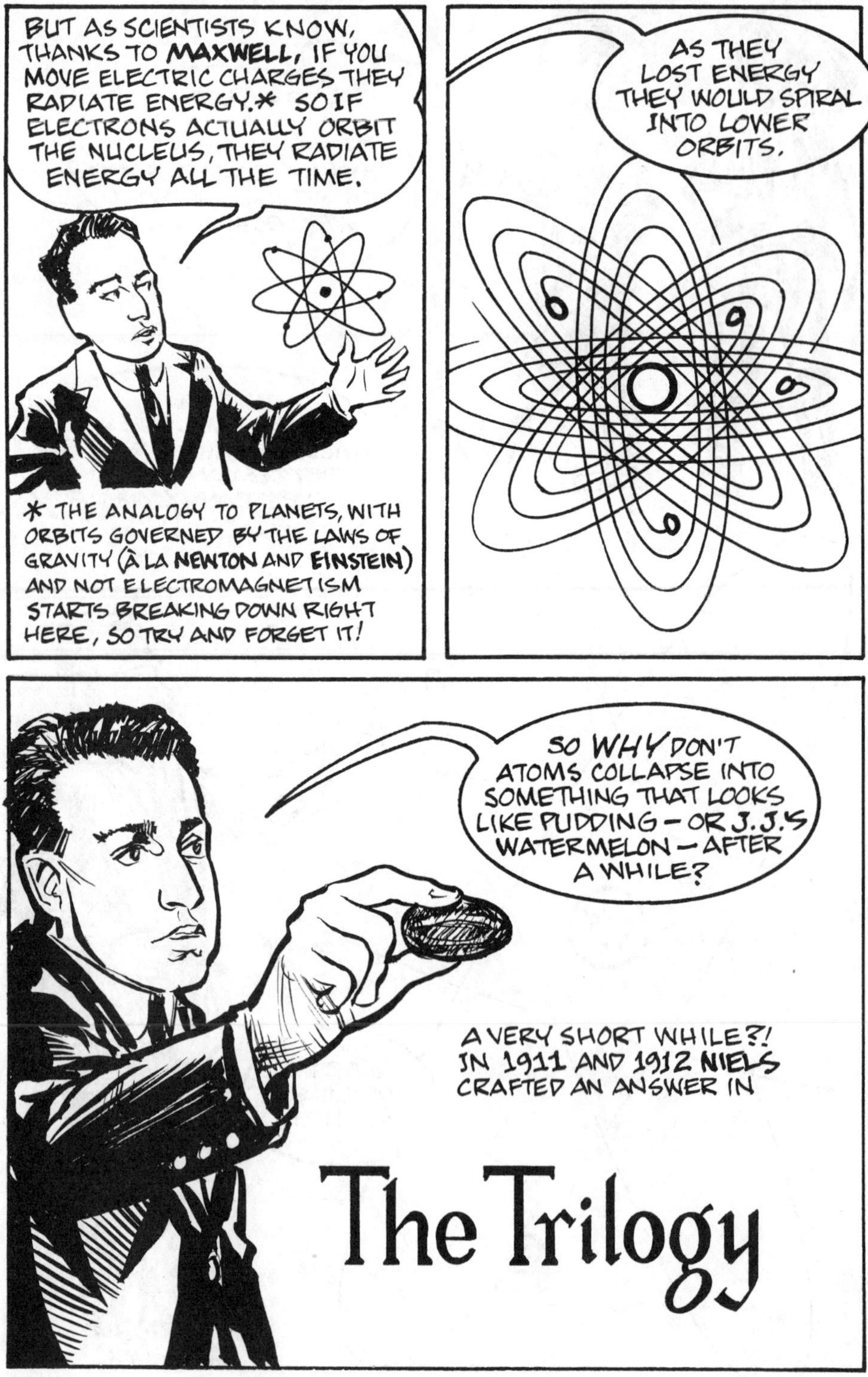
BUT AS SCIENTISTS KNOW, THANKS TO MAXWELL, IF YOU MOVE ELECTRIC CHARGES THEY RADIATE ENERGY.* SO IF ELECTRONS ACTUALLY ORBIT THE NUCLEUS, THEY RADIATE ENERGY ALL THE TIME.
* THE ANALOGY TO PLANETS, WITH ORBITS GOVERNED BY THE LAWS OF GRAVITY (À LA NEWTON AND EINSTEIN) AND NOT ELECTROMAGNETISM STARTS BREAKING DOWN RIGHT HERE, SO TRY AND FORGET IT!
AS THEY LOST ENERGY THEY WOULD SPIRAL INTO LOWER ORBITS.
SO WHY DON'T ATOMS COLLAPSE INTO SOMETHING THAT LOOKS LIKE PUDDING – OR J.J.'S WATERMELON – AFTER A WHILE?
A VERY SHORT WHILE?! IN 1911 AND 1912 NIELS CRAFTED AN ANSWER IN
The Trilogy

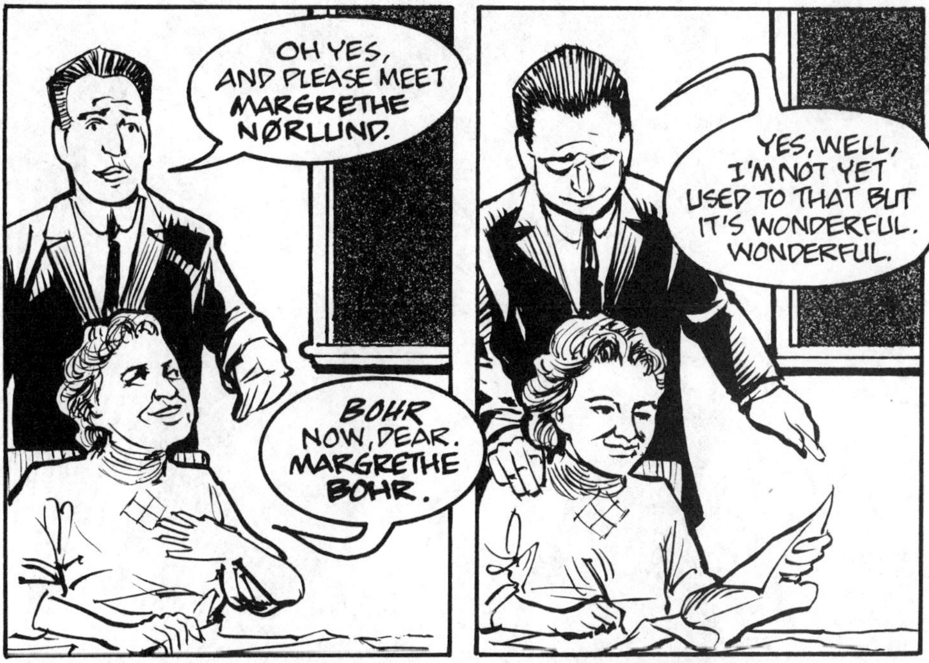
OH YES, AND PLEASE MEET MARGRETHE NØRLUND.
BOHR NOW, DEAR. MARGRETHE BOHR.
YES, WELL, I'M NOT YET USED TO THAT BUT IT'S WONDERFUL. WONDERFUL.

BOHR BEGAN DICTATING THE FIRST PAPER OF *THE TRILOGY* TO HIS NEW BRIDE WHILE ON A 1912 HOLIDAY IN NORWAY* IN IT, HE GAVE A SIMPLE ANSWER TO WHY ATOMS DON'T COLLAPSE:

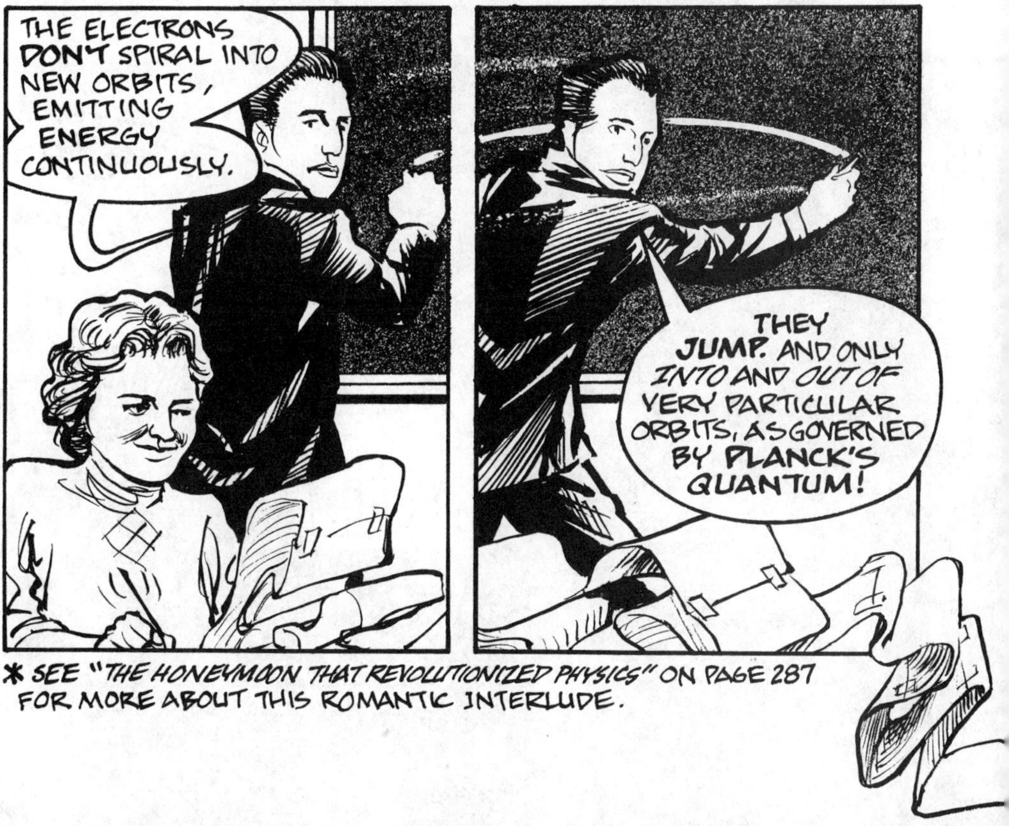
THE ELECTRONS DON'T SPIRAL INTO NEW ORBITS, EMITTING ENERGY CONTINUOUSLY.
THEY JUMP. AND ONLY INTO AND OUT OF VERY PARTICULAR ORBITS, AS GOVERNED BY PLANCK'S QUANTUM!

* *SEE "THE HONEYMOON THAT REVOLUTIONIZED PHYSICS"* ON PAGE 287 FOR MORE ABOUT THIS ROMANTIC INTERLUDE.

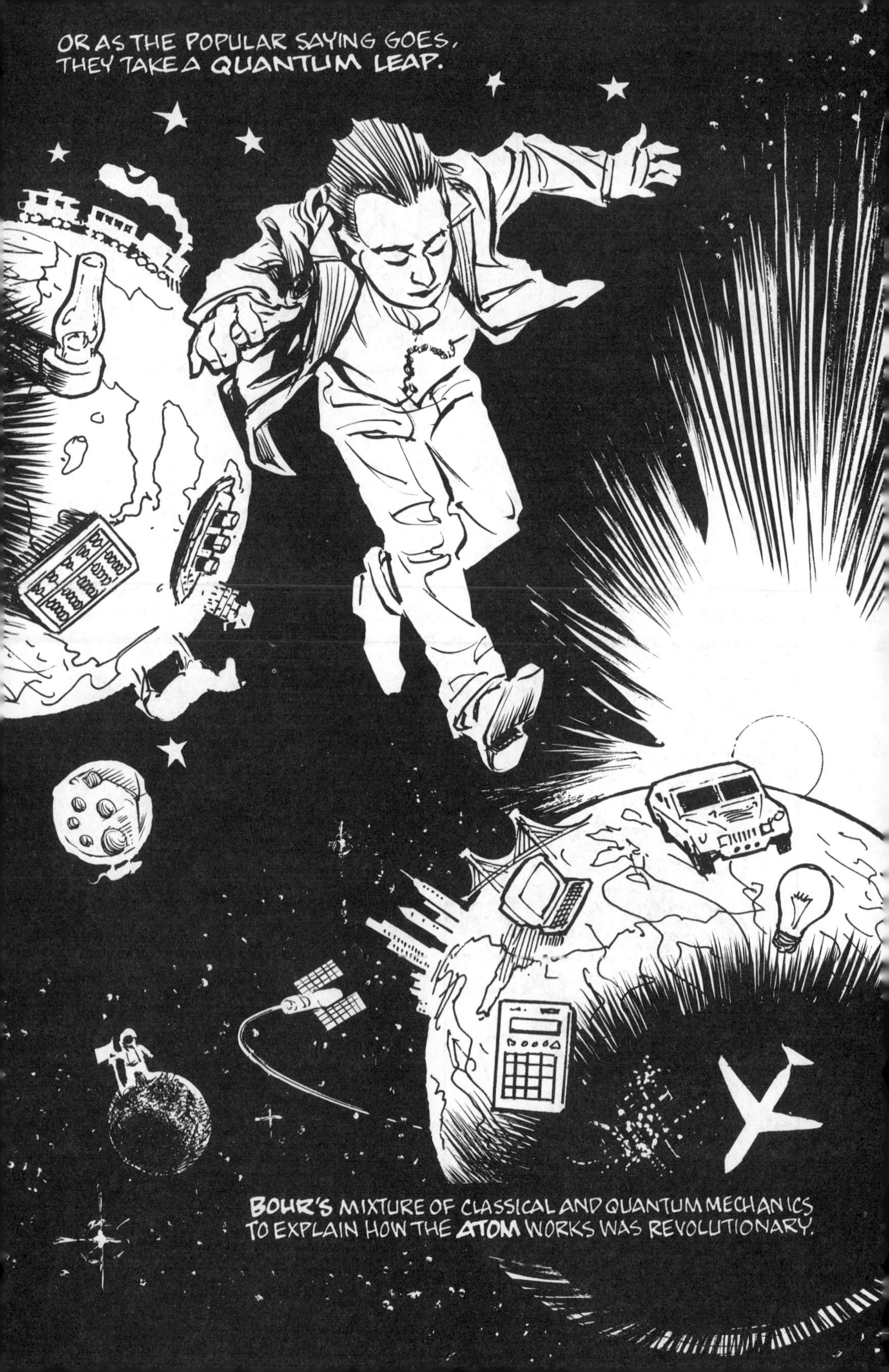
OR AS THE POPULAR SAYING GOES, THEY TAKE A QUANTUM LEAP.
BOUR'S MIXTURE OF CLASSICAL AND QUANTUM MECHANICS TO EXPLAIN HOW THE ATOM WORKS WAS REVOLUTIONARY.

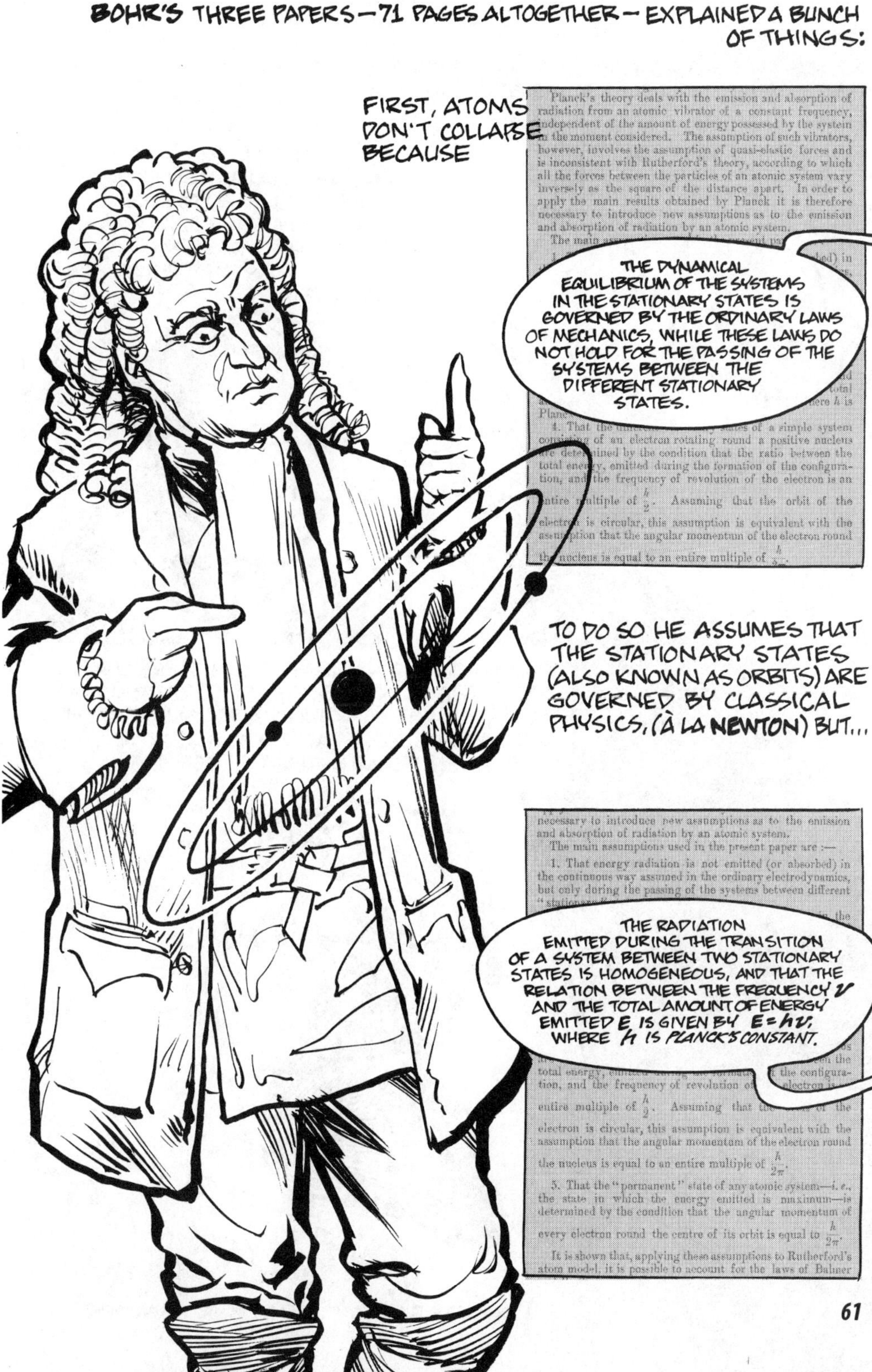
BOHR'S THREE PAPERS—71 PAGES ALTOGETHER—EXPLAINED A BUNCH OF THINGS:
FIRST, ATOMS DON'T COLLAPSE BECAUSE
Planck's theory deals with the emission and absorption of radiation from an atomic vibrator of a constant frequency, independent of the amount of energy possessed by the system in the moment considered. The assumption of such vibrators, however, involves the assumption of quasi-elastic forces and is inconsistent with Rutherford's theory, according to which all the forces between the particles of an atomic system vary inversely as the square of the distance apart. In order to apply the main results obtained by Planck it is therefore necessary to introduce new assumptions as to the emission and absorption of radiation by an atomic system.
THE DYNAMICAL EQUILIBRIUM OF THE SYSTEMS IN THE STATIONARY STATES IS GOVERNED BY THE ORDINARY LAWS OF MECHANICS, WHILE THESE LAWS DO NOT HOLD FOR THE PASSING OF THE SYSTEMS BETWEEN THE DIFFERENT STATIONARY STATES.
4. That the ... states of a simple system ... of an electron rotating round a positive nucleus ... ined by the condition that the ratio between the total energy, emitted during the formation of the configuration, and the frequency of revolution of the electron is an entire multiple of $\frac{h}{2}$. Assuming that the orbit of the electron is circular, this assumption is equivalent with the assumption that the angular momentum of the electron round the nucleus is equal to an entire multiple of
TO DO SO HE ASSUMES THAT THE STATIONARY STATES (ALSO KNOWN AS ORBITS) ARE GOVERNED BY CLASSICAL PHYSICS, (À LA NEWTON) BUT...
necessary to introduce new assumptions as to the emission and absorption of radiation by an atomic system.
The main assumptions used in the present paper are :—
1. That energy radiation is not emitted (or absorbed) in the continuous way assumed in the ordinary electrodynamics, but only during the passing of the systems between different
THE RADIATION EMITTED DURING THE TRANSITION OF A SYSTEM BETWEEN TWO STATIONARY STATES IS HOMOGENEOUS, AND THAT THE RELATION BETWEEN THE FREQUENCY ν AND THE TOTAL AMOUNT OF ENERGY EMITTED E IS GIVEN BY $E = h\nu$, WHERE h IS *PLANCK'S CONSTANT.*
total energy, emitted ... the configuration, and the frequency of revolution ... electron is entire multiple of $\frac{h}{2}$. Assuming that ... of the electron is circular, this assumption is equivalent with the assumption that the angular momentum of the electron round the nucleus is equal to an entire multiple of $\frac{h}{2\pi}$.
5. That the "permanent" state of any atomic system—*i. e.*, the state in which the energy emitted is maximum—is determined by the condition that the angular momentum of every electron round the centre of its orbit is equal to $\frac{h}{2\pi}$.
It is shown that, applying these assumptions to Rutherford's atom model, it is possible to account for the laws of Balmer

BOHR'S WORK ALSO EXPLAINS WHY HYDROGEN ATOMS EMIT A VERY PARTICULAR SPECTRUM OF LIGHT.

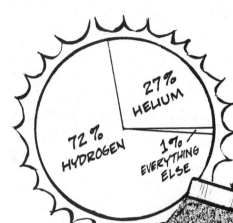

27% HELIUM

72% HYDROGEN

1% EVERYTHING ELSE

SCIENTISTS HAD LONG KNOWN THAT WHEN YOU HEAT UP ELEMENTS LIKE *HYDROGEN* AND *HELIUM*, THE LIGHT THEY EMIT COMES IN VERY PARTICULAR FREQUENCIES.

THOUGH TO THE NAKED EYE (AN IMPRECISE TOOL) THE SUN'S SPECTRUM IS CONTINUOUS, WHEN VIEWED THROUGH A PRISM COMBINED WITH A TELESCOPE AND A NARROW SLIT, IT'S EASY TO SEE THAT IT ISN'T.

A SWISS SCHOOL TEACHER NAMED **JOHN BALMER** HAD PUBLISHED A SIMPLE FORMULA, USING ONLY WHOLE NUMBERS, TO PREDICT THE HYDROGEN LINES IN 1885.*

$$R = 109737.31521 \text{ cm}^{-1}$$
$$\nu = R\left(1/N^2 - 1/M^2\right)$$

* THAT'S RIGHT, THE YEAR BOHR WAS BORN.

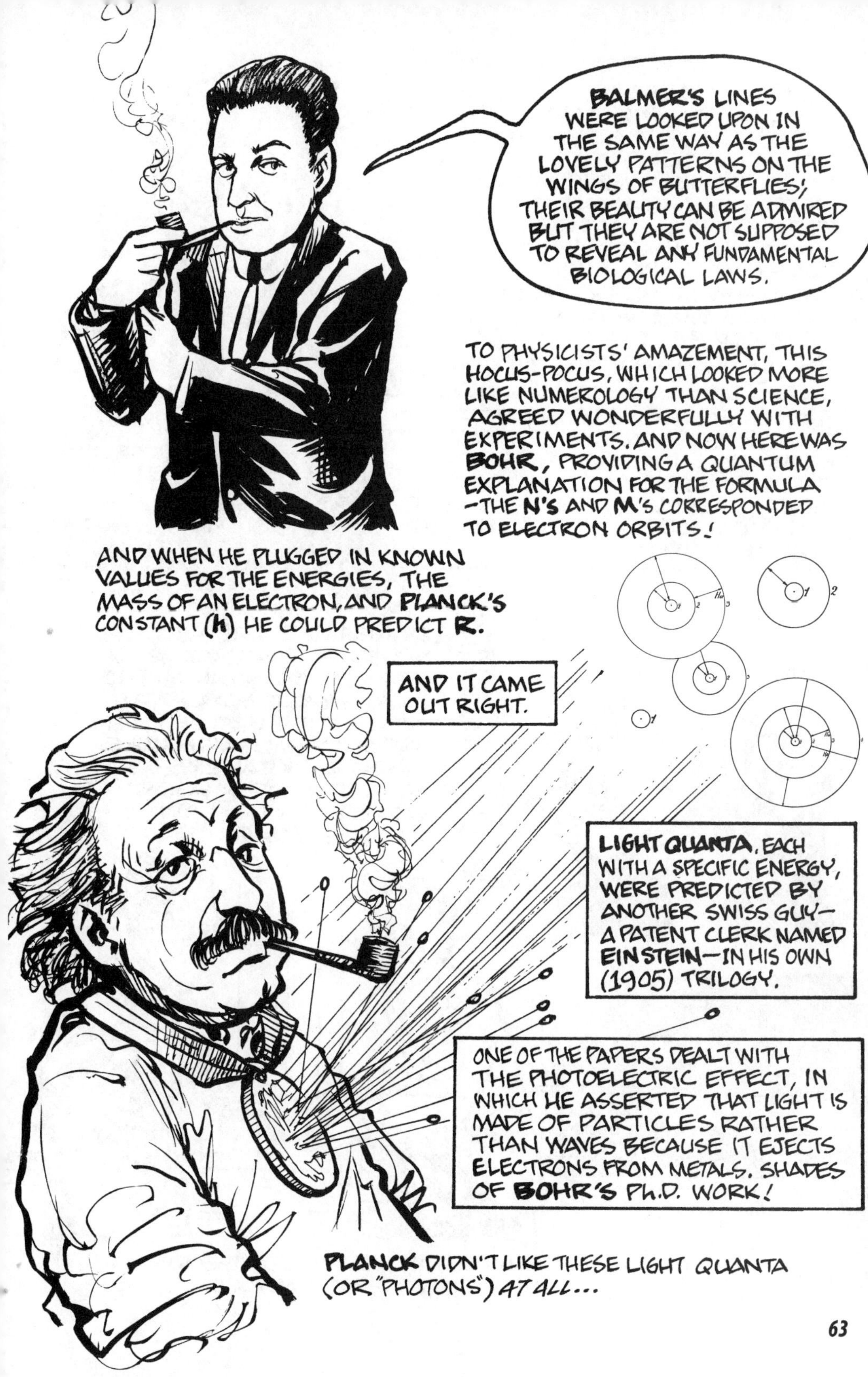
BALMER'S LINES WERE LOOKED UPON IN THE SAME WAY AS THE LOVELY PATTERNS ON THE WINGS OF BUTTERFLIES; THEIR BEAUTY CAN BE ADMIRED BUT THEY ARE NOT SUPPOSED TO REVEAL ANY FUNDAMENTAL BIOLOGICAL LAWS.
TO PHYSICISTS' AMAZEMENT, THIS HOCUS-POCUS, WHICH LOOKED MORE LIKE NUMEROLOGY THAN SCIENCE, AGREED WONDERFULLY WITH EXPERIMENTS. AND NOW HERE WAS BOHR, PROVIDING A QUANTUM EXPLANATION FOR THE FORMULA —THE N'S AND M'S CORRESPONDED TO ELECTRON ORBITS!
AND WHEN HE PLUGGED IN KNOWN VALUES FOR THE ENERGIES, THE MASS OF AN ELECTRON, AND PLANCK'S CONSTANT (h) HE COULD PREDICT R.
AND IT CAME OUT RIGHT.
LIGHT QUANTA, EACH WITH A SPECIFIC ENERGY, WERE PREDICTED BY ANOTHER SWISS GUY— A PATENT CLERK NAMED EINSTEIN—IN HIS OWN (1905) TRILOGY.
ONE OF THE PAPERS DEALT WITH THE PHOTOELECTRIC EFFECT, IN WHICH HE ASSERTED THAT LIGHT IS MADE OF PARTICLES RATHER THAN WAVES BECAUSE IT EJECTS ELECTRONS FROM METALS. SHADES OF BOHR'S Ph.D. WORK!
PLANCK DIDN'T LIKE THESE LIGHT QUANTA (OR "PHOTONS") AT ALL...

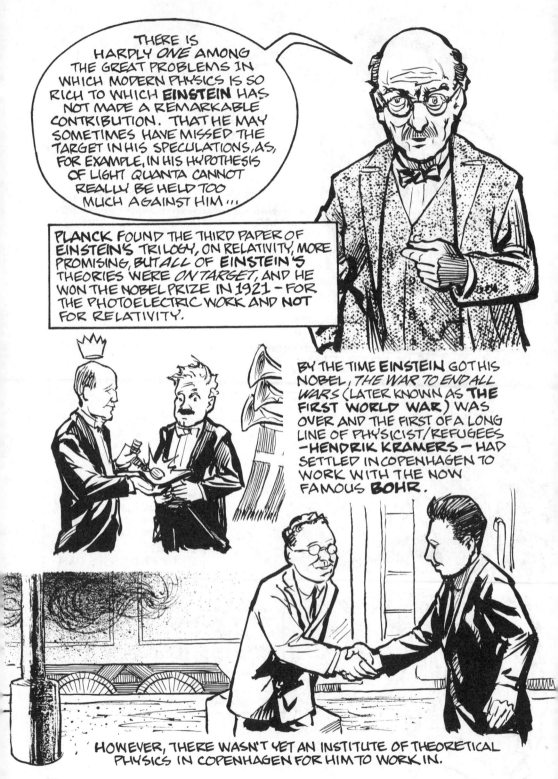

THERE IS HARDLY *ONE* AMONG THE GREAT PROBLEMS IN WHICH MODERN PHYSICS IS SO RICH TO WHICH **EINSTEIN** HAS NOT MADE A REMARKABLE CONTRIBUTION. THAT HE MAY SOMETIMES HAVE MISSED THE TARGET IN HIS SPECULATIONS, AS, FOR EXAMPLE, IN HIS HYPOTHESIS OF LIGHT QUANTA CANNOT REALLY BE HELD TOO MUCH AGAINST HIM ...

PLANCK FOUND THE THIRD PAPER OF EINSTEIN'S TRILOGY, ON RELATIVITY, MORE PROMISING, BUT *ALL* OF EINSTEIN'S THEORIES WERE *ON TARGET*, AND HE WON THE NOBEL PRIZE IN 1921 — FOR THE PHOTOELECTRIC WORK AND **NOT** FOR RELATIVITY.

BY THE TIME **EINSTEIN** GOT HIS NOBEL, *THE WAR TO END ALL WARS* (LATER KNOWN AS **THE FIRST WORLD WAR**) WAS OVER AND THE FIRST OF A LONG LINE OF PHYSICIST/REFUGEES — HENDRIK KRAMERS — HAD SETTLED IN COPENHAGEN TO WORK WITH THE NOW FAMOUS **BOHR**.

HOWEVER, THERE WASN'T YET AN INSTITUTE OF THEORETICAL PHYSICS IN COPENHAGEN FOR HIM TO WORK IN.

Chapter 4

BOHR HAD JUST BEEN MADE A PROFESSOR WHEN **KRAMERS** ARRIVED IN THE FALL OF 1916. PRIOR TO THIS HE'D ONLY BEEN AN INSTRUCTOR (DOCENT), AND HAD DONE MUCH OF HIS THEORETICAL WORK ABROAD.

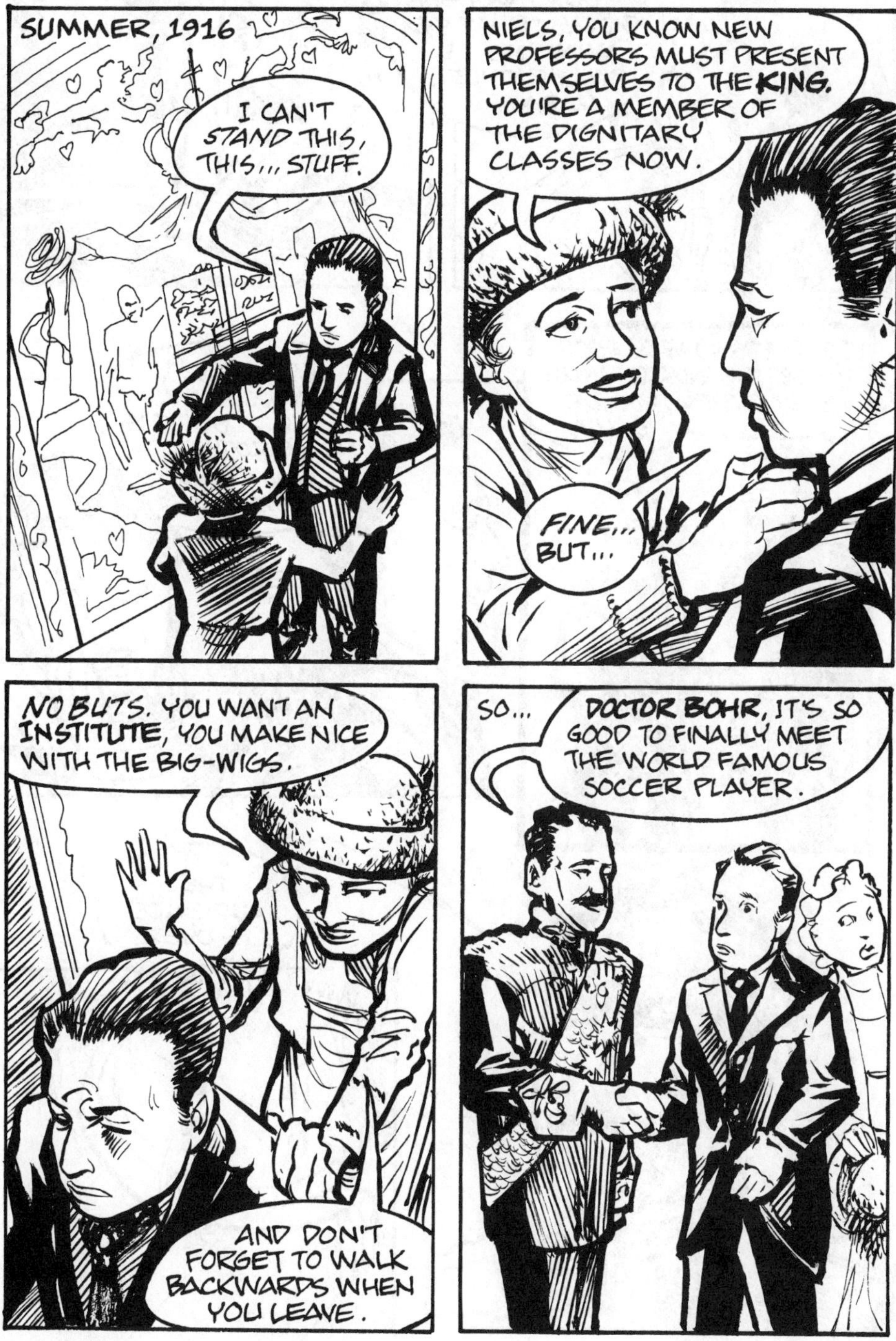
SUMMER, 1916
I CAN'T *STAND* THIS, THIS... STUFF.
NIELS, YOU KNOW NEW PROFESSORS MUST PRESENT THEMSELVES TO THE **KING.** YOU'RE A MEMBER OF THE DIGNITARY CLASSES NOW.
FINE... BUT...
NO BUTS. YOU WANT AN **INSTITUTE**, YOU MAKE NICE WITH THE BIG-WIGS.
AND DON'T FORGET TO WALK BACKWARDS WHEN YOU LEAVE.
SO...
DOCTOR BOHR, IT'S SO GOOD TO FINALLY MEET THE WORLD FAMOUS SOCCER PLAYER.

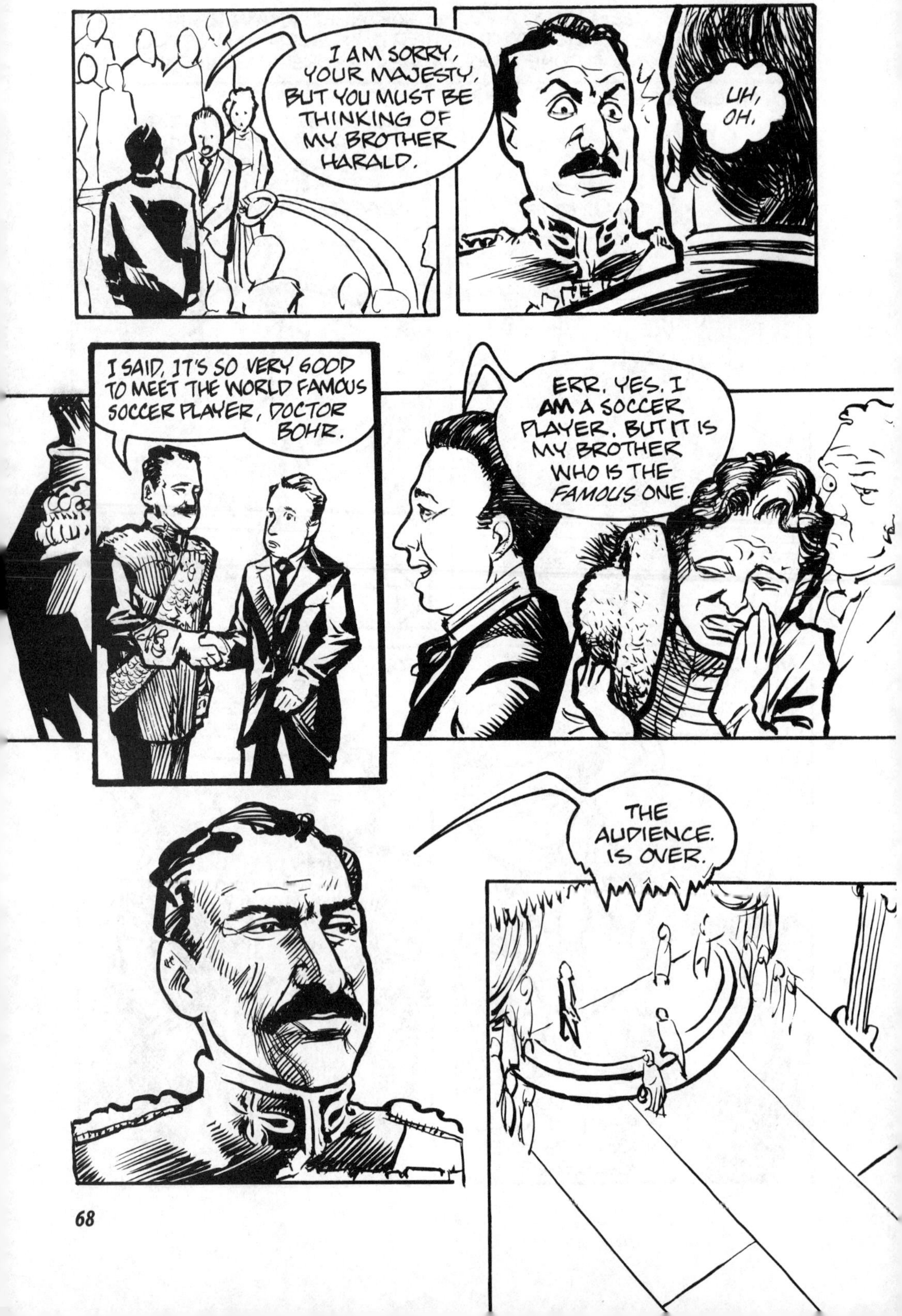
I AM SORRY, YOUR MAJESTY, BUT YOU MUST BE THINKING OF MY BROTHER HARALD.
UH, OH.
I SAID, IT'S SO VERY GOOD TO MEET THE WORLD FAMOUS SOCCER PLAYER, DOCTOR BOHR.
ERR. YES. I **AM** A SOCCER PLAYER. BUT IT IS MY BROTHER WHO IS THE *FAMOUS* ONE.
THE AUDIENCE. IS OVER.

AN AUTHORITY WHO DIDN'T DEAL WELL WITH AUTHORITY, **BOHR** DIDN'T SPARE HIMSELF WHEN IT CAME TO HIS FAMOUS WORK:

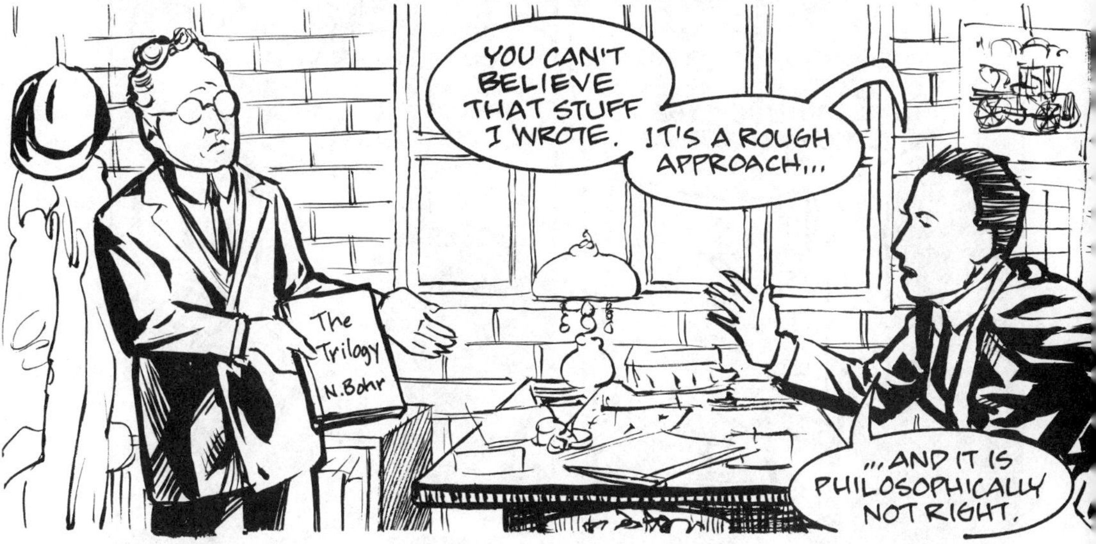

The Trilogy N. Bohr
YOU CAN'T BELIEVE THAT STUFF I WROTE.
IT'S A ROUGH APPROACH,...
...AND IT IS PHILOSOPHICALLY NOT RIGHT.

HIS MODEL ISN'T *PHYSICALLY* RIGHT, EITHER. THE ATOM ISN'T REALLY LIKE A SOLAR SYSTEM. BUT THE METAPHOR HAS STUCK AROUND SINCE IT'S THE LAST PICTURE OF THE ATOM *PHYSICISTS* COULD PRESENT US WITH THAT BEARS ANY RESEMBLANCE TO THE WORLD AS WE KNOW IT.

ANYWAY, EVEN EARLY ON **BOHR** AND **RUTHERFORD** BOTH KNEW THAT HIS MODEL'S FUSION OF CLASSICAL AND MODERN CONCEPTS WAS TRYING TO HAVE IT BOTH WAYS.

THE *BOHR ATOM* IS THE LAST PIECE OF FLOTSAM WE CLING TO BEFORE SINKING INTO AN OCEAN OF PURE MATH.

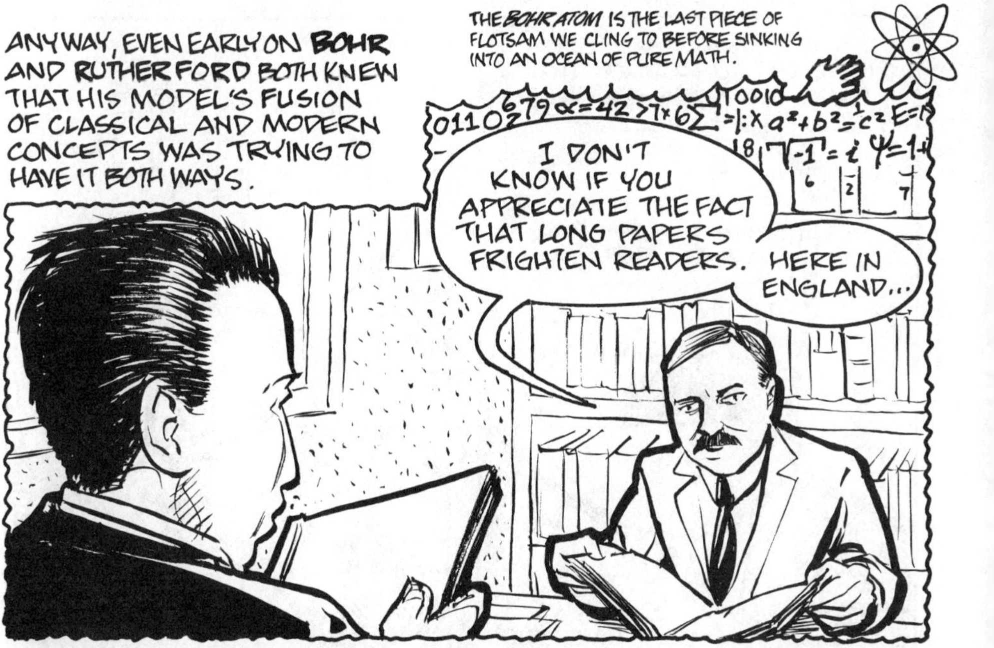

I DON'T KNOW IF YOU APPRECIATE THE FACT THAT LONG PAPERS FRIGHTEN READERS.
HERE IN ENGLAND...

BUT **BOHR'S** PAPERS WERE THE OPENING SHOTS OF THE QUANTUM REVOLUTION. THEY MADE HIS REPUTATION, IF NOT WITH KINGS, AT LEAST IN THE WORLD OF **PHYSICS**. AND NOT ONLY AS A THEORIST, BUT AS A WRITER...

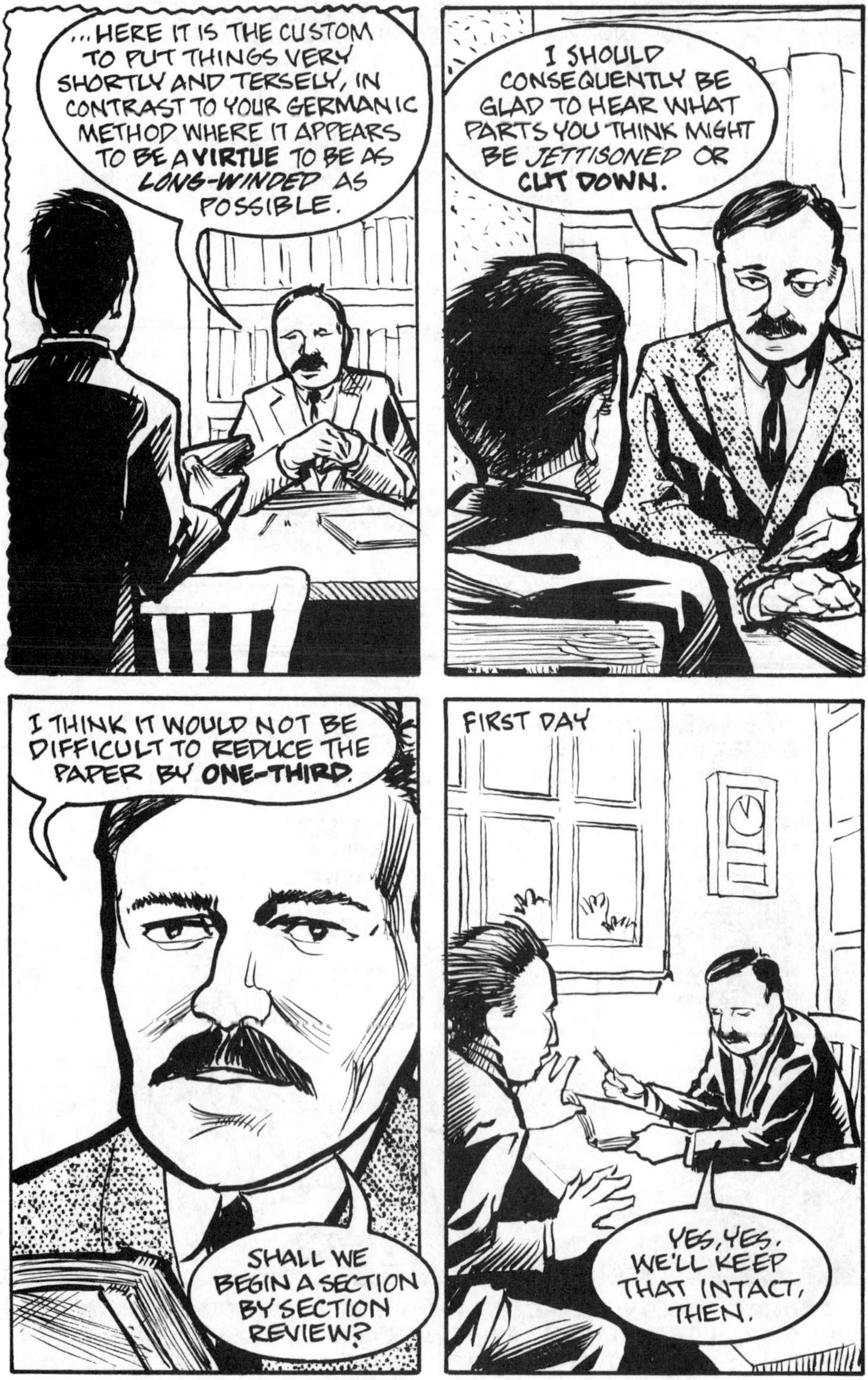
...HERE IT IS THE CUSTOM TO PUT THINGS VERY SHORTLY AND TERSELY, IN CONTRAST TO YOUR GERMANIC METHOD WHERE IT APPEARS TO BE A VIRTUE TO BE AS LONG-WINDED AS POSSIBLE.
I SHOULD CONSEQUENTLY BE GLAD TO HEAR WHAT PARTS YOU THINK MIGHT BE JETTISONED OR CUT DOWN.
I THINK IT WOULD NOT BE DIFFICULT TO REDUCE THE PAPER BY ONE-THIRD.
SHALL WE BEGIN A SECTION BY SECTION REVIEW?
FIRST DAY
YES, YES. WE'LL KEEP THAT INTACT, THEN.

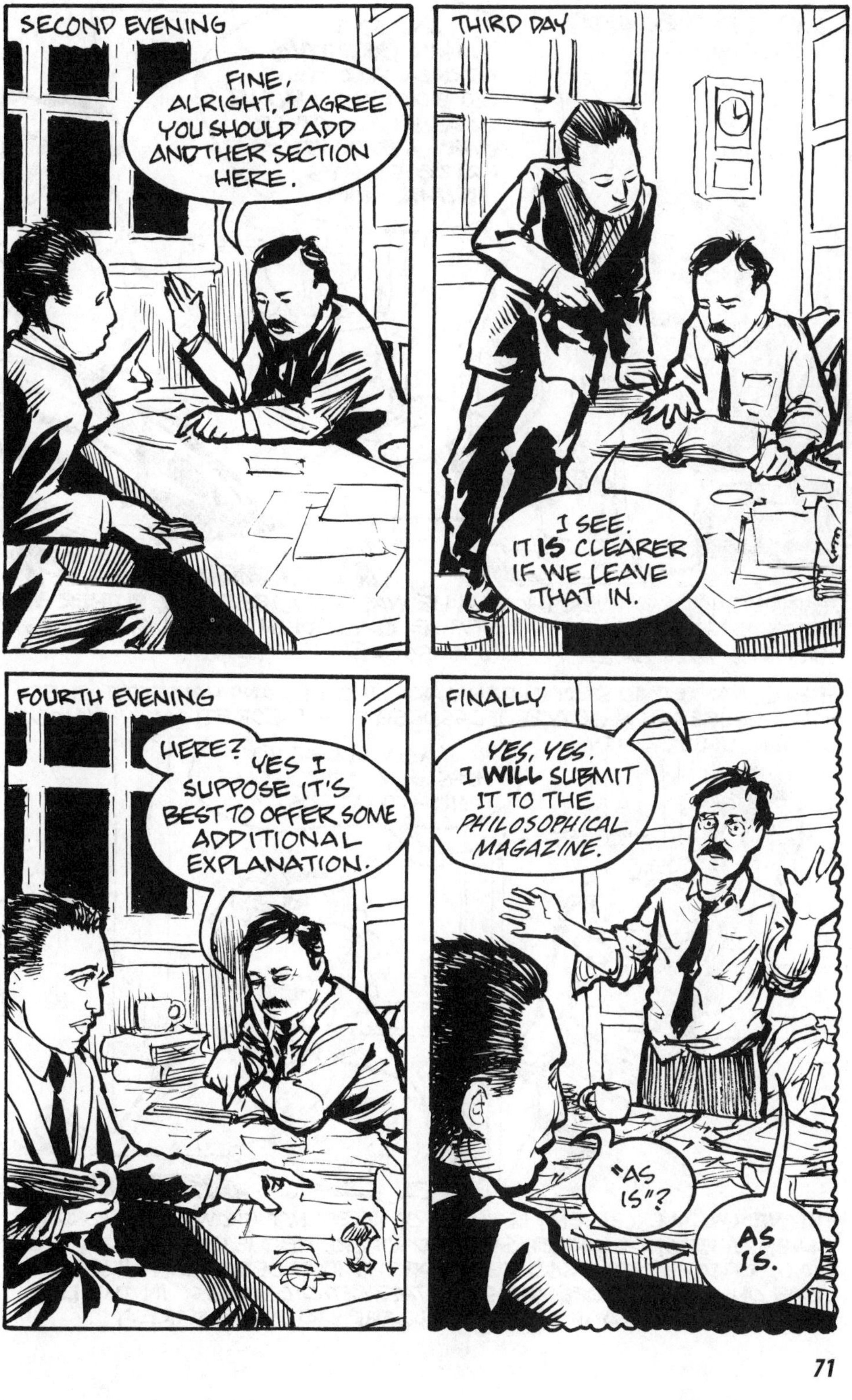
SECOND EVENING
FINE, ALRIGHT, I AGREE YOU SHOULD ADD ANOTHER SECTION HERE.
THIRD DAY
I SEE. IT **IS** CLEARER IF WE LEAVE THAT IN.
FOURTH EVENING
HERE? YES I SUPPOSE IT'S BEST TO OFFER SOME ADDITIONAL EXPLANATION.
FINALLY
YES, YES. I **WILL** SUBMIT IT TO THE *PHILOSOPHICAL MAGAZINE*.
"AS IS"?
AS IS.

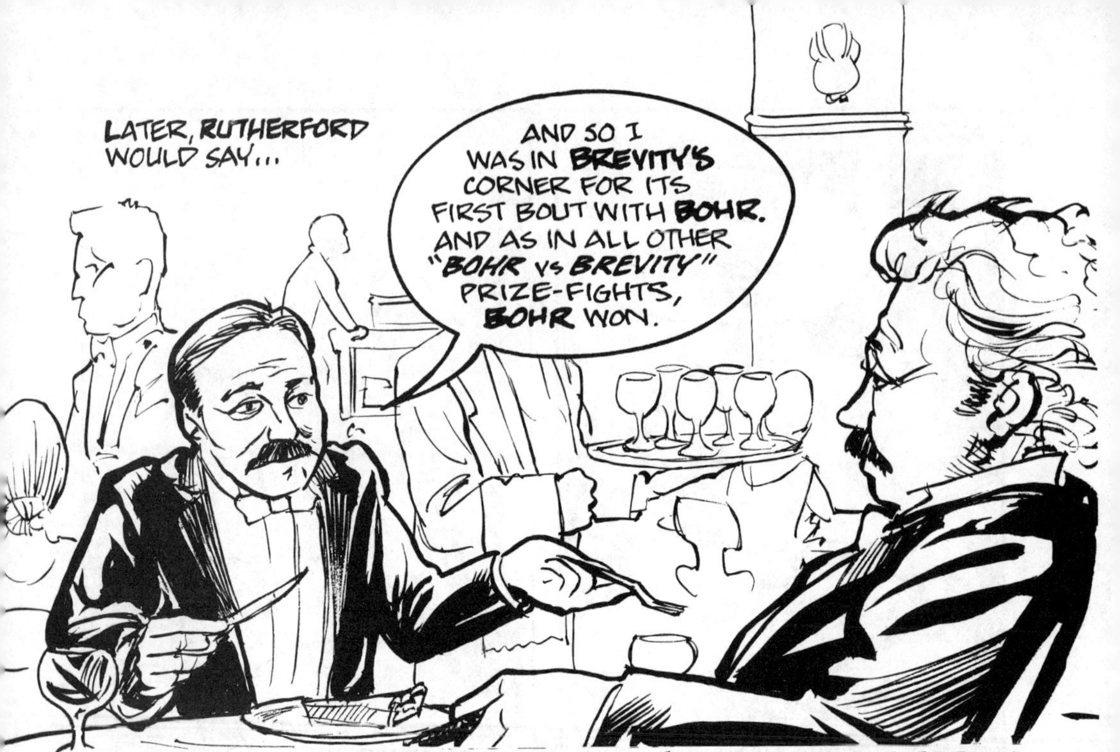
LATER, RUTHERFORD WOULD SAY...
AND SO I WAS IN BREVITY'S CORNER FOR ITS FIRST BOUT WITH BOHR. AND AS IN ALL OTHER "BOHR VS BREVITY" PRIZE-FIGHTS, BOHR WON.

DESPITE THIS, AND EVEN THOUGH HE WAS A *THEORETICIAN*, **RUTHERFORD** OFFERED HIM A POSITION AT THE **CAVENDISH** IN 1914, SAYING, "BOHR'S *DIFFERENT*. HE'S A SOCCER PLAYER!"

NIELS WANTED TO STAY IN DENMARK, THOUGH, AND HAD PETITIONED FOR THE CREATION OF A PROFESSORSHIP IN THEORETICAL PHYSICS AT THE UNIVERSITY.

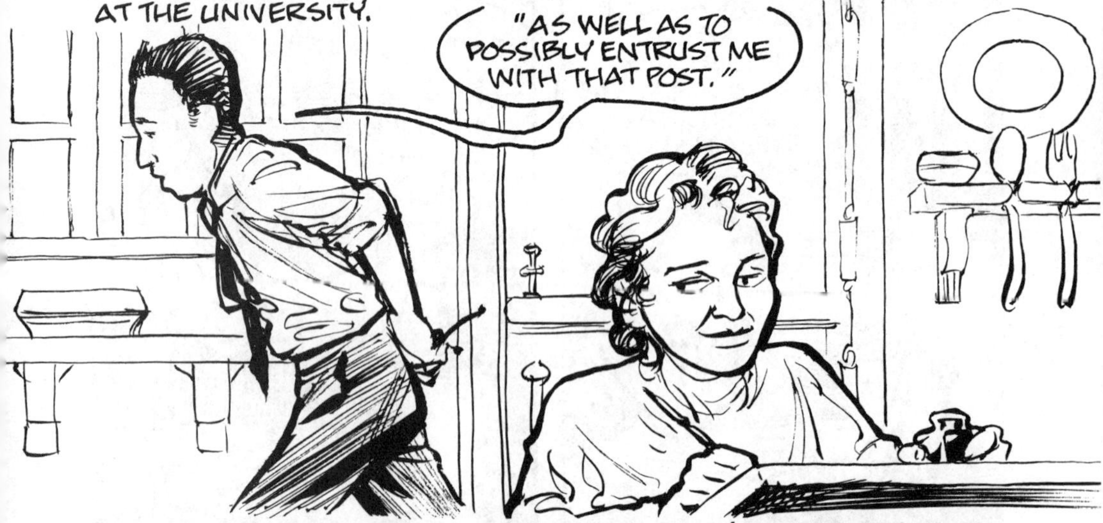
"AS WELL AS TO POSSIBLY ENTRUST ME WITH THAT POST."

BUT EVEN WITH EXCELLENT LETTERS OF REFERENCE (FROM **RUTHERFORD** AND SEVEN OTHERS) THE UNIVERSITY DIDN'T CREATE THE POSITION. THE FIELD WAS, PERHAPS, STILL TOO NEW. (AT THE TURN OF THE CENTURY THERE WERE ONLY **TWO** PROFESSORS OF "*THEORETICAL PHYSICS*" IN THE **U.S.**, **ONE** IN HOLLAND, AND **NONE** IN ALL THE BRITISH EMPIRE.)

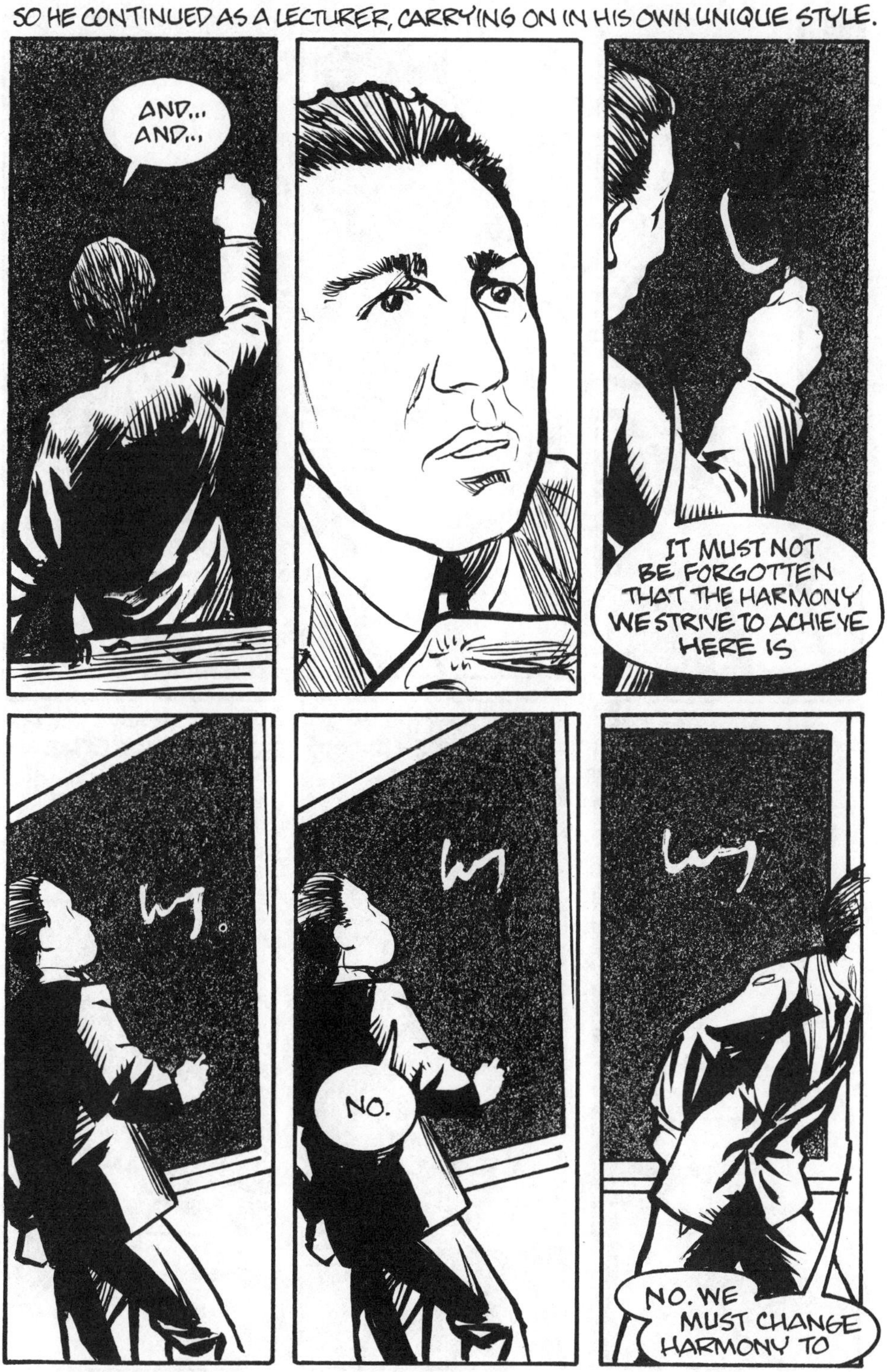
SO HE CONTINUED AS A LECTURER, CARRYING ON IN HIS OWN UNIQUE STYLE.
AND... AND...
IT MUST NOT BE FORGOTTEN THAT THE HARMONY WE STRIVE TO ACHIEVE HERE IS
NO.
NO. WE MUST CHANGE HARMONY TO

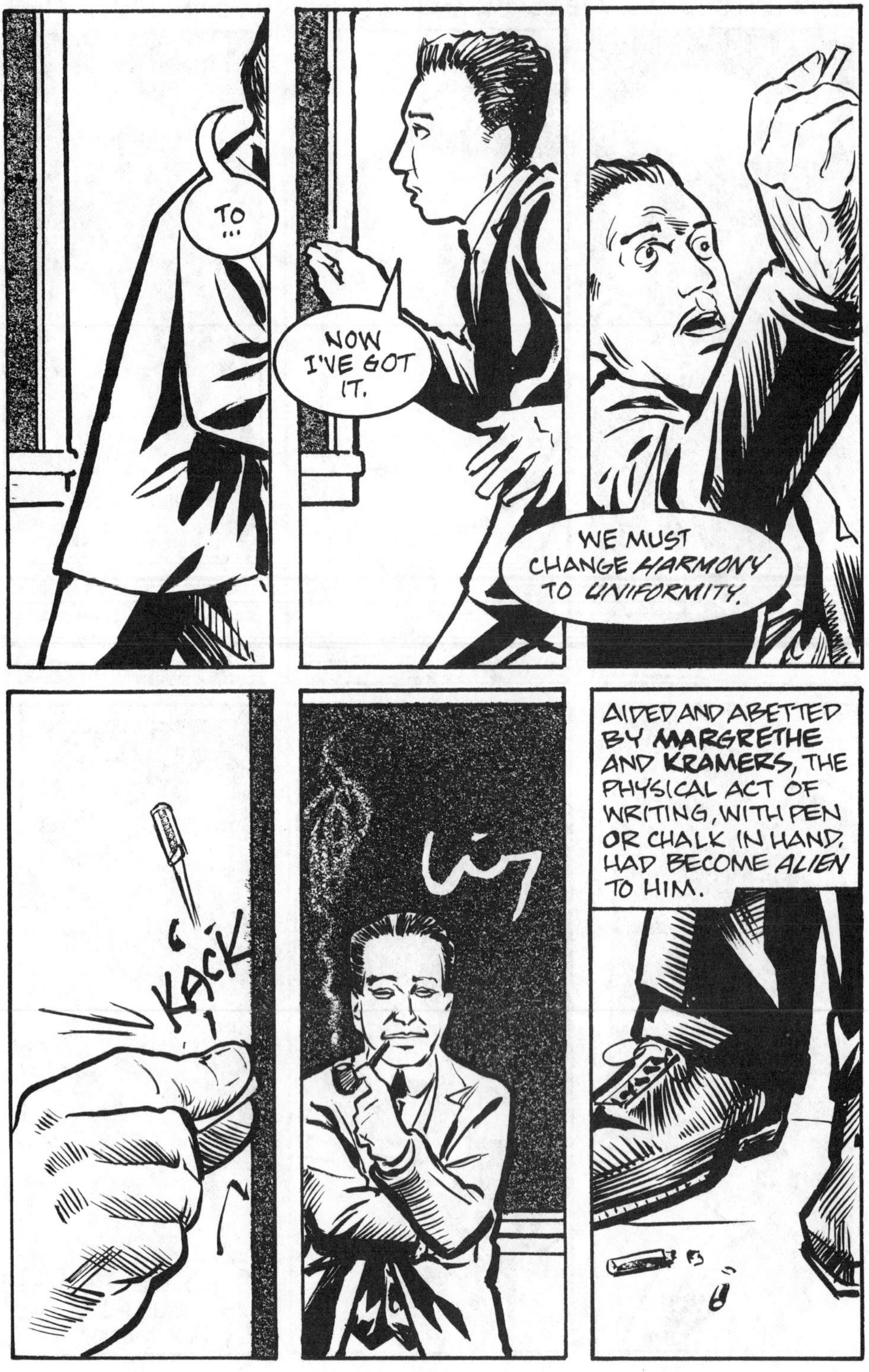
TO ...
NOW I'VE GOT IT.
WE MUST CHANGE *HARMONY* TO *UNIFORMITY*.
KACK
AIDED AND ABETTED BY **MARGRETHE** AND **KRAMERS**, THE PHYSICAL ACT OF WRITING, WITH PEN OR CHALK IN HAND, HAD BECOME *ALIEN* TO HIM.

BY THE END OF 1917 **BOHR** HAD APPROVAL FROM THE DANISH GOVERNMENT TO BUILD THE INSTITUTE HE WANTED — ONE WHOSE SPIRIT HE'D MODEL AFTER **RUTHERFORD'S** LAB. THERE WAS JUST THE MATTER OF GETTING THE *PLANS* FINALIZED.

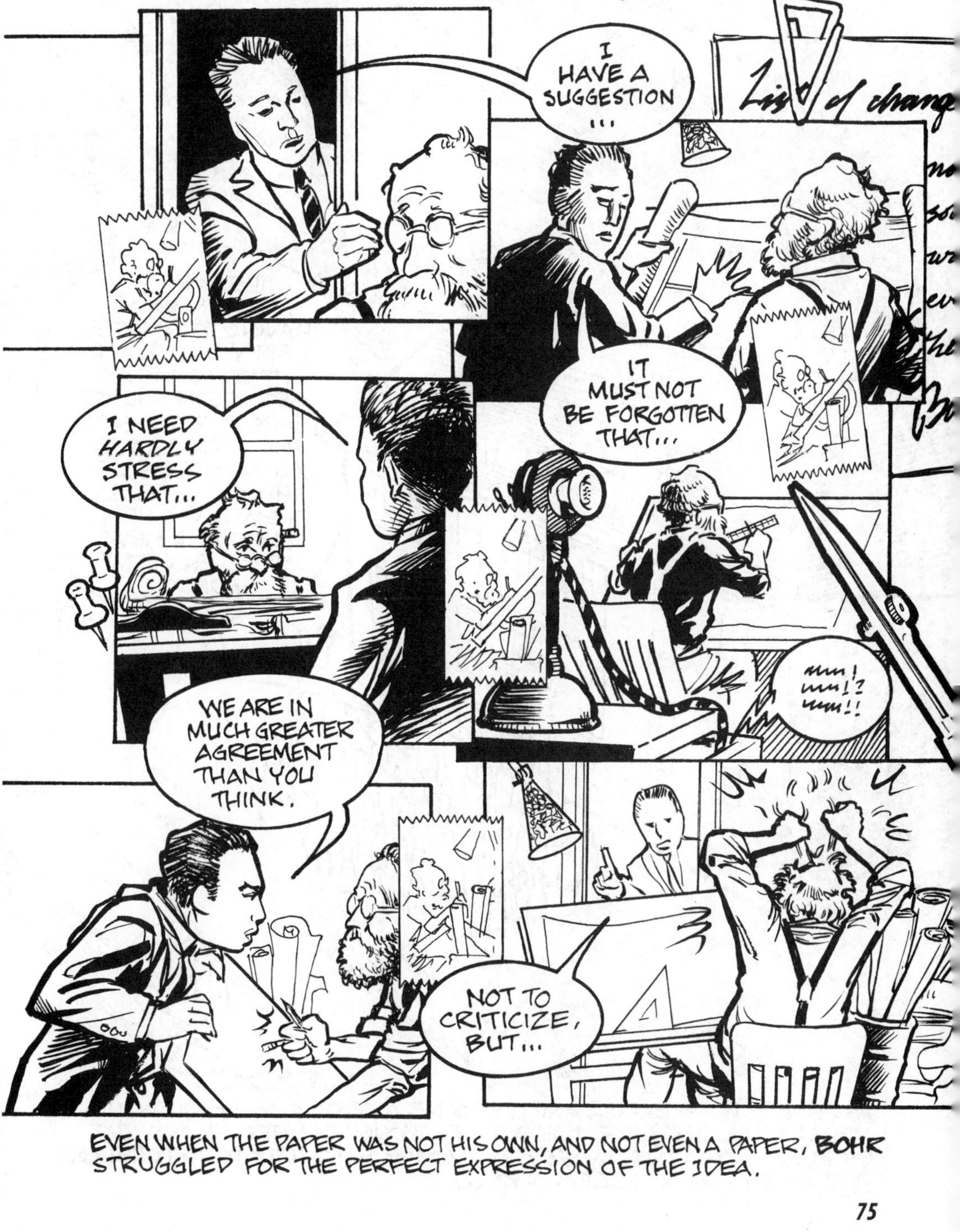
I HAVE A SUGGESTION ...
I NEED *HARDLY* STRESS THAT...
IT MUST NOT BE FORGOTTEN THAT...
WE ARE IN MUCH GREATER AGREEMENT THAN YOU THINK.
NOT TO CRITICIZE, BUT...

EVEN WHEN THE PAPER WAS NOT HIS OWN, AND NOT EVEN A PAPER, **BOHR** STRUGGLED FOR THE PERFECT EXPRESSION OF THE IDEA.

AND SO AN EXHAUSTED **BOHR**—THOUGH NOT *NEARLY* AS EXHAUSTED AS HIS ARCHITECT—DEDICATED THE BUILDING ONLY A COUPLE YEARS PAST SCHEDULE.

AND IT WAS WONDERFUL, AND IT BECAME A CENTER OF THE QUANTUM MECHANICAL UNIVERSE FOR A TIME, THOUGH IN LATER YEARS THE DIFFICULTY OF ACTUALLY *GETTING* TO THE **INSTITUTE FOR THEORETICAL PHYSICS** BECAME LEGENDARY...

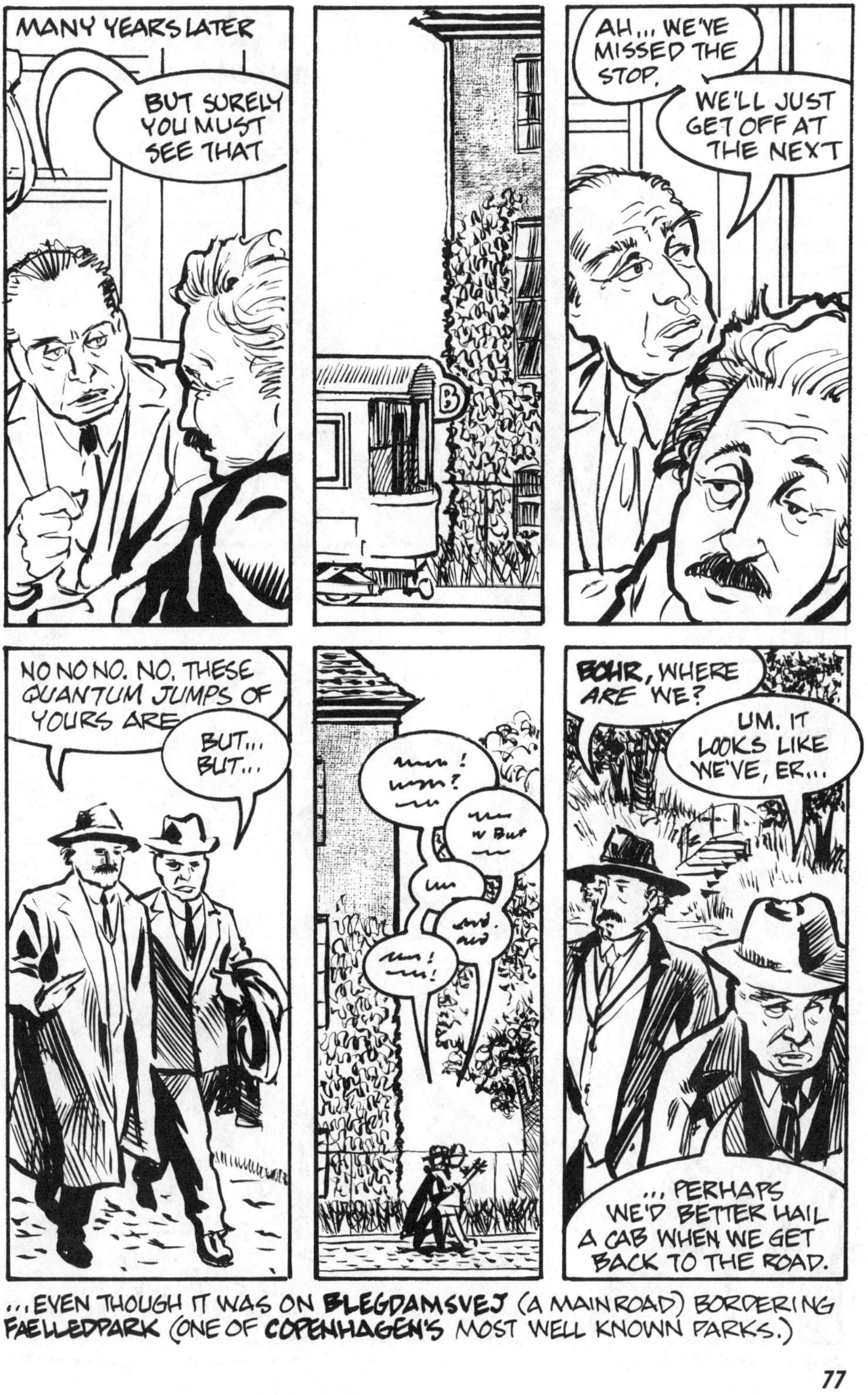
MANY YEARS LATER
BUT SURELY YOU MUST SEE THAT
AH... WE'VE MISSED THE STOP.
WE'LL JUST GET OFF AT THE NEXT
NO NO NO. NO, THESE QUANTUM JUMPS OF YOURS ARE
BUT... BUT...
BOHR, WHERE ARE WE?
UM. IT LOOKS LIKE WE'VE, ER...
... PERHAPS WE'D BETTER HAIL A CAB WHEN WE GET BACK TO THE ROAD.

...EVEN THOUGH IT WAS ON **BLEGDAMSVEJ** (A MAIN ROAD) BORDERING **FAELLEDPARK** (ONE OF **COPENHAGEN'S** MOST WELL KNOWN PARKS.)

BUT WE'VE GOTTEN AHEAD OF OURSELVES, SINCE **BOHR** AND **EINSTEIN** MET IN **BERLIN**, WELL *BEFORE* THE INSTITUTE WAS BUILT.

THIS HISTORIC MEETING HAPPENED IN 1920, WHEN GERMANY WAS STILL RECOVERING FROM **WORLD WAR I**. BUT SCIENCE HAD RESUMED, AND THE NOW FAMOUS **BOHR** HAD ACCEPTED **PLANCK'S** INVITATION TO LECTURE AT THE *PHYSIKALISCHE GESELLSCHAFT.* (PHYSICS SOCIETY)

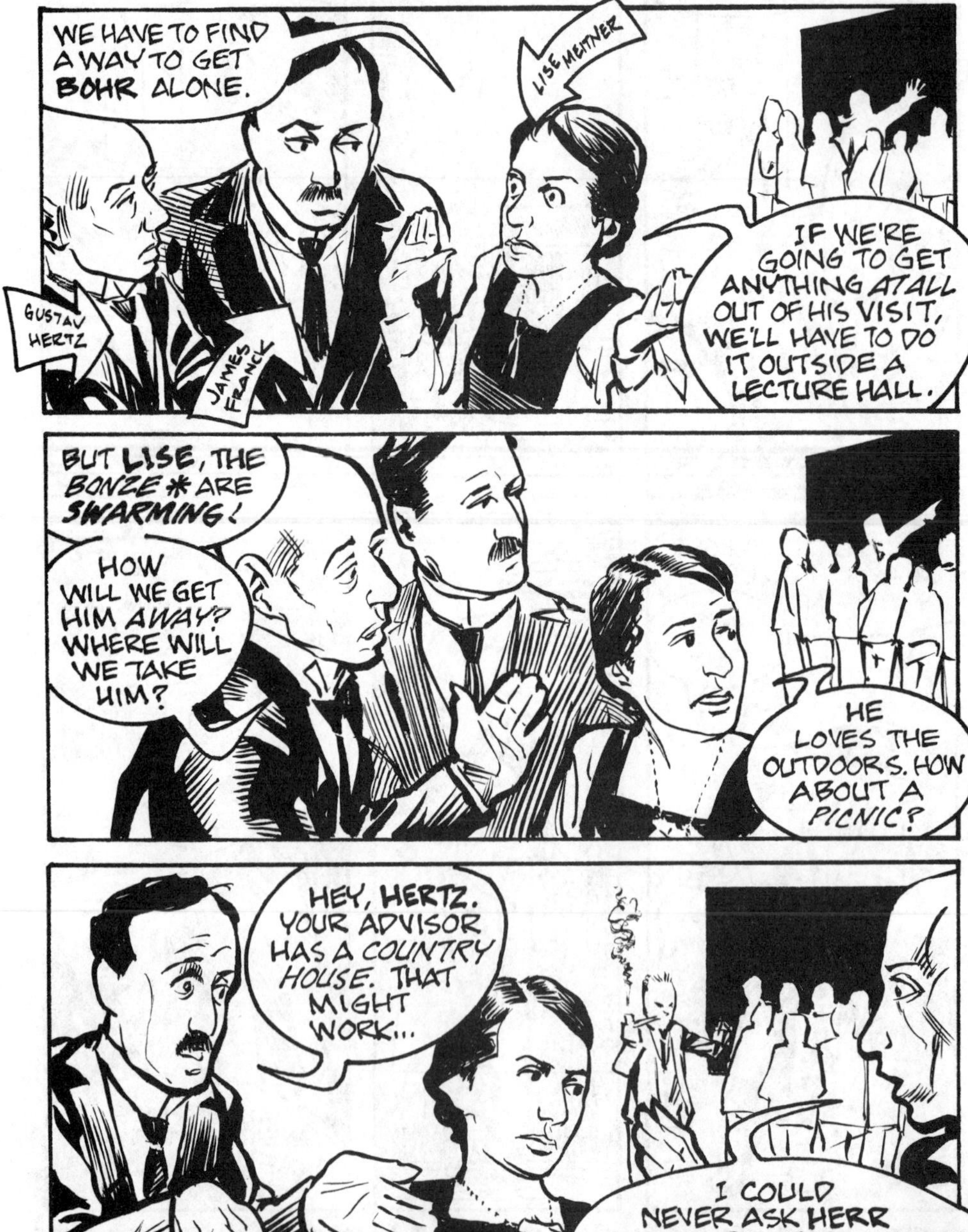
WE HAVE TO FIND A WAY TO GET BOHR ALONE.
LISE MEITNER
GUSTAV HERTZ
JAMES FRANCK
IF WE'RE GOING TO GET ANYTHING AT ALL OUT OF HIS VISIT, WE'LL HAVE TO DO IT OUTSIDE A LECTURE HALL.
BUT LISE, THE BONZE * ARE SWARMING!
HOW WILL WE GET HIM AWAY? WHERE WILL WE TAKE HIM?
HE LOVES THE OUTDOORS. HOW ABOUT A PICNIC?
HEY, HERTZ. YOUR ADVISOR HAS A COUNTRY HOUSE. THAT MIGHT WORK...
I COULD NEVER ASK HERR DOKTOR PROFESSOR HABER THAT! I DON'T HAVE THE NERVE.

*BONZE = 'BIGWIGS'

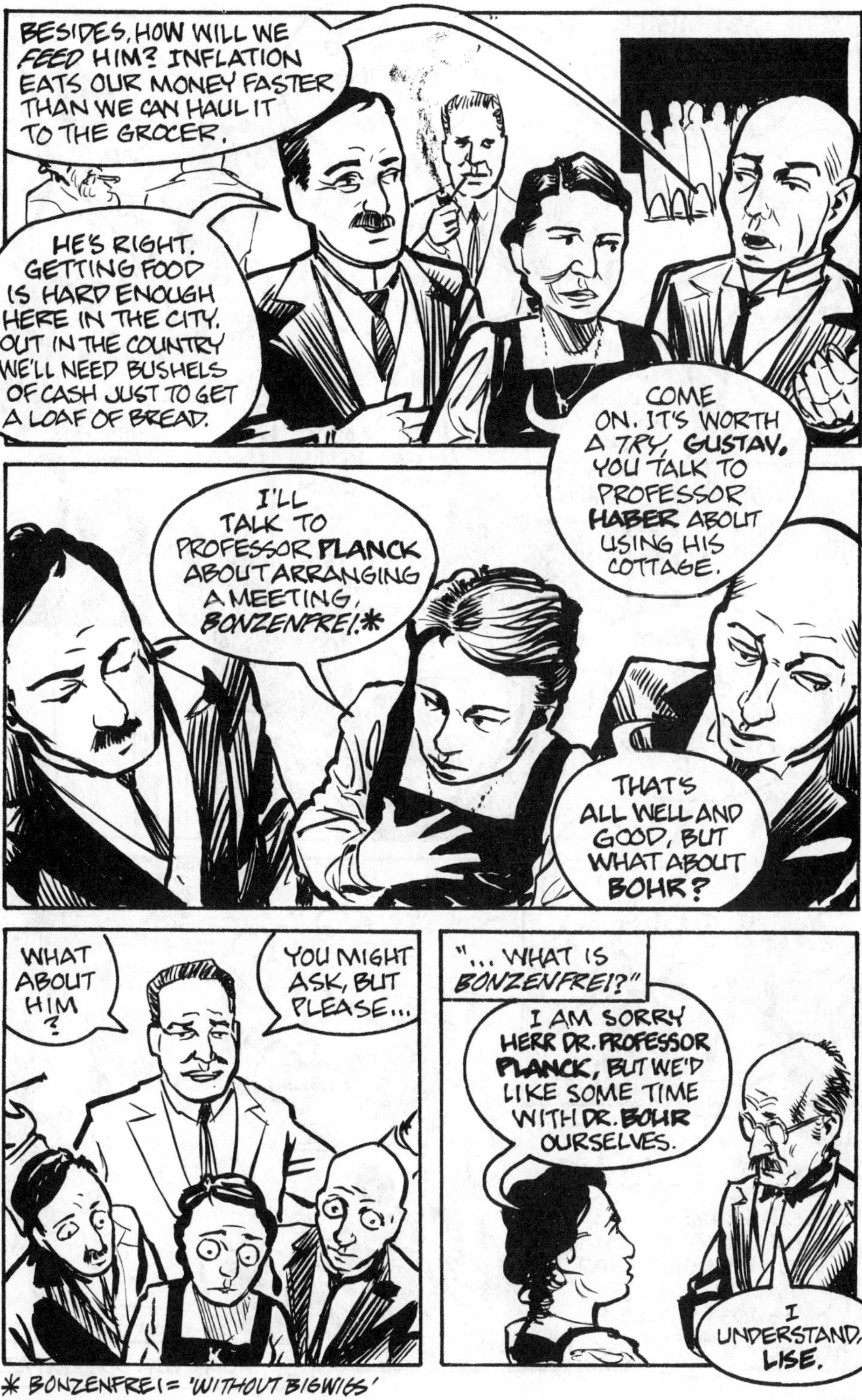
BESIDES, HOW WILL WE *FEED* HIM? INFLATION EATS OUR MONEY FASTER THAN WE CAN HAUL IT TO THE GROCER.
HE'S RIGHT. GETTING FOOD IS HARD ENOUGH HERE IN THE CITY. OUT IN THE COUNTRY WE'LL NEED BUSHELS OF CASH JUST TO GET A LOAF OF BREAD.
COME ON. IT'S WORTH A *TRY*, **GUSTAV.** YOU TALK TO PROFESSOR **HABER** ABOUT USING HIS COTTAGE.
I'LL TALK TO PROFESSOR **PLANCK** ABOUT ARRANGING A MEETING, *BONZENFREI*.*
THAT'S ALL WELL AND GOOD, BUT WHAT ABOUT **BOHR**?
WHAT ABOUT HIM ?
YOU MIGHT ASK, BUT PLEASE...
"... WHAT IS *BONZENFREI*?"
I AM SORRY **HERR DR. PROFESSOR PLANCK**, BUT WE'D LIKE SOME TIME WITH **DR. BOHR** OURSELVES.
I UNDERSTAND, **LISE**.

* BONZENFREI = *'WITHOUT BIGWIGS'*

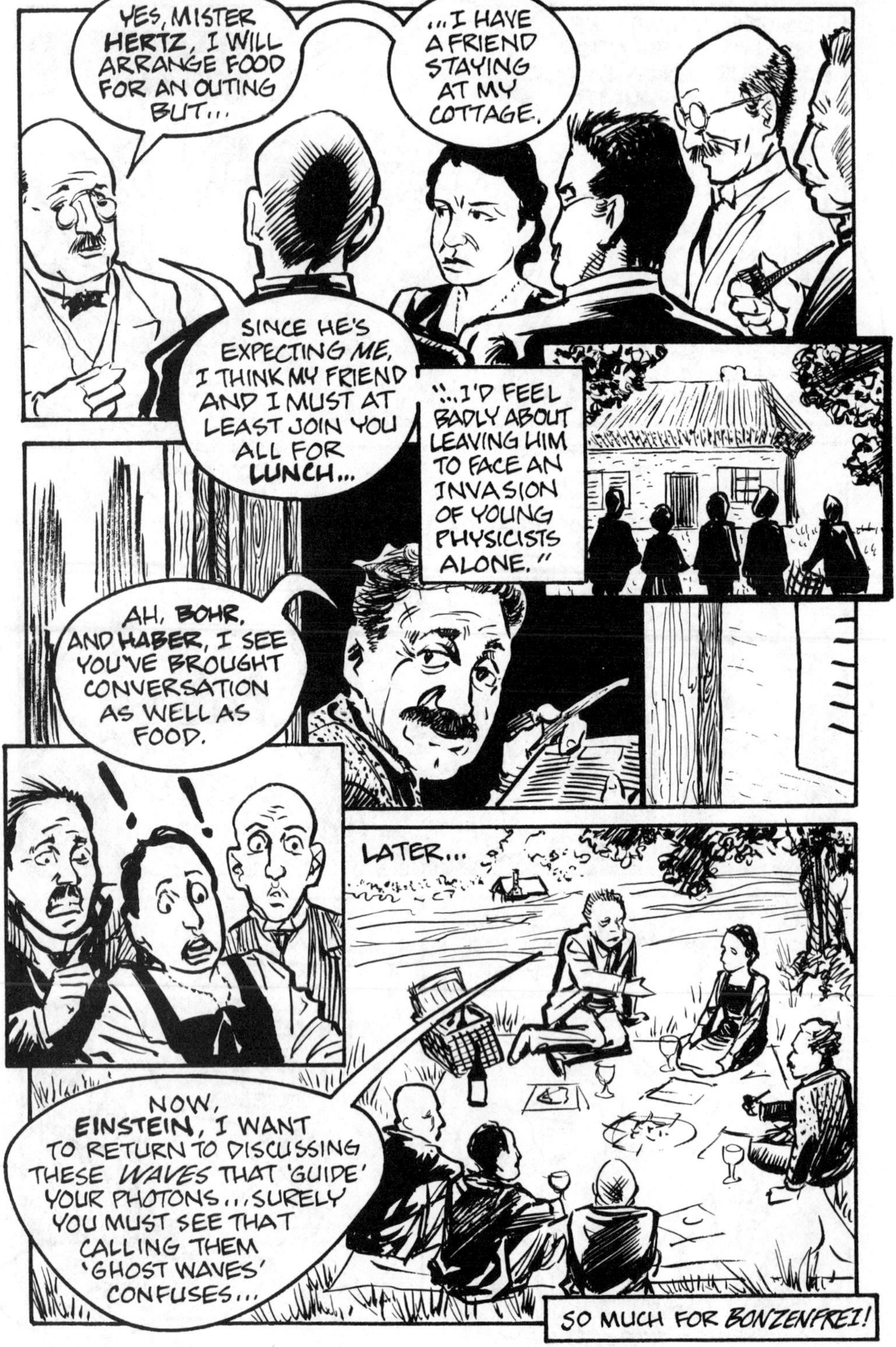
YES, MISTER HERTZ, I WILL ARRANGE FOOD FOR AN OUTING BUT...
...I HAVE A FRIEND STAYING AT MY COTTAGE.
SINCE HE'S EXPECTING ME, I THINK MY FRIEND AND I MUST AT LEAST JOIN YOU ALL FOR LUNCH...
"...I'D FEEL BADLY ABOUT LEAVING HIM TO FACE AN INVASION OF YOUNG PHYSICISTS ALONE."
AH, BOHR. AND HABER, I SEE YOU'VE BROUGHT CONVERSATION AS WELL AS FOOD.
! !
LATER...
NOW, EINSTEIN, I WANT TO RETURN TO DISCUSSING THESE WAVES THAT 'GUIDE' YOUR PHOTONS... SURELY YOU MUST SEE THAT CALLING THEM 'GHOST WAVES' CONFUSES...
SO MUCH FOR BONZENFREI!

Chapter 5

BUT EVEN WITH ALL THE ACCLAIM, **BOHR** SOMETIMES FELT ISOLATED. EVEN IN 1922, THE YEAR HE WON THE *NOBEL PRIZE* *, HE WROTE:

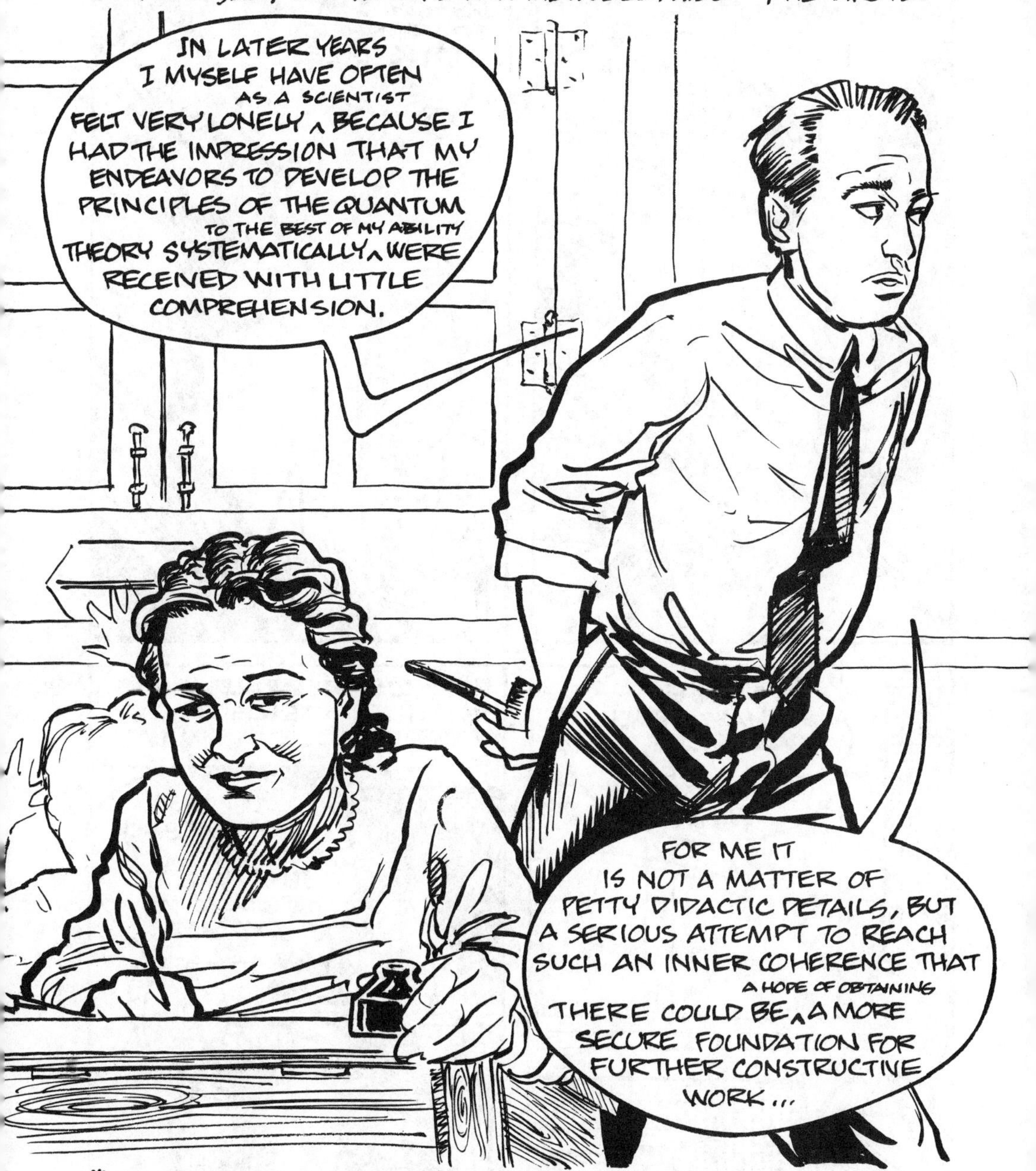
IN LATER YEARS I MYSELF HAVE OFTEN FELT VERY LONELY AS A SCIENTIST BECAUSE I HAD THE IMPRESSION THAT MY ENDEAVORS TO DEVELOP THE PRINCIPLES OF THE QUANTUM THEORY SYSTEMATICALLY TO THE BEST OF MY ABILITY WERE RECEIVED WITH LITTLE COMPREHENSION.
FOR ME IT IS NOT A MATTER OF PETTY DIDACTIC DETAILS, BUT A SERIOUS ATTEMPT TO REACH SUCH AN INNER COHERENCE THAT THERE COULD BE A HOPE OF OBTAINING A MORE SECURE FOUNDATION FOR FURTHER CONSTRUCTIVE WORK...

* WHERE HE LEFT THE NOTES AND SLIDES FOR HIS SPEECH IN HIS HOTEL IN STOCKHOLM, THUS TREATING HIS AUDIENCE TO AN OFF-THE-CUFF SPEECH (UNTIL THE MATERIAL WAS RUSHED OVER FROM HIS ROOM). ALL ACCOUNTS INDICATE THAT, AT LEAST FOR A WHILE, IT WAS CLEARER AND MORE ENTERTAINING THAN THE MUMBLED DELIVERY OF THE PREPARED LECTURE...THE ONE ONLY *HE* WAS RELIEVED TO RETURN TO.

HE DID HOWEVER HAVE A SECURE FOUNDATION AT HOME BY THEN,

HE HAD **MARGRETHE**...

BUT **NIELS**, AND NOT TO CRITICIZE, *SURELY* YOU MUST SEE THAT THIS IS **NOT** LOGICAL.

*UH-OH, I'M STARTING TO **TALK** LIKE HIM.*

I'LL BE *STRAIGHT* BACK, **KRAMERS**, I JUST HAVE TO SPEAK TO MY **WIFE**.

..., FROM WHOM HE TOOK STRENGTH AND INSPIRATION.

HIS BROTHER **HARALD**, WHOSE INSTITUTE WAS RIGHT NEXT DOOR, FULFILLED A SIMILAR ROLE.

I'LL BE *STRAIGHT* BACK, **KRAMERS**, I JUST HAVE TO SPEAK TO MY **BROTHER**.

AND THEN THERE CAME THE CHILDREN. BY THE END OF 1922, **CHRISTIAN**, **HANS ERIK**, AND **AAGE** HAD JOINED THE FAMILY.

WHEN **ERNEST** FOLLOWED A FEW YEARS LATER, THEY HAD WORN OUT THEIR FIRST BABY CARRIAGE.

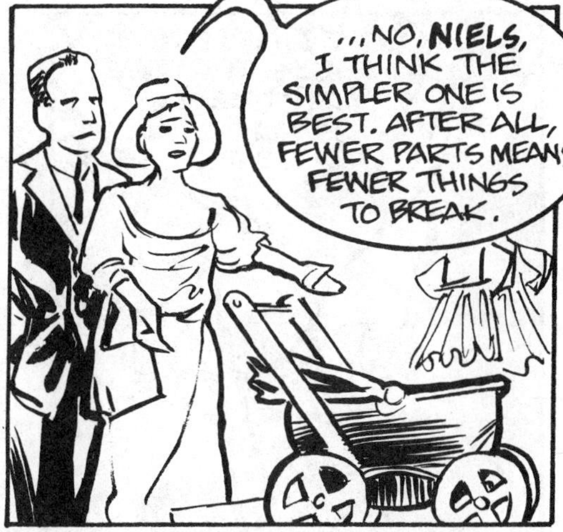
...NO, **NIELS**, I THINK THE SIMPLER ONE IS BEST. AFTER ALL, FEWER PARTS MEANS FEWER THINGS TO BREAK.

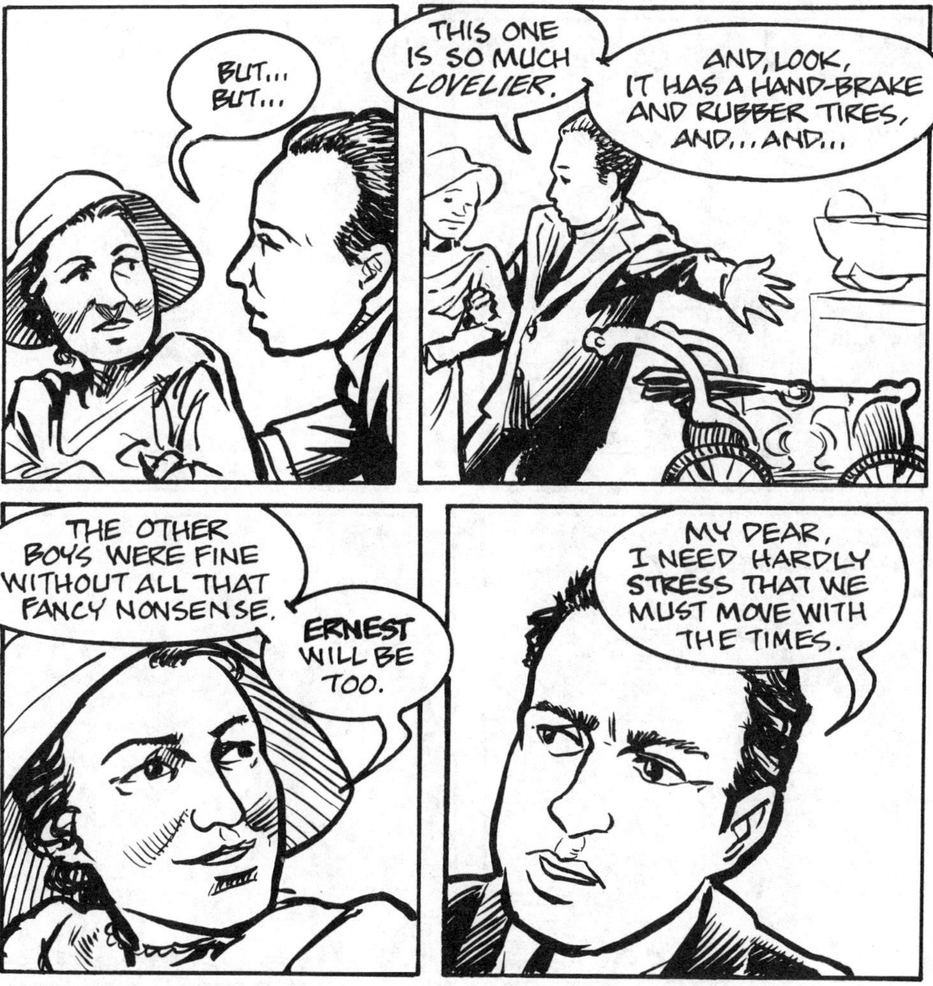
BUT... BUT...
THIS ONE IS SO MUCH *LOVELIER*.
AND, LOOK, IT HAS A HAND-BRAKE AND RUBBER TIRES, AND... AND...
THE OTHER BOYS WERE FINE WITHOUT ALL THAT FANCY NONSENSE.
ERNEST WILL BE TOO.
MY DEAR, I NEED HARDLY STRESS THAT WE MUST MOVE WITH THE TIMES.

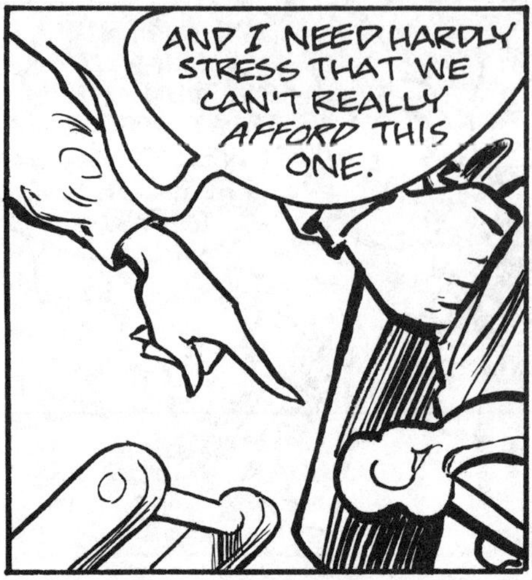
AND I NEED HARDLY STRESS THAT WE CAN'T REALLY AFFORD THIS ONE.

AND SO IT WENT, BACK AND FORTH AND BACK AND FORTH AND SO ON UNTIL...

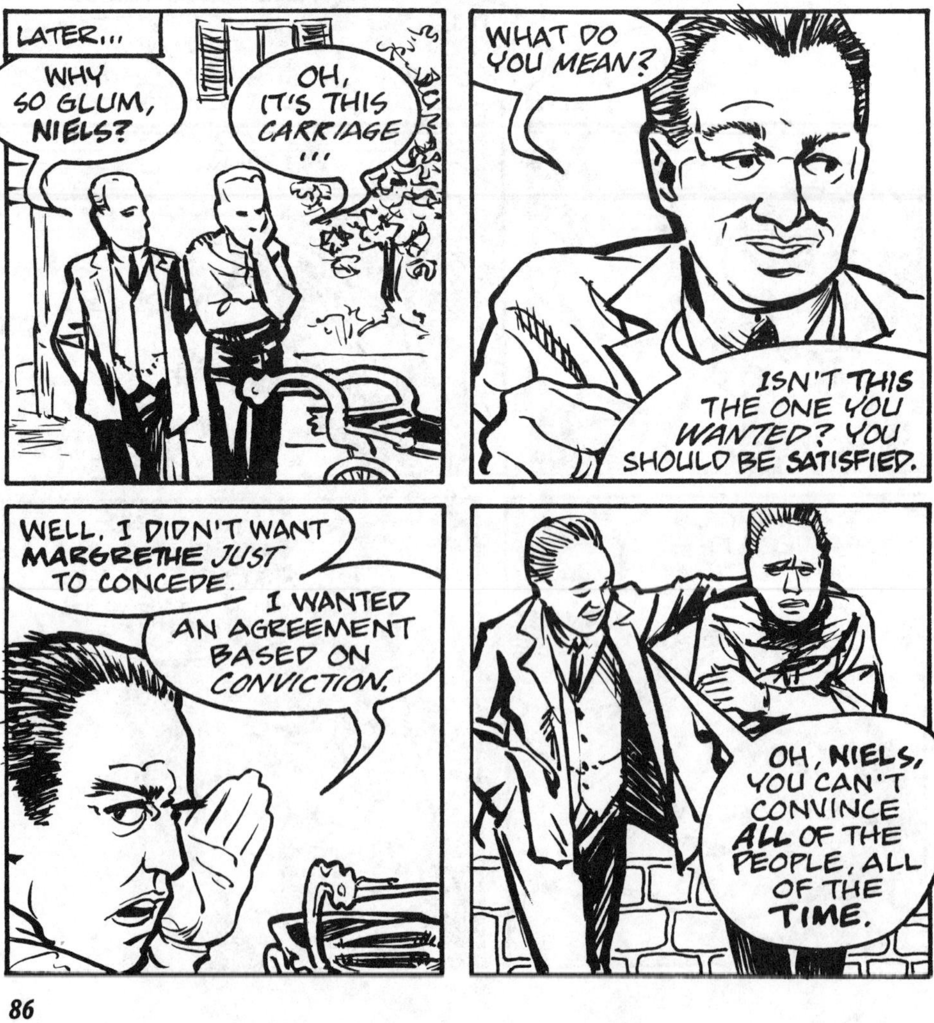
LATER...
WHY SO GLUM, NIELS?
OH, IT'S THIS CARRIAGE ...
WHAT DO YOU MEAN?
ISN'T THIS THE ONE YOU WANTED? YOU SHOULD BE SATISFIED.
WELL, I DIDN'T WANT MARGRETHE JUST TO CONCEDE.
I WANTED AN AGREEMENT BASED ON CONVICTION.
OH, NIELS, YOU CAN'T CONVINCE ALL OF THE PEOPLE, ALL OF THE TIME.

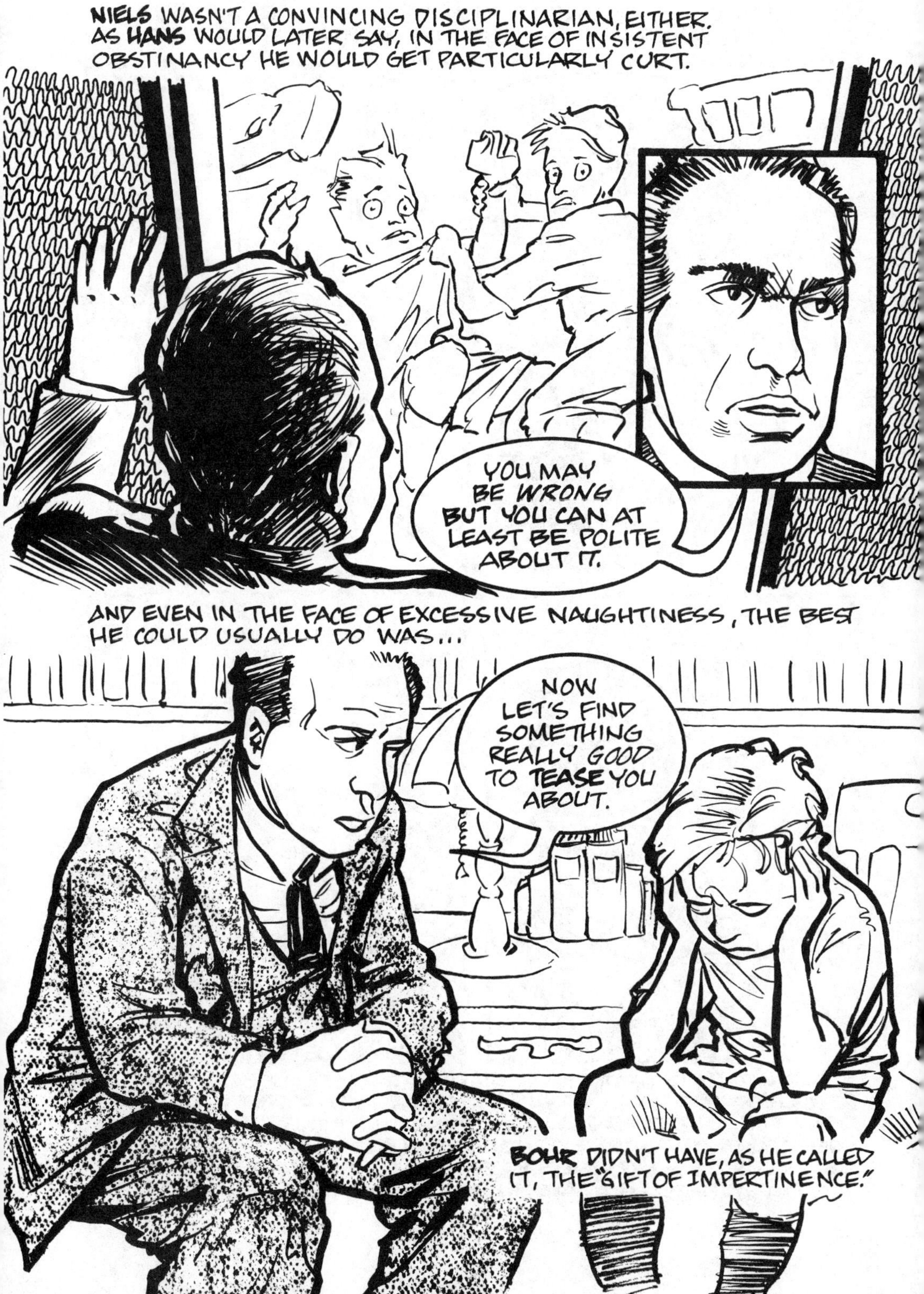
NIELS WASN'T A CONVINCING DISCIPLINARIAN, EITHER. AS HANS WOULD LATER SAY, IN THE FACE OF INSISTENT OBSTINANCY HE WOULD GET PARTICULARLY CURT.
YOU MAY BE WRONG BUT YOU CAN AT LEAST BE POLITE ABOUT IT.
AND EVEN IN THE FACE OF EXCESSIVE NAUGHTINESS, THE BEST HE COULD USUALLY DO WAS...
NOW LET'S FIND SOMETHING REALLY GOOD TO TEASE YOU ABOUT.
BOHR DIDN'T HAVE, AS HE CALLED IT, THE "GIFT OF IMPERTINENCE."

HE HAD THE GIFT OF STORYTELLING*, THOUGH, AND A FAMILIAR TALE TOLD AFTER DINNER OR WHILE PICKING BLACK CURRANTS AT *LYNGHUSET* (THE **BOHR** SUMMER HOME IN *TISVILDE*) WAS A REGULAR FEATURE OF THE HOUSEHOLD.

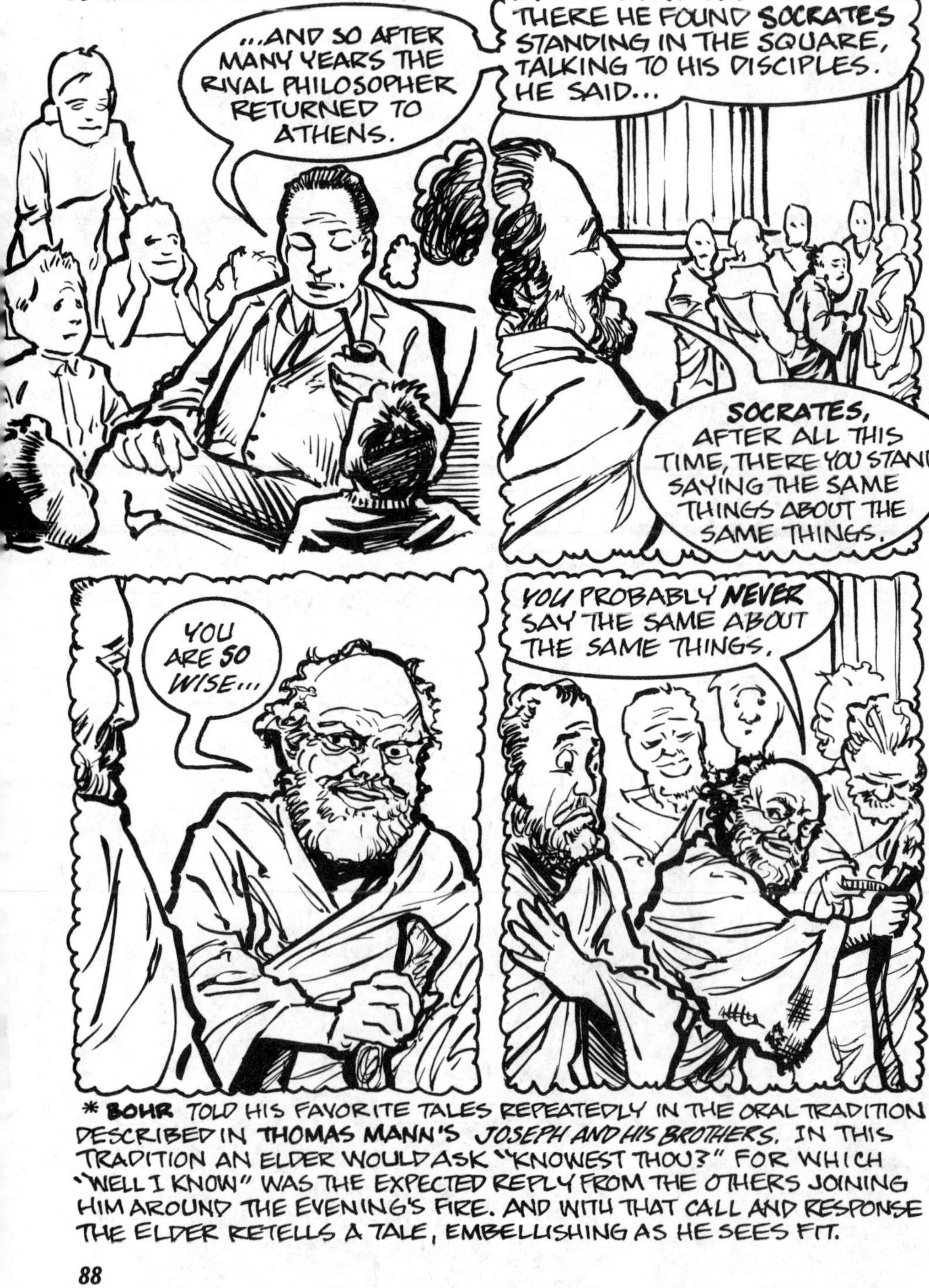

...AND SO AFTER MANY YEARS THE RIVAL PHILOSOPHER RETURNED TO ATHENS.
THERE HE FOUND **SOCRATES** STANDING IN THE SQUARE, TALKING TO HIS DISCIPLES. HE SAID...
SOCRATES, AFTER ALL THIS TIME, THERE YOU STAND SAYING THE SAME THINGS ABOUT THE SAME THINGS.
YOU ARE **SO** *WISE*...
YOU PROBABLY ***NEVER*** SAY THE SAME ABOUT THE SAME THINGS.

* **BOHR** TOLD HIS FAVORITE TALES REPEATEDLY IN THE ORAL TRADITION DESCRIBED IN **THOMAS MANN'S** *JOSEPH AND HIS BROTHERS*. IN THIS TRADITION AN ELDER WOULD ASK "KNOWEST THOU?" FOR WHICH "WELL I KNOW" WAS THE EXPECTED REPLY FROM THE OTHERS JOINING HIM AROUND THE EVENING'S FIRE. AND WITH THAT CALL AND RESPONSE THE ELDER RETELLS A TALE, EMBELLISHING AS HE SEES FIT.

AN INTELLECTUAL UPBRINGING, TO BE SURE.* BUT JUST AS **NIELS** WAS PHYSICALLY ACTIVE THROUGHOUT HIS LIFE, THE BOYS WERE BROUGHT UP *OUTDOORS* AS MUCH AS IN.

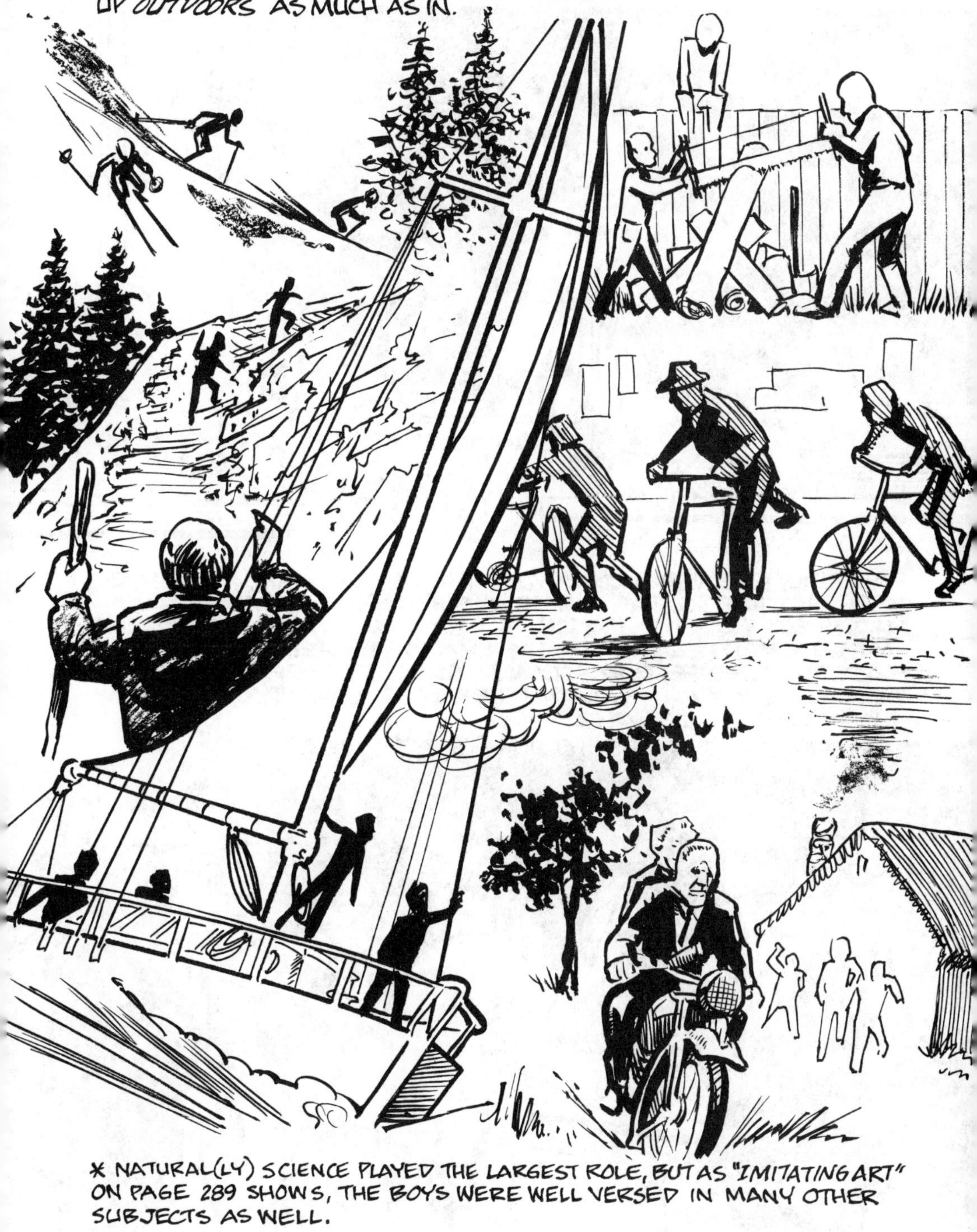

* NATURAL(LY) SCIENCE PLAYED THE LARGEST ROLE, BUT AS "IMITATING ART" ON PAGE 289 SHOWS, THE BOYS WERE WELL VERSED IN MANY OTHER SUBJECTS AS WELL.

IT'S A WONDER HE GOT ANY WORK DONE, BUT IN FACT HE THRIVED ON ALL THE ACTIVITY, AS HE'D SAY TO HIS FRIENDS

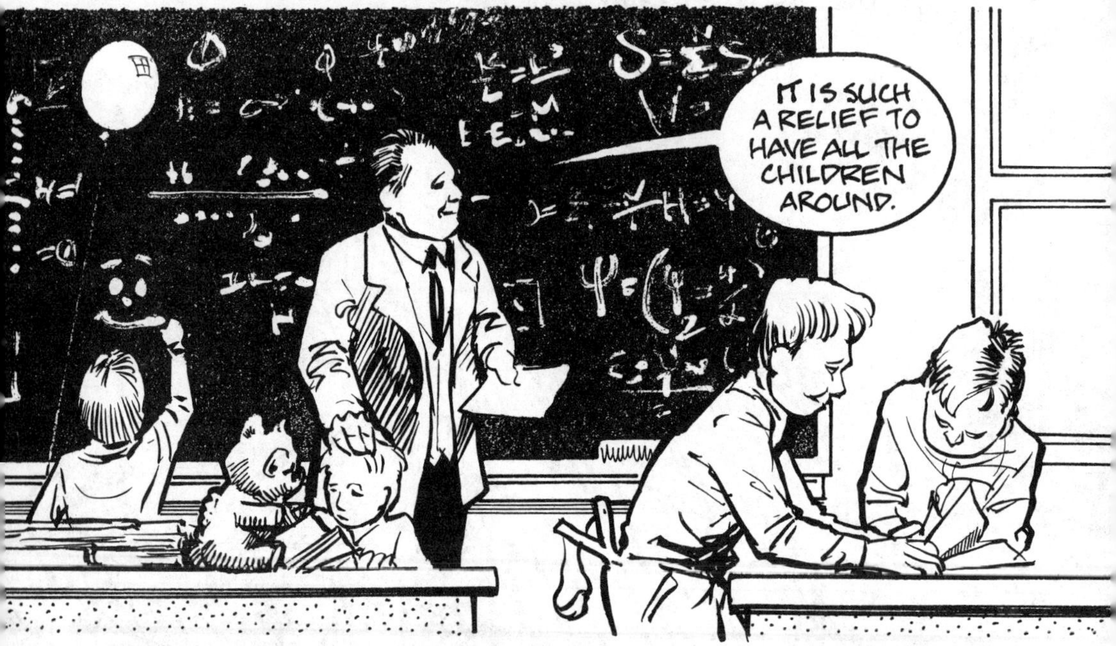
IT IS SUCH A RELIEF TO HAVE ALL THE CHILDREN AROUND.

HIS FAMILY EXTENDED WELL BEYOND THE TIES OF BLOOD, AND VISITORS TO HIS INSTITUTE SUCH AS **BLOCH***, **CASIMIR**, **DELBRÜCK***, **DIRAC*** **EHRENFEST**, **FRANCK***, **FRISCH**, **GAMOW**, **HEVESY***, **KLEIN**, **KRAMERS**, **LANDAU***, **MEITNER**, **MOTT***, **NISHINA**, **OPPENHEIMER**, **PAULI***, **PLACZEK**, **ROSENFELD**, **ROSSELAND**, **SCHRÖDINGER***, **TOLMAN**, **WEIZSÄCKER & C** ... WOULD IN THEIR LATER YEARS PROUDLY CLAIM THEY STUDIED WITH **BOHR**.

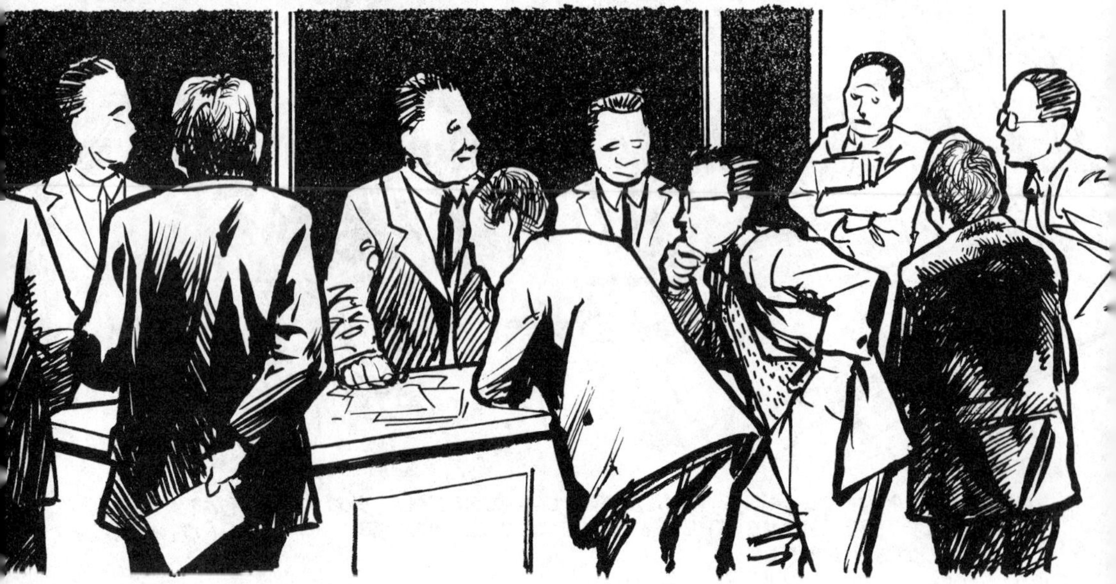

*NOBEL PRIZE WINNERS

MANY CAME FOR WEEKS AND ENDED UP EXTENDING THEIR STAY, FOR TO KNOW **NIELS BOHR**, IN THE WORDS OF **BOHR** AND **EINSTEIN'S** COLLEAGUE (AND PEER) **PAUL EHRENFEST**, WAS "THE MOST IMPORTANT THING TO HAPPEN IN THE LIFE OF A YOUNG PHYSICIST."

BOHR'S FAME DIDN'T PRECEDE HIM OUTSIDE OF SCIENTIFIC CIRCLES, THOUGH, AND **HENDRIK CASIMIR'S** FATHER DIDN'T *BELIEVE* THAT SUCH A THING AS A *FAMOUS PHYSICIST* COULD EXIST, UNTIL...

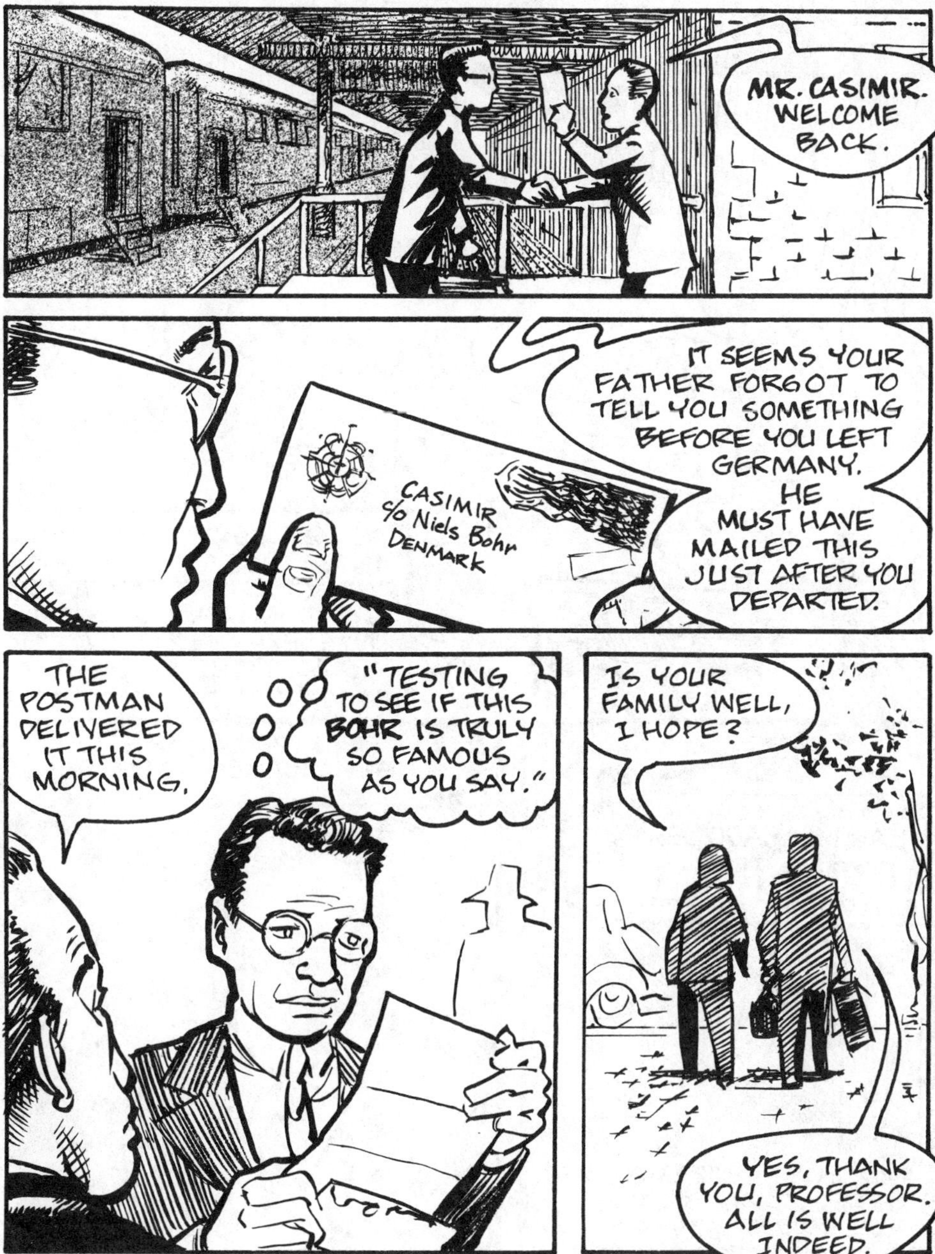
MR. CASIMIR. WELCOME BACK.
IT SEEMS YOUR FATHER FORGOT TO TELL YOU SOMETHING BEFORE YOU LEFT GERMANY. HE MUST HAVE MAILED THIS JUST AFTER YOU DEPARTED.
CASIMIR
c/o Niels Bohr
Denmark
THE POSTMAN DELIVERED IT THIS MORNING.
"TESTING TO SEE IF THIS BOHR IS TRULY SO FAMOUS AS YOU SAY."
IS YOUR FAMILY WELL, I HOPE?
YES, THANK YOU, PROFESSOR. ALL IS WELL INDEED.

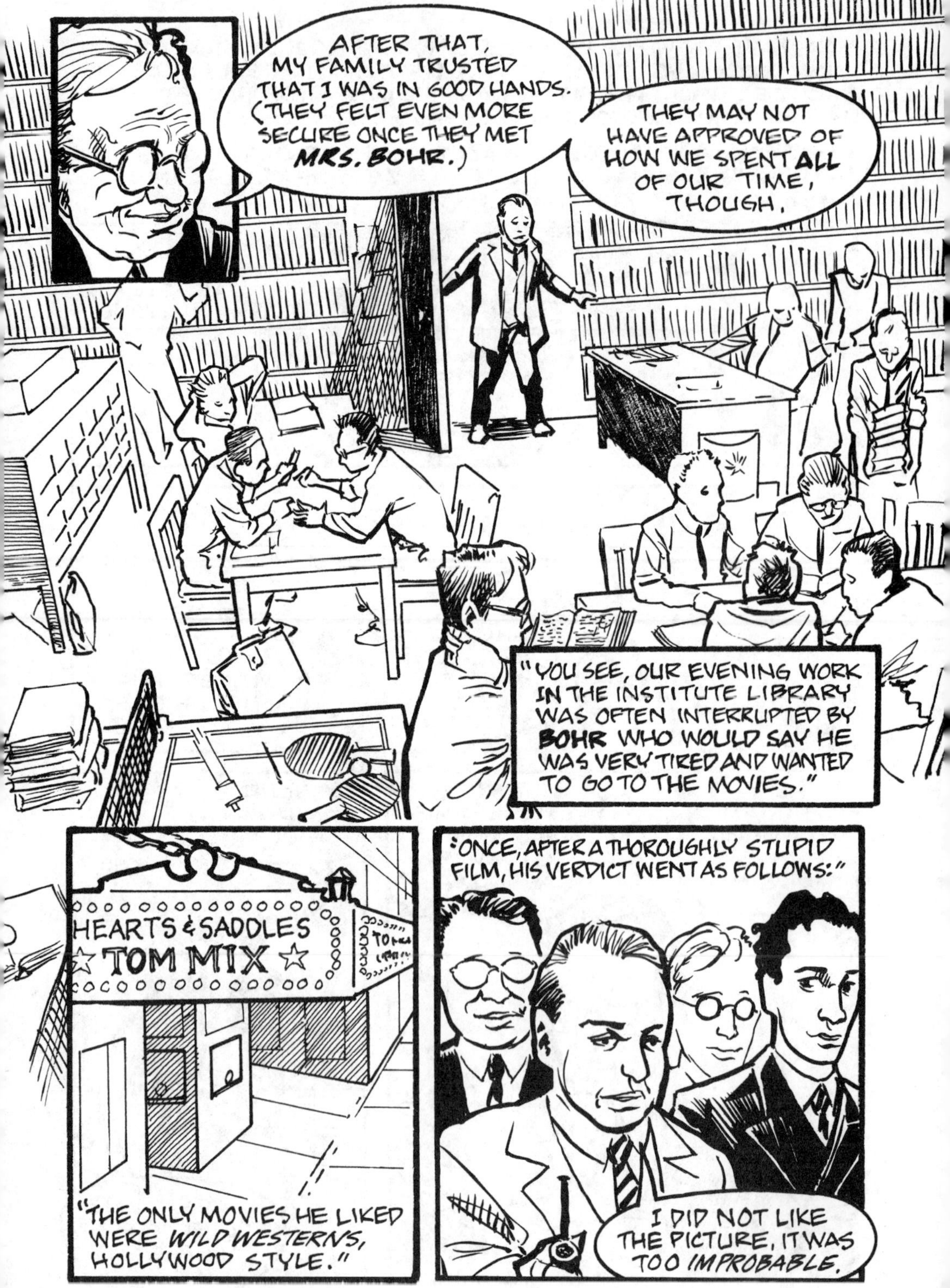
AFTER THAT, MY FAMILY TRUSTED THAT I WAS IN GOOD HANDS. (THEY FELT EVEN MORE SECURE ONCE THEY MET **MRS. BOHR.**)
THEY MAY NOT HAVE APPROVED OF HOW WE SPENT **ALL** OF OUR TIME, THOUGH.
"YOU SEE, OUR EVENING WORK IN THE INSTITUTE LIBRARY WAS OFTEN INTERRUPTED BY **BOHR** WHO WOULD SAY HE WAS VERY TIRED AND WANTED TO GO TO THE MOVIES."
HEARTS & SADDLES
TOM MIX
"THE ONLY MOVIES HE LIKED WERE *WILD WESTERNS*, HOLLYWOOD STYLE."
"ONCE, AFTER A THOROUGHLY STUPID FILM, HIS VERDICT WENT AS FOLLOWS:"
I DID NOT LIKE THE PICTURE, IT WAS TOO *IMPROBABLE*.

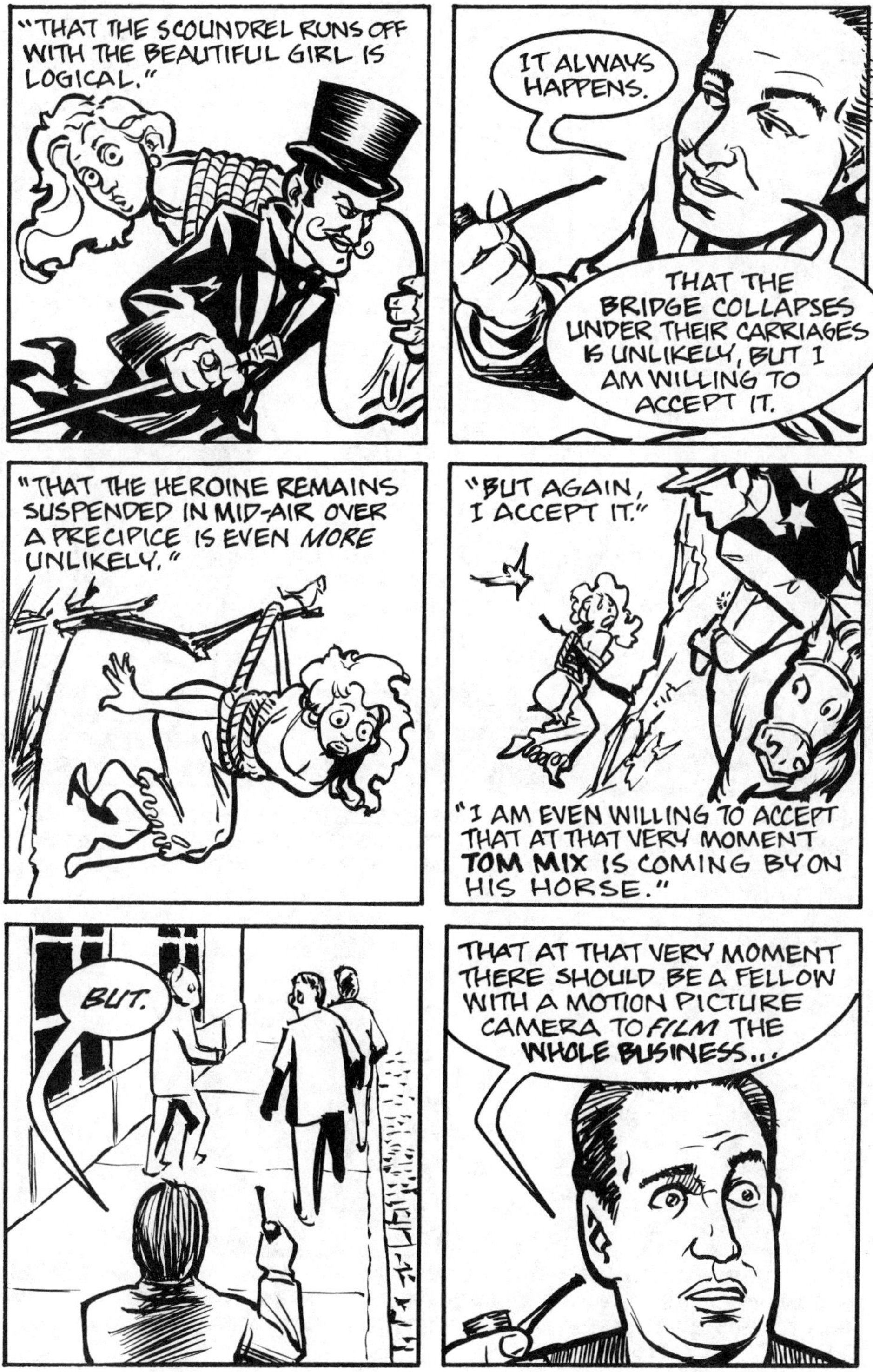
"THAT THE SCOUNDREL RUNS OFF WITH THE BEAUTIFUL GIRL IS LOGICAL."
IT ALWAYS HAPPENS.
THAT THE BRIDGE COLLAPSES UNDER THEIR CARRIAGES IS UNLIKELY, BUT I AM WILLING TO ACCEPT IT.
"THAT THE HEROINE REMAINS SUSPENDED IN MID-AIR OVER A PRECIPICE IS EVEN *MORE* UNLIKELY."
"BUT AGAIN, I ACCEPT IT."
"I AM EVEN WILLING TO ACCEPT THAT AT THAT VERY MOMENT **TOM MIX** IS COMING BY ON HIS HORSE."
BUT.
THAT AT THAT VERY MOMENT THERE SHOULD BE A FELLOW WITH A MOTION PICTURE CAMERA TO *FILM* THE **WHOLE BUSINESS**...

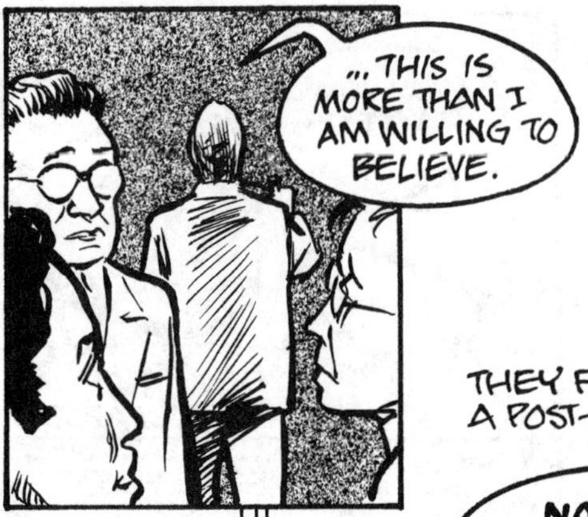
...THIS IS MORE THAN I AM WILLING TO BELIEVE.

BOHR HAD OTHER IDEAS RELATED TO WESTERNS* BUT THIS ONE ON PROBABILITY AND THE ROLE OF THE OBSERVER HAS A PARTICULARLY STRONG RESONANCE FOR PHYSICISTS, SINCE IT RELATES TO THE THEORIES OF **WERNER HEISENBERG**—**BOHR'S** FAVORITE (PHYSICS) SON.

THEY FIRST MET IN GÖTTINGEN DURING A POST-*BONZENFREI* TOUR OF GERMANY...

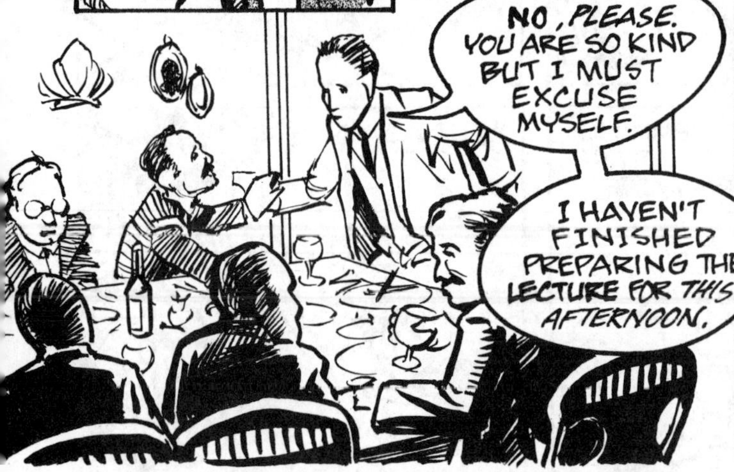
NO, *PLEASE.* YOU ARE SO KIND BUT I MUST EXCUSE MYSELF.
I HAVEN'T FINISHED PREPARING THE **LECTURE** FOR *THIS AFTERNOON.*

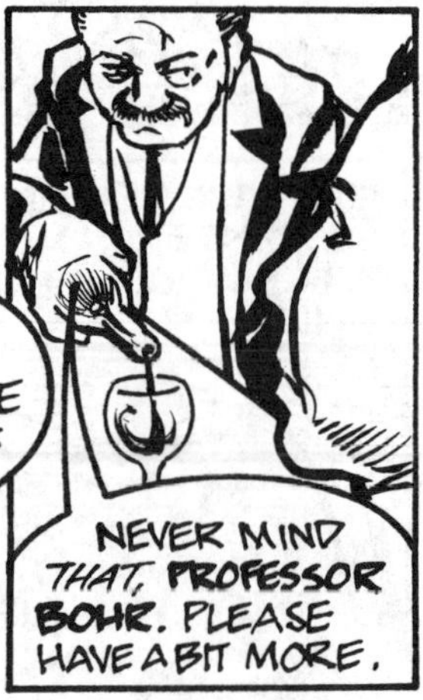
NEVER MIND *THAT,* **PROFESSOR BOHR**. PLEASE HAVE A BIT MORE.

HIS REPUTATION AS A LECTURER HAD PRECEDED HIM—PROBABLY VIA **HARALD**. AS **BOHR** REMEMBERED LATER, **SOMMERFELD** "GAVE A GREAT LUNCH BEFORE THE TALK, AND I WAS AFRAID TO DRINK SO MUCH WINE, BUT THEY SAY IT HELPED."

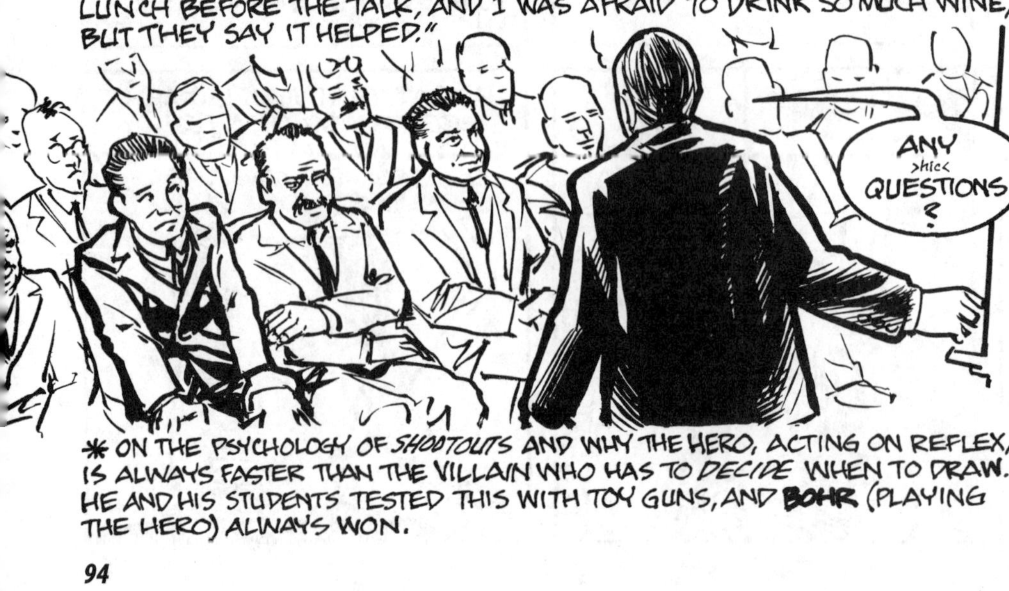
ANY >HIC< QUESTIONS?

* ON THE PSYCHOLOGY OF *SHOOTOUTS* AND WHY THE HERO, ACTING ON REFLEX, IS ALWAYS FASTER THAN THE VILLAIN WHO HAS TO *DECIDE* WHEN TO DRAW. HE AND HIS STUDENTS TESTED THIS WITH TOY GUNS, AND **BOHR** (PLAYING THE HERO) ALWAYS WON.

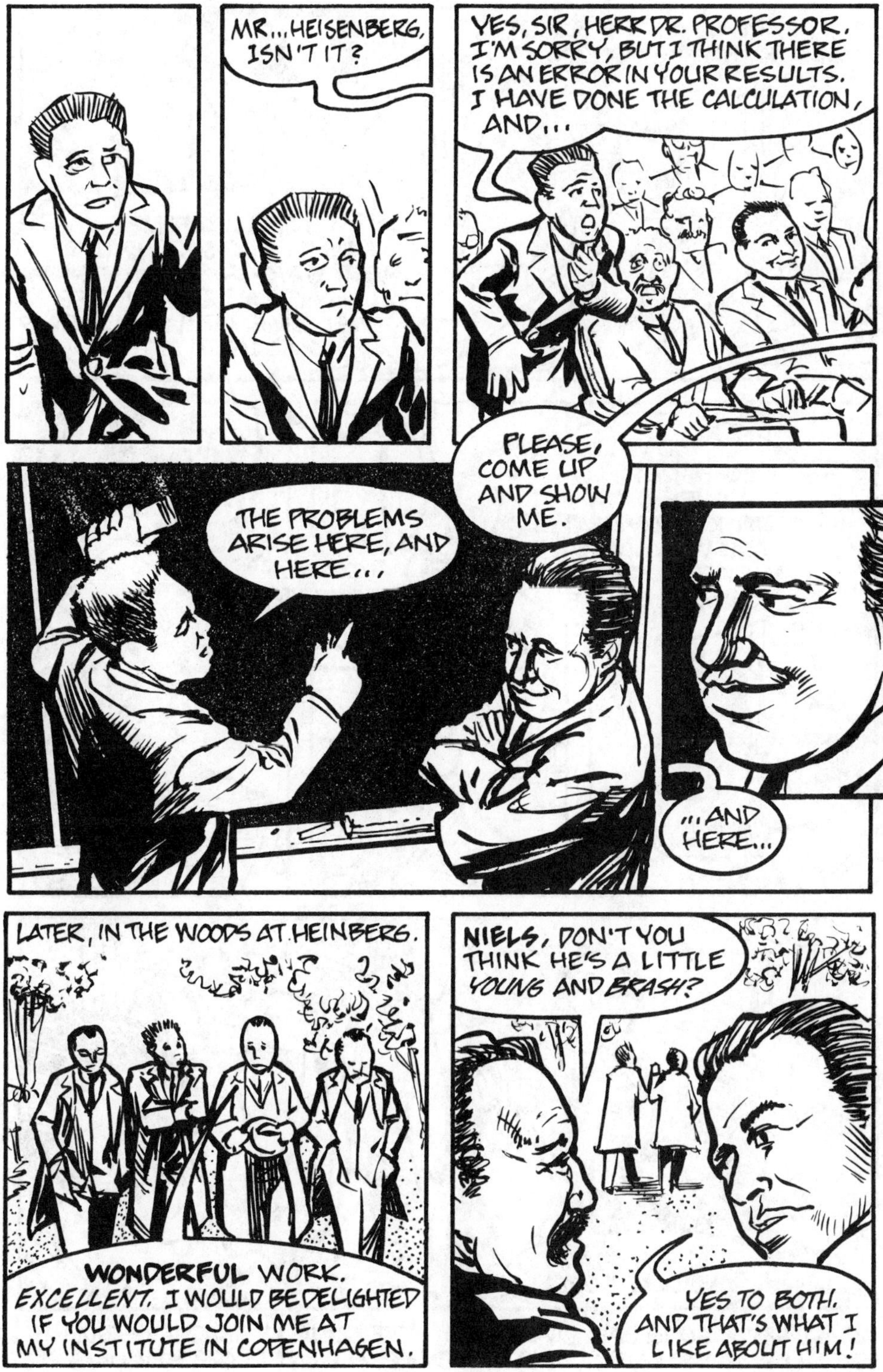

MR... HEISENBERG, ISN'T IT?
YES, SIR, HERR DR. PROFESSOR. I'M SORRY, BUT I THINK THERE IS AN ERROR IN YOUR RESULTS. I HAVE DONE THE CALCULATION, AND...
PLEASE, COME UP AND SHOW ME.
THE PROBLEMS ARISE HERE, AND HERE...
...AND HERE...
LATER, IN THE WOODS AT HEINBERG.
WONDERFUL WORK. EXCELLENT. I WOULD BE DELIGHTED IF YOU WOULD JOIN ME AT MY INSTITUTE IN COPENHAGEN.
NIELS, DON'T YOU THINK HE'S A LITTLE YOUNG AND BRASH?
YES TO BOTH. AND THAT'S WHAT I LIKE ABOUT HIM!

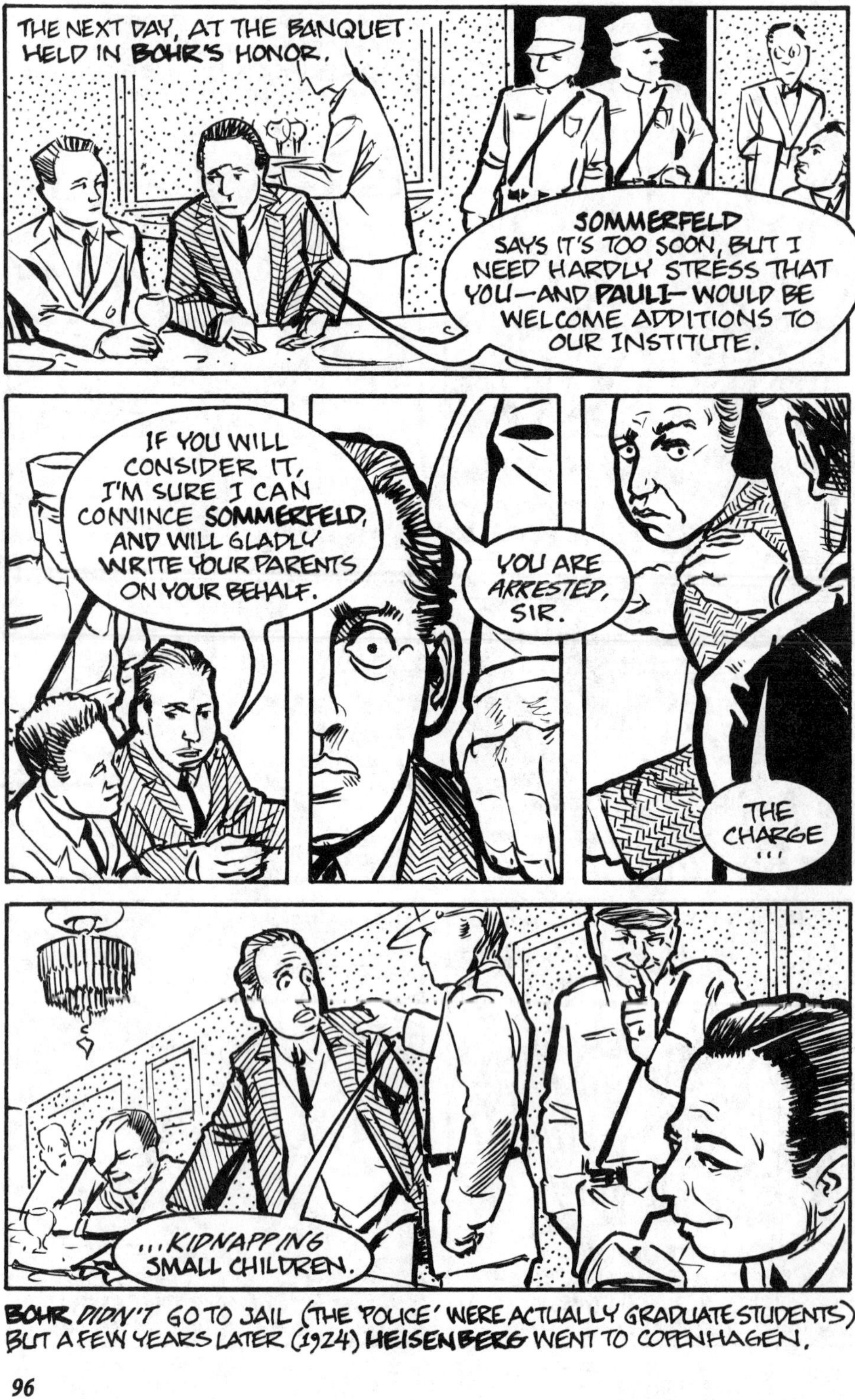
THE NEXT DAY, AT THE BANQUET HELD IN BOHR'S HONOR.
SOMMERFELD SAYS IT'S TOO SOON, BUT I NEED HARDLY STRESS THAT YOU—AND PAULI—WOULD BE WELCOME ADDITIONS TO OUR INSTITUTE.
IF YOU WILL CONSIDER IT, I'M SURE I CAN CONVINCE SOMMERFELD, AND WILL GLADLY WRITE YOUR PARENTS ON YOUR BEHALF.
YOU ARE ARRESTED, SIR.
THE CHARGE ...
...KIDNAPPING SMALL CHILDREN.
BOHR DIDN'T GO TO JAIL (THE 'POLICE' WERE ACTUALLY GRADUATE STUDENTS) BUT A FEW YEARS LATER (1924) HEISENBERG WENT TO COPENHAGEN.

Chapter 6

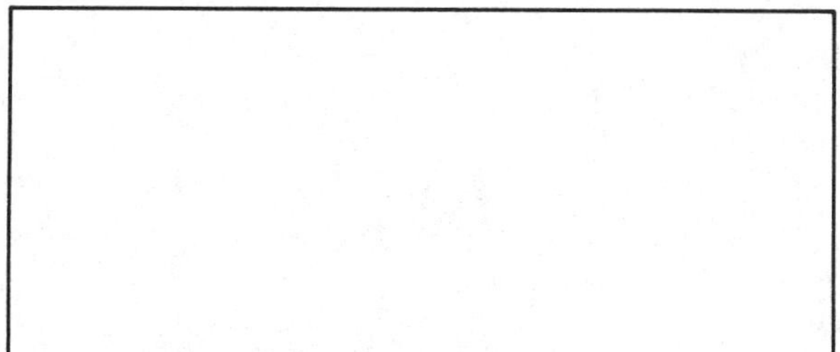

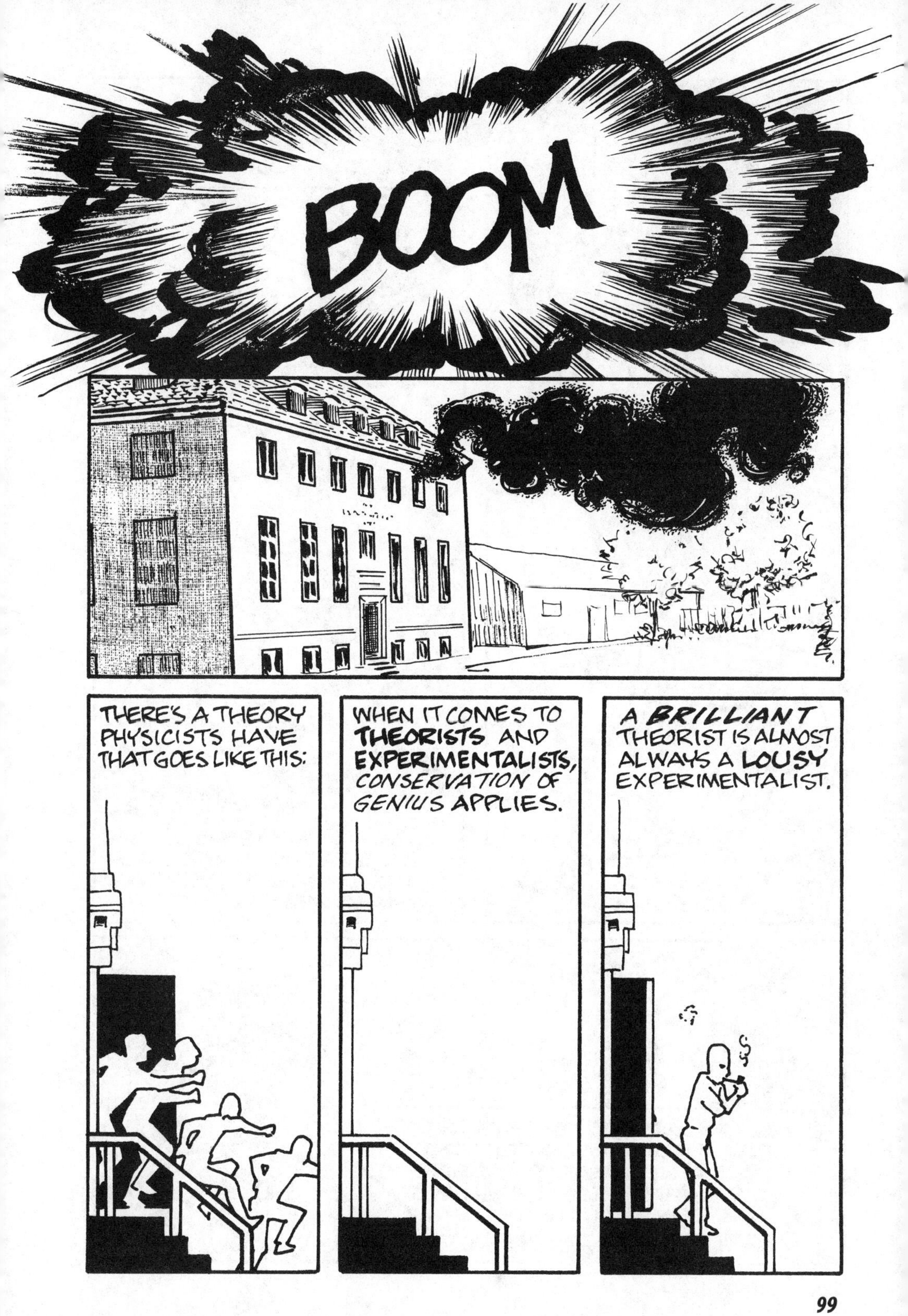
BOOM
THERE'S A THEORY PHYSICISTS HAVE THAT GOES LIKE THIS:
WHEN IT COMES TO **THEORISTS** AND **EXPERIMENTALISTS**, *CONSERVATION OF GENIUS* APPLIES.
A ***BRILLIANT*** THEORIST IS ALMOST ALWAYS A **LOUSY** EXPERIMENTALIST.

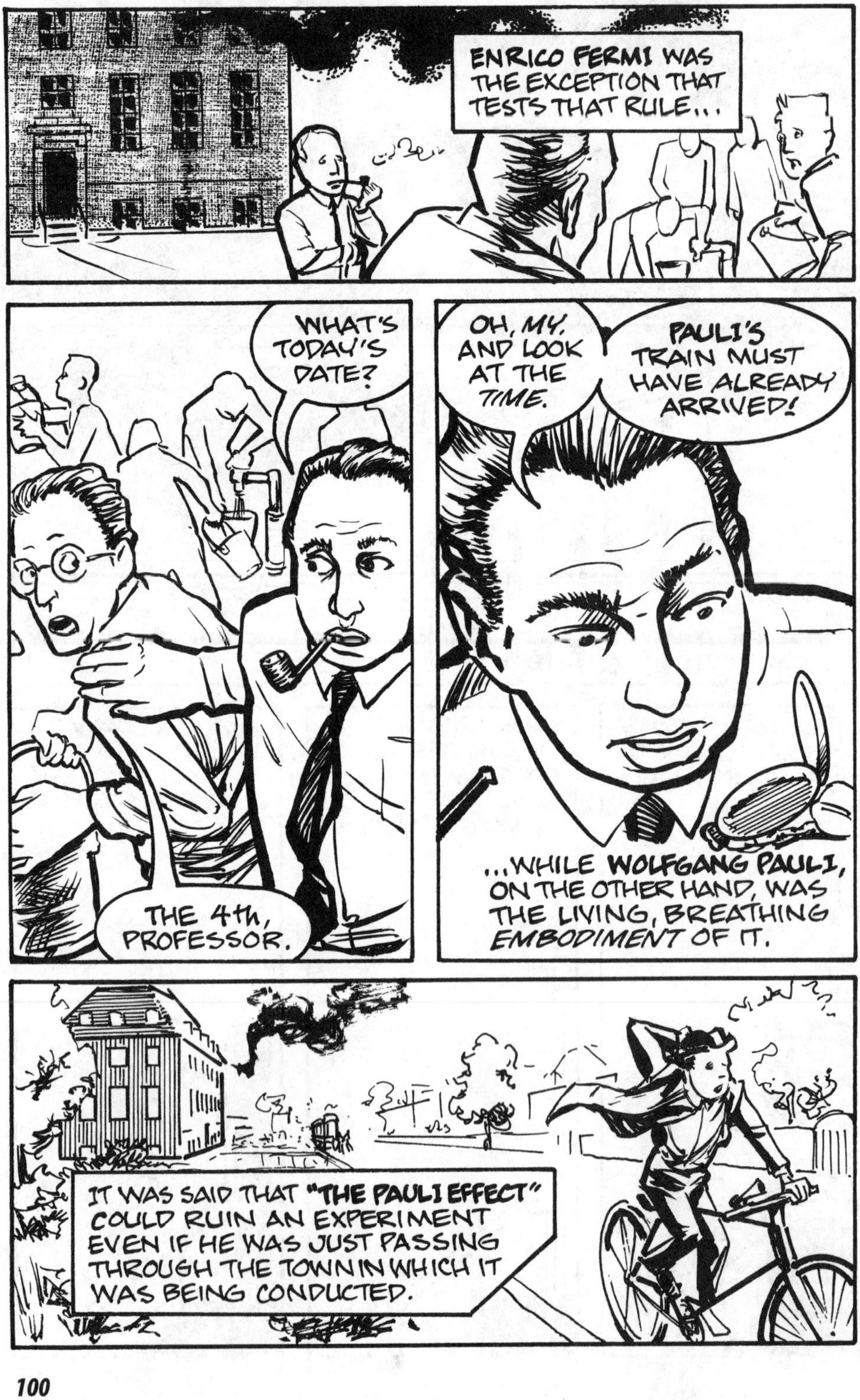
ENRICO FERMI WAS THE EXCEPTION THAT TESTS THAT RULE...
WHAT'S TODAY'S DATE?
THE 4th, PROFESSOR.
OH, MY. AND LOOK AT THE *TIME*.
PAULI'S TRAIN MUST HAVE ALREADY ARRIVED!
...WHILE **WOLFGANG PAULI**, ON THE OTHER HAND, WAS THE LIVING, BREATHING *EMBODIMENT* OF IT.
IT WAS SAID THAT **"THE PAULI EFFECT"** COULD RUIN AN EXPERIMENT EVEN IF HE WAS JUST PASSING THROUGH THE TOWN IN WHICH IT WAS BEING CONDUCTED.

FRIENDS WHO WERE *EXPERIMENTALISTS* WOULD ONLY CONSULT WITH HIM THROUGH **CLOSED DOORS** LEADING TO THEIR LABS.

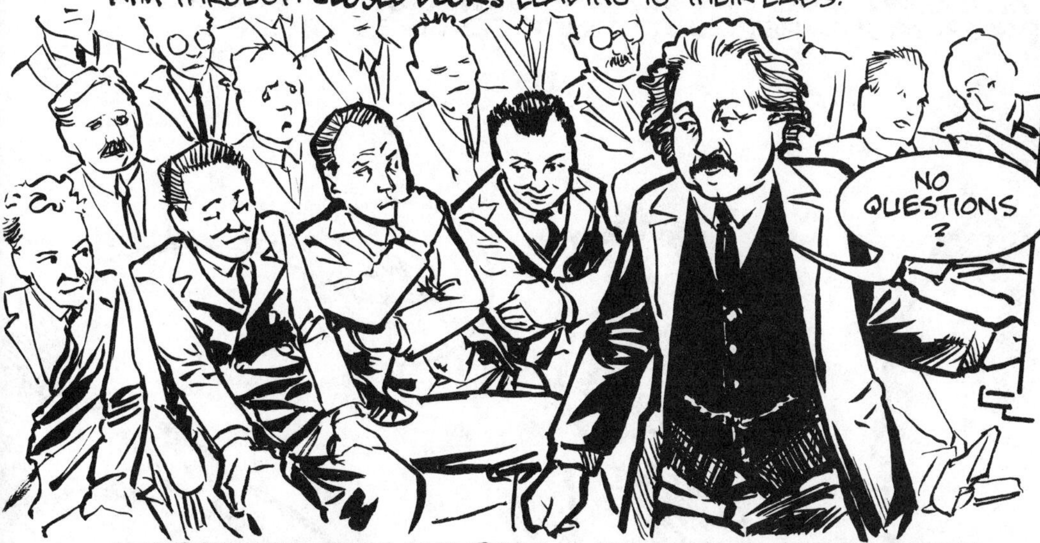
NO QUESTIONS ?

AND BETWEEN **PAULI** AND **BOHR**, A CONSERVATION OF *POLITENESS* PRINCIPLE SEEMED TO OPERATE AS WELL. AS POLITE AS **BOHR** WAS, **PAULI** WAS ... NOT.

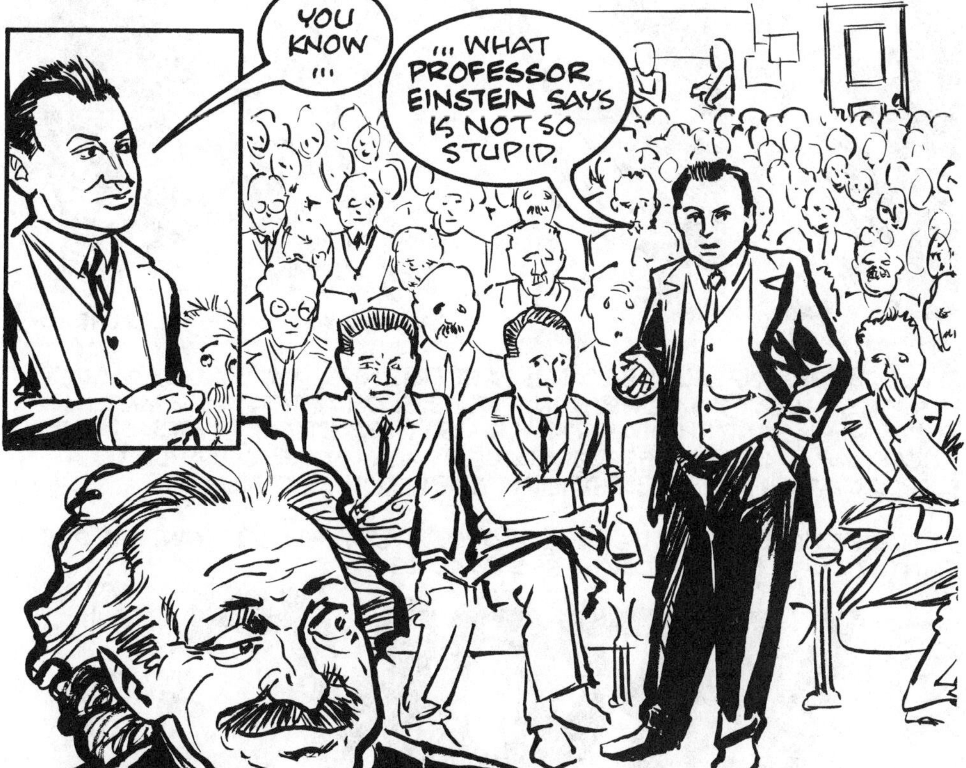
YOU KNOW ...
... WHAT PROFESSOR EINSTEIN SAYS IS NOT SO STUPID.

AND WHERE **BOHR'S** MOST SCATHING CRITICISM WAS "*INTERESTING*" OR "*WE AGREE MUCH MORE THAN YOU THINK,*" WHEN **PAULI** MET WITH A FOOLISH PERSON OR IDEA HE'D RESPOND WITH GENUINE CONTEMPT.

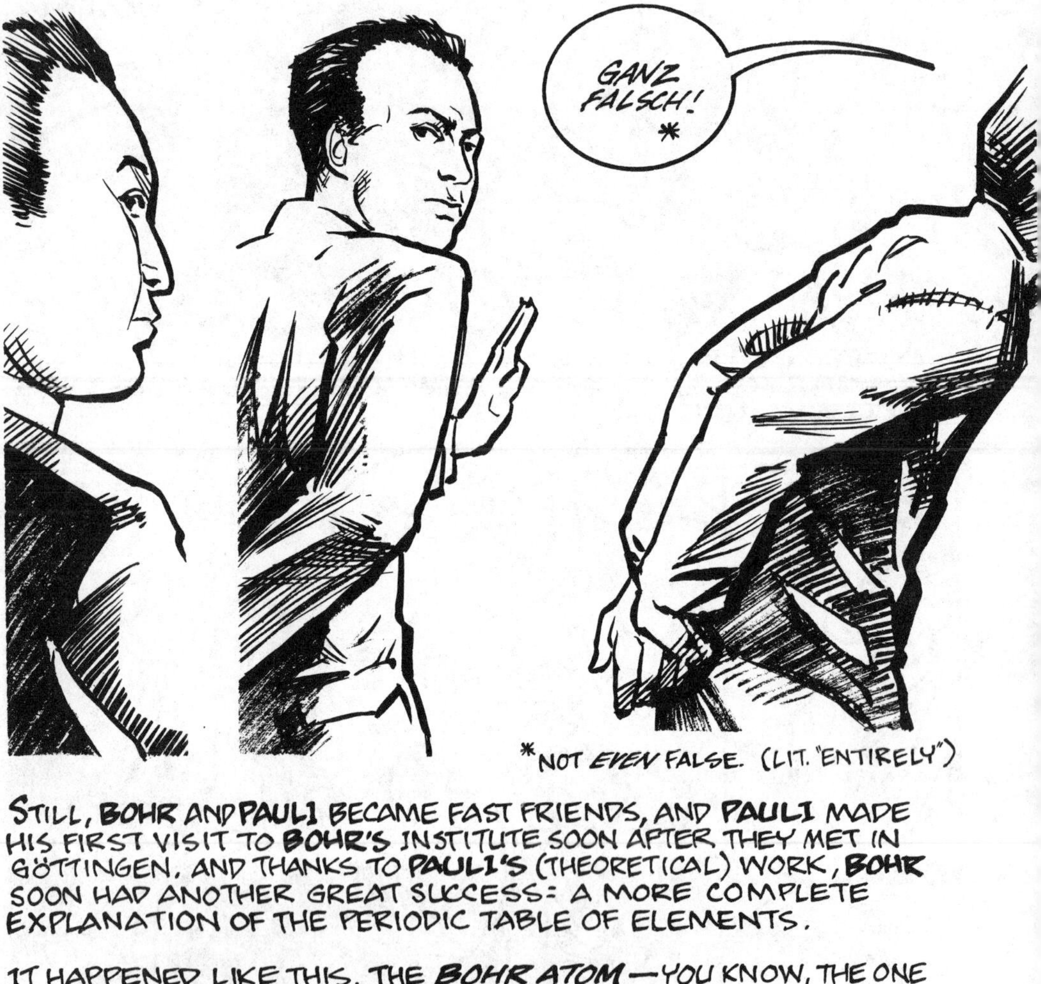
GANZ FALSCH! *

*NOT *EVEN* FALSE. (LIT. "ENTIRELY")

STILL, **BOHR** AND **PAULI** BECAME FAST FRIENDS, AND **PAULI** MADE HIS FIRST VISIT TO **BOHR'S** INSTITUTE SOON AFTER THEY MET IN GÖTTINGEN. AND THANKS TO **PAULI'S** (THEORETICAL) WORK, **BOHR** SOON HAD ANOTHER GREAT SUCCESS: A MORE COMPLETE EXPLANATION OF THE PERIODIC TABLE OF ELEMENTS.

IT HAPPENED LIKE THIS. THE ***BOHR ATOM*** —YOU KNOW, THE ONE THAT LOOKS LIKE A SOLAR SYSTEM—IS

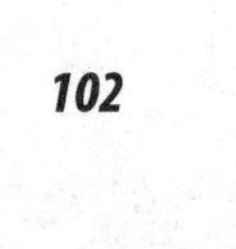

WRONG

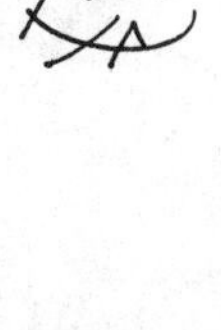

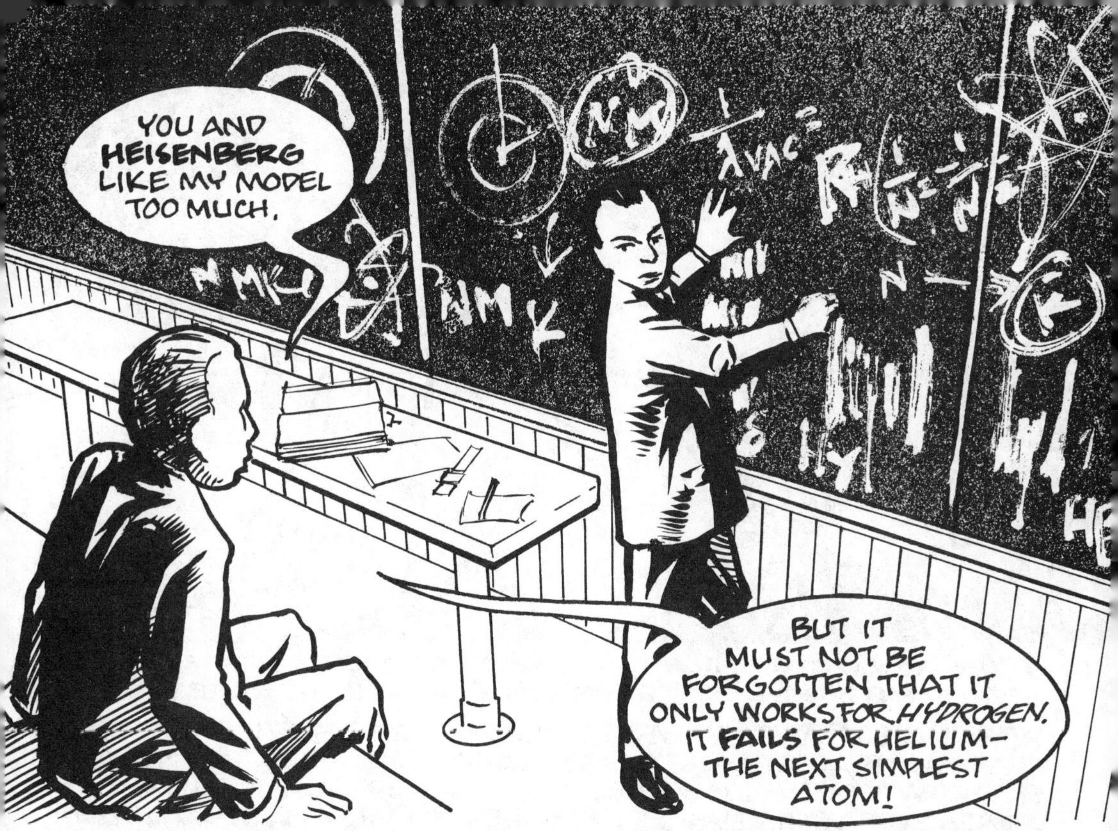
YOU AND **HEISENBERG** LIKE MY MODEL TOO MUCH.
BUT IT MUST NOT BE FORGOTTEN THAT IT ONLY WORKS FOR *HYDROGEN*. IT **FAILS** FOR HELIUM— THE NEXT SIMPLEST ATOM!

TROUBLE. AND HINTS OF MORE TO COME, SINCE BY THIS TIME **BOHR'S** "QUANTUM NUMBERS" (HIS **N**'S AND **M**'S) WEREN'T ENOUGH: THEY'D BEEN JOINED BY **K**'S.

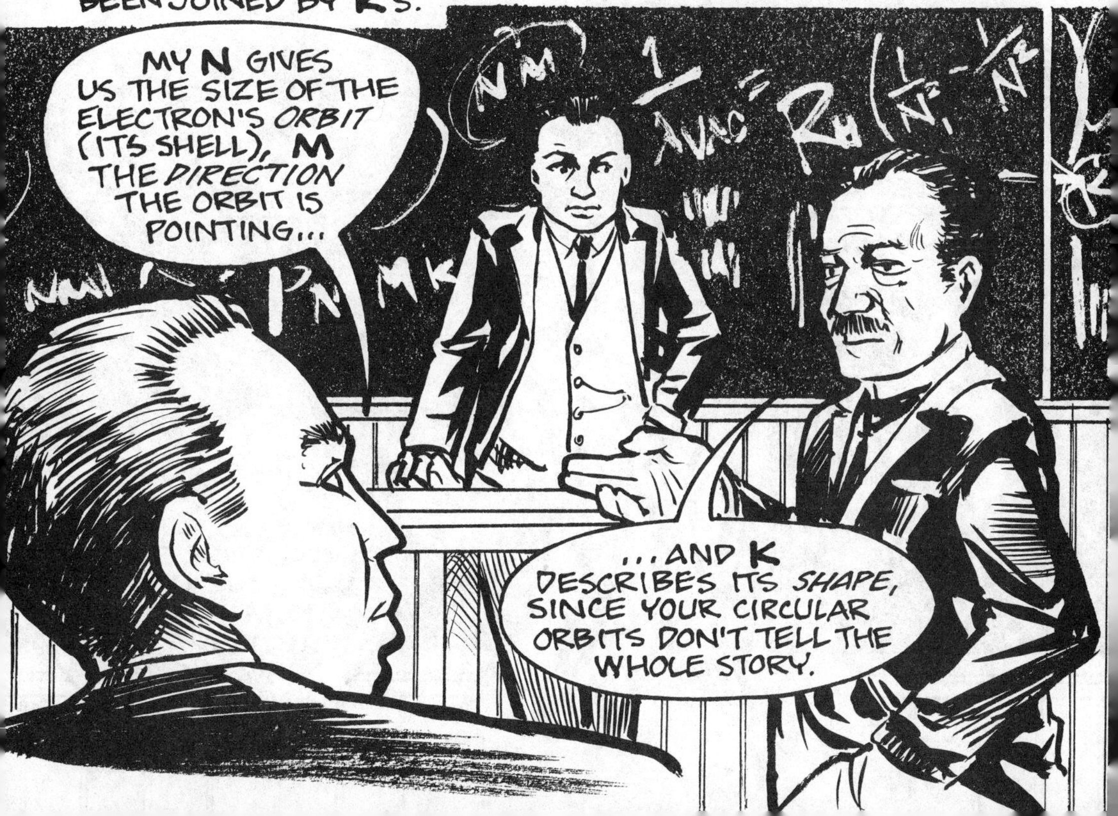
MY **N** GIVES US THE SIZE OF THE ELECTRON'S *ORBIT* (ITS SHELL), **M** THE *DIRECTION* THE ORBIT IS POINTING...
...AND **K** DESCRIBES ITS *SHAPE*, SINCE YOUR CIRCULAR ORBITS DON'T TELL THE WHOLE STORY.

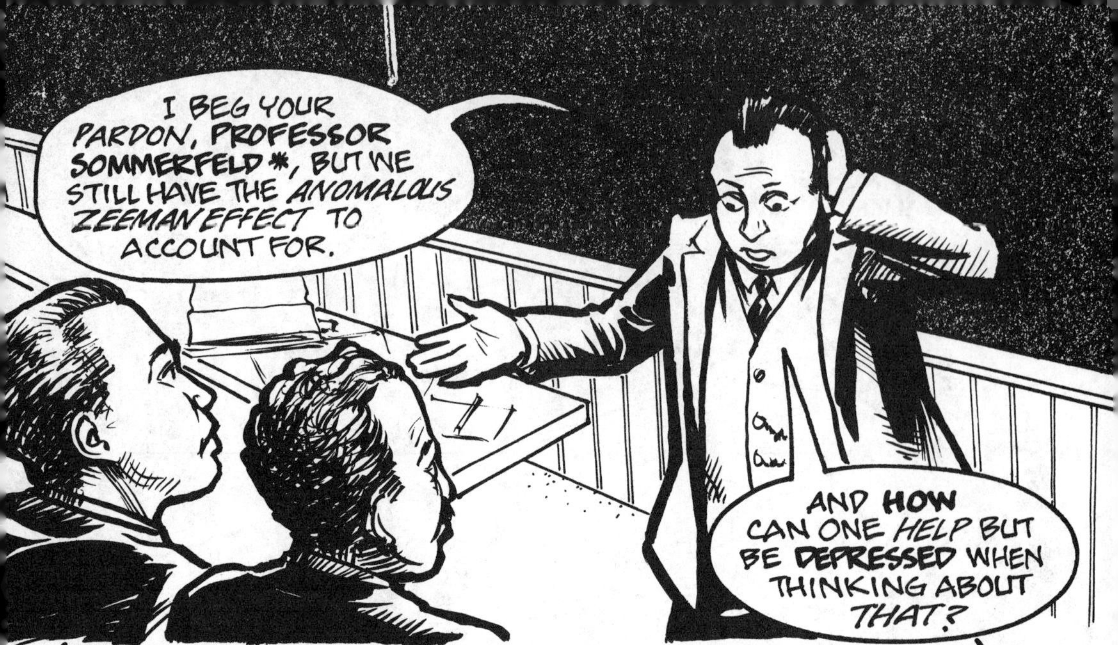
I BEG YOUR PARDON, PROFESSOR SOMMERFELD*, BUT WE STILL HAVE THE *ANOMALOUS ZEEMAN EFFECT* TO ACCOUNT FOR.
AND **HOW** CAN ONE *HELP* BUT BE **DEPRESSED** WHEN THINKING ABOUT *THAT*?

(* "I BEG YOUR PARDON"?! AGAIN, AN EXCEPTION TO TEST THE RULE: *SOMMERFELD* WAS THE ONLY PERSON ANYONE SAW *PAULI* BE POLITE TO.)

HOW INDEED? AND WHAT *IS* THIS WEIRD EFFECT? SUFFICE IT TO SAY THAT WHEN BETTER MEASUREMENTS BECAME AVAILABLE, THE **HYDROGEN SPECTRUM** TURNED OUT TO BE MORE COMPLEX THAN ANYBODY THOUGHT, AND THAT COMPLEXITY MANIFESTED AS THE **ANOMALOUS ZEEMAN EFFECT!**

AN EXPLANATION OF IT TOOK **PAULI** A FEW YEARS (HE HAD LEFT COPENHAGEN BY THEN) AND MOVED OUR PICTURE OF THE ATOM EVEN FURTHER AWAY FROM PHYSICAL REALITY. HIS PROPOSAL:

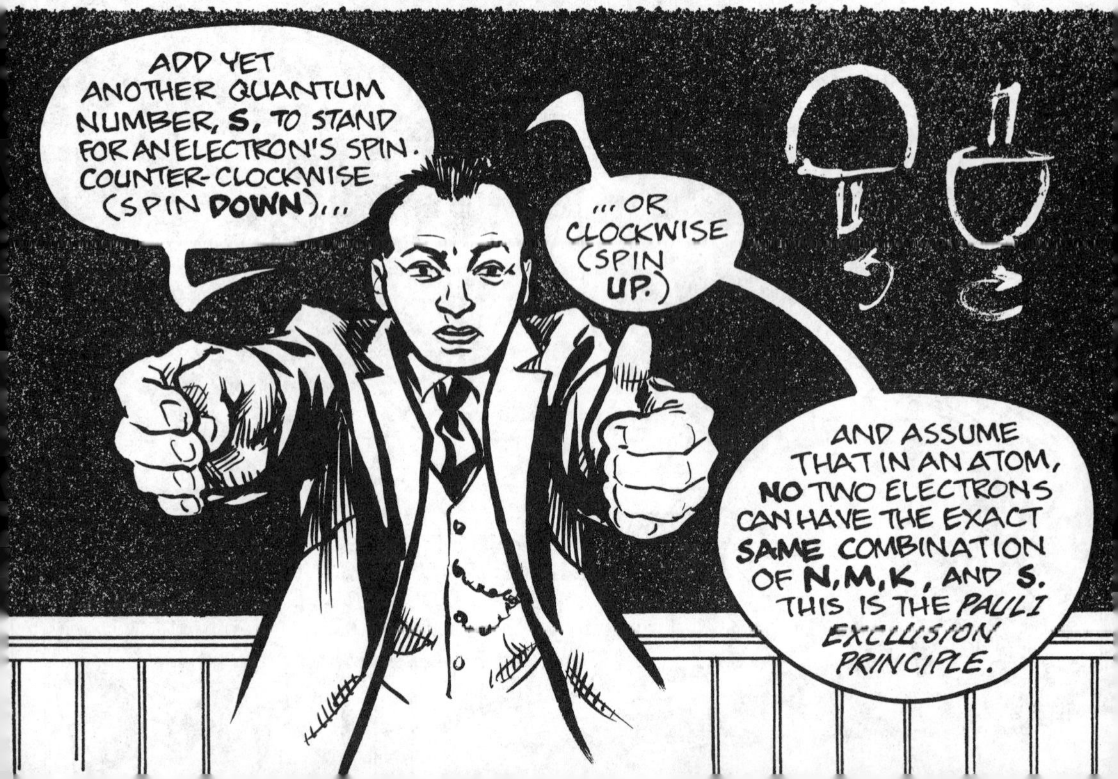
ADD YET ANOTHER QUANTUM NUMBER, **S**, TO STAND FOR AN ELECTRON'S SPIN. COUNTER-CLOCKWISE (SPIN **DOWN**)...
...OR CLOCKWISE (SPIN **UP**.)
AND ASSUME THAT IN AN ATOM, **NO** TWO ELECTRONS CAN HAVE THE EXACT **SAME** COMBINATION OF **N, M, K**, AND **S**. THIS IS THE *PAULI EXCLUSION PRINCIPLE*.

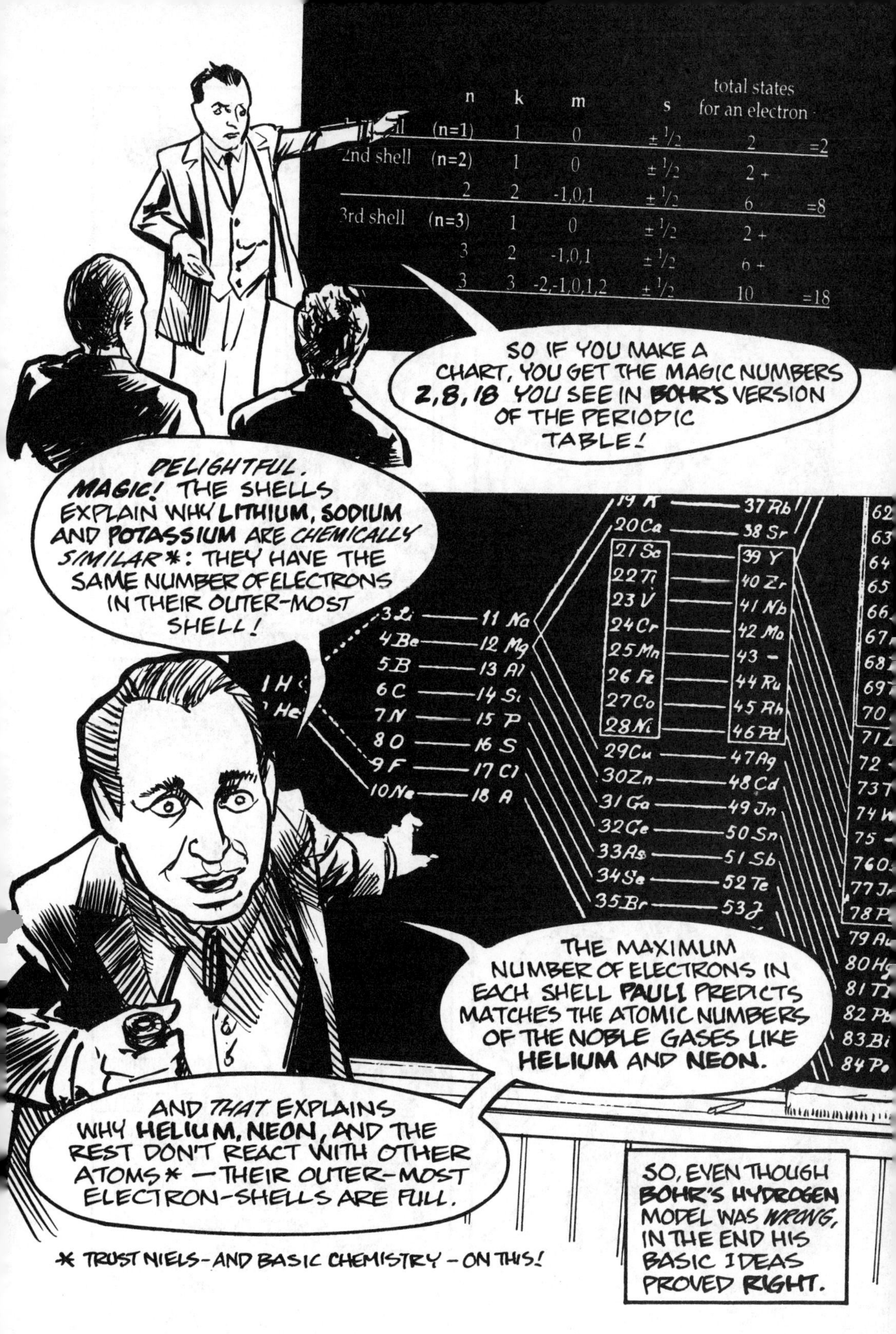
SO IF YOU MAKE A CHART, YOU GET THE MAGIC NUMBERS 2,8,18 YOU SEE IN BOHR'S VERSION OF THE PERIODIC TABLE!
DELIGHTFUL. MAGIC! THE SHELLS EXPLAIN WHY LITHIUM, SODIUM AND POTASSIUM ARE CHEMICALLY SIMILAR*: THEY HAVE THE SAME NUMBER OF ELECTRONS IN THEIR OUTER-MOST SHELL!
THE MAXIMUM NUMBER OF ELECTRONS IN EACH SHELL PAULI PREDICTS MATCHES THE ATOMIC NUMBERS OF THE NOBLE GASES LIKE HELIUM AND NEON.
AND THAT EXPLAINS WHY HELIUM, NEON, AND THE REST DON'T REACT WITH OTHER ATOMS* —THEIR OUTER-MOST ELECTRON-SHELLS ARE FULL.
SO, EVEN THOUGH BOHR'S HYDROGEN MODEL WAS WRONG, IN THE END HIS BASIC IDEAS PROVED RIGHT.
* TRUST NIELS–AND BASIC CHEMISTRY–ON THIS!

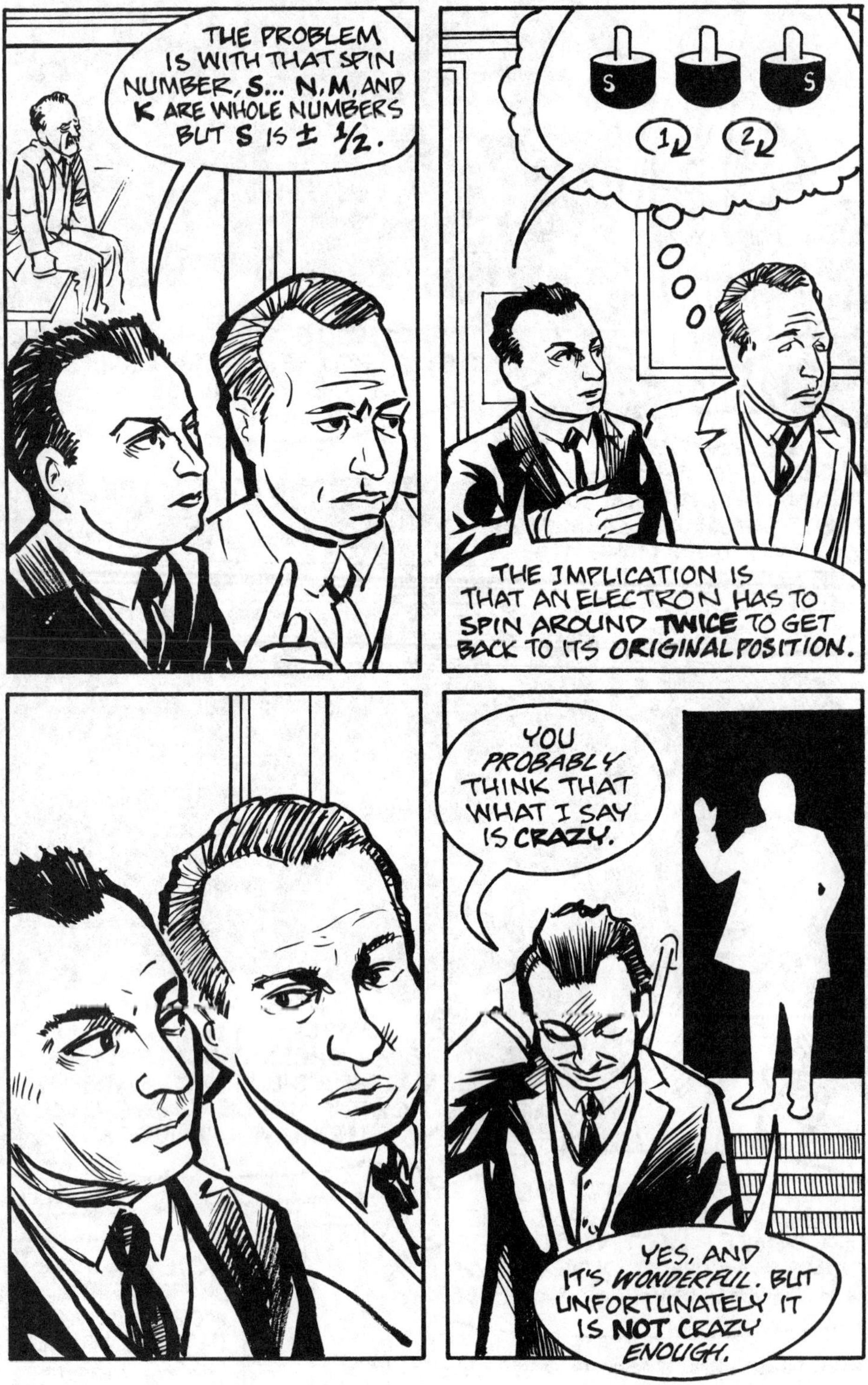
THE PROBLEM IS WITH THAT SPIN NUMBER, S... N, M, AND K ARE WHOLE NUMBERS BUT S IS ± 1/2.
S S
1 2
THE IMPLICATION IS THAT AN ELECTRON HAS TO SPIN AROUND TWICE TO GET BACK TO ITS ORIGINAL POSITION.
YOU PROBABLY THINK THAT WHAT I SAY IS CRAZY.
YES, AND IT'S WONDERFUL. BUT UNFORTUNATELY IT IS NOT CRAZY ENOUGH.

AND IT WASN'T.

ATOMS AND THEIR BUILDING BLOCKS KEPT GETTING STRANGER. **PAULI'S** CRAZY SPIN **QUANTUM NUMBER** IS ONE OF THE ***LEAST*** WEIRD THINGS ABOUT ELECTRONS, FOR INSTANCE.

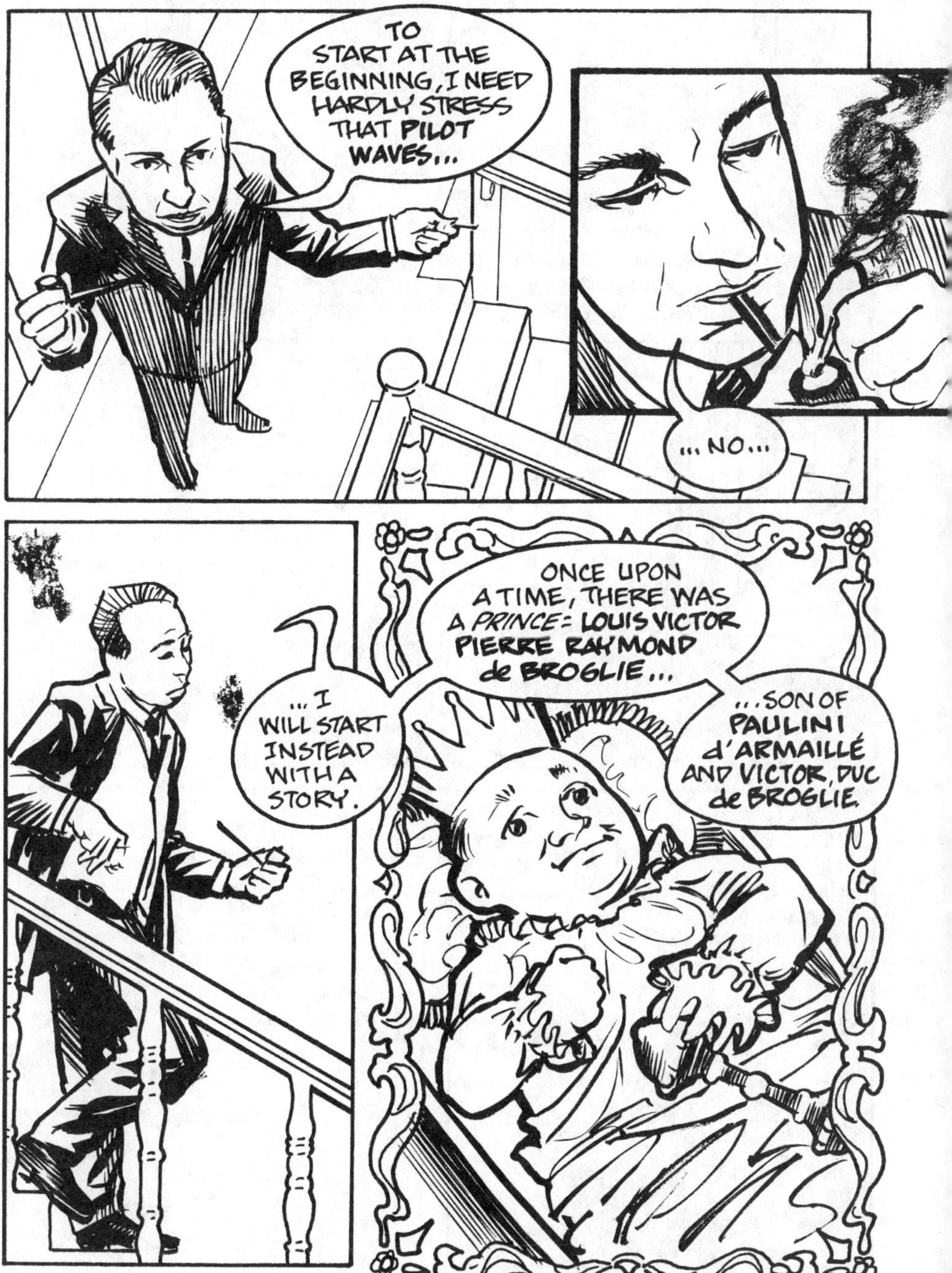
TO START AT THE BEGINNING, I NEED HARDLY STRESS THAT PILOT WAVES...
... NO...
... I WILL START INSTEAD WITH A STORY.
ONCE UPON A TIME, THERE WAS A PRINCE: LOUIS VICTOR PIERRE RAYMOND de BROGLIE...
... SON OF PAULINI d'ARMAILLÉ AND VICTOR, DUC de BROGLIE.

"THE **PRINCE** GOT A DEGREE IN MEDIEVAL HISTORY AT THE SORBONNE.

LIGHT BEHAVES LIKE A **WAVE** *AND A* **PARTICLE?!**

" BUT WHILE HE WAS STATIONED AT THE **EIFFEL TOWER** DURING THE *WAR TO END ALL WARS*, WORKING ON **WIRELESS TRANSMISSIONS**, HIS INTEREST TURNED TO **EINSTEIN'S** *PHOTON THEORIES*."

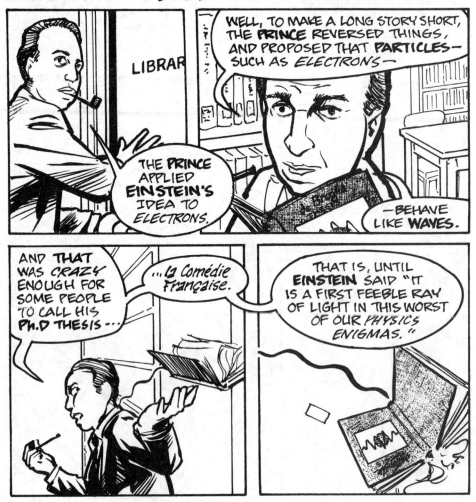

LIBRAR

WELL, TO MAKE A LONG STORY SHORT, THE **PRINCE** REVERSED THINGS, AND PROPOSED THAT **PARTICLES**— SUCH AS *ELECTRONS*—

THE **PRINCE** APPLIED **EINSTEIN'S** IDEA TO ELECTRONS.

—BEHAVE LIKE **WAVES**.

AND **THAT** WAS *CRAZY* ENOUGH FOR SOME PEOPLE TO CALL HIS **Ph.D THESIS**—

"...*la Comédie Française.*

THAT IS, UNTIL **EINSTEIN** SAID "IT IS A FIRST FEEBLE RAY OF LIGHT IN THIS WORST OF OUR *PHYSICS* ENIGMAS."

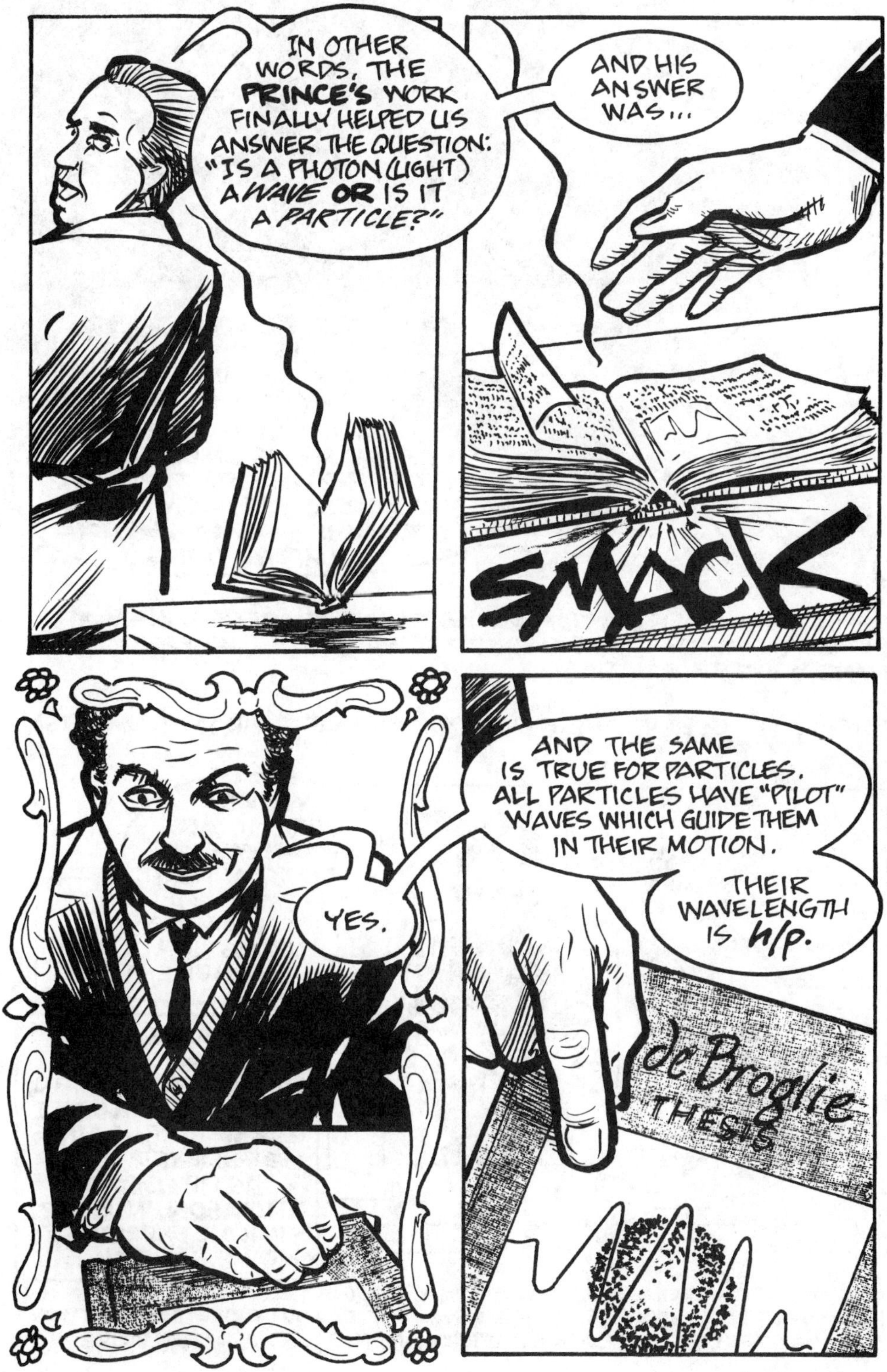
IN OTHER WORDS, THE PRINCE'S WORK FINALLY HELPED US ANSWER THE QUESTION: "IS A PHOTON (LIGHT) A WAVE OR IS IT A PARTICLE?"
AND HIS ANSWER WAS...
SMACK
AND THE SAME IS TRUE FOR PARTICLES. ALL PARTICLES HAVE "PILOT" WAVES WHICH GUIDE THEM IN THEIR MOTION.
THEIR WAVELENGTH IS h/p.
YES.
de Broglie THESIS

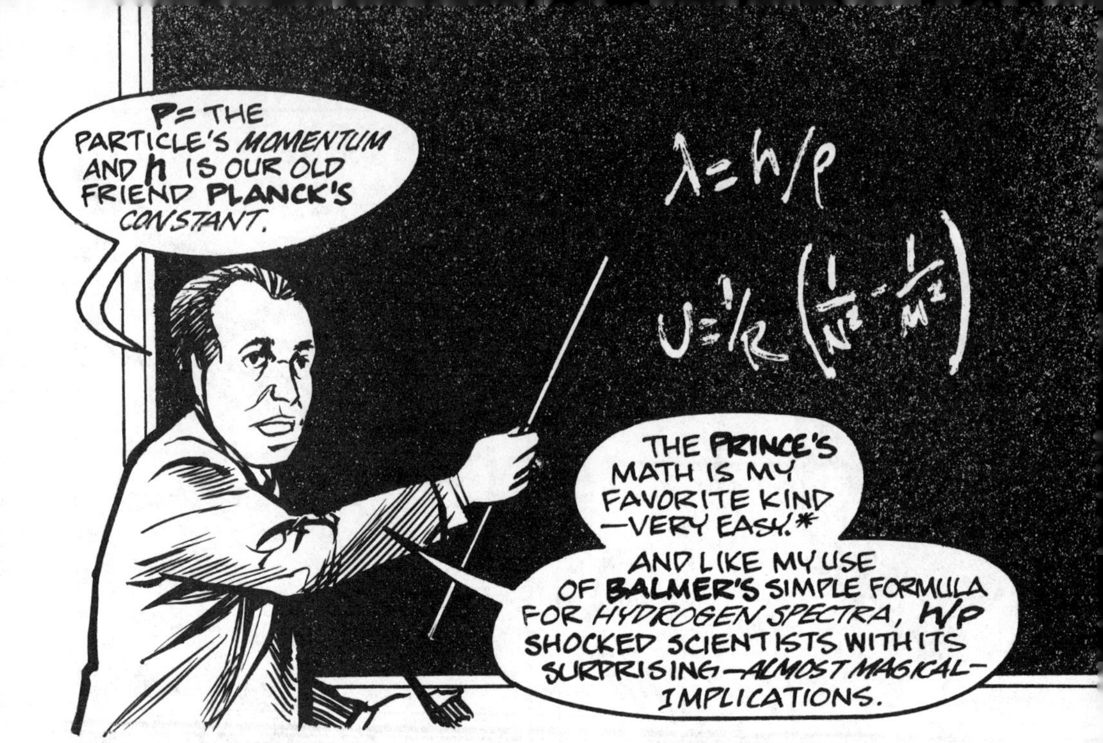
P= THE PARTICLE'S *MOMENTUM* AND *h* IS OUR OLD FRIEND **PLANCK'S** *CONSTANT.*
$\lambda = h/p$
$\nu = 1/R \left(\frac{1}{N^2} - \frac{1}{M^2}\right)$
THE **PRINCE'S** MATH IS MY FAVORITE KIND —VERY EASY!*
AND LIKE MY USE OF **BALMER'S** SIMPLE FORMULA FOR *HYDROGEN SPECTRA*, **h/p** SHOCKED SCIENTISTS WITH ITS SURPRISING—*ALMOST MAGICAL*—IMPLICATIONS.

ESPECIALLY WHEN **CLINTON DAVISSON** AND **CHARLES KUNSMAN** DID EXPERIMENTS THAT SHOWED IT WAS *TRUE* THAT PARTICLES HAVE WAVE PROPERTIES!

THEY DIDN'T BELIEVE THEIR EYES (OR RATHER, THEIR INSTRUMENTS).

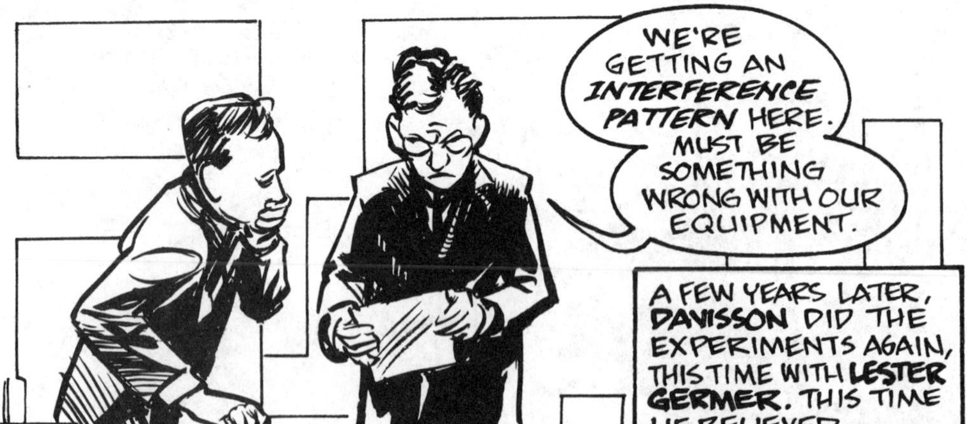
WE'RE GETTING AN ***INTERFERENCE PATTERN*** HERE. MUST BE SOMETHING WRONG WITH OUR EQUIPMENT.
A FEW YEARS LATER, **DAVISSON** DID THE EXPERIMENTS AGAIN, THIS TIME WITH **LESTER GERMER**. THIS TIME HE BELIEVED.
AS DID **GEORGE THOMSON**, WHO DID SIMILAR EXPERIMENTS AT THE SAME TIME.

* "SIMPLE MATH" ON PAGE 292 WILL SHOW YOU, TOO, HOW TO "LIFT THIS GREAT VEIL" (AS *EINSTEIN* PUT IT) AND DERIVE THE EQUATION THAT GOT THE PRINCE A PLACE IN HISTORY, HIS Ph.D., AND A NOBEL PRIZE.

SO EVENTUALLY **THOMSON** AND **DAVISSON** SHARED THE *NOBEL PRIZE* IN **1937**, FOR PROVING THAT ELECTRONS WERE ***WAVES...***
... **31** YEARS AFTER **GEORGE'S** FATHER ***J. J. THOMSON*** GOT THE *NOBEL PRIZE* FOR PROVING THAT ELECTRONS WERE ***PARTICLES.***

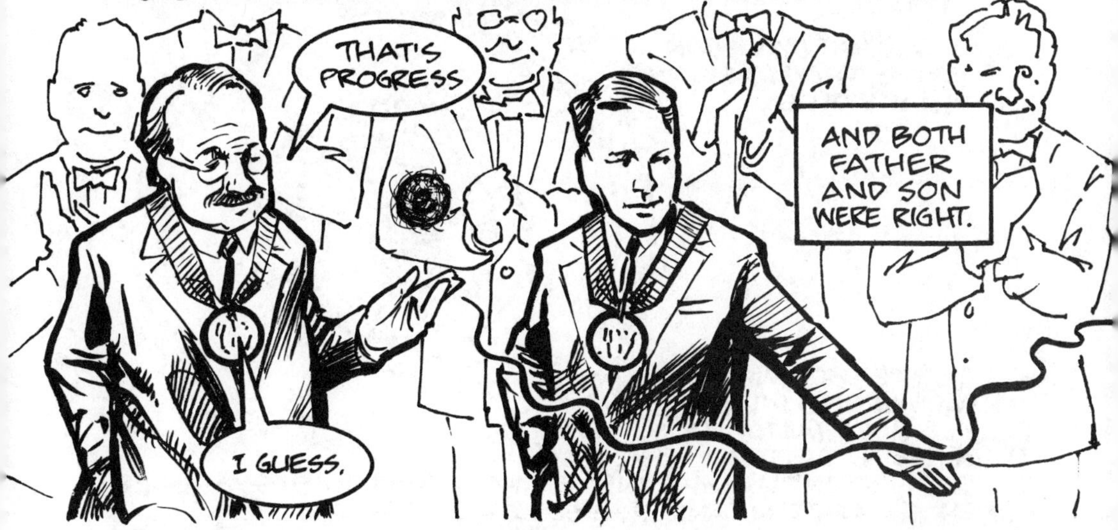
THAT'S PROGRESS
AND BOTH FATHER AND SON WERE RIGHT.
I GUESS.

J.J. PROVED THEY COME IN *LUMPS*, SO IF YOU THINK OF **DAVISSON** AND **GEORGE'S** ELECTRONS AS BALLS FIRED OUT OF A WOBBLY CANNON* TOWARDS A WALL WITH TWO HOLES IN IT**, THEY'D PASS THROUGH EITHER ONE HOLE OR THE OTHER BEFORE HITTING A BACKSTOP.

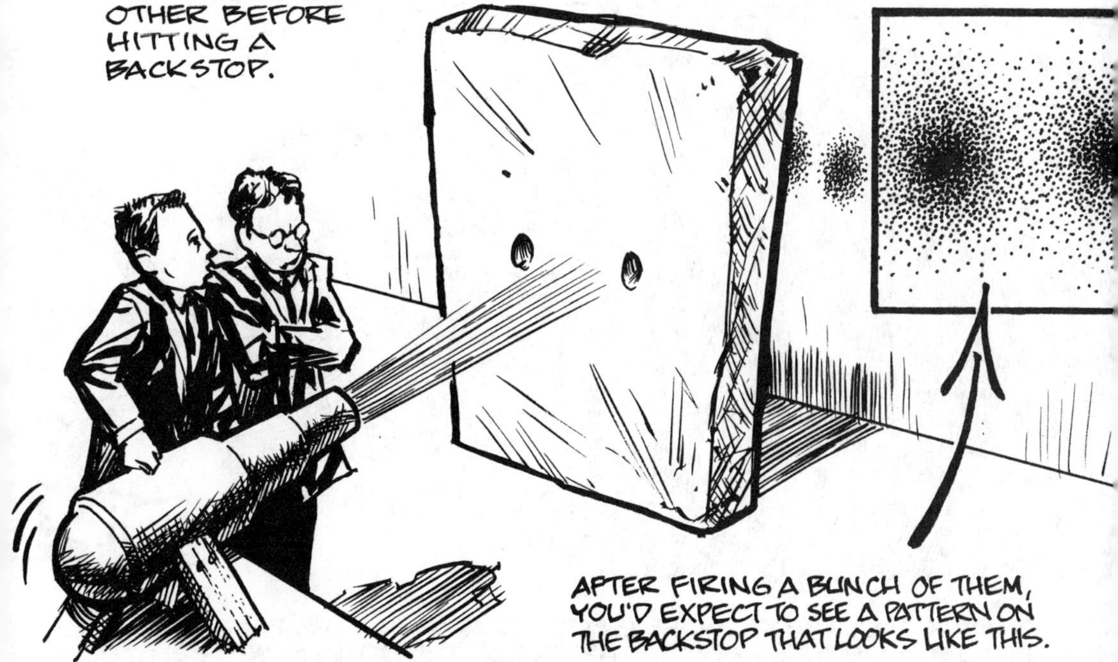

AFTER FIRING A BUNCH OF THEM, YOU'D EXPECT TO SEE A PATTERN ON THE BACKSTOP THAT LOOKS LIKE THIS.

*A HOT FILAMENT OF WIRE **A PURE CRYSTAL.

THAT'S OBVIOUSLY THE SUM OF WHAT WE'D SEE IF ONLY ONE OF
THE HOLES WAS OPEN AT A TIME.

HOWEVER, WHAT **DAVISSON**
AND YOUNG **THOMSON** SAW
LOOKED LIKE THIS:

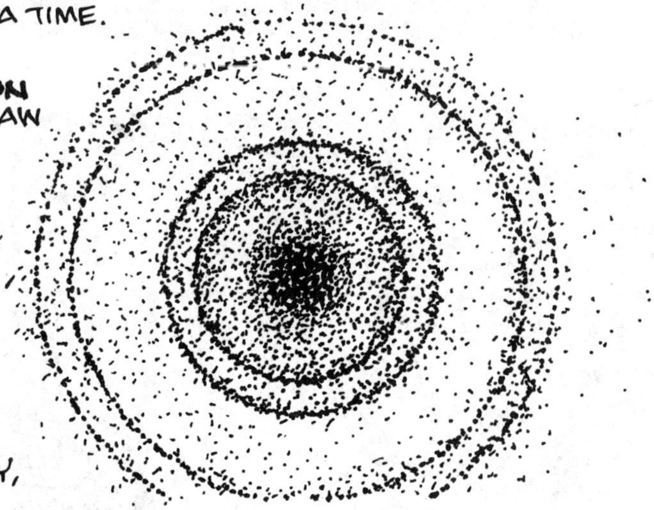

EVER SINCE 1801, WHEN
THOMAS YOUNG DID A
DOUBLE HOLE (ACTUALLY,
THEY WERE SLITS)
EXPERIMENT WITH LIGHT, WE'VE KNOWN THAT THIS IS AN **INTER-
FERENCE PATTERN**, AND IS ASSOCIATED WITH *WAVES*.

THE PATTERNS OF LIGHT AND DARK BANDS RESULT FROM THE
PROBABILITIES THAT THE WAVE PRODUCES *CONSTRUCTIVE
INTERFERENCE* (TWO CRESTS ON TOP OF EACH OTHER) OR *DESTRUCTIVE
INTERFERENCE* (ONE WAVE'S CREST APPEARING AT THE SAME SPOT AS
ANOTHER WAVE'S TROUGH) AT A PARTICULAR SPOT.

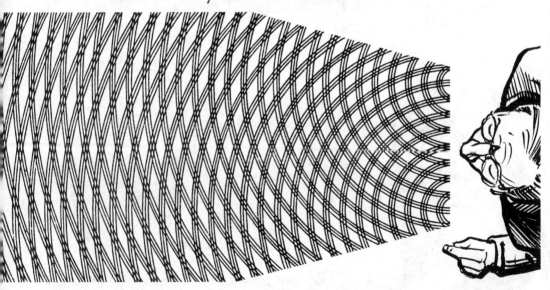

SO EVEN THOUGH WE KNOW THE ELECTRONS ARRIVE AT THE FIRST WALL
IN **LUMPS** (THEY'RE *PARTICLES* AFTER ALL), THE PATTERN WE SEE
THEM PRODUCE ON THE BACKSTOP MAKES US CONCLUDE THEY'RE *WAVES*.

SO, IF WE BUY THIS WAVE STUFF AND WE'RE ONLY SENDING ONE ELECTRON AT A TIME TOWARDS THE HOLES, THEN IT'S INTERFERING WITH... ITSELF.

BUT IT'S A PARTICLE! AS **SIR ARTHUR EDDINGTON** (ONE OF THE BEST POPULAR SCIENCE WRITERS OF THE EARLY 1900'S) SAID: "IT'S LIKE SAYING SOMETHING UNKNOWN IS DOING WE DON'T KNOW WHAT, WHICH DOES NOT SOUND [LIKE] A PARTICULARLY ILLUMINATING THEORY. I HAVE READ SOMETHING LIKE IT ELSEWHERE..."

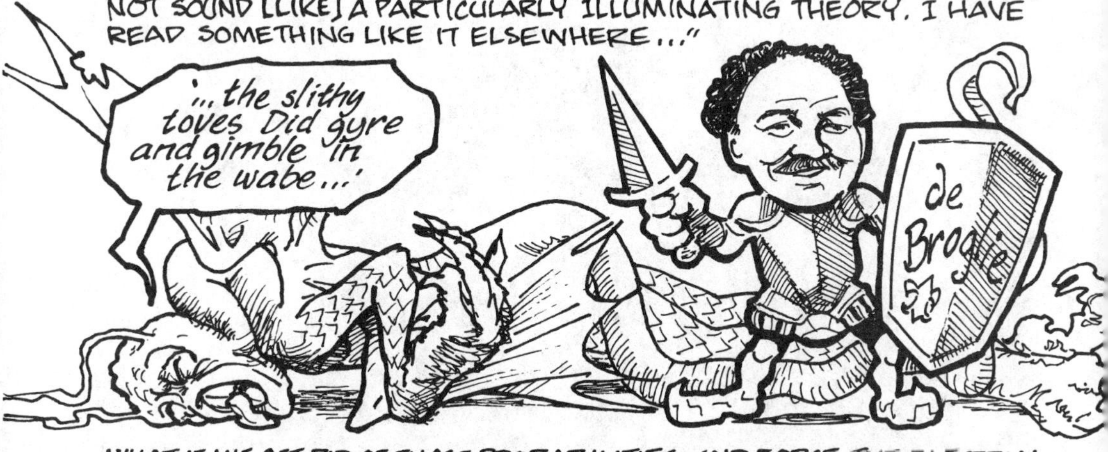
'...the slithy toves Did gyre and gimble in the wabe...'
de Broglie

WHAT IF WE GET RID OF THOSE PROBABILITIES AND FORCE THE ELECTRON TO BEHAVE LIKE A PARTICLE BY MAKING SURE WE SEE EACH ONE **GYRE** AND **GIMBLE** THROUGH A PARTICULAR HOLE?

WELL... SEEING WHERE AN ELECTRON IS MEANS BOUNCING A PHOTON OFF OF IT AND BACK TOWARDS OUR EYES.*

ELECTRONS AREN'T CANNONBALLS, SO BOUNCING LIGHT OFF ONE DISTURBS ITS MOTION.

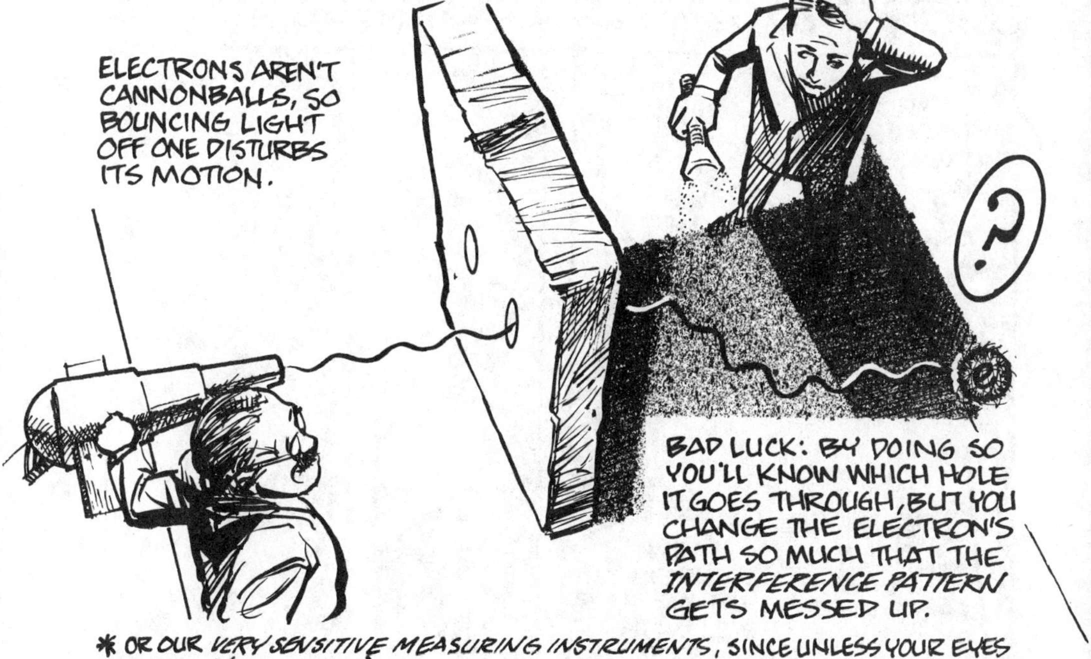
?

BAD LUCK: BY DOING SO YOU'LL KNOW WHICH HOLE IT GOES THROUGH, BUT YOU CHANGE THE ELECTRON'S PATH SO MUCH THAT THE *INTERFERENCE PATTERN* GETS MESSED UP.

* OR OUR *VERY SENSITIVE MEASURING INSTRUMENTS*, SINCE UNLESS YOUR EYES ARE A LOT (LOT, LOT, LOT) BETTER THAN NORMAL, YOU CAN'T SEE ELECTRONS.

SURE, YOU CAN **DIM** THE LIGHT DOWN, IN AN ATTEMPT TO **NOT** KNOCK THE PHOTONS AROUND SO MUCH...

...*BUT* THE PHOTON-ELECTRON INTERACTION **ISN'T** LIKE A TSUNAMI FLATTENING AN ISLAND FULL OF TREES, OR LIKE A GENTLE SWELL WHICH DOESN'T PUSH A BOAT OFF ITS COURSE.

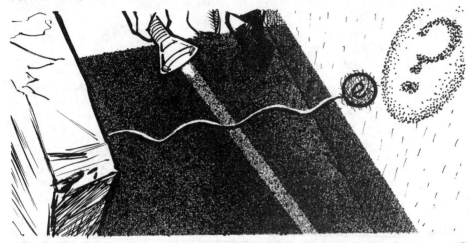

IT'S NOT *WAVELIKE*, IN OTHER WORDS, BUT INSTEAD IT'S LIKE TWO BILLIARD BALLS HITTING ONE ANOTHER. SO A DIMMED LIGHT IN THIS CONTEXT MEANS YOU'RE JUST PUMPING OUT FEWER "BALLS"/PHOTONS.

AND WITH FEWER *PHOTONS*, YOU'LL MISS MORE OF THE *ELECTRONS*, AND IF YOU DON'T GET ANY PHOTONS BOUNCED TOWARDS YOUR *EYE*, YOU CAN'T **SEE** WHICH HOLE THE ELECTRON WENT THROUGH.

AND THE **INTERFERENCE** PATTERN COMES *GALUMPHING* BACK!

HOW WONDERFUL THAT WE HAVE MET WITH A PARADOX.

YES?

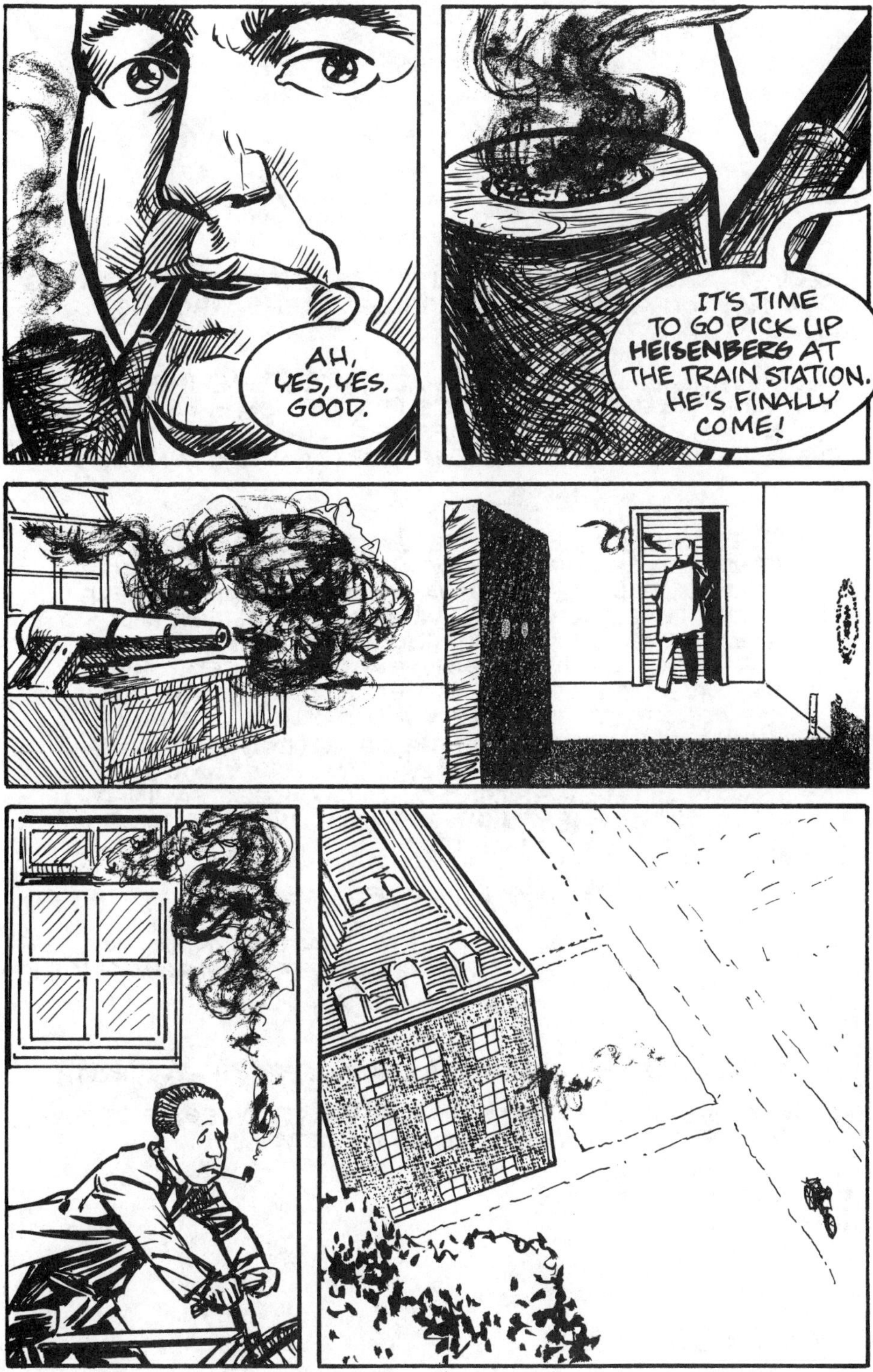
AH, YES, YES. GOOD.
IT'S TIME TO GO PICK UP HEISENBERG AT THE TRAIN STATION. HE'S FINALLY COME!

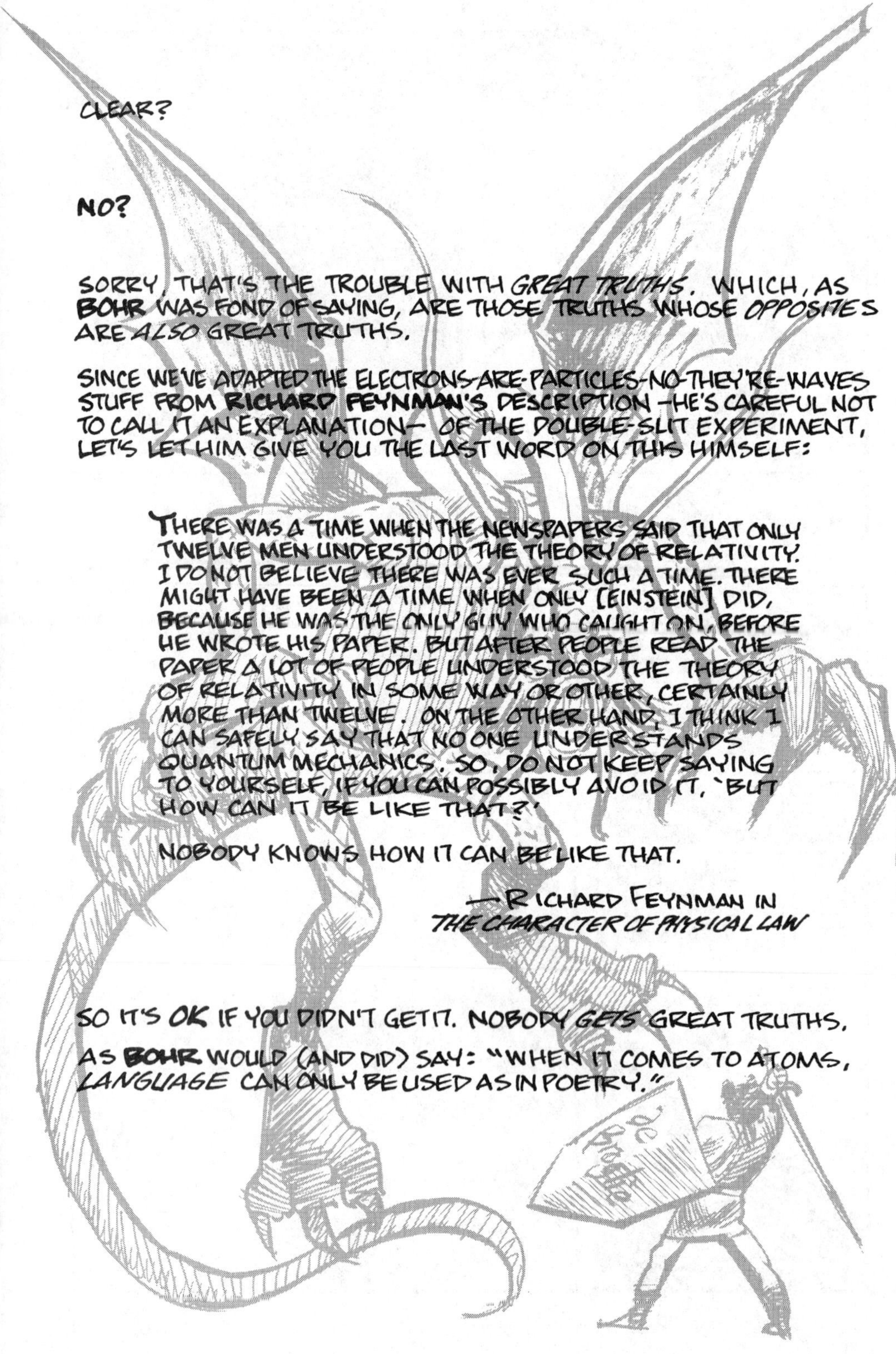

CLEAR?

NO?

SORRY, THAT'S THE TROUBLE WITH *GREAT TRUTHS*. WHICH, AS **BOHR** WAS FOND OF SAYING, ARE THOSE TRUTHS WHOSE *OPPOSITES* ARE *ALSO* GREAT TRUTHS.

SINCE WE'VE ADAPTED THE ELECTRONS-ARE-PARTICLES-NO-THEY'RE-WAVES STUFF FROM **RICHARD FEYNMAN'S** DESCRIPTION —HE'S CAREFUL NOT TO CALL IT AN EXPLANATION— OF THE DOUBLE-SLIT EXPERIMENT, LET'S LET HIM GIVE YOU THE LAST WORD ON THIS HIMSELF:

> THERE WAS A TIME WHEN THE NEWSPAPERS SAID THAT ONLY TWELVE MEN UNDERSTOOD THE THEORY OF RELATIVITY. I DO NOT BELIEVE THERE WAS EVER SUCH A TIME. THERE MIGHT HAVE BEEN A TIME WHEN ONLY [EINSTEIN] DID, BECAUSE HE WAS THE ONLY GUY WHO CAUGHT ON, BEFORE HE WROTE HIS PAPER. BUT AFTER PEOPLE READ THE PAPER A LOT OF PEOPLE UNDERSTOOD THE THEORY OF RELATIVITY IN SOME WAY OR OTHER, CERTAINLY MORE THAN TWELVE. ON THE OTHER HAND, I THINK I CAN SAFELY SAY THAT NO ONE UNDERSTANDS QUANTUM MECHANICS. SO, DO NOT KEEP SAYING TO YOURSELF, IF YOU CAN POSSIBLY AVOID IT, 'BUT HOW CAN IT BE LIKE THAT?'
>
> NOBODY KNOWS HOW IT CAN BE LIKE THAT.
>
> —RICHARD FEYNMAN IN *THE CHARACTER OF PHYSICAL LAW*

SO IT'S **OK** IF YOU DIDN'T GET IT. NOBODY *GETS* GREAT TRUTHS.

AS **BOHR** WOULD (AND DID) SAY: "WHEN IT COMES TO ATOMS, *LANGUAGE* CAN ONLY BE USED AS IN POETRY."

Chapter 7

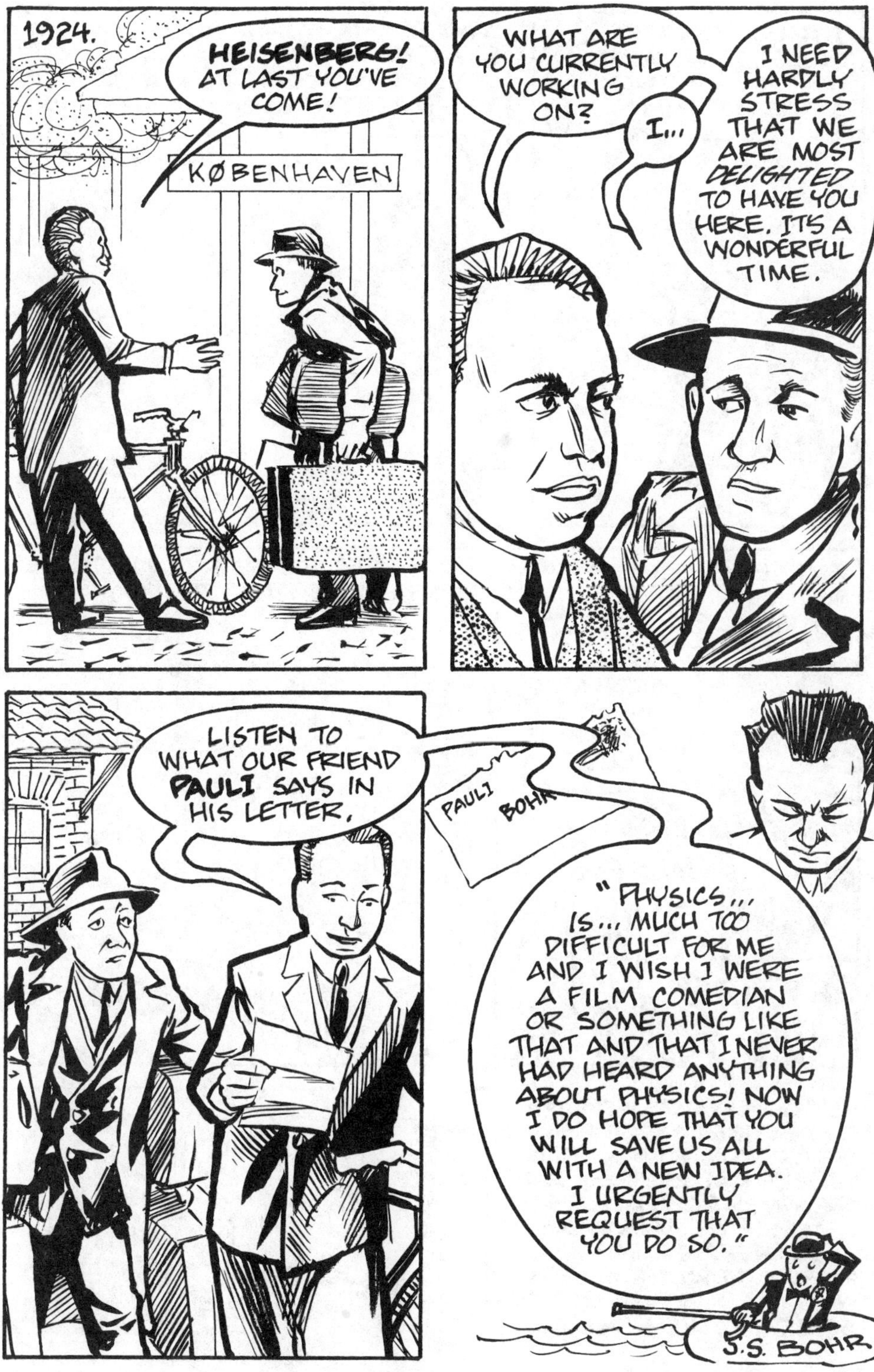
1924.
HEISENBERG! AT LAST YOU'VE COME!
KØBENHAVEN
WHAT ARE YOU CURRENTLY WORKING ON?
I...
I NEED HARDLY STRESS THAT WE ARE MOST *DELIGHTED* TO HAVE YOU HERE. IT'S A WONDERFUL TIME.
LISTEN TO WHAT OUR FRIEND **PAULI** SAYS IN HIS LETTER.
PAULI
BOHR
"PHYSICS... IS... MUCH TOO DIFFICULT FOR ME AND I WISH I WERE A FILM COMEDIAN OR SOMETHING LIKE THAT AND THAT I NEVER HAD HEARD ANYTHING ABOUT PHYSICS! NOW I DO HOPE THAT YOU WILL SAVE US ALL WITH A NEW IDEA. I URGENTLY REQUEST THAT YOU DO SO."
S.S. BOHR

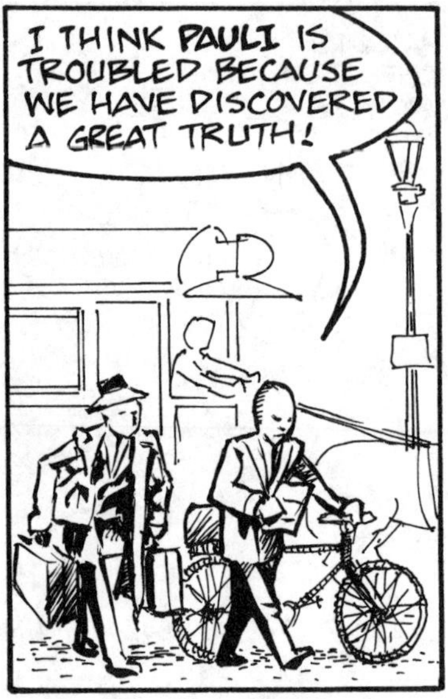
I THINK **PAULI** IS TROUBLED BECAUSE WE HAVE DISCOVERED A GREAT TRUTH!

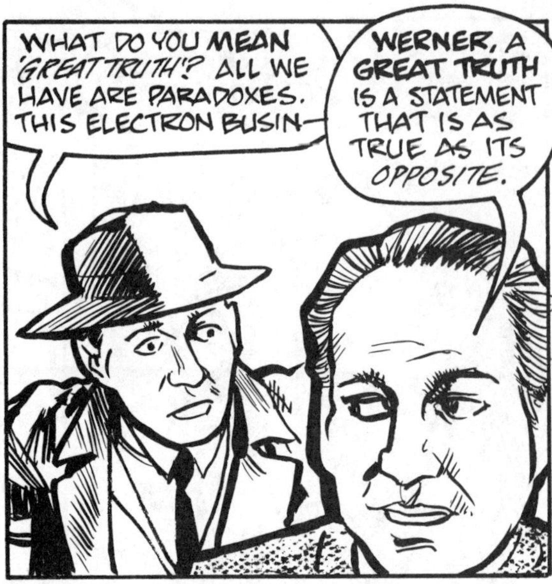
WHAT DO YOU **MEAN** *'GREAT TRUTH'*? ALL WE HAVE ARE PARADOXES. THIS ELECTRON BUSIN—
WERNER, A **GREAT TRUTH** IS A STATEMENT THAT IS AS TRUE AS ITS *OPPOSITE*.

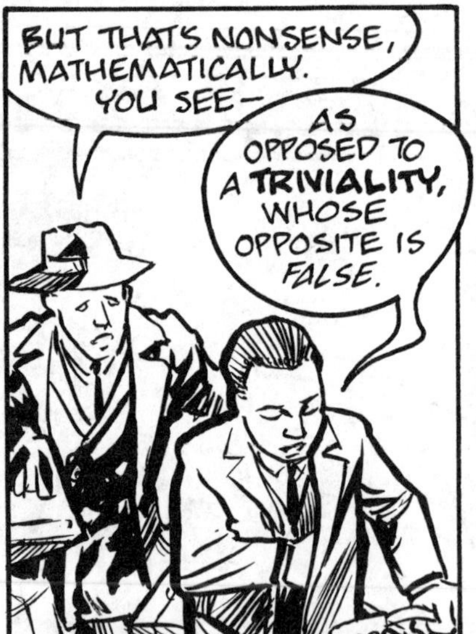
BUT THAT'S NONSENSE, MATHEMATICALLY. YOU SEE—
AS OPPOSED TO A **TRIVIALITY**, WHOSE OPPOSITE IS *FALSE*.

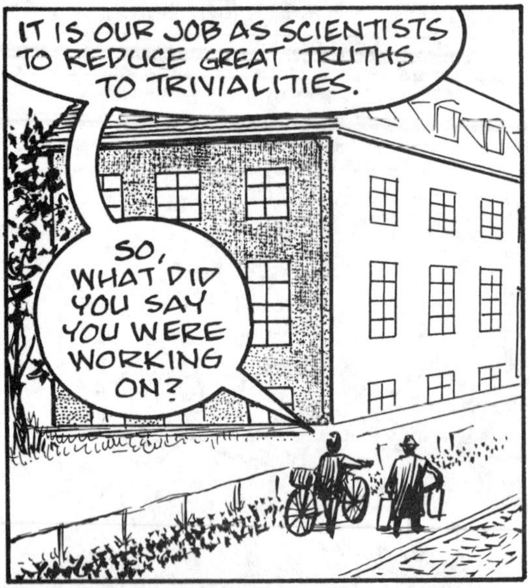
IT IS OUR JOB AS SCIENTISTS TO REDUCE GREAT TRUTHS TO TRIVIALITIES.
SO, WHAT DID YOU SAY YOU WERE WORKING ON?

HEISENBERG WAS WORKING ON A SERIES OF PAPERS WHICH WOULD CULMINATE IN YET ANOTHER UNSUCCESSFUL TREATMENT OF **PAULI'S** NEMESIS, THE **ANOMALOUS ZEEMAN EFFECT**. BUT HIS FIRST ORDER OF BUSINESS WAS TO GET INTO THE SPIRIT OF **COPENHAGEN**.

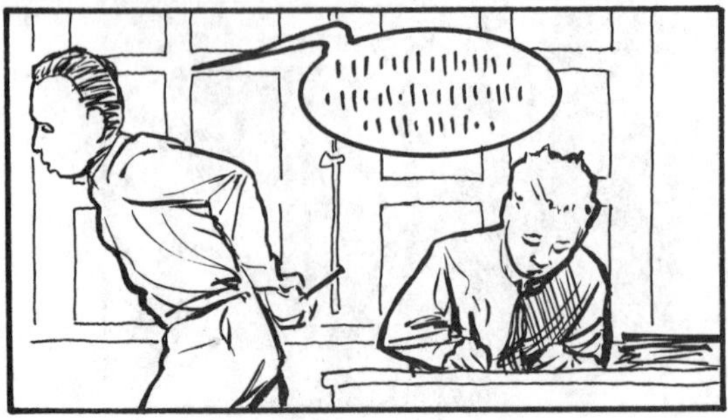

HE WASN'T DOING ANYTHING TRULY REVOLUTIONARY. YET.

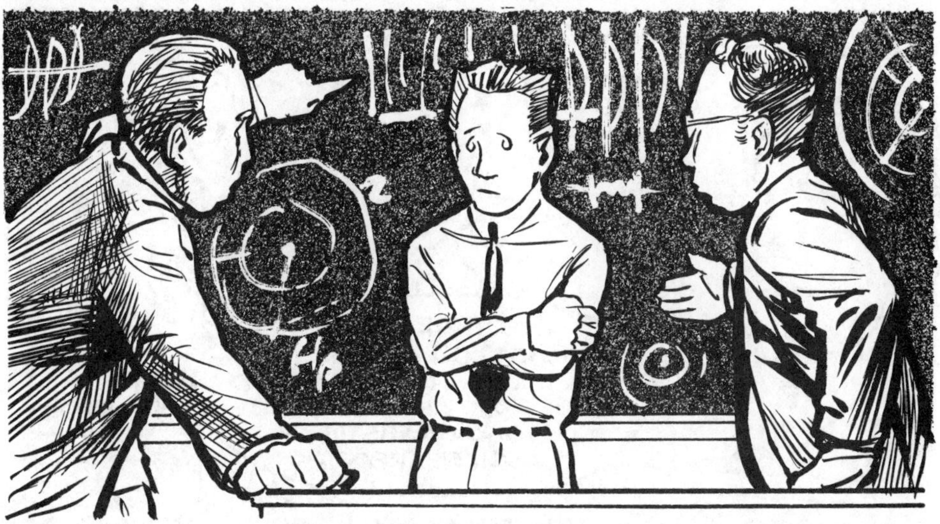

AND NOTHING AS CRAZY AS TRYING TO DEAL WITH THE ELECTRON, OR **BOHR'S** LATEST PROPOSAL FOR THE CONSERVATION OF ENERGY.

OR RATHER, THE **NON-CONSERVATION** OF ENERGY. **BOHR**, ALONG WITH **KRAMERS** AND **JAMES SLATER**, WROTE A PAPER THAT BLENDED PARTICLES WITH WAVES AND RADIATION FIELDS WITH ATOMIC TRANSITIONS.

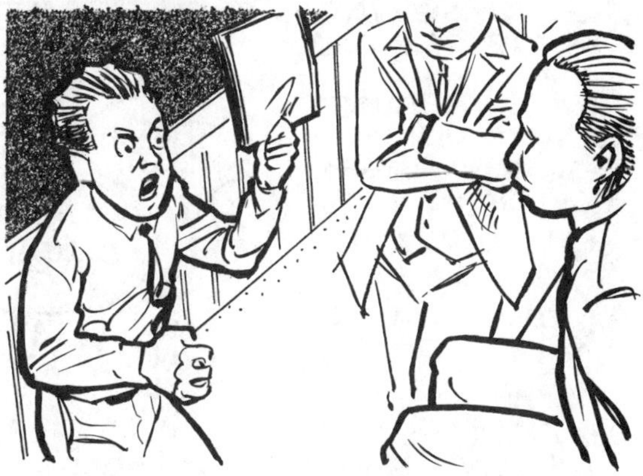

IN IT THEY PROPOSED THAT ATOMS WERE CAPABLE OF *COMMUNICATING* THEIR FUTURE QUANTUM TRANSITIONS WITH OTHER DISTANT ATOMS BY WAY OF A **VIRTUAL RADIATION FIELD.**

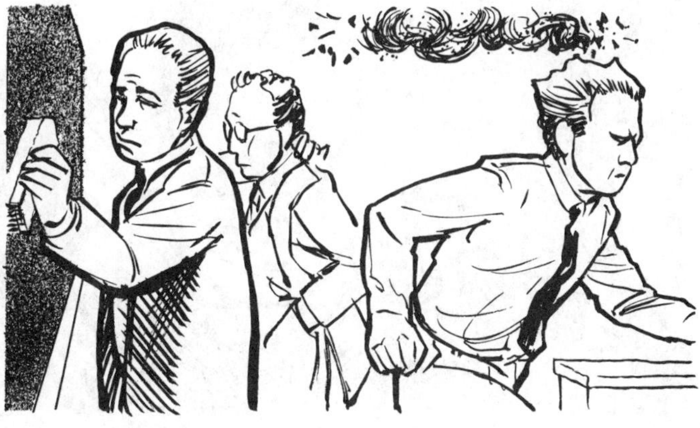

THIS COMMUNICATION BETWEEN ATOMS VIOLATES *CAUSE-AND-EFFECT* AS WE KNOW IT. EVEN WORSE, THE INFAMOUS **BOHR-KRAMERS-SLATER** —OR ***BKS*** — PAPER OFFERED *THIS* CRAZINESS:

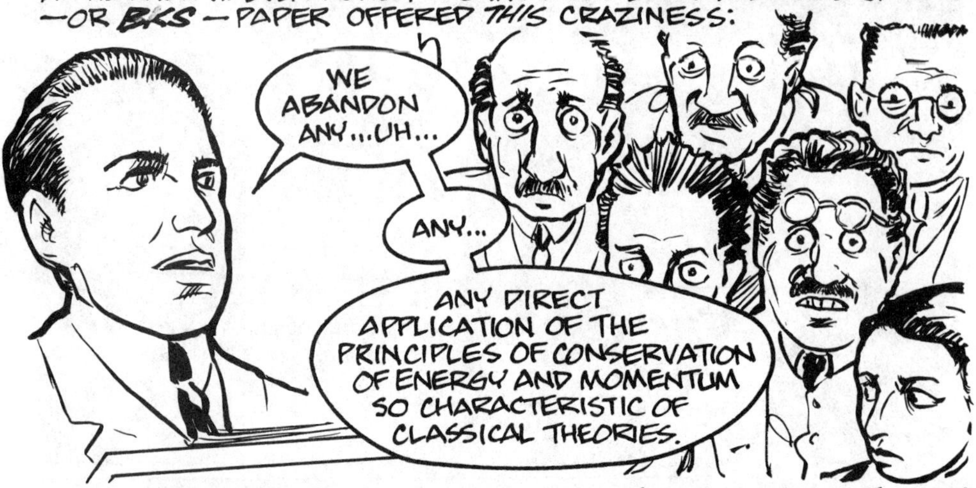
WE ABANDON ANY...UH...
ANY...
ANY DIRECT APPLICATION OF THE PRINCIPLES OF CONSERVATION OF ENERGY AND MOMENTUM SO CHARACTERISTIC OF CLASSICAL THEORIES.

THIS AGREED WITH EXPERIMENTS, ACTUALLY, WHICH UNTIL THEN ONLY SHOWED THAT ENERGY AND MOMENTUM CONSERVATION WORKED AS AN AVERAGE OVER MANY INDIVIDUAL PROCESSES. SO ACCORDING TO **BKS**, CONSERVATION OF ENERGY AND MOMENTUM ARE ONLY *STATISTICAL LAWS!*

NEAR **LYNGHUSET**, **BOHR'S** NEWLY ACQUIRED SUMMER HOME IN **TISVILDE**.

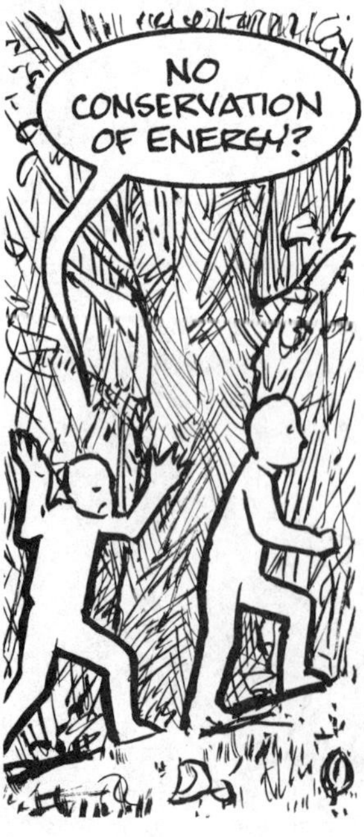
NO CONSERVATION OF ENERGY?

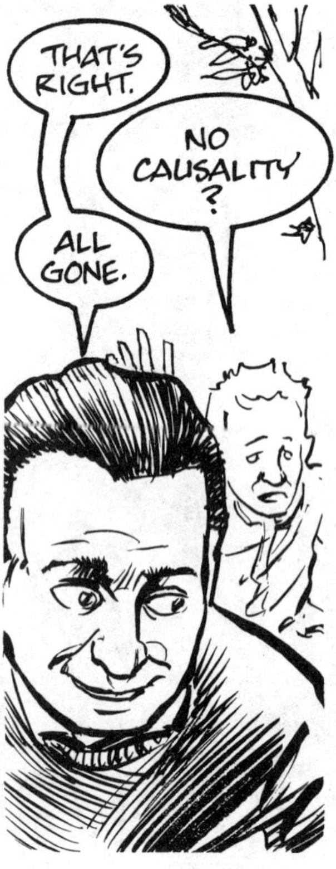
THAT'S RIGHT.
NO CAUSALITY?
ALL GONE.

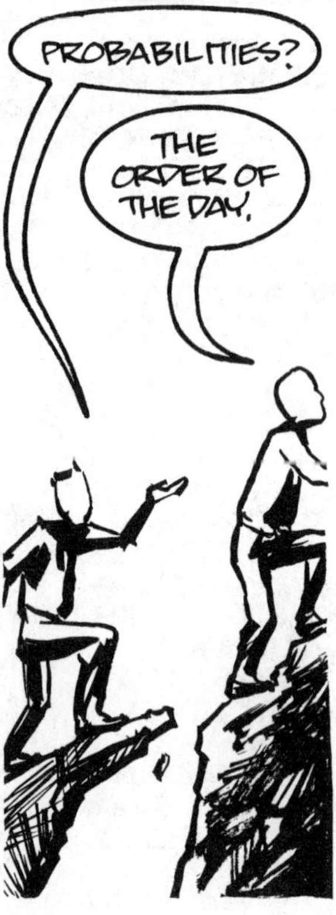
PROBABILITIES?
THE ORDER OF THE DAY.

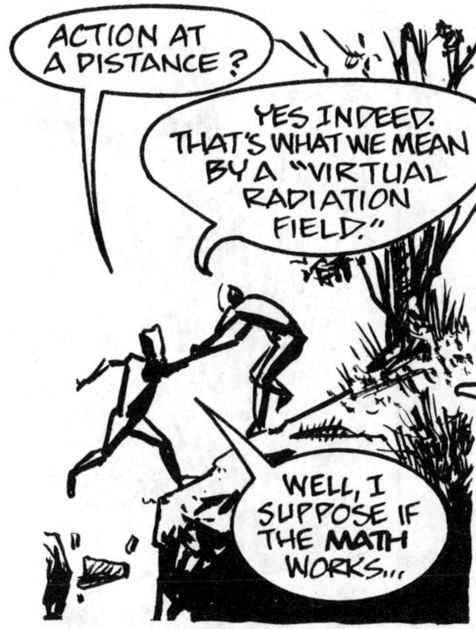
ACTION AT A DISTANCE?
YES INDEED. THAT'S WHAT WE MEAN BY A "VIRTUAL RADIATION FIELD."
WELL, I SUPPOSE IF THE MATH WORKS...

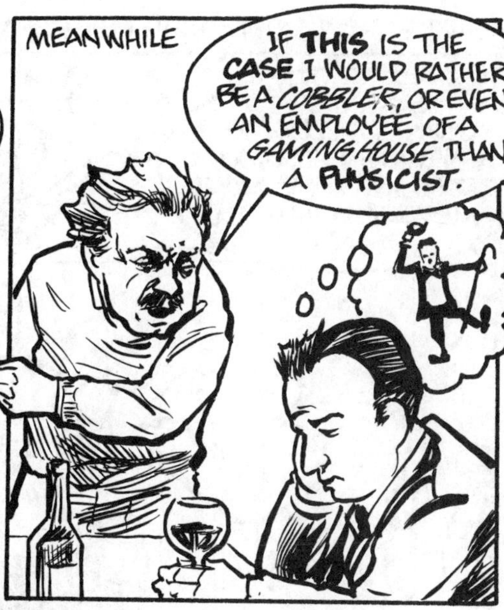
MEANWHILE
IF THIS IS THE CASE I WOULD RATHER BE A *COBBLER*, OR EVEN AN EMPLOYEE OF A *GAMING HOUSE* THAN A PHYSICIST.

GOOD THING FOR **EINSTEIN** THAT **BKS** WAS

WRONG

VERY WRONG, IN FACT. (IT TURNS OUT THAT THE MATH DOESN'T *REALLY* WORK.) SO WRONG THAT IT TOOK THE DISCOVERY OF A NEW PARTICLE, THE **NEUTRINO**, TO FINALLY RESOLVE THE MESS.*

AND YET, EVEN THOUGH **BOHR'S** LEGENDARY INTUITION HAD FAILED HIM ON **CONSERVATION LAWS**, *PROBABILITIES*, *ACTION AT A DISTANCE*, AND *NO MORE CAUSALITY* WERE TRULY THE SHAPE OF THINGS TO COME.

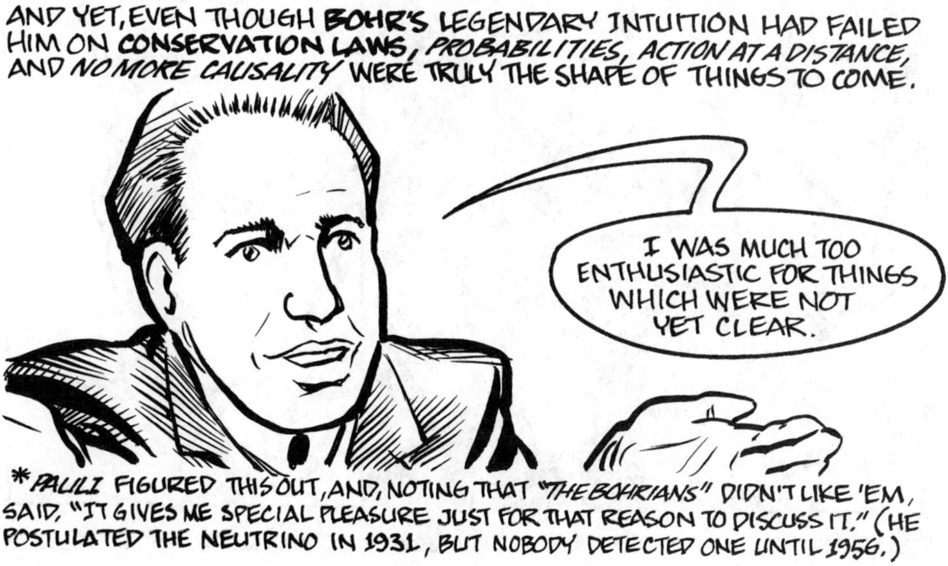
I WAS MUCH TOO ENTHUSIASTIC FOR THINGS WHICH WERE NOT YET CLEAR.

*PAULI FIGURED THIS OUT, AND, NOTING THAT "THE BOHRIANS" DIDN'T LIKE 'EM, SAID, "IT GIVES ME SPECIAL PLEASURE JUST FOR THAT REASON TO DISCUSS IT." (HE POSTULATED THE NEUTRINO IN 1931, BUT NOBODY DETECTED ONE UNTIL 1956.)

THAT'S THE TROUBLE WITH **BOHR'S** METHOD.*

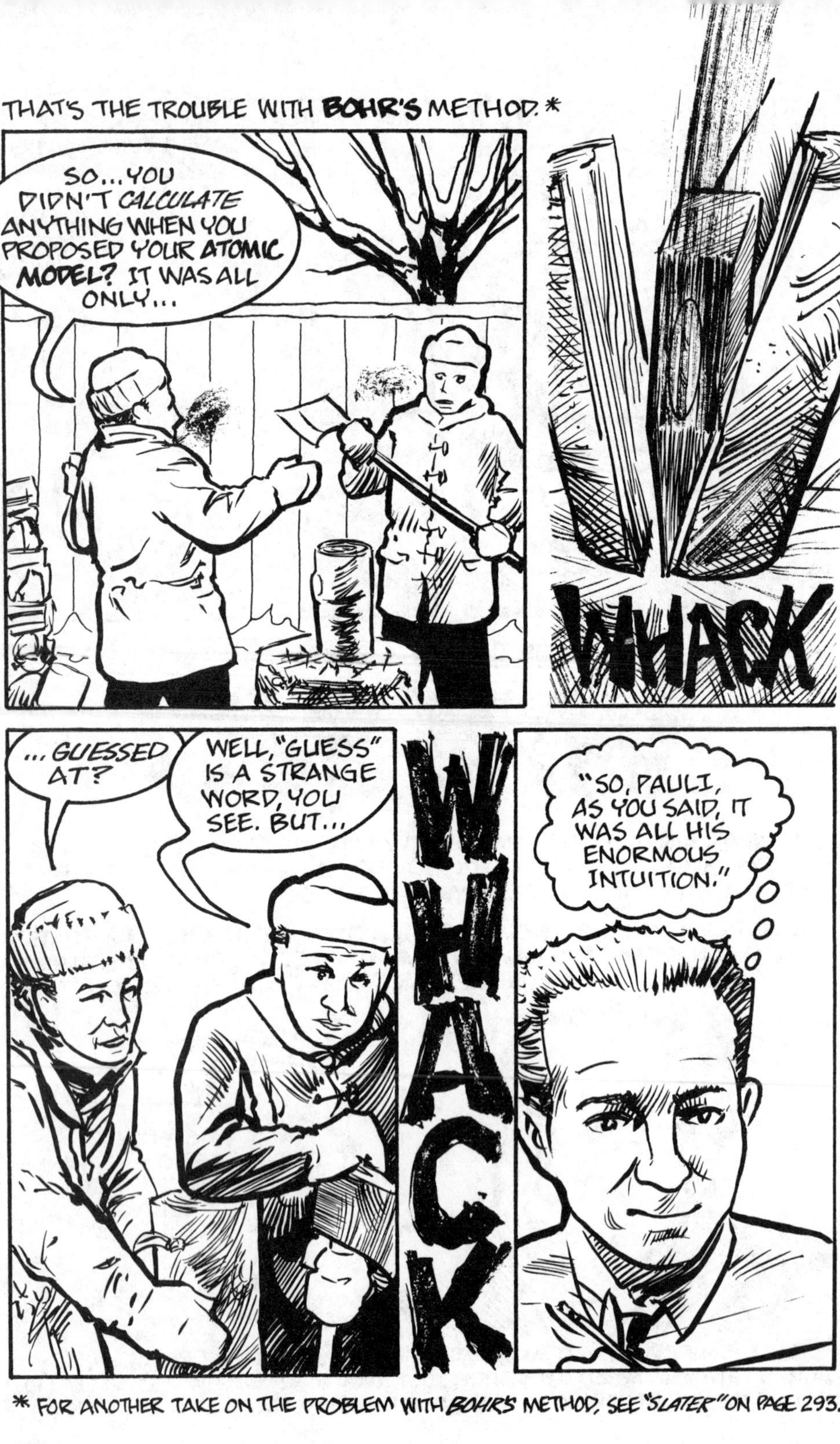
SO... YOU DIDN'T *CALCULATE* ANYTHING WHEN YOU PROPOSED YOUR **ATOMIC MODEL?** IT WAS ALL ONLY...
WHACK
...GUESSED AT?
WELL, "GUESS" IS A STRANGE WORD, YOU SEE. BUT...
WHACK
"SO, PAULI, AS YOU SAID, IT WAS ALL HIS ENORMOUS INTUITION."

* FOR ANOTHER TAKE ON THE PROBLEM WITH *BOHR'S* METHOD, SEE *"SLATER"* ON PAGE 293.

"HE KNEW HOW THINGS WERE, AND THERE WAS NOT ANY WAY OF CALCULATING IT."

AND THIS IS HOW THINGS WERE IN 1925: **HEISENBERG** LEFT **COPENHAGEN** TO TAKE UP HIS PROFESSORSHIP IN **GÖTTINGEN.** (HE HAD BEEN OFFERED IT AT THE TENDER AGE OF 22!)

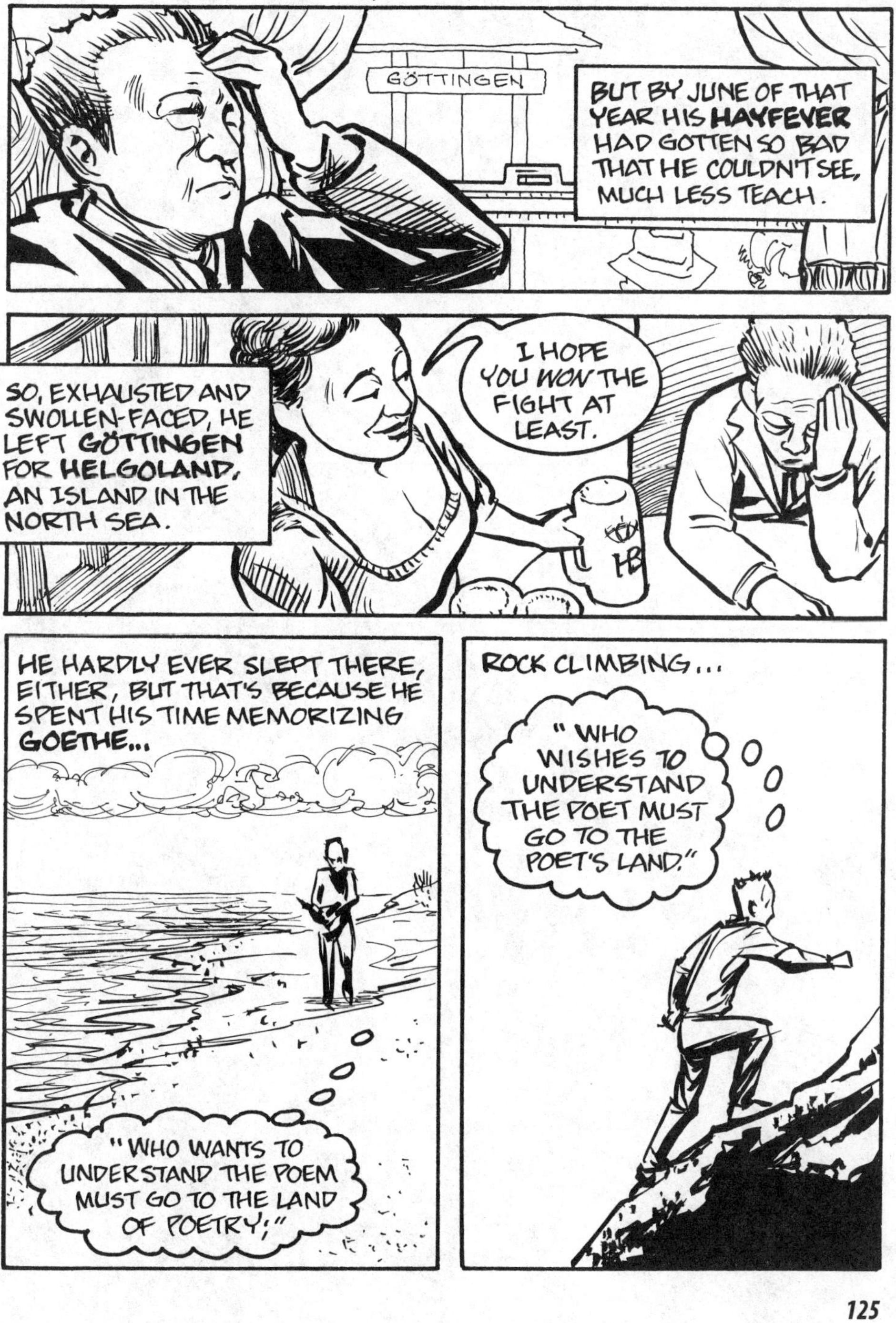
GÖTTINGEN
BUT BY JUNE OF THAT YEAR HIS **HAYFEVER** HAD GOTTEN SO BAD THAT HE COULDN'T SEE, MUCH LESS TEACH.
SO, EXHAUSTED AND SWOLLEN-FACED, HE LEFT **GÖTTINGEN** FOR **HELGOLAND**, AN ISLAND IN THE NORTH SEA.
I HOPE YOU *WON* THE FIGHT AT LEAST.
HE HARDLY EVER SLEPT THERE, EITHER, BUT THAT'S BECAUSE HE SPENT HIS TIME MEMORIZING **GOETHE...**
"WHO WANTS TO UNDERSTAND THE POEM MUST GO TO THE LAND OF POETRY;"
ROCK CLIMBING...
"WHO WISHES TO UNDERSTAND THE POET MUST GO TO THE POET'S LAND."

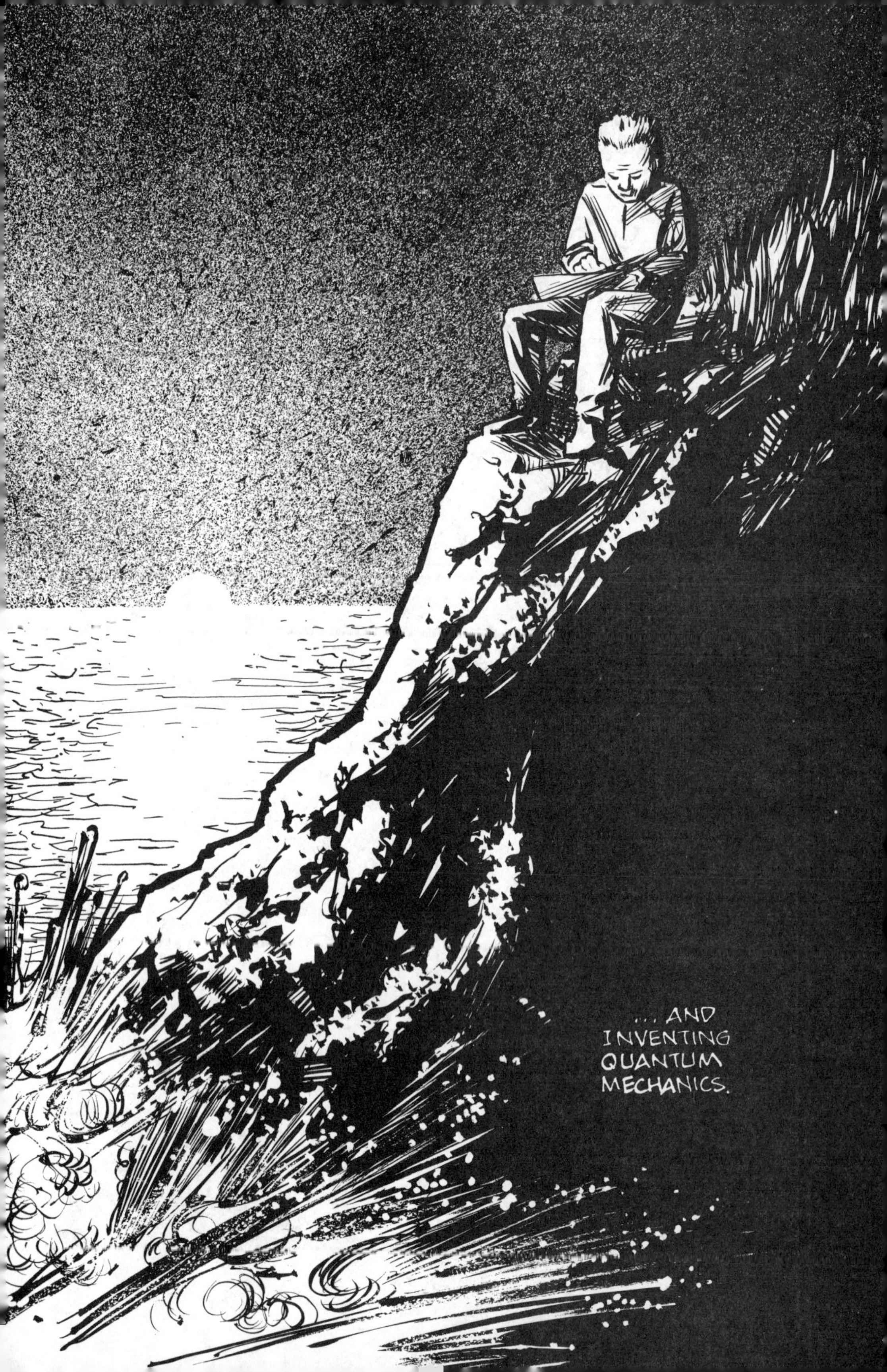
... AND INVENTING QUANTUM MECHANICS.

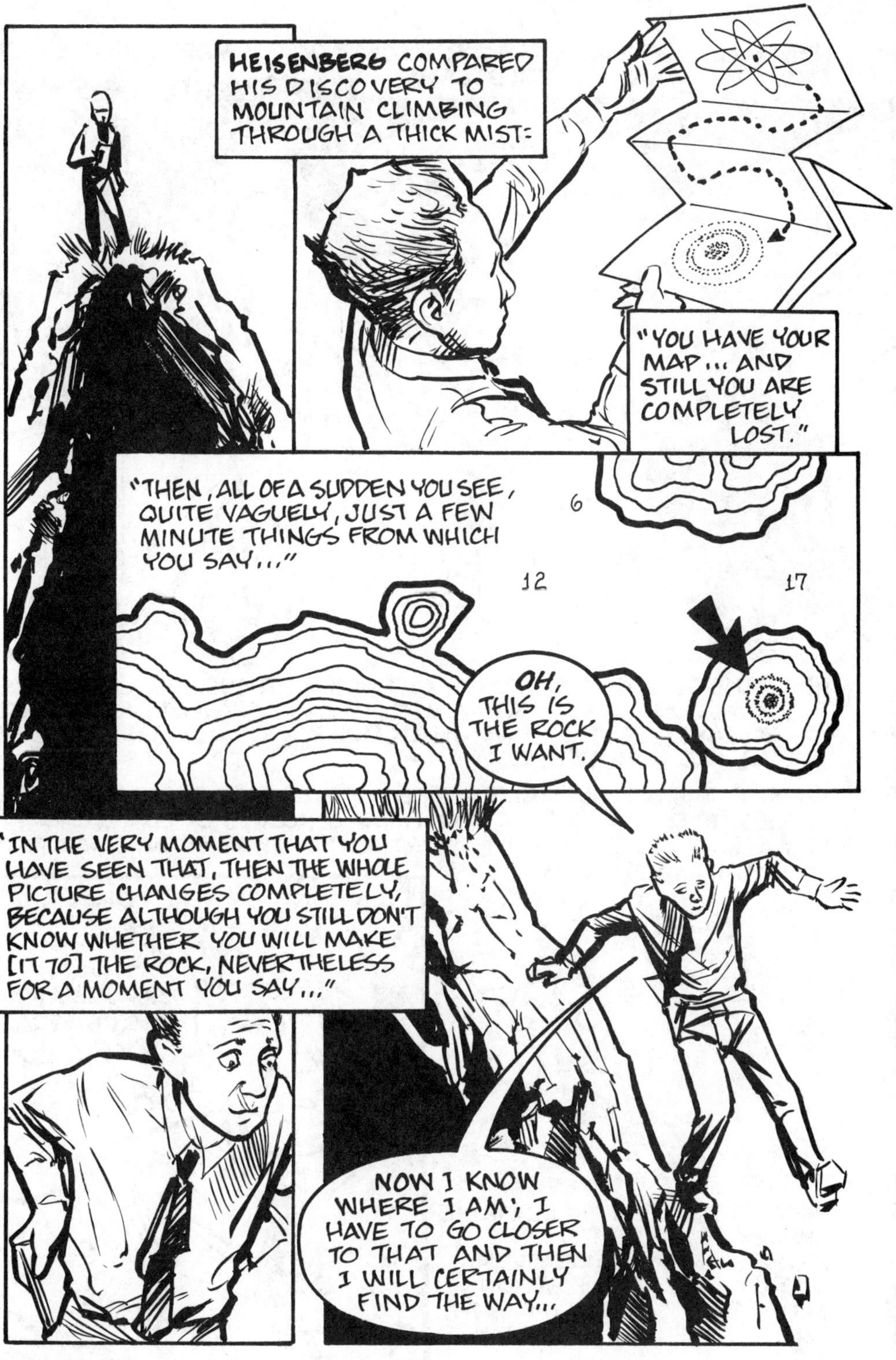
HEISENBERG COMPARED HIS DISCOVERY TO MOUNTAIN CLIMBING THROUGH A THICK MIST:
"YOU HAVE YOUR MAP... AND STILL YOU ARE COMPLETELY LOST."
"THEN, ALL OF A SUDDEN YOU SEE, QUITE VAGUELY, JUST A FEW MINUTE THINGS FROM WHICH YOU SAY..."
6
12
17
OH, THIS IS THE ROCK I WANT.
"IN THE VERY MOMENT THAT YOU HAVE SEEN THAT, THEN THE WHOLE PICTURE CHANGES COMPLETELY, BECAUSE ALTHOUGH YOU STILL DON'T KNOW WHETHER YOU WILL MAKE [IT TO] THE ROCK, NEVERTHELESS FOR A MOMENT YOU SAY..."
NOW I KNOW WHERE I AM; I HAVE TO GO CLOSER TO THAT AND THEN I WILL CERTAINLY FIND THE WAY...

HEISENBERG ABANDONED BOHR'S SOLAR SYSTEM MODEL OF THE ATOM ONCE AND FOR ALL ON HELGOLAND.

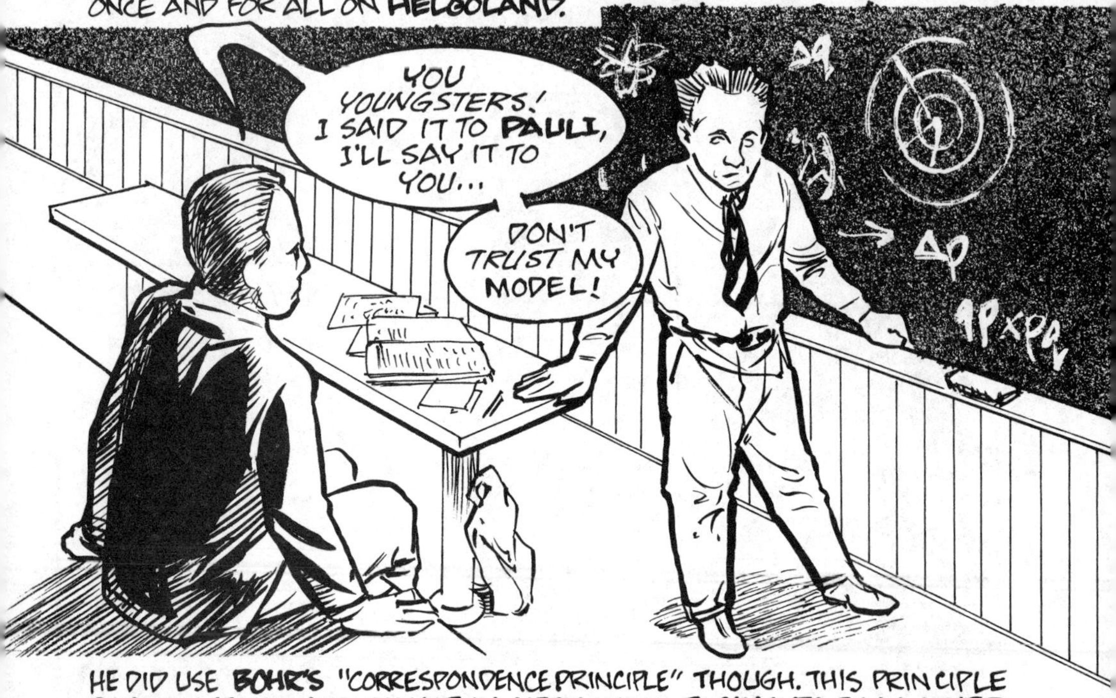
YOU YOUNGSTERS! I SAID IT TO PAULI, I'LL SAY IT TO YOU...
DON'T TRUST MY MODEL!

HE DID USE BOHR'S "CORRESPONDENCE PRINCIPLE" THOUGH. THIS PRINCIPLE SAID CLASSICAL AND QUANTUM MECHANICS *FLOW INTO* EACH OTHER (OR AT LEAST **LOOK** THE SAME) WHEN BOHR'S QUANTUM NUMBERS **N** AND **M** ARE VERY LARGE.

SO WITH THIS IN MIND, HEISENBERG WORKED BACKWARDS FROM THE LARGEST ELECTRON ORBITS, AND USED CONCEPTS OF CLASSICAL PHYSICS TO CALCULATE THE ELECTRON ENERGY FROM QUANTUM JUMPS IN A *NEW* WAY.

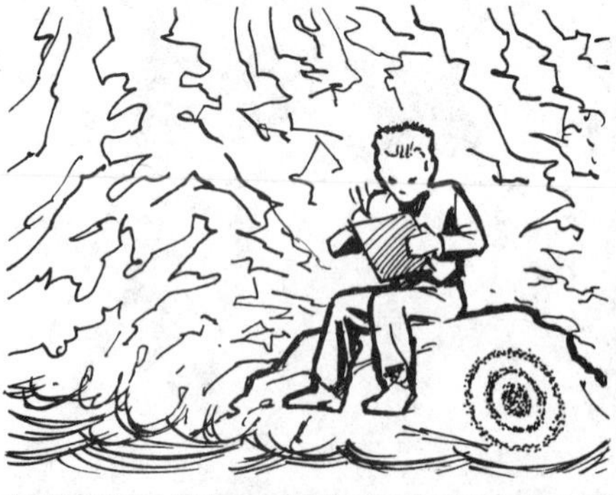

WHEN HE EXPRESSED THE ELECTRON'S ENERGY AS A FUNCTION OF ITS MOMENTUM **p** (REMEMBER *de BROGLIE*?) AND POSITION **q** IN ITS "ORBIT" AND DID THE *MATH*, HE GOT SOMETHING VERY STRANGE.

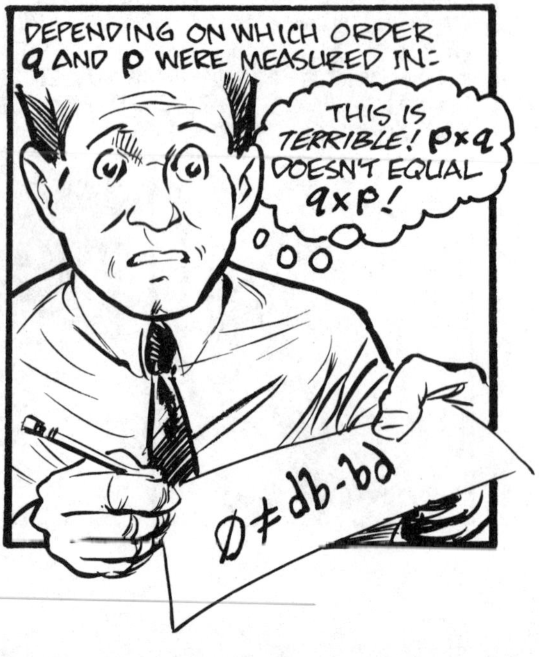
DEPENDING ON WHICH ORDER q AND p WERE MEASURED IN:
THIS IS TERRIBLE! p×q DOESN'T EQUAL q×p!
Ø≠db-bd

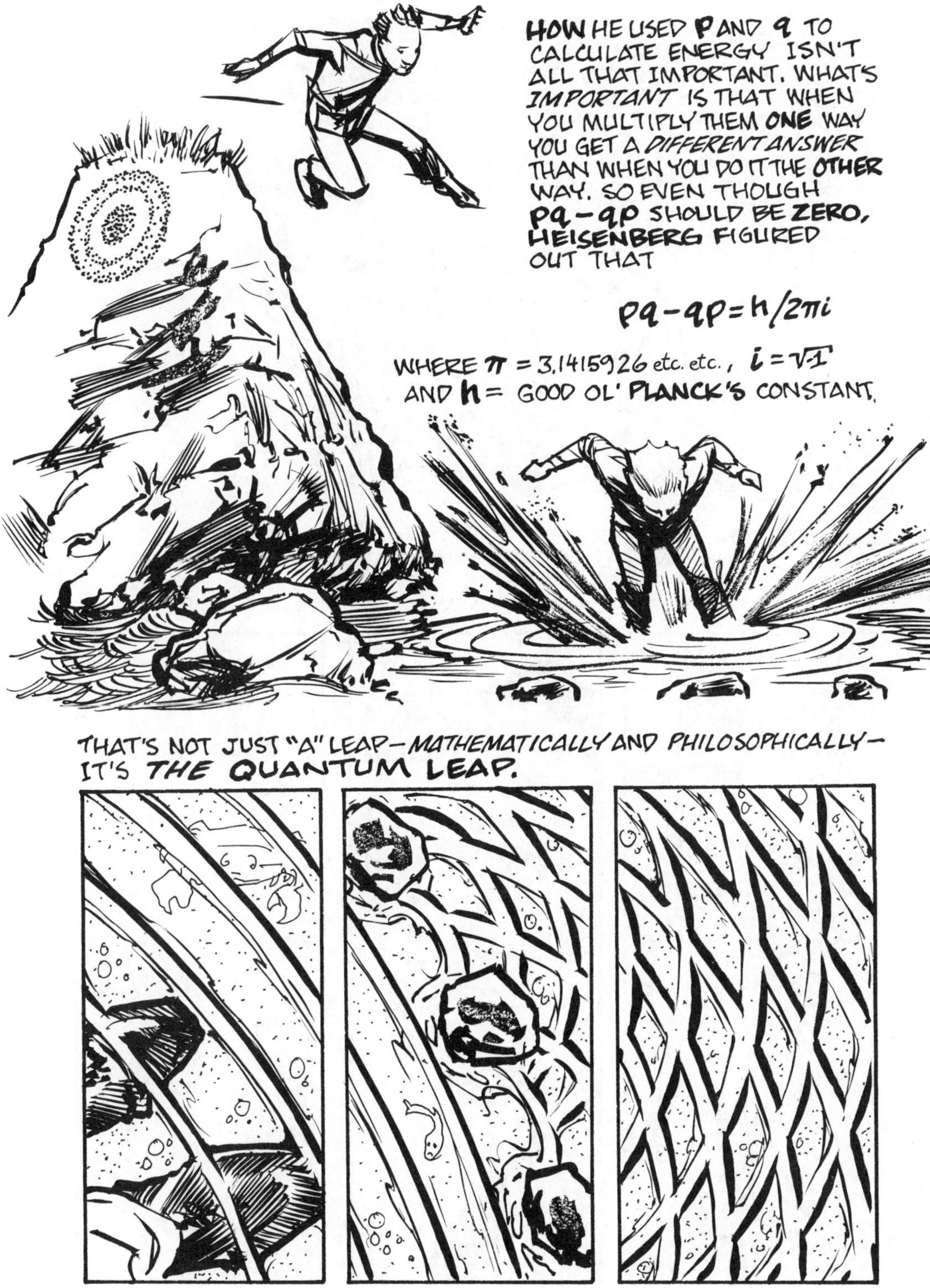
HOW HE USED P AND q TO CALCULATE ENERGY ISN'T ALL THAT IMPORTANT. WHAT'S IMPORTANT IS THAT WHEN YOU MULTIPLY THEM ONE WAY YOU GET A DIFFERENT ANSWER THAN WHEN YOU DO IT THE OTHER WAY. SO EVEN THOUGH pq − qp SHOULD BE ZERO, HEISENBERG FIGURED OUT THAT
$pq - qp = h/2\pi i$
WHERE π = 3.1415926 etc. etc., $i = \sqrt{-1}$ AND h = GOOD OL' PLANCK'S CONSTANT.
THAT'S NOT JUST "A" LEAP—MATHEMATICALLY AND PHILOSOPHICALLY—IT'S THE QUANTUM LEAP.

SKIPPING LOTS OF MATH (TRUST **HEISENBERG** ON THIS) LET'S JUMP TO THE RESULTS:

1) THE *GOOD NEWS* IS, THE ATOM IS **STABLE**... THE *BAD* NEWS IS THAT NOT ONLY **DOESN'T** IT LOOK LIKE **BOHR'S** MINI SOLAR SYSTEM, IT DOESN'T LOOK LIKE ANYTHING *AT ALL*, REALLY.

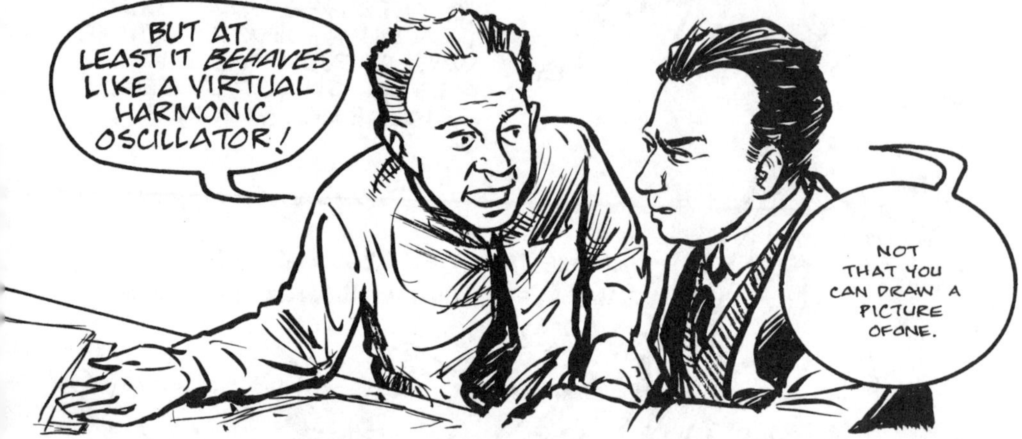
BUT AT LEAST IT *BEHAVES* LIKE A VIRTUAL HARMONIC OSCILLATOR!
NOT THAT YOU CAN DRAW A PICTURE OF ONE.

2) THE *OTHER* **GOOD** NEWS IS THAT THE ANSWER TO THE QUESTION, "ARE ELECTRONS (AND PHOTONS) PARTICLES OR WAVES?" WAS SETTLED AND IS MOST DEFINITELY "*YES*." THE OTHER **BAD** NEWS IS THAT THE ANSWER TO THAT QUESTION ***IS*** MOST DEFINITELY "***YES***."

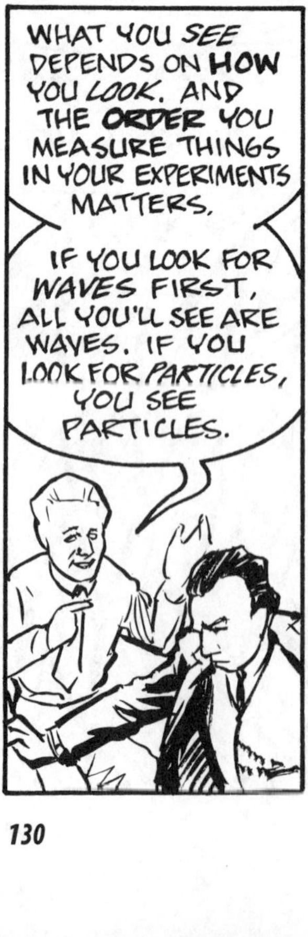
WHAT YOU *SEE* DEPENDS ON **HOW** YOU *LOOK*. AND THE **ORDER** YOU MEASURE THINGS IN YOUR EXPERIMENTS MATTERS.
IF YOU LOOK FOR *WAVES* FIRST, ALL YOU'LL SEE ARE WAVES. IF YOU LOOK FOR *PARTICLES*, YOU SEE PARTICLES.

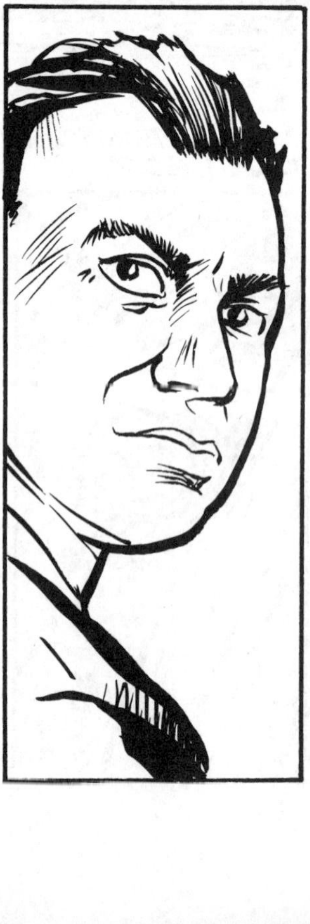

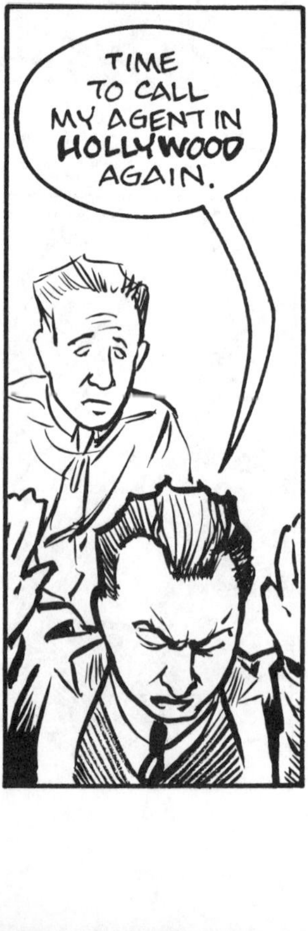
TIME TO CALL MY AGENT IN **HOLLYWOOD** AGAIN.

BUT SOON **PAULI**, ALONG WITH **MAX BORN**, **PASCUAL JORDAN**, AND **PAUL DIRAC** (WORKING INDEPENDENTLY) HAD WORKED OUT THE MATH.

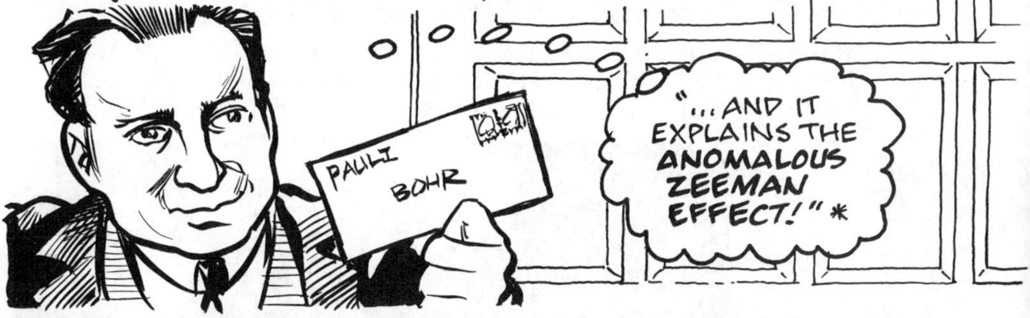
PAULI
BOHR
"...AND IT EXPLAINS THE **ANOMALOUS ZEEMAN EFFECT!**" *

BORN AND **JORDAN** CALLED IT *"MATRIX MECHANICS"* AND -MONTHS LATER- **HEISENBERG** FINALLY WORKED UP THE NERVE TO TALK WITH **BOHR** ABOUT IT.

* REMEMBER THAT, FROM CHAPTER 6? WE KNOW YOU'RE RELIEVED TO HAVE THIS CLEARED UP.

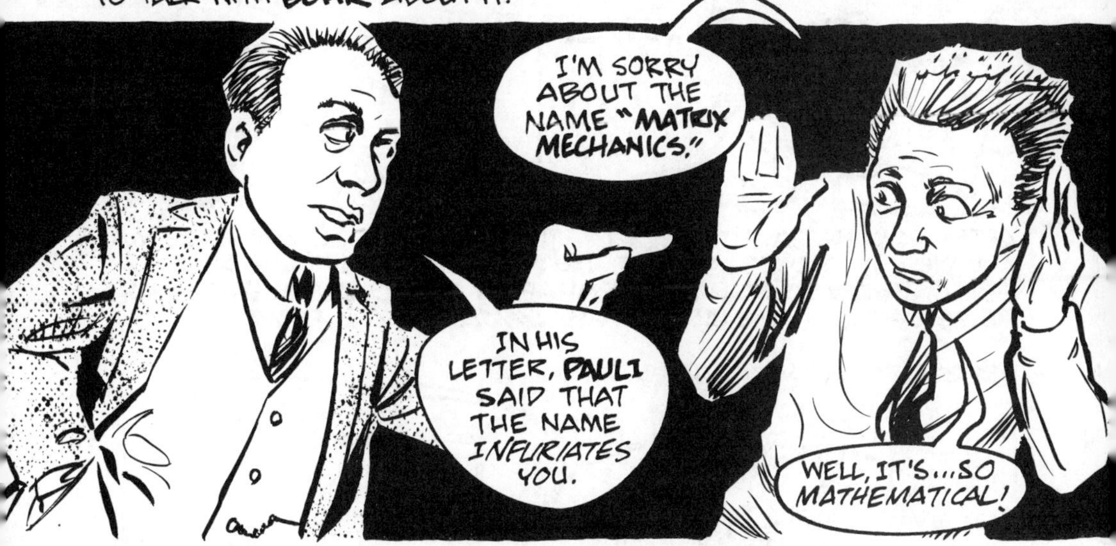
I'M SORRY ABOUT THE NAME "**MATRIX MECHANICS**."
IN HIS LETTER, **PAULI** SAID THAT THE NAME *INFURIATES* YOU.
WELL, IT'S...SO *MATHEMATICAL!*

HEISENBERG WAS BACK IN **COPENHAGEN** IN 1926, AND TOGETHER, HE AND **BOHR** TACKLED THE PHILOSOPHICAL PROBLEM:

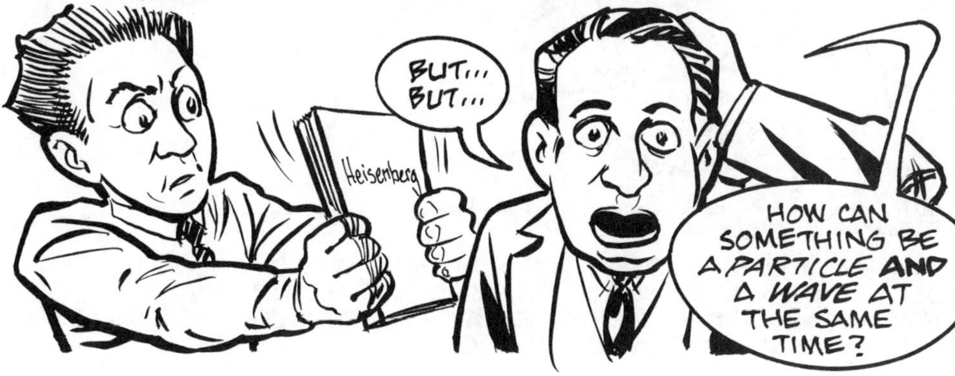
BUT... BUT...
Heisenberg
HOW CAN SOMETHING BE A *PARTICLE* **AND** A *WAVE* AT THE SAME TIME?

FOR MONTHS, **BOHR** TRIED TO EXPLAIN THE *WHY* BEHIND THE SIMULTANEOUS EXISTENCE OF BOTH, SINCE BOTH WERE NEEDED FOR A COMPLETE DESCRIPTION – EVEN THOUGH THEY'RE MUTUALLY EXCLUSIVE.

HEISENBERG MAINTAINED THAT IF ALL THE MEASURABLE QUANTITIES (THE **P**'S AND **Q**'S, FOR INSTANCE) CAN PROVIDE A COMPLETE DESCRIPTION OF WHAT'S THERE, AND THE MATH IS CONSISTENT, THAT'S ENOUGH.

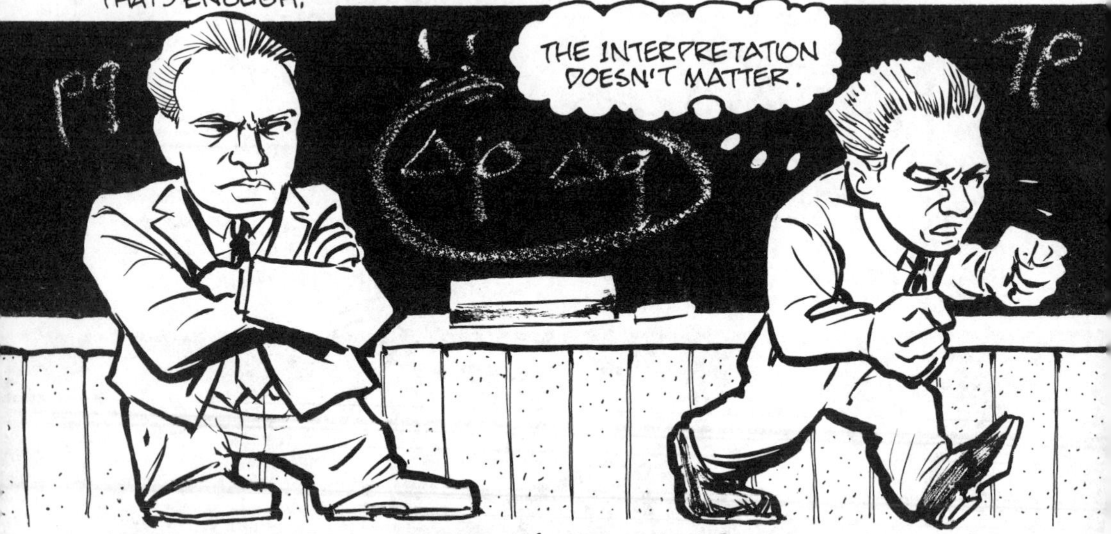

THE INTERPRETATION DOESN'T MATTER.

AFTER DRIVING EACH OTHER *CRAZY* THROUGH THE FALL, PAST CHRISTMAS, AND WELL INTO 1927, **BOHR** WENT SKIING IN **NORWAY** AND **HEISENBERG** STAYED IN **COPENHAGEN**. WHILE **BOHR** WAS AWAY, **HEISENBERG** CAME UP WITH HIS *UNCERTAINTY PRINCIPLE*.

HERE'S (ROUGHLY) WHAT HE DID.

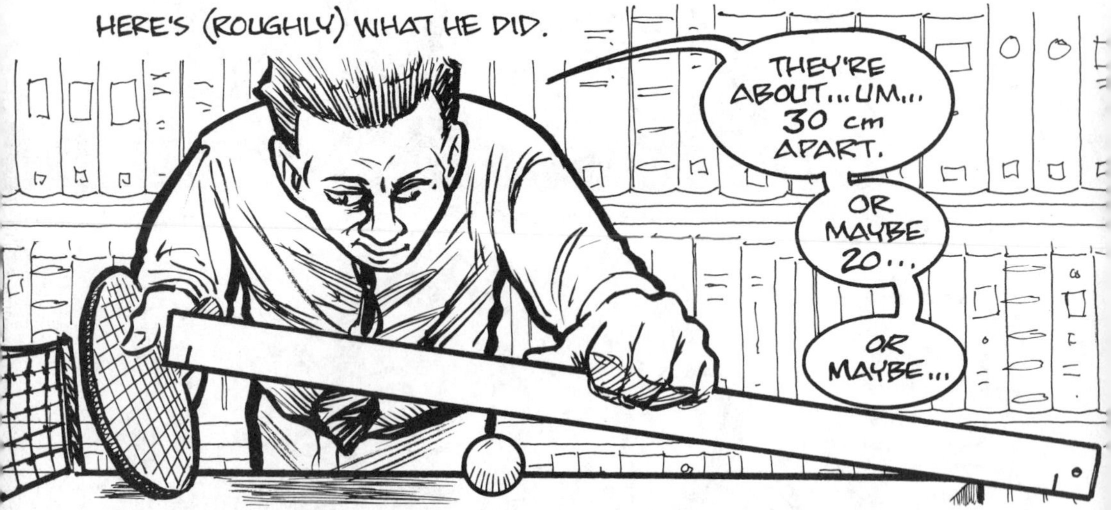

THEY'RE ABOUT... UM... 30 cm APART.
OR MAYBE 20...
OR MAYBE...

FIRST, **HEISENBERG** NOTED THAT YOU CAN'T MEASURE SOMETHING'S POSITION TO AN ACCURACY OF, SAY, ONE CENTIMETER IF YOUR RULER ONLY HAS MARKINGS THAT ARE *ONE HUNDRED* CENTIMETERS APART. YOU CAN ONLY MAKE A ROUGH GUESS.

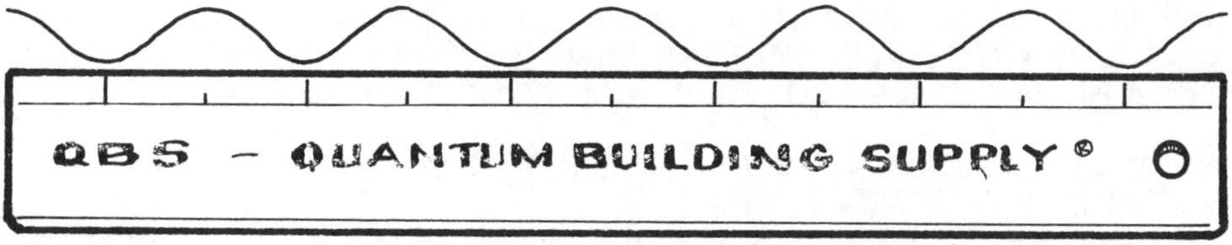
QBS – QUANTUM BUILDING SUPPLY®

MEASURING MEANS **LOOKING**, SO IF YOU MEASURE AN OBJECT'S POSITION *q* BY BOUNCING LIGHT OF WAVELENGTH λ OFF OF IT, THAT MEANS TWO THINGS.

FIRST, IT MEANS YOU CAN'T KNOW *q* MORE ACCURATELY THAN λ, SINCE THE WAVELENGTH IS LIKE THE MARKINGS ON YOUR RULER.

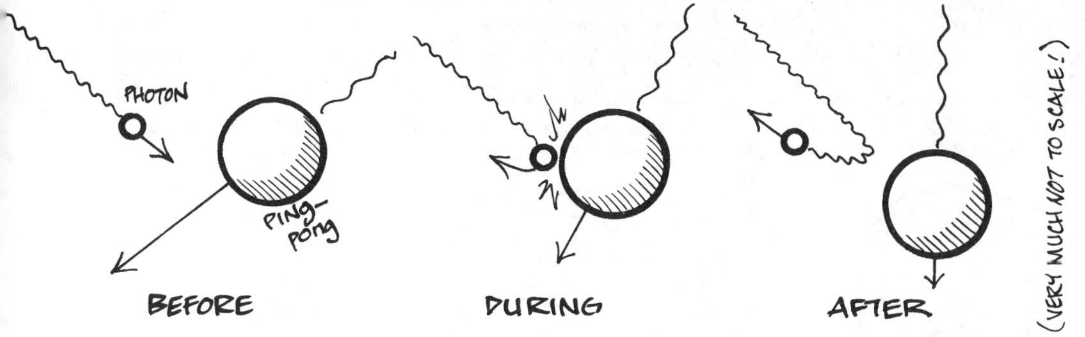
PHOTON
PING-PONG
BEFORE
DURING
AFTER
(VERY MUCH NOT TO SCALE!)

SECOND. SINCE LIGHT COMES IN BUNDLES (PHOTONS), THEY KNOCK EVEN LARGE OBJECTS LIKE *PING-PONG* BALLS AROUND, AT LEAST A LITTLE. THE SMALLER THE WAVELENGTH, THE MORE ENERGETIC THE PHOTON— OR OBJECT.

THAT MEANS THAT THE MORE ACCURATELY A *PHOTON* CAN PINPOINT AN OBJECT'S LOCATION (*q*) AT A PARTICULAR TIME, THE MORE THE PHOTON KNOCKS IT AWAY FROM THAT LOCATION.

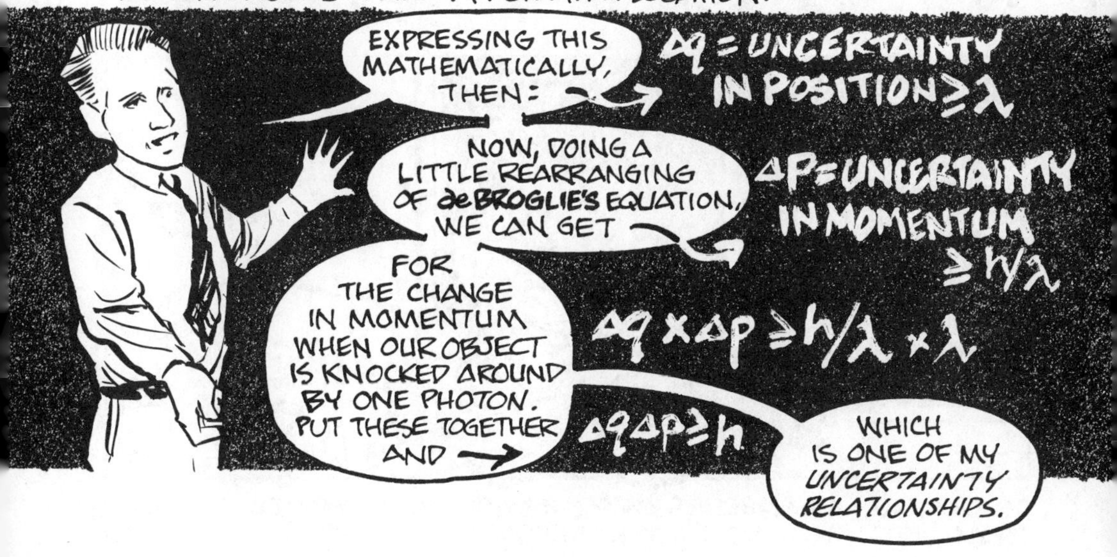
EXPRESSING THIS MATHEMATICALLY, THEN:
Δq = UNCERTAINTY IN POSITION ≥ λ
NOW, DOING A LITTLE REARRANGING OF deBROGLIE'S EQUATION, WE CAN GET
ΔP = UNCERTAINTY IN MOMENTUM ≥ h/λ
FOR THE CHANGE IN MOMENTUM WHEN OUR OBJECT IS KNOCKED AROUND BY ONE PHOTON. PUT THESE TOGETHER AND
Δq × Δp ≥ h/λ × λ
ΔqΔp ≥ h
WHICH IS ONE OF MY *UNCERTAINTY RELATIONSHIPS.*

THE OTHER UNCERTAINTY RELATIONSHIP, $\Delta E \Delta t \geq h$, HAS TO DO WITH A PARTICLE'S ENERGY (**E**) AND THE TIME (**t**) THAT IT HAS THAT ENERGY. (IT'S A BIT MORE SUBTLE, AND WILL COME BACK TO HAUNT US.)

WHEN **BOHR** RETURNED ABOUT A MONTH LATER, **HEISENBERG** SHOWED HIM THE RESULTS.

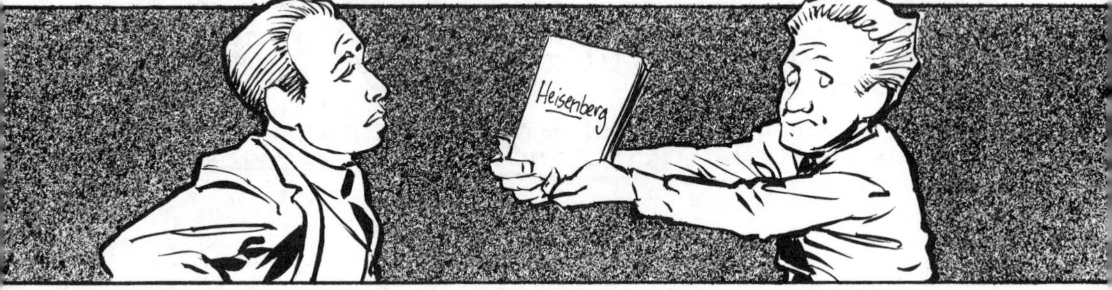
Heisenberg

THOUGH INITIALLY ENTHUSIASTIC, **BOHR** SOON THOUGHT HE FOUND FLAWS IN THE ARGUMENT, AND SUGGESTED MANY REVISIONS.

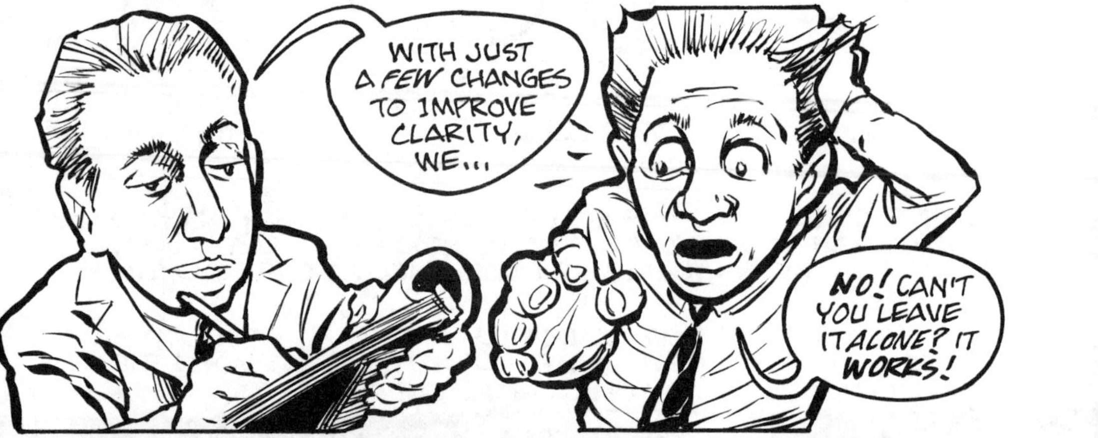
WITH JUST A *FEW* CHANGES TO IMPROVE CLARITY, WE...
NO! CAN'T YOU LEAVE IT ALONE? IT **WORKS!**

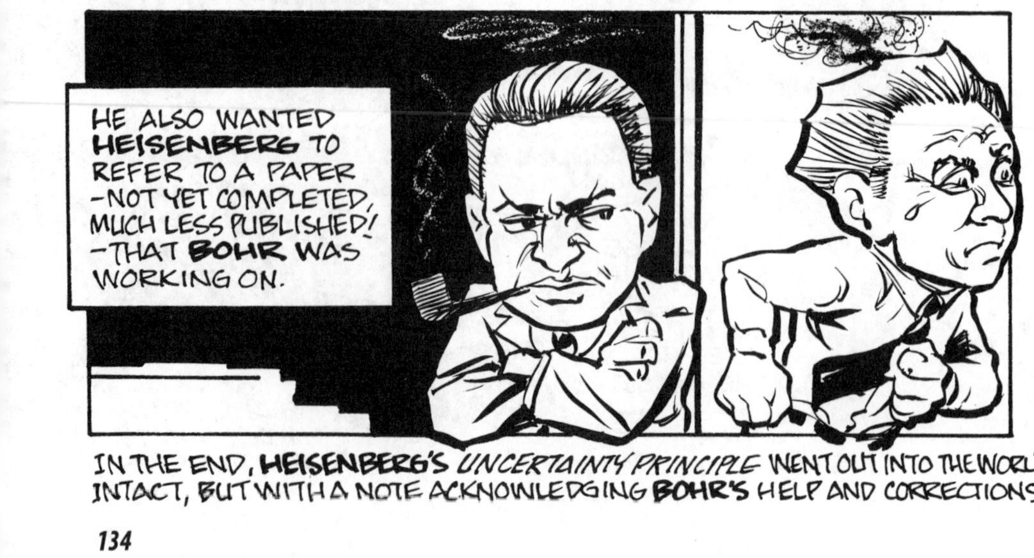
HE ALSO WANTED **HEISENBERG** TO REFER TO A PAPER -NOT YET COMPLETED, MUCH LESS PUBLISHED! -THAT **BOHR** WAS WORKING ON.

IN THE END, **HEISENBERG'S** *UNCERTAINTY PRINCIPLE* WENT OUT INTO THE WORLD INTACT, BUT WITH A NOTE ACKNOWLEDGING **BOHR'S** HELP AND CORRECTIONS.

AFTER RETURNING TO GERMANY, HE WROTE **BOHR**:

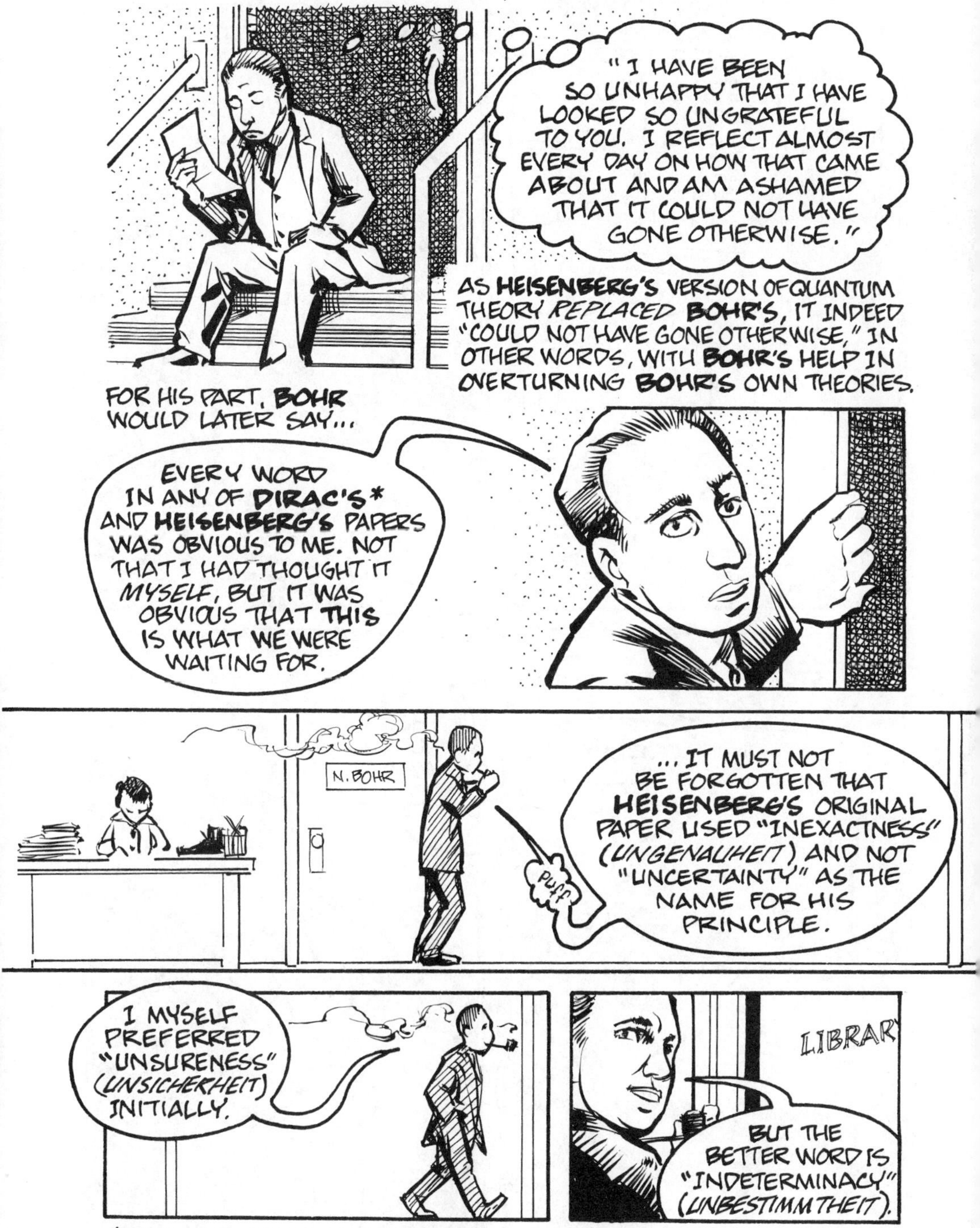

"I HAVE BEEN SO UNHAPPY THAT I HAVE LOOKED SO UNGRATEFUL TO YOU. I REFLECT ALMOST EVERY DAY ON HOW THAT CAME ABOUT AND AM ASHAMED THAT IT COULD NOT HAVE GONE OTHERWISE."
AS **HEISENBERG'S** VERSION OF QUANTUM THEORY *REPLACED* **BOHR'S**, IT INDEED "COULD NOT HAVE GONE OTHERWISE," IN OTHER WORDS, WITH **BOHR'S** HELP IN OVERTURNING **BOHR'S** OWN THEORIES.
FOR HIS PART, **BOHR** WOULD LATER SAY...
EVERY WORD IN ANY OF **DIRAC'S*** AND **HEISENBERG'S** PAPERS WAS OBVIOUS TO ME. NOT THAT I HAD THOUGHT IT *MYSELF*, BUT IT WAS OBVIOUS THAT **THIS** IS WHAT WE WERE WAITING FOR.
N. BOHR
PUFF
...IT MUST NOT BE FORGOTTEN THAT **HEISENBERG'S** ORIGINAL PAPER USED "INEXACTNESS" (*UNGENAUHEIT*) AND NOT "UNCERTAINTY" AS THE NAME FOR HIS PRINCIPLE.
I MYSELF PREFERRED "UNSURENESS" (*UNSICHERHEIT*) INITIALLY.
LIBRARY
BUT THE BETTER WORD IS "INDETERMINACY" (*UNBESTIMMTHEIT*).

* HIM AGAIN! WHO IS THIS GUY?
SEE "OH, THAT DIRAC!" ON PAGE 294 TO FIND OUT.

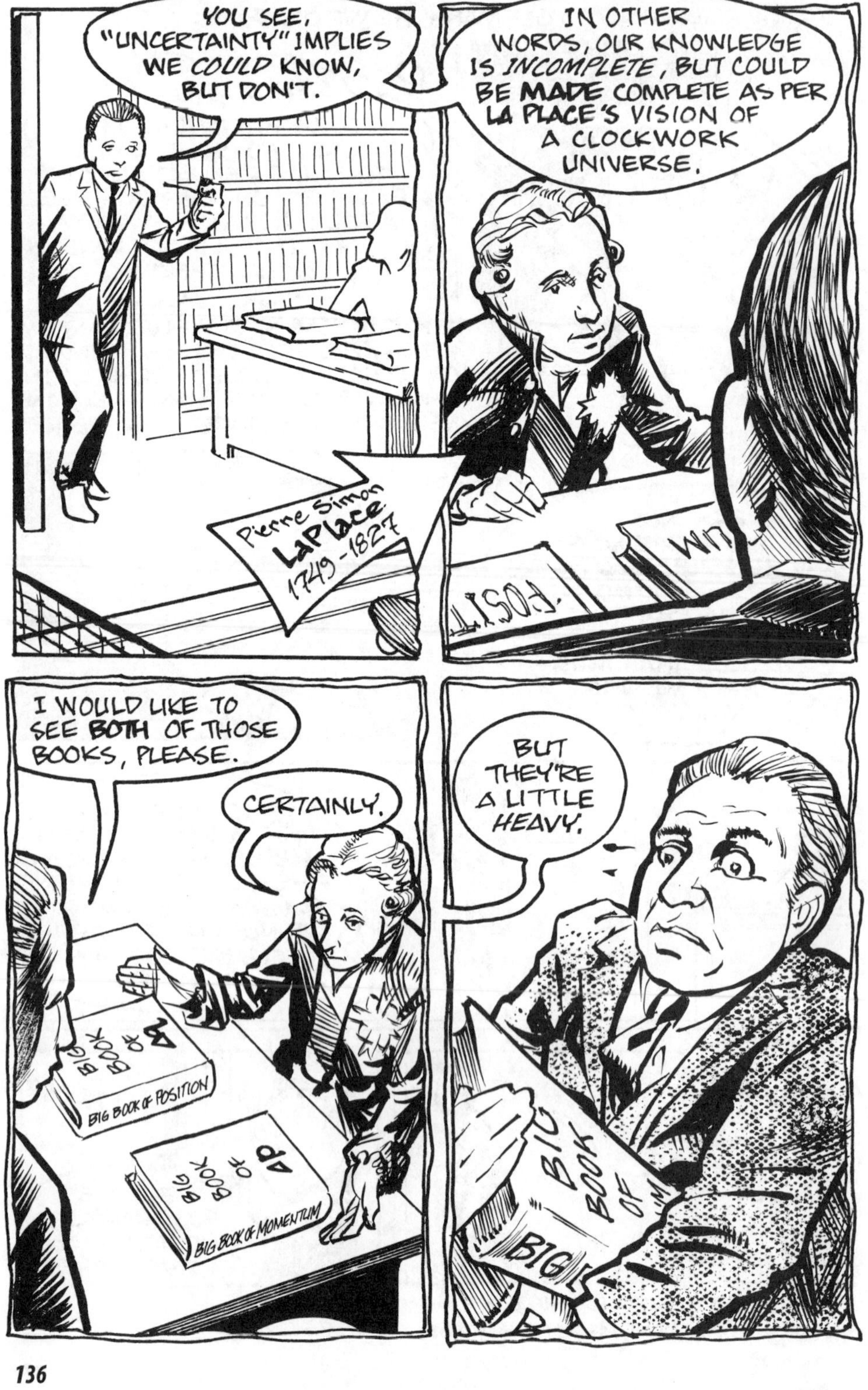
YOU SEE, "UNCERTAINTY" IMPLIES WE COULD KNOW, BUT DON'T.
IN OTHER WORDS, OUR KNOWLEDGE IS INCOMPLETE, BUT COULD BE MADE COMPLETE AS PER LA PLACE'S VISION OF A CLOCKWORK UNIVERSE.
Pierre Simon LaPlace 1749-1827
I WOULD LIKE TO SEE BOTH OF THOSE BOOKS, PLEASE.
CERTAINLY.
BIG BOOK OF ΔX
BIG BOOK OF POSITION
BIG BOOK OF ΔP
BIG BOOK OF MOMENTUM
BUT THEY'RE A LITTLE HEAVY.
BIG BOOK OF

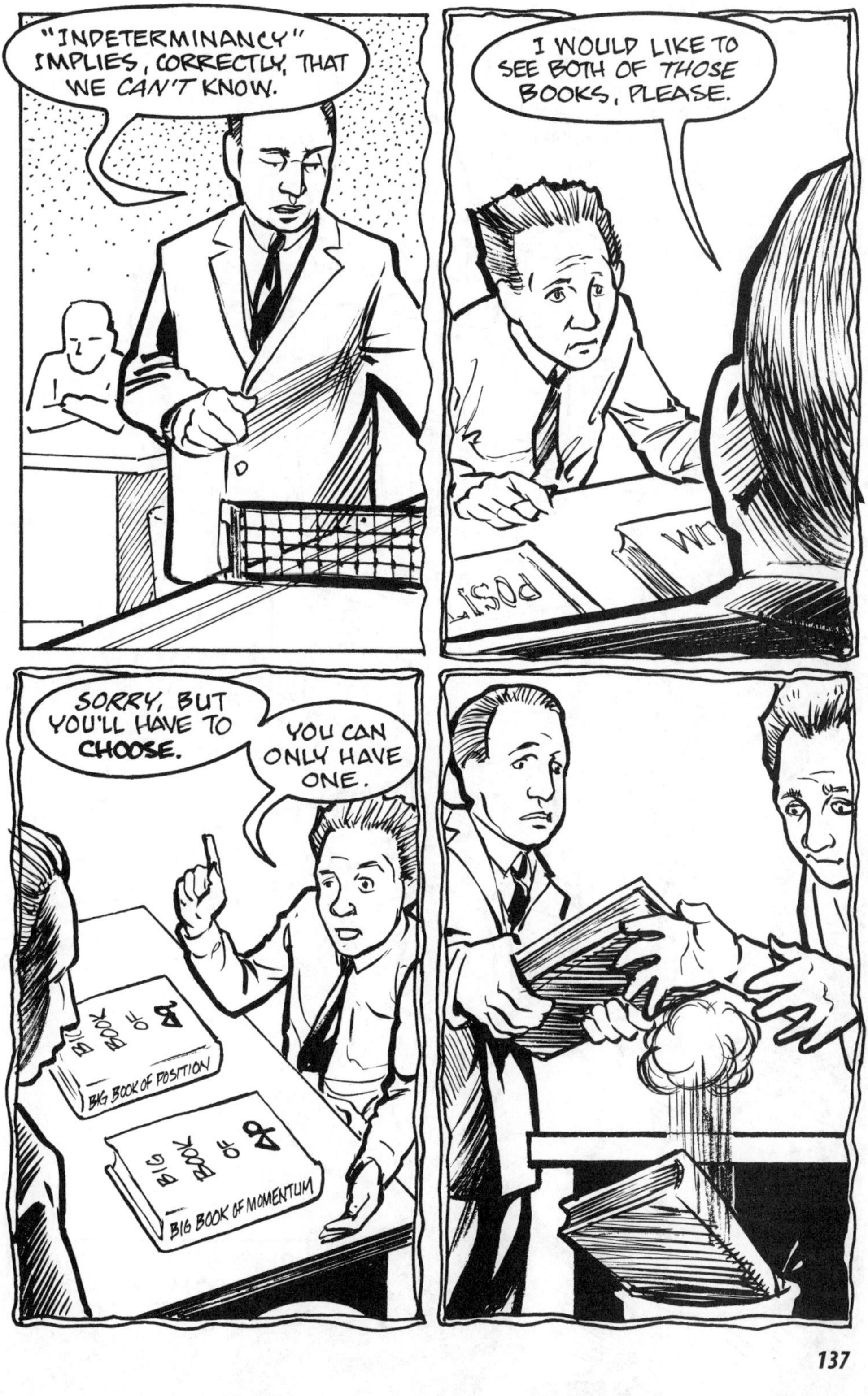
"INDETERMINANCY" IMPLIES, CORRECTLY, THAT WE CAN'T KNOW.
I WOULD LIKE TO SEE BOTH OF THOSE BOOKS, PLEASE.
POSI
SORRY, BUT YOU'LL HAVE TO CHOOSE.
YOU CAN ONLY HAVE ONE.
BIG BOOK OF Δq
BIG BOOK OF POSITION
BIG BOOK OF Δp
BIG BOOK OF MOMENTUM

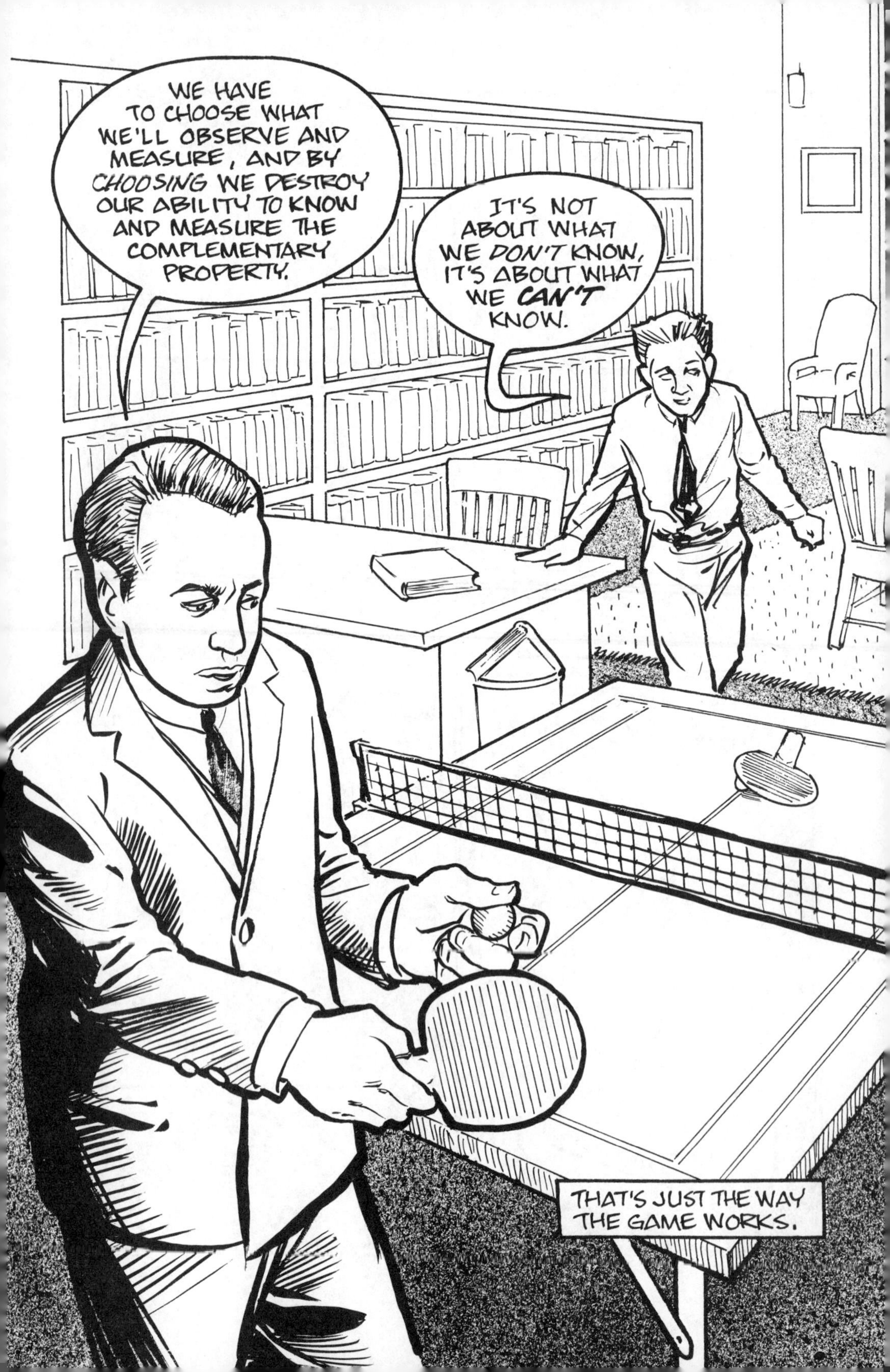
WE HAVE TO CHOOSE WHAT WE'LL OBSERVE AND MEASURE, AND BY *CHOOSING* WE DESTROY OUR ABILITY TO KNOW AND MEASURE THE COMPLEMENTARY PROPERTY.
IT'S NOT ABOUT WHAT WE *DON'T* KNOW, IT'S ABOUT WHAT WE ***CAN'T*** KNOW.
THAT'S JUST THE WAY THE GAME WORKS.

Chapter 8

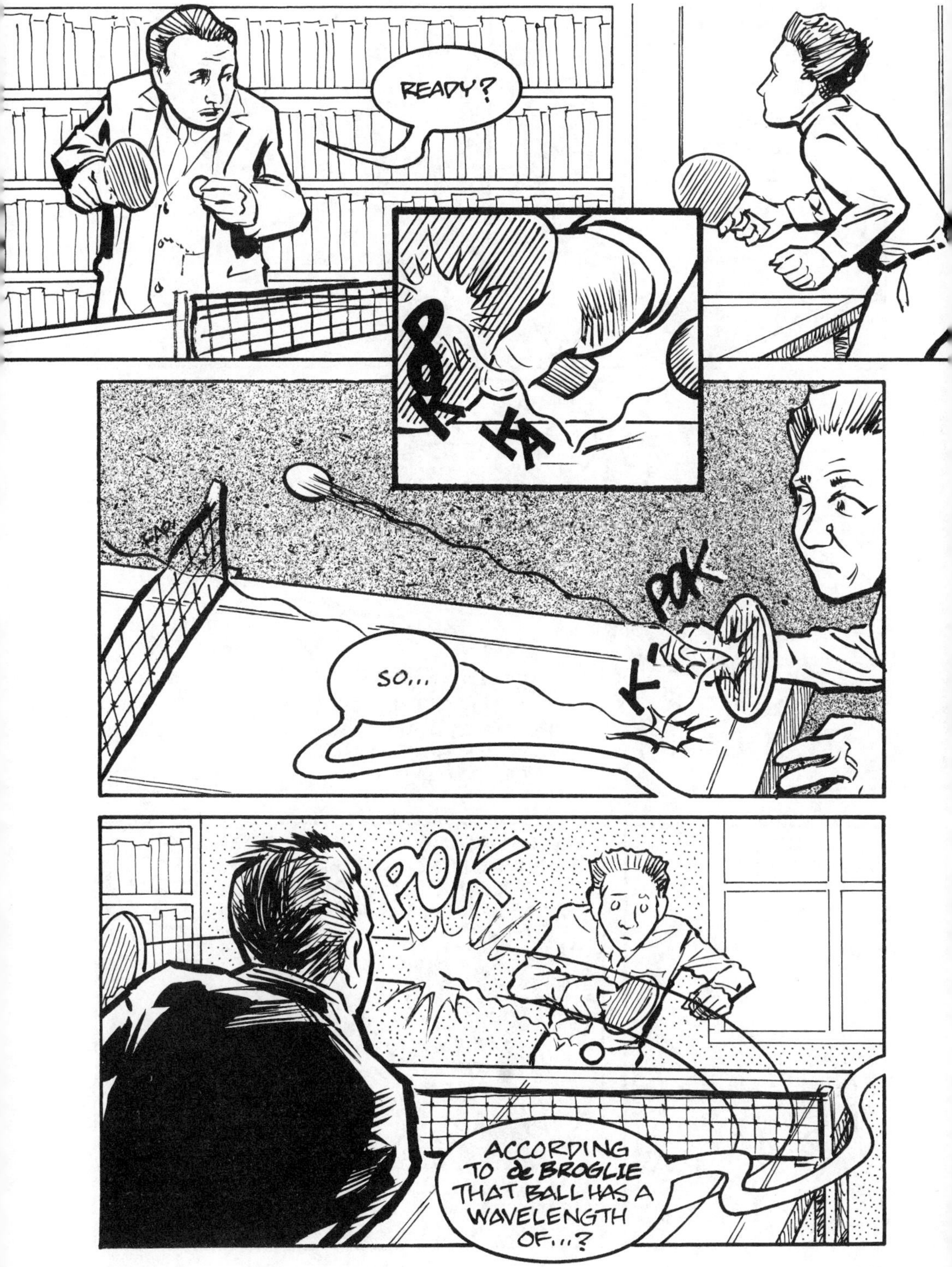
READY?
KA
POK
SO...
POK
ACCORDING TO de BROGLIE THAT BALL HAS A WAVELENGTH OF...?

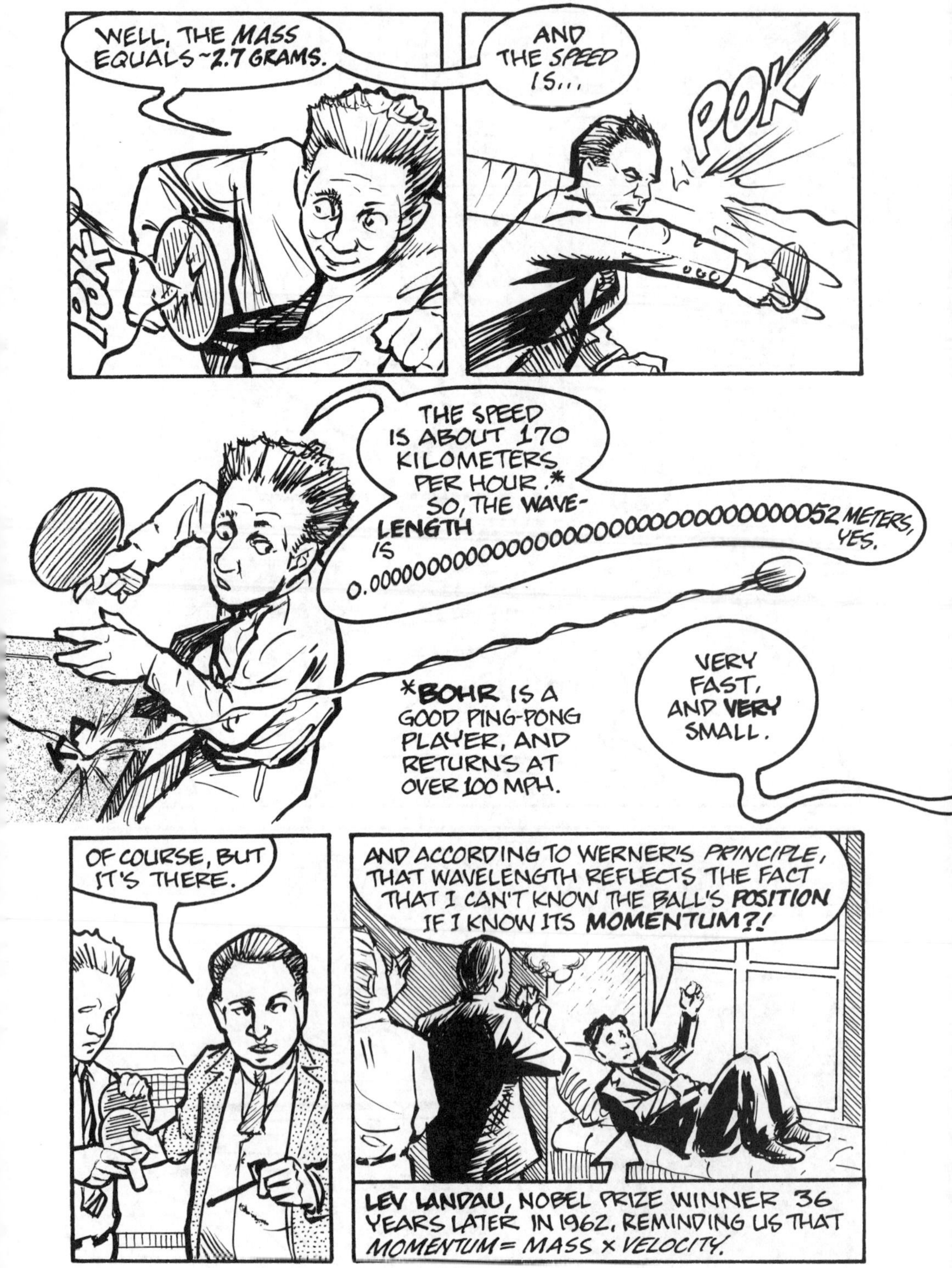
WELL, THE *MASS* EQUALS ~2.7 GRAMS.
POK
AND THE *SPEED* IS...
POK
THE SPEED IS ABOUT 170 KILOMETERS PER HOUR.* SO, THE WAVE-**LENGTH** IS 0.00000000000000000000000000000000052 METERS, YES.
VERY FAST, AND **VERY** SMALL.
***BOHR** IS A GOOD PING-PONG PLAYER, AND RETURNS AT OVER 100 MPH.
OF COURSE, BUT IT'S THERE.
AND ACCORDING TO WERNER'S *PRINCIPLE*, THAT WAVELENGTH REFLECTS THE FACT THAT I CAN'T KNOW THE BALL'S **POSITION** IF I KNOW ITS **MOMENTUM?!**
LEV LANDAU, NOBEL PRIZE WINNER 36 YEARS LATER IN 1962, REMINDING US THAT *MOMENTUM* = *MASS* × *VELOCITY*.

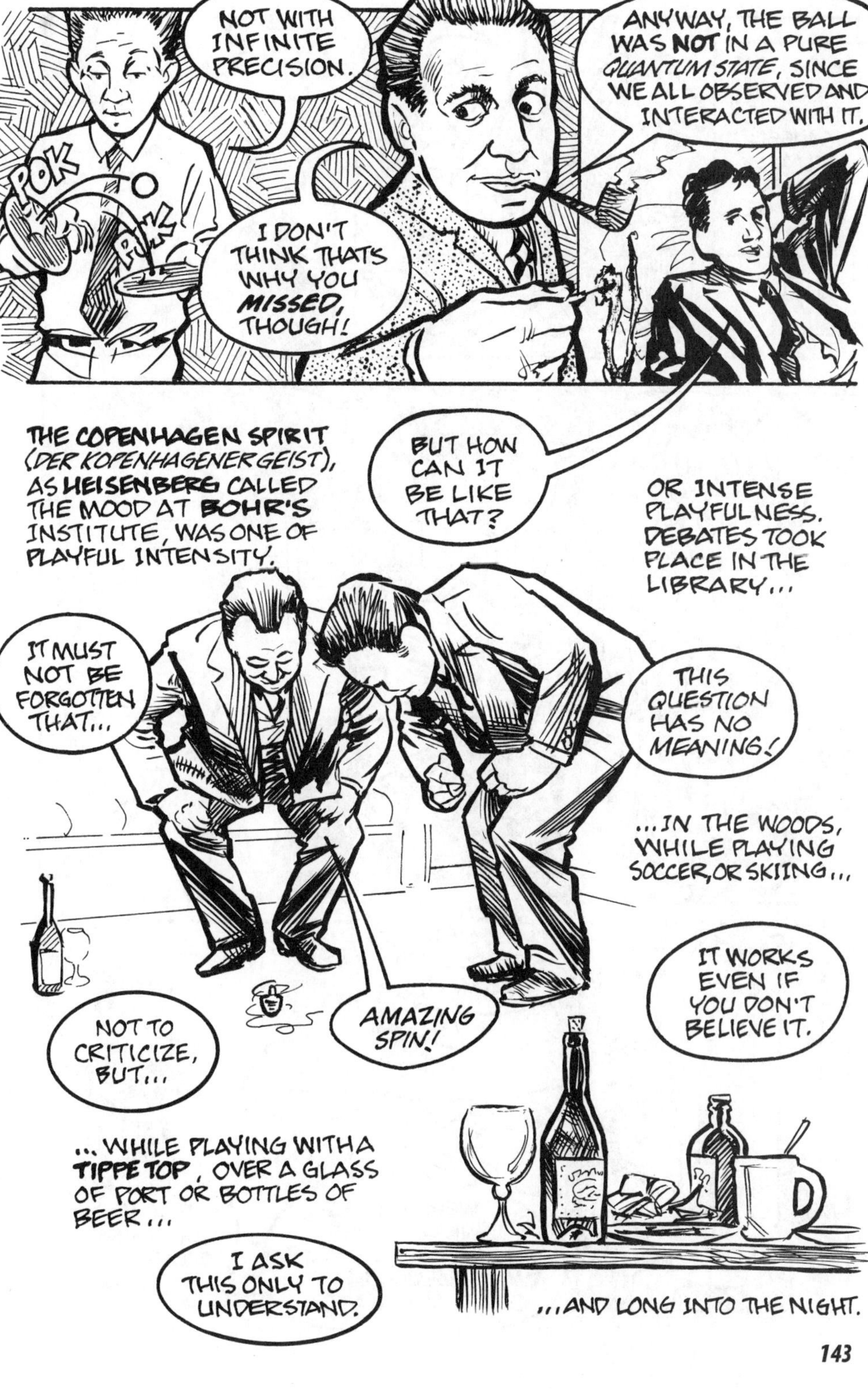
POK
POK
NOT WITH INFINITE PRECISION.
I DON'T THINK THAT'S WHY YOU MISSED, THOUGH!
ANYWAY, THE BALL WAS NOT IN A PURE QUANTUM STATE, SINCE WE ALL OBSERVED AND INTERACTED WITH IT.
THE COPENHAGEN SPIRIT (DER KOPENHAGENERGEIST), AS HEISENBERG CALLED THE MOOD AT BOHR'S INSTITUTE, WAS ONE OF PLAYFUL INTENSITY,
BUT HOW CAN IT BE LIKE THAT?
OR INTENSE PLAYFULNESS. DEBATES TOOK PLACE IN THE LIBRARY...
IT MUST NOT BE FORGOTTEN THAT...
THIS QUESTION HAS NO MEANING!
...IN THE WOODS, WHILE PLAYING SOCCER, OR SKIING...
IT WORKS EVEN IF YOU DON'T BELIEVE IT.
NOT TO CRITICIZE, BUT...
AMAZING SPIN!
... WHILE PLAYING WITH A TIPPE TOP, OVER A GLASS OF PORT OR BOTTLES OF BEER...
I ASK THIS ONLY TO UNDERSTAND.
...AND LONG INTO THE NIGHT.

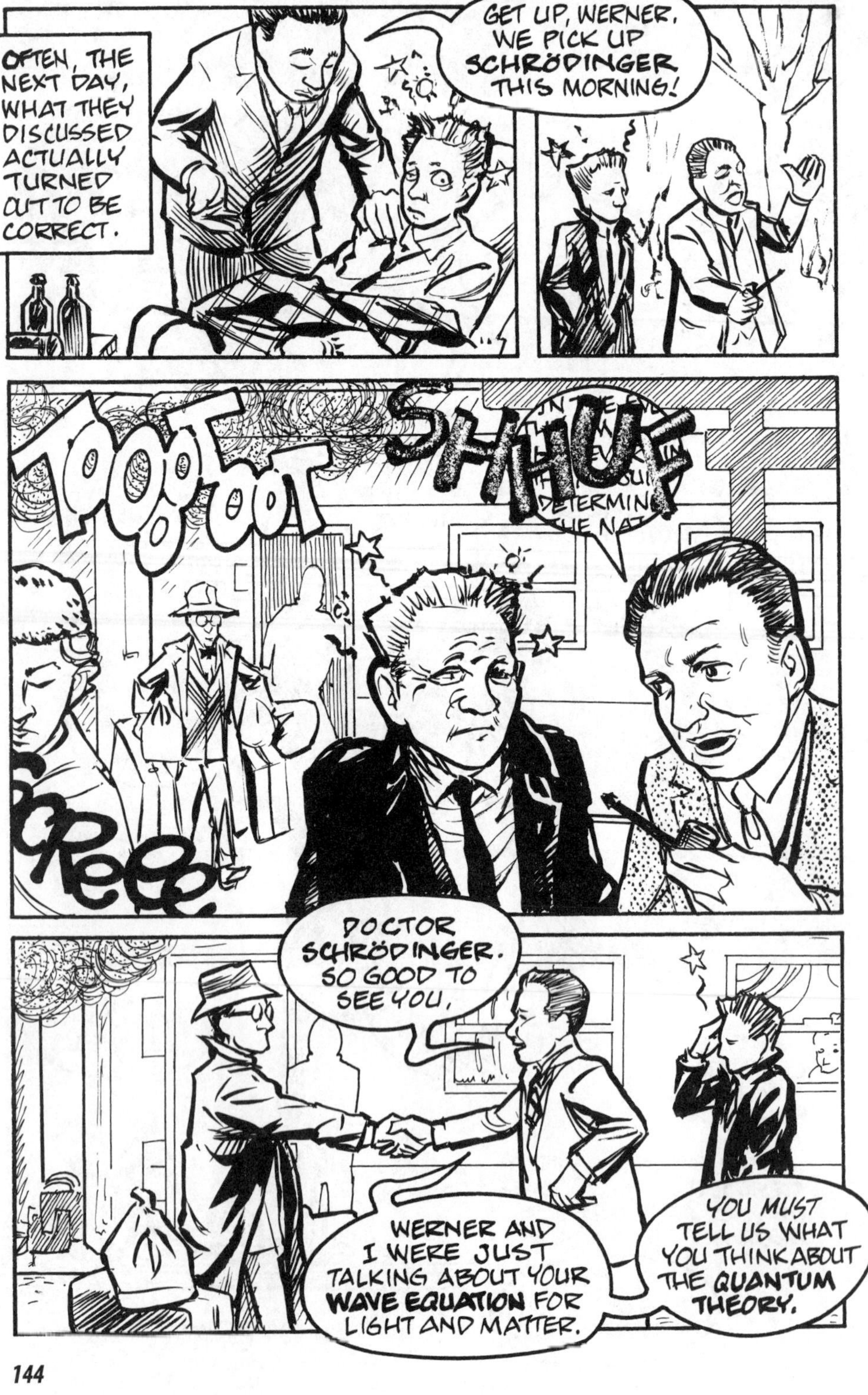
OFTEN, THE NEXT DAY, WHAT THEY DISCUSSED ACTUALLY TURNED OUT TO BE CORRECT.
GET UP, WERNER. WE PICK UP SCHRÖDINGER THIS MORNING!
TOOOT OOT
SHHUF
DETERMIN
SCREEE
DOCTOR SCHRÖDINGER. SO GOOD TO SEE YOU.
WERNER AND I WERE JUST TALKING ABOUT YOUR WAVE EQUATION FOR LIGHT AND MATTER.
YOU MUST TELL US WHAT YOU THINK ABOUT THE QUANTUM THEORY.

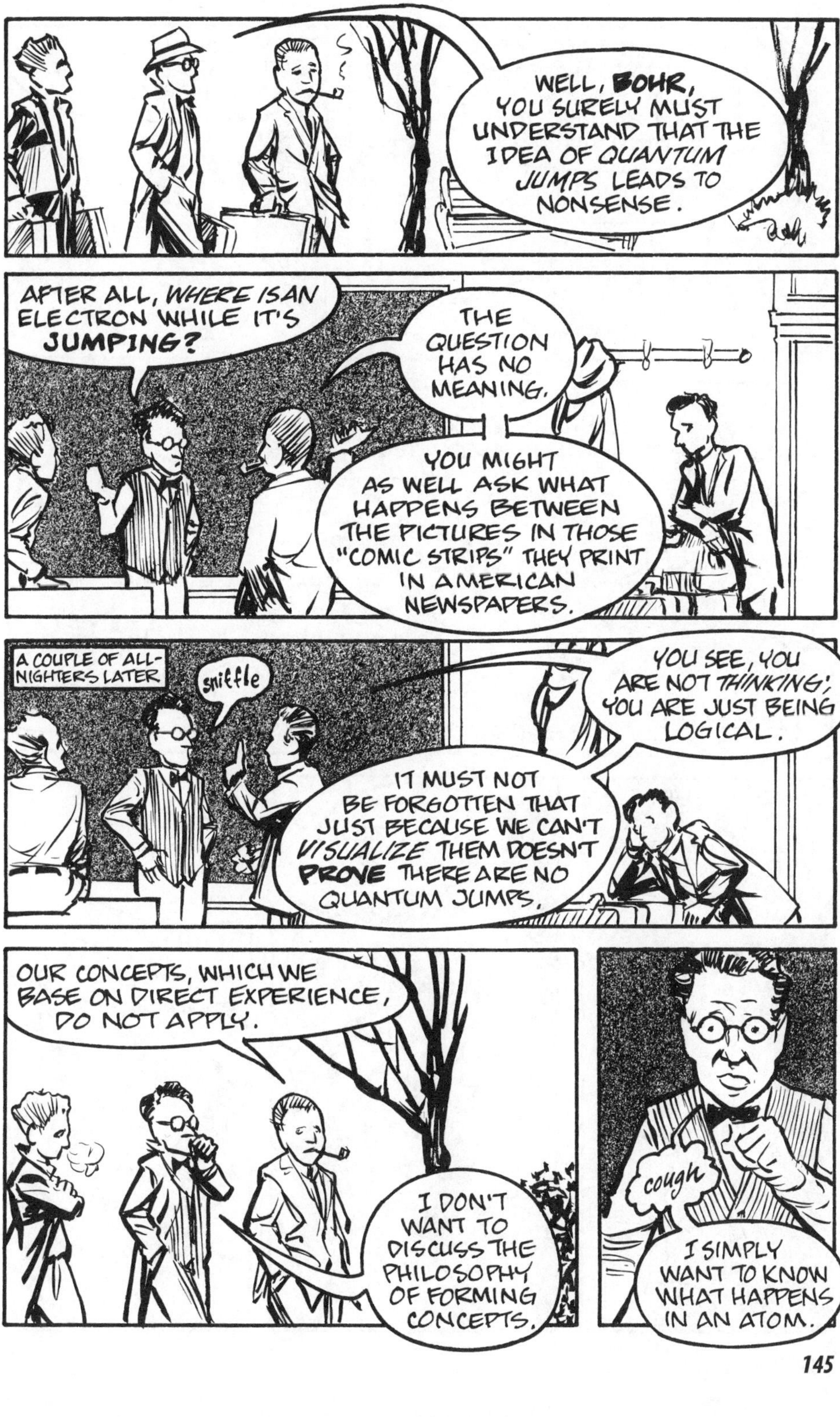
WELL, BOHR, YOU SURELY MUST UNDERSTAND THAT THE IDEA OF QUANTUM JUMPS LEADS TO NONSENSE.
AFTER ALL, WHERE IS AN ELECTRON WHILE IT'S JUMPING?
THE QUESTION HAS NO MEANING.
YOU MIGHT AS WELL ASK WHAT HAPPENS BETWEEN THE PICTURES IN THOSE "COMIC STRIPS" THEY PRINT IN AMERICAN NEWSPAPERS.
A COUPLE OF ALL-NIGHTERS LATER
sniffle
YOU SEE, YOU ARE NOT THINKING; YOU ARE JUST BEING LOGICAL.
IT MUST NOT BE FORGOTTEN THAT JUST BECAUSE WE CAN'T VISUALIZE THEM DOESN'T PROVE THERE ARE NO QUANTUM JUMPS.
OUR CONCEPTS, WHICH WE BASE ON DIRECT EXPERIENCE, DO NOT APPLY.
I DON'T WANT TO DISCUSS THE PHILOSOPHY OF FORMING CONCEPTS.
cough
I SIMPLY WANT TO KNOW WHAT HAPPENS IN AN ATOM.

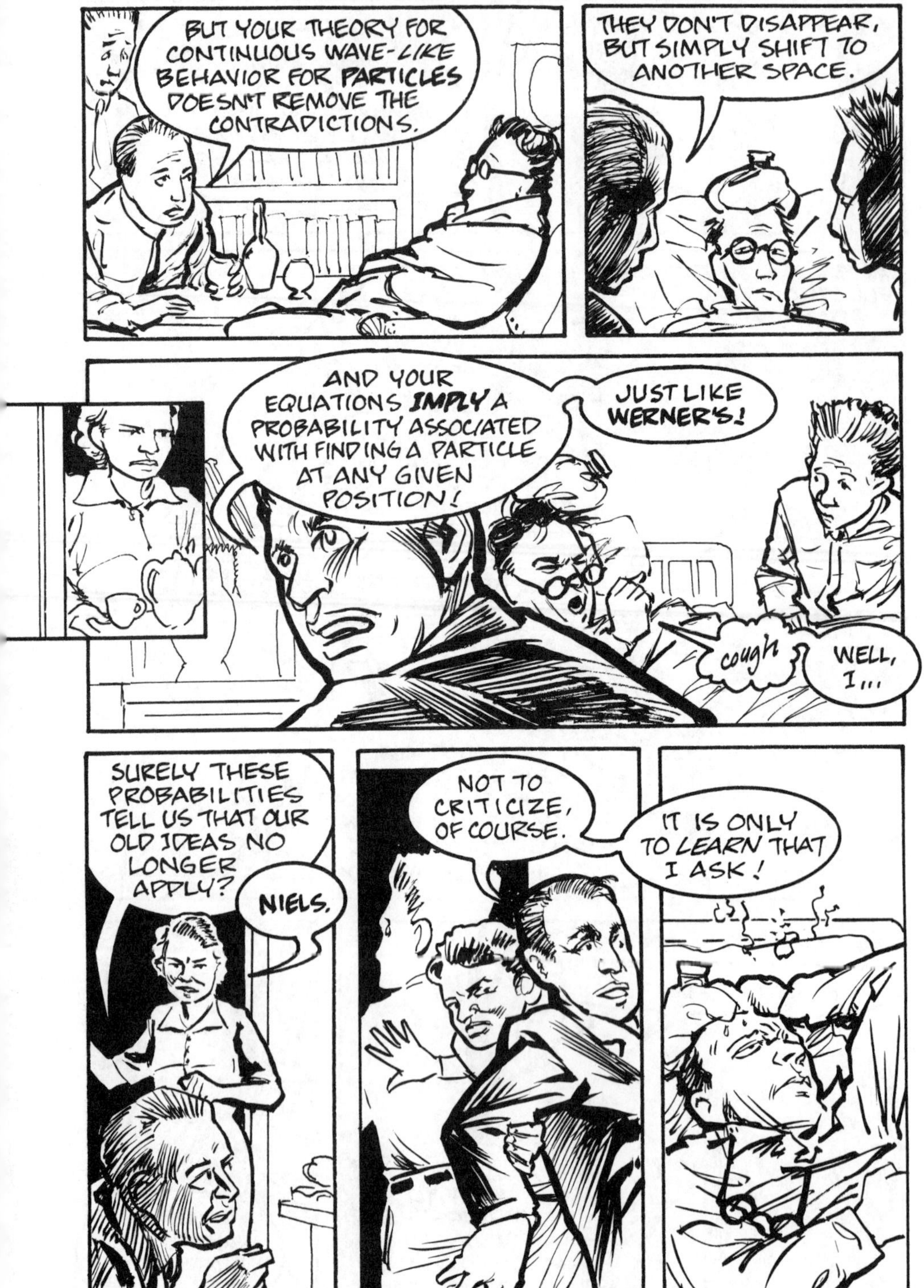
BUT YOUR THEORY FOR CONTINUOUS WAVE-*LIKE* BEHAVIOR FOR **PARTICLES** DOESN'T REMOVE THE CONTRADICTIONS.
THEY DON'T DISAPPEAR, BUT SIMPLY SHIFT TO ANOTHER SPACE.
AND YOUR EQUATIONS ***IMPLY*** A PROBABILITY ASSOCIATED WITH FINDING A PARTICLE AT ANY GIVEN POSITION!
JUST LIKE **WERNER'S!**
cough
WELL, I...
SURELY THESE PROBABILITIES TELL US THAT OUR OLD IDEAS NO LONGER APPLY?
NIELS.
NOT TO CRITICIZE, OF COURSE.
IT IS ONLY TO *LEARN* THAT I ASK!

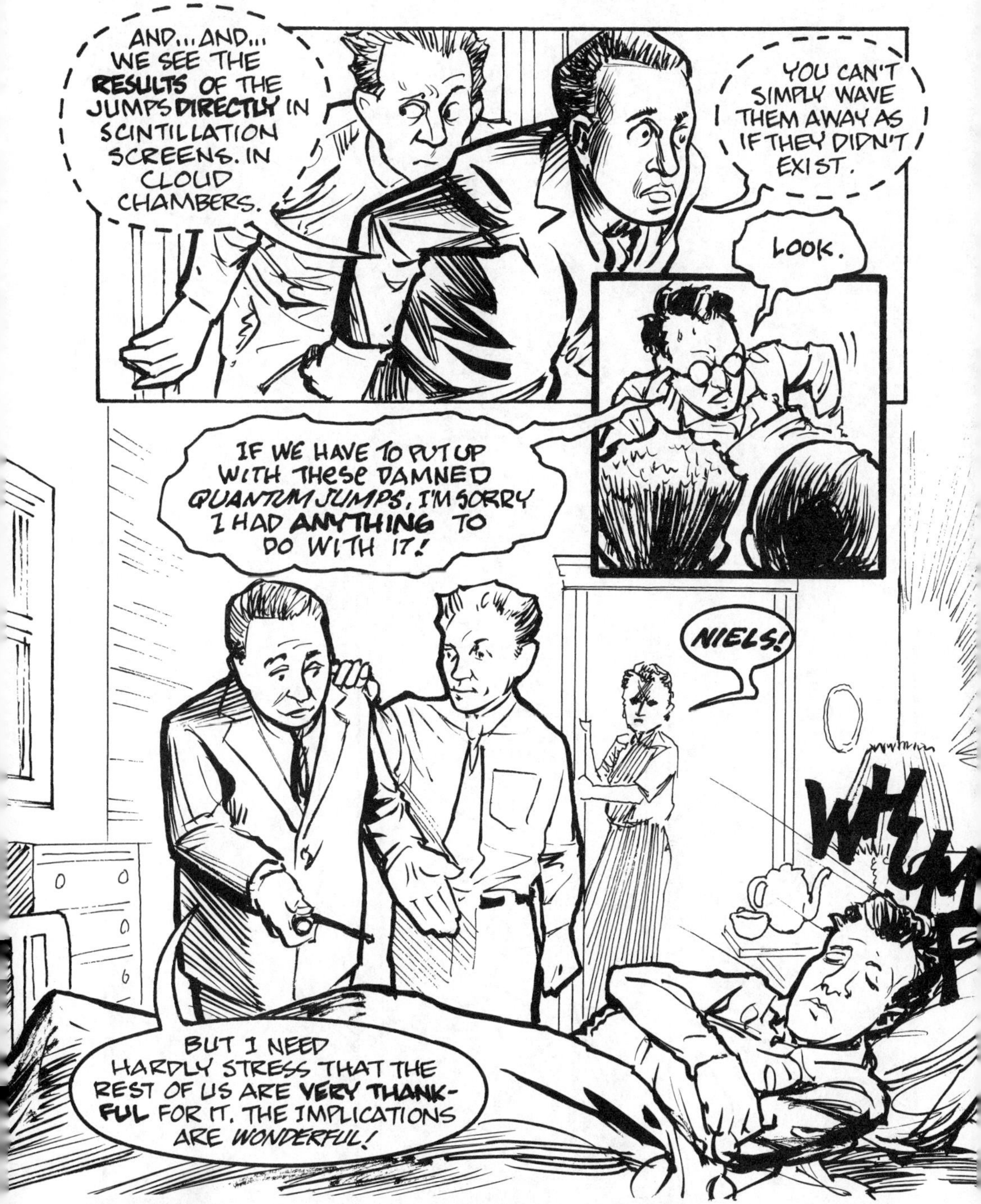
AND... AND... WE SEE THE **RESULTS** OF THE JUMPS **DIRECTLY** IN SCINTILLATION SCREENS. IN CLOUD CHAMBERS.
YOU CAN'T SIMPLY WAVE THEM AWAY AS IF THEY DIDN'T EXIST.
LOOK.
IF WE HAVE TO PUT UP WITH THESE DAMNED *QUANTUM JUMPS*, I'M SORRY I HAD **ANYTHING** TO DO WITH IT!
NIELS!
BUT I NEED HARDLY STRESS THAT THE REST OF US ARE **VERY THANKFUL** FOR IT. THE IMPLICATIONS ARE *WONDERFUL!*

THE SPIRIT OF COPENHAGEN HAD A CERTAIN *RELENTLESS* ASPECT TO ITS PLAYFUL NATURE.

WHAT BECAME KNOWN AS THE COPENHAGEN INTERPRETATION OF **QUANTUM MECHANICS** EMERGED FROM ALL THESE DEBATES.

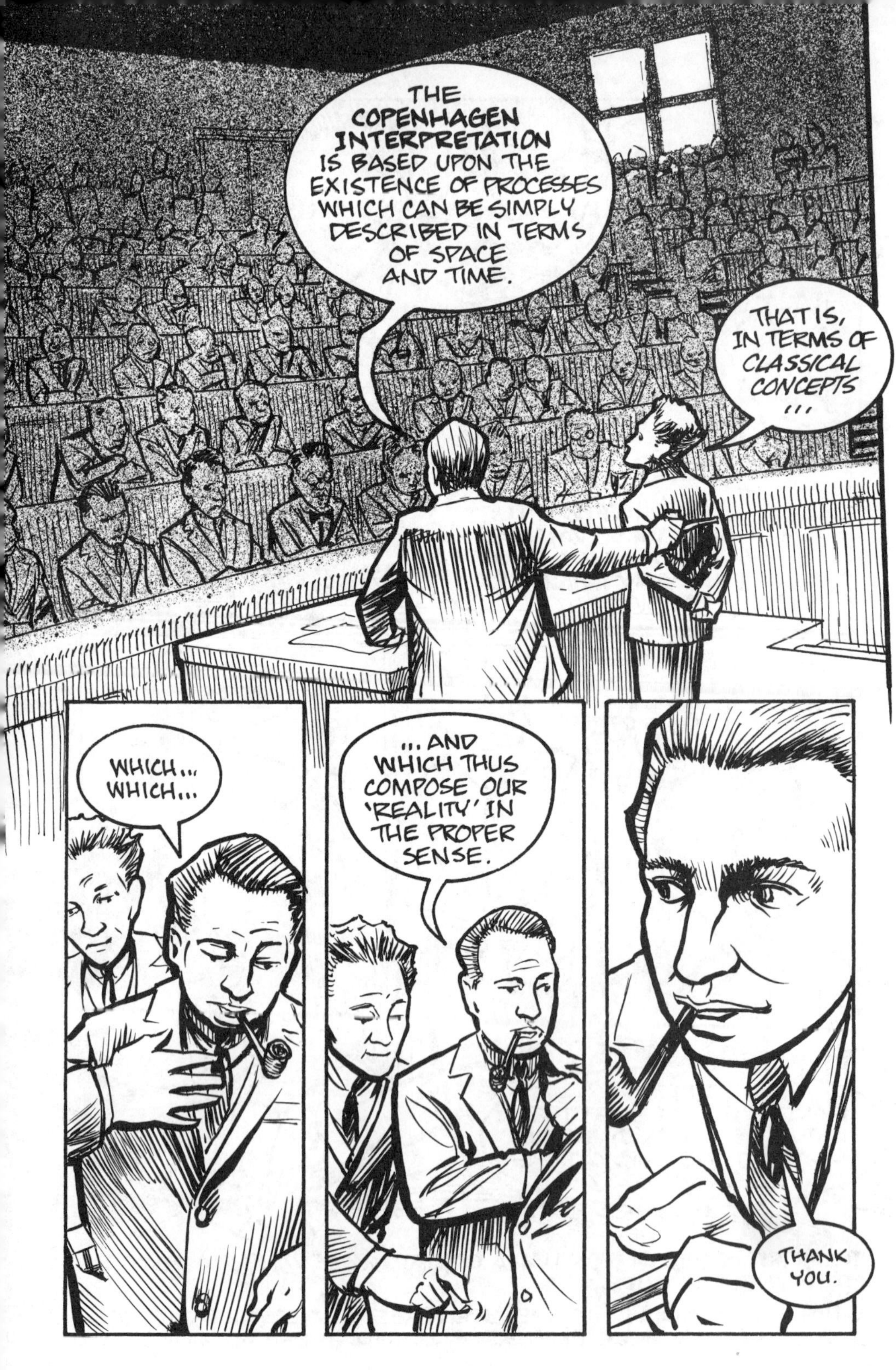
THE COPENHAGEN INTERPRETATION IS BASED UPON THE EXISTENCE OF PROCESSES WHICH CAN BE SIMPLY DESCRIBED IN TERMS OF SPACE AND TIME.
THAT IS, IN TERMS OF CLASSICAL CONCEPTS ...
WHICH... WHICH...
...AND WHICH THUS COMPOSE OUR 'REALITY' IN THE PROPER SENSE.
THANK YOU.

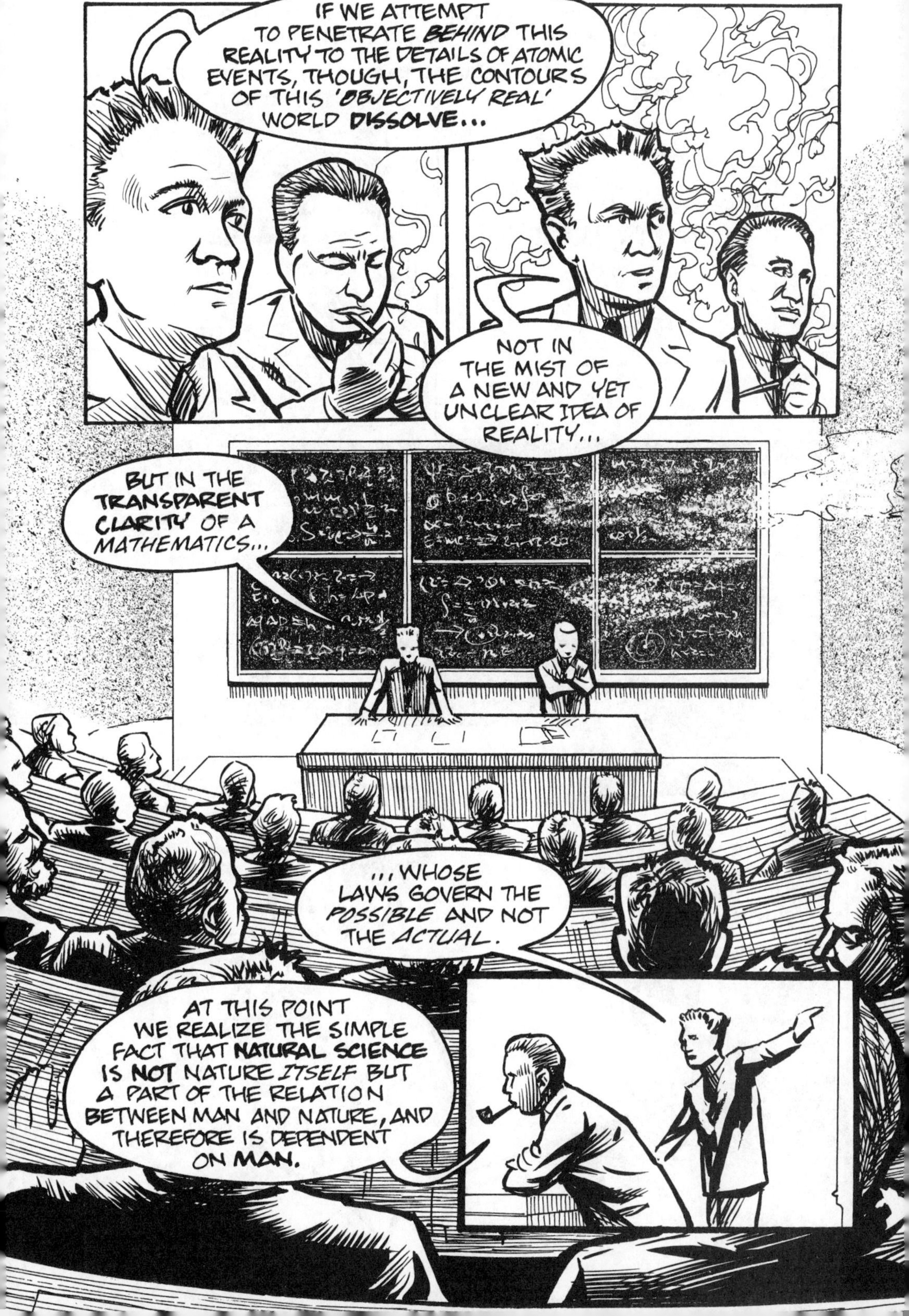
IF WE ATTEMPT TO PENETRATE *BEHIND* THIS REALITY TO THE DETAILS OF ATOMIC EVENTS, THOUGH, THE CONTOURS OF THIS *'OBJECTIVELY REAL'* WORLD **DISSOLVE...**
NOT IN THE MIST OF A NEW AND YET UNCLEAR IDEA OF REALITY...
BUT IN THE **TRANSPARENT CLARITY** OF A *MATHEMATICS...*
...WHOSE LAWS GOVERN THE *POSSIBLE* AND NOT THE *ACTUAL*.
AT THIS POINT WE REALIZE THE SIMPLE FACT THAT **NATURAL SCIENCE** IS **NOT** NATURE *ITSELF* BUT A PART OF THE RELATION BETWEEN MAN AND NATURE, AND THEREFORE IS DEPENDENT ON **MAN.**

THE *COPENHAGEN INTERPRETATION* COMBINED **FOUR** THINGS: **FIRST**, FROM THE LAST CHAPTER, **HEISENBERG'S** *UNCERTAINTY* (INDETERMINACY) *PRINCIPLE*.

SECOND, AND RELATED TO IT, THE IDEA THAT A SYSTEM IS AFFECTED BY AN OBSERVER.

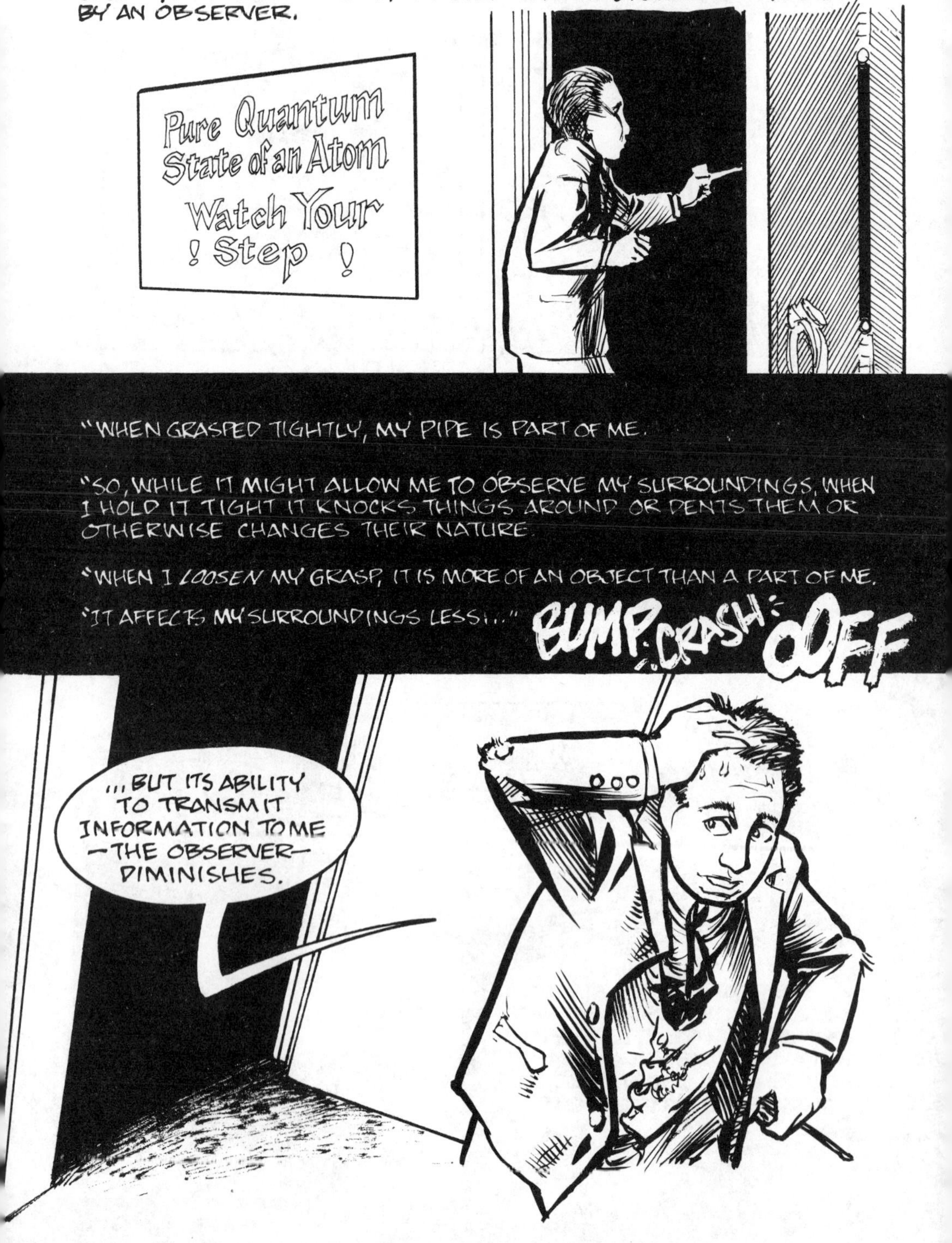

Pure Quantum State of an Atom
Watch Your ! Step !
"WHEN GRASPED TIGHTLY, MY PIPE IS PART OF ME.
"SO, WHILE IT MIGHT ALLOW ME TO OBSERVE MY SURROUNDINGS, WHEN I HOLD IT TIGHT IT KNOCKS THINGS AROUND OR DENTS THEM OR OTHERWISE CHANGES THEIR NATURE.
"WHEN I *LOOSEN* MY GRASP, IT IS MORE OF AN OBJECT THAN A PART OF ME.
"IT AFFECTS MY SURROUNDINGS LESS..."
BUMP
CRASH
OOFF
...BUT ITS ABILITY TO TRANSMIT INFORMATION TO ME —THE OBSERVER— DIMINISHES.

THE **THIRD** FACET OF *THE COPENHAGEN INTERPRETATION* WAS THE **PROBABILISTIC** NATURE OF QUANTUM EFFECTS, A FUNDAMENTAL IMPLICATION OF BOTH **SCHRÖDINGER'S** WAVE EQUATION AND **HEISENBERG'S** MATRIX MECHANICS.

EVEN THOUGH THEY LOOK (VERY) DIFFERENT!

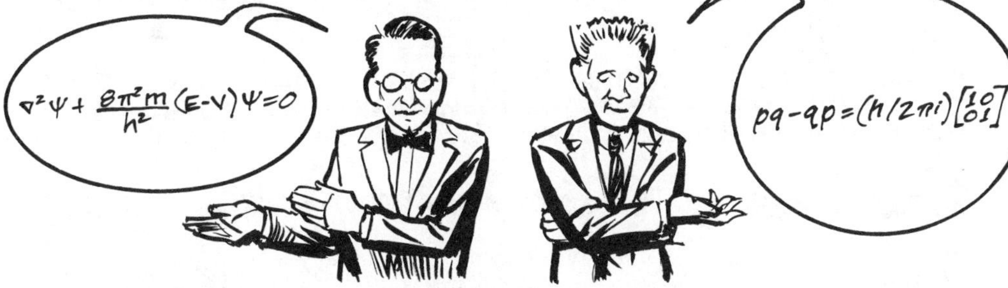

$\nabla^2\psi + \frac{8\pi^2 m}{h^2}(E-V)\psi=0$
$pq-qp=(h/2\pi i)\begin{bmatrix}1&0\\0&1\end{bmatrix}$

THE **FOURTH** AND FINAL PIECE WAS SOMETHING **BOHR** CALLED "COMPLEMENTARITY":

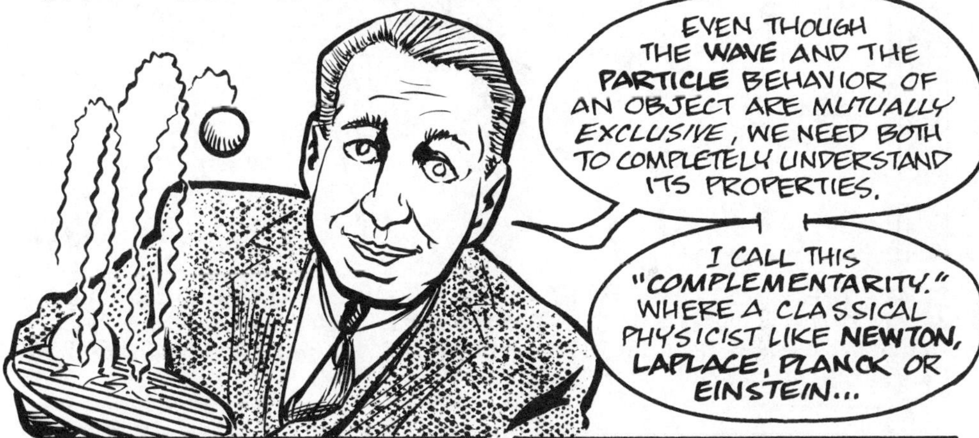

EVEN THOUGH THE **WAVE** AND THE **PARTICLE** BEHAVIOR OF AN OBJECT ARE MUTUALLY *EXCLUSIVE*, WE NEED BOTH TO COMPLETELY UNDERSTAND ITS PROPERTIES.
I CALL THIS **"COMPLEMENTARITY."** WHERE A CLASSICAL PHYSICIST LIKE **NEWTON, LAPLACE, PLANCK** OR **EINSTEIN...**

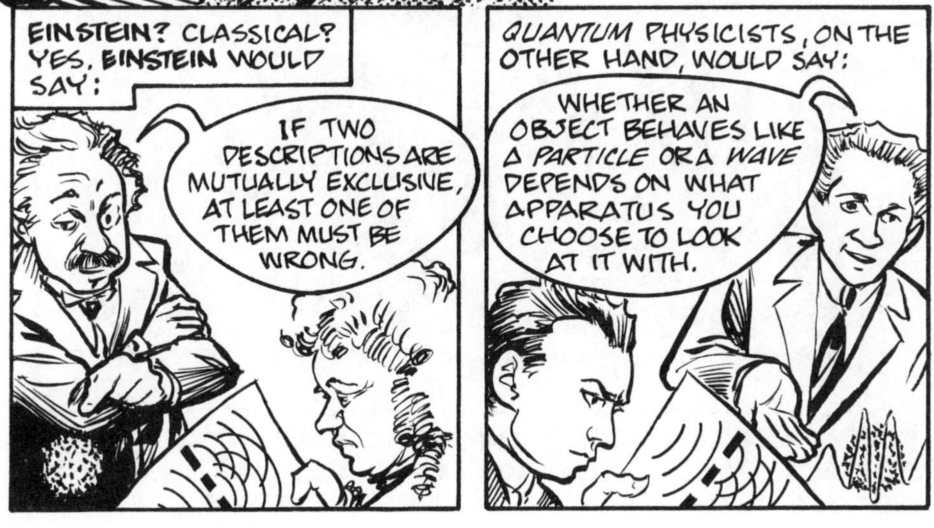

EINSTEIN? CLASSICAL? YES. **EINSTEIN** WOULD SAY:
IF TWO DESCRIPTIONS ARE MUTUALLY EXCLUSIVE, AT LEAST ONE OF THEM MUST BE WRONG.
QUANTUM PHYSICISTS, ON THE OTHER HAND, WOULD SAY:
WHETHER AN OBJECT BEHAVES LIKE A *PARTICLE* OR A *WAVE* DEPENDS ON WHAT APPARATUS YOU CHOOSE TO LOOK AT IT WITH.

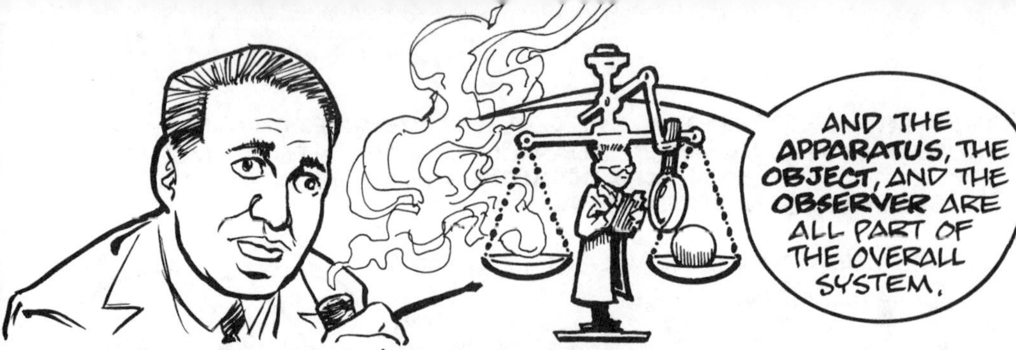
AND THE **APPARATUS**, THE **OBJECT**, AND THE **OBSERVER** ARE ALL PART OF THE OVERALL SYSTEM.

SO THESE **FOUR** IDEAS (AND THE EXPERIMENTS AND MATH THAT SUPPORT THEM) THAT MAKE UP *THE COPENHAGEN INTERPRETATION* ARE WHAT **BOHR, HEISENBERG**, AND OTHER *BOHRIANS* BROUGHT TO THE...

Solvay Conference, 1927

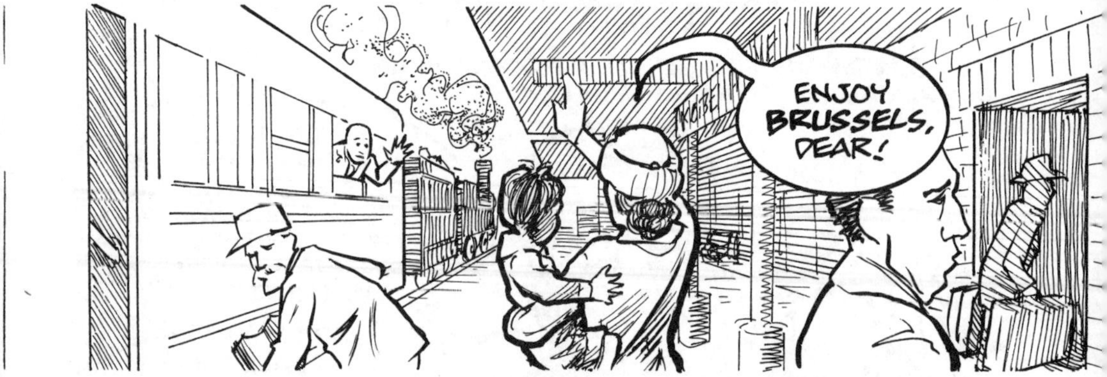
ENJOY **BRUSSELS**, DEAR!

IT WAS THE FIRST TIME **BOHR** ATTENDED ONE OF THESE MEETINGS, AND NOT COINCIDENTALLY THIS CONFERENCE TURNED OUT TO BE THE *ALLSTAR GAME, WOODSTOCK*, AND THE *OLYMPICS* OF **THEORETICAL PHYSICS**, ALL ROLLED INTO ONE.

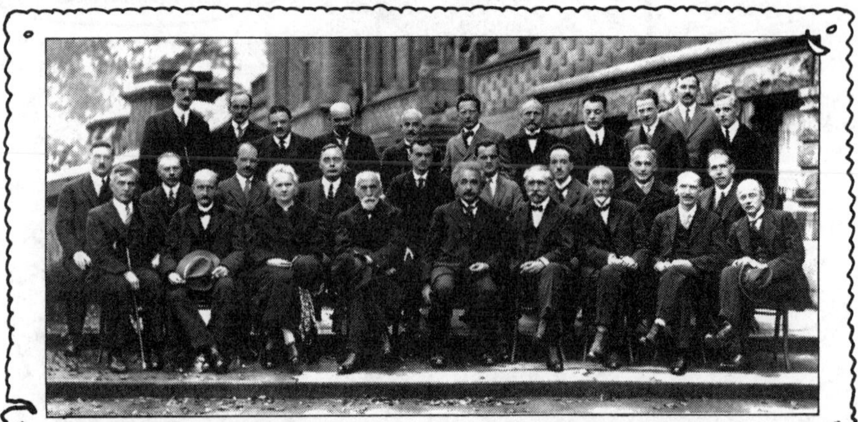

SCHRÖDINGER, PAULI, HEISENBERG, KRAMERS, DIRAC, COMPTON, de BROGLIE, BORN, BOHR, PLANCK, Mme CURIE, EINSTEIN AND MORE... EVERYBODY WHO WAS ANYBODY WAS THERE. AND THERE, THEY ARGUED.

NOT AT THE FORMAL SESSIONS, WHERE MODEST ASSENT AND POLITE DISAGREEMENT WERE THE NORM.

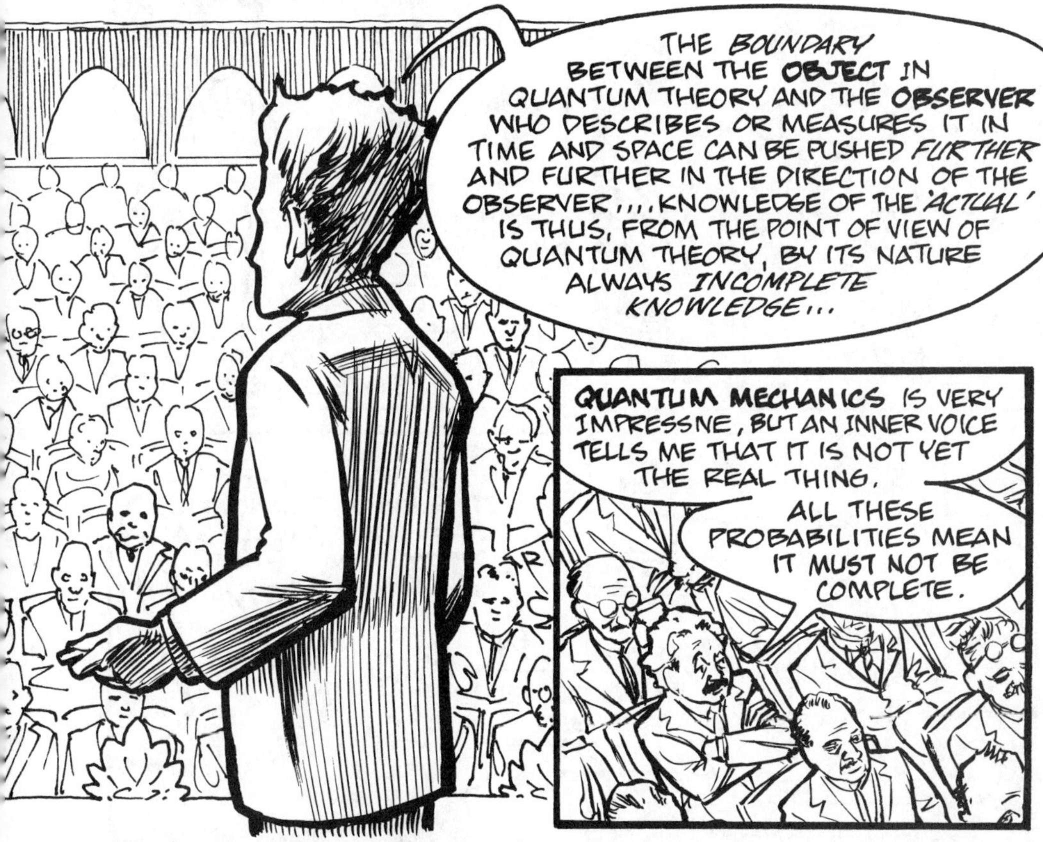
THE *BOUNDARY* BETWEEN THE **OBJECT** IN QUANTUM THEORY AND THE **OBSERVER** WHO DESCRIBES OR MEASURES IT IN TIME AND SPACE CAN BE PUSHED *FURTHER* AND FURTHER IN THE DIRECTION OF THE OBSERVER.... KNOWLEDGE OF THE *'ACTUAL'* IS THUS, FROM THE POINT OF VIEW OF QUANTUM THEORY, BY ITS NATURE ALWAYS *INCOMPLETE KNOWLEDGE*...
QUANTUM MECHANICS IS VERY IMPRESSIVE, BUT AN INNER VOICE TELLS ME THAT IT IS NOT YET THE REAL THING.
ALL THESE PROBABILITIES MEAN IT MUST NOT BE COMPLETE.

EVERY MORNING AT BREAKFAST, **EINSTEIN** WOULD PRESENT A NEW OBJECTION TO THE **COPENHAGEN INTERPRETATION**, USUALLY BY WAY OF A *GEDANKENEXPERIMENT.* *

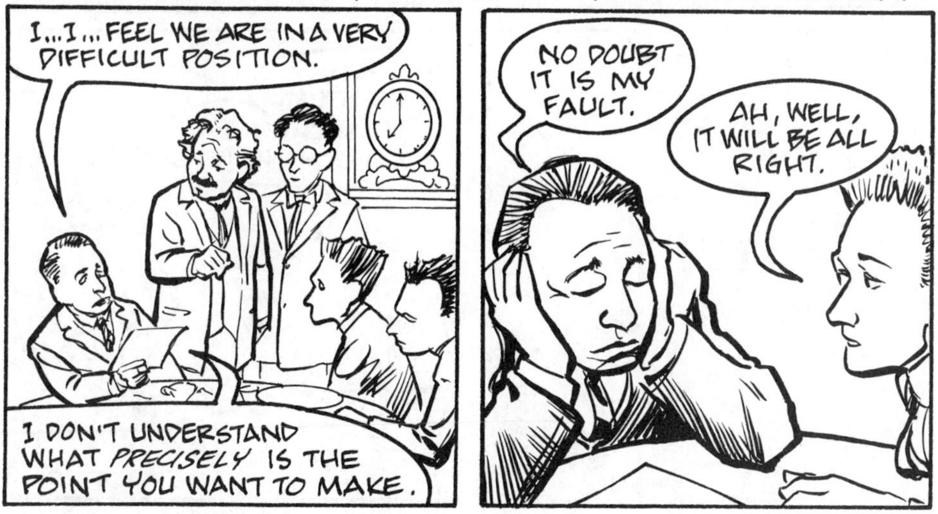
I...I... FEEL WE ARE IN A VERY DIFFICULT POSITION.
I DON'T UNDERSTAND WHAT *PRECISELY* IS THE POINT YOU WANT TO MAKE.
NO DOUBT IT IS MY FAULT.
AH, WELL, IT WILL BE ALL RIGHT.

* *GEDANKENEXPERIMENT* = "THOUGHT EXPERIMENT"

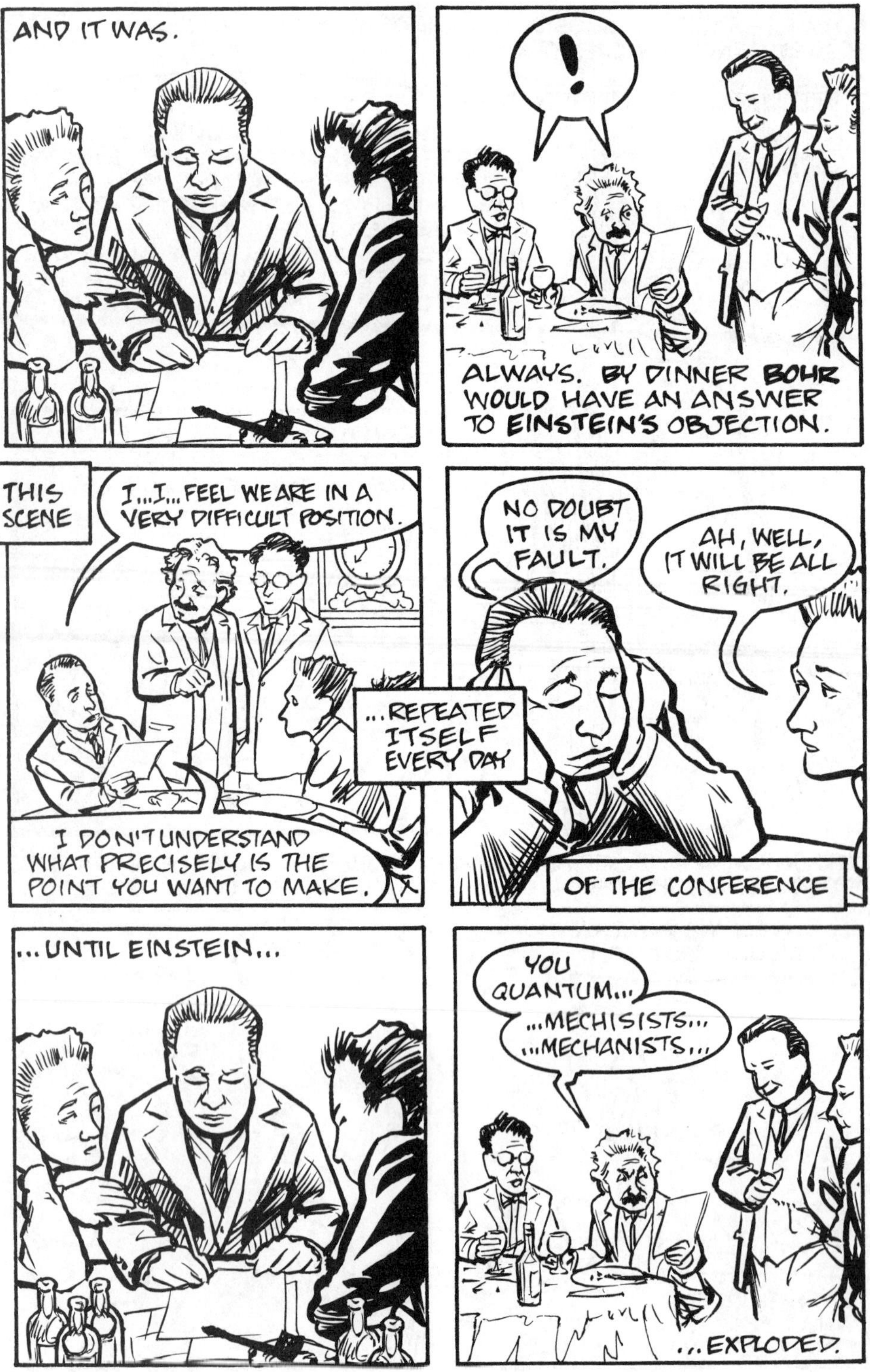
AND IT WAS.
!
ALWAYS. BY DINNER BOHR WOULD HAVE AN ANSWER TO EINSTEIN'S OBJECTION.
THIS SCENE
I...I... FEEL WE ARE IN A VERY DIFFICULT POSITION.
I DON'T UNDERSTAND WHAT PRECISELY IS THE POINT YOU WANT TO MAKE.
...REPEATED ITSELF EVERY DAY
NO DOUBT IT IS MY FAULT.
AH, WELL, IT WILL BE ALL RIGHT.
OF THE CONFERENCE
...UNTIL EINSTEIN...
YOU QUANTUM...
...MECHISISTS... ...MECHANISTS...
...EXPLODED.

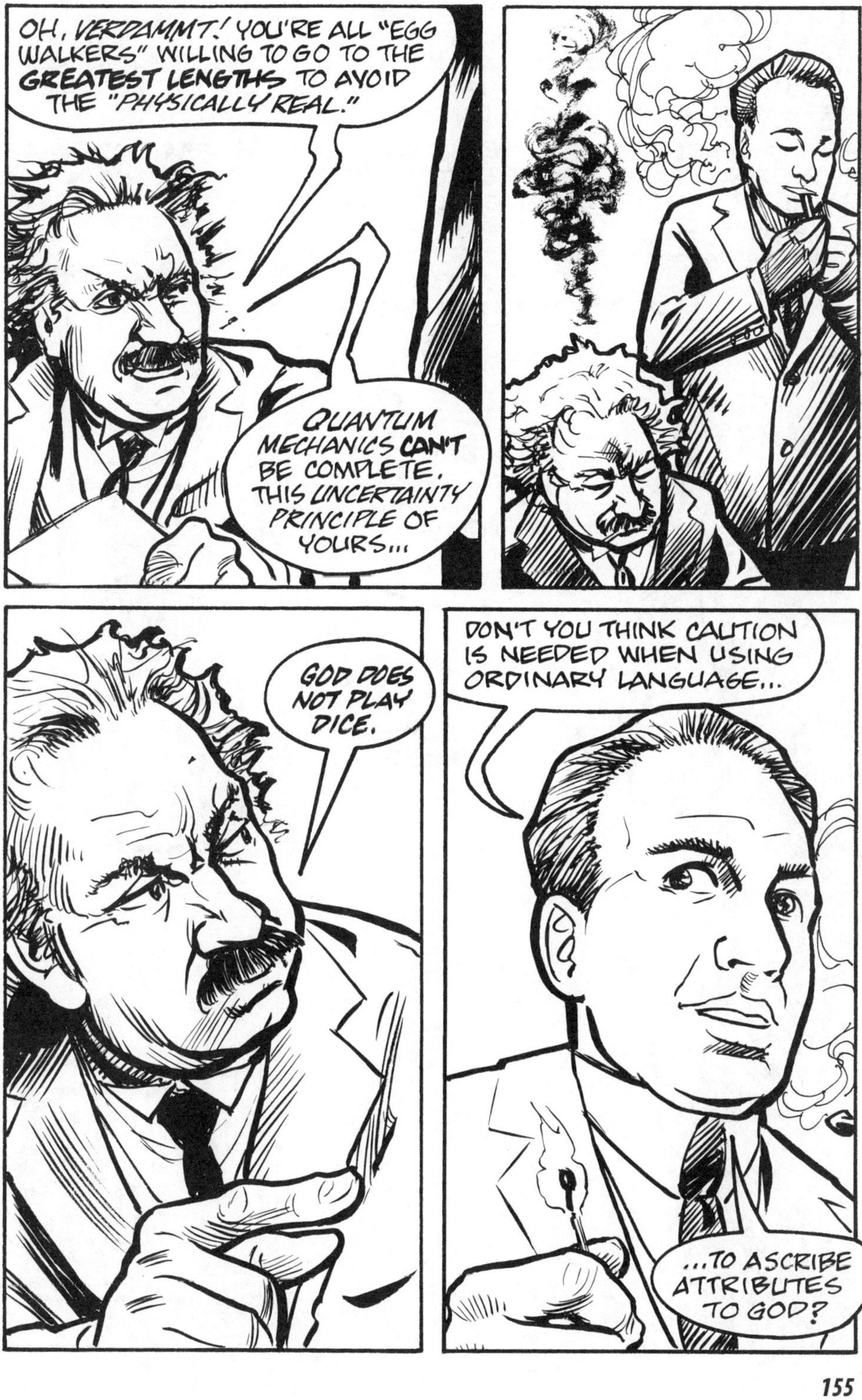
OH, VERDAMMT! YOU'RE ALL "EGG WALKERS" WILLING TO GO TO THE GREATEST LENGTHS TO AVOID THE "PHYSICALLY REAL."
QUANTUM MECHANICS CAN'T BE COMPLETE. THIS UNCERTAINTY PRINCIPLE OF YOURS...
GOD DOES NOT PLAY DICE.
DON'T YOU THINK CAUTION IS NEEDED WHEN USING ORDINARY LANGUAGE...
...TO ASCRIBE ATTRIBUTES TO GOD?

EINSTEIN WOULD LATER WRITE TO **SCHRÖDINGER**: "THE **HEISENBERG-BOHR** SOOTHING PHILOSOPHY— OR RELIGION?— IS SO FINELY CHISELED THAT IT PROVIDES A SOFT PILLOW FOR BELIEVERS FROM WHICH THEY CAN'T VERY EASILY BE AROUSED. SO LET THEM LIE THERE. THIS RELIGION DOES DAMNED LITTLE FOR ME."

HE HAD CLEARLY *NOT* BECOME A CONVERT. AND THE DEBATE CONTINUED AT THE NEXT ***SOLVAY CONFERENCE*** IN 1930. THERE, **EINSTEIN** DELIVERED HIS FINAL CHALLENGE TO **BOHR**.

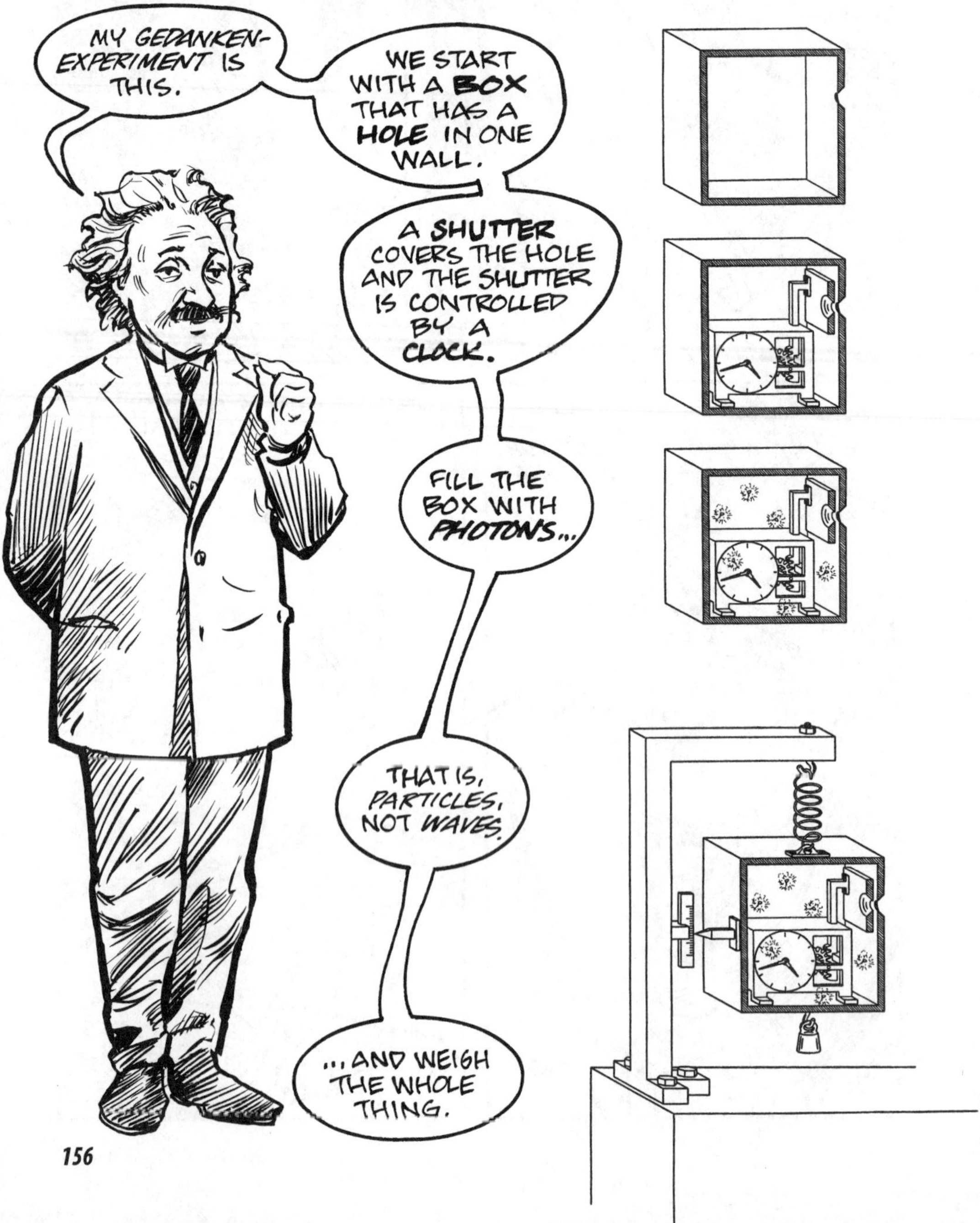

MY GEDANKEN-EXPERIMENT IS THIS.
WE START WITH A BOX THAT HAS A HOLE IN ONE WALL.
A SHUTTER COVERS THE HOLE AND THE SHUTTER IS CONTROLLED BY A CLOCK.
FILL THE BOX WITH PHOTONS...
THAT IS, PARTICLES, NOT WAVES.
...AND WEIGH THE WHOLE THING.

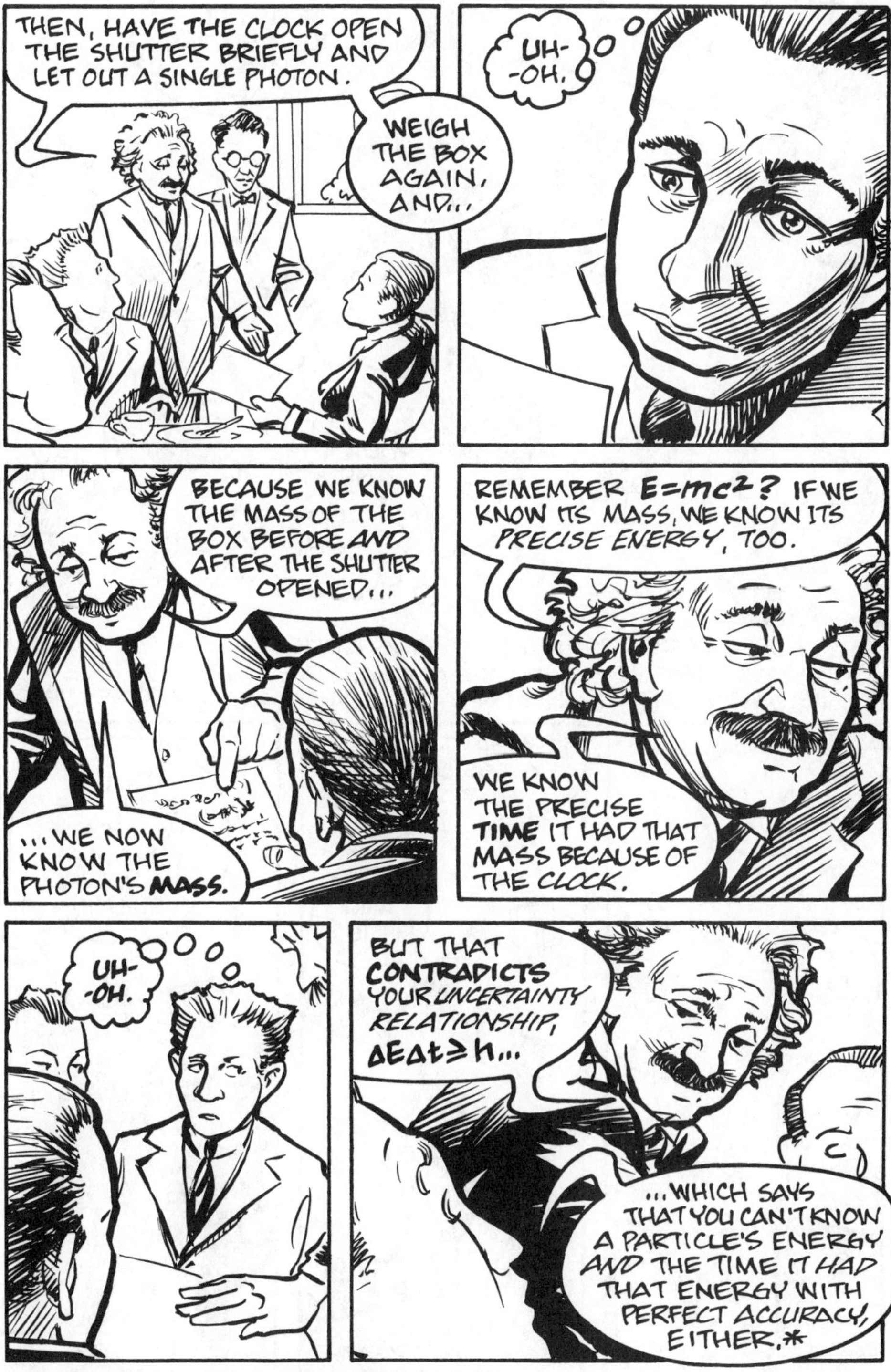
THEN, HAVE THE CLOCK OPEN THE SHUTTER BRIEFLY AND LET OUT A SINGLE PHOTON.
WEIGH THE BOX AGAIN, AND...
UH- -OH.
BECAUSE WE KNOW THE MASS OF THE BOX BEFORE *AND* AFTER THE SHUTTER OPENED...
...WE NOW KNOW THE PHOTON'S **MASS.**
REMEMBER **$E=mc^2$?** IF WE KNOW ITS MASS, WE KNOW ITS *PRECISE ENERGY*, TOO.
WE KNOW THE PRECISE **TIME** IT HAD THAT MASS BECAUSE OF THE *CLOCK*.
UH- -OH.
BUT THAT **CONTRADICTS** YOUR *UNCERTAINTY RELATIONSHIP*, **$\Delta E \Delta t \geq h$...**
...WHICH SAYS THAT YOU CAN'T KNOW A PARTICLE'S ENERGY *AND* THE TIME IT *HAD* THAT ENERGY WITH PERFECT ACCURACY, EITHER.*

* REMEMBER IN THE LAST CHAPTER WHEN WE SAID THIS WOULD COME BACK TO HAUNT US?

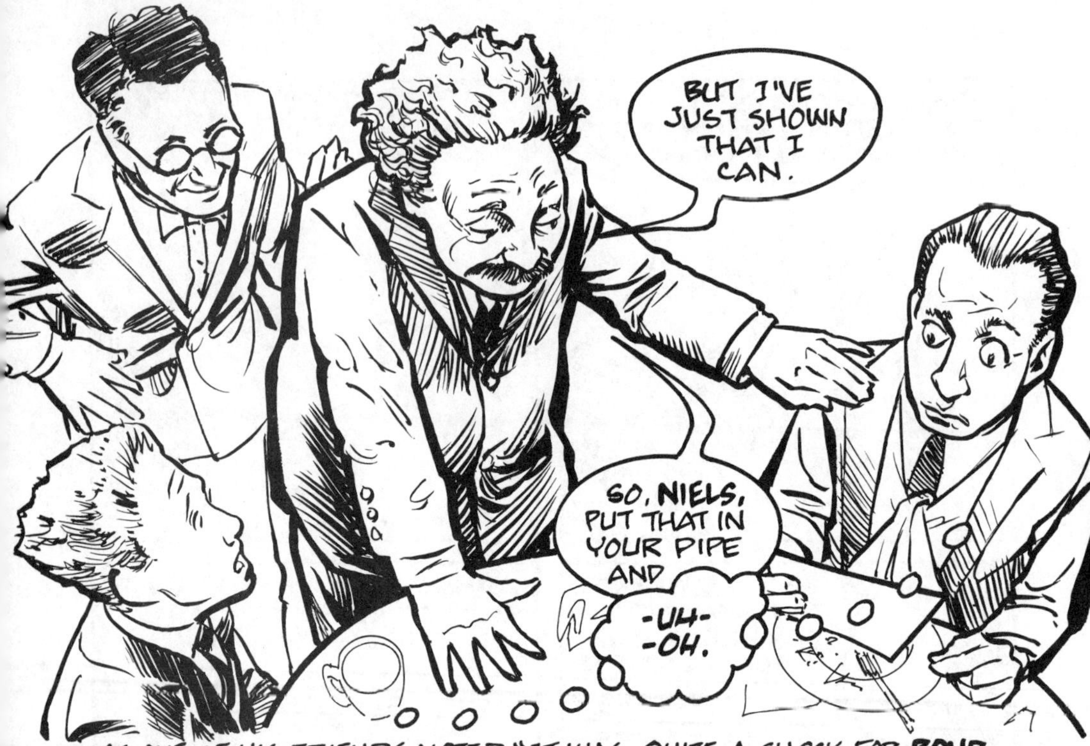
BUT I'VE JUST SHOWN THAT I CAN.
SO, NIELS, PUT THAT IN YOUR PIPE AND
-UH- -OH.

AS ONE OF HIS FRIENDS NOTED, "IT WAS QUITE A SHOCK FOR **BOHR**... HE DID NOT SEE THE SOLUTION AT ONCE. DURING THE WHOLE EVENING HE WAS EXTREMELY UNHAPPY, GOING FROM ONE TO THE OTHER:"

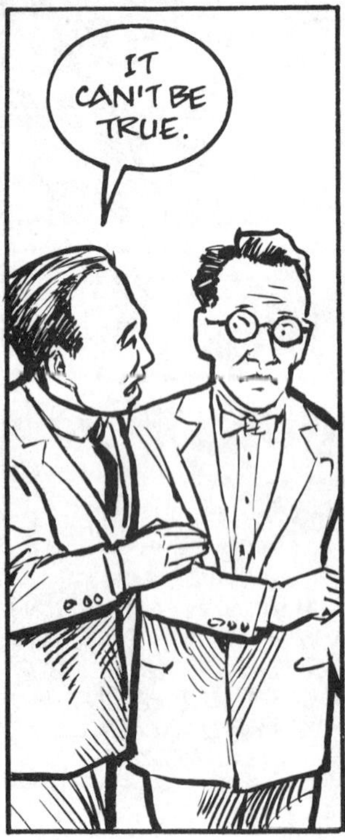
IT CAN'T BE TRUE.

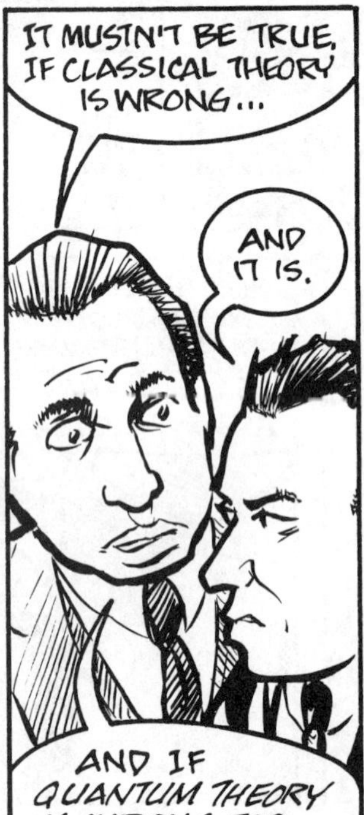
IT MUSTN'T BE TRUE, IF CLASSICAL THEORY IS WRONG...
AND IT IS.
AND IF QUANTUM THEORY IS WRONG TOO...

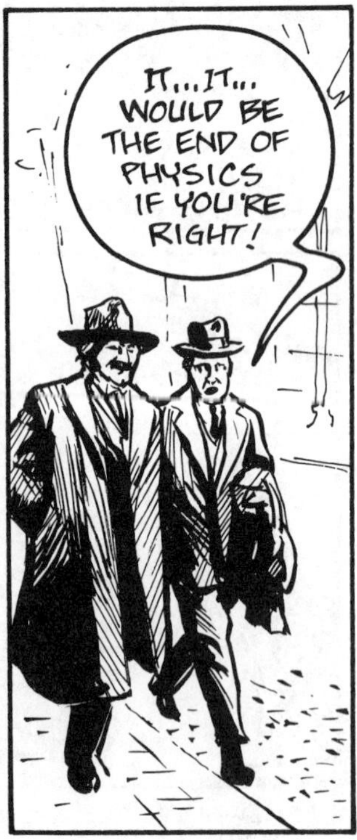
IT... IT... WOULD BE THE END OF PHYSICS IF YOU'RE RIGHT!

MAYBE NOT, BUT THE NIGHT THAT FOLLOWED PASSED — IN THE TRADITION OF COMPLEMENTARITY — BOTH SLOWLY AND QUICKLY FOR **BOHR** AND **HEISENBERG**.

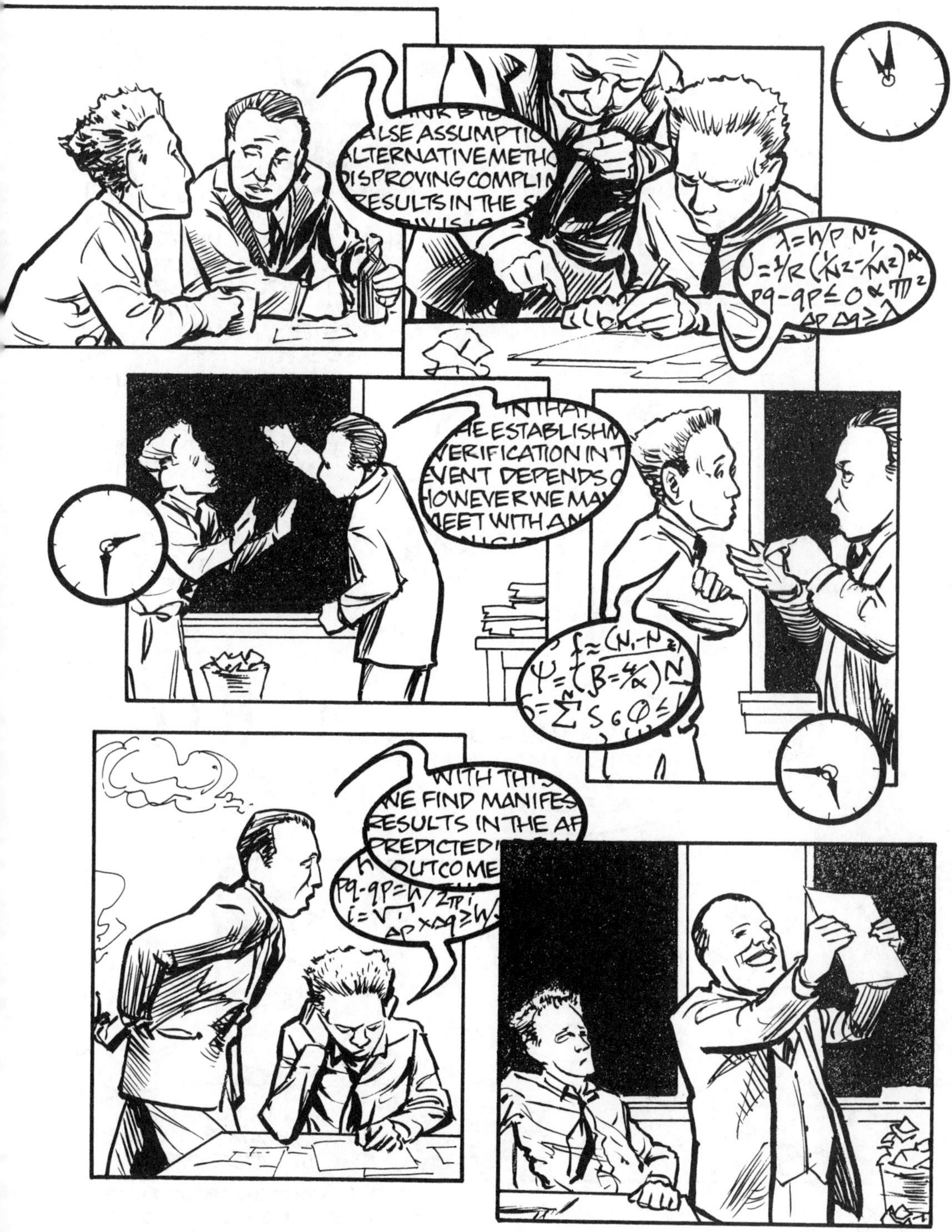
ALSE ASSUMPTIO
ALTERNATIVEMETHO
DISPROVINGCOMPLIN
RESULTS IN THE S
HE ESTABLISHM
VERIFICATION IN T
EVENT DEPENDS
HOWEVER WE MA
MEET WITH AN
WITH TH
WE FIND MANIFES
RESULTS IN THE AF
PREDICTED
OUTCOME

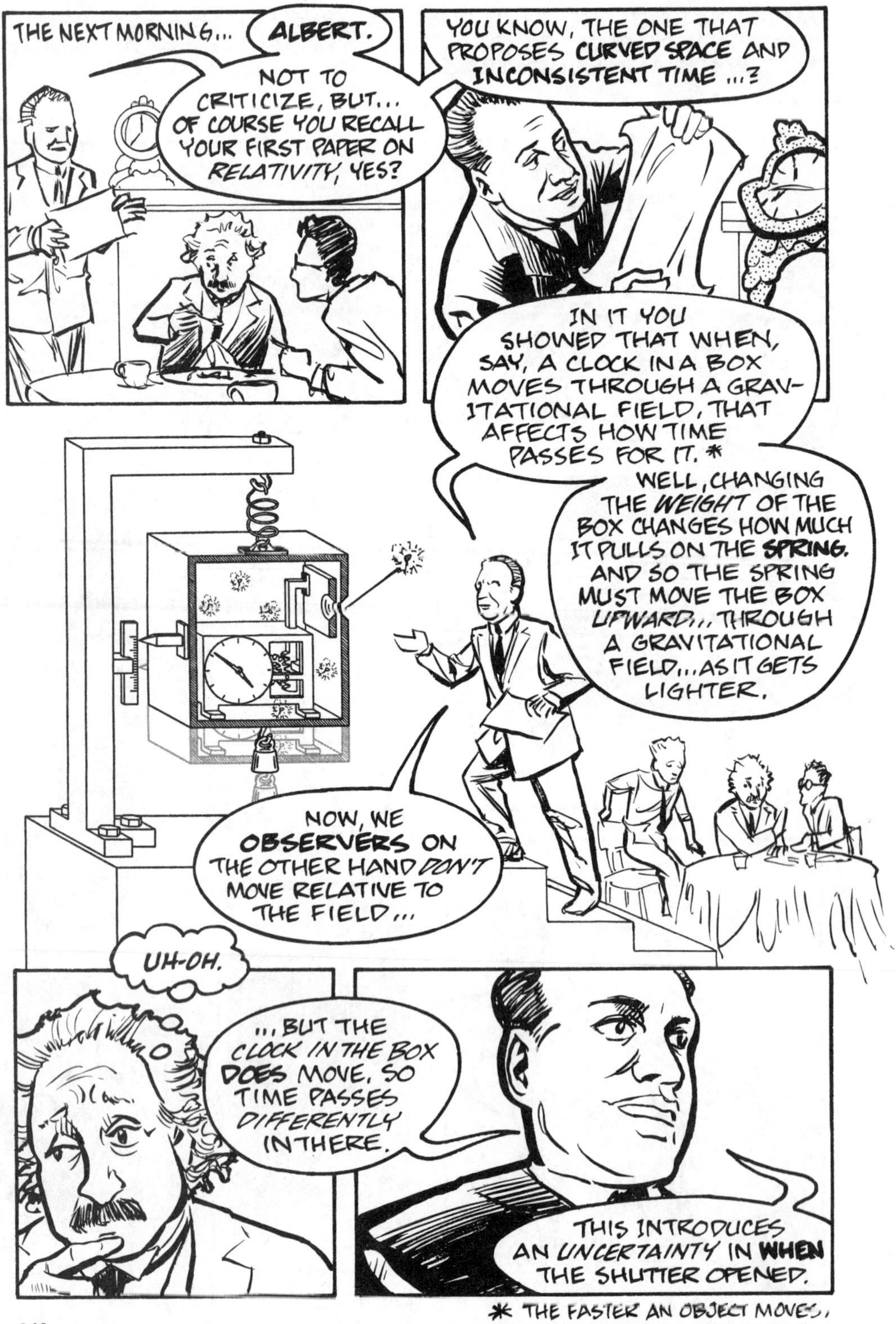
THE NEXT MORNING...
ALBERT.
NOT TO CRITICIZE, BUT... OF COURSE YOU RECALL YOUR FIRST PAPER ON RELATIVITY, YES?
YOU KNOW, THE ONE THAT PROPOSES CURVED SPACE AND INCONSISTENT TIME ...?
IN IT YOU SHOWED THAT WHEN, SAY, A CLOCK IN A BOX MOVES THROUGH A GRAVITATIONAL FIELD, THAT AFFECTS HOW TIME PASSES FOR IT. *
WELL, CHANGING THE WEIGHT OF THE BOX CHANGES HOW MUCH IT PULLS ON THE SPRING. AND SO THE SPRING MUST MOVE THE BOX UPWARD... THROUGH A GRAVITATIONAL FIELD... AS IT GETS LIGHTER.
NOW, WE OBSERVERS ON THE OTHER HAND DON'T MOVE RELATIVE TO THE FIELD...
UH-OH.
...BUT THE CLOCK IN THE BOX DOES MOVE, SO TIME PASSES DIFFERENTLY IN THERE.
THIS INTRODUCES AN UNCERTAINTY IN WHEN THE SHUTTER OPENED.

* THE FASTER AN OBJECT MOVES, THE MORE TIME SLOWS FOR IT.

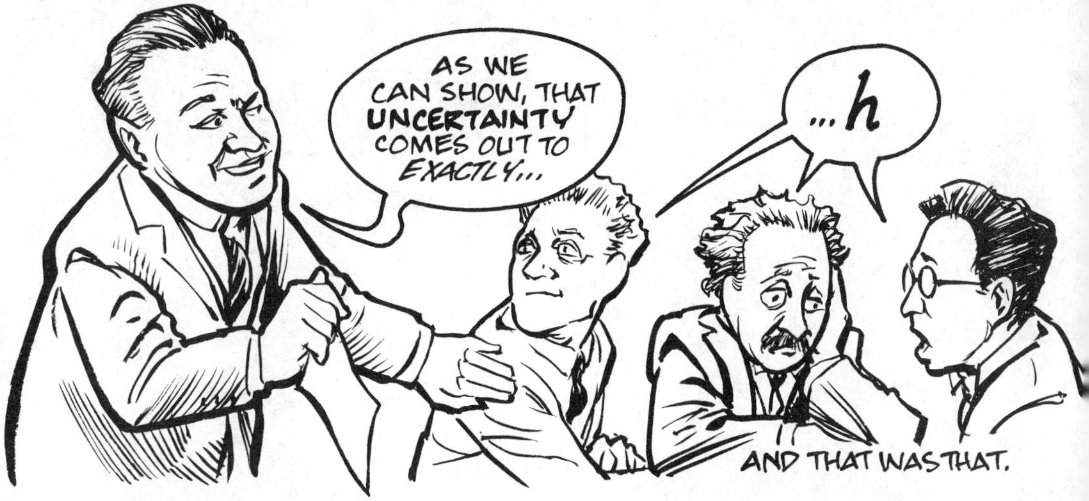
AS WE CAN SHOW, THAT **UNCERTAINTY** COMES OUT TO *EXACTLY*...
...*h*
AND THAT WAS THAT.

ALMOST. **EINSTEIN** TOOK ONE MORE SHOT AT QUANTUM *THEORY* FIVE YEARS LATER FROM HIS NEW HOME IN PRINCETON, NEW JERSEY. *

THIS TIME **EINSTEIN** (WORKING WITH **BORIS PODOLSKY** AND **NATHAN ROSEN**) DIDN'T BASE HIS CHALLENGE ON **HEISENBERG'S** *UNCERTAINTY PRINCIPLE*,

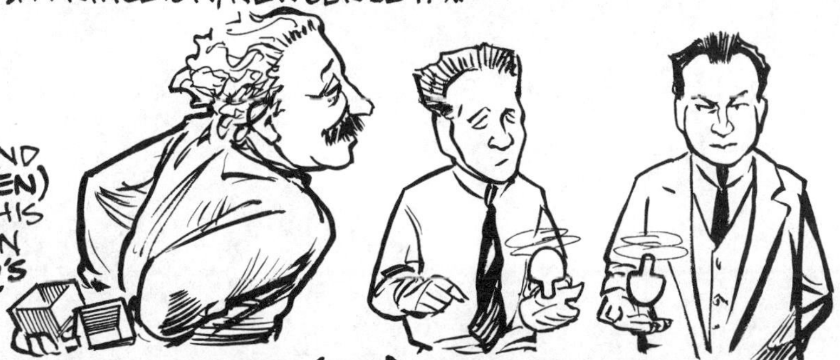

EINSTEIN, **PODOLSKY**, AND **ROSEN (EPR)** INSTEAD FOCUSED ON EXPERIMENTS THAT SHOWED YOU COULD CREATE *PAIRS* OF PARTICLES IN "ENTANGLED" STATES. FOR INSTANCE, IF ONE ELECTRON HAS A PARTICULAR SPIN, THE OTHER *MUST* HAVE A MATCHING SPIN.

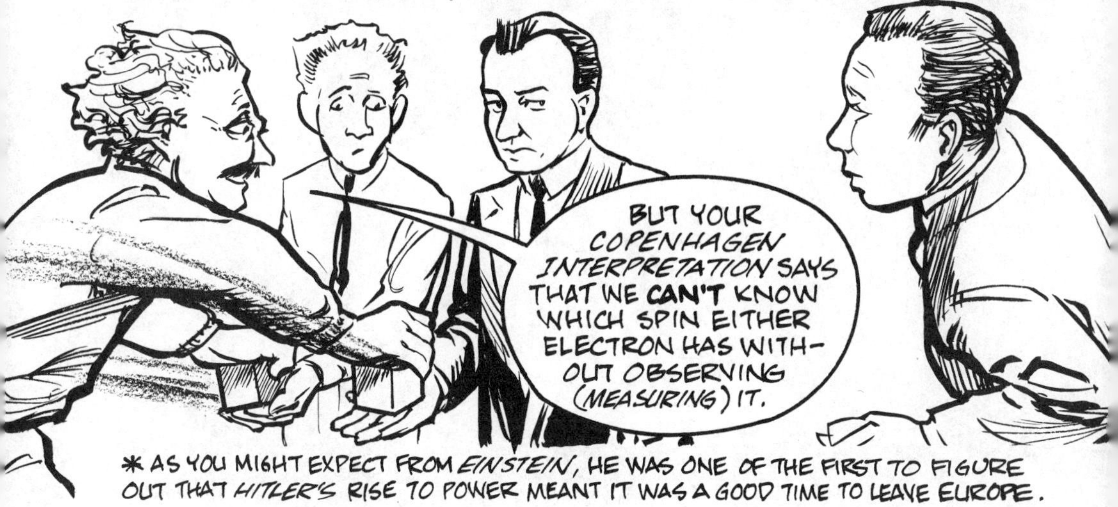
BUT YOUR *COPENHAGEN INTERPRETATION* SAYS THAT WE **CAN'T** KNOW WHICH SPIN EITHER ELECTRON HAS WITH-OUT OBSERVING (*MEASURING*) IT.

* AS YOU MIGHT EXPECT FROM *EINSTEIN*, HE WAS ONE OF THE FIRST TO FIGURE OUT THAT *HITLER'S* RISE TO POWER MEANT IT WAS A GOOD TIME TO LEAVE EUROPE.

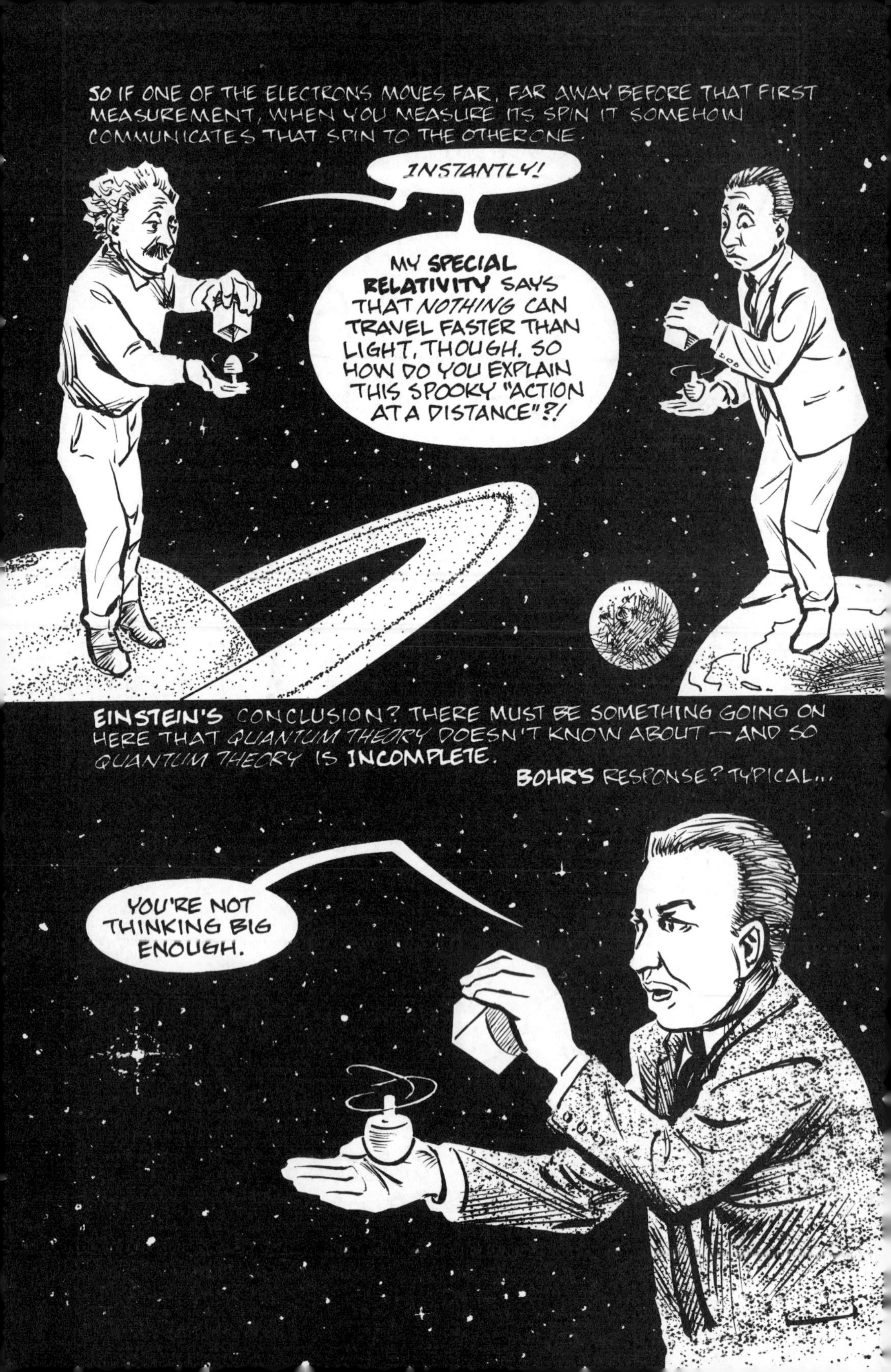
SO IF ONE OF THE ELECTRONS MOVES FAR, FAR AWAY BEFORE THAT FIRST MEASUREMENT, WHEN YOU MEASURE ITS SPIN IT SOMEHOW COMMUNICATES THAT SPIN TO THE OTHER ONE.
INSTANTLY!
MY SPECIAL RELATIVITY SAYS THAT NOTHING CAN TRAVEL FASTER THAN LIGHT, THOUGH. SO HOW DO YOU EXPLAIN THIS SPOOKY "ACTION AT A DISTANCE"?!
EINSTEIN'S CONCLUSION? THERE MUST BE SOMETHING GOING ON HERE THAT QUANTUM THEORY DOESN'T KNOW ABOUT — AND SO QUANTUM THEORY IS INCOMPLETE.
BOHR'S RESPONSE? TYPICAL...
YOU'RE NOT THINKING BIG ENOUGH.

IN HIS RESPONSE, WHICH HE MISCHIEVOUSLY GAVE THE EXACT SAME TITLE AS THE **EPR** PAPER (*"CAN QUANTUM-MECHANICAL DESCRIPTION OF PHYSICAL REALITY BE CONSIDERED COMPLETE?"*) **BOHR** POINTED OUT:

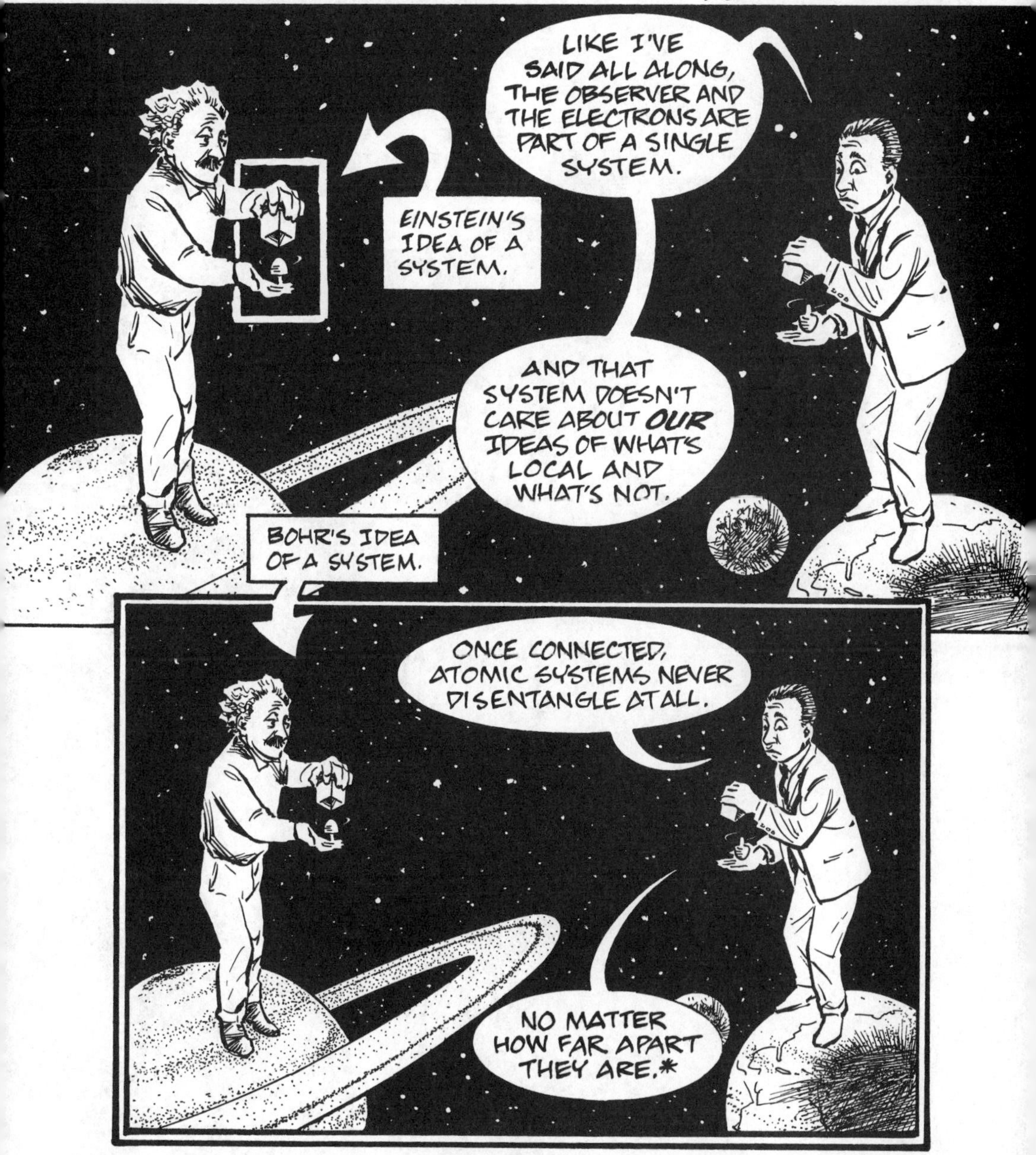

EINSTEIN'S IDEA OF A SYSTEM.
LIKE I'VE SAID ALL ALONG, THE OBSERVER AND THE ELECTRONS ARE PART OF A SINGLE SYSTEM.
AND THAT SYSTEM DOESN'T CARE ABOUT OUR IDEAS OF WHAT'S LOCAL AND WHAT'S NOT.
BOHR'S IDEA OF A SYSTEM.
ONCE CONNECTED, ATOMIC SYSTEMS NEVER DISENTANGLE AT ALL.
NO MATTER HOW FAR APART THEY ARE.*

* IT'S TRUE. THIS INSTANT COMMUNICATION, WHICH APPARENTLY VIOLATES EINSTEIN'S FUNDAMENTAL UPPER LIMIT ON THE SPEED OF ANYTHING, HAS BEEN DEMONSTRATED EXPERIMENTALLY. SEE THE COLOR SUPPLEMENT *"QUANTUM ENTANGLEMENT, SPOOKY ACTION AT A DISTANCE, TELEPORTATION, AND YOU"* FOR ONE OF ITS MANY USES AROUND THE HOME.

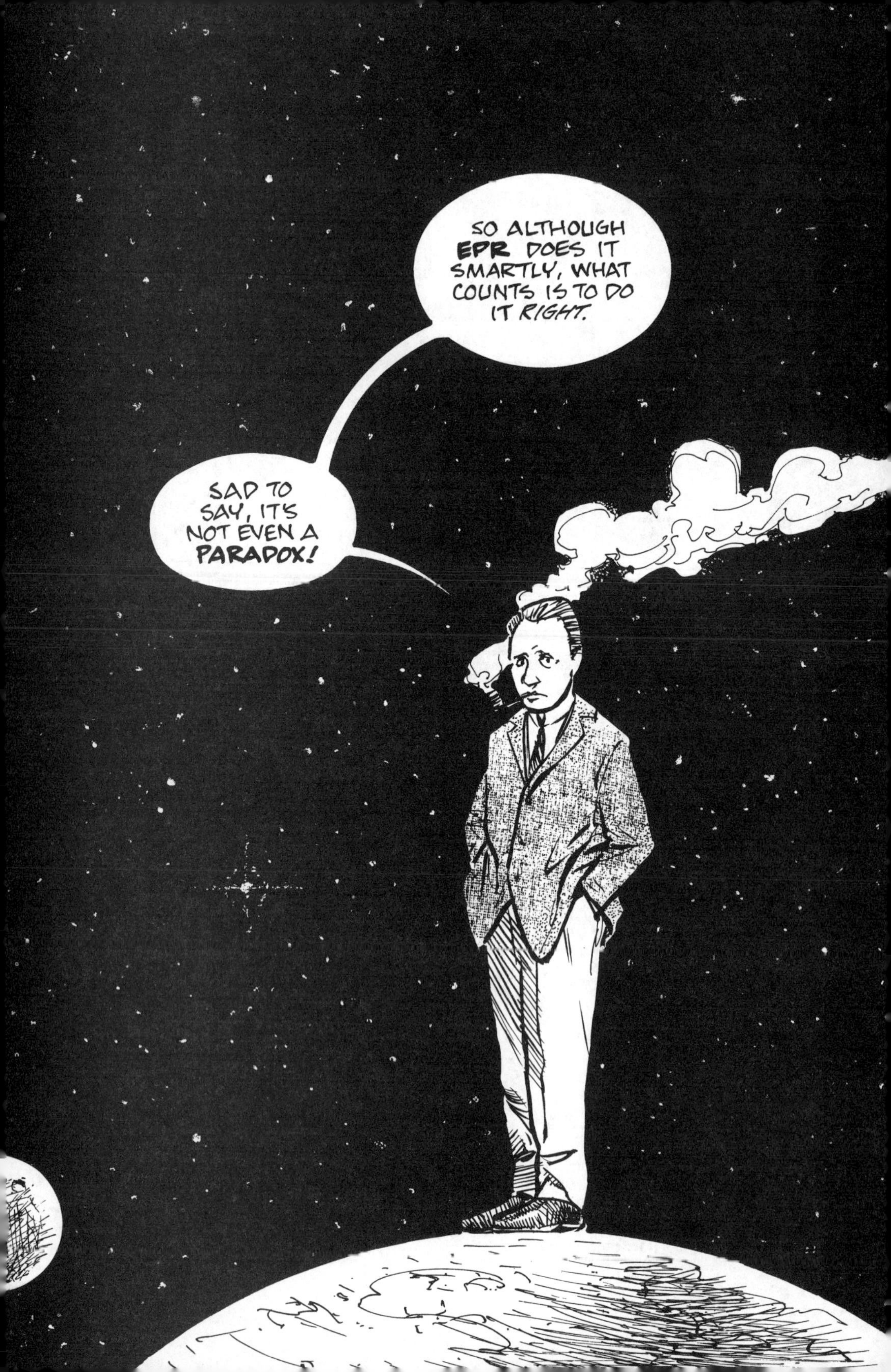
SAD TO SAY, IT'S NOT EVEN A PARADOX!
SO ALTHOUGH EPR DOES IT SMARTLY, WHAT COUNTS IS TO DO IT RIGHT.

Chapter 9

EINSTEIN REMAINED UNCONVINCED TO THE END. UPON BOHR'S RETURN, COPENHAGEN DEVOTED ITS ATTENTION TO THE OVERALL STRUCTURE OF THE ATOM.

MAKE THAT *ATTENTIONS*, AS A STEADY STREAM OF VISITORS—SOME OF THEM REFUGEES FROM THE INCREASINGLY BAD POLITICAL SITUATION ON THE CONTINENT— WALKED THE INSTITUTE'S HALLS.

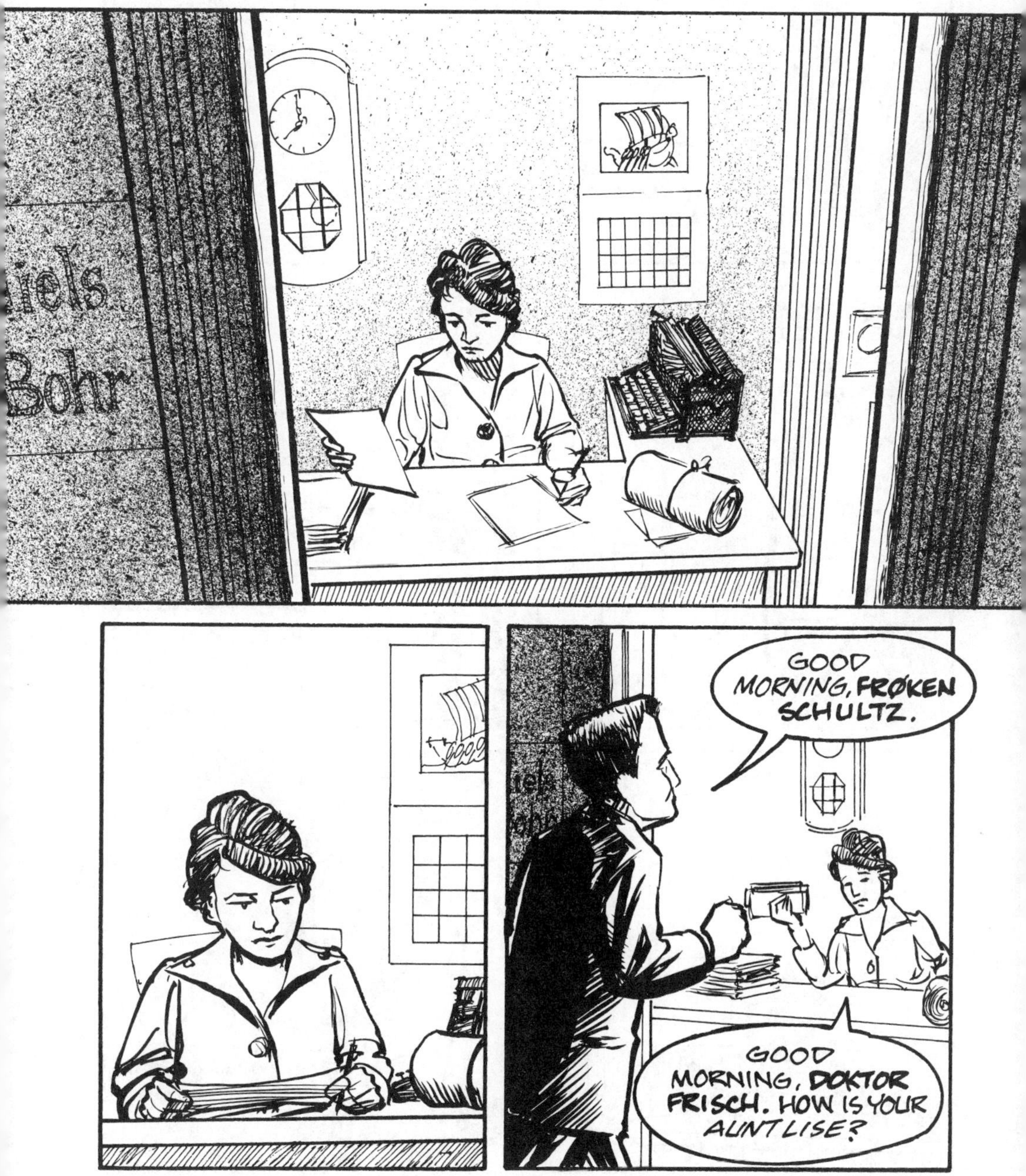

Bohr
GOOD MORNING, FRØKEN SCHULTZ.
GOOD MORNING, DOKTOR FRISCH. HOW IS YOUR AUNT LISE?

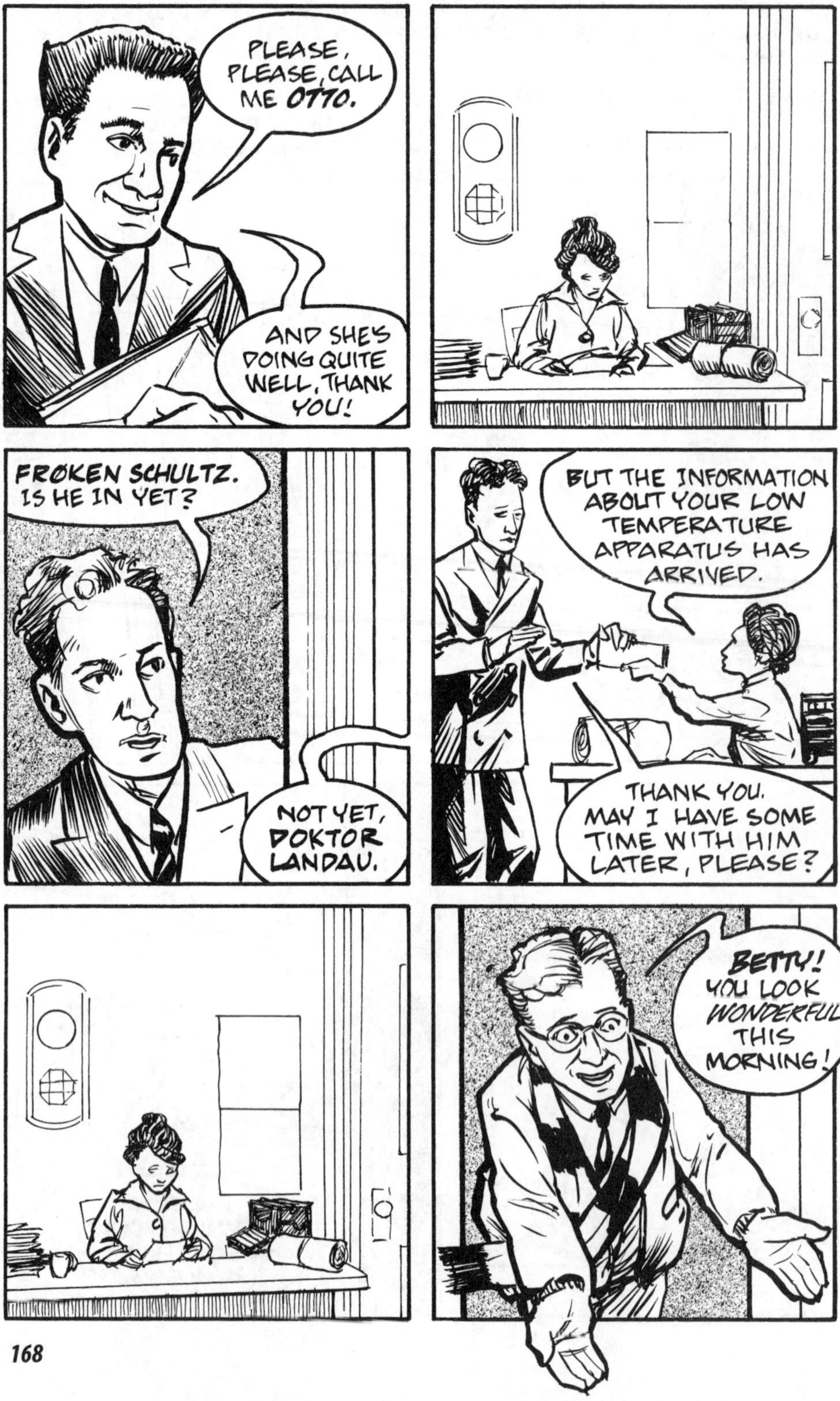
PLEASE, PLEASE, CALL ME OTTO.
AND SHE'S DOING QUITE WELL, THANK YOU!
FRØKEN SCHULTZ. IS HE IN YET?
NOT YET, DOKTOR LANDAU.
BUT THE INFORMATION ABOUT YOUR LOW TEMPERATURE APPARATUS HAS ARRIVED.
THANK YOU. MAY I HAVE SOME TIME WITH HIM LATER, PLEASE?
BETTY! YOU LOOK WONDERFUL THIS MORNING!

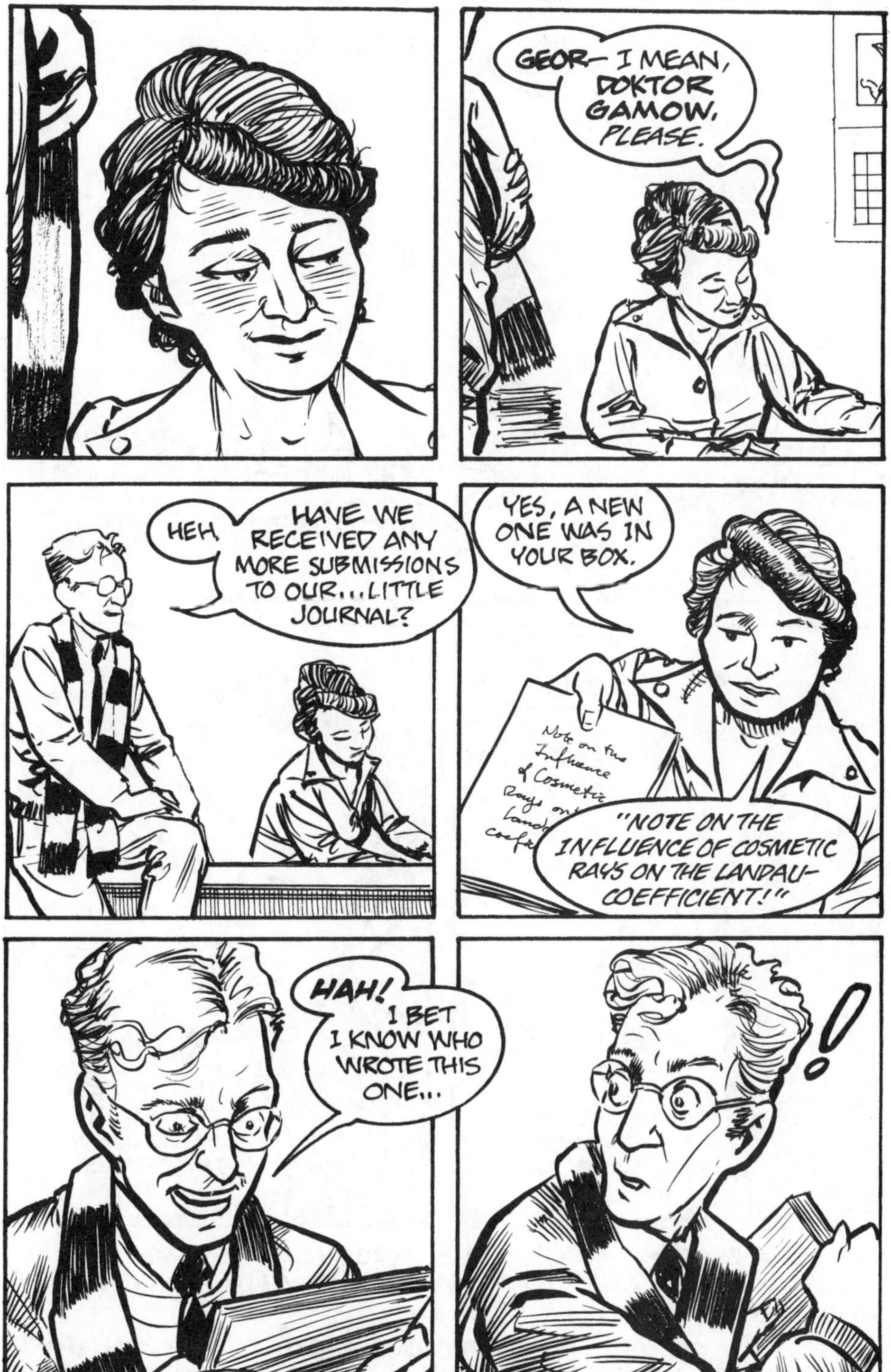
GEOR— I MEAN, DOKTOR GAMOW, PLEASE.
HEH.
HAVE WE RECEIVED ANY MORE SUBMISSIONS TO OUR...LITTLE JOURNAL?
YES, A NEW ONE WAS IN YOUR BOX.
Note on the Influence of Cosmetic Rays on the Landau coeffi
"NOTE ON THE INFLUENCE OF COSMETIC RAYS ON THE LANDAU-COEFFICIENT!"
HAH!
I BET I KNOW WHO WROTE THIS ONE...
!

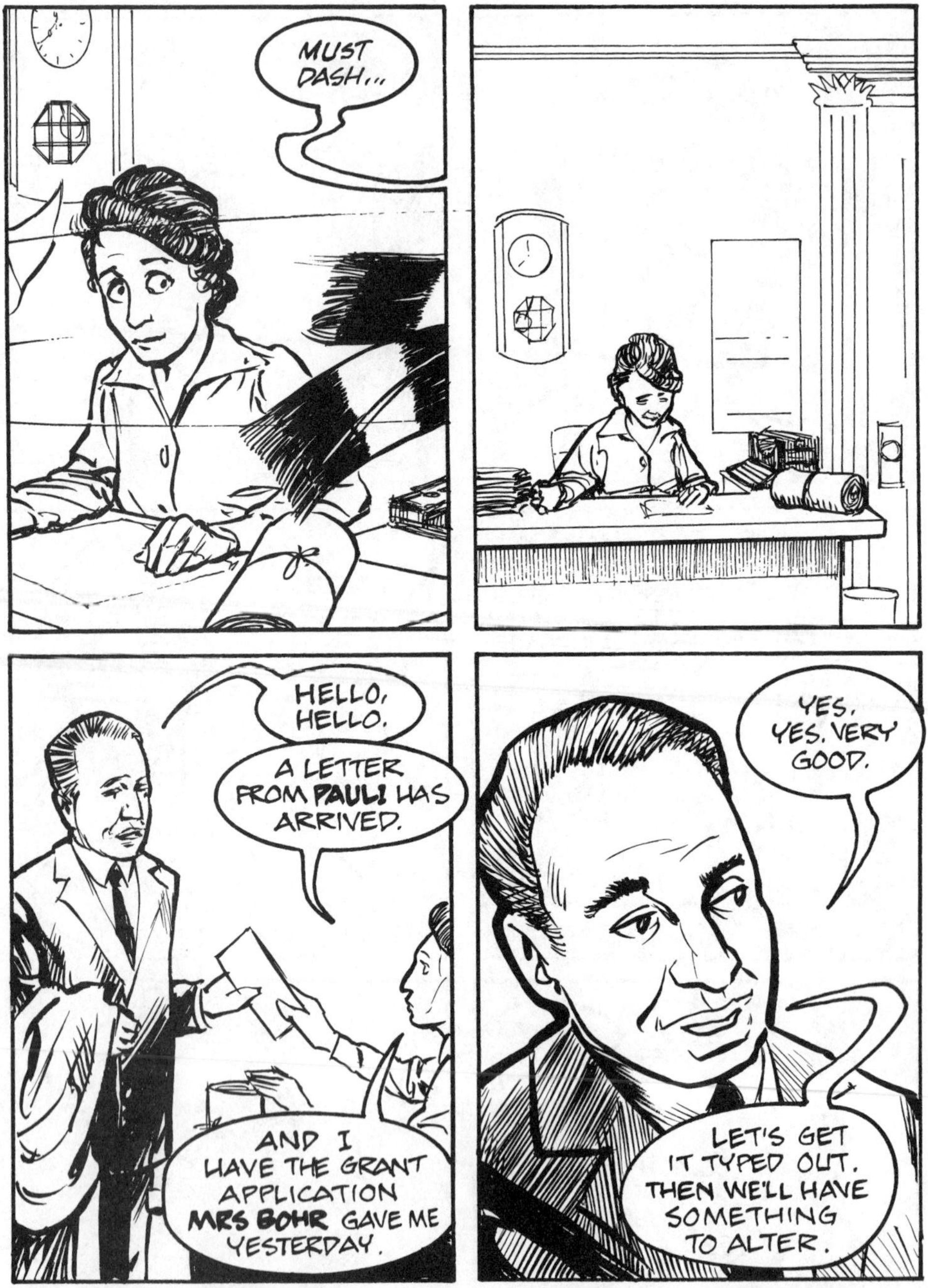
MUST DASH...
HELLO, HELLO.
A LETTER FROM PAULI HAS ARRIVED.
AND I HAVE THE GRANT APPLICATION MRS BOHR GAVE ME YESTERDAY.
YES. YES. VERY GOOD.
LET'S GET IT TYPED OUT. THEN WE'LL HAVE SOMETHING TO ALTER.

ALL **BOHR'S** GRANT APPLICATIONS WERE ACCOMPANIED BY LENGTHY (*QUEL SURPRISE*) WRITTEN APPLICATIONS, WHICH HE ALWAYS FOLLOWED UP WITH A PERSONAL VISIT.

BE IT TO THE **ROCKEFELLER** OR THE **CARLSBERG** FOUNDATION, **BOHR** ALWAYS GOT WHAT HE ASKED FOR.

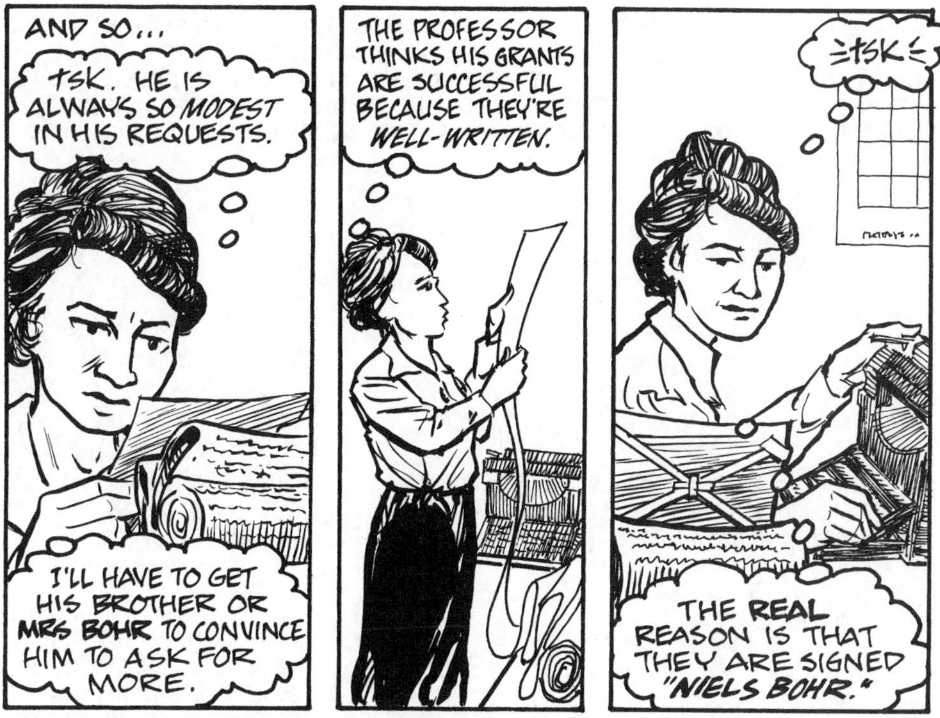
AND SO...
TSK. HE IS ALWAYS SO *MODEST* IN HIS REQUESTS.
I'LL HAVE TO GET HIS BROTHER OR **MRS BOHR** TO CONVINCE HIM TO ASK FOR MORE.
THE PROFESSOR THINKS HIS GRANTS ARE SUCCESSFUL BECAUSE THEY'RE *WELL-WRITTEN*.
TSK
THE **REAL** REASON IS THAT THEY ARE SIGNED ***"NIELS BOHR."***

THE *ROCKEFELLER FOUNDATION* FUNDED BIOLOGICAL RESEARCH, ABOUT WHICH **BOHR** HAD BECOME "EXCEEDINGLY FASCINATED, ELECTRIFIED." THE *CARLSBERG FOUNDATION* GAVE MONEY FOR WORK ON BASIC PHYSICS.

THEY ALSO PROVIDED **BOHR** WITH HIS NEW HOME: **ÆRESBOLIG.**

(RESIDENCE OF HONOR)

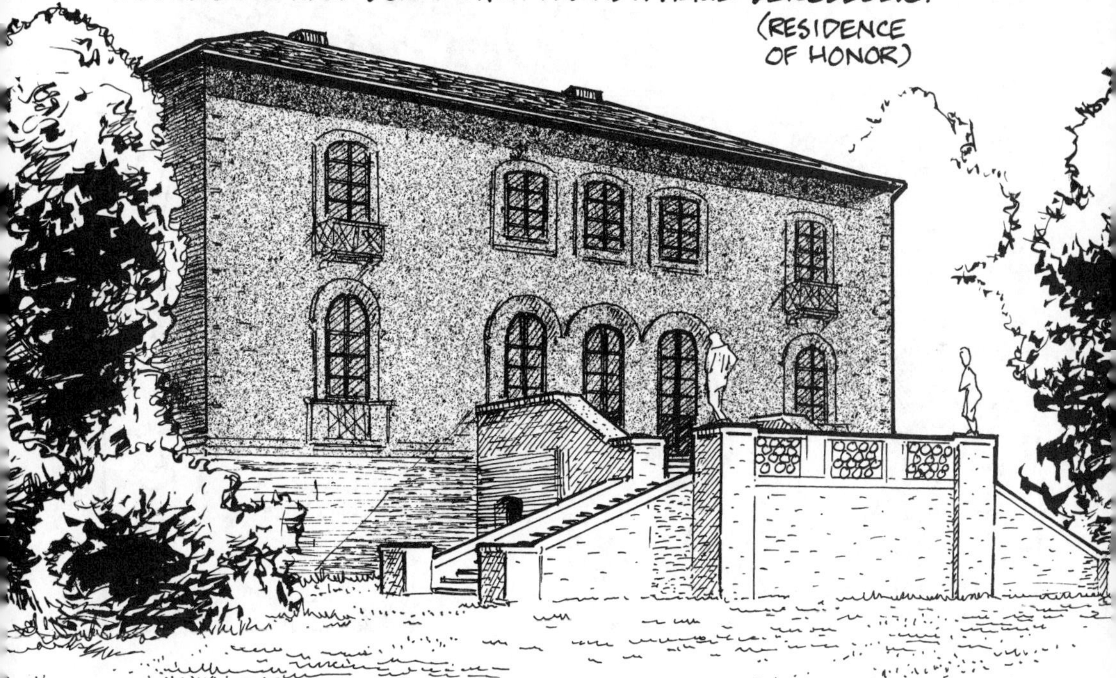

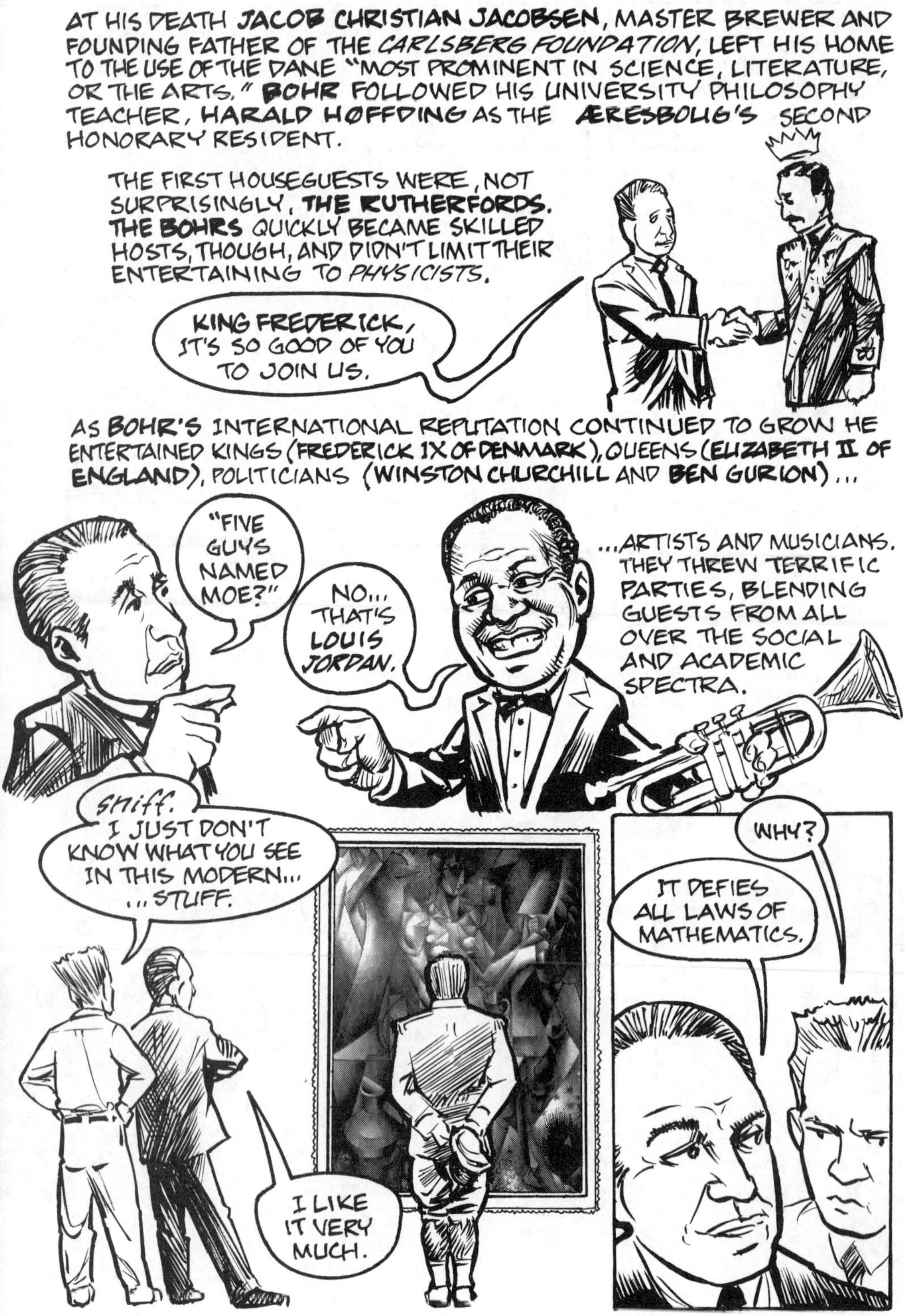
AT HIS DEATH JACOB CHRISTIAN JACOBSEN, MASTER BREWER AND FOUNDING FATHER OF THE CARLSBERG FOUNDATION, LEFT HIS HOME TO THE USE OF THE DANE "MOST PROMINENT IN SCIENCE, LITERATURE, OR THE ARTS." BOHR FOLLOWED HIS UNIVERSITY PHILOSOPHY TEACHER, HARALD HØFFDING AS THE ÆRESBOLIG'S SECOND HONORARY RESIDENT.
THE FIRST HOUSEGUESTS WERE, NOT SURPRISINGLY, THE RUTHERFORDS. THE BOHRS QUICKLY BECAME SKILLED HOSTS, THOUGH, AND DIDN'T LIMIT THEIR ENTERTAINING TO PHYSICISTS.
KING FREDERICK, IT'S SO GOOD OF YOU TO JOIN US.
AS BOHR'S INTERNATIONAL REPUTATION CONTINUED TO GROW HE ENTERTAINED KINGS (FREDERICK IX OF DENMARK), QUEENS (ELIZABETH II OF ENGLAND), POLITICIANS (WINSTON CHURCHILL AND BEN GURION)...
"FIVE GUYS NAMED MOE?"
NO... THAT'S LOUIS JORDAN.
...ARTISTS AND MUSICIANS. THEY THREW TERRIFIC PARTIES, BLENDING GUESTS FROM ALL OVER THE SOCIAL AND ACADEMIC SPECTRA.
SNIFF. I JUST DON'T KNOW WHAT YOU SEE IN THIS MODERN... ...STUFF.
I LIKE IT VERY MUCH.
WHY?
IT DEFIES ALL LAWS OF MATHEMATICS.

THE **BOHR** FAMILY'S RISE TO SOCIAL PROMINENCE COINCIDED WITH RISING FEAR AND INTOLERANCE IN EUROPE. SO THOUGH SCIENCE WAS STILL THE FOCUS, THE WORLD SCENE BEGAN TO PLAY A BIGGER PART IN **BOHR'S** LIFE.

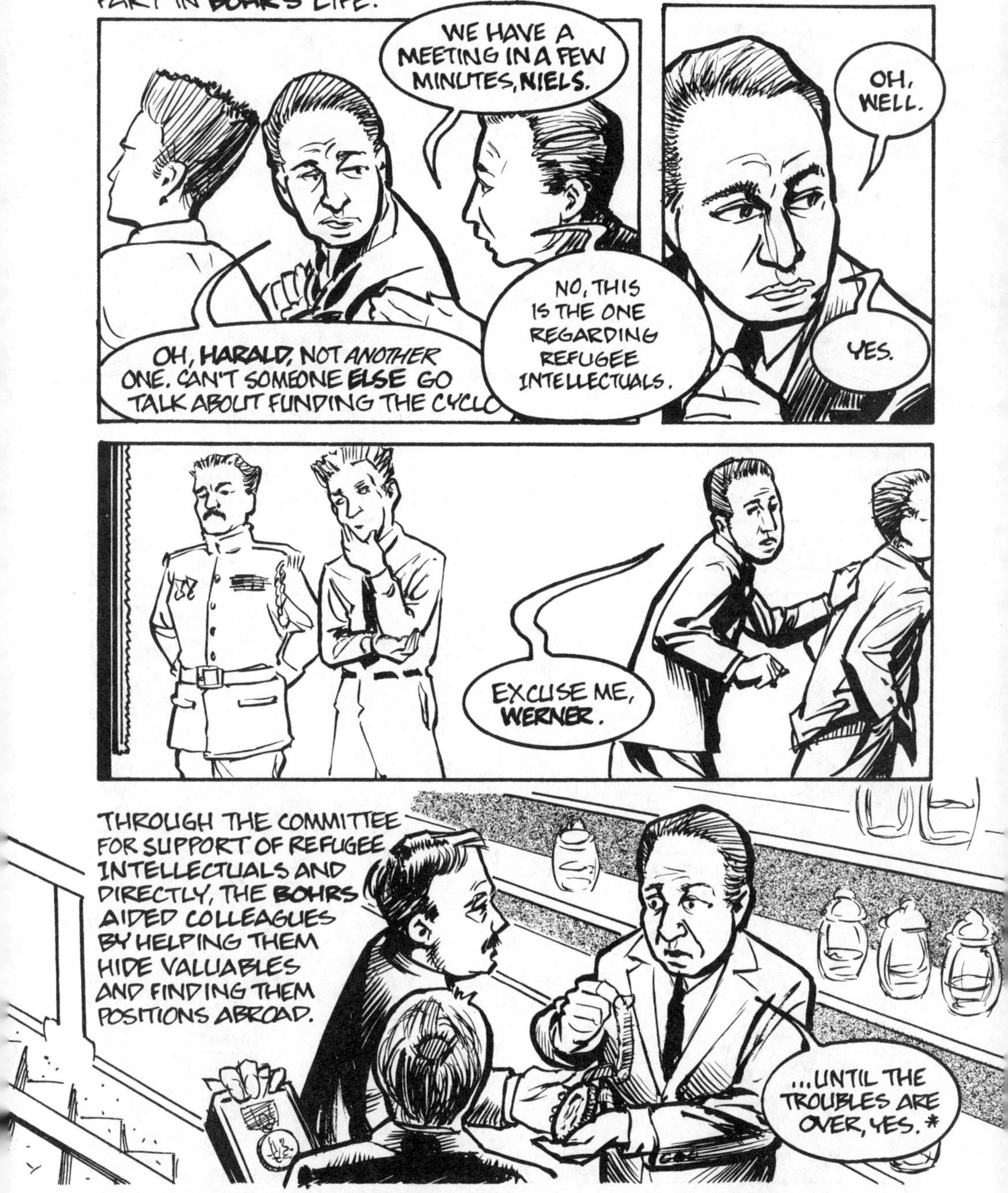
WE HAVE A MEETING IN A FEW MINUTES, NIELS.
OH, HARALD, NOT ANOTHER ONE. CAN'T SOMEONE ELSE GO TALK ABOUT FUNDING THE CYCLO
NO, THIS IS THE ONE REGARDING REFUGEE INTELLECTUALS.
OH, WELL.
YES.
EXCUSE ME, WERNER.
THROUGH THE COMMITTEE FOR SUPPORT OF REFUGEE INTELLECTUALS AND DIRECTLY, THE BOHRS AIDED COLLEAGUES BY HELPING THEM HIDE VALUABLES AND FINDING THEM POSITIONS ABROAD.
...UNTIL THE TROUBLES ARE OVER, YES. *

* BOHR DISSOLVED SOME OF THE *NOBEL* MEDALS IN ACID TO BETTER HIDE THEM. HE SENT HIS OWN TO **FINNISH** WAR AID ONCE FIGHTING BROKE OUT.

PERSONAL SADNESS ALSO TOUCHED THE **BOHR FAMILY** IN THIS PERIOD. CLOSE FRIEND AND GIFTED PHYSICIST **PAUL EHRENFEST** COMMITTED SUICIDE, AND **BOHR'S** OLDEST SON **CHRISTIAN** DIED IN A BOATING ACCIDENT IN 1934. *

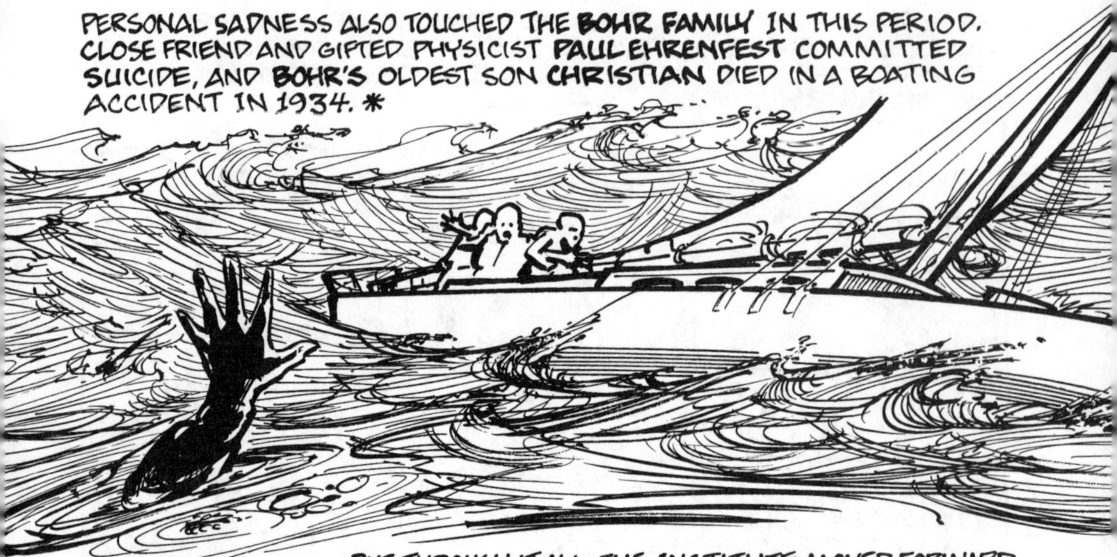

BUT THROUGH IT ALL, THE INSTITUTE MOVED FORWARD.

VISITORS – REFUGEES AND OTHERWISE – WERE IMPRESSED THAT GRANT MONEY NEVER WENT TOWARDS COSMETIC IMPROVEMENTS TO THE BUILDINGS BUT ALWAYS WENT TOWARDS THE WORK AND SUPPORTING STUDENTS.

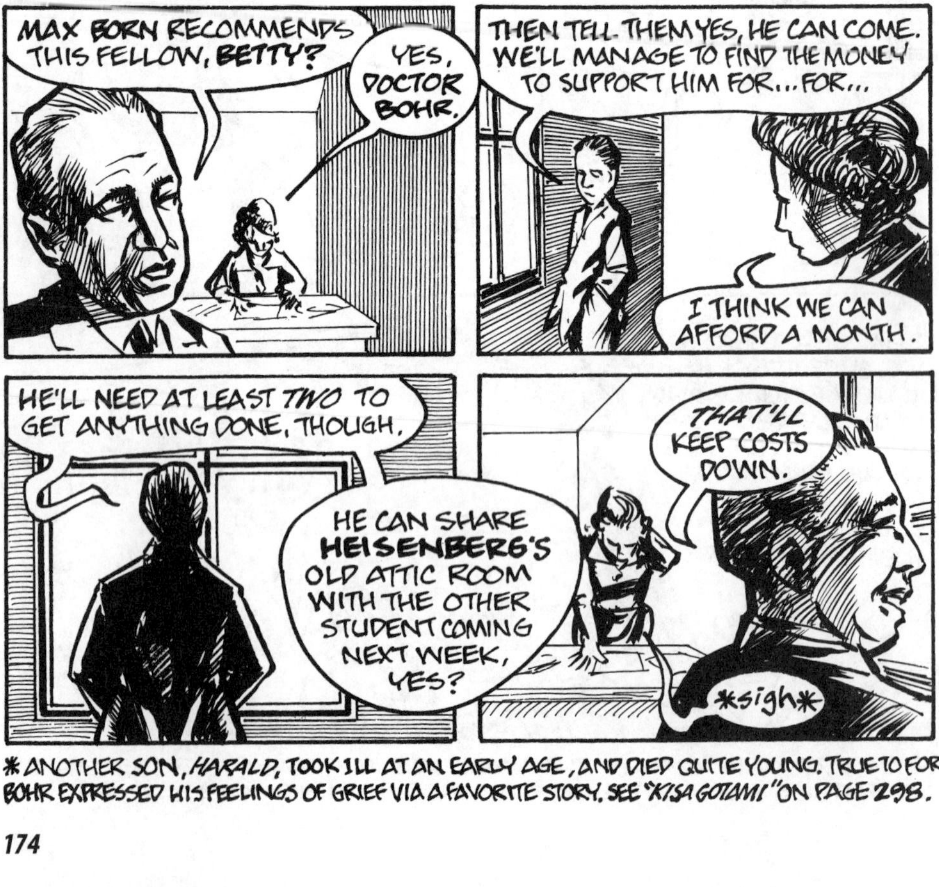
MAX BORN RECOMMENDS THIS FELLOW, BETTY?
YES, DOCTOR BOHR.
THEN TELL THEM YES, HE CAN COME. WE'LL MANAGE TO FIND THE MONEY TO SUPPORT HIM FOR... FOR...
I THINK WE CAN AFFORD A MONTH.
HE'LL NEED AT LEAST *TWO* TO GET ANYTHING DONE, THOUGH.
HE CAN SHARE **HEISENBERG'S** OLD ATTIC ROOM WITH THE OTHER STUDENT COMING NEXT WEEK, YES?
THAT'LL KEEP COSTS DOWN.
sigh

* ANOTHER SON, *HARALD*, TOOK ILL AT AN EARLY AGE, AND DIED QUITE YOUNG. TRUE TO FORM, BOHR EXPRESSED HIS FEELINGS OF GRIEF VIA A FAVORITE STORY. SEE "*KISA GOTAMI*" ON PAGE 298.

AND **FRØKEN SCHULTZ** ALSO KEPT COSTS DOWN, IN PART BY KEEPING **BOHR** FROM MEETING TOO MANY UNANNOUNCED GUESTS—BECAUSE EVEN THE CRACKPOTS WOULD GET SOMETHING IF THEY SPUN HIM A GOOD YARN.

NOT THAT THERE WASN'T OCCASION FOR CRACKPOT THEORIES TO COME FROM THE INSTITUTE ITSELF. AND, NO, THAT'S NOT A REFERENCE TO **B.K.S.** OR SOME OF **BOHR'S** OTHER FAILED THEORIES. RATHER:

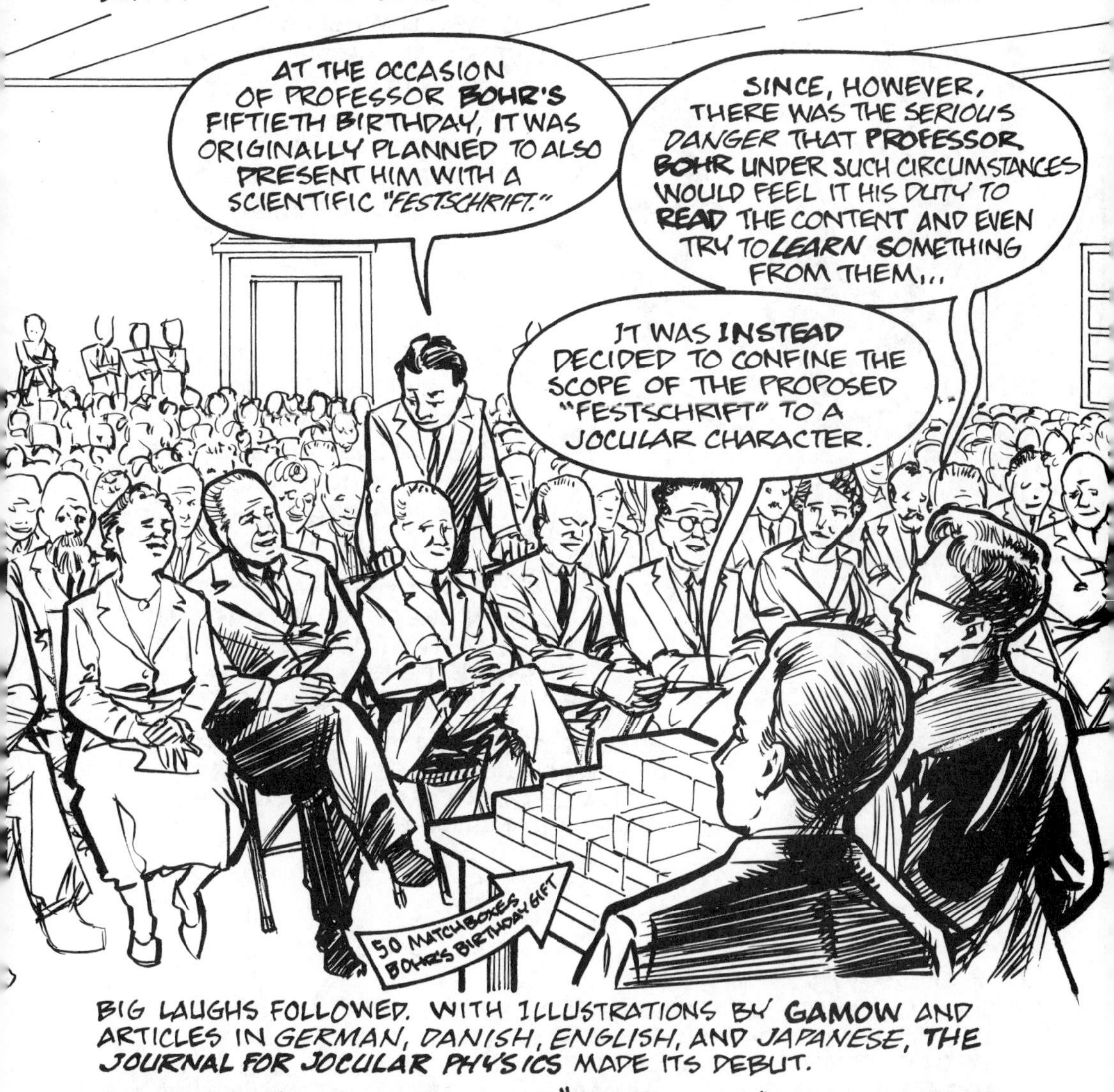
AT THE OCCASION OF PROFESSOR BOHR'S FIFTIETH BIRTHDAY, IT WAS ORIGINALLY PLANNED TO ALSO PRESENT HIM WITH A SCIENTIFIC "FESTSCHRIFT."
SINCE, HOWEVER, THERE WAS THE SERIOUS DANGER THAT PROFESSOR BOHR UNDER SUCH CIRCUMSTANCES WOULD FEEL IT HIS DUTY TO READ THE CONTENT AND EVEN TRY TO LEARN SOMETHING FROM THEM...
IT WAS INSTEAD DECIDED TO CONFINE THE SCOPE OF THE PROPOSED "FESTSCHRIFT" TO A JOCULAR CHARACTER.
50 MATCHBOXES BOHR'S BIRTHDAY GIFT

BIG LAUGHS FOLLOWED. WITH ILLUSTRATIONS BY **GAMOW** AND ARTICLES IN *GERMAN, DANISH, ENGLISH,* AND *JAPANESE*, ***THE JOURNAL FOR JOCULAR PHYSICS*** MADE ITS DEBUT.

IT FEATURED THE AFOREMENTIONED *"COSMETIC RAYS"*, PIECES BY **EDWARD TELLER** AND **HANS BETHE, OTTO FRISCH**, AND **VICTOR WEISSKOPF.**

OVER THE YEARS TWO MORE VOLUMES APPEARED, PUBLISHING ARTICLES LIKE *"THE NEW ELEPHANT'S CHILD"* (BY A FROG), *"A VOYAGE TO LA PLACIA"* BY **LEON ROSENFELD**, AND A REPORT IN 1955 ON THE *"ALCOHOL FOR PEACE"* CONFERENCE IN GENEVA.

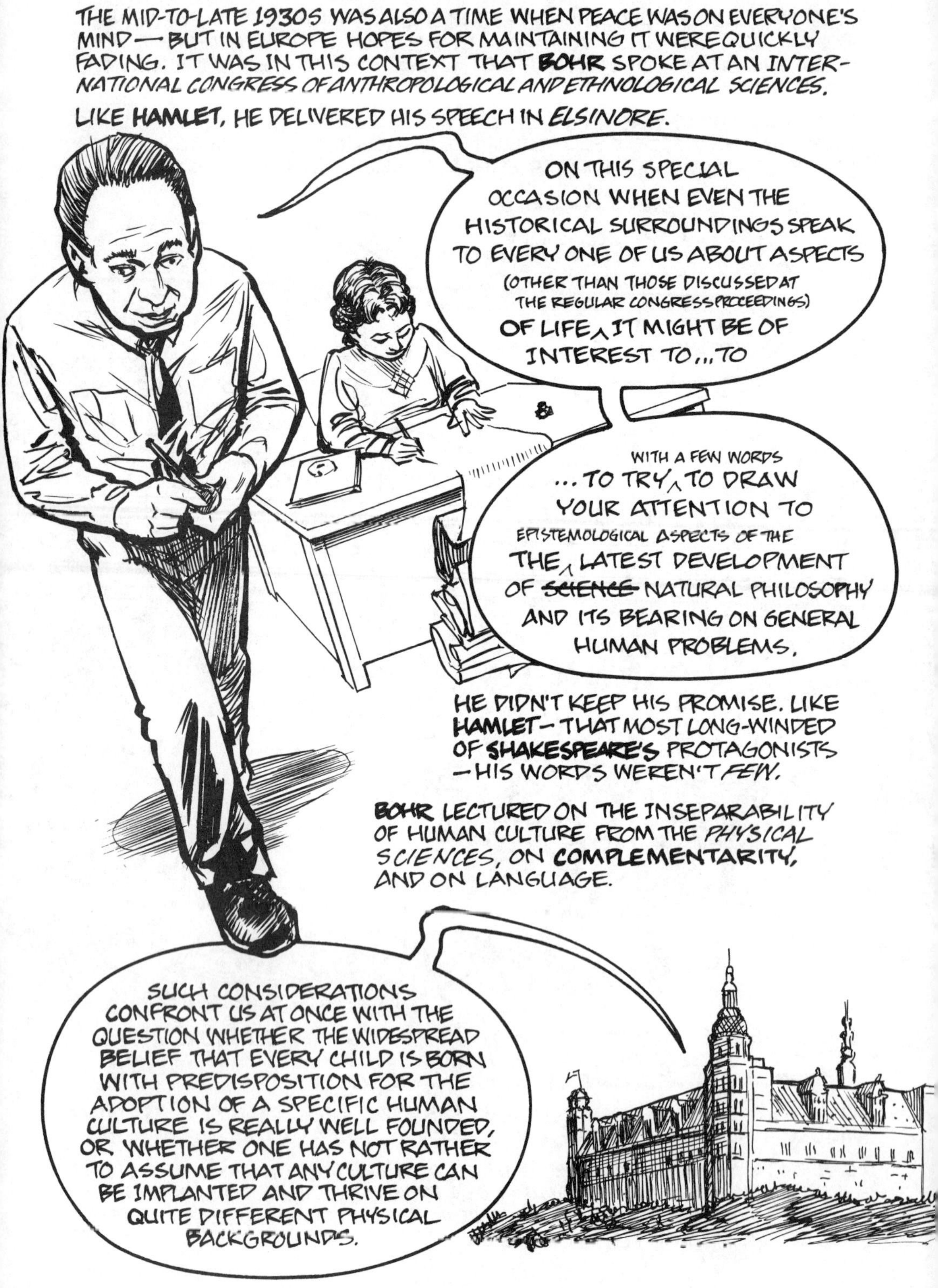

THE MID-TO-LATE 1930S WAS ALSO A TIME WHEN PEACE WAS ON EVERYONE'S MIND — BUT IN EUROPE HOPES FOR MAINTAINING IT WERE QUICKLY FADING. IT WAS IN THIS CONTEXT THAT **BOHR** SPOKE AT AN INTER-NATIONAL CONGRESS OF ANTHROPOLOGICAL AND ETHNOLOGICAL SCIENCES.
LIKE **HAMLET**, HE DELIVERED HIS SPEECH IN *ELSINORE*.
ON THIS SPECIAL OCCASION WHEN EVEN THE HISTORICAL SURROUNDINGS SPEAK TO EVERY ONE OF US ABOUT ASPECTS (OTHER THAN THOSE DISCUSSED AT THE REGULAR CONGRESS PROCEEDINGS) OF LIFE^ IT MIGHT BE OF INTEREST TO... TO
...TO TRY^ (WITH A FEW WORDS) TO DRAW YOUR ATTENTION TO EPISTEMOLOGICAL ASPECTS OF THE THE^ LATEST DEVELOPMENT OF ~~SCIENCE~~ NATURAL PHILOSOPHY AND ITS BEARING ON GENERAL HUMAN PROBLEMS.
HE DIDN'T KEEP HIS PROMISE. LIKE **HAMLET** — THAT MOST LONG-WINDED OF **SHAKESPEARE'S** PROTAGONISTS — HIS WORDS WEREN'T *FEW*.
BOHR LECTURED ON THE INSEPARABILITY OF HUMAN CULTURE FROM THE *PHYSICAL SCIENCES*, ON **COMPLEMENTARITY**, AND ON LANGUAGE.
SUCH CONSIDERATIONS CONFRONT US AT ONCE WITH THE QUESTION WHETHER THE WIDESPREAD BELIEF THAT EVERY CHILD IS BORN WITH PREDISPOSITION FOR THE ADOPTION OF A SPECIFIC HUMAN CULTURE IS REALLY WELL FOUNDED, OR WHETHER ONE HAS NOT RATHER TO ASSUME THAT ANY CULTURE CAN BE IMPLANTED AND THRIVE ON QUITE DIFFERENT PHYSICAL BACKGROUNDS.

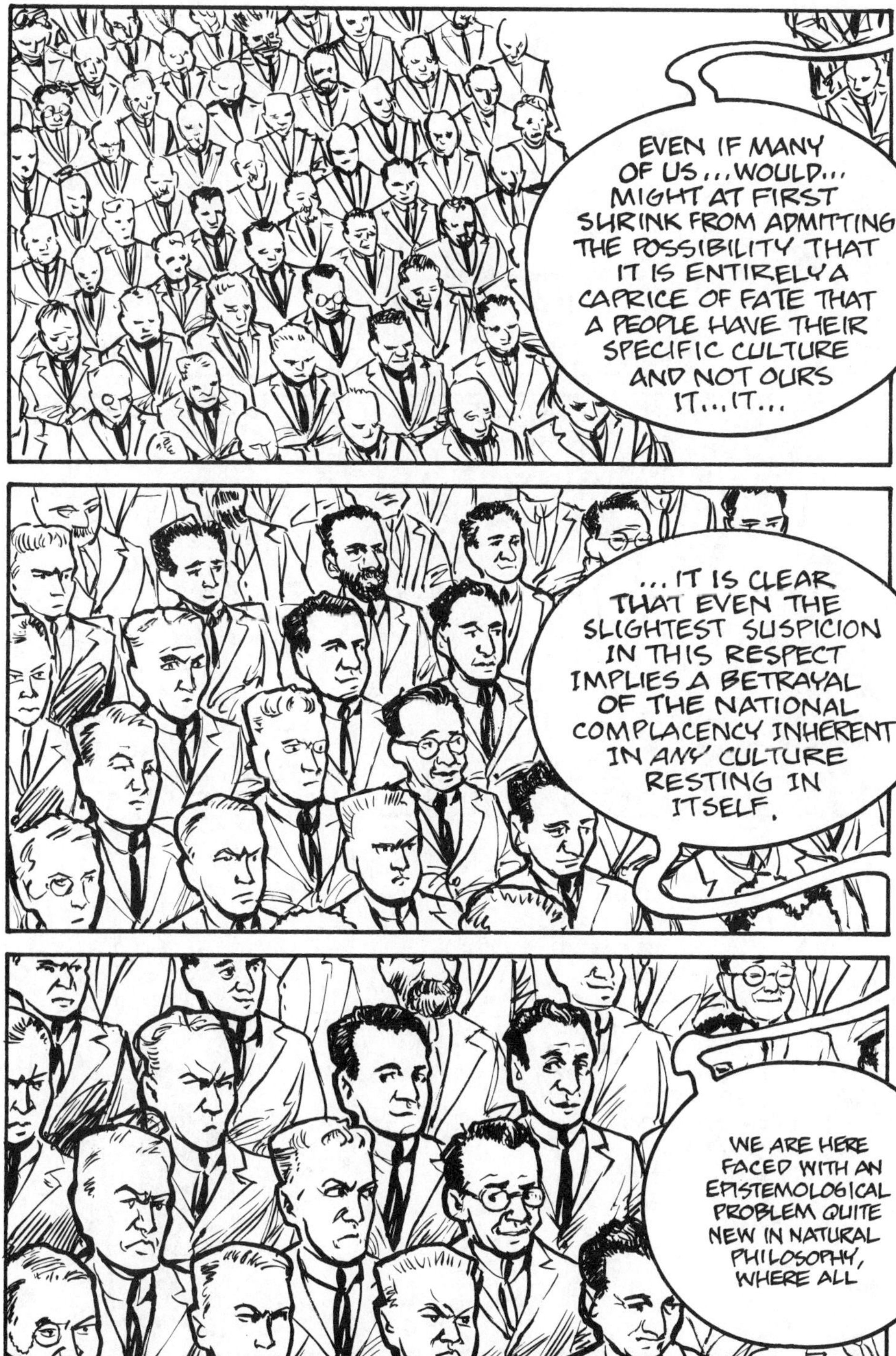
EVEN IF MANY OF US ... WOULD... MIGHT AT FIRST SHRINK FROM ADMITTING THE POSSIBILITY THAT IT IS ENTIRELY A CAPRICE OF FATE THAT A PEOPLE HAVE THEIR SPECIFIC CULTURE AND NOT OURS IT..., IT...
...IT IS CLEAR THAT EVEN THE SLIGHTEST SUSPICION IN THIS RESPECT IMPLIES A BETRAYAL OF THE NATIONAL COMPLACENCY INHERENT IN *ANY* CULTURE RESTING IN ITSELF.
WE ARE HERE FACED WITH AN EPISTEMOLOGICAL PROBLEM QUITE NEW IN NATURAL PHILOSOPHY, WHERE ALL

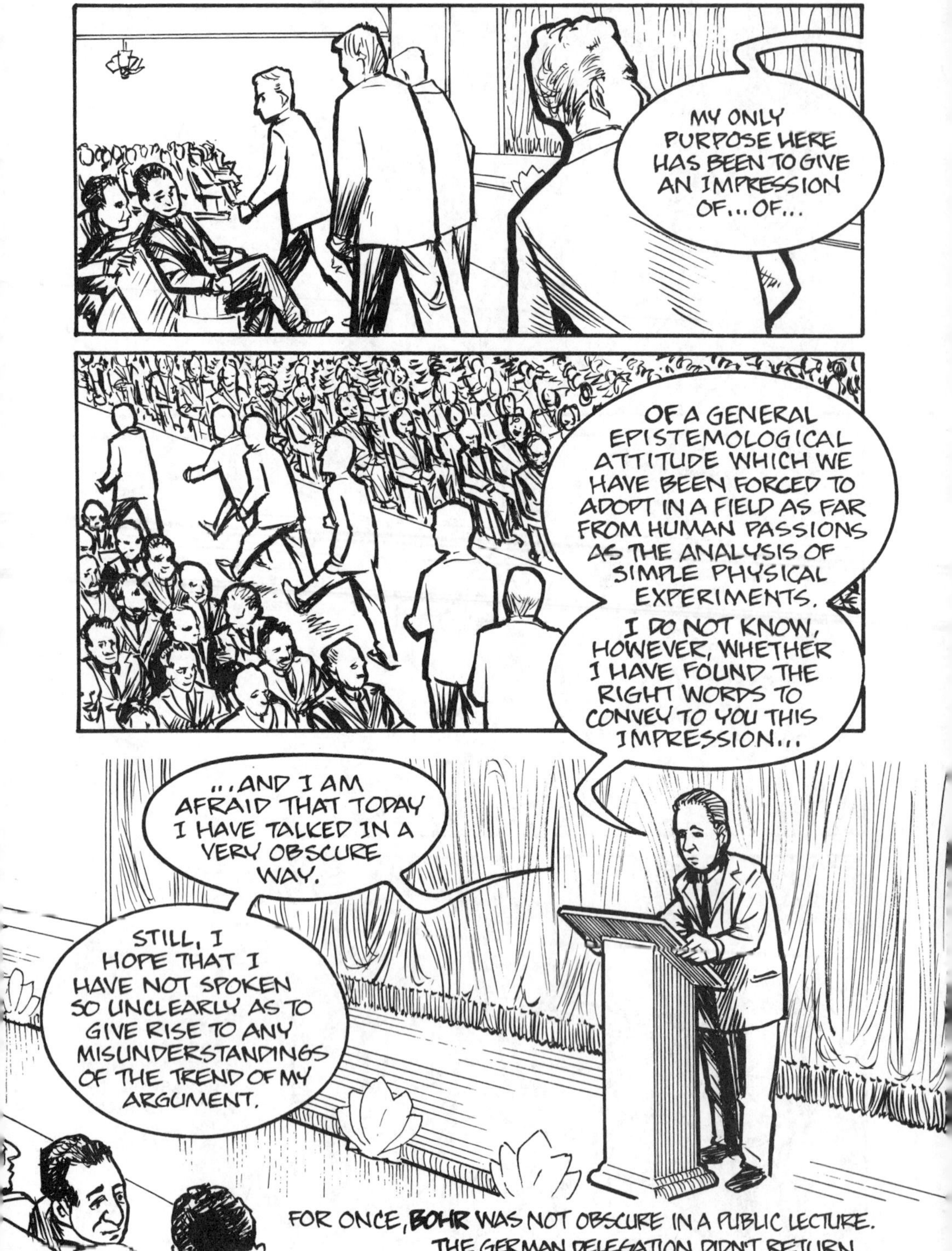
MY ONLY PURPOSE HERE HAS BEEN TO GIVE AN IMPRESSION OF... OF...
OF A GENERAL EPISTEMOLOGICAL ATTITUDE WHICH WE HAVE BEEN FORCED TO ADOPT IN A FIELD AS FAR FROM HUMAN PASSIONS AS THE ANALYSIS OF SIMPLE PHYSICAL EXPERIMENTS.
I DO NOT KNOW, HOWEVER, WHETHER I HAVE FOUND THE RIGHT WORDS TO CONVEY TO YOU THIS IMPRESSION...
...AND I AM AFRAID THAT TODAY I HAVE TALKED IN A VERY OBSCURE WAY.
STILL, I HOPE THAT I HAVE NOT SPOKEN SO UNCLEARLY AS TO GIVE RISE TO ANY MISUNDERSTANDINGS OF THE TREND OF MY ARGUMENT.
FOR ONCE, BOHR WAS NOT OBSCURE IN A PUBLIC LECTURE.
THE GERMAN DELEGATION DIDN'T RETURN.

Chapter 10

BOHR HAD INITIATED **LÉON ROSENFELD** — HIS CHIEF COLLABORATOR THROUGH THE 1930s — AT AN **EARLIER** CONFERENCE.

ROSENFELD DESCRIBED IT THIS WAY:

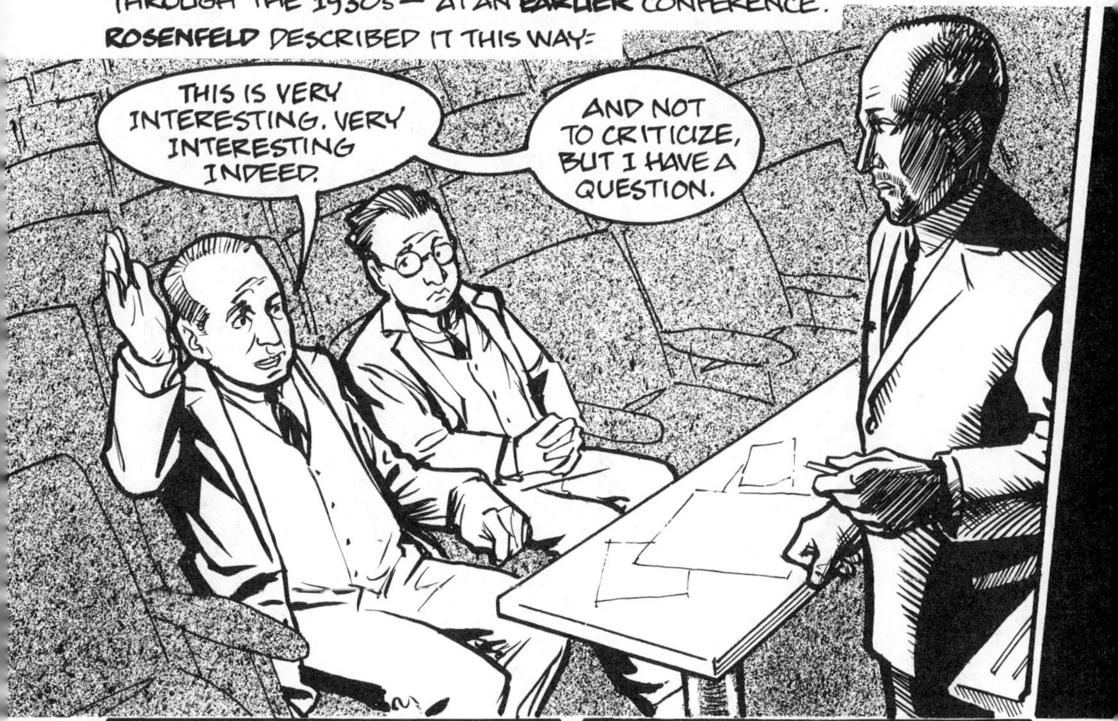

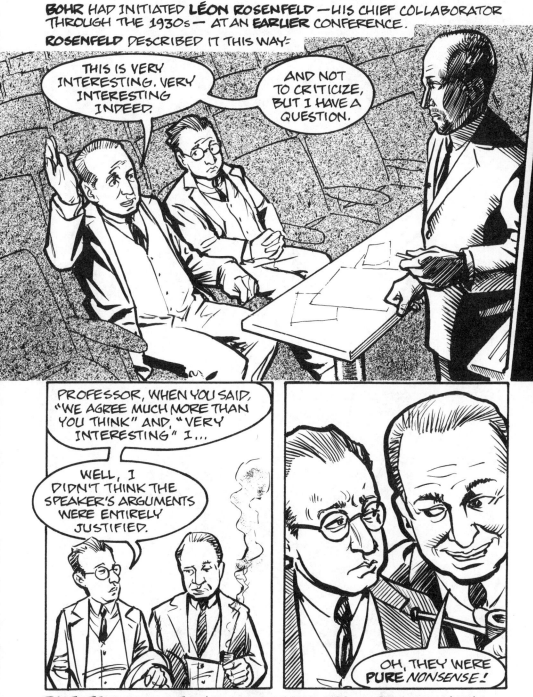

THIS IS VERY INTERESTING. VERY INTERESTING INDEED.
AND NOT TO CRITICIZE, BUT I HAVE A QUESTION.

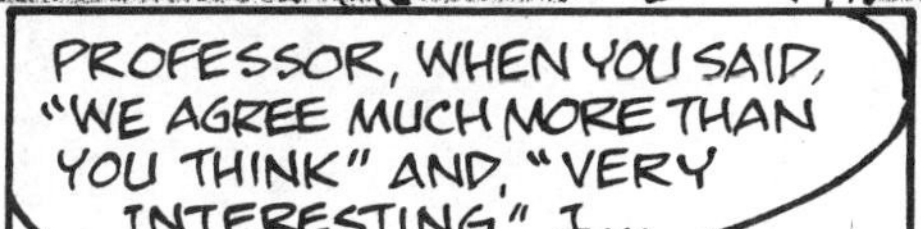

PROFESSOR, WHEN YOU SAID, "WE AGREE MUCH MORE THAN YOU THINK" AND, "VERY INTERESTING" I...
WELL, I DIDN'T THINK THE SPEAKER'S ARGUMENTS WERE ENTIRELY JUSTIFIED.

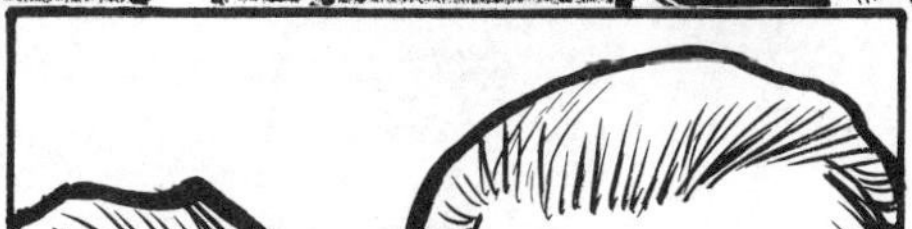

OH, THEY WERE **PURE** *NONSENSE*!

ROSENFELD SAID LATER, "SO I KNEW I HAD BEEN LED ASTRAY BY A MERE MATTER OF TERMINOLOGY." AND WITH THAT WARM-UP EXERCISE OVER, THE REAL INITIATION BEGAN...

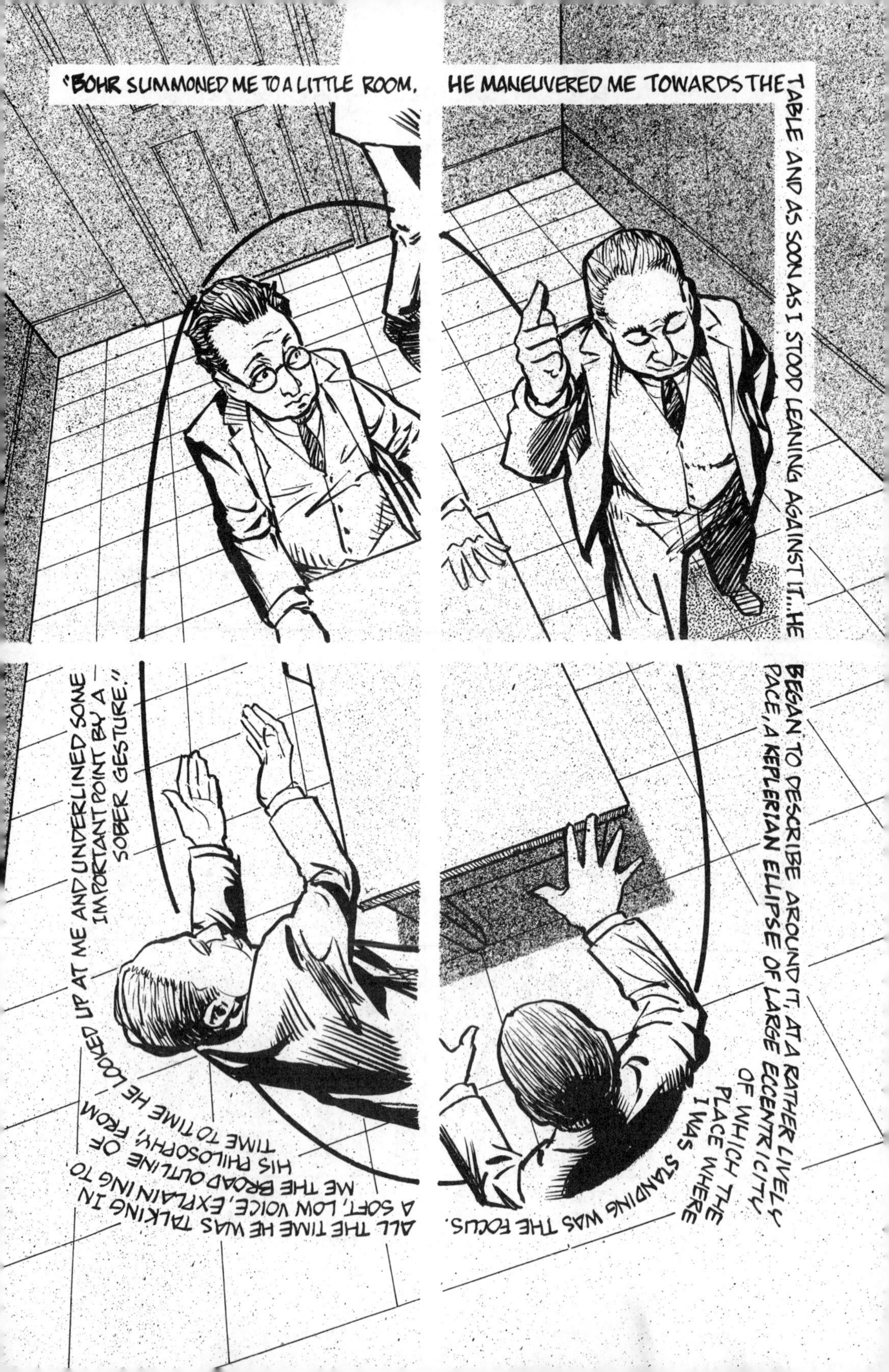
"BOHR SUMMONED ME TO A LITTLE ROOM.
HE MANEUVERED ME TOWARDS THE TABLE AND AS SOON AS I STOOD LEANING AGAINST IT...HE
BEGAN TO DESCRIBE AROUND IT, AT A RATHER LIVELY PACE, A KEPLERIAN ELLIPSE OF LARGE ECCENTRICITY, OF WHICH THE PLACE WHERE I WAS STANDING WAS THE FOCUS.
ALL THE TIME HE WAS TALKING IN A SOFT, LOW VOICE, EXPLAINING TO ME THE BROAD OUTLINE OF HIS PHILOSOPHY. FROM TIME TO TIME HE LOOKED UP AT ME AND UNDERLINED SOME IMPORTANT POINT BY A SOBER GESTURE."

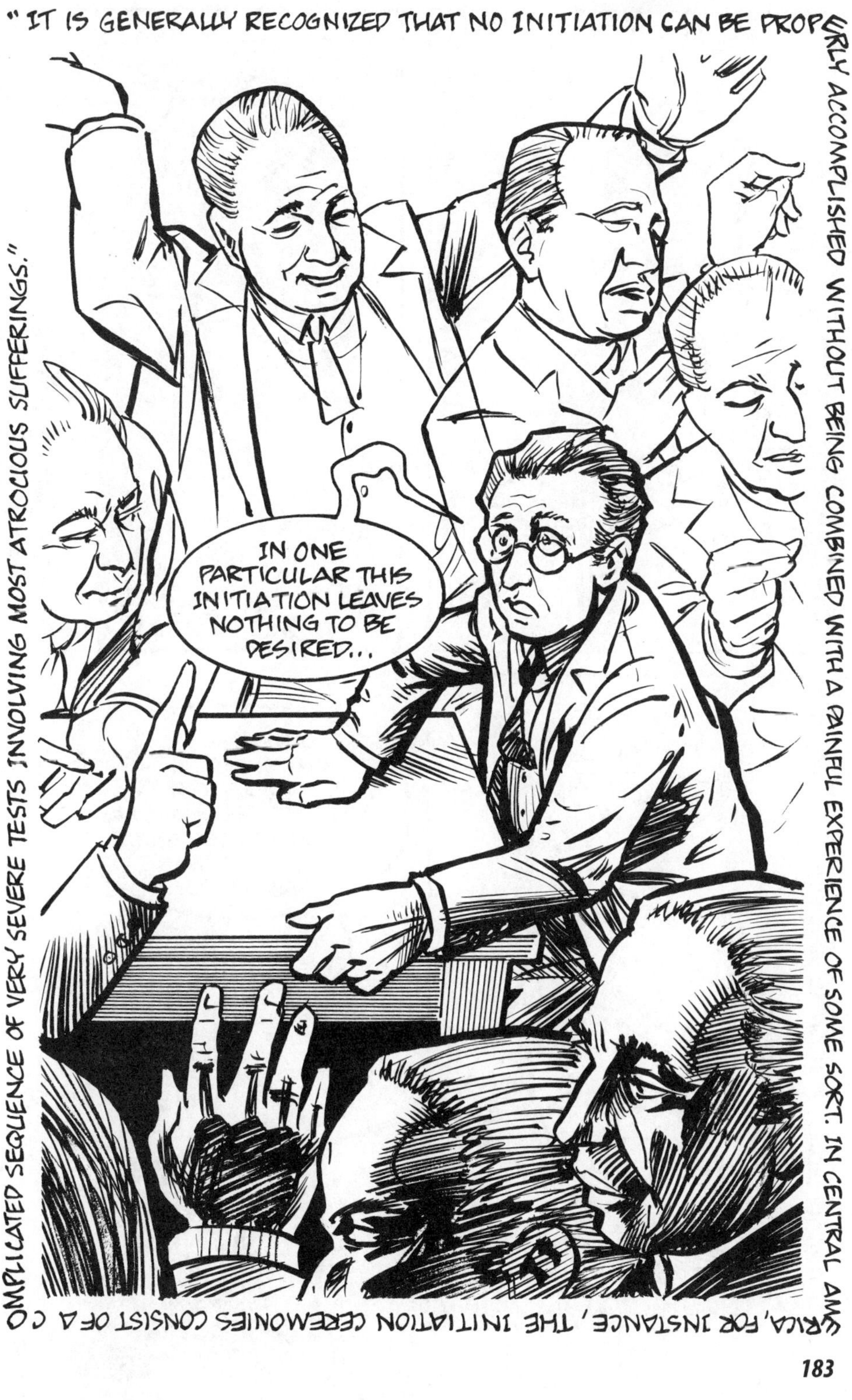
"IT IS GENERALLY RECOGNIZED THAT NO INITIATION CAN BE PROPERLY ACCOMPLISHED WITHOUT BEING COMBINED WITH A PAINFUL EXPERIENCE OF SOME SORT. IN CENTRAL AMERICA, FOR INSTANCE, THE INITIATION CEREMONIES CONSIST OF A COMPLICATED SEQUENCE OF VERY SEVERE TESTS INVOLVING MOST ATROCIOUS SUFFERINGS."
IN ONE PARTICULAR THIS INITIATION LEAVES NOTHING TO BE DESIRED...

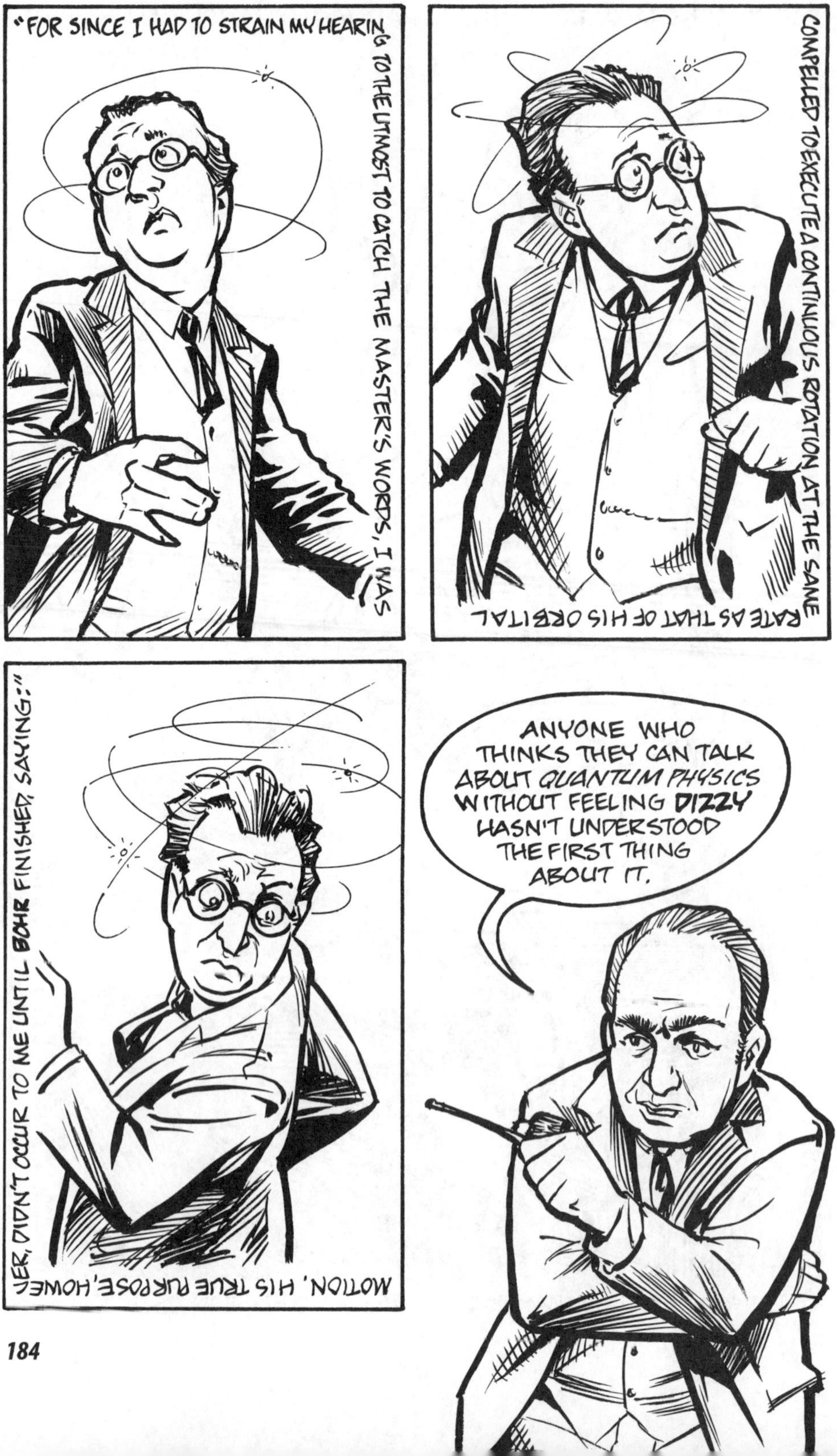

"FOR SINCE I HAD TO STRAIN MY HEARING TO THE UTMOST TO CATCH THE MASTER'S WORDS, I WAS
COMPELLED TO EXECUTE A CONTINUOUS ROTATION AT THE SAME RATE AS THAT OF HIS ORBITAL
MOTION, HIS TRUE PURPOSE, HOWEVER, DIDN'T OCCUR TO ME UNTIL BOHR FINISHED, SAYING:"
ANYONE WHO THINKS THEY CAN TALK ABOUT *QUANTUM PHYSICS* WITHOUT FEELING **DIZZY** HASN'T UNDERSTOOD THE FIRST THING ABOUT IT.

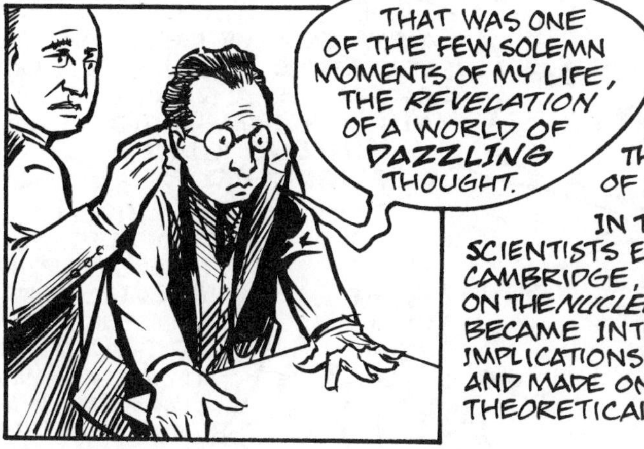
THAT WAS ONE OF THE FEW SOLEMN MOMENTS OF MY LIFE, THE *REVELATION* OF A WORLD OF **DAZZLING** THOUGHT.

AS FOR **BOHR** AND HIS INSTITUTE, THE *THOUGHT* TURNED INCREASINGLY TOWARDS THE OVERALL STRUCTURE OF THE **ATOM.**

IN THE MID 1930s, AS SCIENTISTS ELSEWHERE (BERLIN, CAMBRIDGE, AND ROME) FOCUSED ON THE *NUCLEUS*, **BOHR** OF COURSE BECAME INTERESTED IN THE IMPLICATIONS OF THEIR EXPERIMENTS, AND MADE ONE OF HIS LAST MAJOR THEORETICAL CONTRIBUTIONS.

This is the atom that Bohr built:

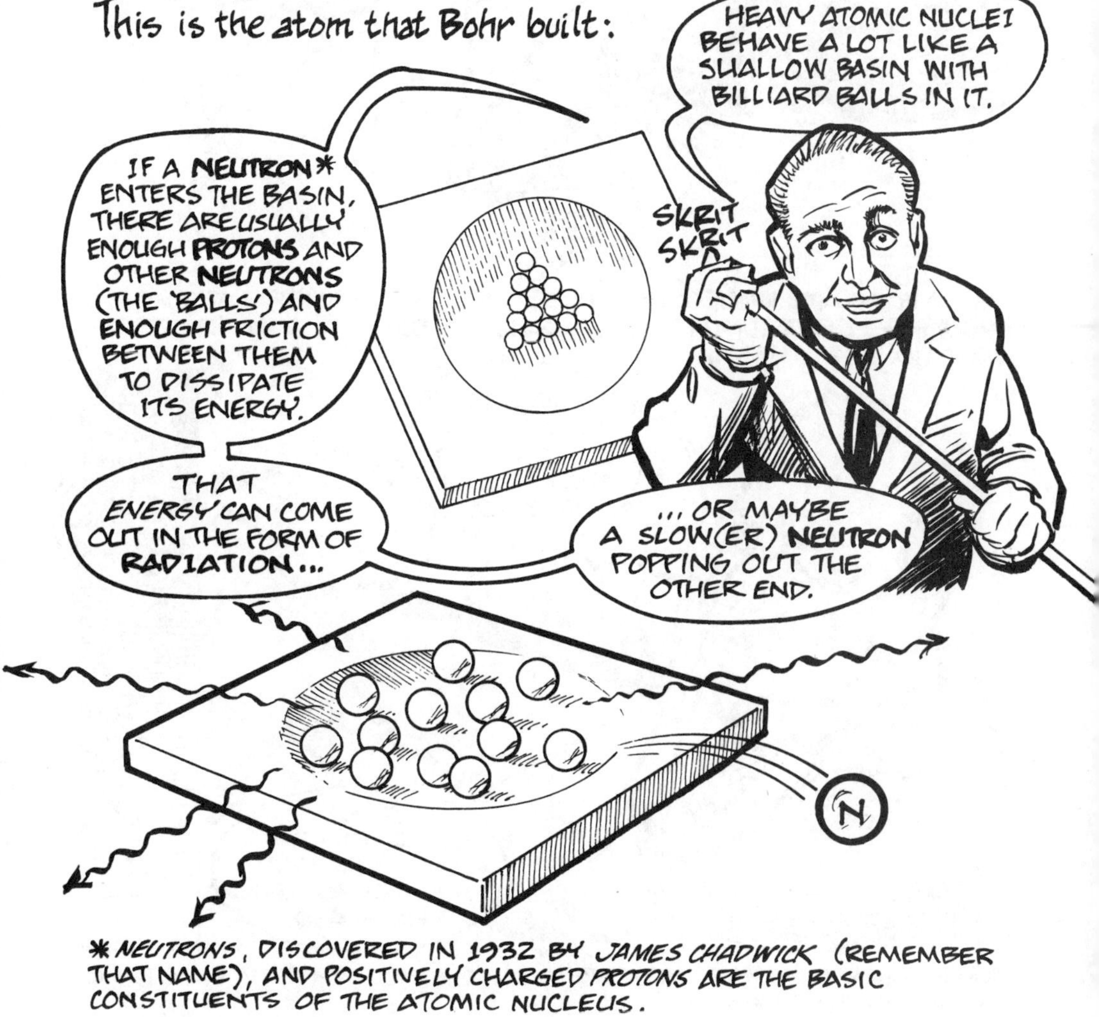
HEAVY ATOMIC NUCLEI BEHAVE A LOT LIKE A SHALLOW BASIN WITH BILLIARD BALLS IN IT.
SKRIT SKRIT SKR
IF A **NEUTRON*** ENTERS THE BASIN, THERE ARE USUALLY ENOUGH **PROTONS** AND OTHER **NEUTRONS** (THE 'BALLS') AND ENOUGH FRICTION BETWEEN THEM TO DISSIPATE ITS ENERGY.
THAT *ENERGY* CAN COME OUT IN THE FORM OF **RADIATION...**
...OR MAYBE A SLOW(ER) **NEUTRON** POPPING OUT THE OTHER END.
N

* *NEUTRONS*, DISCOVERED IN 1932 BY *JAMES CHADWICK* (REMEMBER THAT NAME), AND POSITIVELY CHARGED *PROTONS* ARE THE BASIC CONSTITUENTS OF THE ATOMIC NUCLEUS.

This is the drop
That looks like the nucleus
That sits in the atom
That Bohr built.

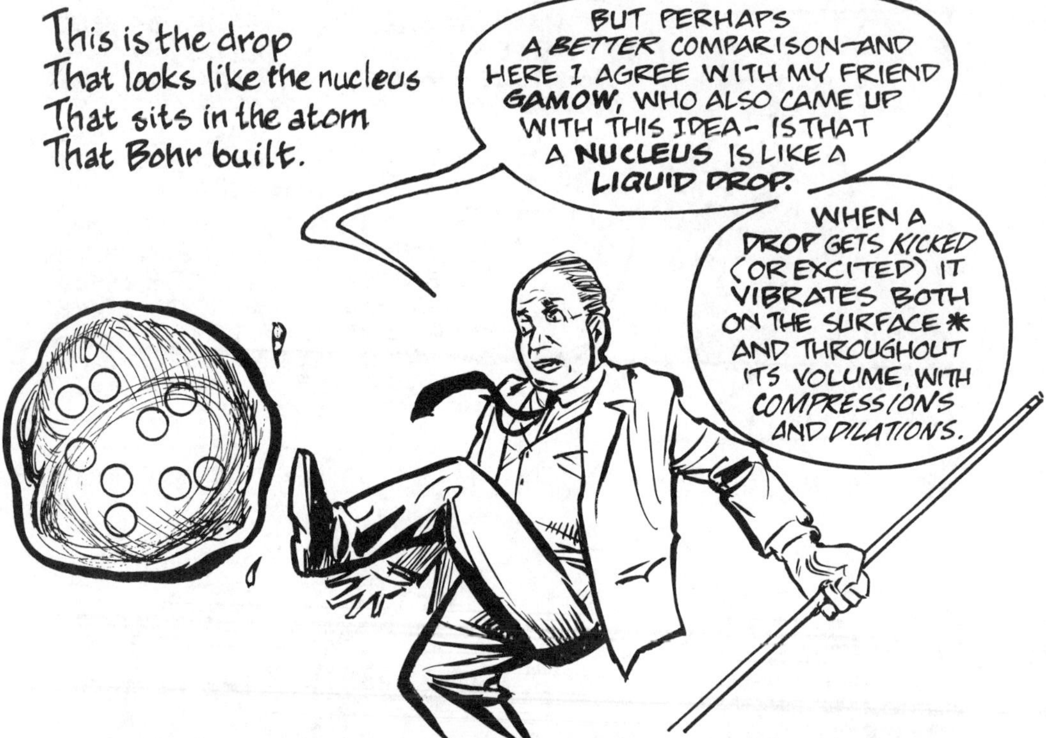
BUT PERHAPS A *BETTER* COMPARISON—AND HERE I AGREE WITH MY FRIEND **GAMOW**, WHO ALSO CAME UP WITH THIS IDEA- IS THAT A **NUCLEUS** IS LIKE A **LIQUID DROP.**
WHEN A **DROP** GETS *KICKED* (OR EXCITED) IT VIBRATES BOTH ON THE SURFACE * AND THROUGHOUT ITS VOLUME, WITH *COMPRESSIONS* AND *DILATIONS.*

VIBRATIONS ARE **WAVES**, OF COURSE, AND WHERE THERE ARE *WAVES* THERE'S THE OPPORTUNITY TO APPLY **HEISENBERG'S** OR **SCHRÖDINGER'S** EQUATIONS *TO* THEM.

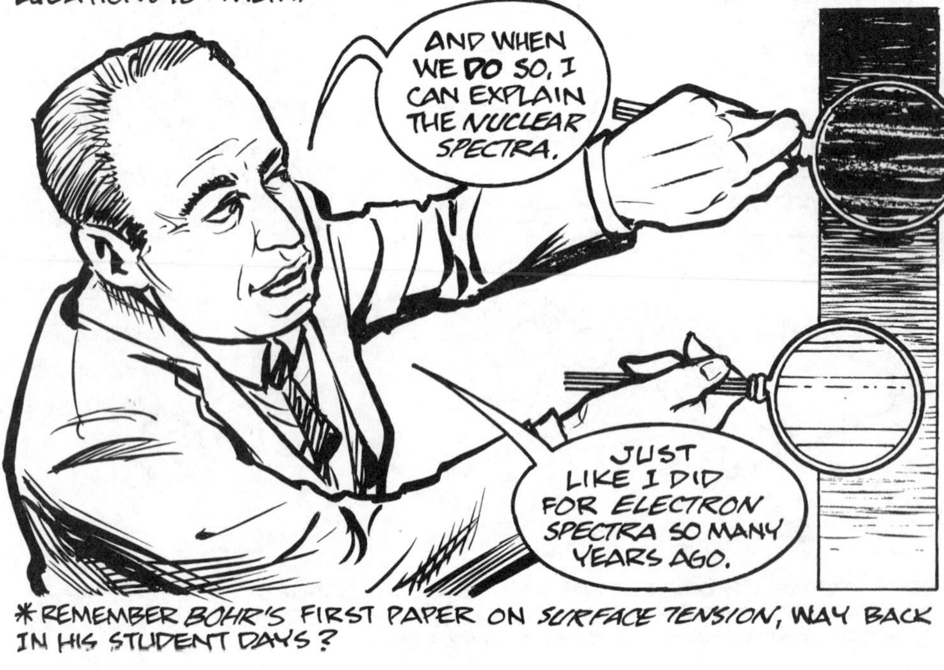
AND WHEN WE **DO** SO, I CAN EXPLAIN THE *NUCLEAR SPECTRA.*
JUST LIKE I DID FOR *ELECTRON SPECTRA* SO MANY YEARS AGO.

* REMEMBER *BOHR'S* FIRST PAPER ON *SURFACE TENSION*, WAY BACK IN HIS STUDENT DAYS?

SO, WAS THIS ANOTHER ONE OF **BOHR'S** GROUND-BREAKING —BUT ULTIMATELY WRONG— MODELS?

WELL, SCIENTISTS EVERYWHERE WERE SHOOTING **NEUTRONS** INTO **HEAVY ATOMS** LIKE *RADIUM* AND *URANIUM*. THE GREAT EXPERIMENTALIST **FERMI** WAS DOING SO IN ROME...

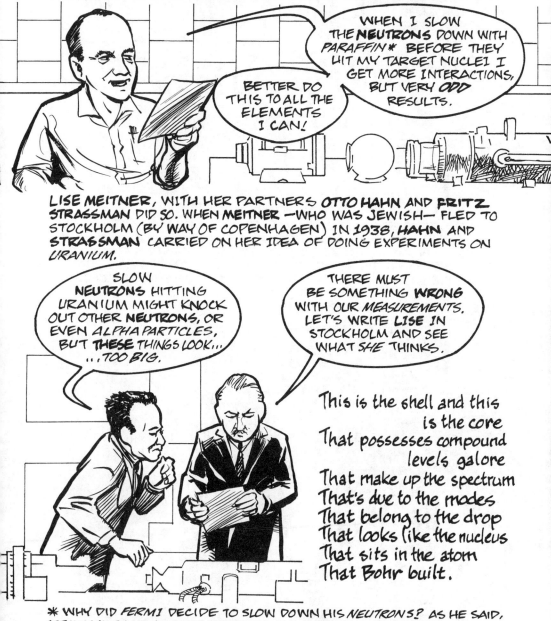

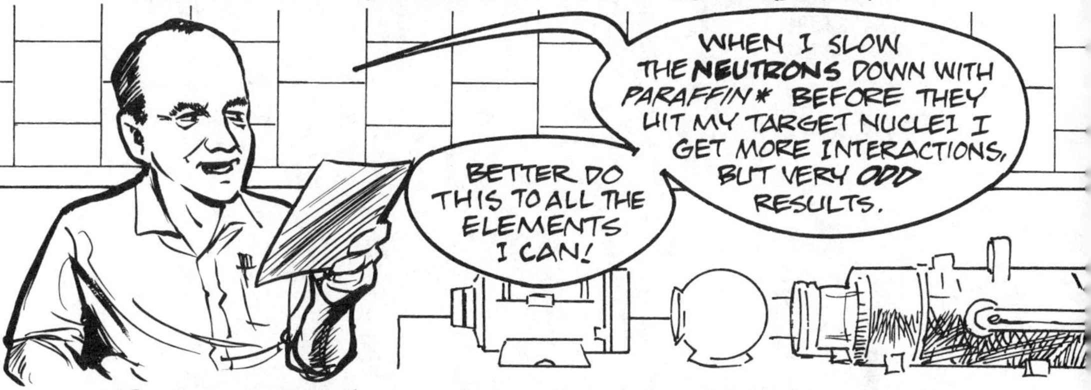
WHEN I SLOW THE **NEUTRONS** DOWN WITH *PARAFFIN** BEFORE THEY HIT MY TARGET NUCLEI I GET MORE INTERACTIONS, BUT VERY ***ODD*** RESULTS.
BETTER DO THIS TO ALL THE ELEMENTS I CAN!

LISE MEITNER, WITH HER PARTNERS **OTTO HAHN** AND **FRITZ STRASSMAN** DID SO. WHEN **MEITNER** —WHO WAS JEWISH— FLED TO STOCKHOLM (BY WAY OF COPENHAGEN) IN **1938**, **HAHN** AND **STRASSMAN** CARRIED ON HER IDEA OF DOING EXPERIMENTS ON *URANIUM*.

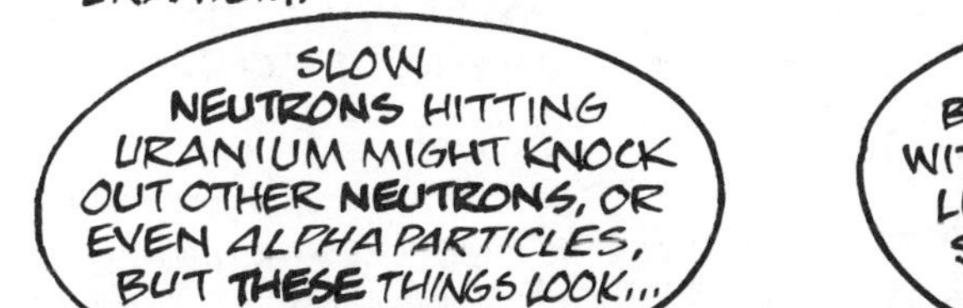
SLOW **NEUTRONS** HITTING URANIUM MIGHT KNOCK OUT OTHER **NEUTRONS**, OR EVEN *ALPHA PARTICLES*, BUT **THESE** THINGS LOOK... ...*TOO BIG*.
THERE MUST BE SOMETHING **WRONG** WITH OUR *MEASUREMENTS*. LET'S WRITE **LISE** IN STOCKHOLM AND SEE WHAT *SHE* THINKS.

This is the shell and this
is the core
That possesses compound
levels galore
That make up the spectrum
That's due to the modes
That belong to the drop
That looks like the nucleus
That sits in the atom
That Bohr built.

* WHY DID *FERMI* DECIDE TO SLOW DOWN HIS *NEUTRONS*? AS HE SAID, "IT WAS WITH NO ADVANCE WARNING, NO CONSCIOUS PRIOR REASONING..." WHICH ON THE EXPERIMENTAL SIDE CORRESPONDS TO (OR SHOULD WE SAY *COMPLEMENTS*?) BOHR'S LEGENDARY THEORETICAL INTUITION.

BACK IN COPENHAGEN, **BOHR'S** EXPERIMENTAL TEAM WAS TESTING **NEUTRON** ABSORPTION IN *CADMIUM, BORON...*

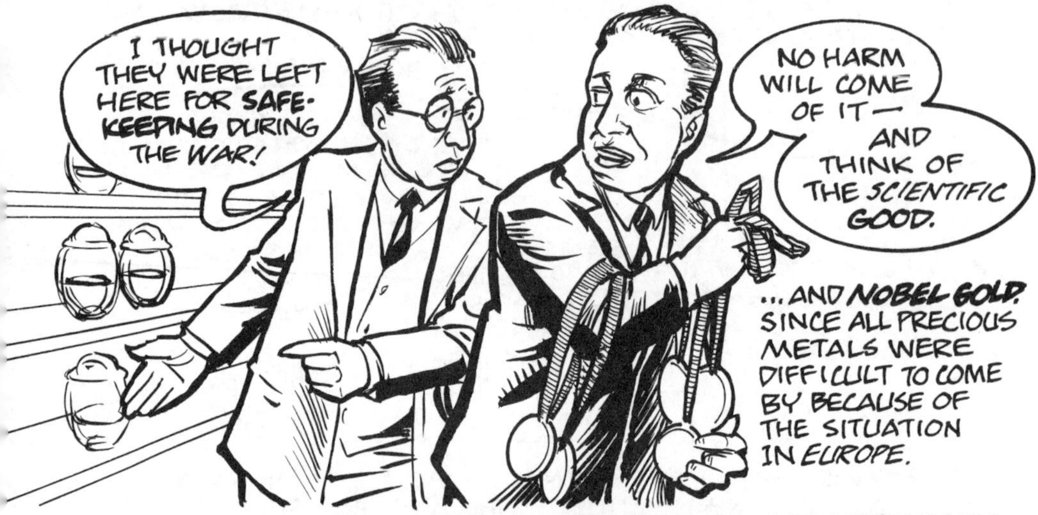
I THOUGHT THEY WERE LEFT HERE FOR **SAFE-KEEPING** DURING THE *WAR!*
NO HARM WILL COME OF IT— AND THINK OF THE *SCIENTIFIC* **GOOD.**
...AND ***NOBEL GOLD.*** SINCE ALL PRECIOUS METALS WERE DIFFICULT TO COME BY BECAUSE OF THE SITUATION IN *EUROPE.*

THIS SITUATION BROUGHT **ENRICO FERMI** BRIEFLY TO *COPENHAGEN* IN 1938. EARLIER THAT YEAR **BOHR** HAD BROKEN PROTOCOL AND HINTED TO **FERMI** THAT HE WAS UNDER CONSIDERATION FOR THE *NOBEL PRIZE*. WHEN HE WENT TO *STOCKHOLM* THAT DECEMBER TO RECEIVE HIS MEDAL —AND THE EVEN MORE IMPORTANT MONEY THAT WENT WITH IT— **FERMI**, HIS (JEWISH) WIFE, AND CHILDREN CAME PREPARED FOR A *LONG* TRIP.

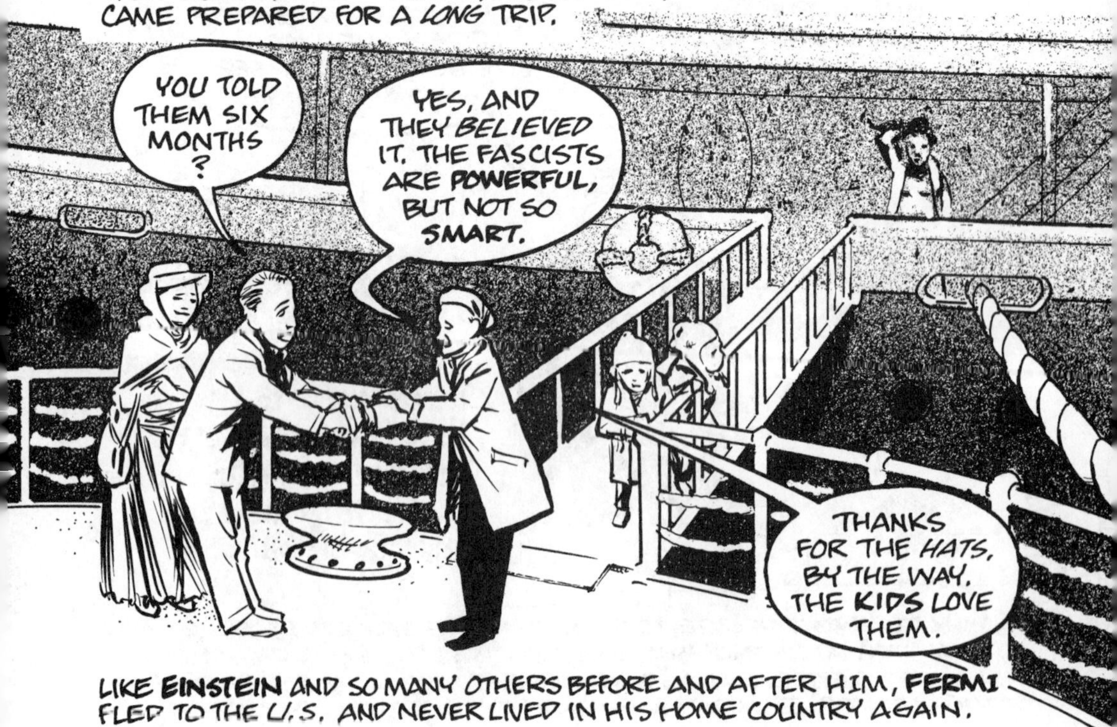
YOU TOLD THEM SIX MONTHS?
YES, AND THEY *BELIEVED* IT. THE FASCISTS ARE **POWERFUL**, BUT NOT SO **SMART.**
THANKS FOR THE *HATS*, BY THE WAY. THE **KIDS** LOVE THEM.

LIKE **EINSTEIN** AND SO MANY OTHERS BEFORE AND AFTER HIM, **FERMI** FLED TO THE *U.S.* AND NEVER LIVED IN HIS HOME COUNTRY AGAIN.

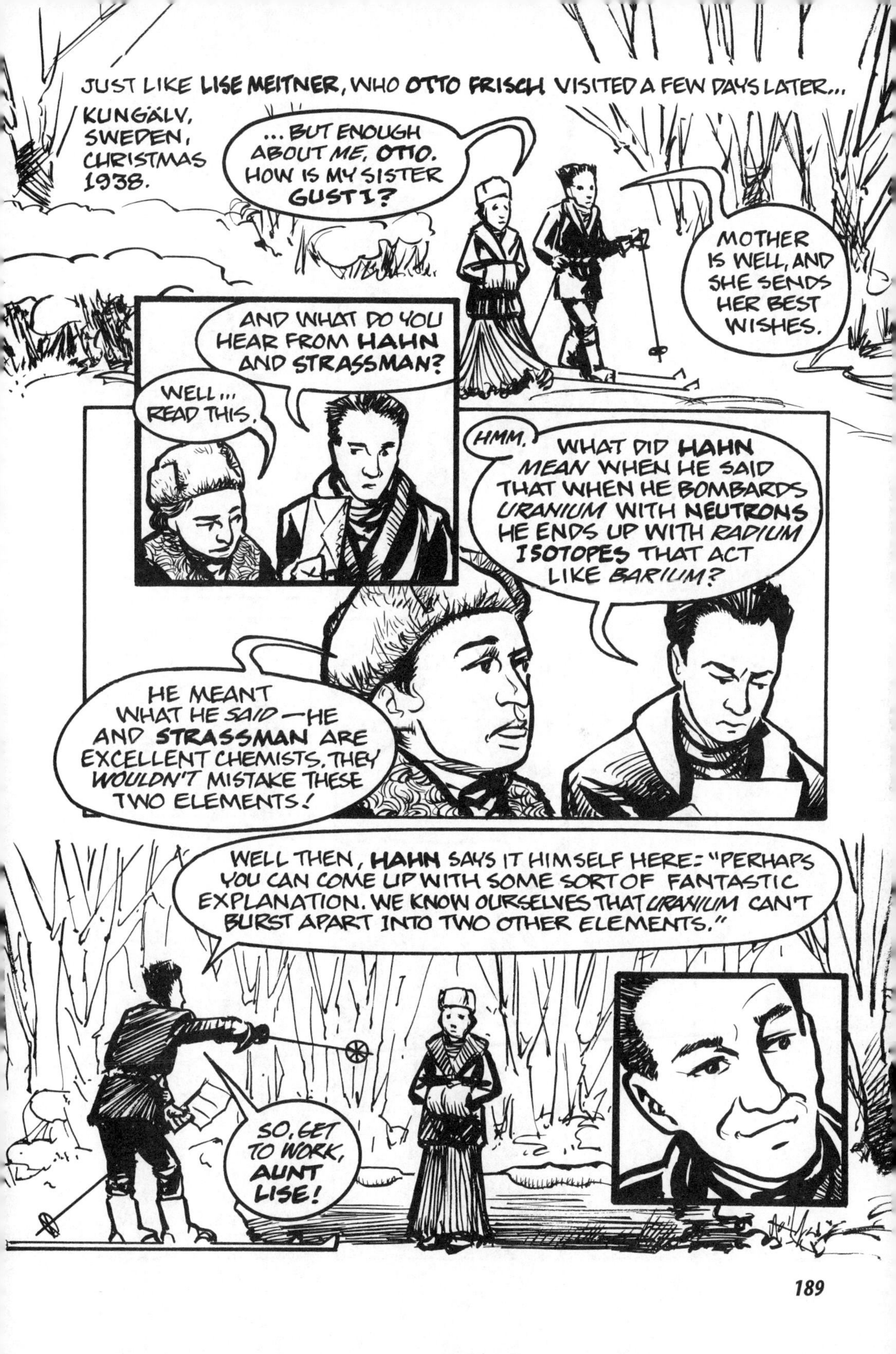
JUST LIKE LISE MEITNER, WHO OTTO FRISCH VISITED A FEW DAYS LATER...
KUNGÄLV, SWEDEN, CHRISTMAS 1938.
... BUT ENOUGH ABOUT ME, OTTO. HOW IS MY SISTER GUSTI?
MOTHER IS WELL, AND SHE SENDS HER BEST WISHES.
AND WHAT DO YOU HEAR FROM HAHN AND STRASSMAN?
WELL... READ THIS.
HMM.
WHAT DID HAHN MEAN WHEN HE SAID THAT WHEN HE BOMBARDS URANIUM WITH NEUTRONS HE ENDS UP WITH RADIUM ISOTOPES THAT ACT LIKE BARIUM?
HE MEANT WHAT HE SAID—HE AND STRASSMAN ARE EXCELLENT CHEMISTS. THEY WOULDN'T MISTAKE THESE TWO ELEMENTS!
WELL THEN, HAHN SAYS IT HIMSELF HERE: "PERHAPS YOU CAN COME UP WITH SOME SORT OF FANTASTIC EXPLANATION. WE KNOW OURSELVES THAT URANIUM CAN'T BURST APART INTO TWO OTHER ELEMENTS."
SO, GET TO WORK, AUNT LISE!

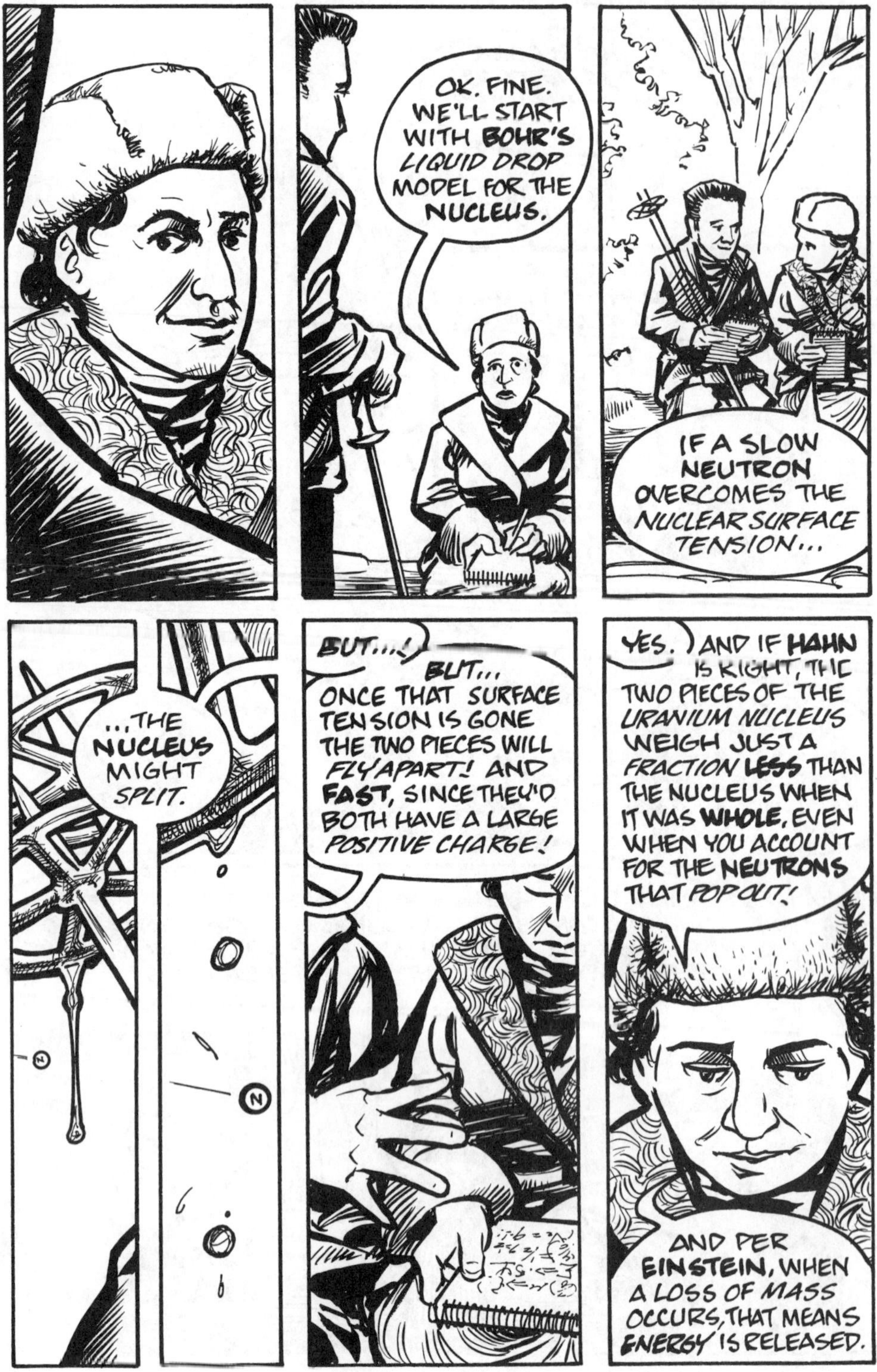
OK. FINE. WE'LL START WITH BOHR'S LIQUID DROP MODEL FOR THE NUCLEUS.
IF A SLOW NEUTRON OVERCOMES THE NUCLEAR SURFACE TENSION...
...THE NUCLEUS MIGHT SPLIT.
BUT...!
BUT... ONCE THAT SURFACE TENSION IS GONE THE TWO PIECES WILL FLY APART! AND FAST, SINCE THEY'D BOTH HAVE A LARGE POSITIVE CHARGE!
YES.
AND IF HAHN IS RIGHT, THE TWO PIECES OF THE URANIUM NUCLEUS WEIGH JUST A FRACTION LESS THAN THE NUCLEUS WHEN IT WAS WHOLE, EVEN WHEN YOU ACCOUNT FOR THE NEUTRONS THAT POP OUT!
AND PER EINSTEIN, WHEN A LOSS OF MASS OCCURS, THAT MEANS ENERGY IS RELEASED.

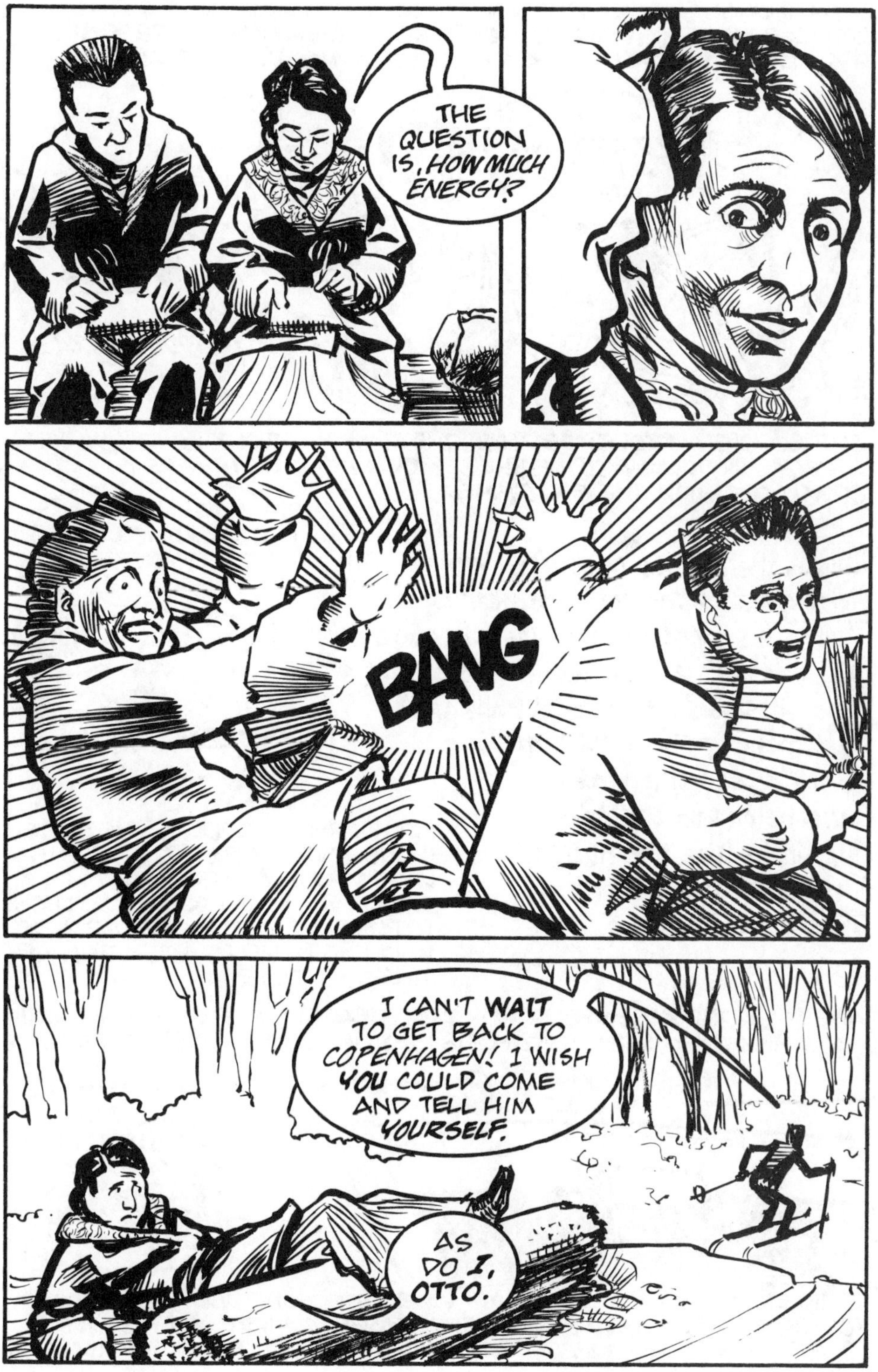
THE QUESTION IS, HOW MUCH ENERGY?
BANG
I CAN'T WAIT TO GET BACK TO COPENHAGEN! I WISH YOU COULD COME AND TELL HIM YOURSELF.
AS DO I, OTTO.

EVEN THOUGH **BOHR** (LIKE EVERYONE ELSE) HAD MISSED THE IMPLICATIONS OF HIS WORK (THIS ONE TIME), WHEN **FRISCH** PRESENTED HIS AUNT'S THEORY, **BOHR** (AS USUAL) WAS DELIGHTED.

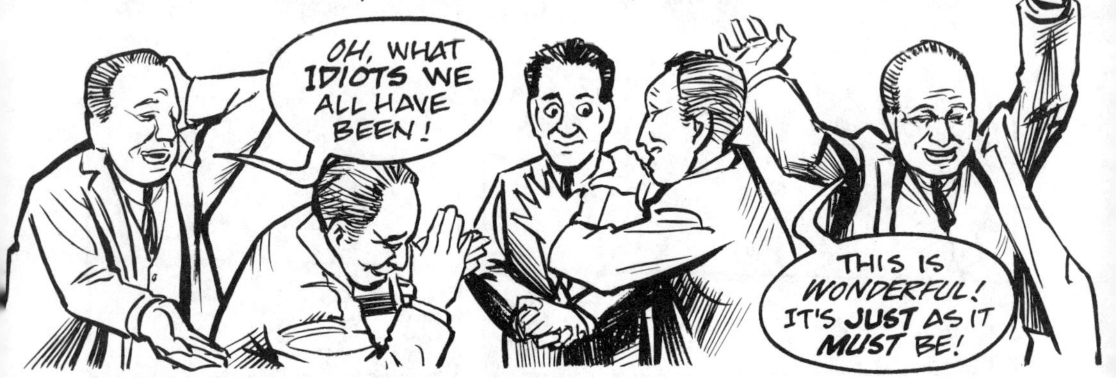
OH, WHAT **IDIOTS** WE ALL HAVE BEEN!
THIS IS *WONDERFUL!* IT'S **JUST** AS IT ***MUST*** BE!

AND SO, IT'S APPROPRIATE THAT "THE ATOM THAT BOHR BUILT", WHICH APPEARS IN VOLUME III OF THE *JOURNAL OF JOCULAR PHYSICS* CONCLUDES WITH THE FOLLOWING:

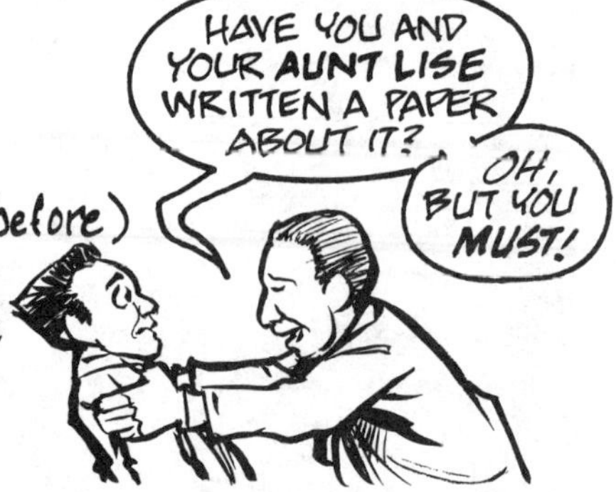
HAVE YOU AND YOUR **AUNT LISE** WRITTEN A PAPER ABOUT IT?
OH, BUT YOU **MUST!**

This is the day we celebrate Bohr
Who gave us the complementarity
That gives correspondence (as Bohr said before)
That holds in the shell, as well as the core
That possesses the compound levels galore
That make up the spectrum
That's due to the modes
That belong to the drop
That looks like the nucleus
That sits in the atom
That Bohr built.

FOR **BOHR'S** MODEL OF THE NUCLEUS, THOUGH NOT PERFECT*, WAS HIS LAST MAJOR CONTRIBUTION IN A *LONG LINE* OF MAJOR CONTRIBUTIONS TO **PHYSICS.** AND HIS *LIQUID DROP* MODEL STILL HELPS SCIENTISTS GET THE JOB DONE.

AND SO HE AND **ROSENFELD** TOOK **MEITNER'S** AND **FRISCH'S** RESULTS —AND HIS OWN— WITH HIM ON HIS JANUARY 1939 TRIP TO THE ***U.S.***

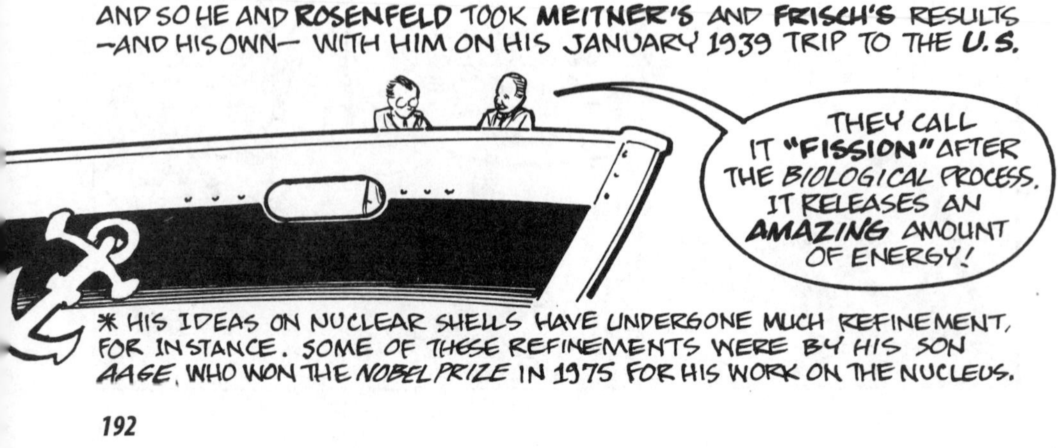
THEY CALL IT **"FISSION"** AFTER THE *BIOLOGICAL PROCESS.* IT RELEASES AN ***AMAZING*** AMOUNT OF ENERGY!

* HIS IDEAS ON NUCLEAR SHELLS HAVE UNDERGONE MUCH REFINEMENT, FOR INSTANCE. SOME OF THESE REFINEMENTS WERE BY HIS SON *AAGE*, WHO WON THE *NOBEL PRIZE* IN 1975 FOR HIS WORK ON THE NUCLEUS.

AND WHEN THEY ARRIVED, **ROSENFELD** TOLD **JOHN WHEELER**.

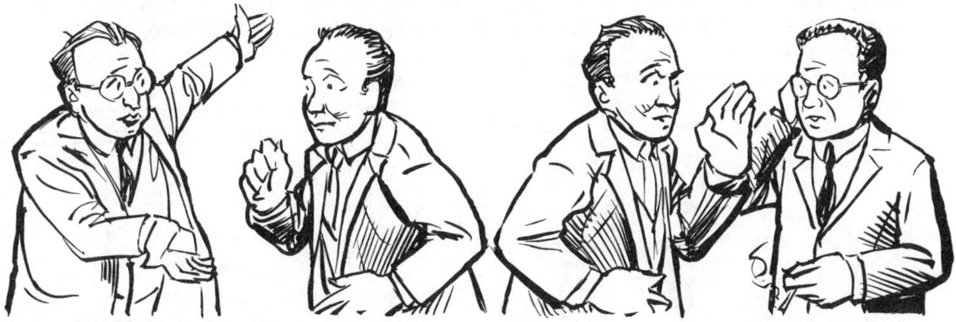

WHEELER MENTIONED IT TO **I.I. RABI**, WHO TOOK THE NEWS BACK TO *COLUMBIA UNIVERSITY*...

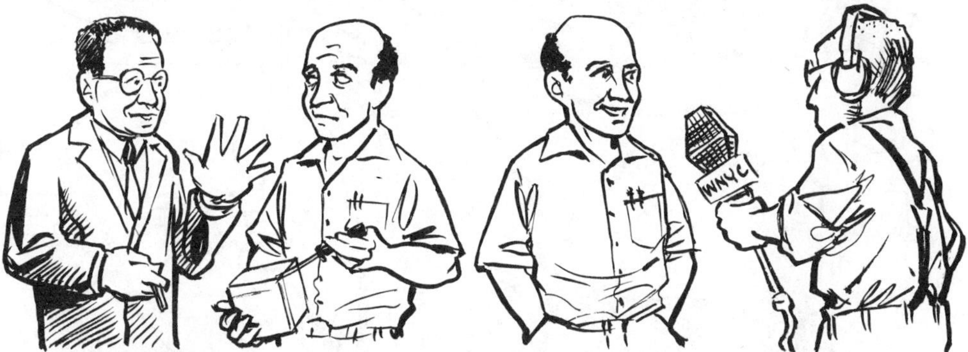
WNYC

...WHERE **FERMI** HAD SETTLED. **FERMI** MENTIONED **FISSION** ON THE *RADIO*, AND...

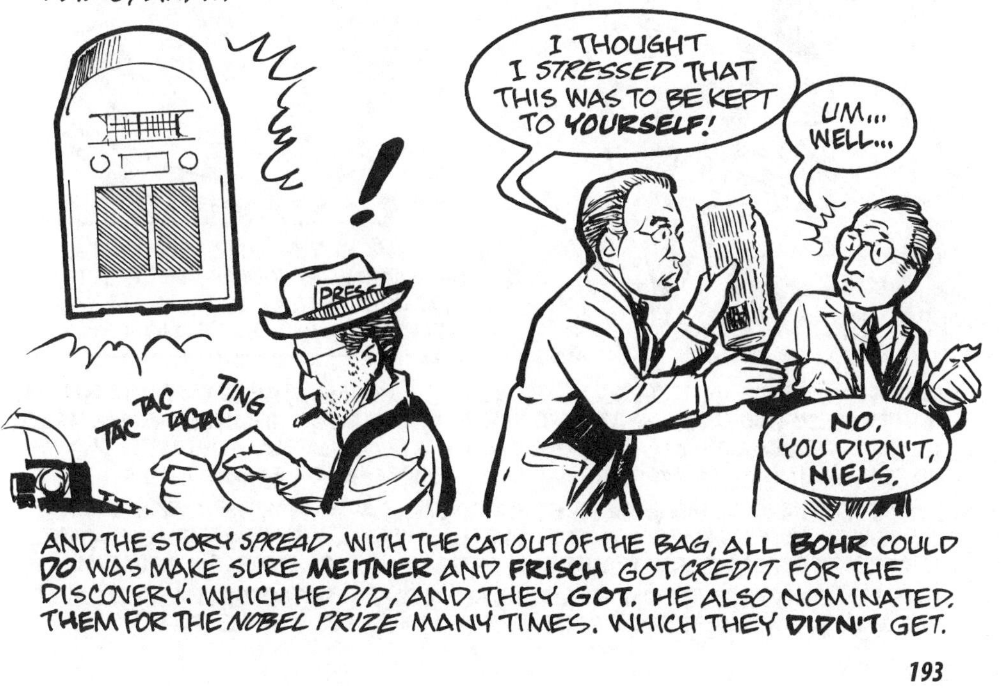
!
PRESS
TAC TAC TACTAC TING
I THOUGHT I *STRESSED* THAT THIS WAS TO BE KEPT TO **YOURSELF**!
UM... WELL...
NO, YOU DIDN'T, NIELS.

AND THE STORY *SPREAD*. WITH THE CAT OUT OF THE BAG, ALL **BOHR** COULD **DO** WAS MAKE SURE **MEITNER** AND **FRISCH** GOT *CREDIT* FOR THE DISCOVERY. WHICH HE *DID*, AND THEY **GOT**. HE ALSO NOMINATED **THEM** FOR THE *NOBEL PRIZE* MANY TIMES. WHICH THEY **DIDN'T** GET.

THINGS HAPPENED FAST AFTER THIS: **BOHR** SOON RECOGNIZED THAT *FISSION* ONLY HAPPENED WITH *SLOW* **NEUTRONS** IN **U-235**, A RARE* ISOTOPE OF *URANIUM* WITH **143 NEUTRONS** AND 92 **PROTONS** IN ITS NUCLEUS. TO HIS GREAT IRRITATION NOT EVERYONE ACCEPTED THIS RIGHT AWAY.

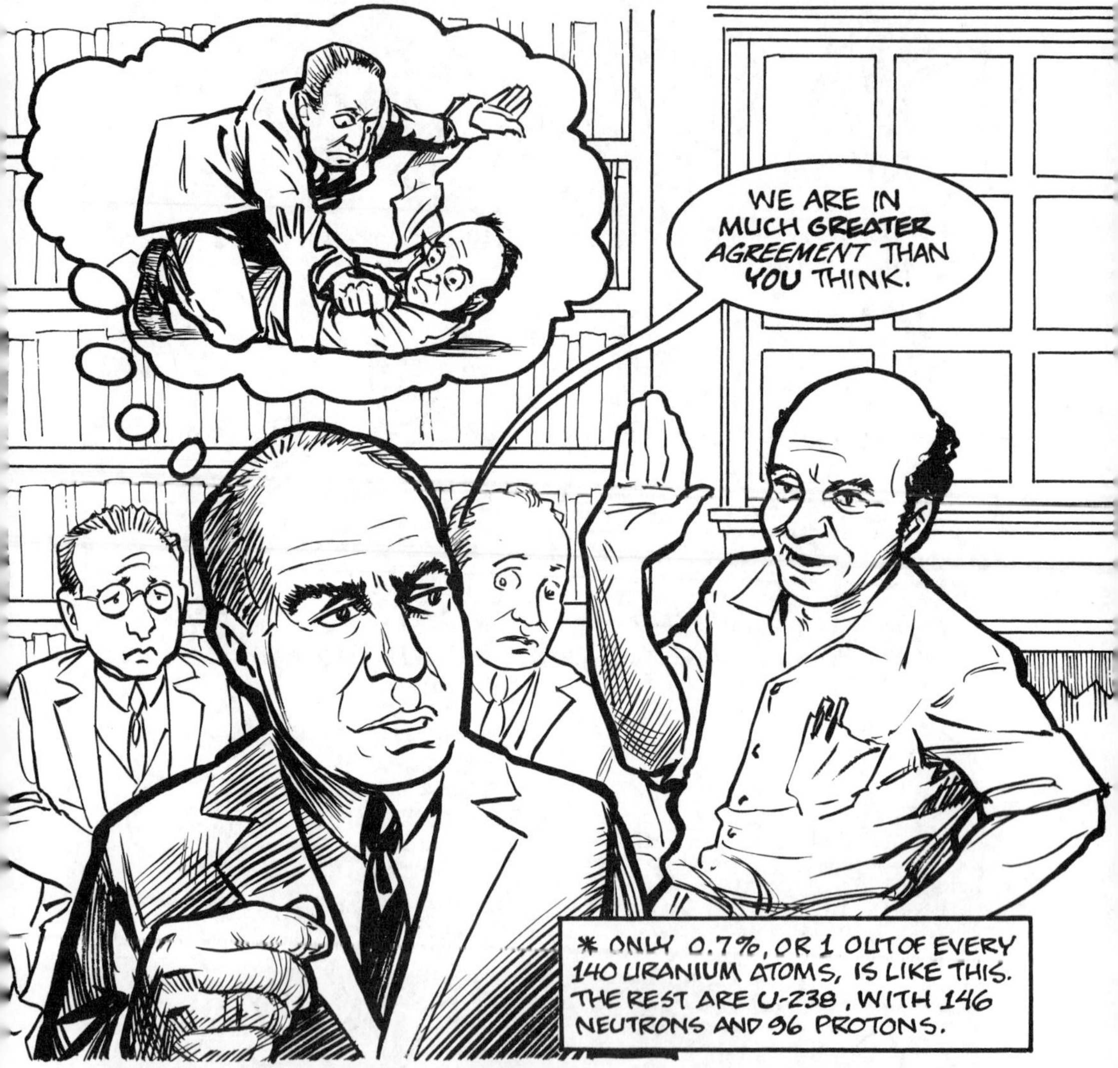
WE ARE IN MUCH **GREATER** *AGREEMENT* THAN **YOU** THINK.
* ONLY 0.7%, OR 1 OUT OF EVERY 140 URANIUM ATOMS, IS LIKE THIS. THE REST ARE U-238, WITH 146 NEUTRONS AND 96 PROTONS.

REGARDLESS OF WHICH ISOTOPE WAS SPLITTING, ONE DAY AFTER **HITLER** "LIBERATED" **SLOVAKIA** AND **RUTHENIA** TO INCORPORATE **CZECHOSLOVAKIA** IN THE *GERMAN REICH*, **FERMI'S** GROUP AT COLUMBIA SUBMITTED A PAPER OUTLINING **FISSION'S** HUGE ENERGY RELEASE...

...AND **BOHR** AND **WHEELER** SENT THEIR PAPER *"THE MECHANISM OF NUCLEAR FISSION"* TO THE PUBLISHER A FEW MONTHS LATER. IT APPEARED IN THE SEPTEMBER 1, 1939 ISSUE OF *PHYSICAL REVIEW*.

THIS TIME HISTORY DIDN'T WAIT EVEN A DAY —**HITLER'S** INVASION OF **POLAND** STARTED *WORLD WAR II* ON THAT VERY SAME DAY.

Chapter 11

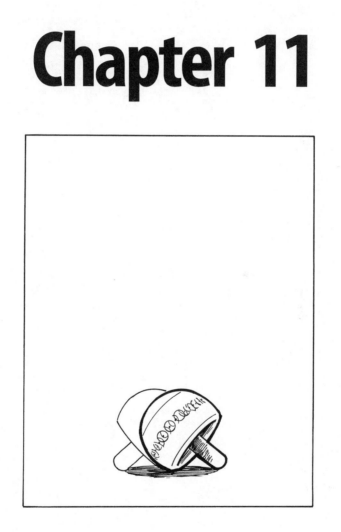

THE WAR IN EUROPE DIDN'T SLOW NUCLEAR PHYSICS RESEARCH APPRECIABLY—ESPECIALLY SINCE SO MANY TOP PHYSICISTS HAD HEADED *WEST.* **OTTO FRISCH** AND **RUDOLPH PEIERLS*** HAD SETTLED IN *ENGLAND* WHILE OTHERS, LIKE **FERMI** AND **EINSTEIN** BEFORE THEM, ENDED UP IN THE *U.S.*

BUT THE WAR **DID** LEND SOME *URGENCY* TO THAT RESEARCH, EVEN THOUGH THE PREDOMINANT VIEW WAS STILL MUCH LIKE **RUTHERFORD'S** IN 1933:

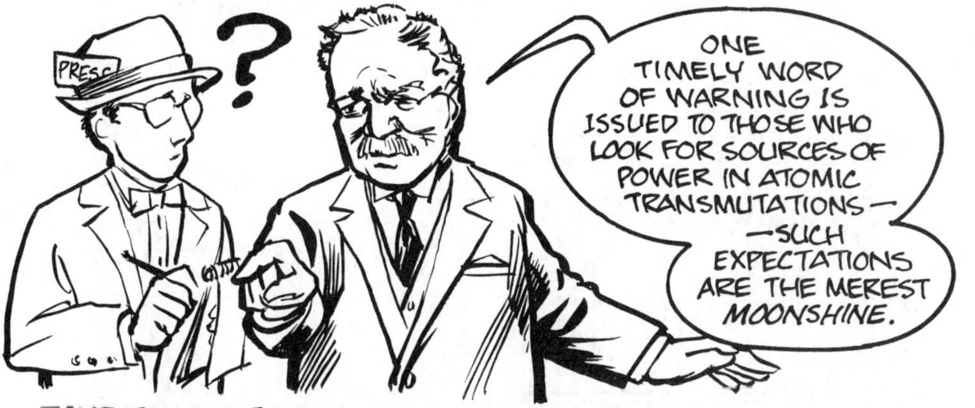
PRESS
?
ONE TIMELY WORD OF WARNING IS ISSUED TO THOSE WHO LOOK FOR SOURCES OF POWER IN ATOMIC TRANSMUTATIONS— —SUCH EXPECTATIONS ARE THE MEREST *MOONSHINE.*

BOHR *SHARED* THIS VIEW, THOUGH FOR *ENGINEERING* RATHER THAN SCIENTIFIC/THEORETICAL REASONS.

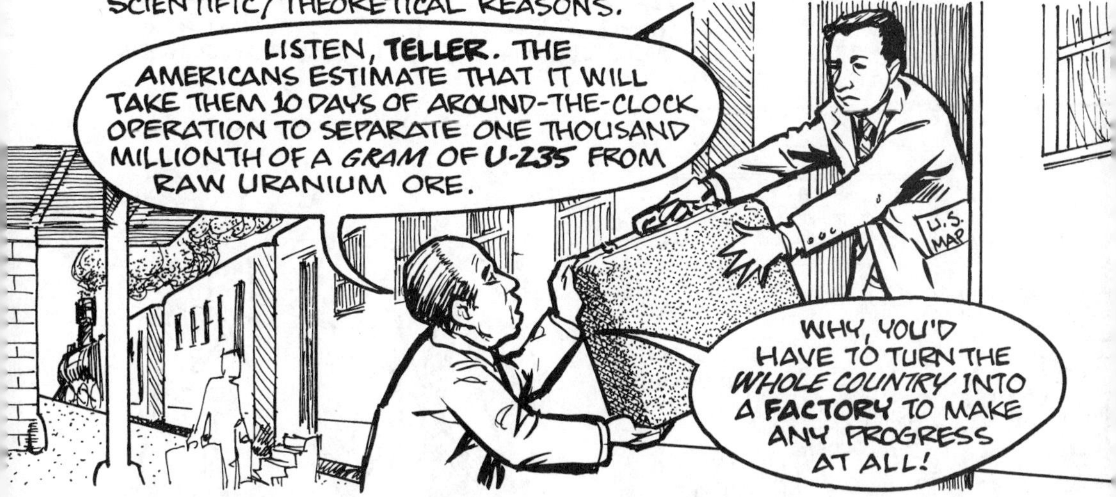
LISTEN, **TELLER**. THE AMERICANS ESTIMATE THAT IT WILL TAKE THEM 10 DAYS OF AROUND-THE-CLOCK OPERATION TO SEPARATE ONE THOUSAND MILLIONTH OF A *GRAM* OF **U-235** FROM RAW URANIUM ORE.
U.S. MAP
WHY, YOU'D HAVE TO TURN THE *WHOLE COUNTRY* INTO A **FACTORY** TO MAKE ANY PROGRESS AT ALL!

ABOUT A MONTH AFTER **FRISCH** AND **PEIERLS** MADE PUBLIC THEIR CALCULATIONS ON THE CRITICAL MASS OF *U-235* NEEDED FOR A *BOMB*— IT WAS *NOT* **TONS**, BUT IT *WAS* A LOT MORE THAN ONE THOUSAND MILLIONTH OF A GRAM! — *GERMANY* OCCUPIED *DENMARK* TO ENSURE THAT THE COUNTRY WOULD "ACCEPT THE PROTECTION OF THE REICH."

* RUDOLPH E. PEIERLS WAS (YET ANOTHER) OF *BOHR'S* COLLABORATORS. A TOP-NOTCH MATHEMATICIAN, A REFUGEE ... AND THE AUTHOR OF "*THE ATOM THAT BOHR BUILT.*"

BOHR HAD JUST COME FROM *NORWAY*, WHERE HE HAD REPORTED ON THE CONFIRMATION OF HIS **U-235** THEORY.

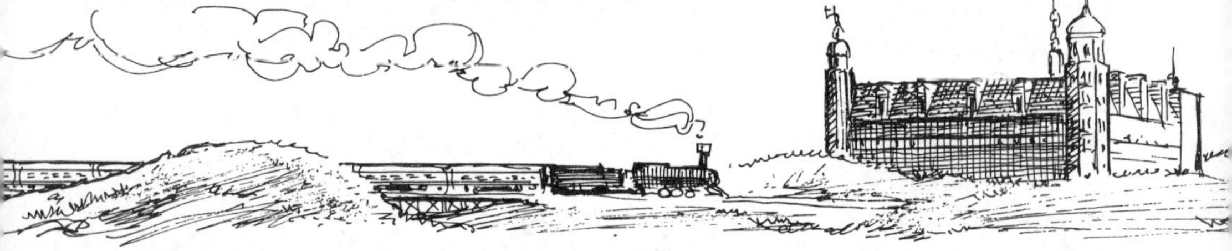

UPON HIS RETURN TO *COPENHAGEN*, HE WAS EFFECTIVELY UNDER HOUSE ARREST.

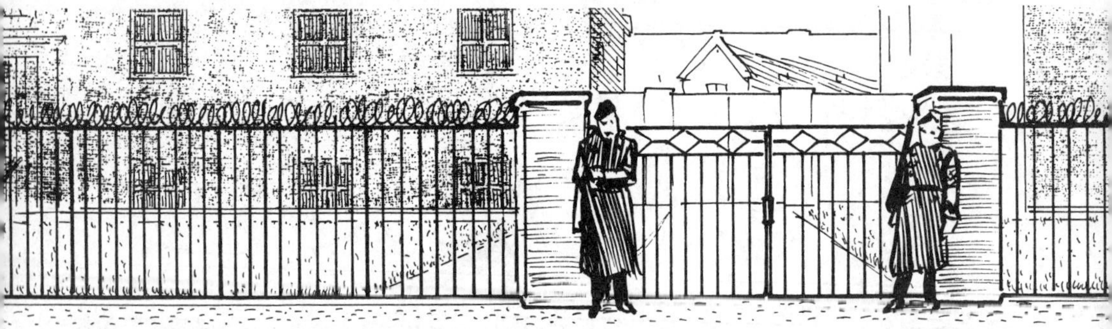

MESSAGES URGING **BOHR** TO *LEAVE IMMEDIATELY* BEGAN TO ARRIVE AT THE INSTITUTE. WITH A JEWISH MOTHER AND THEIR WORK ON PLACING REFUGEE INTELLECTUALS WELL KNOWN, **NIELS**, **HARALD** AND THEIR FAMILIES WERE TARGETS.

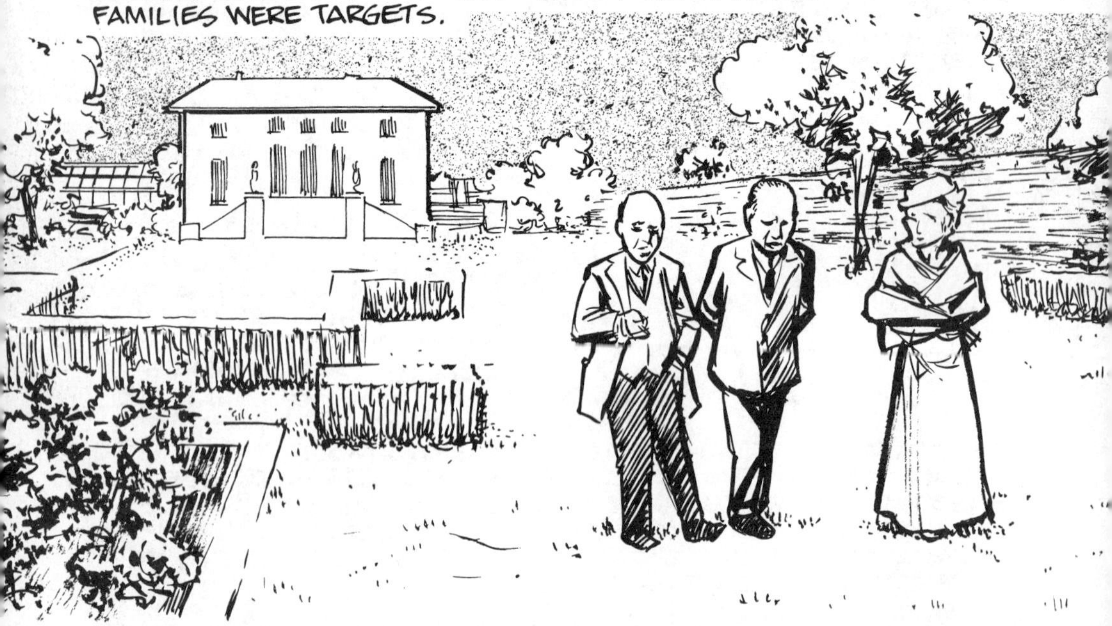

BUT THEY DECIDED TO STAY, SINCE THE **BOHR** BROTHERS WERE ALSO SYMBOLS OF *DANISH CULTURE* IN THE FACE OF **NAZI** EFFORTS TO ESTABLISH DOMINANCE. NOT SO MUCH BY PHYSICAL MEANS (YET), BUT MORE SUBTLY.

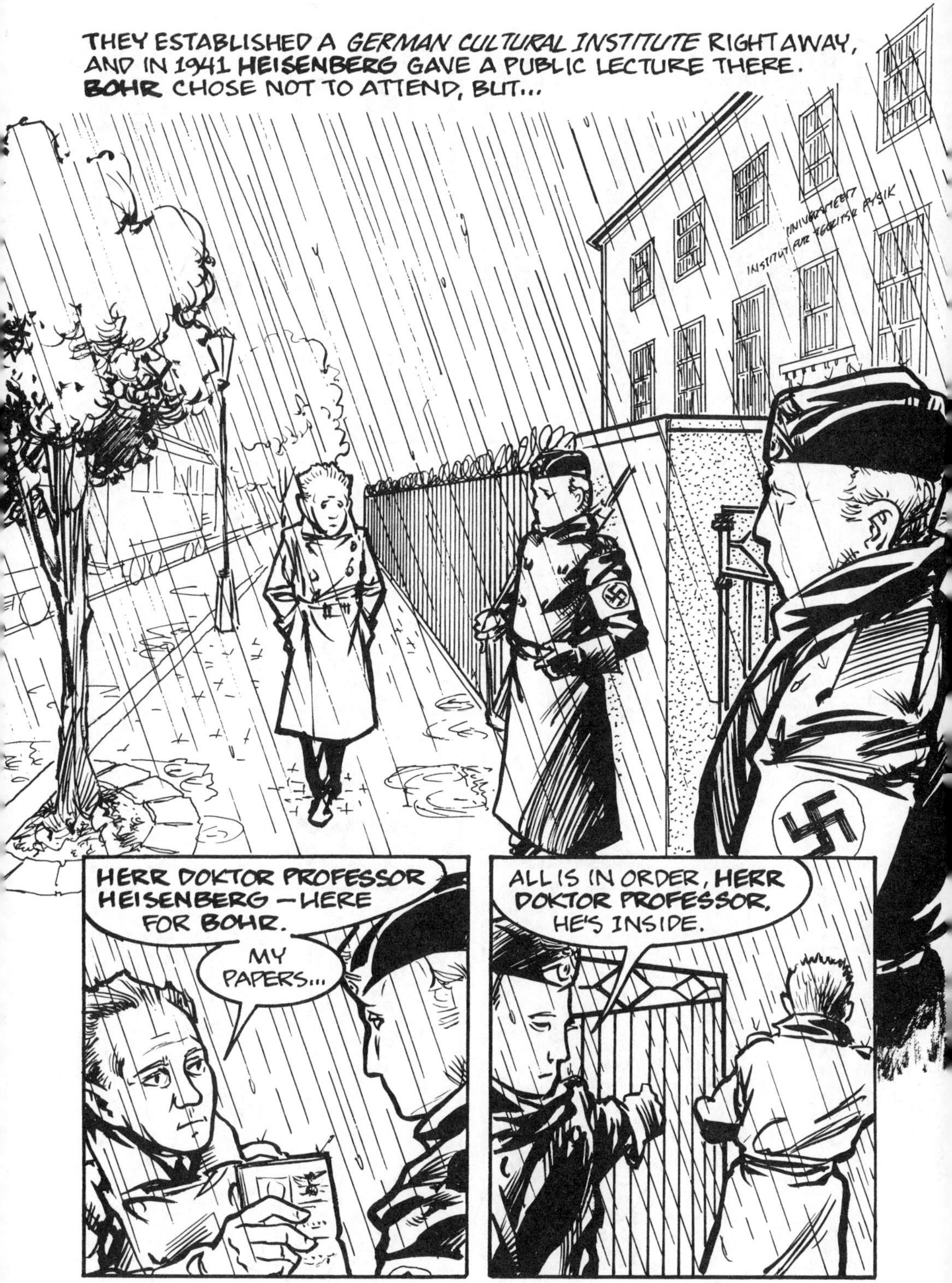
THEY ESTABLISHED A *GERMAN CULTURAL INSTITUTE* RIGHT AWAY, AND IN 1941 **HEISENBERG** GAVE A PUBLIC LECTURE THERE. **BOHR** CHOSE NOT TO ATTEND, BUT...
HERR DOKTOR PROFESSOR HEISENBERG—HERE FOR BOHR.
MY PAPERS...
ALL IS IN ORDER, HERR DOKTOR PROFESSOR. HE'S INSIDE.

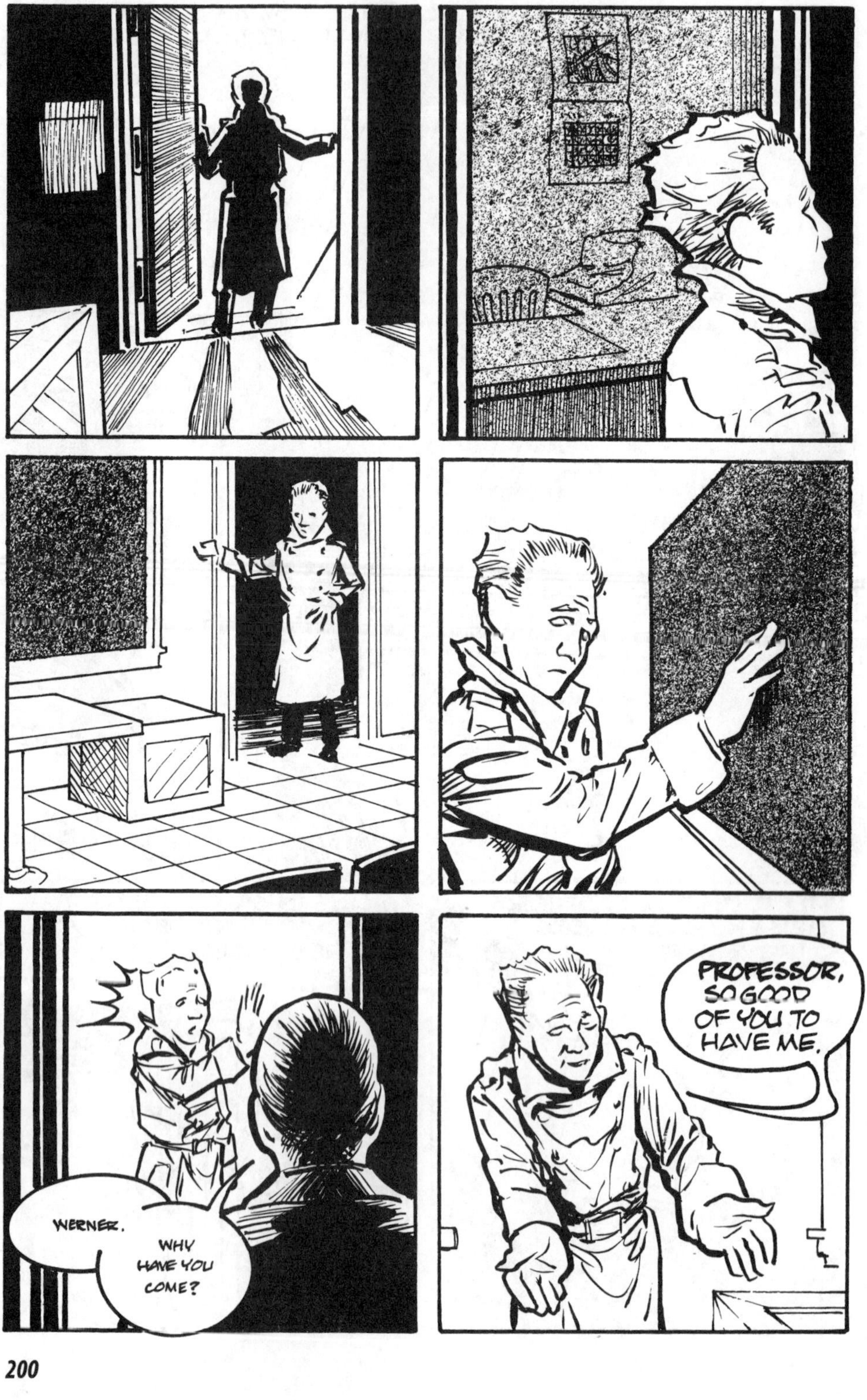
WERNER.
WHY HAVE YOU COME?
PROFESSOR, SO GOOD OF YOU TO HAVE ME.

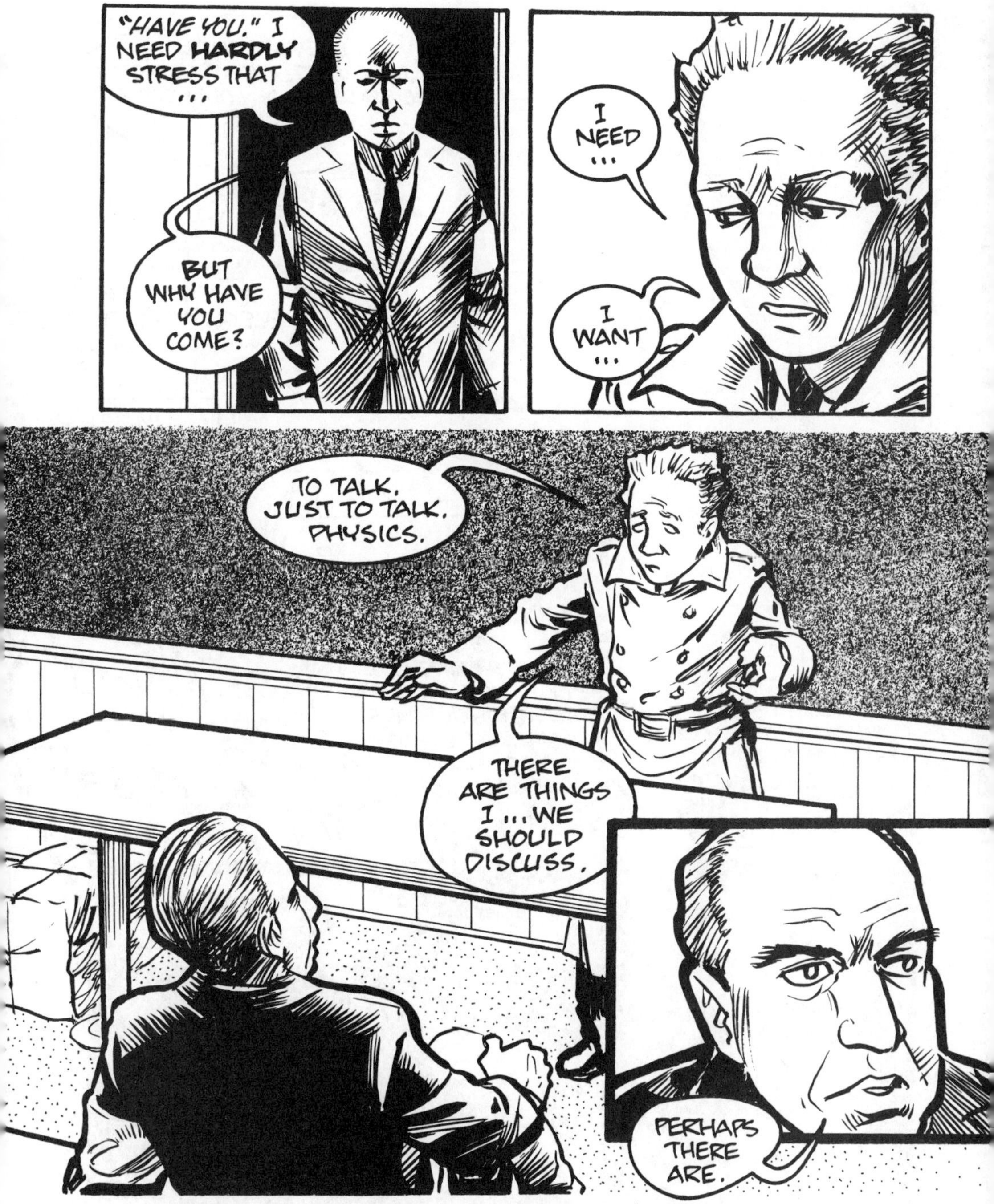
"HAVE YOU." I NEED **HARDLY** STRESS THAT ...
BUT WHY HAVE YOU COME?
I NEED ...
I WANT ...
TO TALK. JUST TO TALK. PHYSICS.
THERE ARE THINGS I ... WE SHOULD DISCUSS.
PERHAPS THERE ARE.

AND SO THEY TALKED, JUST AS THEY HAD IN THE PAST. AND... *NOT* JUST LIKE IN THE PAST, FOR **HEISENBERG** HAD STAYED IN *GERMANY* AND IN DOING SO HAD — IN THE MINDS OF MANY — TACITLY ENDORSED THE NAZIS.

HE SAW IT DIFFERENTLY, OF COURSE.

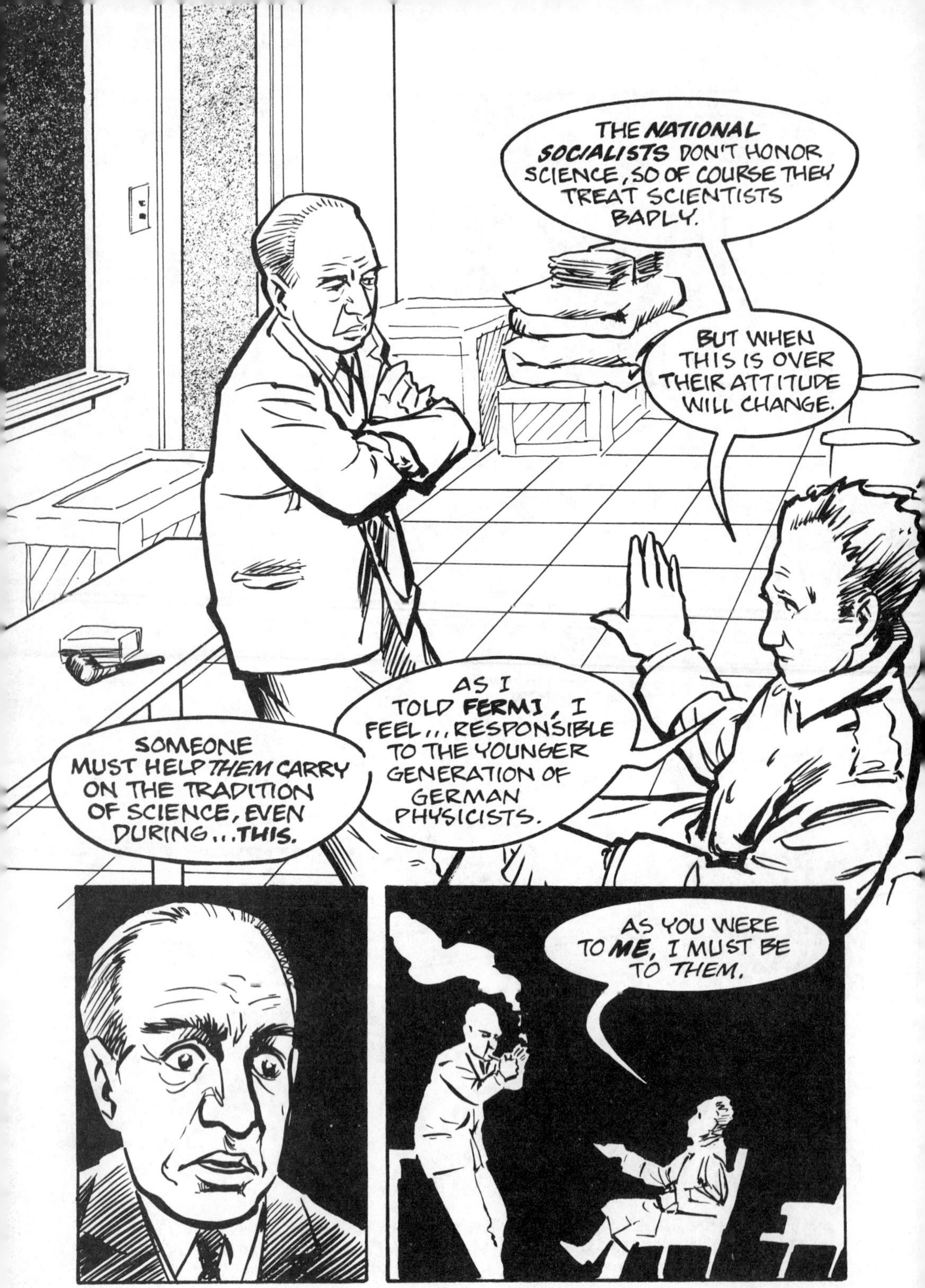
THE NATIONAL SOCIALISTS DON'T HONOR SCIENCE, SO OF COURSE THEY TREAT SCIENTISTS BADLY.
BUT WHEN THIS IS OVER THEIR ATTITUDE WILL CHANGE.
AS I TOLD FERMI, I FEEL... RESPONSIBLE TO THE YOUNGER GENERATION OF GERMAN PHYSICISTS.
SOMEONE MUST HELP THEM CARRY ON THE TRADITION OF SCIENCE, EVEN DURING... THIS.
AS YOU WERE TO ME, I MUST BE TO THEM.

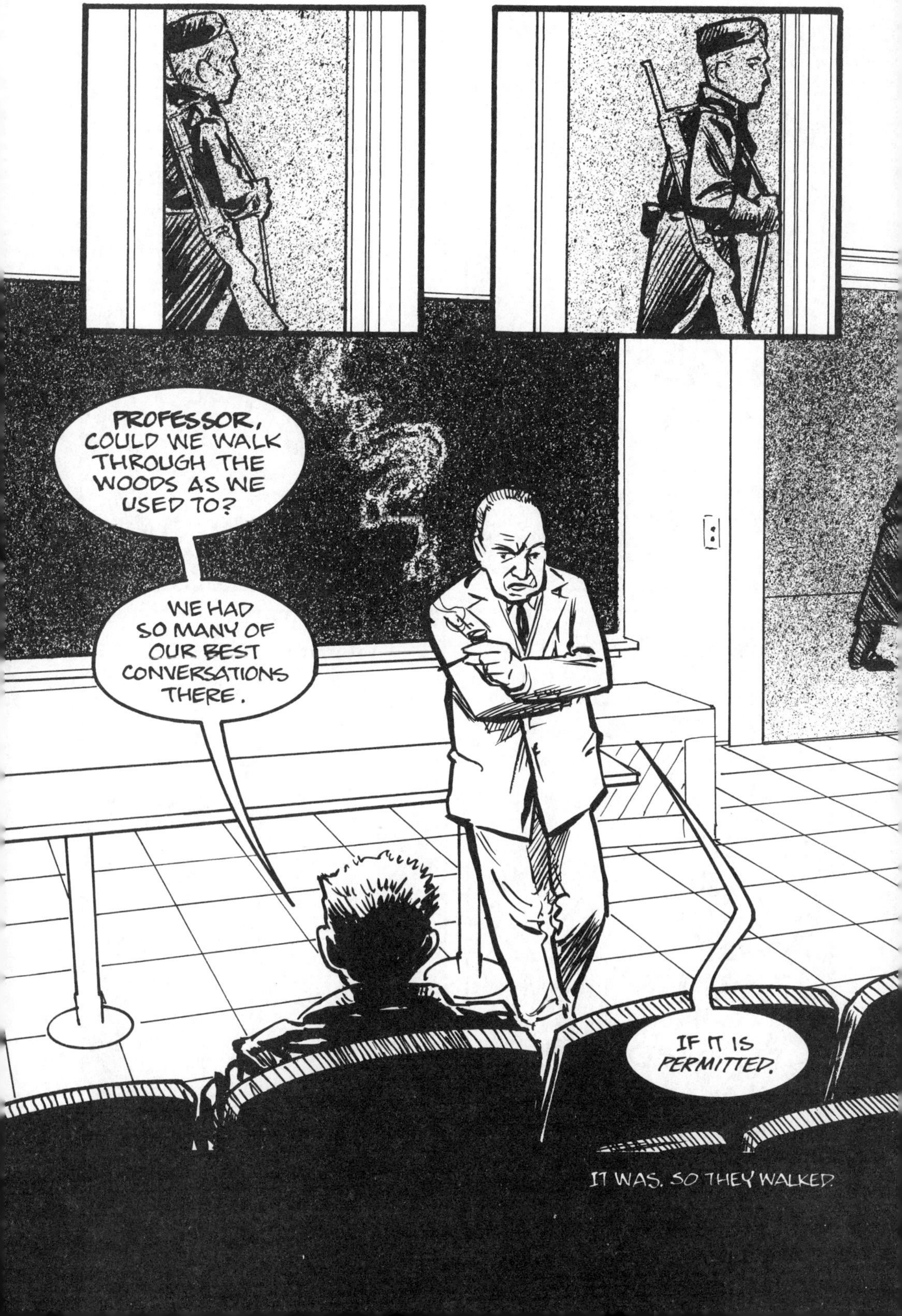
PROFESSOR, COULD WE WALK THROUGH THE WOODS AS WE USED TO?
WE HAD SO MANY OF OUR BEST CONVERSATIONS THERE.
IF IT IS PERMITTED.
IT WAS. SO THEY WALKED.

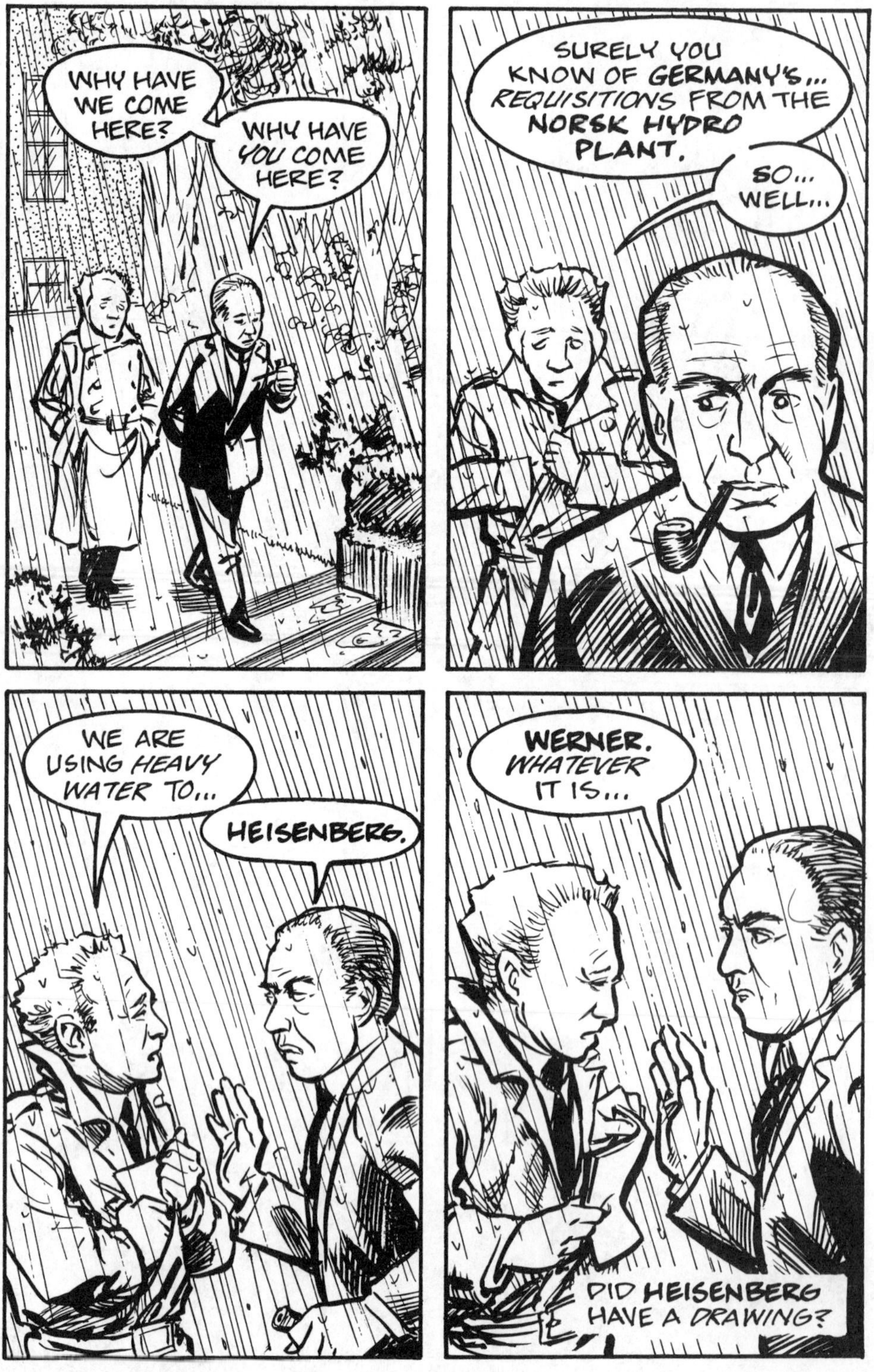
WHY HAVE WE COME HERE?
WHY HAVE YOU COME HERE?
SURELY YOU KNOW OF GERMANY'S... REQUISITIONS FROM THE NORSK HYDRO PLANT.
SO... WELL...
WE ARE USING HEAVY WATER TO...
HEISENBERG.
WERNER. WHATEVER IT IS...
DID HEISENBERG HAVE A DRAWING?

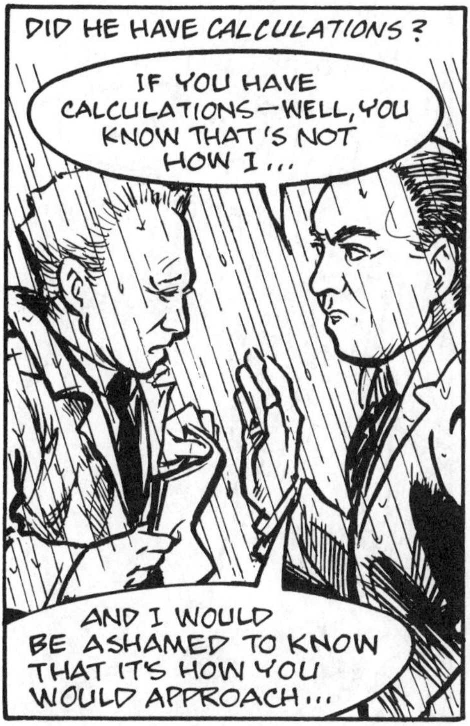
DID HE HAVE *CALCULATIONS*?
IF YOU HAVE CALCULATIONS—WELL, YOU KNOW THAT'S NOT HOW I...
AND I WOULD BE ASHAMED TO KNOW THAT IT'S HOW YOU WOULD APPROACH...

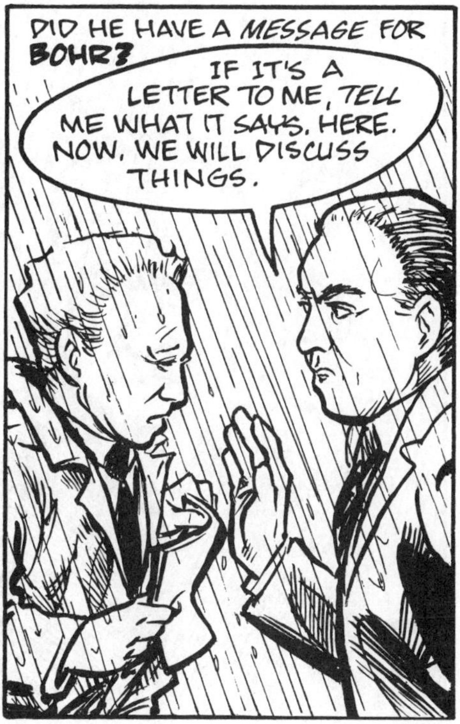
DID HE HAVE A *MESSAGE* FOR **BOHR**?
IF IT'S A LETTER TO ME, *TELL* ME WHAT IT SAYS. HERE. NOW. WE WILL DISCUSS THINGS.

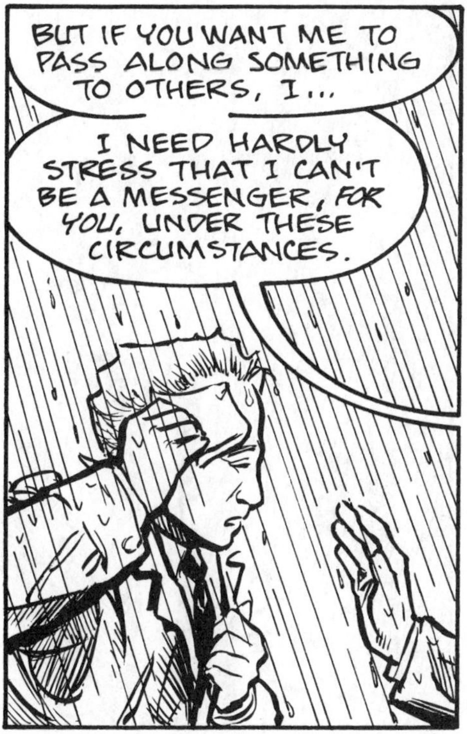
BUT IF YOU WANT ME TO PASS ALONG SOMETHING TO OTHERS, I...
I NEED HARDLY STRESS THAT I CAN'T BE A MESSENGER, *FOR YOU*, UNDER THESE CIRCUMSTANCES.

WAS THERE EVEN A PIECE OF PAPER *AT ALL*? WHAT HAPPENED IS **UN-CLEAR** TO THIS DAY, SINCE NEITHER SPOKE OF THEIR MEETING IN DETAIL TO ANYONE.

AND THEY WERE ALONE IN THE WOODS.

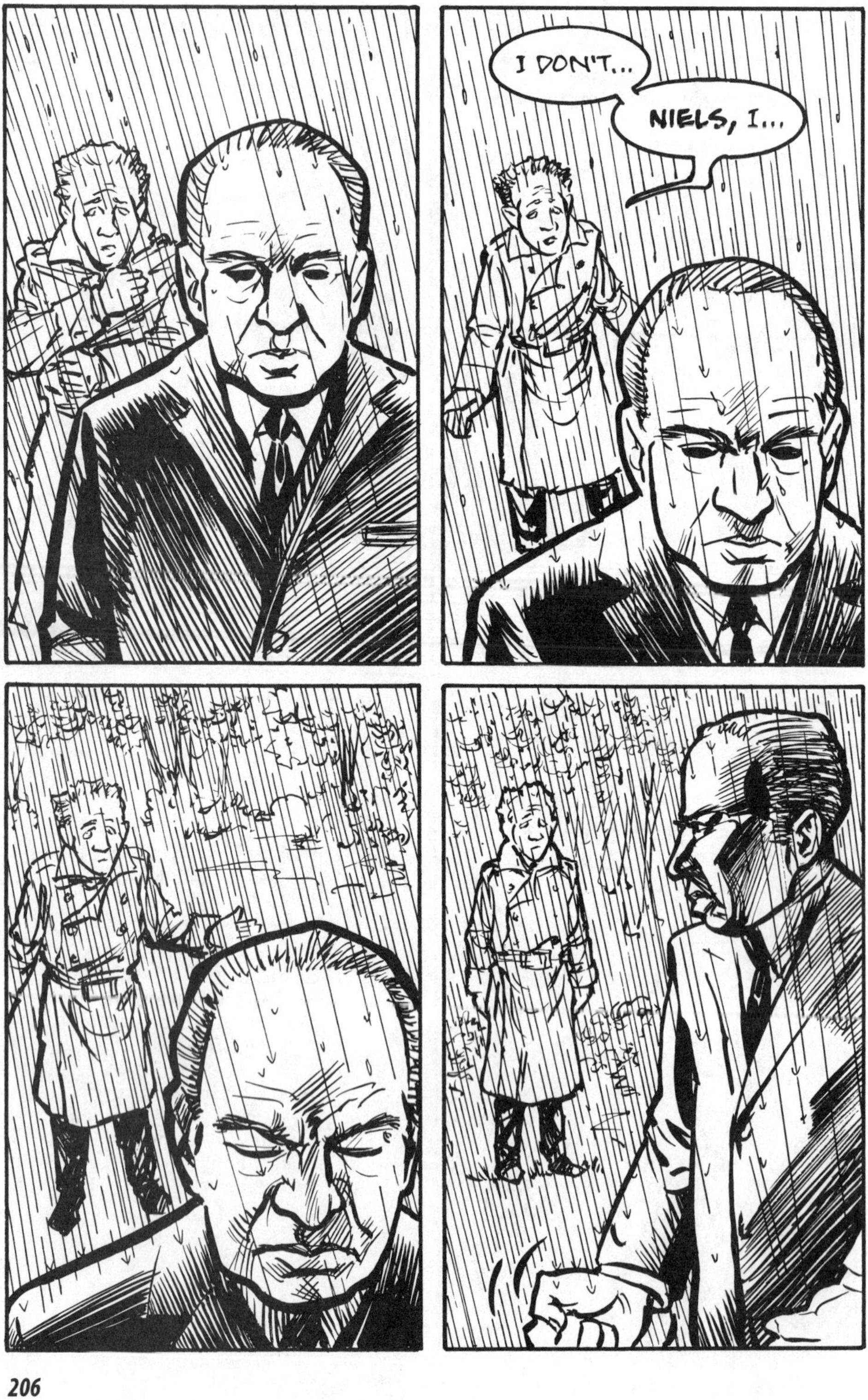
I DON'T...
NIELS, I...

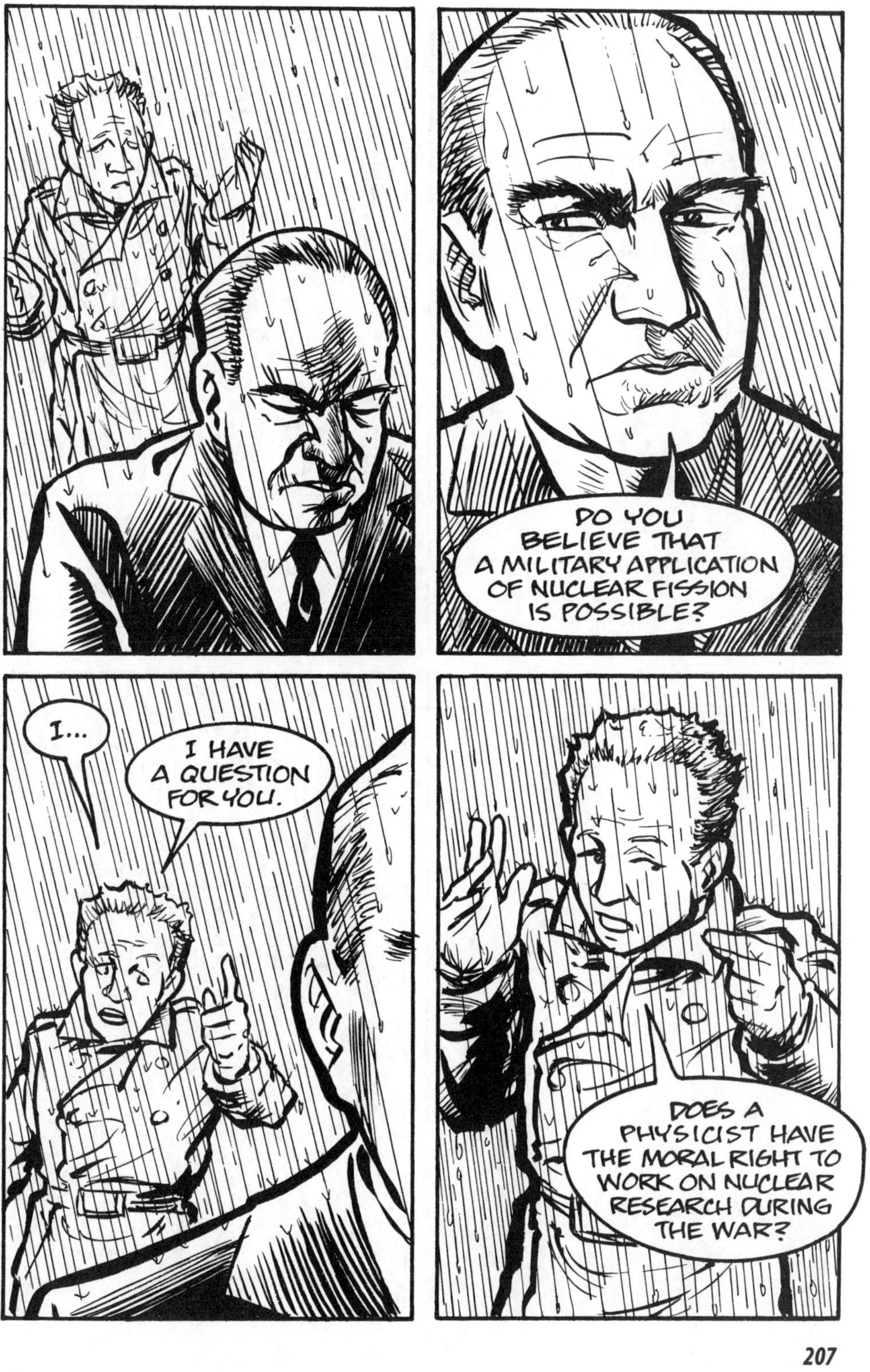
DO YOU BELIEVE THAT A MILITARY APPLICATION OF NUCLEAR FISSION IS POSSIBLE?
I...
I HAVE A QUESTION FOR YOU.
DOES A PHYSICIST HAVE THE MORAL RIGHT TO WORK ON NUCLEAR RESEARCH DURING THE WAR?

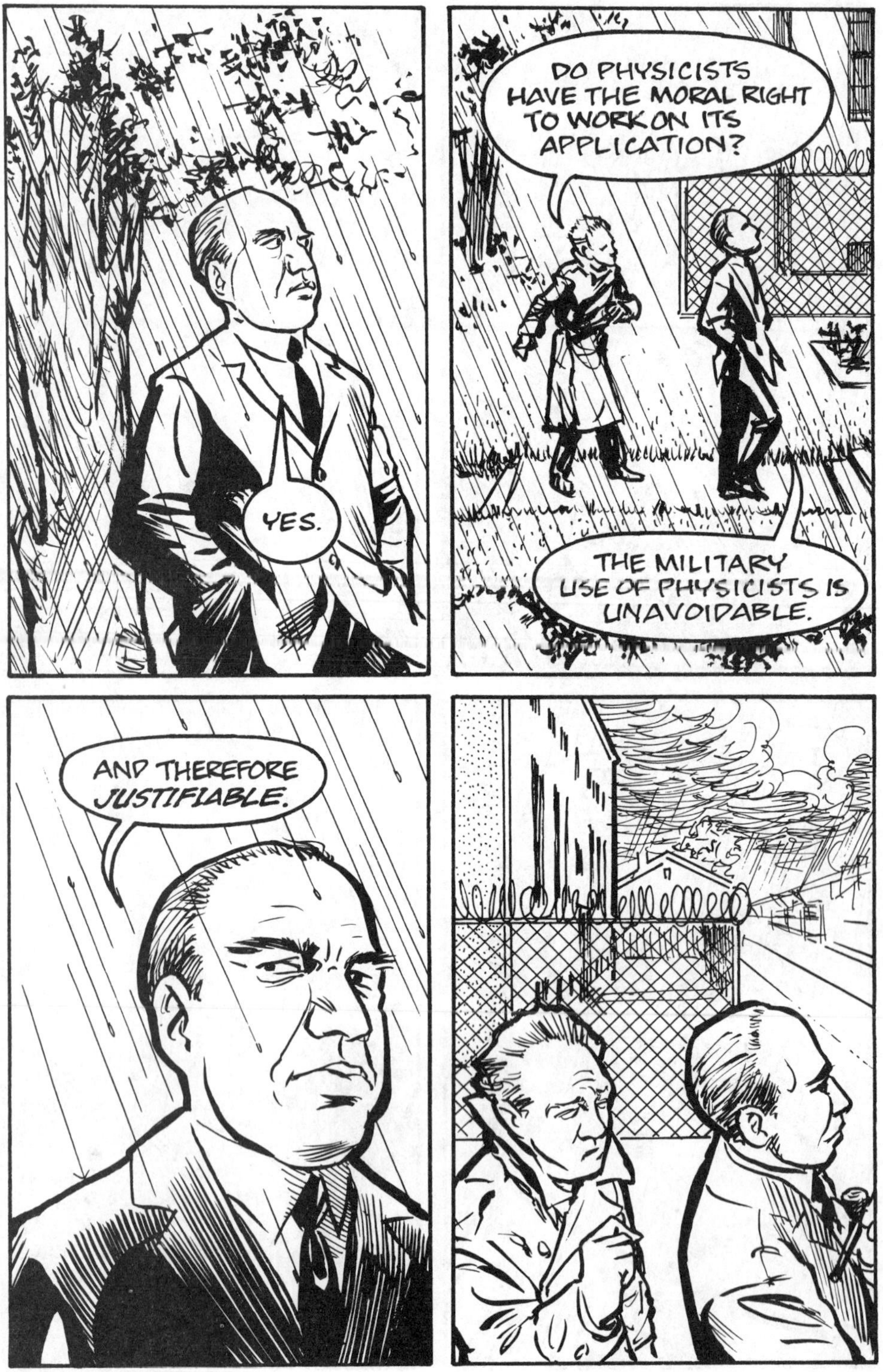
YES.
DO PHYSICISTS HAVE THE MORAL RIGHT TO WORK ON ITS APPLICATION?
THE MILITARY USE OF PHYSICISTS IS UNAVOIDABLE.
AND THEREFORE *JUSTIFIABLE.*

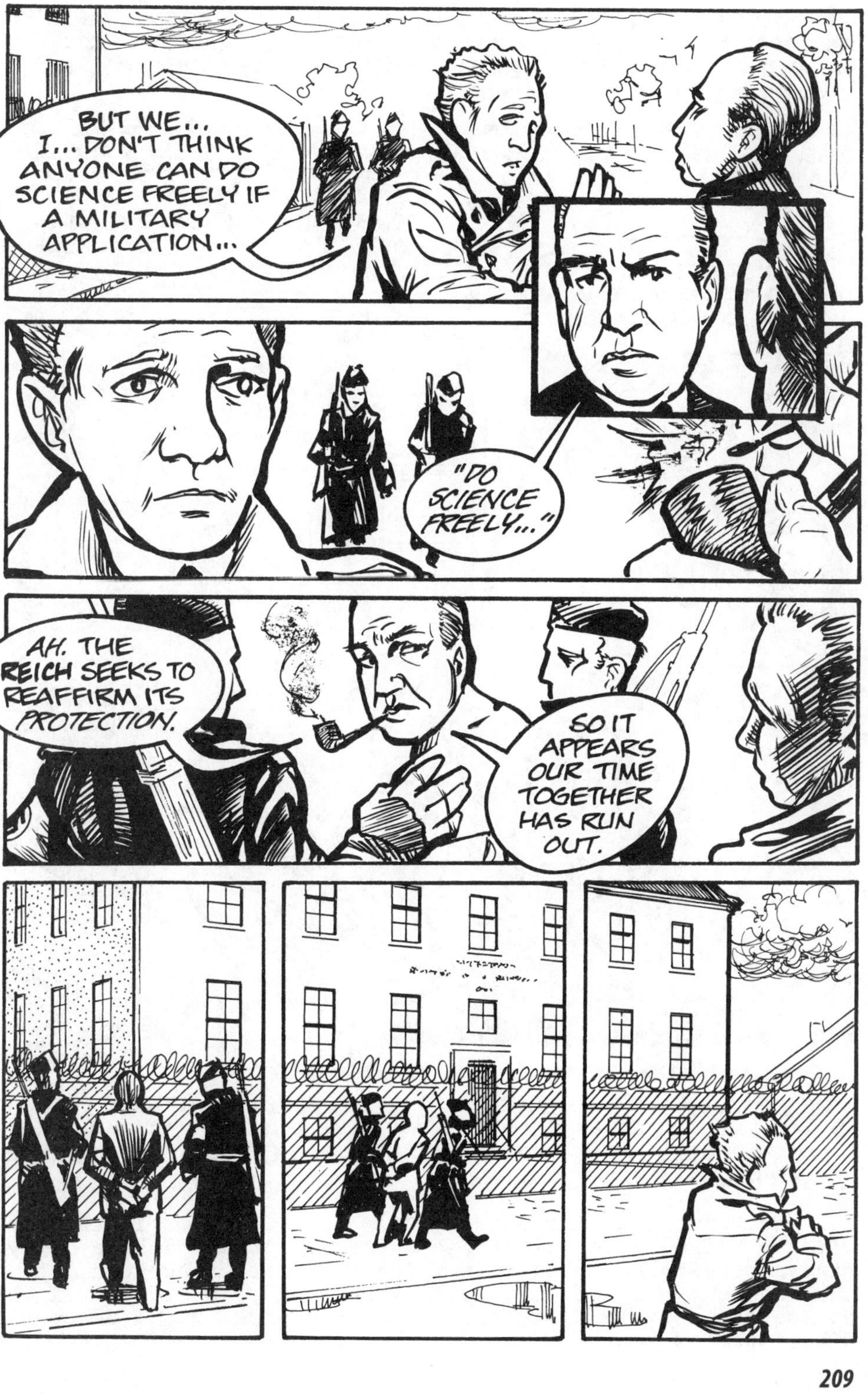
BUT WE... I... DON'T THINK ANYONE CAN DO SCIENCE FREELY IF A MILITARY APPLICATION...
"DO SCIENCE FREELY..."
AH. THE REICH SEEKS TO REAFFIRM ITS PROTECTION.
SO IT APPEARS OUR TIME TOGETHER HAS RUN OUT.

INFORMATION ON **FISSION** (AND ALMOST ALL OTHER ATOMIC RESEARCH) BEGAN TO DISAPPEAR FROM THE SCIENTIFIC LITERATURE AT ABOUT THIS TIME — WHEN **BOHR** AND HIS COLLEAGUES AT THE INSTITUTE CRAVED IT MOST.

THEY KNEW **FERMI**, **PAULI**, AND OTHER COLLEAGUES IN *ENGLAND* AND THE U.S. WERE AT WORK, BUT BY EARLY 1943 IT SEEMED NOBODY WAS WRITING AT ALL.

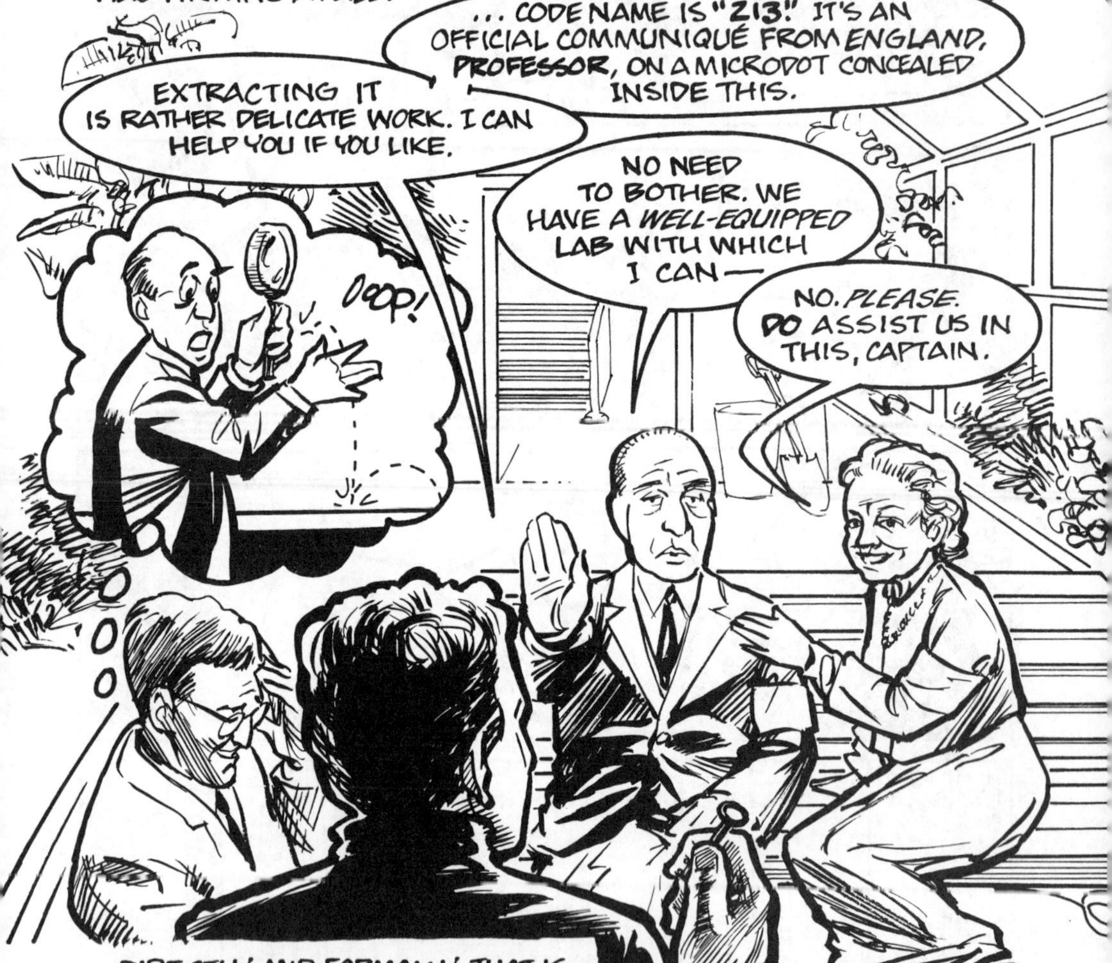

... CODE NAME IS "213." IT'S AN OFFICIAL COMMUNIQUÉ FROM ENGLAND, PROFESSOR, ON A MICRODOT CONCEALED INSIDE THIS.
EXTRACTING IT IS RATHER DELICATE WORK. I CAN HELP YOU IF YOU LIKE.
OOOP!
NO NEED TO BOTHER. WE HAVE A WELL-EQUIPPED LAB WITH WHICH I CAN —
NO. PLEASE. DO ASSIST US IN THIS, CAPTAIN.

...DIRECTLY AND FORMALLY, THAT IS.

THE MESSAGE WAS AN INVITATION FROM **JAMES CHADWICK** (THE DISCOVERER OF THE *NEUTRON*), WHO SUGGESTED THAT IF **BOHR** WAS PREPARED TO **ESCAPE** FROM *DENMARK* HE WOULD BE WELCOMED IN *ENGLAND*. INDEED:

A factor which may influence you in your decision is that you will work freely in scientific matters. Indeed I have in my mind a particular problem in which your assistance would be of the greatest help ... You will, I hope, appreciate that I can not be specific in my reference to this work, but I am sure it will interest you.

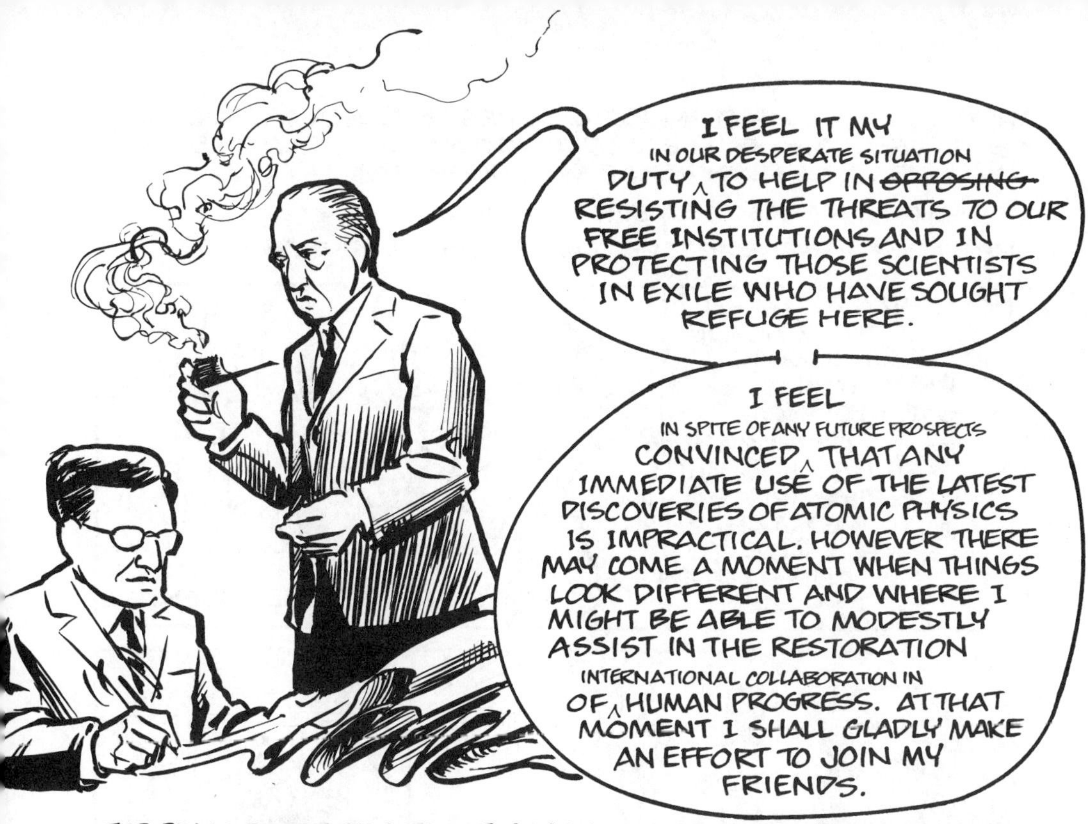
I FEEL IT MY
IN OUR DESPERATE SITUATION
DUTY ^ TO HELP IN ~~OPPOSING~~
RESISTING THE THREATS TO OUR FREE INSTITUTIONS AND IN PROTECTING THOSE SCIENTISTS IN EXILE WHO HAVE SOUGHT REFUGE HERE.
I FEEL
IN SPITE OF ANY FUTURE PROSPECTS
CONVINCED ^ THAT ANY IMMEDIATE USE ^ OF THE LATEST DISCOVERIES OF ATOMIC PHYSICS IS IMPRACTICAL. HOWEVER THERE MAY COME A MOMENT WHEN THINGS LOOK DIFFERENT AND WHERE I MIGHT BE ABLE TO MODESTLY ASSIST IN THE RESTORATION
INTERNATIONAL COLLABORATION IN
OF ^ HUMAN PROGRESS. AT THAT MOMENT I SHALL GLADLY MAKE AN EFFORT TO JOIN MY FRIENDS.

THE FINAL DRAFT WAS *TWICE AS LONG*, OF COURSE, AND EVEN REDUCED GREATLY IT MAY HAVE GIVEN THE DANISH UNDERGROUND'S DENTIST A HARD TIME FITTING INTO THE HOLLOW TOOTH OF THE COURIER. BUT THE MESSAGE MADE IT TO *ENGLAND* POSTHASTE.

(AS DID A REVISED MESSAGE, SENT VIA LESS DRAMATIC MEANS BY **CAPTAIN GYTH.**)

AND THE TIME TO JOIN HIS FRIENDS CAME ONLY A FEW MONTHS LATER.

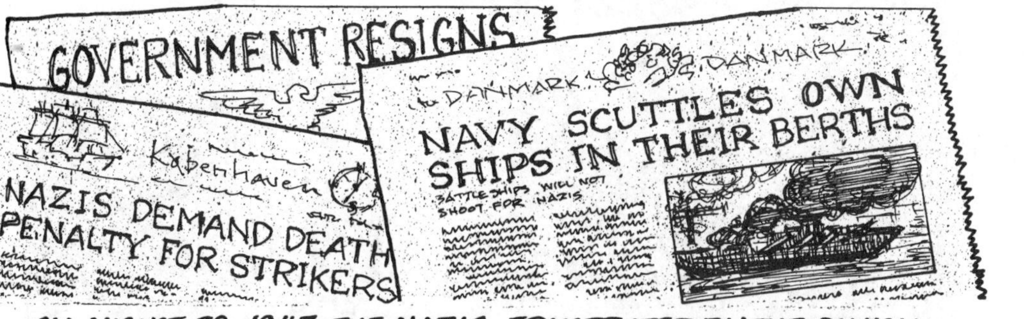
GOVERNMENT RESIGNS
København
NAZIS DEMAND DEATH PENALTY FOR STRIKERS
DANMARK
DANMARK
NAVY SCUTTLES OWN SHIPS IN THEIR BERTHS
BATTLESHIPS WILL NOT SHOOT FOR NAZIS

ON AUGUST 28, 1943 THE **NAZIS**, FRUSTRATED BY THE *DANISH UNDERGROUND'S* INCREASED SABOTAGE ACTIVITY, DEMANDED **CAPITAL PUNISHMENT** FOR SABOTEURS. THE GOVERNMENT RESIGNED, WITH ITS LAST OFFICIAL ACT BEING THE *REJECTION* OF THAT ULTIMATUM. THE *DANES* DESTROYED THEIR **BATTLESHIPS** TO PREVENT THEIR MISUSE...

...AND DROPPED THE PRETENSE OF INDEPENDENCE AND DECLARED THE LONG OCCUPATION AN **ACT OF WAR.**

THE **NAZIS** INITIALLY PLANNED TO ARREST **NIELS** AND **HARALD** ON SEPTEMBER **28th** BUT DECIDED TO WAIT AN EXTRA TWO DAYS AND DO IT WHEN THEY ROUNDED UP THE *DANISH* **JEWS**.

IT WOULD CAUSE LESS OF A STIR THAT WAY.

THE **BOHRS** LEARNED OF THE PLAN ON SEPTEMBER **28**.

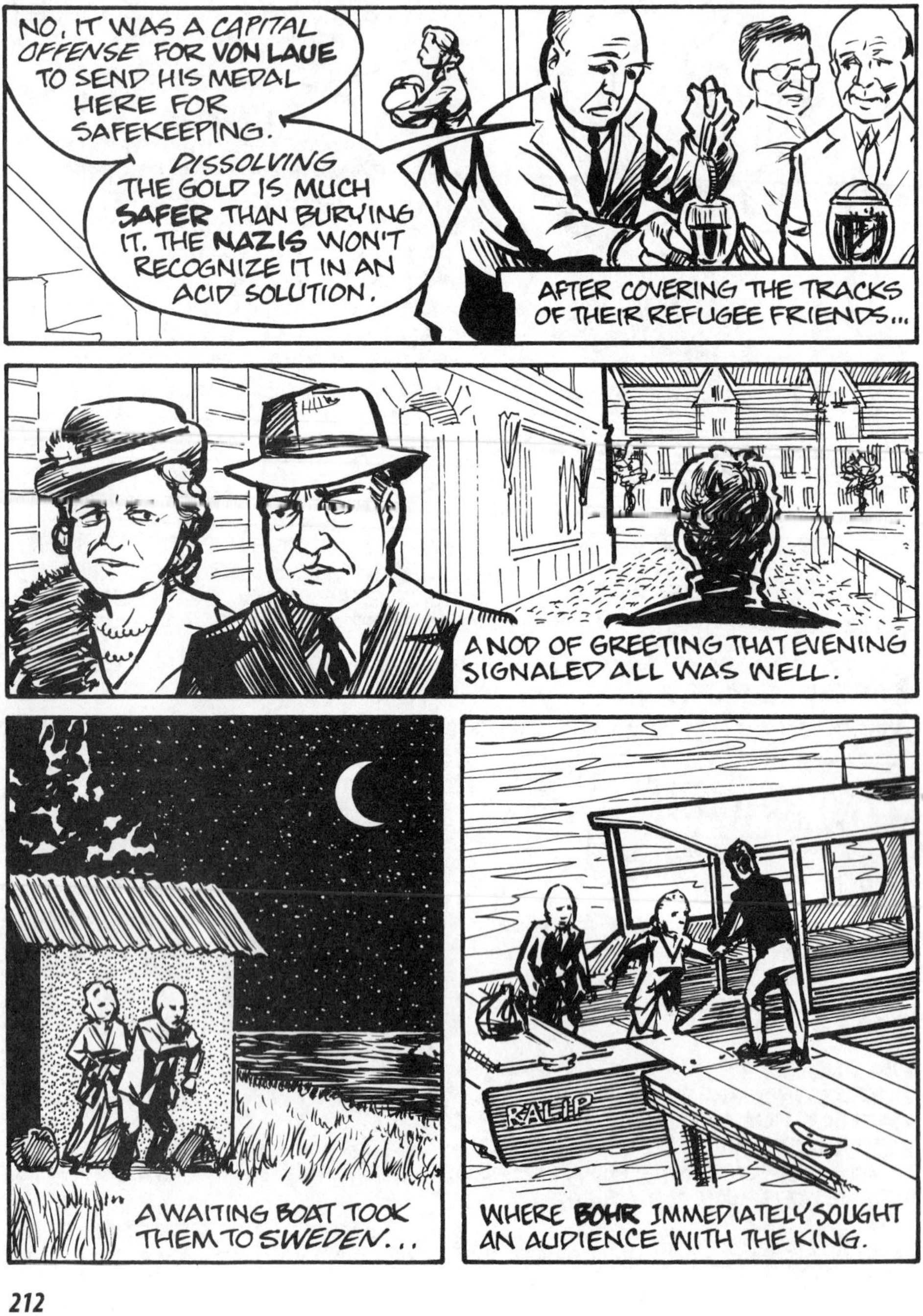

NO, IT WAS A CAPITAL OFFENSE FOR VON LAUE TO SEND HIS MEDAL HERE FOR SAFEKEEPING.
DISSOLVING THE GOLD IS MUCH SAFER THAN BURYING IT. THE NAZIS WON'T RECOGNIZE IT IN AN ACID SOLUTION.
AFTER COVERING THE TRACKS OF THEIR REFUGEE FRIENDS...
A NOD OF GREETING THAT EVENING SIGNALED ALL WAS WELL.
A WAITING BOAT TOOK THEM TO SWEDEN...
RALIP
WHERE BOHR IMMEDIATELY SOUGHT AN AUDIENCE WITH THE KING.

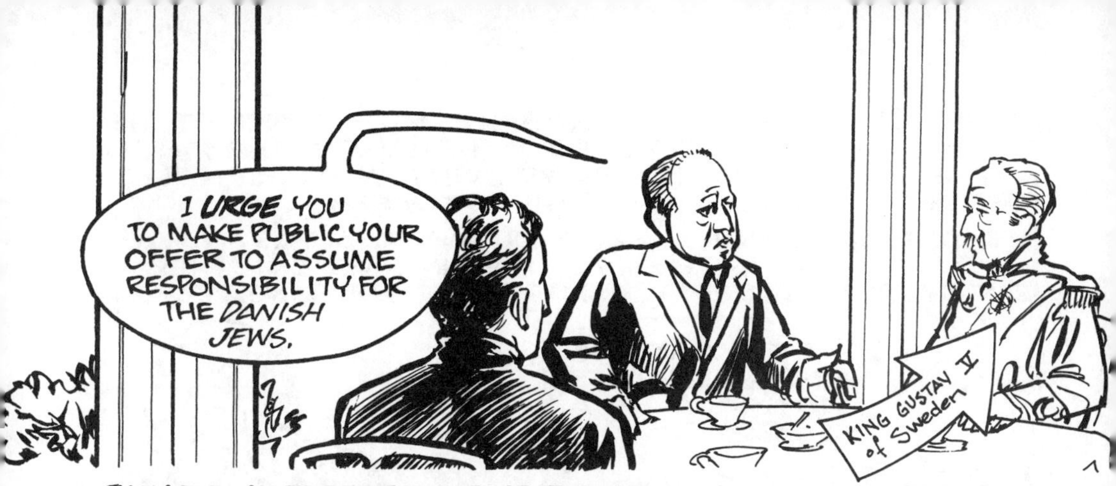
I URGE YOU TO MAKE PUBLIC YOUR OFFER TO ASSUME RESPONSIBILITY FOR THE DANISH JEWS.
KING GUSTAV V of Sweden

THEY DID, IN PART BECAUSE OF **BOHR'S** INTENSE LOBBYING.* *STOCKHOLM* HAD MORE THAN ITS SHARE OF *GERMAN AGENTS*, THOUGH, SO **NIELS** COULDN'T STAY LONG. HE ACCEPTED AN OFFER TO GO TO *ENGLAND*, AND LEFT ALMOST IMMEDIATELY IN THE **BOMB BAY** OF A *MOSQUITO BOMBER*.

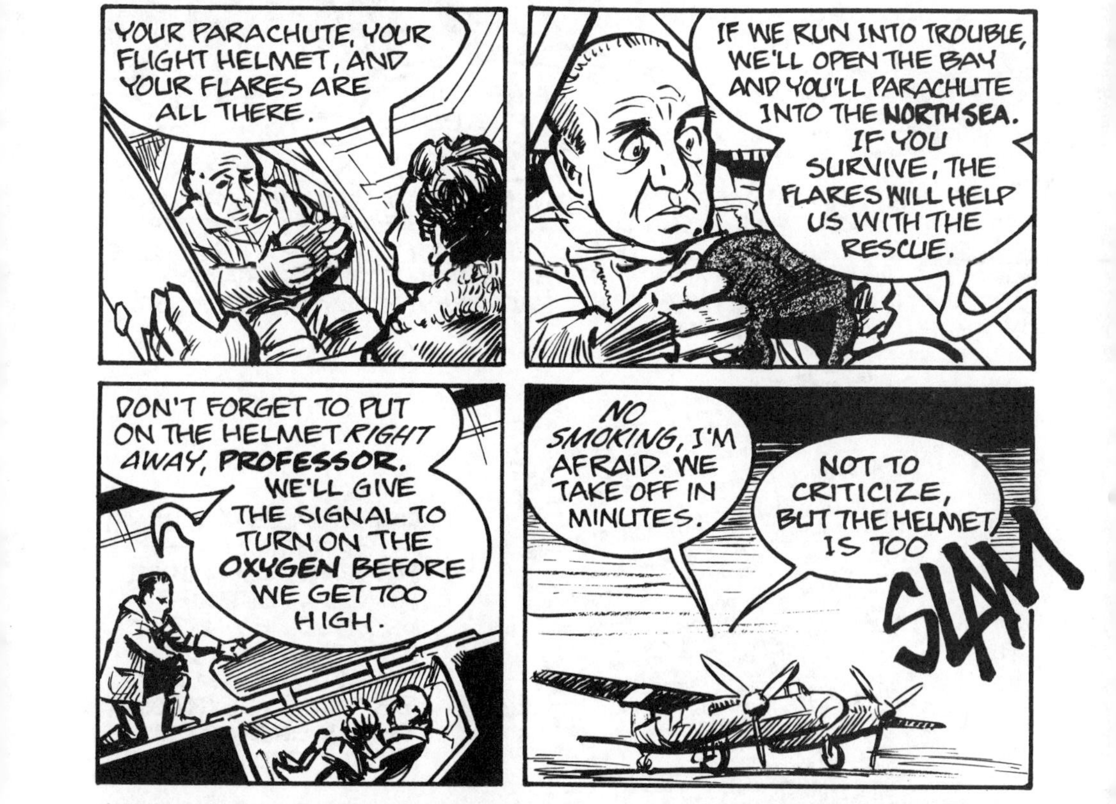
YOUR PARACHUTE, YOUR FLIGHT HELMET, AND YOUR FLARES ARE ALL THERE.
IF WE RUN INTO TROUBLE, WE'LL OPEN THE BAY AND YOU'LL PARACHUTE INTO THE NORTH SEA. IF YOU SURVIVE, THE FLARES WILL HELP US WITH THE RESCUE.
DON'T FORGET TO PUT ON THE HELMET RIGHT AWAY, PROFESSOR. WE'LL GIVE THE SIGNAL TO TURN ON THE OXYGEN BEFORE WE GET TOO HIGH.
NO SMOKING, I'M AFRAID. WE TAKE OFF IN MINUTES.
NOT TO CRITICIZE, BUT THE HELMET IS TOO
SLAM

* WITHIN 24 HOURS OF HIS ARRIVAL IN *SWEDEN*, *BOHR* MET WITH SWEDISH FOREIGN MINISTER GUNTHER, THE KING, THE CROWN PRINCE, AND NUMEROUS OTHER OFFICIALS. THOUGH NOT *100%* SUCCESSFUL. "ARMBANDS" (PAGE 301) TELLS MORE ABOUT *DENMARK'S* REMARKABLE RECORD OF SAVING ITS JEWISH CITIZENS.

THE HELMET *WAS* TOO SMALL FOR **BOHR**, SO HE DIDN'T GET THE SIGNAL. WHEN HE DIDN'T RESPOND (HE HAD *PASSED OUT* FROM LACK OF OXYGEN) THE PILOT CAME DOWN LOW AND FLEW THE REST OF THE WAY JUST ABOVE THE *NORTH SEA*.

HE RECOVERED QUICKLY, AND **AAGE** FOLLOWED TO ACT AS AN AIDE WHILE THE REST OF THE FAMILY STAYED IN SWEDEN. AFTER LEARNING OF THE ALLIED PROGRESS TOWARDS BUILDING A BOMB...

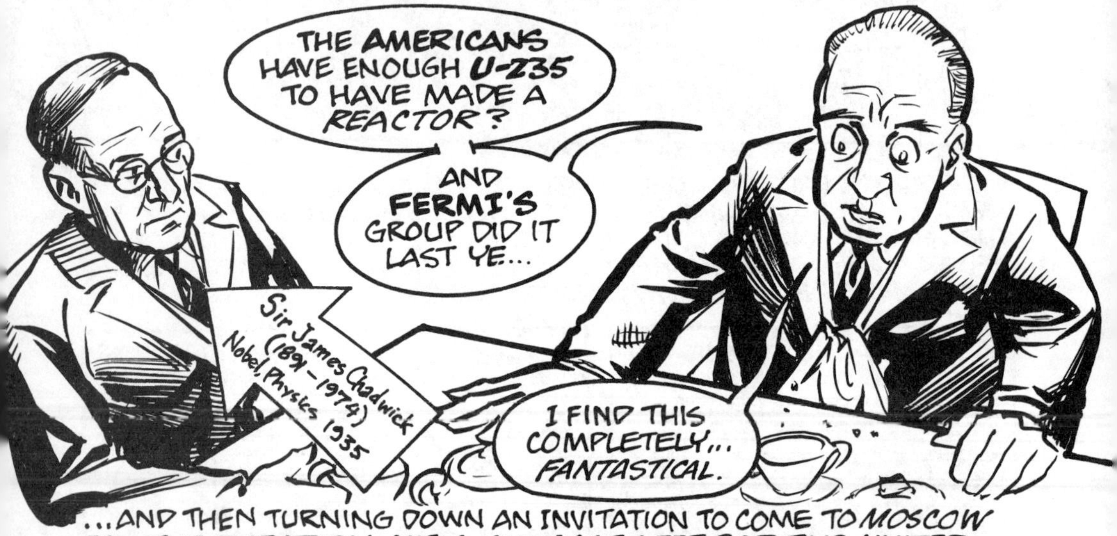
THE AMERICANS HAVE ENOUGH U-235 TO HAVE MADE A REACTOR?
AND FERMI'S GROUP DID IT LAST YE...
Sir James Chadwick (1891-1974) Nobel, Physics 1935
I FIND THIS COMPLETELY... FANTASTICAL.

...AND THEN TURNING DOWN AN INVITATION TO COME TO *MOSCOW* FOR THE DURATION, **NIELS** AND **AAGE** LEFT FOR THE *UNITED STATES* ON NOVEMBER 28. THE COVER STORY WAS THAT **BOHR'S** PURPOSE IN VISITING WAS TO PAVE THE WAY FOR POST-WAR COOPERATION. *THE NEW YORK TIMES* HAD PREVIOUSLY SPECULATED ON HIS FUTURE ROLE AS WELL.

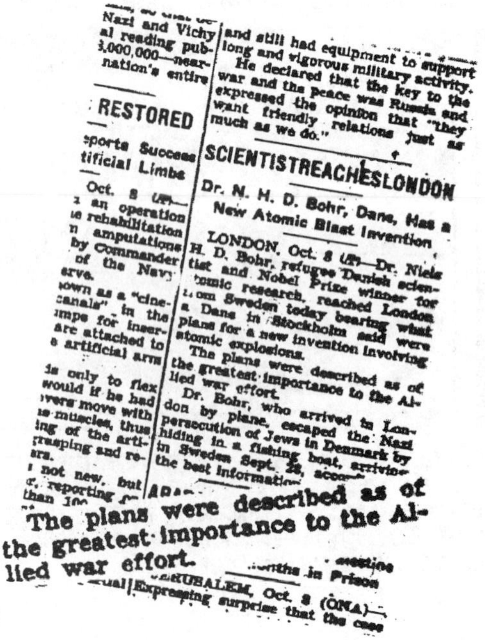

Nazi and Vichy
al reading pub-
3,000,000—near-
nation's entire

RESTORED

eports Success
tificial Limbs

Oct. 8 (UP)—
an operation
e rehabilitation
n amputations
by Commander
of the Navy
erve.
own as a "cine-
canals" in the
umps for inser-
are attached to
e artificial arm

is only to flex
would if he had
vers move with
e muscles, thus
ing of the arti-
grasping and re-
ars.
not new, but
r, reporting
than 100

and still had equipment to support long and vigorous military activity.

He declared that the key to the war and the peace was Russia and expressed the opinion that "they want friendly relations just as much as we do."

SCIENTIST REACHES LONDON

Dr. N. H. D. Bohr, Dane, Has a New Atomic Blast Invention

LONDON, Oct. 8 (UP)—Dr. Niels H. D. Bohr, refugee Danish scientist and Nobel Prize winner for atomic research, reached London from Sweden today bearing what a Dane in Stockholm said were plans for a new invention involving atomic explosions.

The plans were described as of the greatest importance to the Allied war effort.

Dr. Bohr, who arrived in London by plane, escaped the Nazi persecution of Jews in Denmark by hiding in a fishing boat, arriving in Sweden Sept. 28, according to the best information

The plans were described as of the greatest importance to the Allied war effort.

...nths in Prison

JERUSALEM, Oct. 8 (ONA)—Expressing surprise that the case

REGARDLESS OF WHAT — IF ANYTHING — **HEISENBERG** SHOWED HIM, OR PERHAPS BECAUSE OF WHAT HE DIDN'T, **BOHR** DID INDEED HAVE PLANS FOR "ATOMIC EXPLOSIONS." THEY WEREN'T TECHNICAL, THOUGH.

THEY WERE POLITICAL.

Chapter 12

THOUGH FAR FRIENDLIER WITH *EACH OTHER* THAN WITH THE **SOVIETS**, THE **AMERICANS** AND THE **BRITISH** STILL DIDN'T TRUST EACH OTHER ABSOLUTELY, AND *BOTH* HOPED TO SNAG **BOHR** FOR THEIR OWN BOMB EFFORTS — THE **BRITISH** FOR THEIR *TUBE ALLOYS PROJECT*, AND THE **AMERICANS** FOR ITS COUNTERPART, *THE MANHATTAN PROJECT.*

BUT AS HIS MINDERS IN *WASHINGTON* SOON FOUND OUT, **BOHR** DIDN'T MAKE A GOOD PAWN.

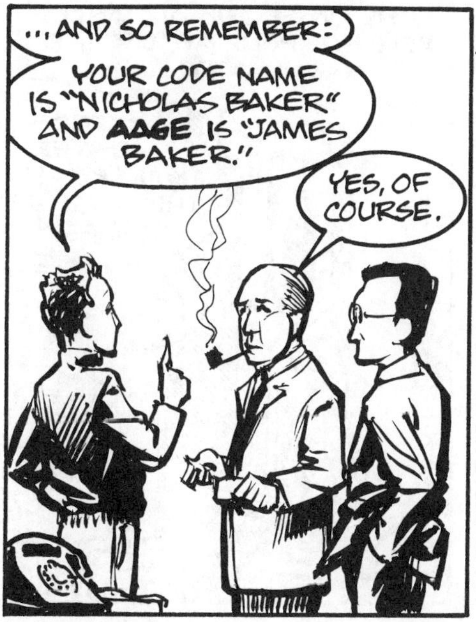
...AND SO REMEMBER:
YOUR CODE NAME IS "NICHOLAS BAKER" AND **AAGE** IS "JAMES BAKER."
YES, OF COURSE.

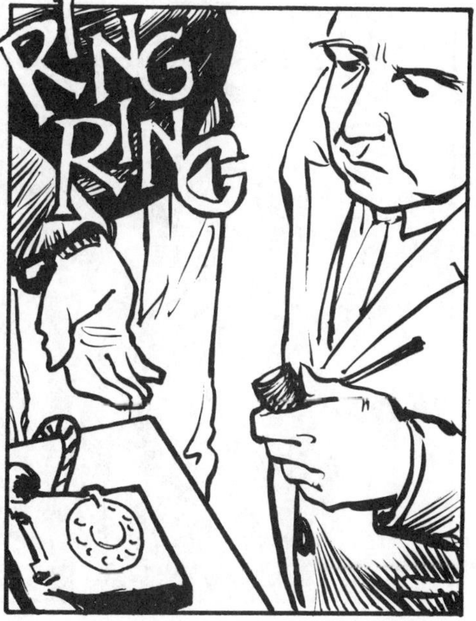
RING
RING

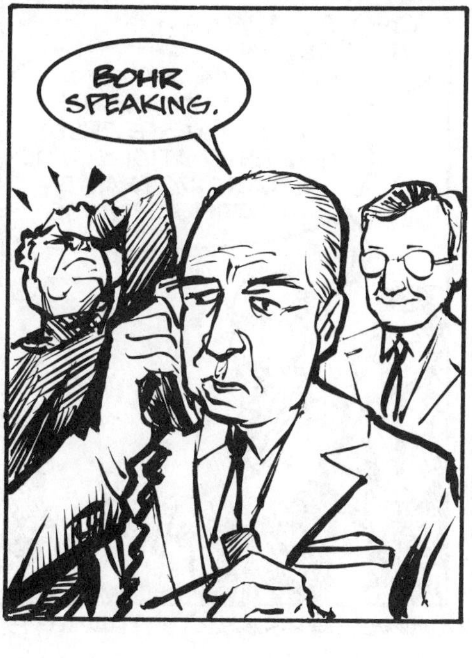
BOHR SPEAKING.

OR A GOOD SECRET AGENT.

AND HE WOULDN'T COMMIT TO ONE SIDE AT THE EXPENSE OF ANOTHER. AS HE SAW IT, HIS MISSION WAS NOT TO HELP BUILD A BOMB BUT — TO PUT A SPIN ON THE BREATHLESS *NEW YORK TIMES* STORY — TO MAKE THE CASE FOR AN OPEN WORLD.

BOHR WASN'T POLITICALLY NAIVE: HE'D BEEN AROUND, VISITED THE **SOVIET UNION**, KNEW HOW THE *THIRD ALLY'S SYSTEM* WORKED, AND HAD INTERVENED PERSONALLY (AND UNSUCCESSFULLY) WITH **STALIN** TO FREE HIS FRIEND **LEV LANDAU*** FROM PRISON.

BUT **BOHR** WAS **BOHR**, AND SO HE BELIEVED THAT AN ATOMIC *BOMB* HAD A COMPLEMENTARY NATURE: IT WAS A PROBLEM THAT PROVIDED AN OPPORTUNITY.

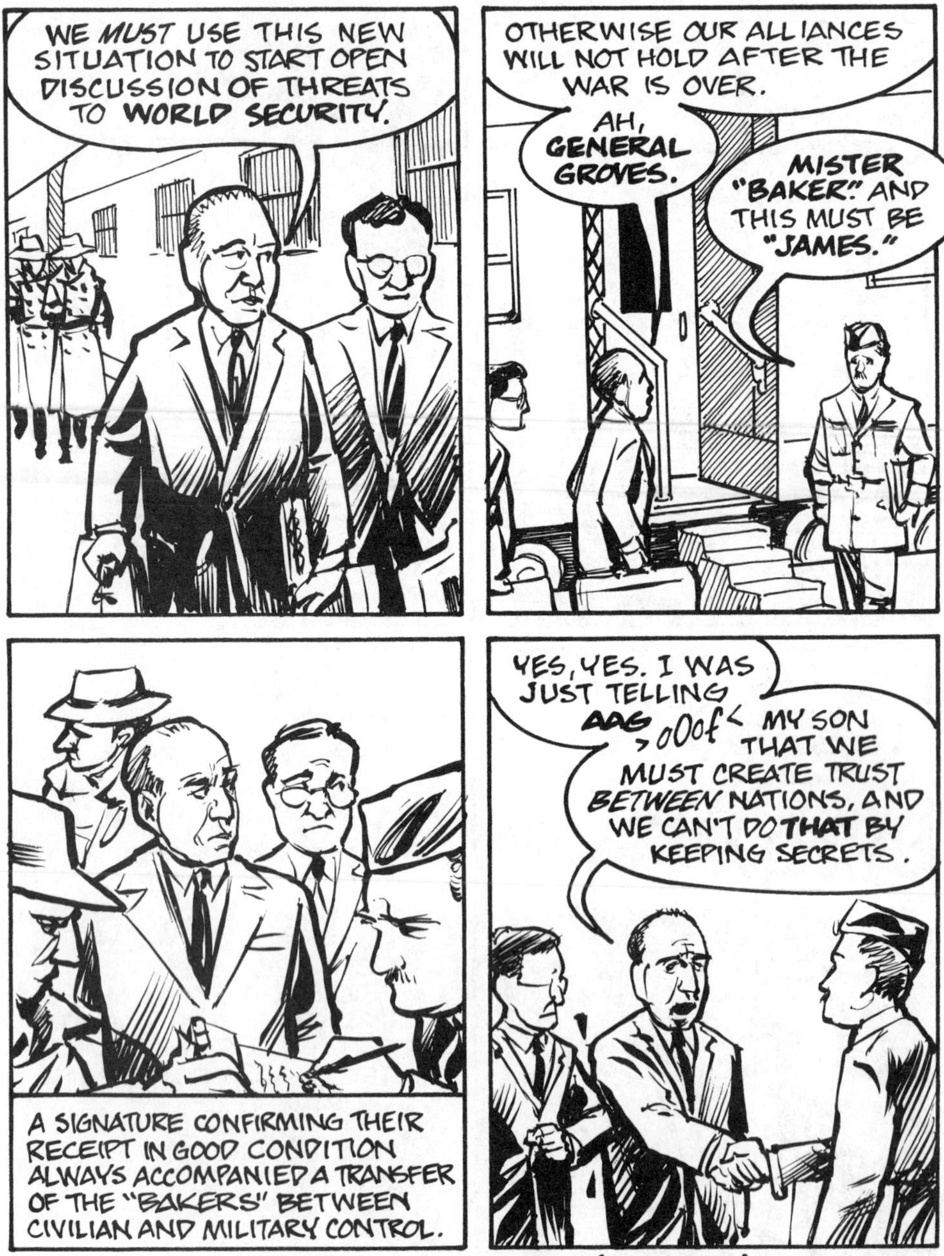

WE MUST USE THIS NEW SITUATION TO START OPEN DISCUSSION OF THREATS TO WORLD SECURITY.
OTHERWISE OUR ALLIANCES WILL NOT HOLD AFTER THE WAR IS OVER.
AH, GENERAL GROVES.
MISTER "BAKER." AND THIS MUST BE "JAMES."
A SIGNATURE CONFIRMING THEIR RECEIPT IN GOOD CONDITION ALWAYS ACCOMPANIED A TRANSFER OF THE "BAKERS" BETWEEN CIVILIAN AND MILITARY CONTROL.
YES, YES. I WAS JUST TELLING
AAG >oOof<
MY SON THAT WE MUST CREATE TRUST BETWEEN NATIONS, AND WE CAN'T DO THAT BY KEEPING SECRETS.

*WE LAST SAW *LANDAU* (ON HIS BACK) IN CHAPTER 8.

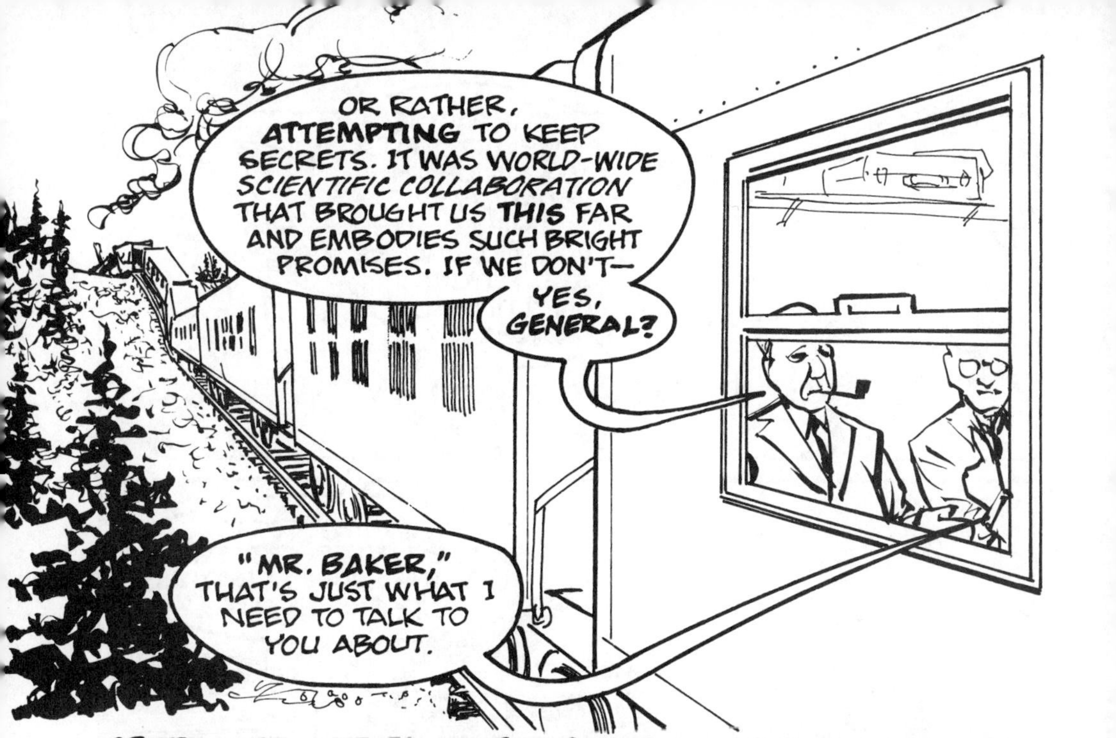
OR RATHER, **ATTEMPTING** TO KEEP SECRETS. IT WAS WORLD-WIDE *SCIENTIFIC COLLABORATION* THAT BROUGHT US **THIS** FAR AND EMBODIES SUCH BRIGHT PROMISES. IF WE DON'T—
YES, GENERAL?
"MR. BAKER," THAT'S JUST WHAT I NEED TO TALK TO YOU ABOUT.

GROVES ATTEMPTED TO USE THE TRIP FROM *WASHINGTON D.C.* TO *LOS ALAMOS* TO BRIEF **NIELS** AND **AAGE**... ER, MAKE THAT **NICHOLAS** AND **JAMES**... ON WHAT THEY *COULD* TALK ABOUT AND WHAT THEY *COULDN'T* WHEN THEY ARRIVED AT THE NERVE CENTER OF THE ***MANHATTAN PROJECT.***

BUT AS THE TRAIN MADE ITS WAY WEST, THE CONVERSATION SHIFTED.

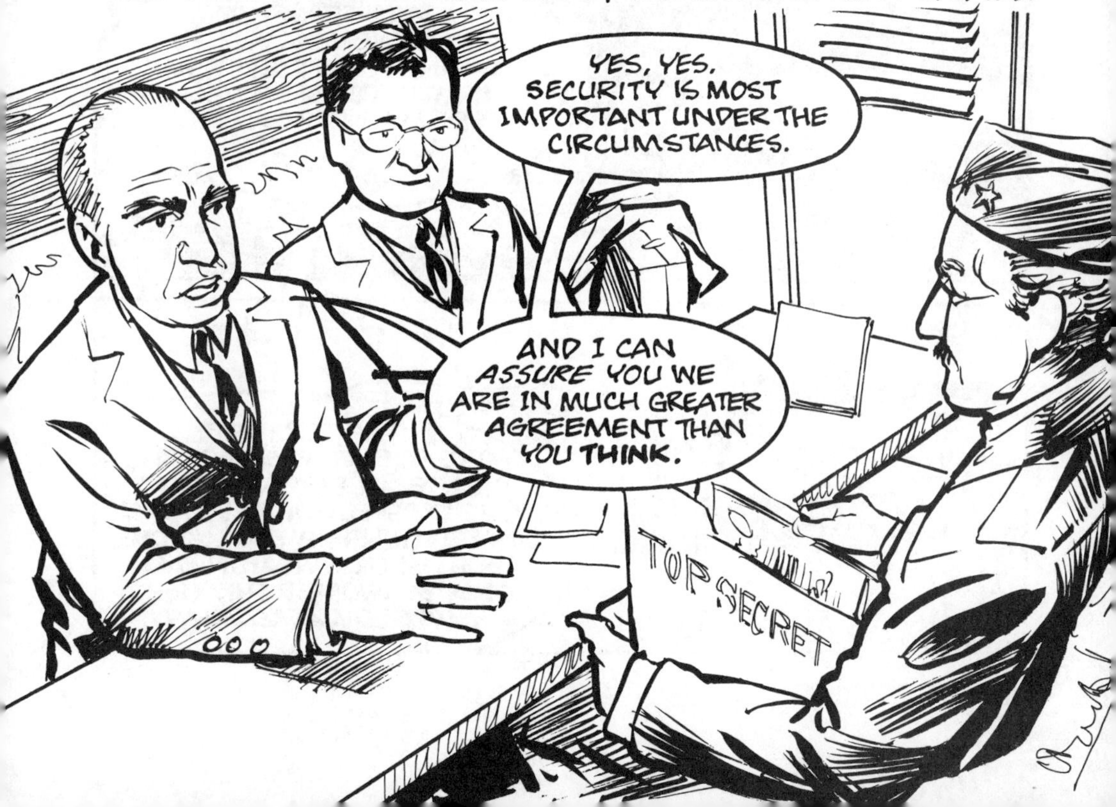
YES, YES. SECURITY IS MOST IMPORTANT UNDER THE CIRCUMSTANCES.
AND I CAN *ASSURE* YOU WE ARE IN MUCH GREATER AGREEMENT THAN YOU **THINK.**
TOP SECRET

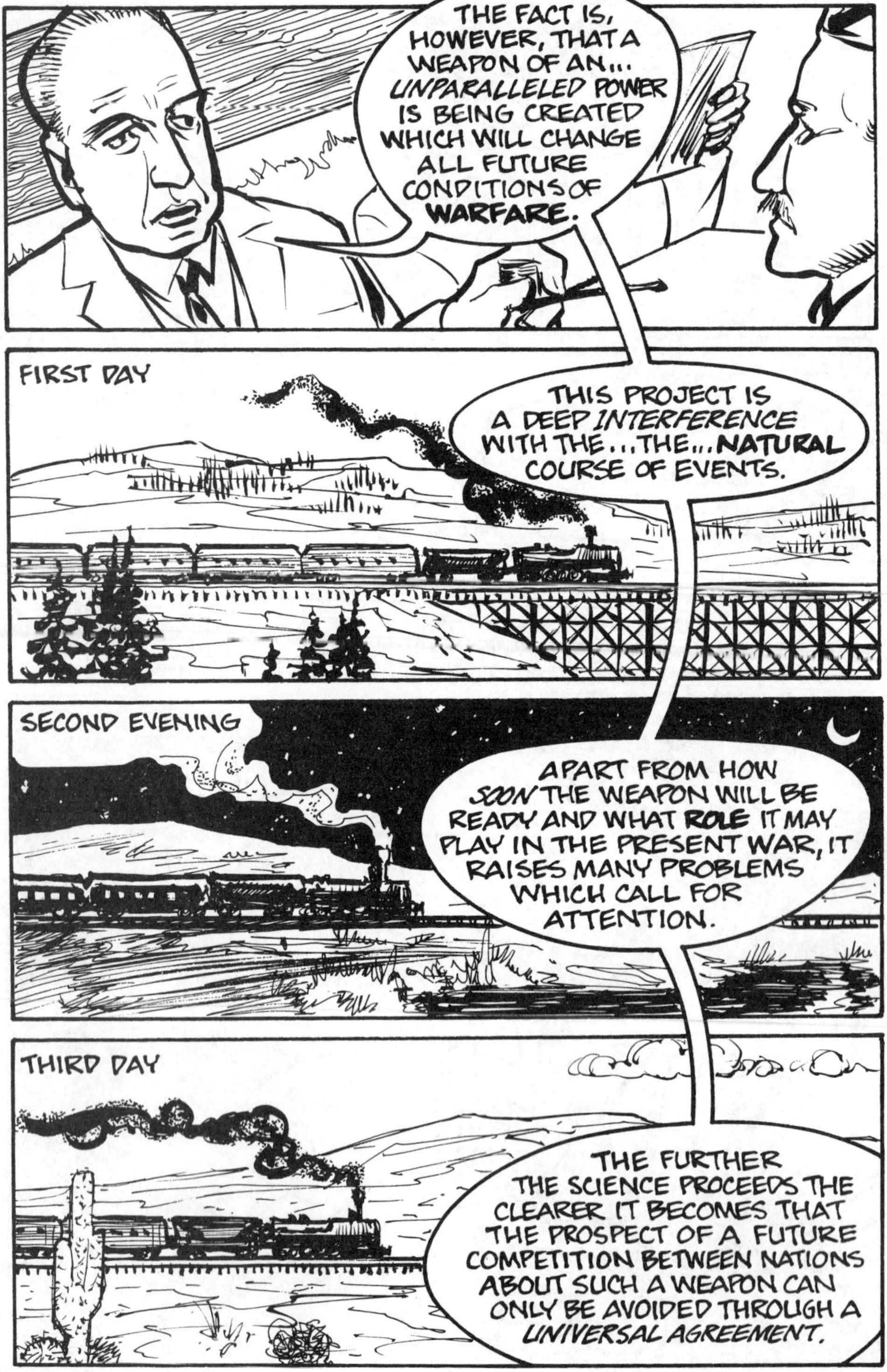
THE FACT IS, HOWEVER, THAT A WEAPON OF AN... UNPARALLELED POWER IS BEING CREATED WHICH WILL CHANGE ALL FUTURE CONDITIONS OF WARFARE.
FIRST DAY
THIS PROJECT IS A DEEP INTERFERENCE WITH THE...THE...NATURAL COURSE OF EVENTS.
SECOND EVENING
APART FROM HOW SOON THE WEAPON WILL BE READY AND WHAT ROLE IT MAY PLAY IN THE PRESENT WAR, IT RAISES MANY PROBLEMS WHICH CALL FOR ATTENTION.
THIRD DAY
THE FURTHER THE SCIENCE PROCEEDS THE CLEARER IT BECOMES THAT THE PROSPECT OF A FUTURE COMPETITION BETWEEN NATIONS ABOUT SUCH A WEAPON CAN ONLY BE AVOIDED THROUGH A UNIVERSAL AGREEMENT.

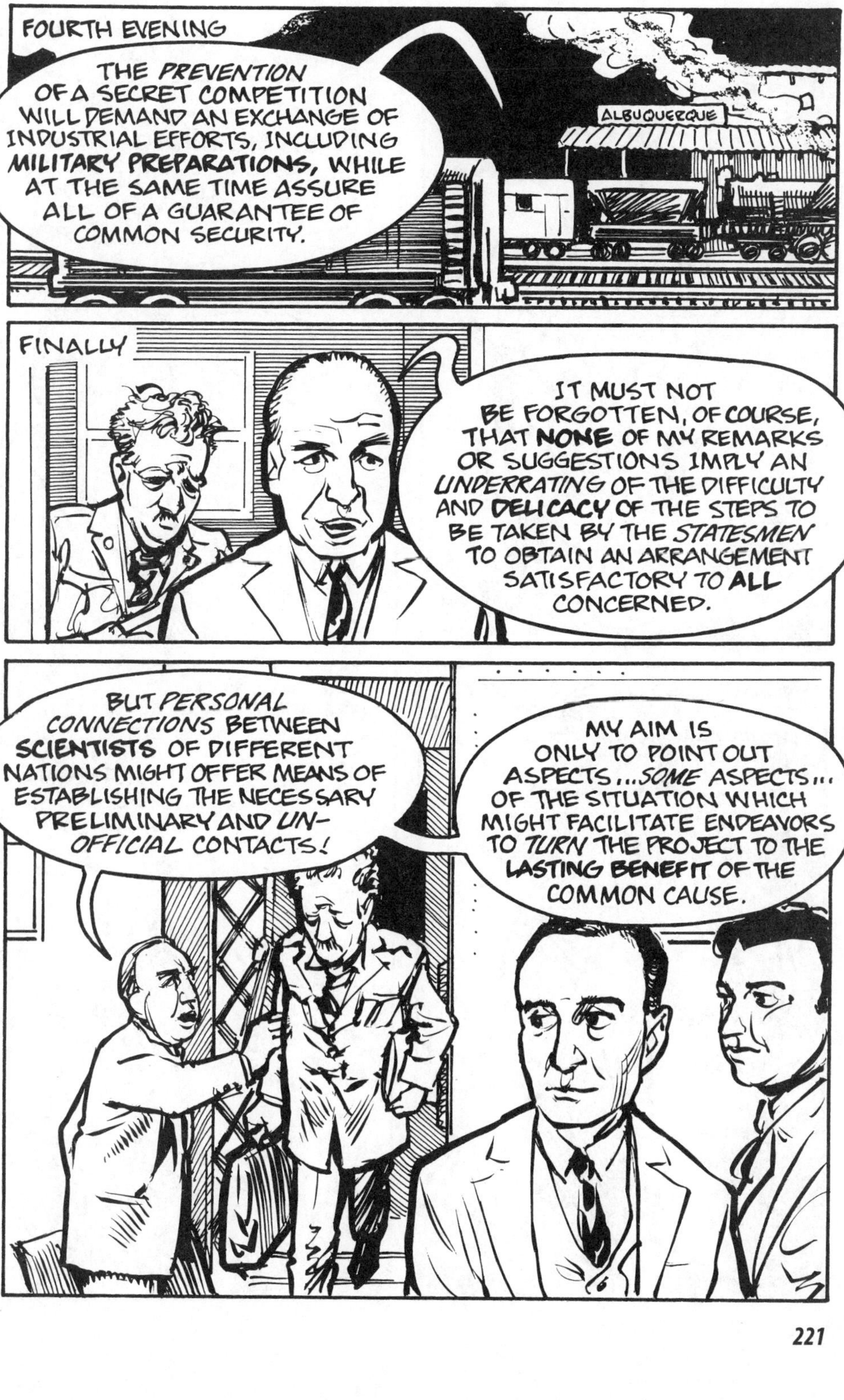
FOURTH EVENING
THE PREVENTION OF A SECRET COMPETITION WILL DEMAND AN EXCHANGE OF INDUSTRIAL EFFORTS, INCLUDING MILITARY PREPARATIONS, WHILE AT THE SAME TIME ASSURE ALL OF A GUARANTEE OF COMMON SECURITY.
ALBUQUERQUE
FINALLY
IT MUST NOT BE FORGOTTEN, OF COURSE, THAT NONE OF MY REMARKS OR SUGGESTIONS IMPLY AN UNDERRATING OF THE DIFFICULTY AND DELICACY OF THE STEPS TO BE TAKEN BY THE STATESMEN TO OBTAIN AN ARRANGEMENT SATISFACTORY TO ALL CONCERNED.
BUT PERSONAL CONNECTIONS BETWEEN SCIENTISTS OF DIFFERENT NATIONS MIGHT OFFER MEANS OF ESTABLISHING THE NECESSARY PRELIMINARY AND UN-OFFICIAL CONTACTS!
MY AIM IS ONLY TO POINT OUT ASPECTS... SOME ASPECTS... OF THE SITUATION WHICH MIGHT FACILITATE ENDEAVORS TO TURN THE PROJECT TO THE LASTING BENEFIT OF THE COMMON CAUSE.

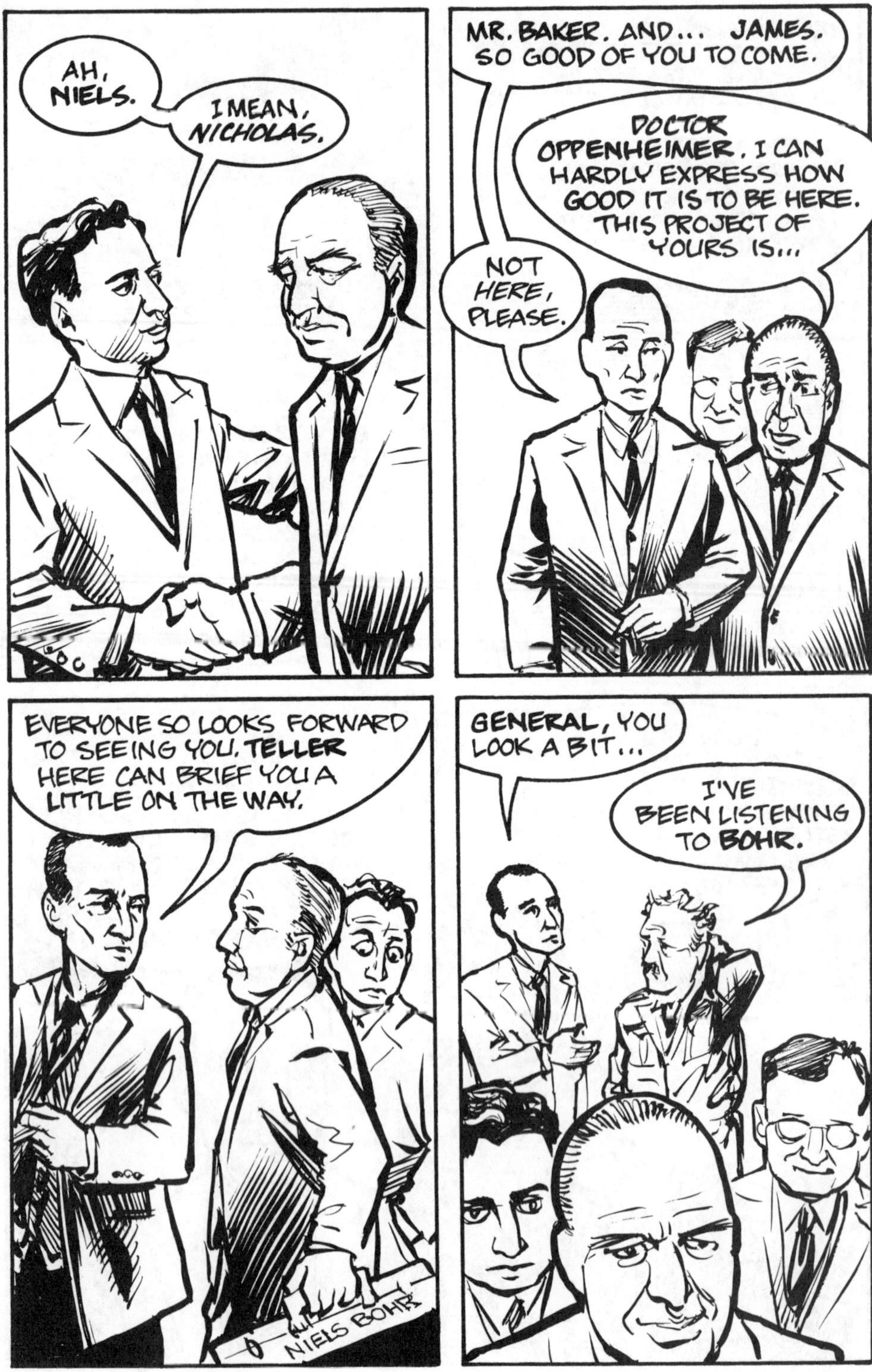
AH, NIELS.
I MEAN, NICHOLAS.
MR. BAKER. AND... JAMES. SO GOOD OF YOU TO COME.
DOCTOR OPPENHEIMER. I CAN HARDLY EXPRESS HOW GOOD IT IS TO BE HERE. THIS PROJECT OF YOURS IS...
NOT HERE, PLEASE.
EVERYONE SO LOOKS FORWARD TO SEEING YOU. TELLER HERE CAN BRIEF YOU A LITTLE ON THE WAY.
NIELS BOHR
GENERAL, YOU LOOK A BIT...
I'VE BEEN LISTENING TO BOHR.

YES, I'M SURE YOU HAVE.
SO, UNCLE NICK, REMEMBER WHAT YOU SAID ABOUT TURNING THE *WHOLE COUNTRY* INTO A FACTORY?

WELL, NOW YOU MUST SEE THAT WASN'T NEC—
NO, NO. I'VE BEEN TRAVELLING AROUND THIS COUNTRY.

YOU HAVE DONE JUST THAT!
HANFORD, WA
CHICAGO, IL
NYC
LOS ALAMOS, NM
OAK RIDGE, TN

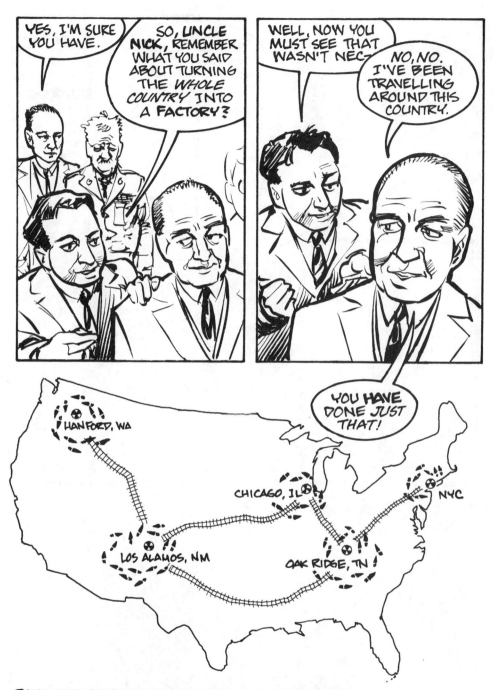

BOHR HADN'T BEEN EVERYWHERE, BUT HE *HAD* BEEN BUSY.

AND EVERYWHERE HE WENT HE TOOK HIS ARMS CONTROL MESSAGE, THE SCIENTISTS, BOTH THOSE WHO HAD ALREADY WORKED WITH HIM AND THOSE WHO HAD NEVER MET HIM, TOOK TO **BOHR** LIKE HE WAS...

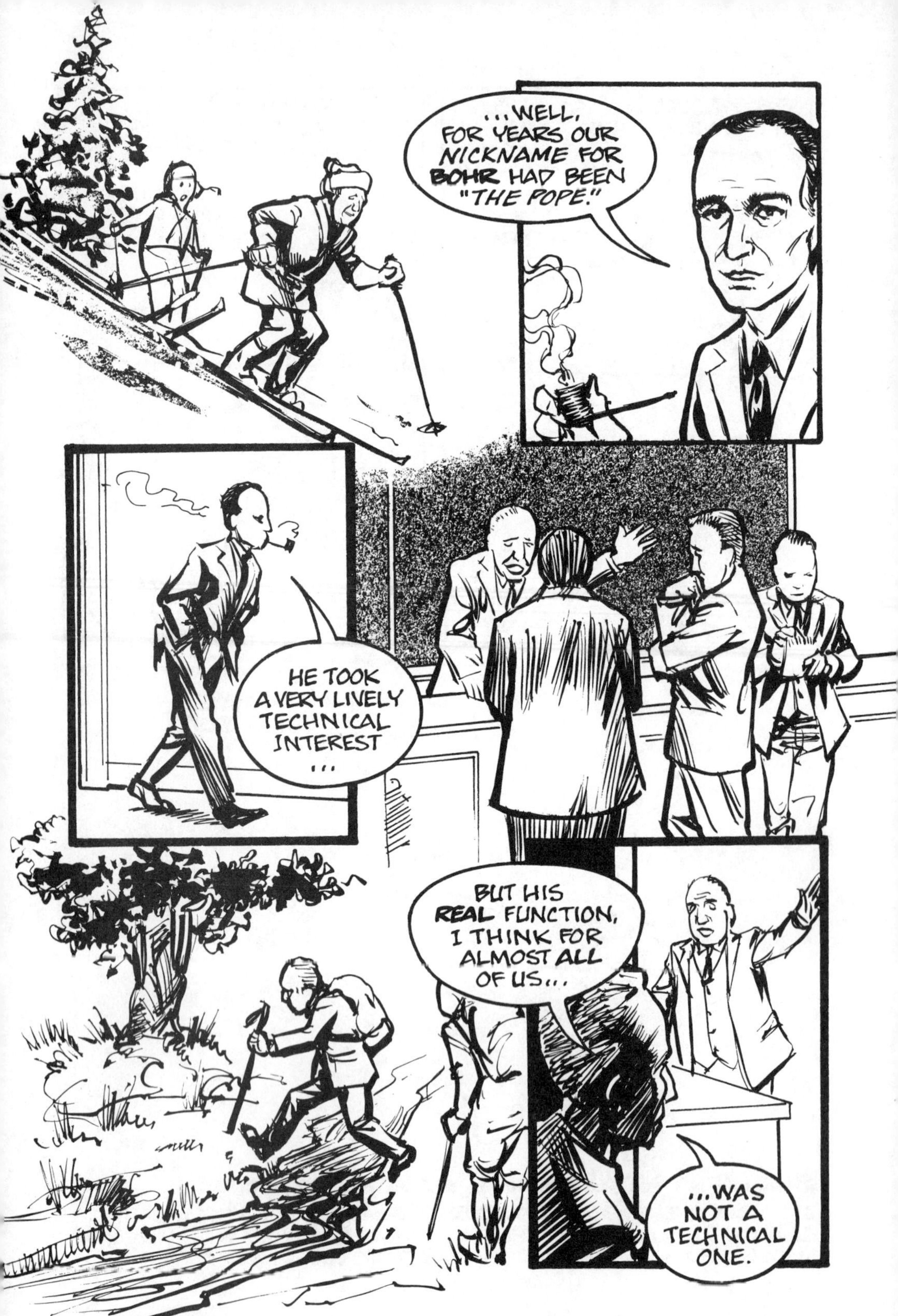
...WELL, FOR YEARS OUR NICKNAME FOR BOHR HAD BEEN "THE POPE."
HE TOOK A VERY LIVELY TECHNICAL INTEREST ...
BUT HIS REAL FUNCTION, I THINK FOR ALMOST ALL OF US...
...WAS NOT A TECHNICAL ONE.

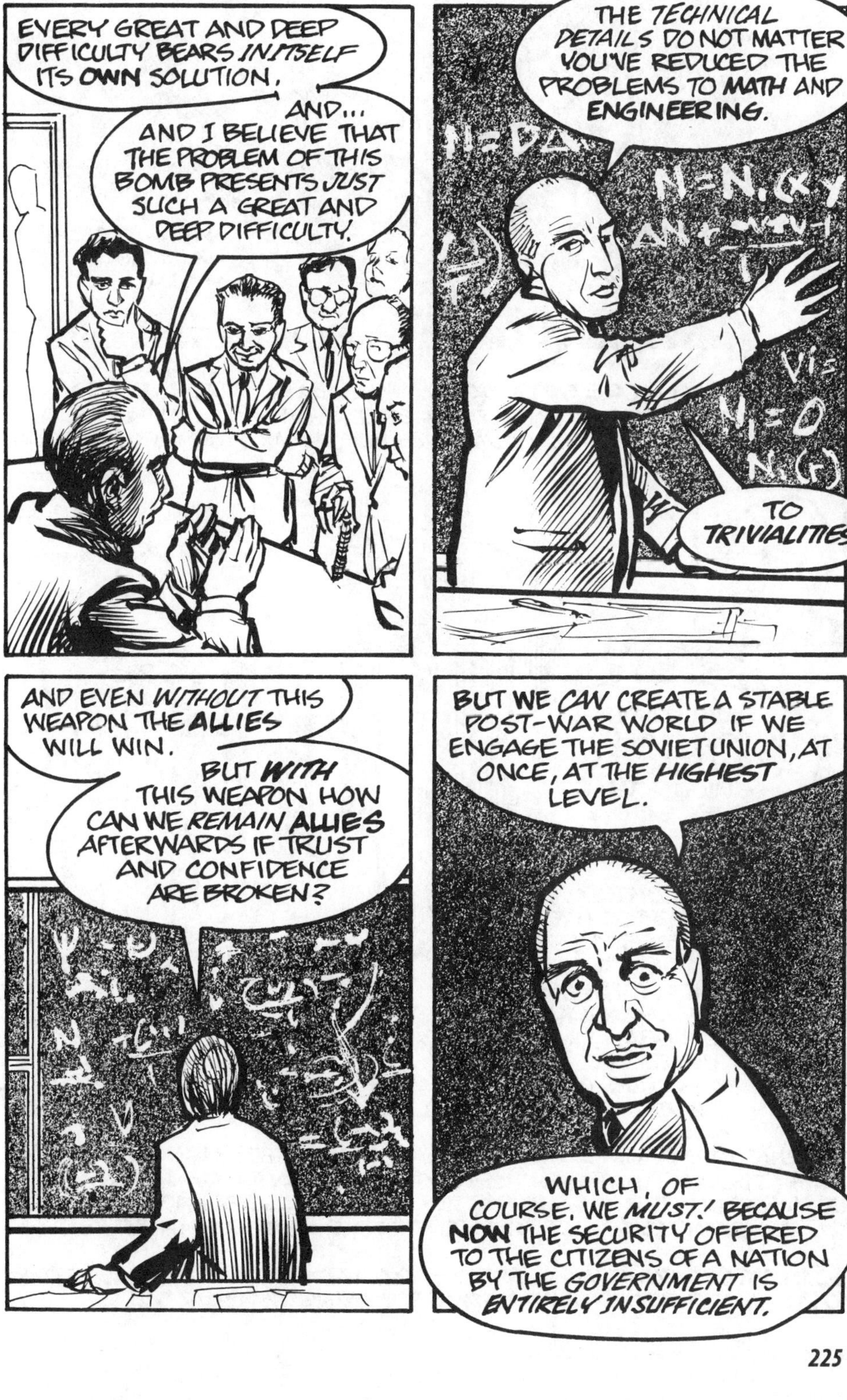
EVERY GREAT AND DEEP DIFFICULTY BEARS IN ITSELF ITS OWN SOLUTION.
AND... AND I BELIEVE THAT THE PROBLEM OF THIS BOMB PRESENTS JUST SUCH A GREAT AND DEEP DIFFICULTY.
THE TECHNICAL DETAILS DO NOT MATTER. YOU'VE REDUCED THE PROBLEMS TO MATH AND ENGINEERING.
TO TRIVIALITIES.
AND EVEN WITHOUT THIS WEAPON THE ALLIES WILL WIN.
BUT WITH THIS WEAPON HOW CAN WE REMAIN ALLIES AFTERWARDS IF TRUST AND CONFIDENCE ARE BROKEN?
BUT WE CAN CREATE A STABLE POST-WAR WORLD IF WE ENGAGE THE SOVIET UNION, AT ONCE, AT THE HIGHEST LEVEL.
WHICH, OF COURSE, WE MUST! BECAUSE NOW THE SECURITY OFFERED TO THE CITIZENS OF A NATION BY THE GOVERNMENT IS ENTIRELY INSUFFICIENT.

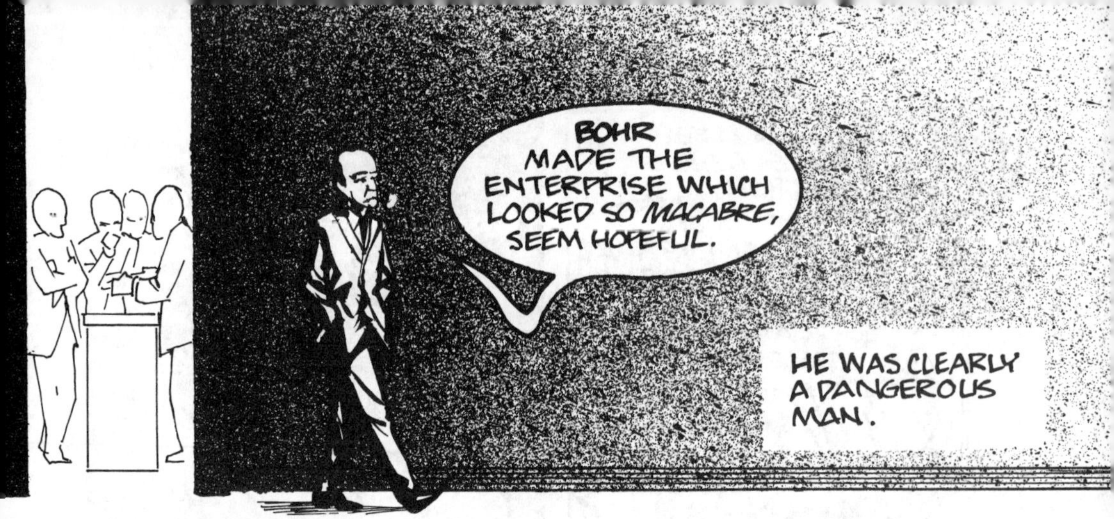
BOHR MADE THE ENTERPRISE WHICH LOOKED SO *MACABRE*, SEEM HOPEFUL.
HE WAS CLEARLY A DANGEROUS MAN.

AND GETTING MORE SO EVERY DAY. WHEN HE RETURNED TO WASHINGTON **BOHR** EXPRESSED THE NEED FOR ARMS CONTROL TO HIS FRIEND, AND *SUPREME COURT JUSTICE*, **FELIX FRANKFURTER**.

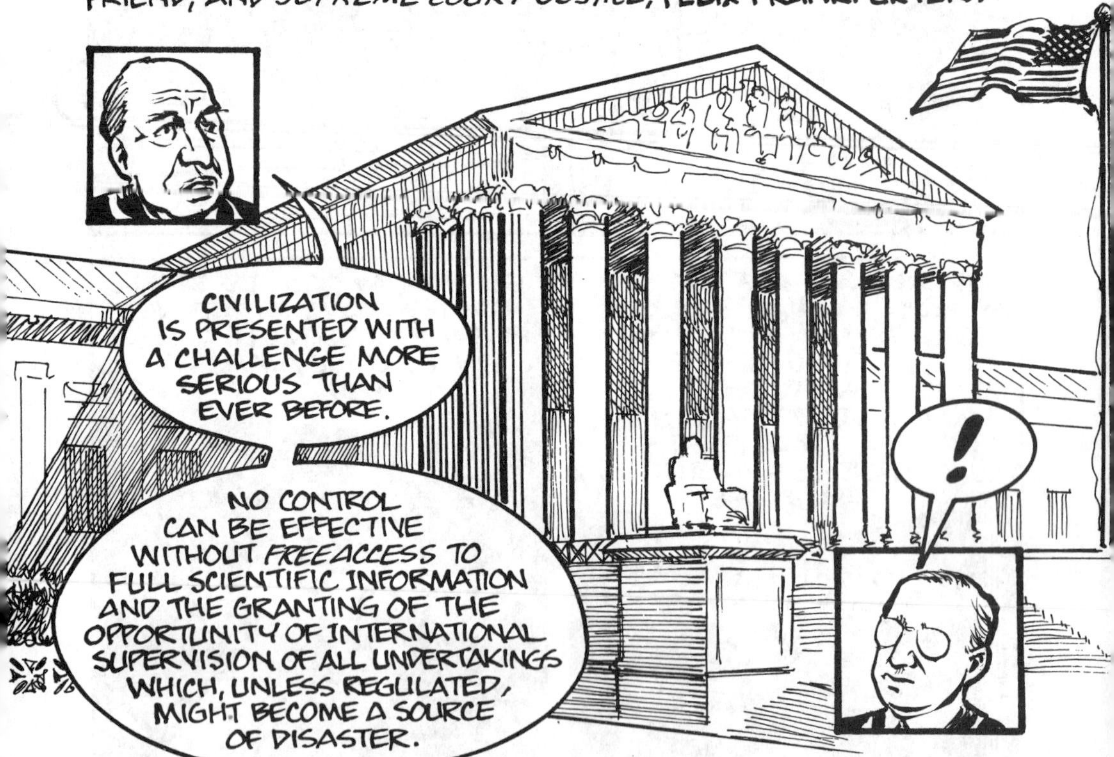
CIVILIZATION IS PRESENTED WITH A CHALLENGE MORE SERIOUS THAN EVER BEFORE.
NO CONTROL CAN BE EFFECTIVE WITHOUT *FREE ACCESS* TO FULL SCIENTIFIC INFORMATION AND THE GRANTING OF THE OPPORTUNITY OF INTERNATIONAL SUPERVISION OF ALL UNDERTAKINGS WHICH, UNLESS REGULATED, MIGHT BECOME A SOURCE OF DISASTER.
!

THIS WAS POTENTIALLY A SERIOUS BREACH, SINCE THE **MANHATTAN PROJECT** WAS *SO* SECRET THAT EVEN VICE-PRESIDENT **HARRY TRUMAN** KNEW *NOTHING* OF IT. FORTUNATELY **FRANKFURTER** WAS A CLOSE FRIEND AND ADVISOR TO ***PRESIDENT ROOSEVELT***. BETTER STILL, HE AGREED WITH **BOHR**.

SO IN THE END **BOHR** WAS SENT OFF TO *LONDON* WITH AN OFFICIAL LETTER TO DELIVER TO *BRITISH PRIME MINISTER* **WINSTON CHURCHILL**.

CHURCHILL KEPT HIM WAITING FOR *WEEKS*, DURING WHICH TIME AN INVITATION TO **EMIGRATE** TO *RUSSIA* –MANY MONTHS AFTER IT WAS SENT– FOUND ITS WAY FROM HIS FRIEND **KAPITZA** IN MOSCOW TO **MARGRETHE** IN STOCKHOLM TO **CHURCHILL'S** AGENTS IN *LONDON* TO **BOHR**.

BAD TIMING.

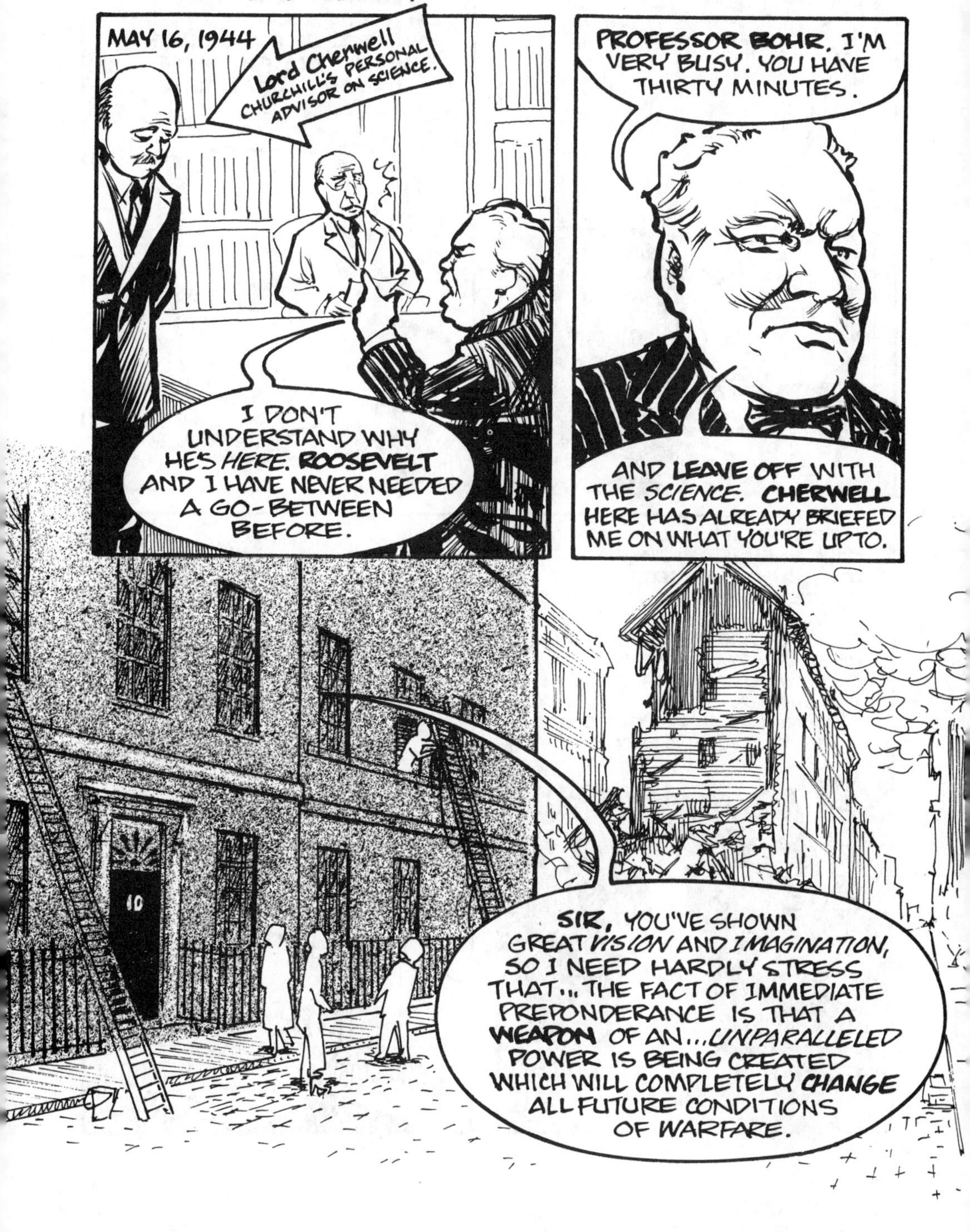

MAY 16, 1944
Lord Cherwell CHURCHILL'S PERSONAL ADVISOR ON SCIENCE.
I DON'T UNDERSTAND WHY HE'S *HERE*. **ROOSEVELT** AND I HAVE NEVER NEEDED A GO-BETWEEN BEFORE.
PROFESSOR **BOHR**. I'M VERY BUSY. YOU HAVE THIRTY MINUTES.
AND **LEAVE OFF** WITH THE *SCIENCE*. **CHERWELL** HERE HAS ALREADY BRIEFED ME ON WHAT YOU'RE UP TO.
10
SIR, YOU'VE SHOWN GREAT *VISION* AND *IMAGINATION*, SO I NEED HARDLY STRESS THAT... THE FACT OF IMMEDIATE PREPONDERANCE IS THAT A **WEAPON** OF AN... *UNPARALLELED* POWER IS BEING CREATED WHICH WILL COMPLETELY **CHANGE** ALL FUTURE CONDITIONS OF WARFARE.

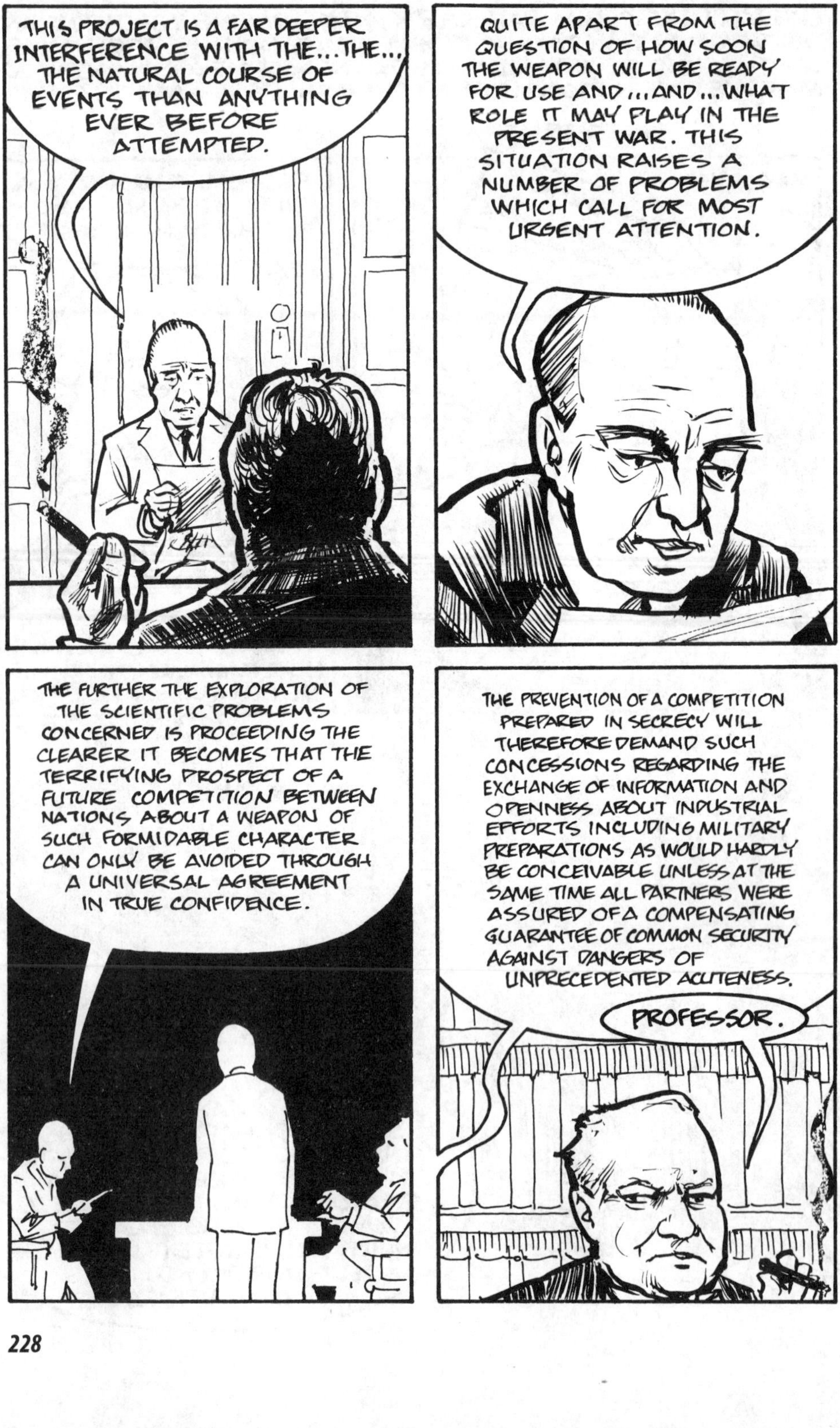
THIS PROJECT IS A FAR DEEPER INTERFERENCE WITH THE... THE... THE NATURAL COURSE OF EVENTS THAN ANYTHING EVER BEFORE ATTEMPTED.
QUITE APART FROM THE QUESTION OF HOW SOON THE WEAPON WILL BE READY FOR USE AND... AND... WHAT ROLE IT MAY PLAY IN THE PRESENT WAR. THIS SITUATION RAISES A NUMBER OF PROBLEMS WHICH CALL FOR MOST URGENT ATTENTION.
THE FURTHER THE EXPLORATION OF THE SCIENTIFIC PROBLEMS CONCERNED IS PROCEEDING THE CLEARER IT BECOMES THAT THE TERRIFYING PROSPECT OF A FUTURE COMPETITION BETWEEN NATIONS ABOUT A WEAPON OF SUCH FORMIDABLE CHARACTER CAN ONLY BE AVOIDED THROUGH A UNIVERSAL AGREEMENT IN TRUE CONFIDENCE.
THE PREVENTION OF A COMPETITION PREPARED IN SECRECY WILL THEREFORE DEMAND SUCH CONCESSIONS REGARDING THE EXCHANGE OF INFORMATION AND OPENNESS ABOUT INDUSTRIAL EFFORTS INCLUDING MILITARY PREPARATIONS AS WOULD HARDLY BE CONCEIVABLE UNLESS AT THE SAME TIME ALL PARTNERS WERE ASSURED OF A COMPENSATING GUARANTEE OF COMMON SECURITY AGAINST DANGERS OF UNPRECEDENTED ACUTENESS.
PROFESSOR.

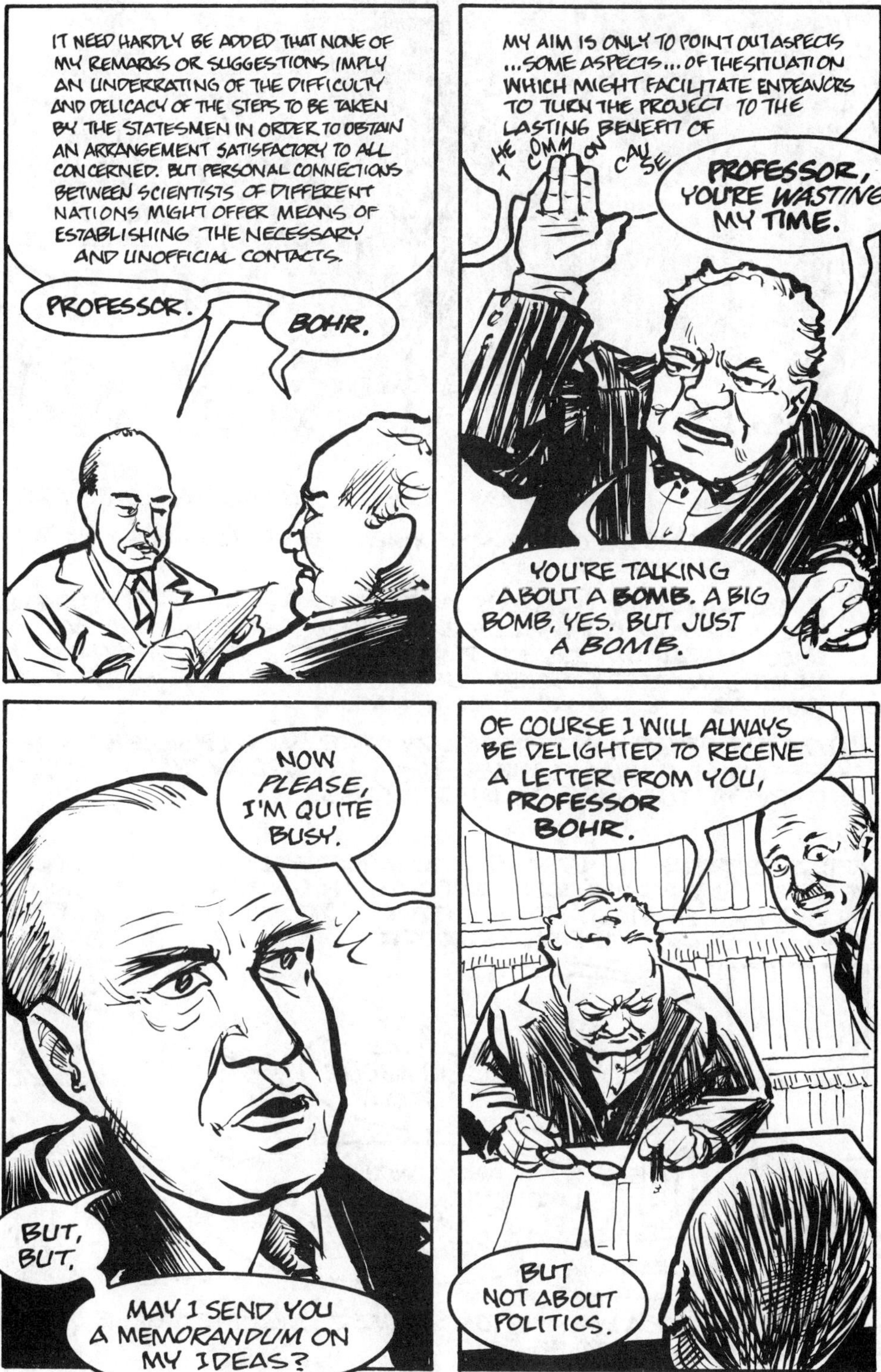

IT NEED HARDLY BE ADDED THAT NONE OF MY REMARKS OR SUGGESTIONS IMPLY AN UNDERRATING OF THE DIFFICULTY AND DELICACY OF THE STEPS TO BE TAKEN BY THE STATESMEN IN ORDER TO OBTAIN AN ARRANGEMENT SATISFACTORY TO ALL CONCERNED. BUT PERSONAL CONNECTIONS BETWEEN SCIENTISTS OF DIFFERENT NATIONS MIGHT OFFER MEANS OF ESTABLISHING THE NECESSARY AND UNOFFICIAL CONTACTS.
PROFESSOR.
BOHR.
MY AIM IS ONLY TO POINT OUT ASPECTS ...SOME ASPECTS... OF THE SITUATION WHICH MIGHT FACILITATE ENDEAVORS TO TURN THE PROJECT TO THE LASTING BENEFIT OF
THE COMMON CAUSE
PROFESSOR, YOU'RE *WASTING* MY TIME.
YOU'RE TALKING ABOUT A **BOMB**. A BIG BOMB, YES. BUT JUST A *BOMB*.
NOW *PLEASE*, I'M QUITE BUSY.
BUT, BUT,
MAY I SEND YOU A MEMORANDUM ON MY IDEAS?
OF COURSE I WILL ALWAYS BE DELIGHTED TO RECEIVE A LETTER FROM YOU, PROFESSOR BOHR.
BUT NOT ABOUT POLITICS.

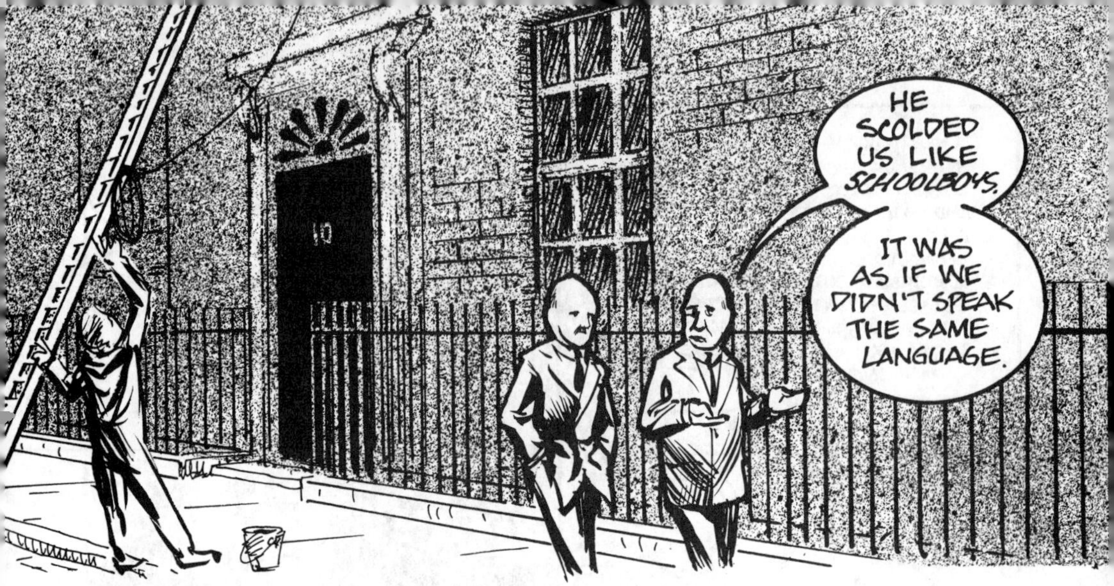
HE SCOLDED US LIKE SCHOOLBOYS.
IT WAS AS IF WE DIDN'T SPEAK THE SAME LANGUAGE.
10

WHY DID **BOHR** FAIL HERE? MANY REASONS, BUT THE MAIN ONES ARE:

1) **BOHR** WAS NEVER COMPELLING WHEN IT CAME TO DELIVERING A PREPARED SPEECH.

2) **CHURCHILL** KNEW FROM **LORD CHERWELL** THAT AT THIS POINT THERE WAS NO BOMB, IT WAS ALL STILL *THEORY*. THERE WASN'T EVEN ENOUGH **URANIUM-235** OR **PLUTONIUM** TO *BUILD* ONE! AND WHAT'S MORE, THE SCIENTISTS DIDN'T HAVE A CLEAR IDEA OF HOW MUCH "ENOUGH" REALLY WAS.

3) ON THE *OTHER* HAND, ON THE DAY THEY MET, **CHURCHILL** KNEW —BECAUSE HE WAS PLANNING IT— THAT **D-DAY** WAS ABOUT TO HAPPEN. FOR SURE. IN A FEW WEEKS.

AFTER PREPARING A LENGTHY *POLITICAL* NOTE TO **CHURCHILL**, **BOHR** RETURNED TO WASHINGTON AND TURNED HIS ATTENTION TO THE MUCH MORE GENIAL AND RECEPTIVE ***FDR***. WHO HAD BEEN FORE-WARNED BY **JUSTICE FRANKFURTER**.

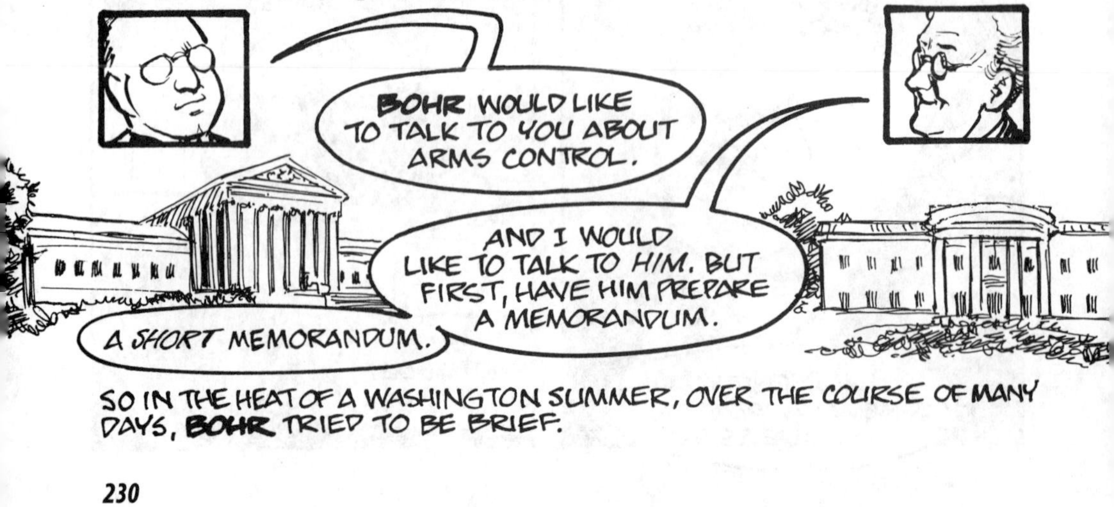
BOHR WOULD LIKE TO TALK TO YOU ABOUT ARMS CONTROL.
AND I WOULD LIKE TO TALK TO *HIM*. BUT FIRST, HAVE HIM PREPARE A MEMORANDUM.
A *SHORT* MEMORANDUM.

SO IN THE HEAT OF A WASHINGTON SUMMER, OVER THE COURSE OF MANY DAYS, **BOHR** TRIED TO BE BRIEF.

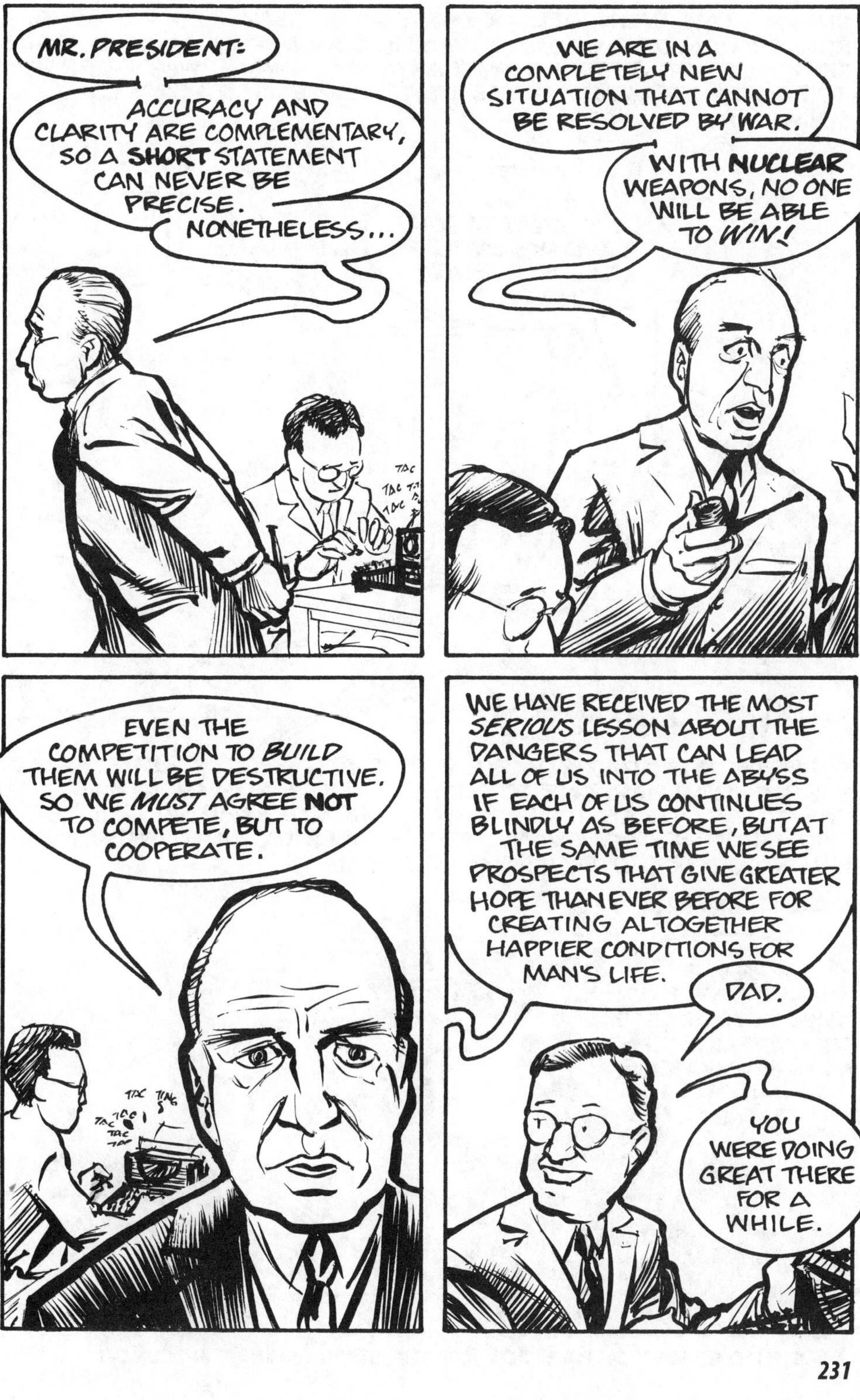
MR. PRESIDENT:
ACCURACY AND CLARITY ARE COMPLEMENTARY, SO A **SHORT** STATEMENT CAN NEVER BE PRECISE.
NONETHELESS...
TAC TAC TAC
WE ARE IN A COMPLETELY NEW SITUATION THAT CANNOT BE RESOLVED BY WAR.
WITH **NUCLEAR** WEAPONS, NO ONE WILL BE ABLE TO *WIN*!
EVEN THE COMPETITION TO *BUILD* THEM WILL BE DESTRUCTIVE. SO WE *MUST* AGREE **NOT** TO COMPETE, BUT TO COOPERATE.
TAC TING TAC TAC TAC TAC
WE HAVE RECEIVED THE MOST *SERIOUS* LESSON ABOUT THE DANGERS THAT CAN LEAD ALL OF US INTO THE ABYSS IF EACH OF US CONTINUES BLINDLY AS BEFORE, BUT AT THE SAME TIME WE SEE PROSPECTS THAT GIVE GREATER HOPE THAN EVER BEFORE FOR CREATING ALTOGETHER HAPPIER CONDITIONS FOR MAN'S LIFE.
DAD.
YOU WERE DOING GREAT THERE FOR A WHILE.

THIS MEETING WENT WELL. **ROOSEVELT** WAS AMUSED BY **BOHR'S** DESCRIPTION OF HIS TIME WITH **CHURCHILL** —HE ASSURED **BOHR** THAT THIS WAS JUST THE *PRIME MINISTER'S* WAY— WAS RECEPTIVE TO **BOHR'S** IDEAS, AND THEY ENTERTAINED EACH OTHER WITH FOLKSY ANECDOTES.

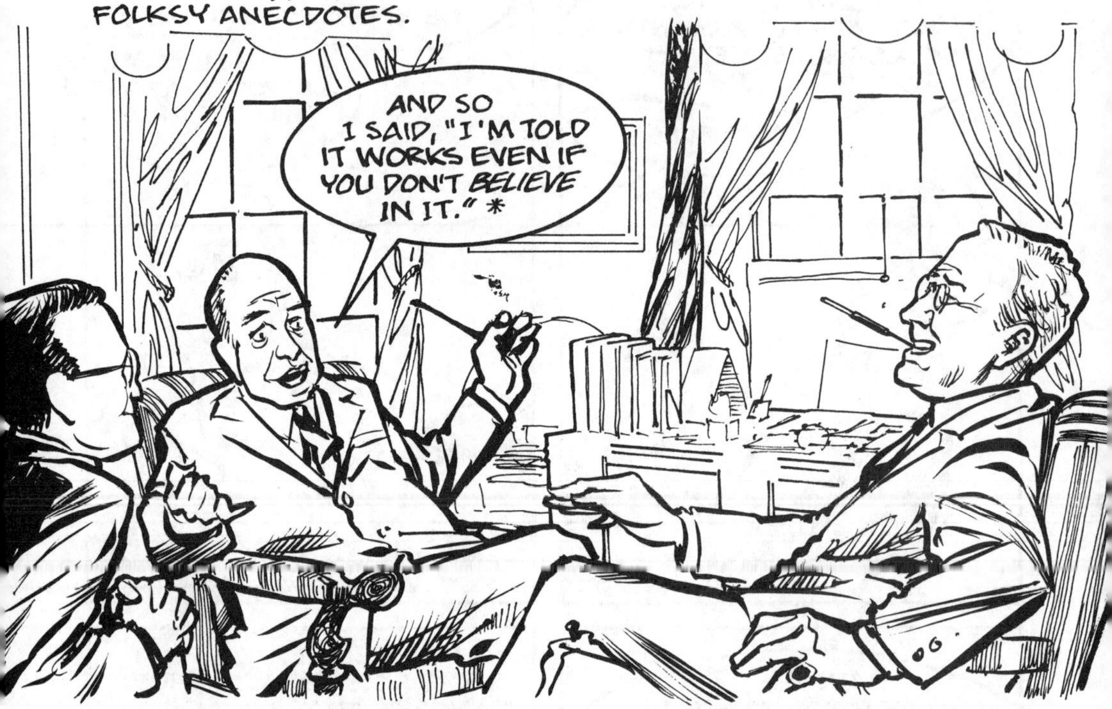
AND SO I SAID, "I'M TOLD IT WORKS EVEN IF YOU DON'T *BELIEVE* IN IT." *

BUT BEFORE **BOHR** HAD A CHANCE TO SEND **FDR** A FOLLOW-UP MESSAGE, THE PRESIDENT HAD GONE TO QUEBEC TO MEET WITH **CHURCHILL**. BY THIS TIME (LATE SEPTEMBER, 1944) THE **ALLIES** HAD LIBERATED *PARIS*, AND HAD ENTERED *GERMANY*. THINGS WERE LOOKING UP, THOUGH NOT FOR **BOHR'S** *OPEN WORLD* PROPOSAL.

OR FOR HIMSELF.

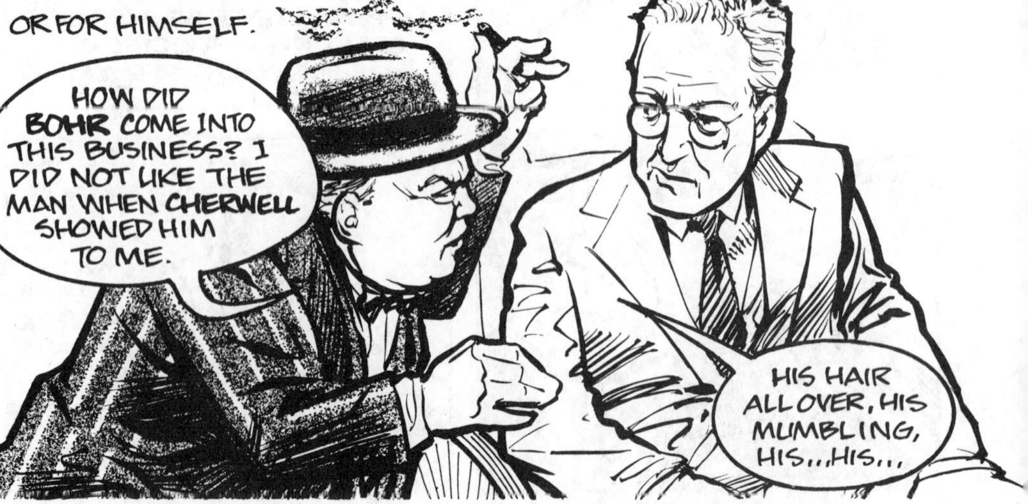
HOW DID **BOHR** COME INTO THIS BUSINESS? I DID NOT LIKE THE MAN WHEN **CHERWELL** SHOWED HIM TO ME.
HIS HAIR ALL OVER, HIS MUMBLING, HIS...HIS...

* SEE "HORSESHOES" ON PAGE 302 FOR THE STORY BEHIND THE PUNCHLINE.

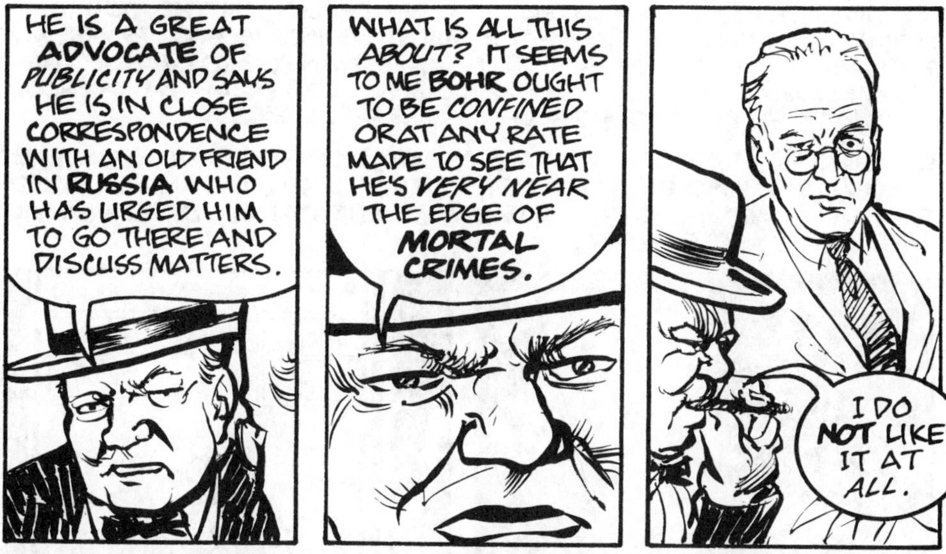
HE IS A GREAT ADVOCATE OF PUBLICITY AND SAYS HE IS IN CLOSE CORRESPONDENCE WITH AN OLD FRIEND IN RUSSIA WHO HAS URGED HIM TO GO THERE AND DISCUSS MATTERS.
WHAT IS ALL THIS ABOUT? IT SEEMS TO ME BOHR OUGHT TO BE CONFINED OR AT ANY RATE MADE TO SEE THAT HE'S VERY NEAR THE EDGE OF MORTAL CRIMES.
I DO NOT LIKE IT AT ALL.

IN THE END, NEITHER DID **FDR**, AND AS A RESULT THE TWO ISSUED THE *"AIDE MÉMOIRE OF THE CONVERSATION BETWEEN THE PRESIDENT AND THE PRIME MINISTER AT HYDE PARK, 19th SEPTEMBER, 1944."* IT HAD THREE THESES:

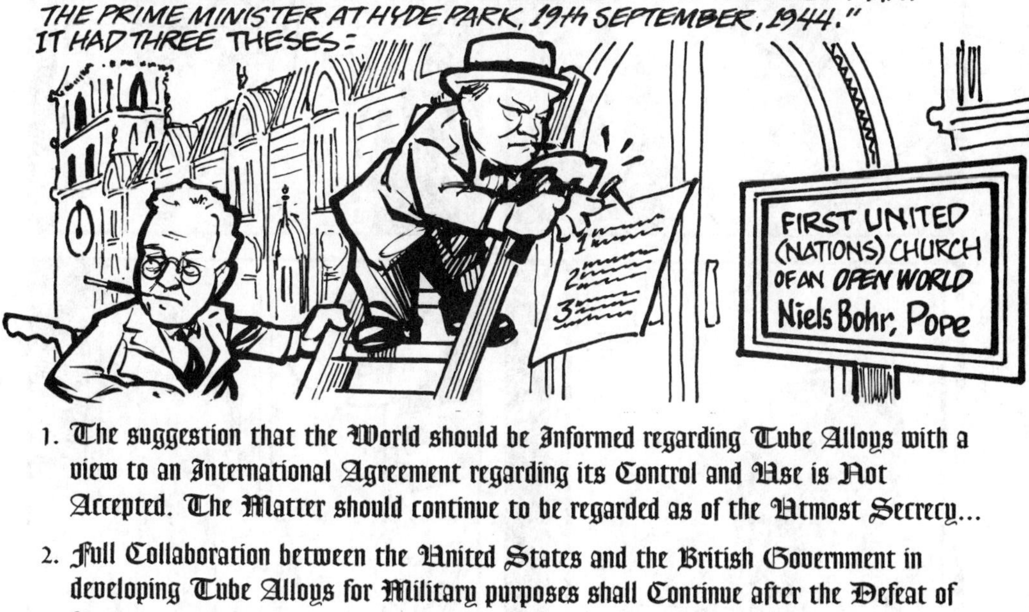
1
2
3
FIRST UNITED (NATIONS) CHURCH OF AN OPEN WORLD
Niels Bohr, Pope

1. The suggestion that the World should be Informed regarding Tube Alloys with a view to an International Agreement regarding its Control and Use is Not Accepted. The Matter should continue to be regarded as of the Utmost Secrecy...
2. Full Collaboration between the United States and the British Government in developing Tube Alloys for Military purposes shall Continue after the Defeat of Japan...
3. Enquiries should be made regarding the Activities of Professor Bohr and Steps Taken to Ensure he is responsible for No Leakage of Information, Particularly to the Russians.

RECALL THAT *"TUBE ALLOYS"* WAS THE **BRITISH** NAME FOR THE *MANHATTAN PROJECT*, AND **BRITISH** SPELLING PREVAILED THROUGHOUT THE REST OF THE DOCUMENT—AN UNSUBTLE INDICATION OF ITS AUTHOR'S IDENTITY.

AS OPPENHEIMER SAID LATER, "OUR MONOPOLY [ON THE ATOMIC BOMB] IS LIKE A CAKE OF ICE MELTING IN THE SUN. BOHR WAS FOR *ACTION*, AND TIMELY ACTION ... HE WANTED TO CHANGE THE FRAMEWORK IN WHICH THE PROBLEM WOULD APPEAR *EARLY* ENOUGH SO THAT THE PROBLEM ITSELF WOULD BE ALTERED."

SO WHEN AN *INTERIM COMMITTEE* ON ARMS CONTROL FINALLY CONVENED IN MAY, 1945, AND MET, AND MET, AND MET, AND MET AND IN THE END RECOMMENDED *NOTHING* OF SUBSTANCE, OPPENHEIMER WENT TO CONSOLE BOHR.

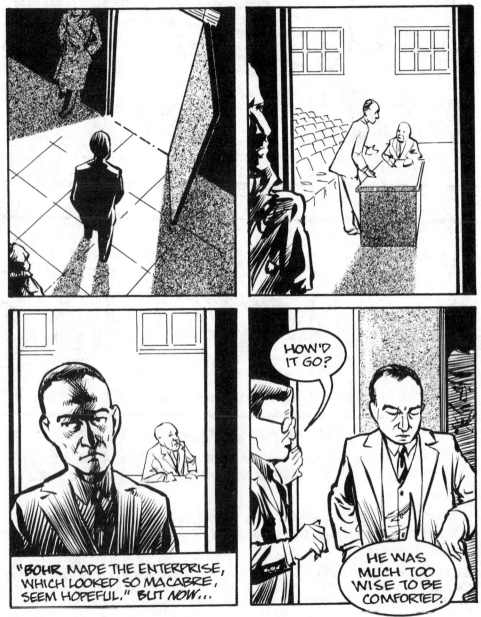

HOW'D IT GO?

"BOHR MADE THE ENTERPRISE, WHICH LOOKED SO MACABRE, SEEM HOPEFUL." BUT *NOW*...

HE WAS MUCH TOO WISE TO BE COMFORTED.

Chapter 13

BECAUSE OF ITS SPECIAL PROPORTIONS THE **TIPPE TOP**, WHEN SPUN HARD, ENDS UP SPINNING AROUND THE AXIS CORRESPONDING TO ITS SMALLEST MOMENT OF INERTIA..., AND WITH ITS HEAVIEST PART UP. THE FRICTIONAL FORCE BETWEEN THE **TOP** AND THE SURFACE IT SPINS ON DOES THE TRICK: THIS FORCE PROVIDES A *TORQUE* WHICH FLIPS THE TOP OVER. (IT SPINS MORE SLOWLY ONCE IT FLIPS, SINCE ITS CENTER OF GRAVITY IS THEN MUCH HIGHER THAN AT THE START. SO SOME KINETIC ENERGY IS CONVERTED INTO POTENTIAL ENERGY IN THE PROCESS.)

IN THE 1950s A NUMBER OF PHYSICISTS — INCLUDING **BOHR**, WHO ALWAYS HAD AN INTEREST IN ROTATING THINGS, BE THEY ELECTRONS OR ATOMS OR TOPS — TRIED TO UNDERSTAND THE BEHAVIOR OF THE TIPPE TOP IN BOTH PHYSICAL AND MATHEMATICAL TERMS. THE EQUATIONS (FIRST PUT FORTH IN **J.H. JELLETT'S** 1872 BOOK ENTITLED *TREATISE ON THE THEORY OF FRICTION*) ARE DIFFICULT TO SOLVE, THOUGH. MORE THAN 100 YEARS AFTER **JELLETT'S** BOOK APPEARED **STEFAN EBENFELD** AND **FLORIAN SCHECK**, WITH THE HELP OF COMPUTER ANALYSIS, CAME UP WITH AN ELEGANT SOLUTION TO THE PROBLEM IN *"A NEW ANALYSIS OF THE TIPPE TOP: ASYMPTOTIC STATES AND LIUPANOV STABILITY"* (ANNALS OF PHYSICS, vol 243, p. 195, 1995).

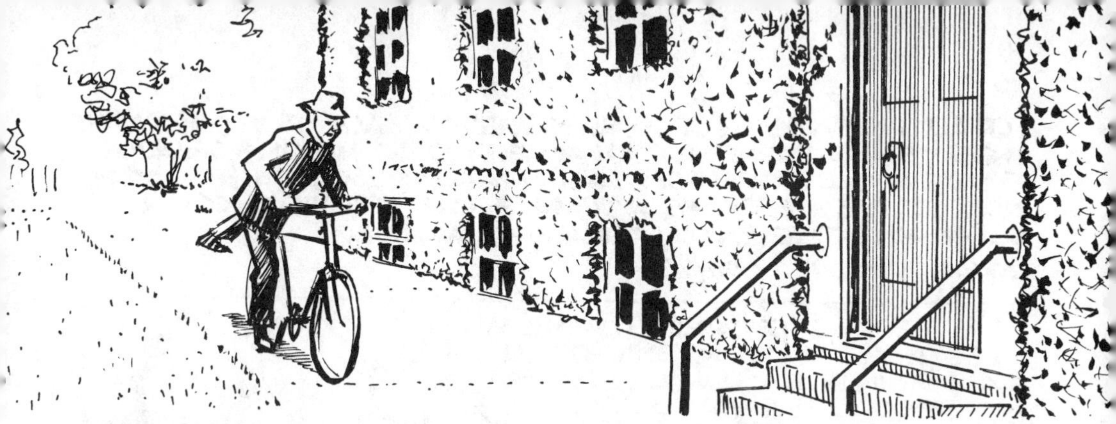

BEFORE **BOHR** RETURNED TO HIS INSTITUTE IN *AUGUST, 1945* – AND EVEN BEFORE *JAPAN* HAD SURRENDERED – HE TOOK HIS CASE FOR *ARMS CONTROL* AND AN *OPEN WORLD* TO THE **PUBLIC**... AND RIGHT ON **CHURCHILL'S** HOME TURF, IN A LETTER TO THE *LONDON TIMES* HE TITLED "SCIENCE AND CIVILIZATION."

IN IT HE SAID THE SAME ABOUT THE SAME THINGS, AND THEN HE SAID THE SAME AGAIN IN AN ARTICLE FOR THE JOURNAL *SCIENCE*.

NEITHER ATTRACTED MUCH PUBLIC ATTENTION, REALLY. THE WORLD AT LARGE WASN'T READY TO THINK ABOUT ARMS CONTROL. BUT THE *RUSSIANS* FINALLY CAUGHT UP WITH HIM IN *COPENHAGEN* UNDER THE PRETENSE OF DELIVERING A LETTER FROM HIS FRIEND **PETER KAPITZA**, WHO WAS NOT PERMITTED TO LEAVE THE **SOVIET UNION**.

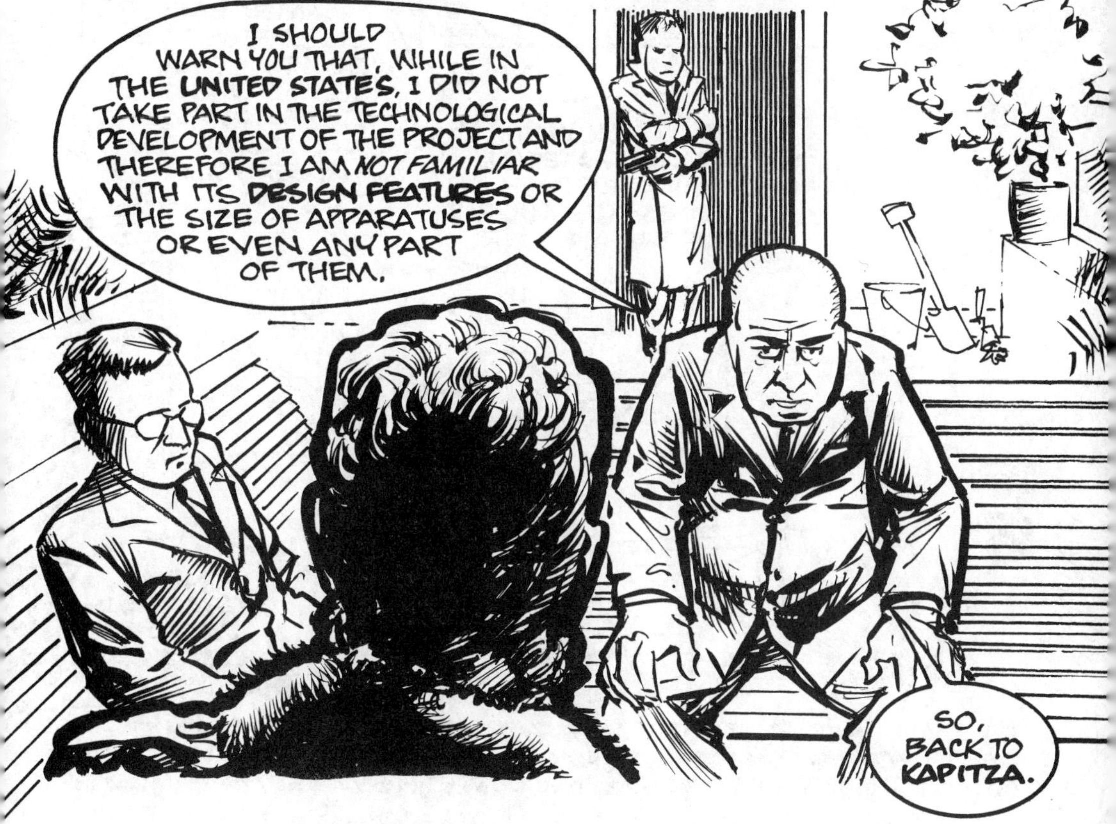
I SHOULD WARN YOU THAT, WHILE IN THE UNITED STATES, I DID NOT TAKE PART IN THE TECHNOLOGICAL DEVELOPMENT OF THE PROJECT AND THEREFORE I AM NOT FAMILIAR WITH ITS DESIGN FEATURES OR THE SIZE OF APPARATUSES OR EVEN ANY PART OF THEM.
SO, BACK TO KAPITZA.

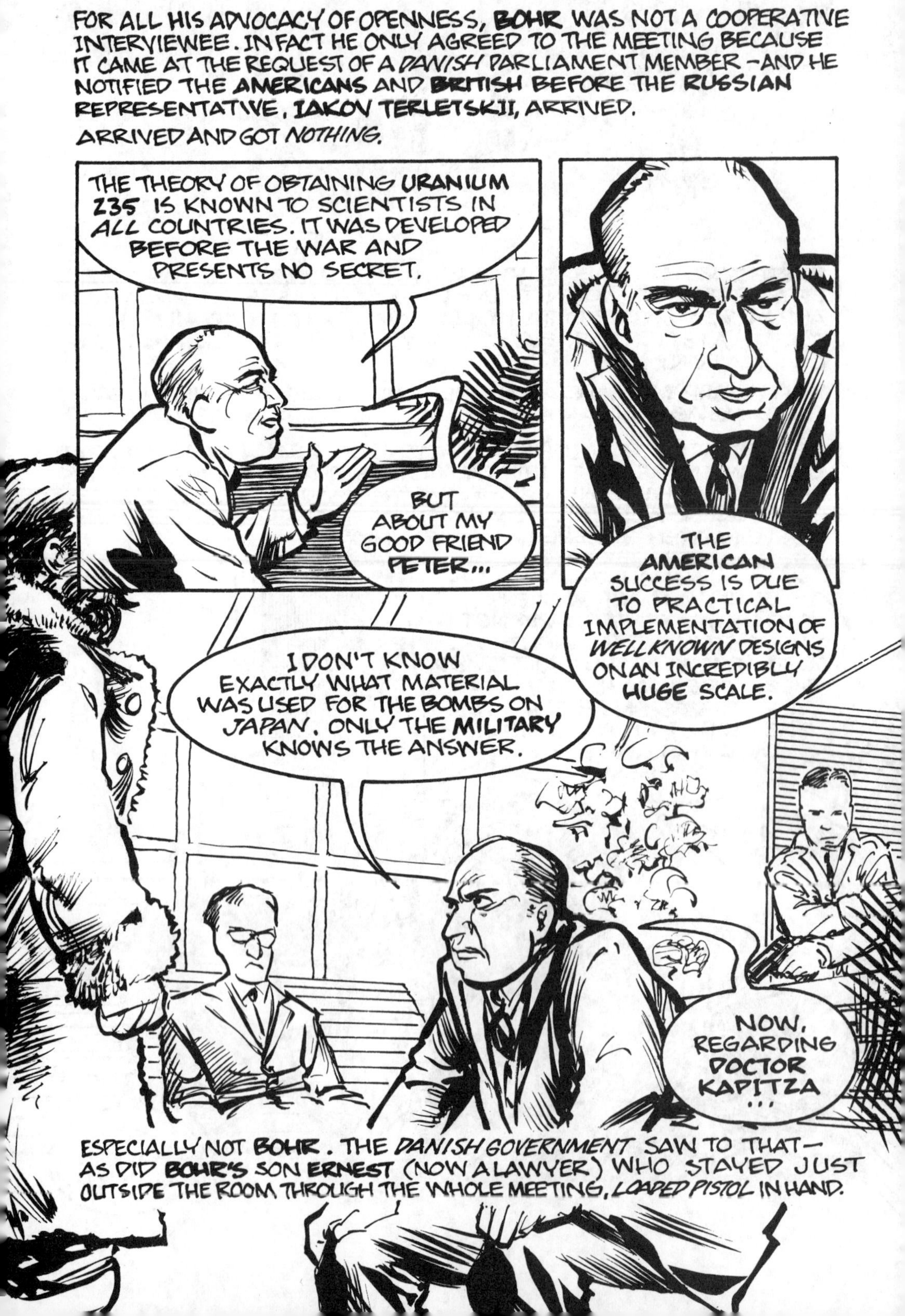
FOR ALL HIS ADVOCACY OF OPENNESS, BOHR WAS NOT A COOPERATIVE INTERVIEWEE. IN FACT HE ONLY AGREED TO THE MEETING BECAUSE IT CAME AT THE REQUEST OF A DANISH PARLIAMENT MEMBER -AND HE NOTIFIED THE AMERICANS AND BRITISH BEFORE THE RUSSIAN REPRESENTATIVE, IAKOV TERLETSKII, ARRIVED.
ARRIVED AND GOT NOTHING.
THE THEORY OF OBTAINING URANIUM 235 IS KNOWN TO SCIENTISTS IN ALL COUNTRIES. IT WAS DEVELOPED BEFORE THE WAR AND PRESENTS NO SECRET.
BUT ABOUT MY GOOD FRIEND PETER...
THE AMERICAN SUCCESS IS DUE TO PRACTICAL IMPLEMENTATION OF WELLKNOWN DESIGNS ON AN INCREDIBLY HUGE SCALE.
I DON'T KNOW EXACTLY WHAT MATERIAL WAS USED FOR THE BOMBS ON JAPAN. ONLY THE MILITARY KNOWS THE ANSWER.
NOW, REGARDING DOCTOR KAPITZA ...
ESPECIALLY NOT BOHR. THE DANISH GOVERNMENT SAW TO THAT— AS DID BOHR'S SON ERNEST (NOW A LAWYER) WHO STAYED JUST OUTSIDE THE ROOM THROUGH THE WHOLE MEETING, LOADED PISTOL IN HAND.

THE CAUTION WAS JUSTIFIABLE SINCE SCIENTISTS WERE NOW SPOILS OF WAR.

BOHR KNEW OF THE RACE WITH THE *SOVIETS* TO MAKE **WERNER VON BRAUN** AND OTHER *GERMAN ROCKET EXPERTS* OFFERS THEY COULDN'T REFUSE. AND HE ALMOST CERTAINLY HAD WORD OF **HEISENBERG'S** REMOVAL TO *FARM HALL* IN THE ENGLISH COUNTRYSIDE WHERE HE WAS STAYING *"AT HER MAJESTY'S PLEASURE."**

THE WORLD SITUATION WAS PRECARIOUS, AND SCIENTISTS WERE AT THE CENTER OF THE MAELSTROM. SO **BOHR** GOT TO WORK.

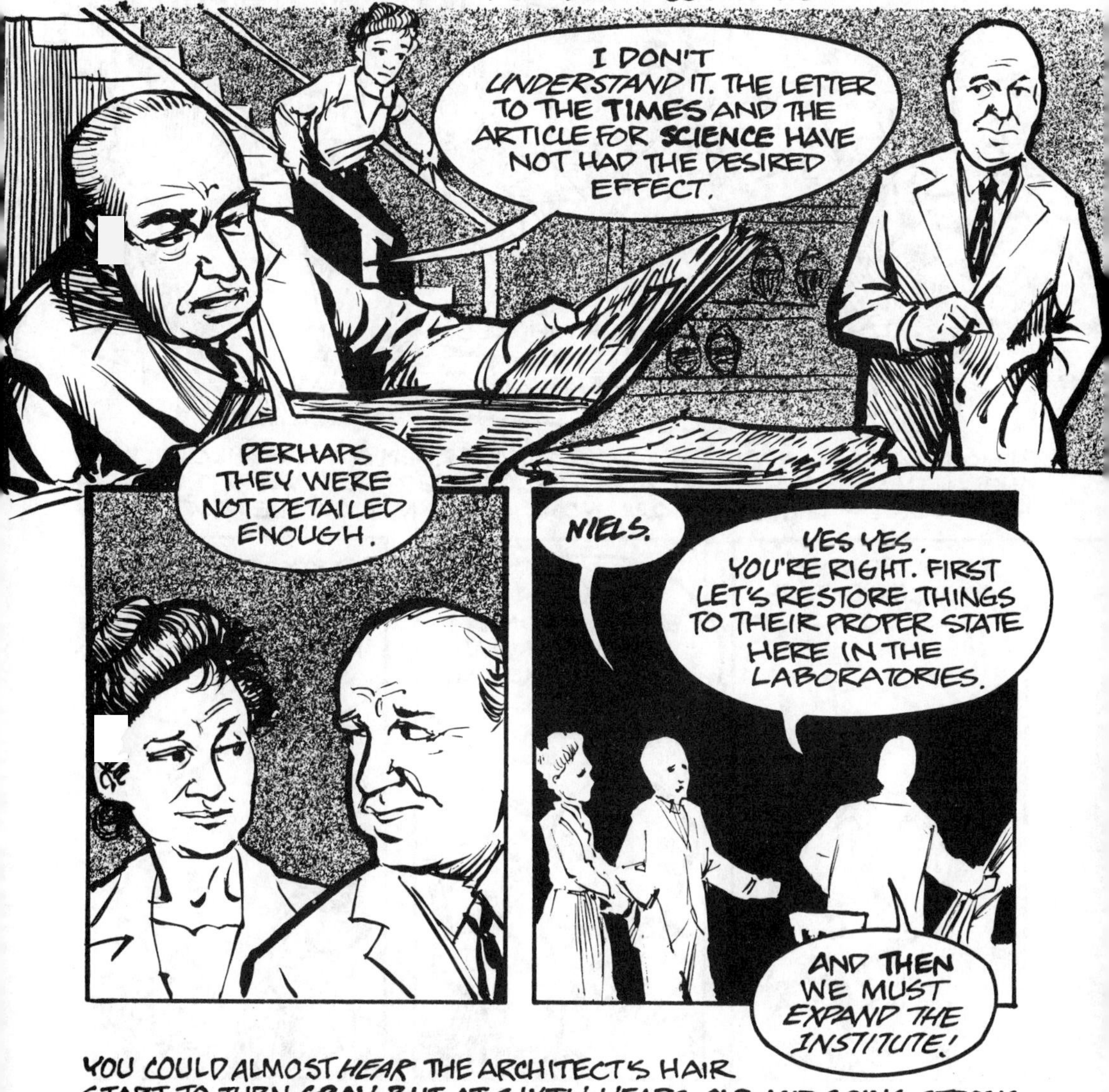
I DON'T UNDERSTAND IT. THE LETTER TO THE TIMES AND THE ARTICLE FOR SCIENCE HAVE NOT HAD THE DESIRED EFFECT.
PERHAPS THEY WERE NOT DETAILED ENOUGH.
NIELS.
YES YES. YOU'RE RIGHT. FIRST LET'S RESTORE THINGS TO THEIR PROPER STATE HERE IN THE LABORATORIES.
AND THEN WE MUST EXPAND THE INSTITUTE!

YOU COULD ALMOST *HEAR* THE ARCHITECT'S HAIR START TO TURN **GRAY**. BUT AT SIXTY YEARS OLD AND GOING STRONG, HE WAS READY FOR NEW CHALLENGES.

* IN OTHER WORDS: *HEISENBERG* WAS UNDER ARREST UNTIL THEY FOUND OUT WHAT HE AND HIS GROUP KNEW, AND HAD DONE. NOT MUCH AND VERY LITTLE, IT TURNED OUT.

AND *THE DANISH ORDER OF THE ELEPHANT* —USUALLY AWARDED ONLY TO ROYALTY AND HEADS OF STATE— GAVE AN OFFICIAL IMPRIMATUR TO BOHR'S INTERNATIONAL ROLE, BOTH WITHIN AND OUTSIDE OF PHYSICS.

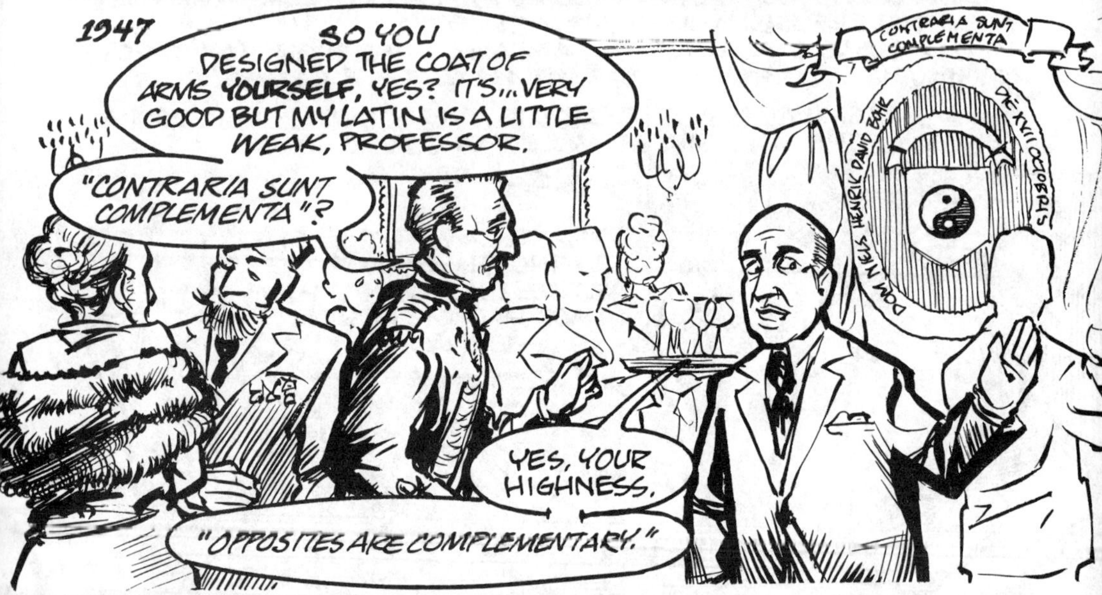
1947
SO YOU DESIGNED THE COAT OF ARMS **YOURSELF**, YES? IT'S... VERY GOOD BUT MY LATIN IS A LITTLE *WEAK*, PROFESSOR.
"CONTRARIA SUNT COMPLEMENTA"?
CONTRARIA SUNT COMPLEMENTA
YES, YOUR HIGHNESS.
"OPPOSITES ARE COMPLEMENTARY."

HIS COLLEAGUES, WHOM THE FASCISTS HAD DRIVEN OUT OF EUROPE, WERE INSTRUMENTAL IN MAKING THE **BOMB** THAT ENDED THE WAR. BUT WITH THE EXCEPTION OF **LEO SZILARD*** NONE OF THEM TOOK THE NEXT STEP.

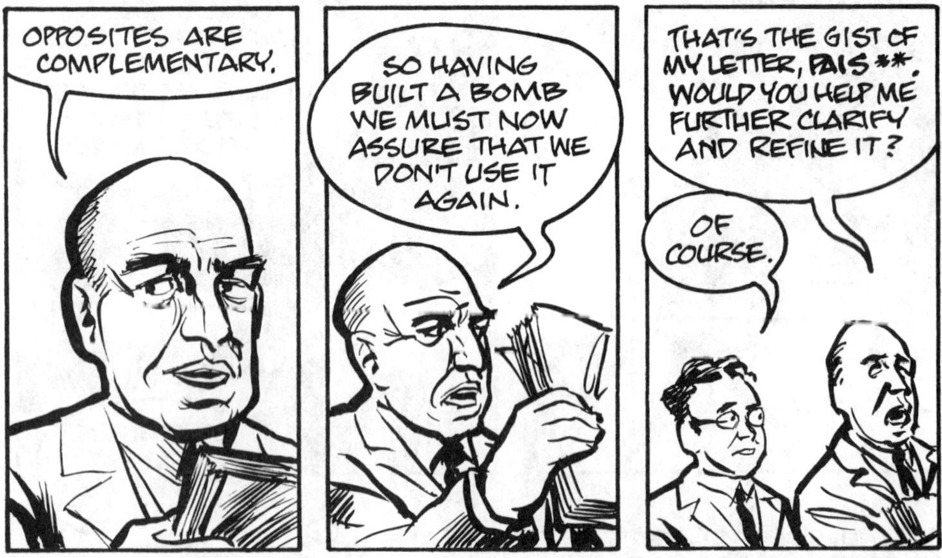
OPPOSITES ARE COMPLEMENTARY.
SO HAVING BUILT A BOMB WE MUST NOW ASSURE THAT WE DON'T USE IT AGAIN.
THAT'S THE GIST OF MY LETTER, **PAIS****. WOULD YOU HELP ME FURTHER CLARIFY AND REFINE IT?
OF COURSE.

* SZILARD DIDN'T HAVE *BOHR'S* STATURE, THOUGH, AND AS SUCH HAD VERY LITTLE CHANCE OF GETTING HIS MESSAGE HEARD.

** *ABRAHAM PAIS*, BOHR'S FRIEND AND EVENTUAL BIOGRAPHER. SEE "REFERENCES" BEGINNING ON PAGE 305 FOR A DESCRIPTION OF HIS AND OTHER BOOKS THAT WILL DEEPEN YOUR UNDERSTANDING OF BOHR AND HIS WORK.

BOHR HAD STARTED THIS LETTER MONTHS BEFORE. ACTUALLY, YOU COULD SAY *YEARS BEFORE*, SINCE HE QUOTED HIS OWN MEMORANDA TO **ROOSEVELT** AND **CHURCHILL** EXTENSIVELY. HE WORKED ON IT ALL THROUGH HIS 1950 VISIT TO *PRINCETON*.

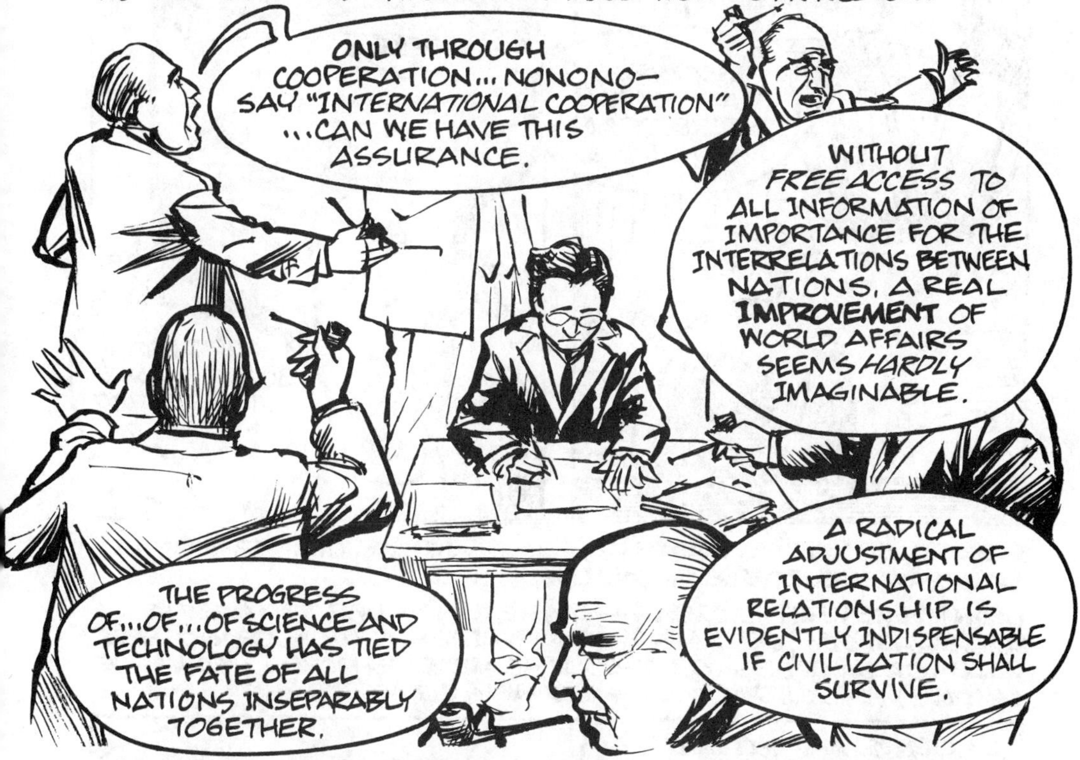
ONLY THROUGH COOPERATION... NONONO- SAY "INTERNATIONAL COOPERATION" ...CAN WE HAVE THIS ASSURANCE.
WITHOUT FREE ACCESS TO ALL INFORMATION OF IMPORTANCE FOR THE INTERRELATIONS BETWEEN NATIONS, A REAL IMPROVEMENT OF WORLD AFFAIRS SEEMS HARDLY IMAGINABLE.
THE PROGRESS OF...OF...OF SCIENCE AND TECHNOLOGY HAS TIED THE FATE OF ALL NATIONS INSEPARABLY TOGETHER.
A RADICAL ADJUSTMENT OF INTERNATIONAL RELATIONSHIP IS EVIDENTLY INDISPENSABLE IF CIVILIZATION SHALL SURVIVE.

HE TOOK ONLY BRIEF BREAKS TO MEET WITH HIGH LEVEL POLITICAL OFFICIALS, SUCH AS *U.S. SECRETARY OF STATE* **DEAN ACHESON**.

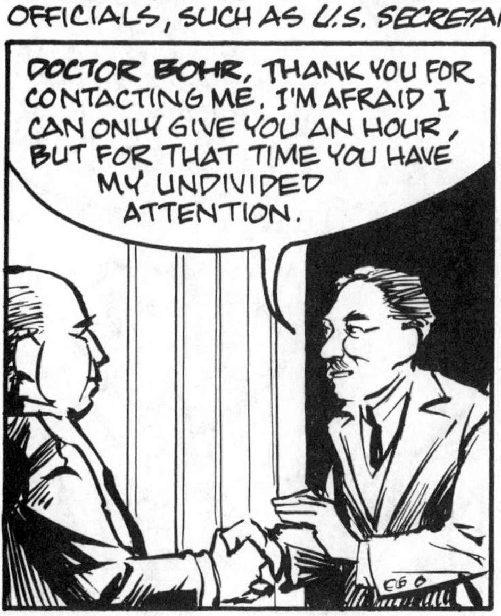
DOCTOR BOHR, THANK YOU FOR CONTACTING ME. I'M AFRAID I CAN ONLY GIVE YOU AN HOUR, BUT FOR THAT TIME YOU HAVE MY UNDIVIDED ATTENTION.

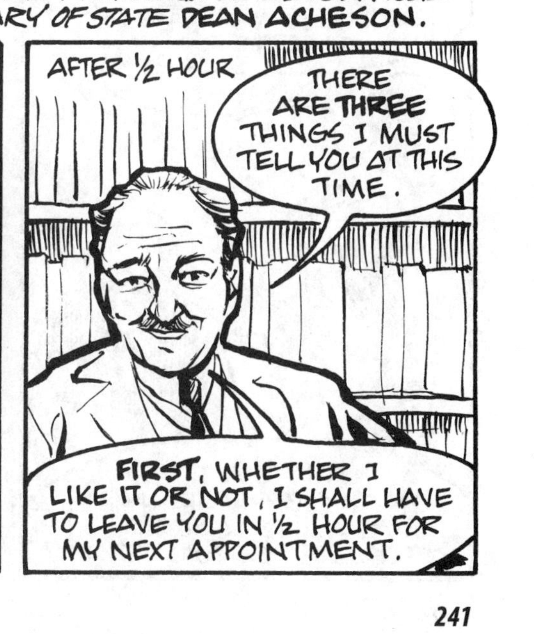
AFTER 1/2 HOUR
THERE ARE THREE THINGS I MUST TELL YOU AT THIS TIME.
FIRST, WHETHER I LIKE IT OR NOT, I SHALL HAVE TO LEAVE YOU IN 1/2 HOUR FOR MY NEXT APPOINTMENT.

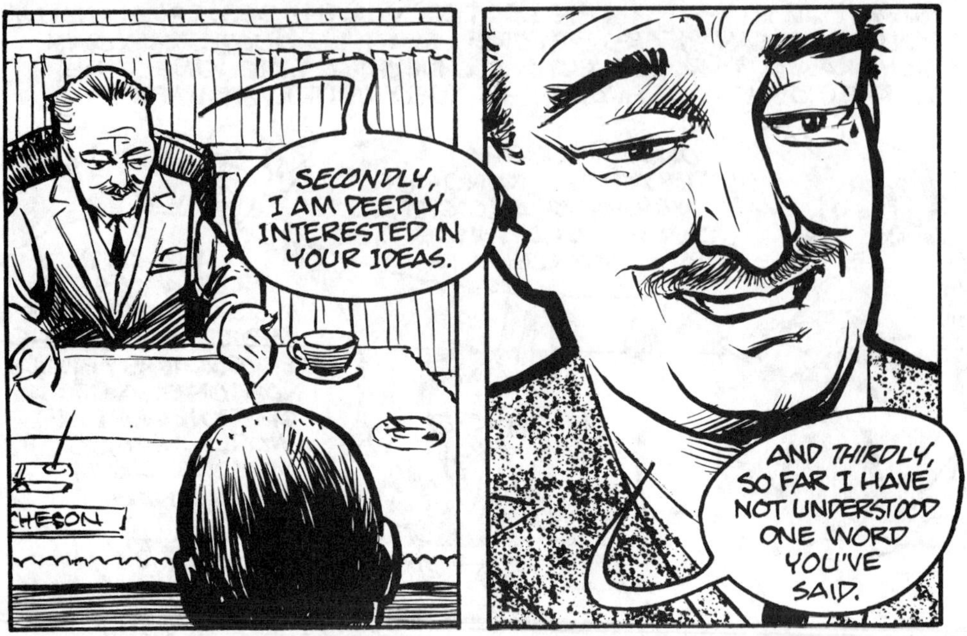
SECONDLY, I AM DEEPLY INTERESTED IN YOUR IDEAS.
CHESON
AND *THIRDLY*, SO FAR I HAVE NOT UNDERSTOOD ONE WORD YOU'VE SAID.

BOHR FILLED HIS REMAINING HALF HOUR WITH AN UNINTERRUPTED (AND UNINTERRUPTIBLE) MONOLOGUE.

UPON HIS RETURN TO *COPENHAGEN*, HE CONTINUED TO MAKE THE LETTER *LONGER*, CERTAIN THAT WITH THE ADDITION OF ANOTHER DOZEN OR SO PAGES (OR SHOULD HE ADD EVEN MORE? *YES, YES HE SHOULD!*) HE COULD MAKE HIS MEANING CLEAR.

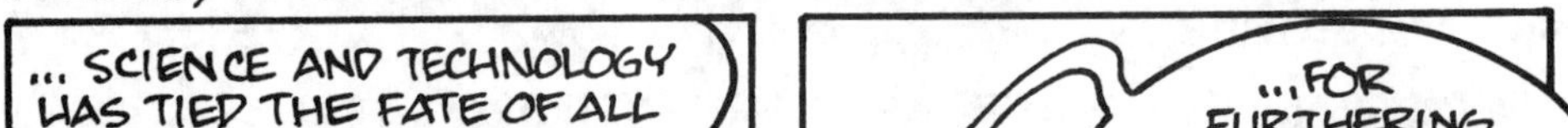
... SCIENCE AND TECHNOLOGY HAS TIED THE FATE OF ALL NATIONS INSEPARABLY TOGETHER.
IT IS JUST ON THIS BACKGROUND THAT QUITE UNIQUE OPPORTUNITIES EXIST TODAY.
...FOR FURTHERING COOPERATION BETWEEN NATIONS ON THE PROGRESS OF HUMAN CULTURE IN ALL ITS ASPECTS.

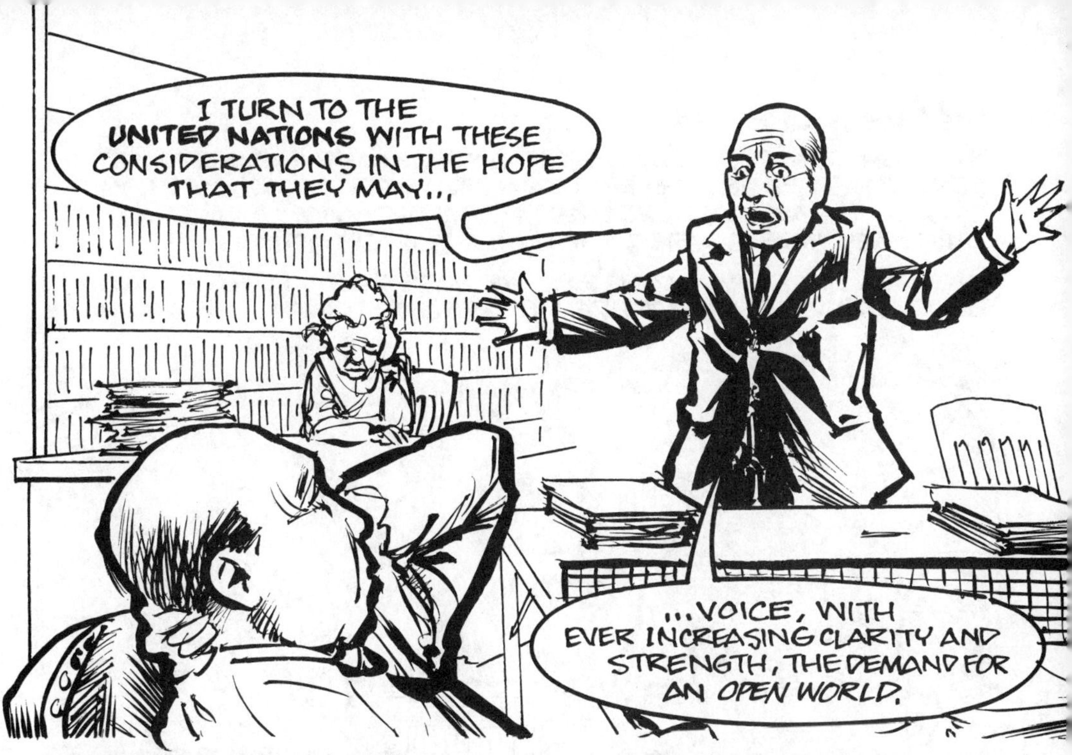
I TURN TO THE **UNITED NATIONS** WITH THESE CONSIDERATIONS IN THE HOPE THAT THEY MAY...
...VOICE, WITH EVER INCREASING CLARITY AND STRENGTH, THE DEMAND FOR AN *OPEN WORLD.*

DELIVERED TO THE *U.N.* ON JUNE 9, *1950*, WITH THOUSANDS OF ADDITIONAL COPIES PRINTED AND IN CIRCULATION AT HIS OWN EXPENSE, **BOHR'S** LETTER CHANGED THE COURSE OF HISTORY AND THE **COLD WAR** CEASED ALMOST IMMEDIATELY.

NO, OF COURSE IT DIDN'T.

WHAT *DID* HAPPEN WAS THAT THE **KOREAN WAR** BROKE OUT JUST TWO WEEKS LATER, AND A FEW MONTHS AFTER THAT THE **U.S.** EXPLODED ITS FIRST HYDROGEN BOMB.
...***1000 TIMES*** MORE POWERFUL THAN THE *FISSION BOMBS* DROPPED ON **JAPAN**, IT OBLITERATED AN ENTIRE ISLAND.

HISTORY IS LIKE THAT.

THOUGH TRUMPED, **BOHR** NEVER GAVE UP, AND THROUGHOUT THE REST OF HIS LIFE HE LOBBIED FOR AN OPEN WORLD. IN RECOGNITION OF THIS, HE WAS AWARDED THE FIRST *"ATOMS FOR PEACE"* AWARD IN 1957, JUST A FEW WEEKS AFTER THE LAUNCH OF **SPUTNIK**.

WITH HIS LATEST AWARD IN HAND HE MADE THE CALL FOR GREATER UNDERSTANDING AND CONFIDENCE BETWEEN NATIONS YET AGAIN.

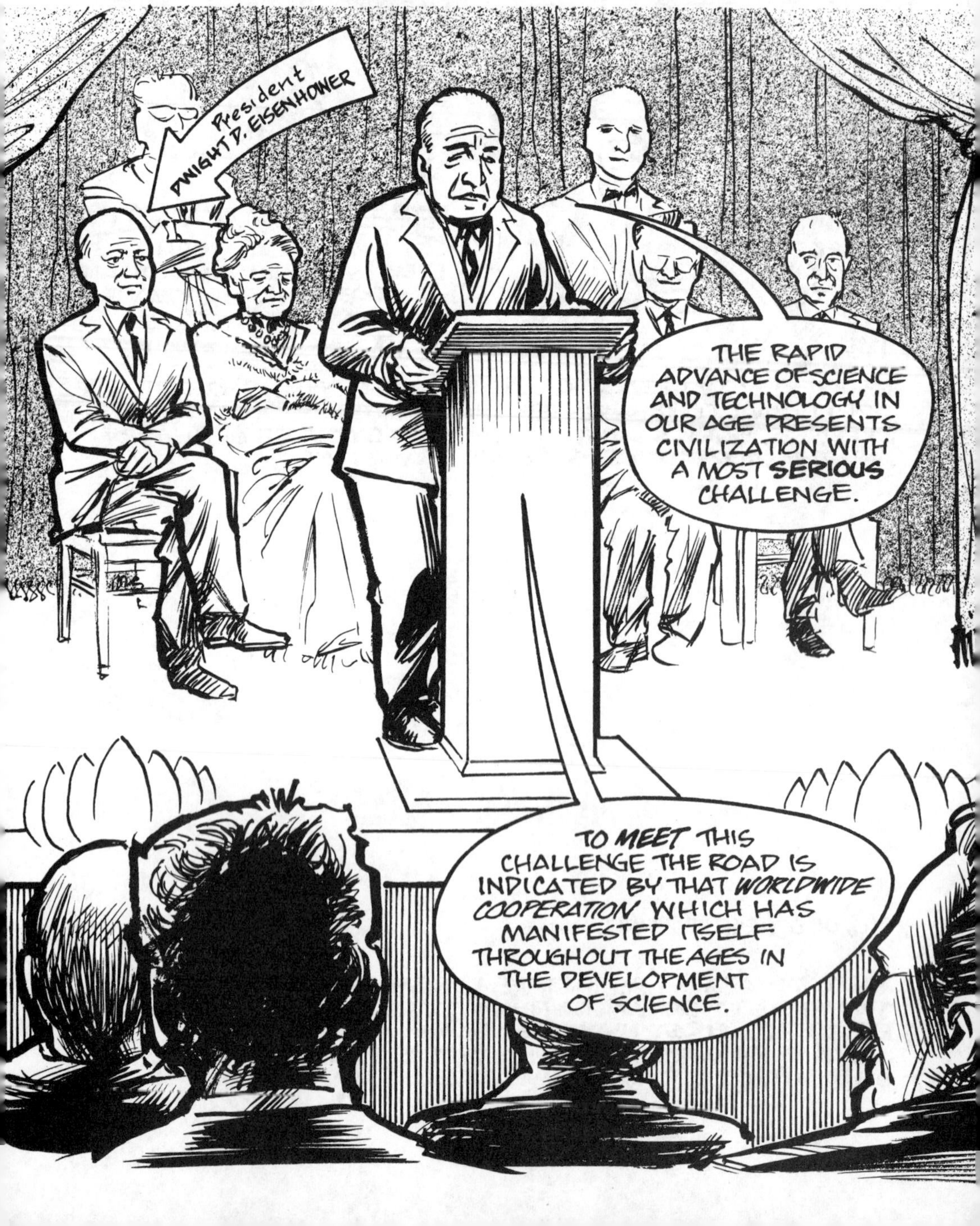
President DWIGHT D. EISENHOWER
THE RAPID ADVANCE OF SCIENCE AND TECHNOLOGY IN OUR AGE PRESENTS CIVILIZATION WITH A MOST SERIOUS CHALLENGE.
TO MEET THIS CHALLENGE THE ROAD IS INDICATED BY THAT WORLDWIDE COOPERATION WHICH HAS MANIFESTED ITSELF THROUGHOUT THE AGES IN THE DEVELOPMENT OF SCIENCE.

BOHR'S POST-WAR, POST-OPEN LETTER TO THE *U.N.* YEARS WEREN'T ALL PHILOSOPHY AND STATESMANSHIP, BUT HIS SCIENTIFIC WORK *DID* TAKE ON A MORE INTERNATIONAL AND ADMINISTRATIVE THAN THEORETICAL ROLE.

FOR INSTANCE, IN 1952 HE BECAME THE FIRST HEAD OF THE *THEORY GROUP* AT **CERN** (EUROPEAN ORGANIZATION FOR NUCLEAR RESEARCH.)

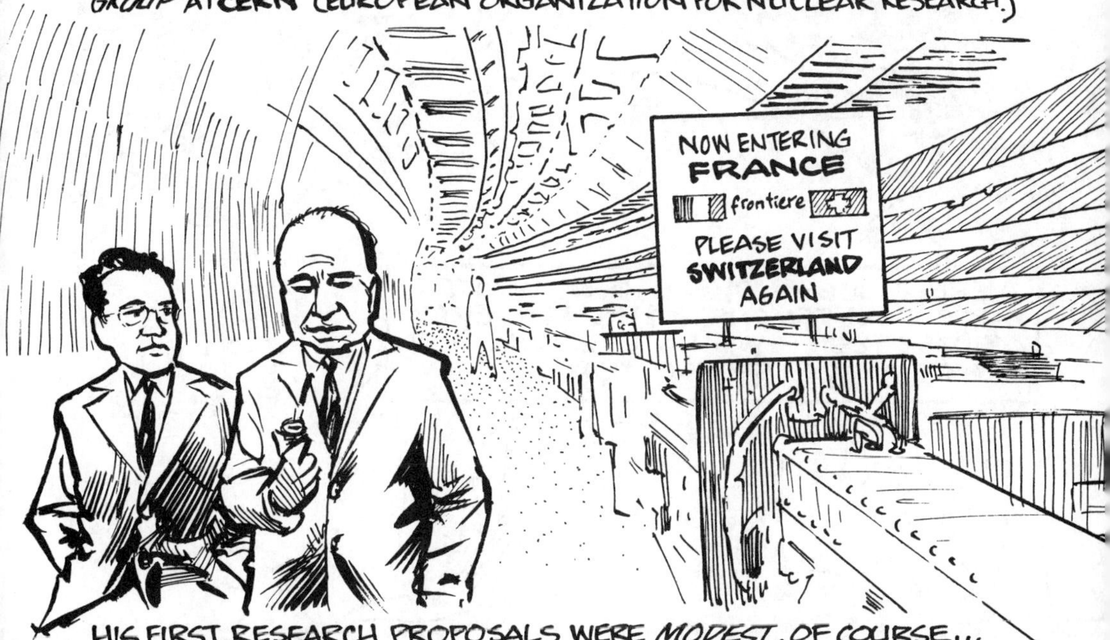
NOW ENTERING
FRANCE
frontiere
PLEASE VISIT
SWITZERLAND
AGAIN

HIS FIRST RESEARCH PROPOSALS WERE *MODEST*, OF COURSE...

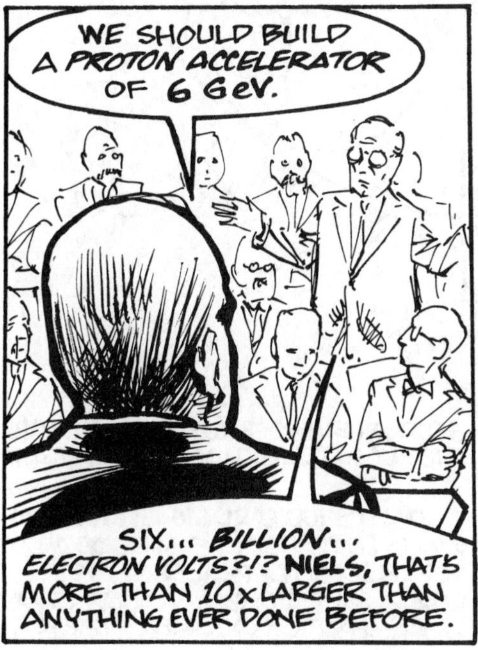
WE SHOULD BUILD A *PROTON ACCELERATOR* OF 6 GeV.
SIX... *BILLION*... *ELECTRON VOLTS?!?* **NIELS**, THAT'S MORE THAN 10x LARGER THAN ANYTHING EVER DONE BEFORE.

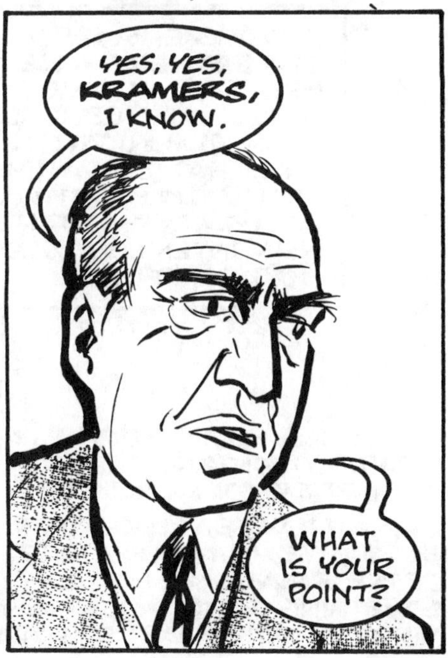
YES, YES, **KRAMERS**, I KNOW.
WHAT IS YOUR POINT?

CERN'S MAIN LABORATORIES CROSS THE BORDER BETWEEN *SWITZERLAND* AND *FRANCE*, AND ELEVEN COUNTRIES TOOK PART IN BUILDING IT.

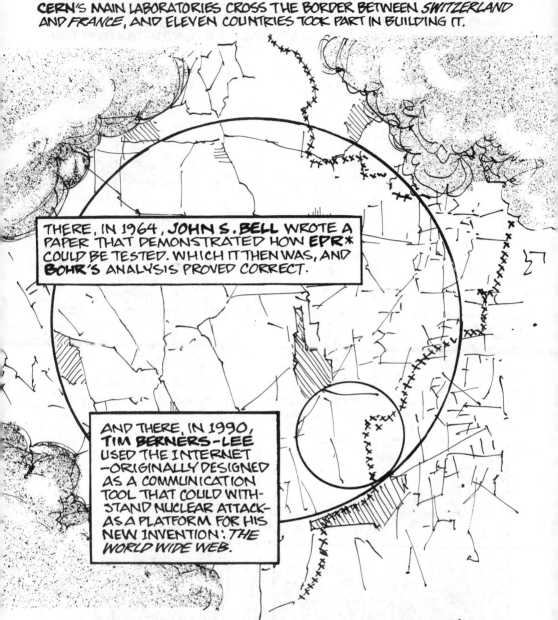

THERE, IN 1964, **JOHN S. BELL** WROTE A PAPER THAT DEMONSTRATED HOW **EPR*** COULD BE TESTED. WHICH IT THEN WAS, AND **BOHR'S** ANALYSIS PROVED CORRECT.

AND THERE, IN 1990, **TIM BERNERS-LEE** USED THE INTERNET —ORIGINALLY DESIGNED AS A COMMUNICATION TOOL THAT COULD WITH-STAND NUCLEAR ATTACK— AS A PLATFORM FOR HIS NEW INVENTION: *THE WORLD WIDE WEB.*

IS THE **WEB** PROOF OF **BOHR'S** ADAGE THAT EVERY PROBLEM (ATOMIC WEAPONS) CONTAINS ITS *OWN* SOLUTION (INTERNATIONAL COOPERATION VIA BETTER COMMUNICATION)?

OK, THAT MAY BE A REACH. AND RIGHT NOW ITS TOO EARLY TO TELL ANYWAY. BUT THE WEB'S MAIN FEATURE — HOW IT LETS PEOPLE SHARE A LOT OF INFORMATION GLOBALLY, AND PERSON-TO-PERSON, IS SOMETHING **BOHR** WOULD HAVE LIKED. (HE PROBABLY WOULDN'T HAVE MINDED ITS NON-LINEAR, SOMETIMES EVEN CHAOTIC NATURE EITHER.)

* REMEMBER SPOOKY ACTION-AT-A-DISTANCE?

BOHR'S FAITH IN THE IDEA OF INTERNATIONAL COOPERATION AND AN OPEN WORLD BORDERED ON THE *RELIGIOUS*. HE HAD LEFT THE LUTHERAN CHURCH IN 1912, BUT WRITINGS ON FAITH AND PHILOSOPHY STILL INFLUENCED HIS WORLD VIEW. AND IN THESE LATER YEARS HIS EARLY INTEREST IN PHILOSOPHICAL MATTERS RETURNED TO CENTER STAGE.

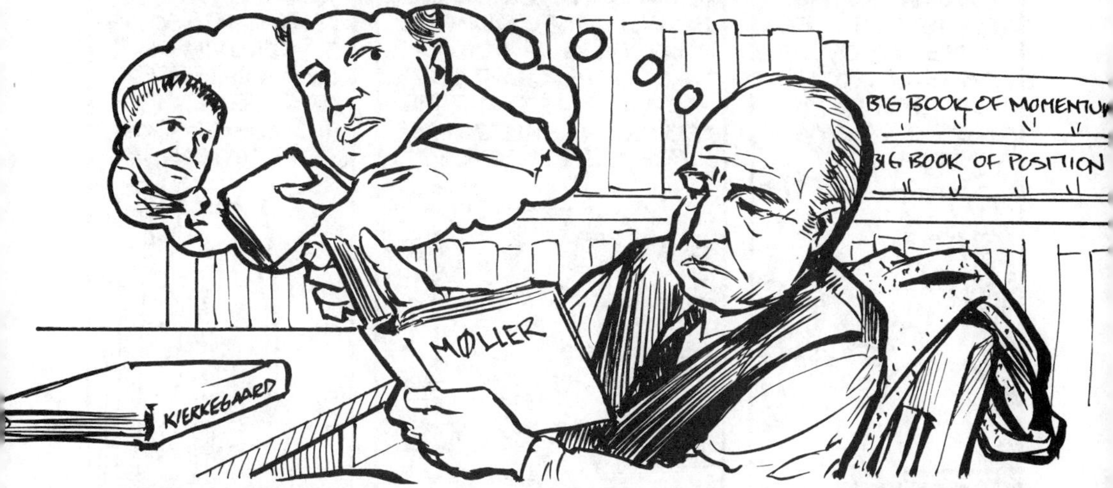
BIG BOOK OF MOMENTU
BIG BOOK OF POSITION
MØLLER
KIERKEGAARD

HIS ENDLESS REVISIONS, COMPLICATED SENTENCES, AND IDEAS ABOUT *COMPLEMENTARITY AND CONTRADICTION* HAD THEIR ORIGINS IN **MØLLER'S** *TALE OF A DANISH STUDENT*, WHERE HE HAD READ:

"I TORTURE MYSELF TO SOLVE THE UNACCOUNTABLE PUZZLE, HOW ONE CAN THINK, TALK, OR WRITE... THE MIND CANNOT PROCEED WITHOUT MOVING ALONG A CERTAIN LINE; BUT BEFORE FOLLOWING THIS LINE, IT MUST ALREADY HAVE THOUGHT IT. THEREFORE ONE HAS ALREADY THOUGHT EVERY THOUGHT BEFORE ONE THINKS IT. THUS EVERY THOUGHT, WHICH SEEMS THE WORK OF THE MOMENT, PRESUPPOSES AN ETERNITY.

"THE INSIGHT INTO THE IMPOSSIBILITY OF THINKING CONTAINS ITSELF AN IMPOSSIBILITY, THE RECOGNITION OF WHICH AGAIN IMPLIES AN INEXPLICABLE CONTRADICTION."

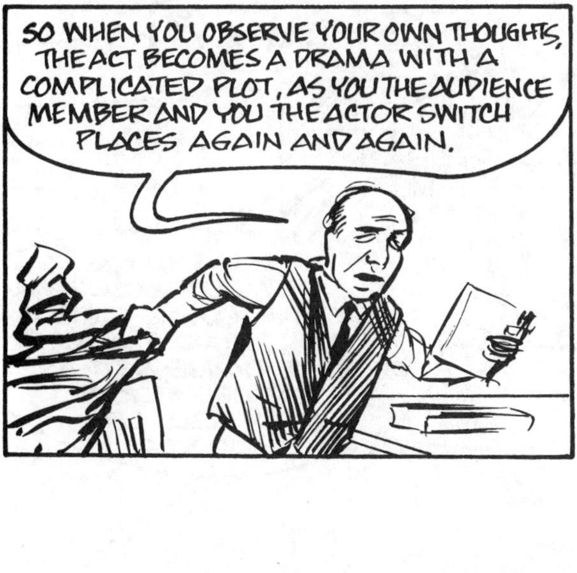
SO WHEN YOU OBSERVE YOUR OWN THOUGHTS, THE ACT BECOMES A DRAMA WITH A COMPLICATED PLOT, AS YOU THE AUDIENCE MEMBER AND YOU THE ACTOR SWITCH PLACES AGAIN AND AGAIN.

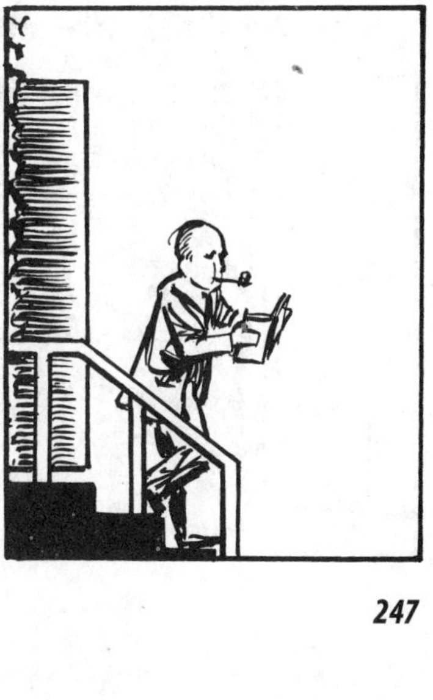

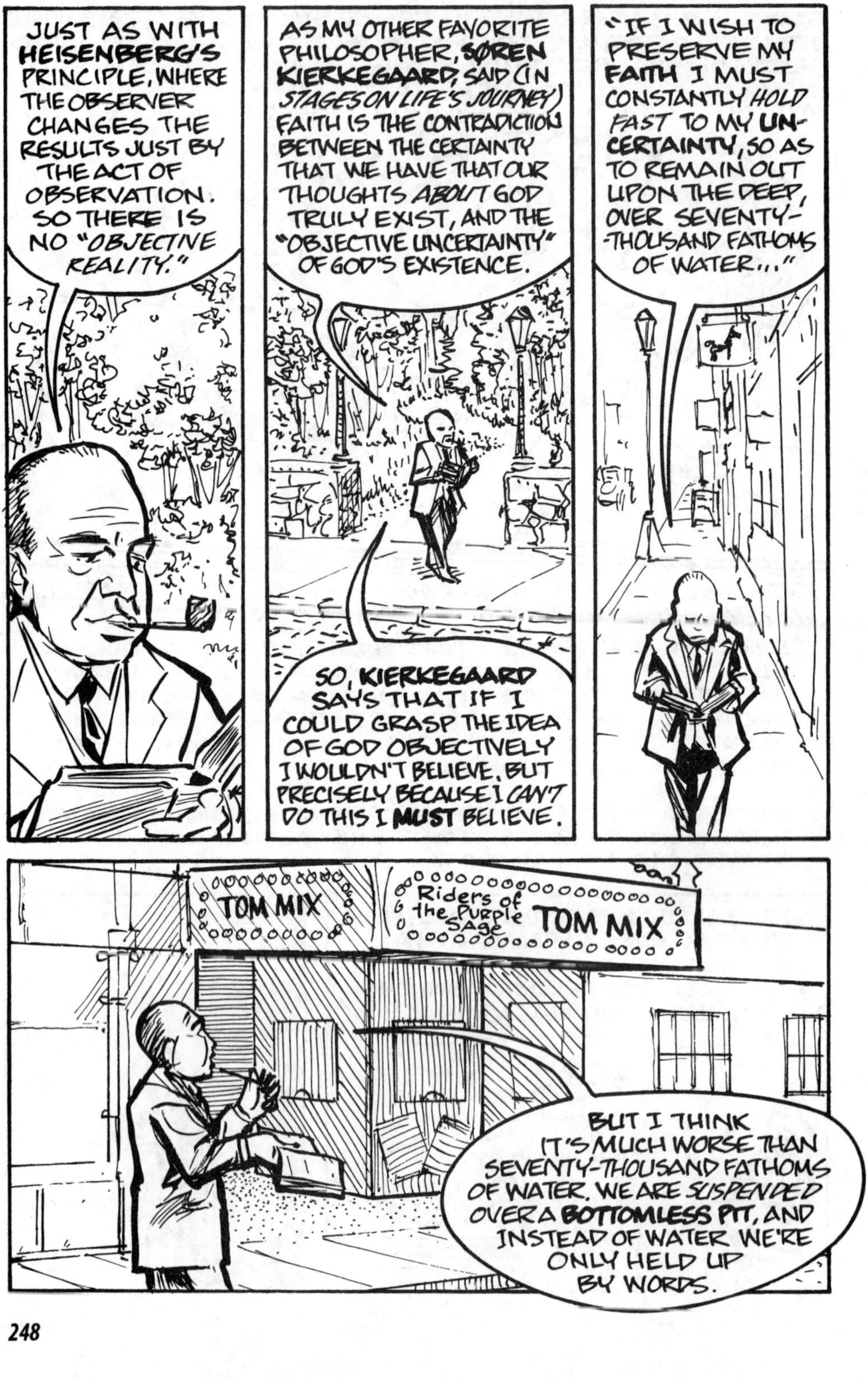
JUST AS WITH HEISENBERG'S PRINCIPLE, WHERE THE OBSERVER CHANGES THE RESULTS JUST BY THE ACT OF OBSERVATION. SO THERE IS NO "OBJECTIVE REALITY."
AS MY OTHER FAVORITE PHILOSOPHER, SØREN KIERKEGAARD, SAID (IN STAGES ON LIFE'S JOURNEY) FAITH IS THE CONTRADICTION BETWEEN THE CERTAINTY THAT WE HAVE THAT OUR THOUGHTS ABOUT GOD TRULY EXIST, AND THE "OBJECTIVE UNCERTAINTY" OF GOD'S EXISTENCE.
SO, KIERKEGAARD SAYS THAT IF I COULD GRASP THE IDEA OF GOD OBJECTIVELY I WOULDN'T BELIEVE. BUT PRECISELY BECAUSE I CAN'T DO THIS I MUST BELIEVE.
"IF I WISH TO PRESERVE MY FAITH I MUST CONSTANTLY HOLD FAST TO MY UN-CERTAINTY, SO AS TO REMAIN OUT UPON THE DEEP, OVER SEVENTY-THOUSAND FATHOMS OF WATER..."
TOM MIX
Riders of the Purple Sage
TOM MIX
BUT I THINK IT'S MUCH WORSE THAN SEVENTY-THOUSAND FATHOMS OF WATER. WE ARE SUSPENDED OVER A BOTTOMLESS PIT, AND INSTEAD OF WATER WE'RE ONLY HELD UP BY WORDS.

(AND IN **BOHR'S** PHILOSOPHY THERE WAS NO ROOM FOR **KIERKEGAARD'S** "OBJECTIVE UNCERTAINTY" EITHER, AFTER ALL, SINCE HE FOUND BOTH OF THOSE WORDS TROUBLESOME.)

THE TROUBLE WITH WORDS DIDN'T STOP **BOHR** FROM CONTINUING TO *WRITE*, AND *REWRITE*, EXTENSIVELY IN THE POSTWAR YEARS. BETWEEN 1946 AND HIS DEATH IN 1962, HE WROTE MORE THAN A PAPER A YEAR ON PHILOSOPHICAL TOPICS WITH TITLES SUCH AS:

ON THE NOTIONS OF CAUSALITY AND COMPLEMENTARITY (1948)
PHYSICAL SCIENCE AND THE PROBLEM OF LIFE (1949)
PHYSICAL SCIENCE AND THE STUDY OF RELIGIONS (1953)
ATOMS AND HUMAN KNOWLEDGE (1955)
PHYSICAL SCIENCE AND MAN'S POSITION (1956)
QUANTUM PHYSICS AND PHILOSOPHY —CAUSALITY AND COMPLEMENTARITY (1958)
QUANTUM PHYSICS AND BIOLOGY (1960)
THE UNITY OF HUMAN KNOWLEDGE (1960)
PHYSICAL MODELS AND LIVING ORGANISMS (1961)
LIGHT AND LIFE REVISITED (UNFINISHED) (1962, BASED ON A 1932 LECTURE OF THE SAME NAME)

IN THEM HE REVISED HIS IDEAS ON COMPLEMENTARITY ALMOST CONSTANTLY. THEY WEREN'T JUST REFINEMENTS, SINCE HIS DEBATE WITH **EINSTEIN** ABOUT *EPR* CHANGED HIS THINKING SO MUCH THAT HE DECIDED TO ACTUALLY LEAVE OUT A NUMBER OF ESSAYS FROM THE *1930s* AND *1940s* THAT WOULD OTHERWISE HAVE APPEARED IN HIS SELF-EDITED COLLECTION OF PHILOSOPHICAL WRITINGS.

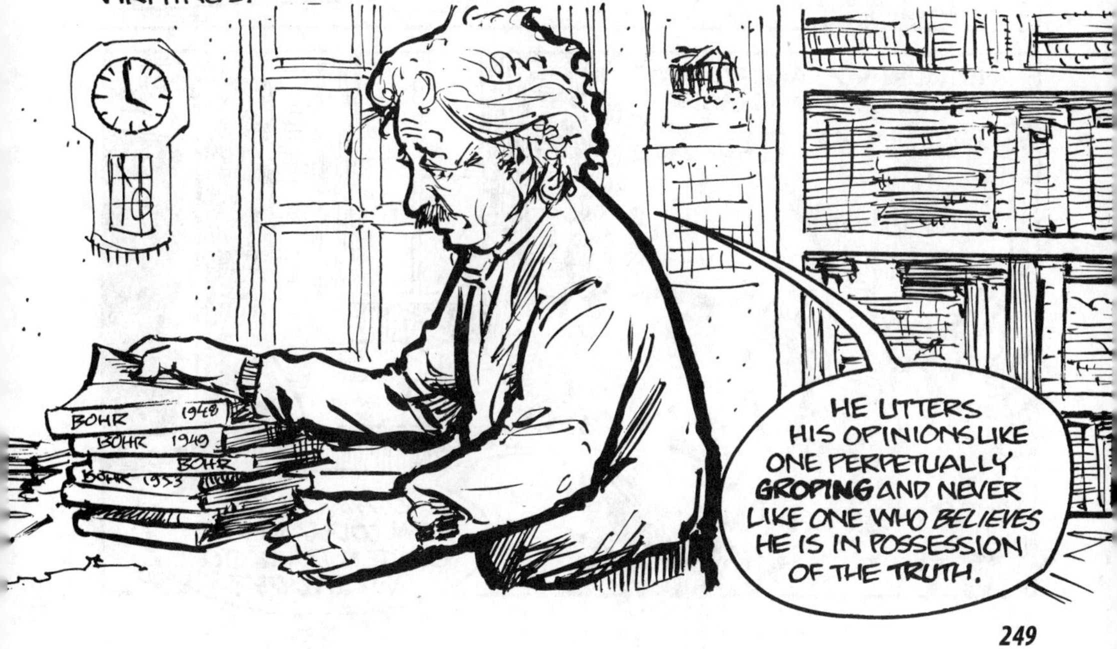
BOHR 1948
BOHR 1949
BOHR
BOHR 1953
HE UTTERS HIS OPINIONS LIKE ONE PERPETUALLY GROPING AND NEVER LIKE ONE WHO BELIEVES HE IS IN POSSESSION OF THE TRUTH.

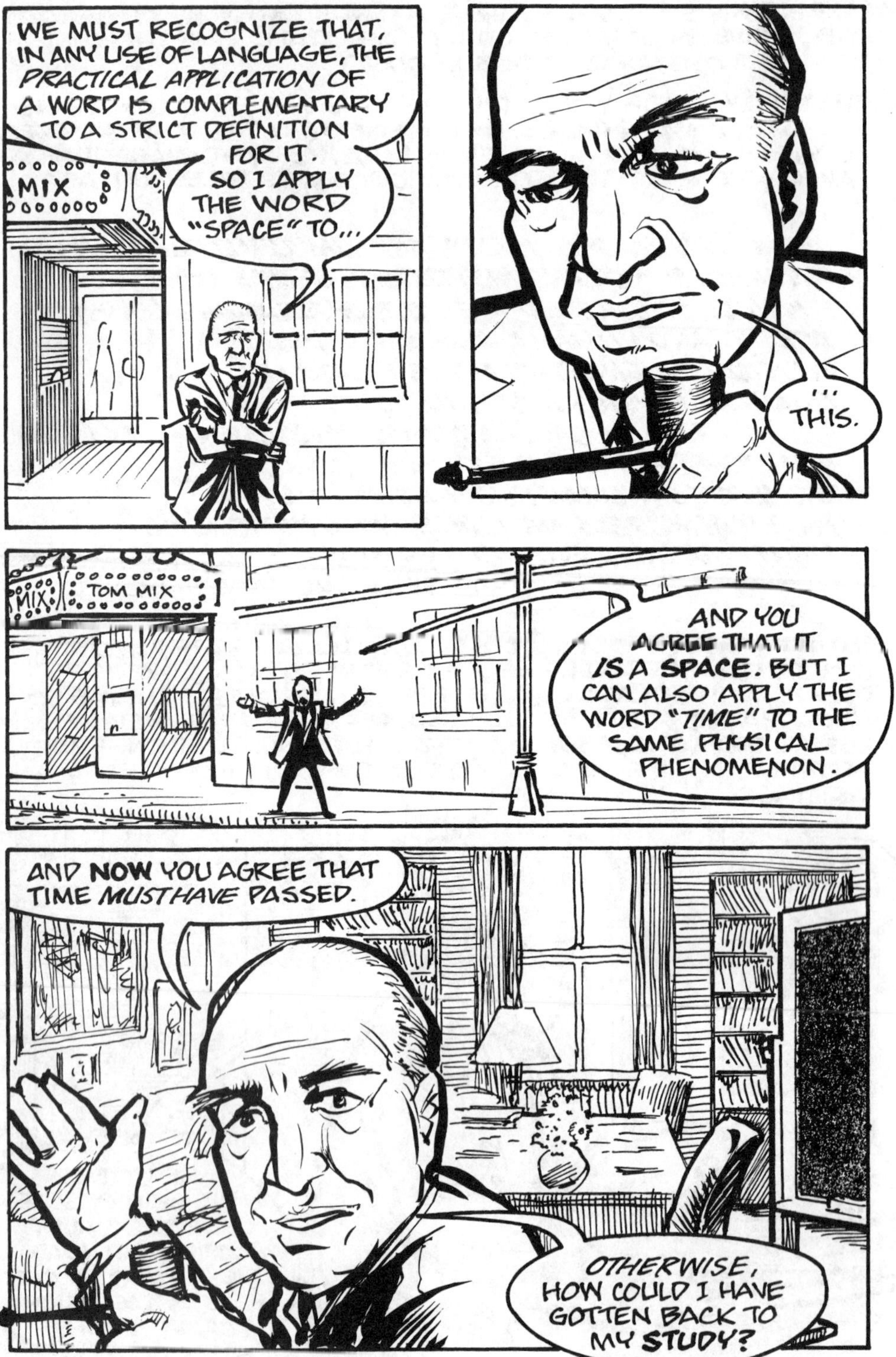
WE MUST RECOGNIZE THAT, IN ANY USE OF LANGUAGE, THE *PRACTICAL APPLICATION* OF A WORD IS COMPLEMENTARY TO A STRICT DEFINITION FOR IT.
SO I APPLY THE WORD "SPACE" TO...
MIX
... THIS.
TOM MIX
AND YOU AGREE THAT IT *IS* A **SPACE**. BUT I CAN ALSO APPLY THE WORD "*TIME*" TO THE SAME PHYSICAL PHENOMENON.
AND **NOW** YOU AGREE THAT TIME *MUST HAVE* PASSED.
OTHERWISE, HOW COULD I HAVE GOTTEN BACK TO MY **STUDY**?

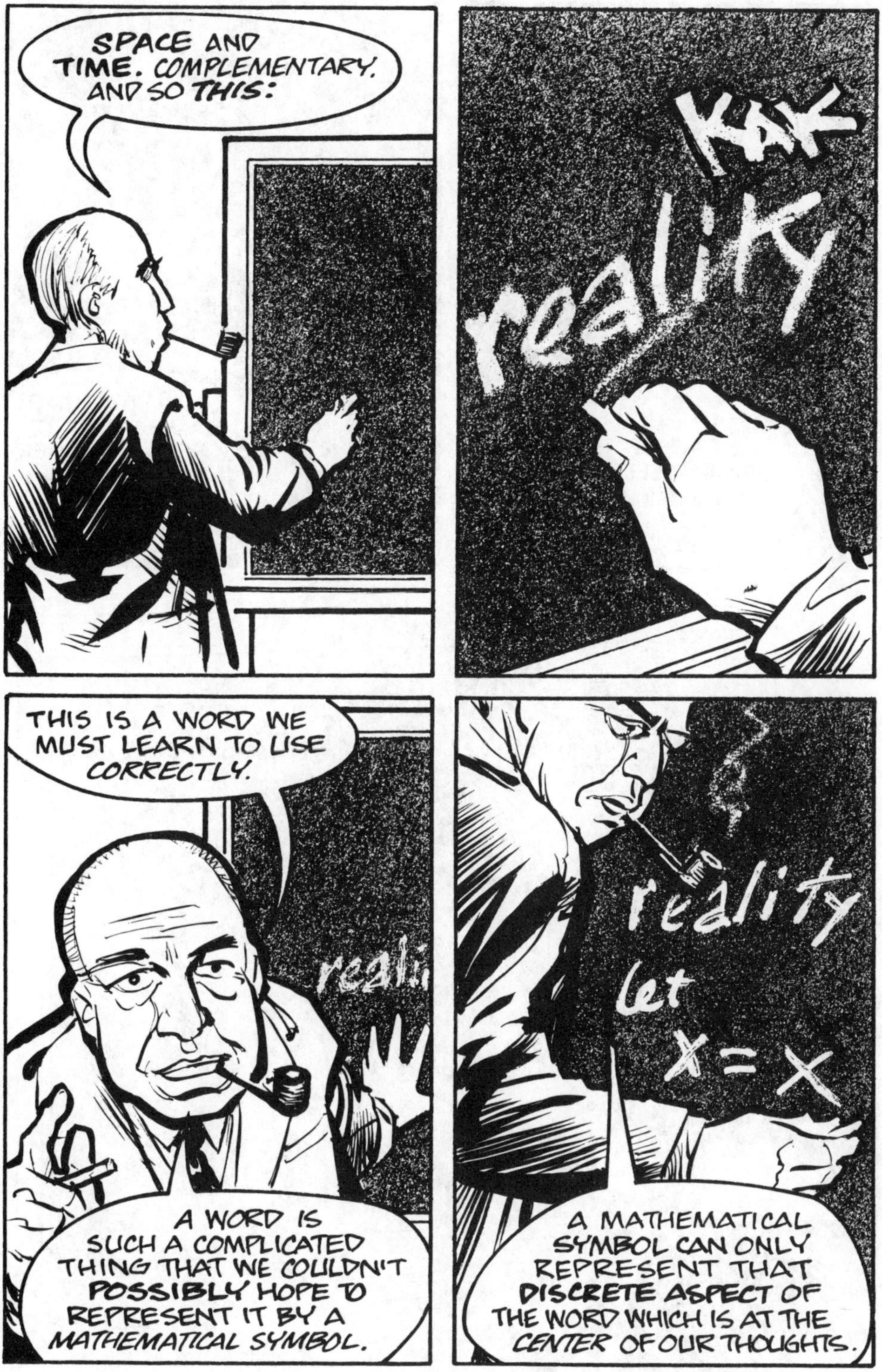
SPACE AND TIME. COMPLEMENTARY. AND SO THIS:
KAK
reality
THIS IS A WORD WE MUST LEARN TO USE CORRECTLY.
reali
A WORD IS SUCH A COMPLICATED THING THAT WE COULDN'T POSSIBLY HOPE TO REPRESENT IT BY A MATHEMATICAL SYMBOL.
reality
let
x = x
A MATHEMATICAL SYMBOL CAN ONLY REPRESENT THAT DISCRETE ASPECT OF THE WORD WHICH IS AT THE CENTER OF OUR THOUGHTS.

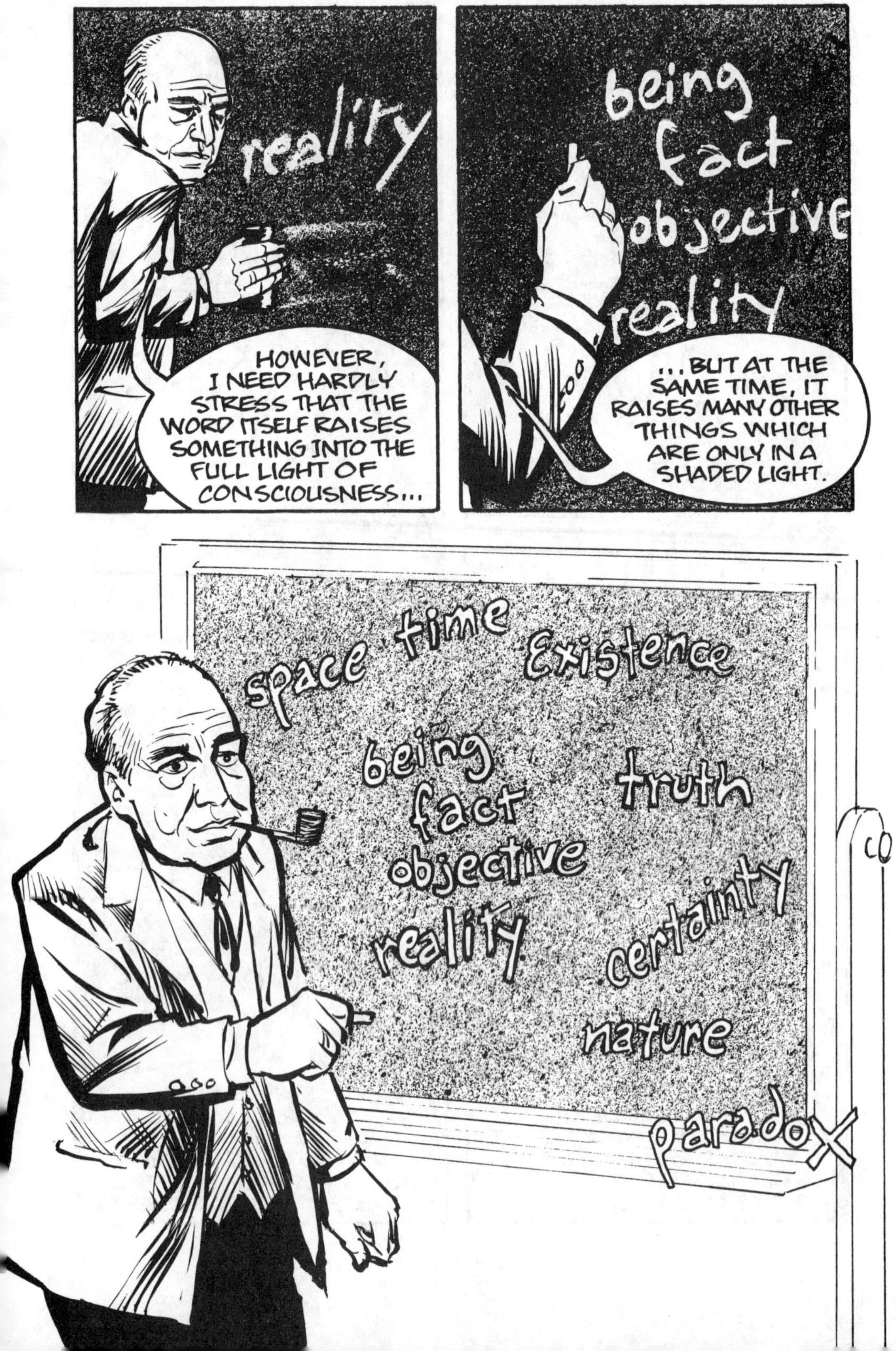
reality
HOWEVER, I NEED HARDLY STRESS THAT THE WORD ITSELF RAISES SOMETHING INTO THE FULL LIGHT OF CONSCIOUSNESS...
being
fact
objective
reality
...BUT AT THE SAME TIME, IT RAISES MANY OTHER THINGS WHICH ARE ONLY IN A SHADED LIGHT.
space time
Existence
being
fact
objective
reality
truth
certainty
nature
paradox

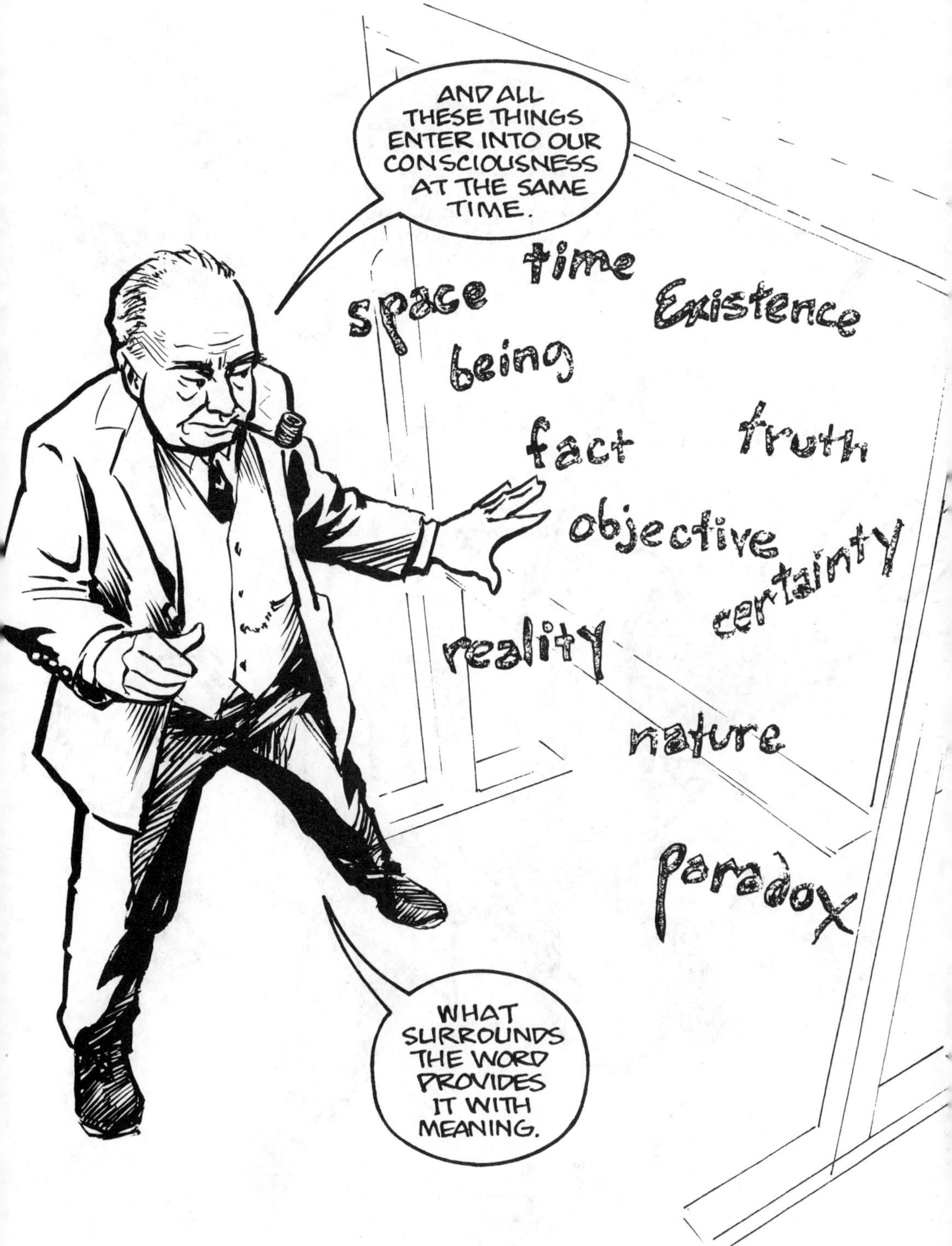
AND ALL THESE THINGS ENTER INTO OUR CONSCIOUSNESS AT THE SAME TIME.
space
time
Existence
being
fact
truth
objective
certainty
reality
nature
paradox
WHAT SURROUNDS THE WORD PROVIDES IT WITH MEANING.

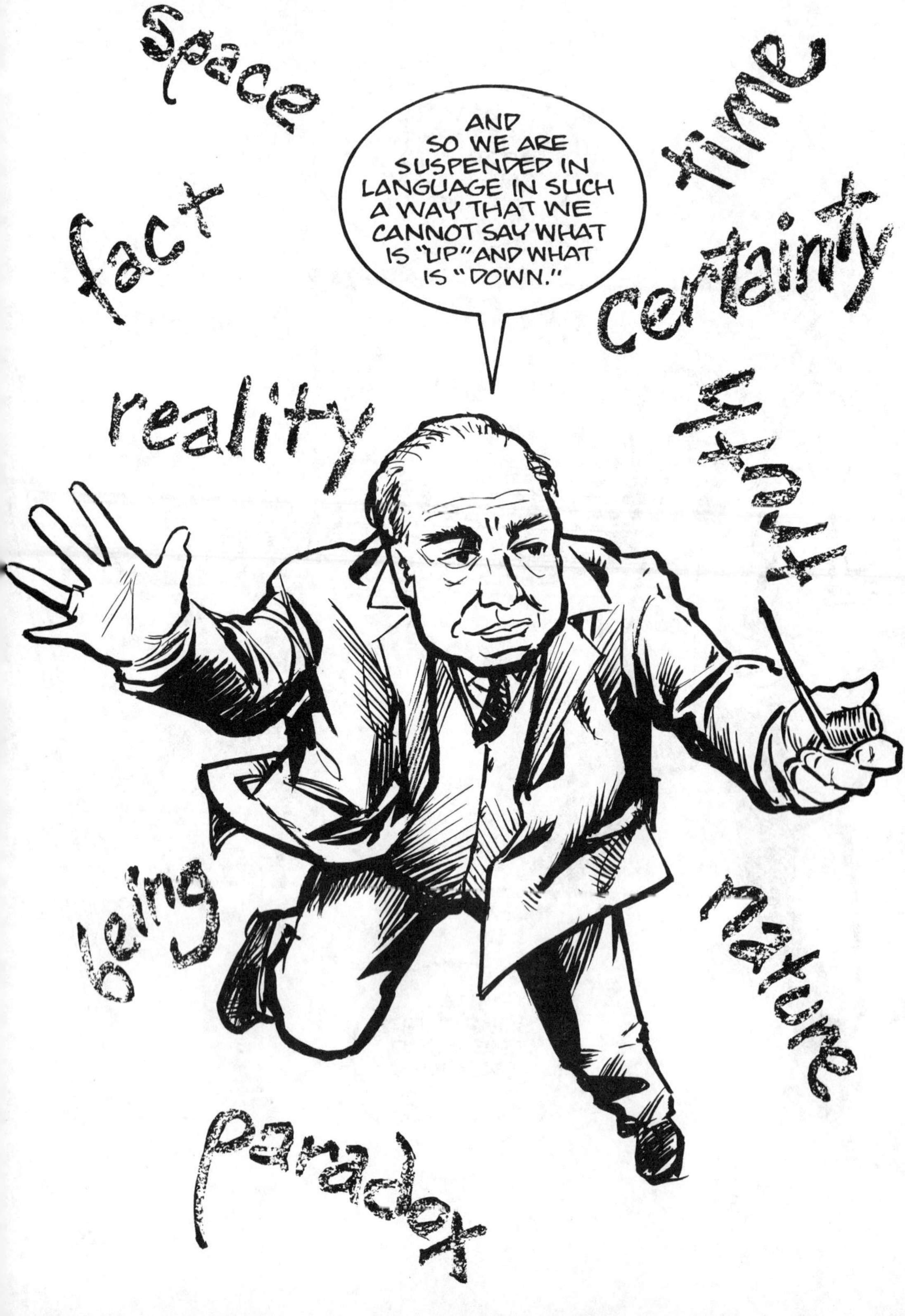
space
time
fact
certainty
AND SO WE ARE SUSPENDED IN LANGUAGE IN SUCH A WAY THAT WE CANNOT SAY WHAT IS "UP" AND WHAT IS "DOWN."
reality
truth
being
nature
paradox

Chapter 14

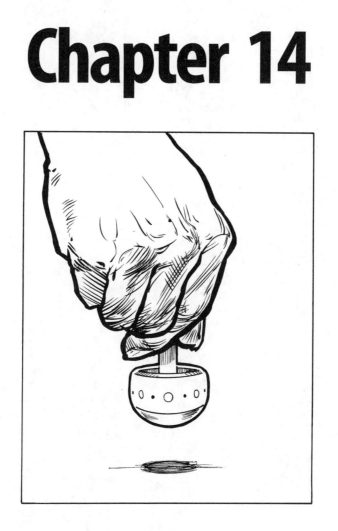

257

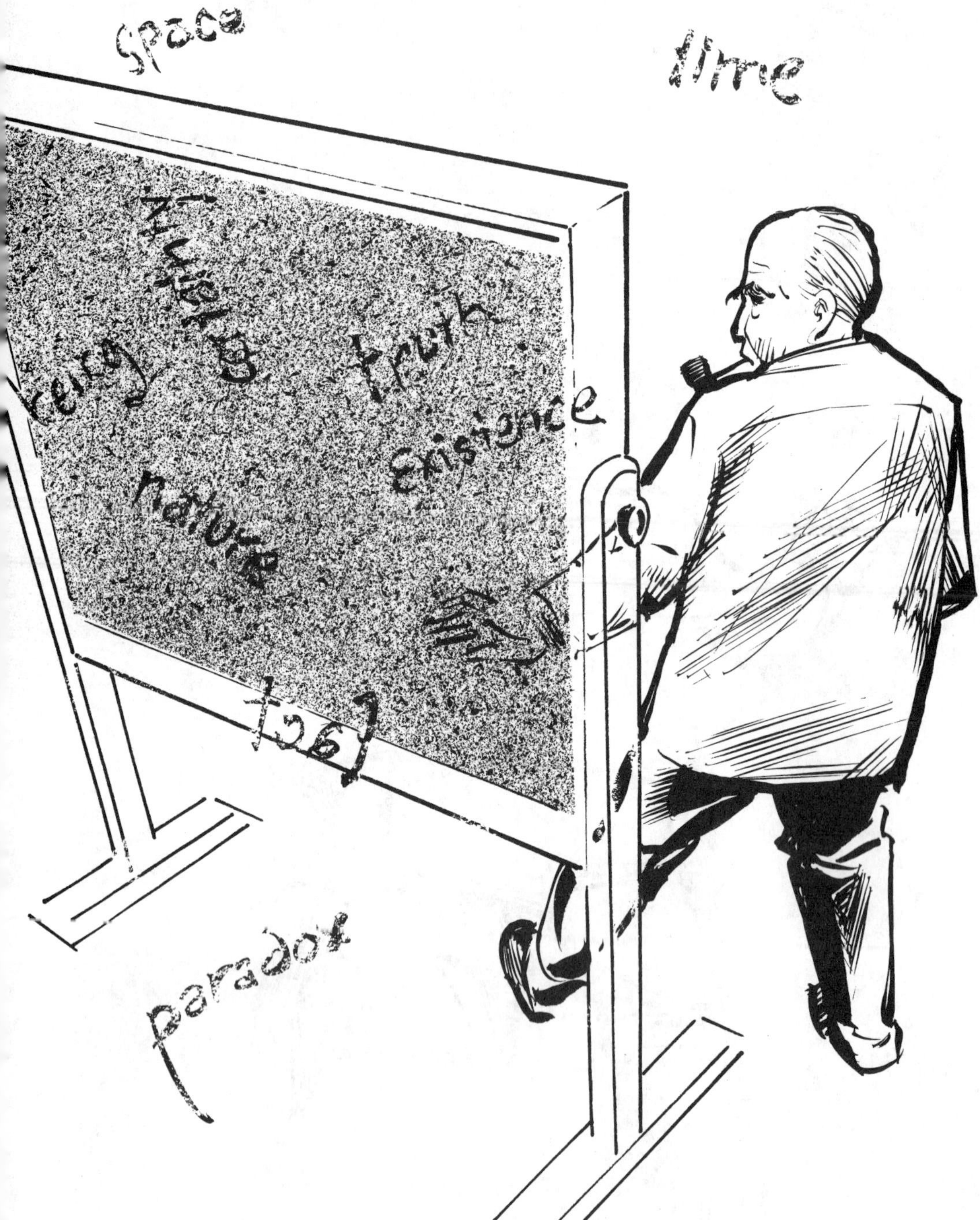
space
time
truth
Existence
nature
paradox

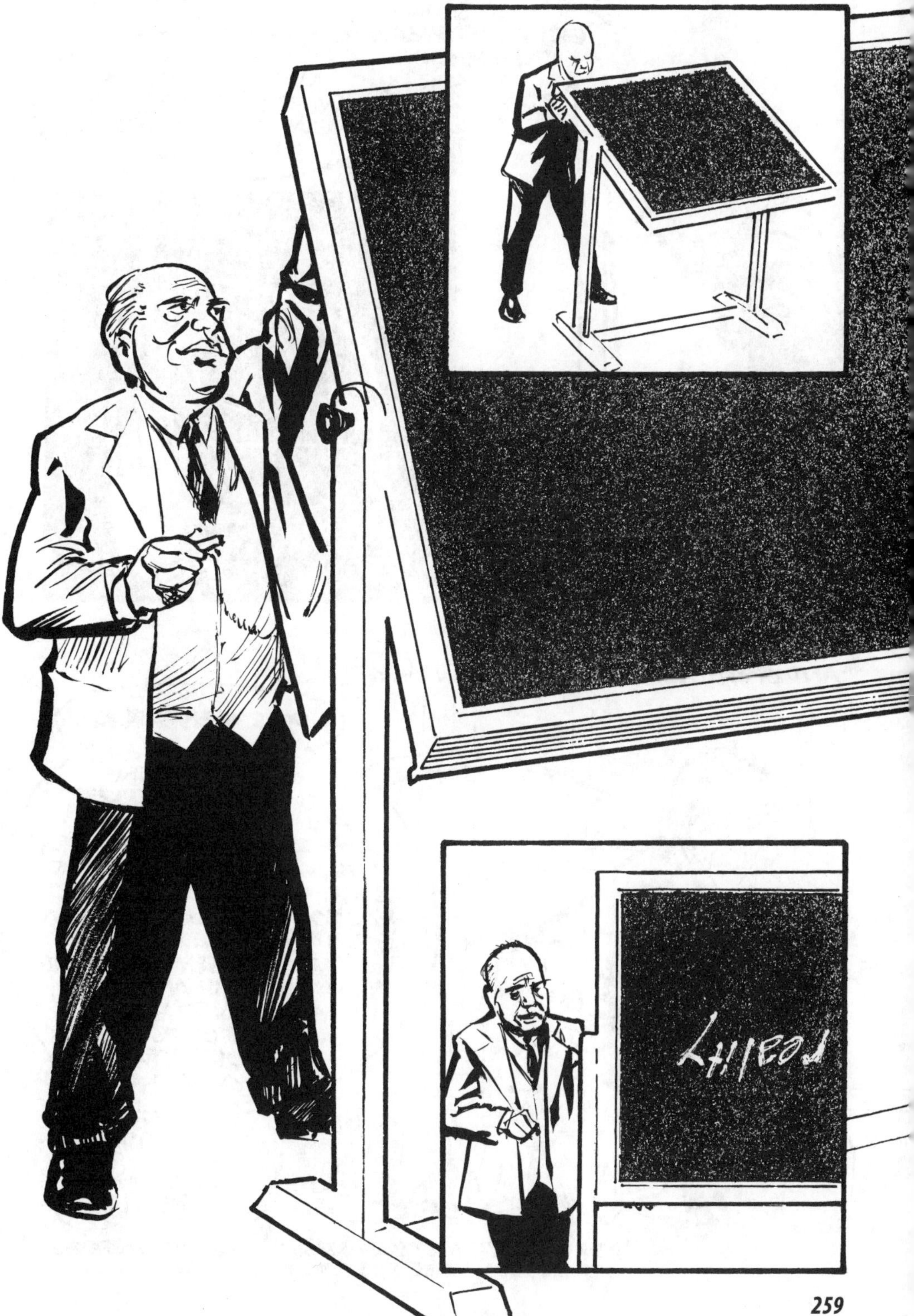
reality

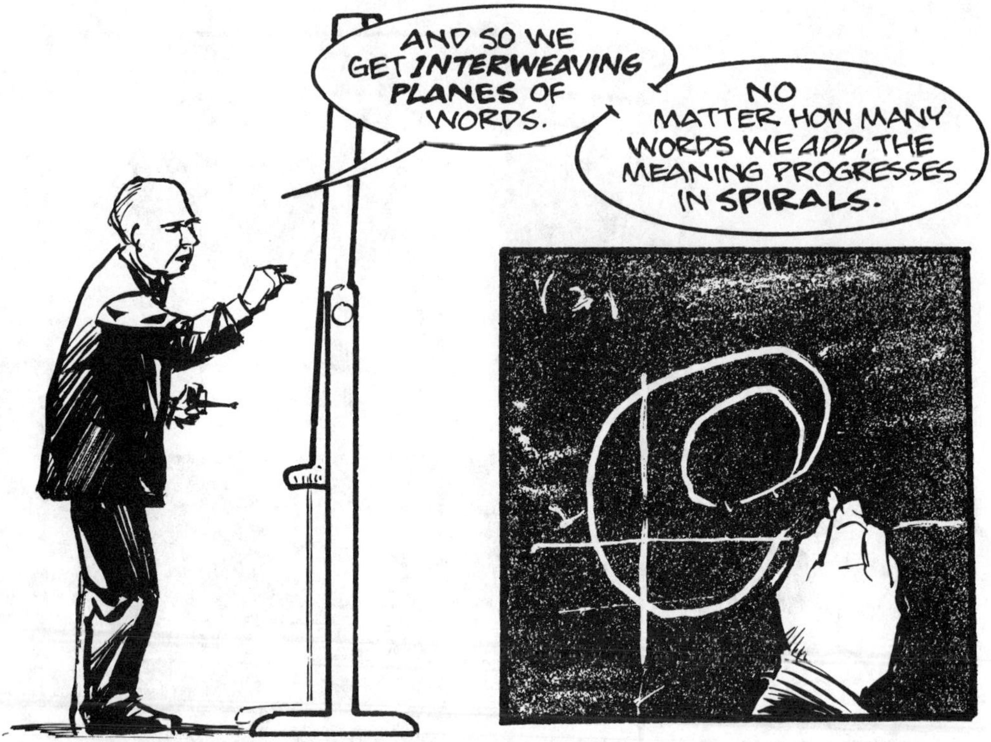
AND SO WE GET **INTERWEAVING PLANES** OF WORDS.
NO MATTER HOW MANY WORDS WE *ADD*, THE MEANING PROGRESSES IN **SPIRALS.**

"AND OPPOSITES ARE COMPLEMENTARY."

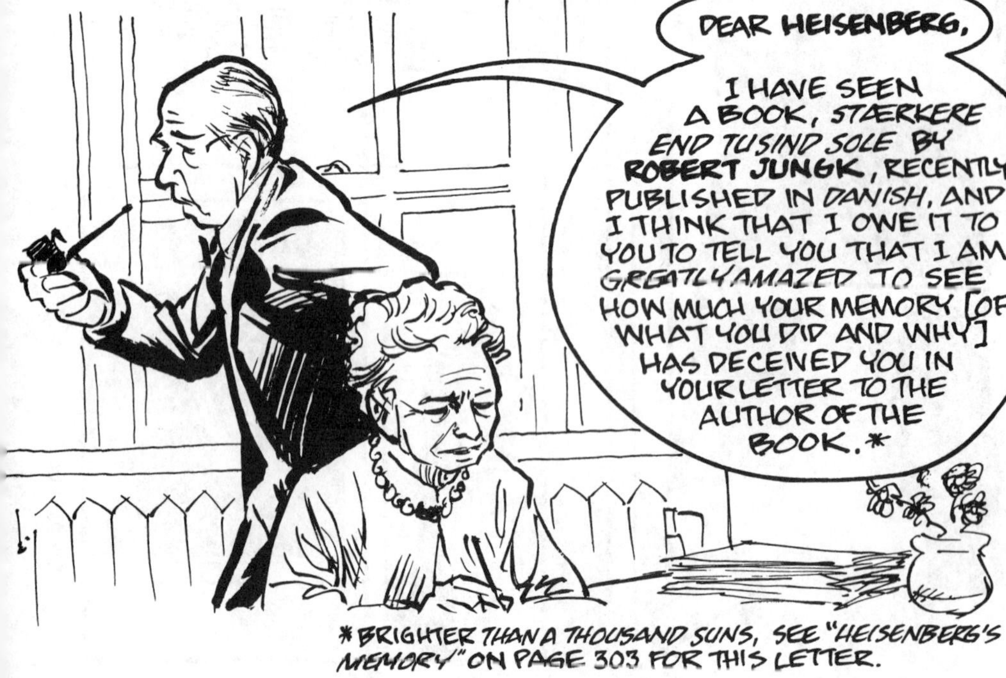
DEAR **HEISENBERG,**
I HAVE SEEN A BOOK, *STÆRKERE END TUSIND SOLE* BY **ROBERT JUNGK**, RECENTLY PUBLISHED IN *DANISH*, AND I THINK THAT I OWE IT TO YOU TO TELL YOU THAT I AM *GREATLY* AMAZED TO SEE HOW MUCH YOUR MEMORY [OF WHAT YOU DID AND WHY] HAS DECEIVED YOU IN YOUR LETTER TO THE AUTHOR OF THE BOOK.*

* *BRIGHTER THAN A THOUSAND SUNS*, SEE "*HEISENBERG'S MEMORY*" ON PAGE 303 FOR THIS LETTER.

AND SO BEGAN THE FIRST OF ALMOST A DOZEN DRAFTS OF A LETTER ABOUT THEIR MEETING IN 1941. **BOHR** WROTE TO HEISENBERG BETWEEN 1957 AND HIS DEATH IN 1962.

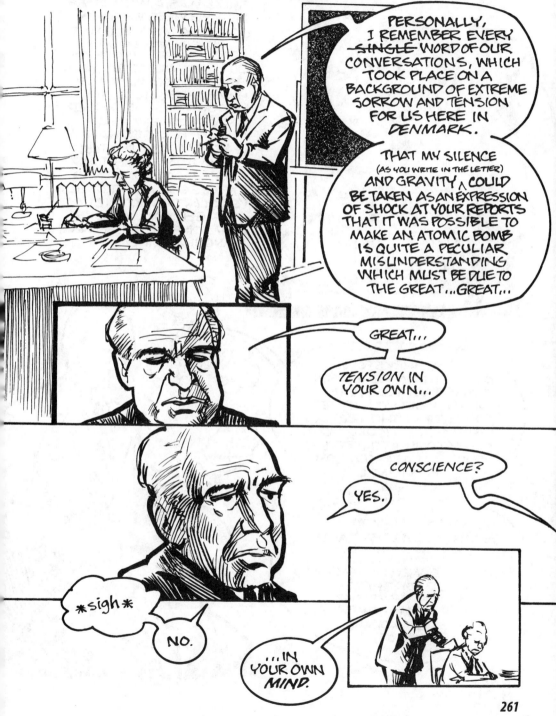

PERSONALLY, I REMEMBER EVERY ~~SINGLE~~ WORD OF OUR CONVERSATIONS, WHICH TOOK PLACE ON A BACKGROUND OF EXTREME SORROW AND TENSION FOR US HERE IN DENMARK.

THAT MY SILENCE (AS YOU WRITE IN THE LETTER) AND GRAVITY ∧ COULD BE TAKEN AS AN EXPRESSION OF SHOCK AT YOUR REPORTS THAT IT WAS POSSIBLE TO MAKE AN ATOMIC BOMB IS QUITE A PECULIAR MISUNDERSTANDING WHICH MUST BE DUE TO THE GREAT...GREAT...

GREAT...

TENSION IN YOUR OWN...

CONSCIENCE?

YES.

sigh

NO.

...IN YOUR OWN *MIND*.

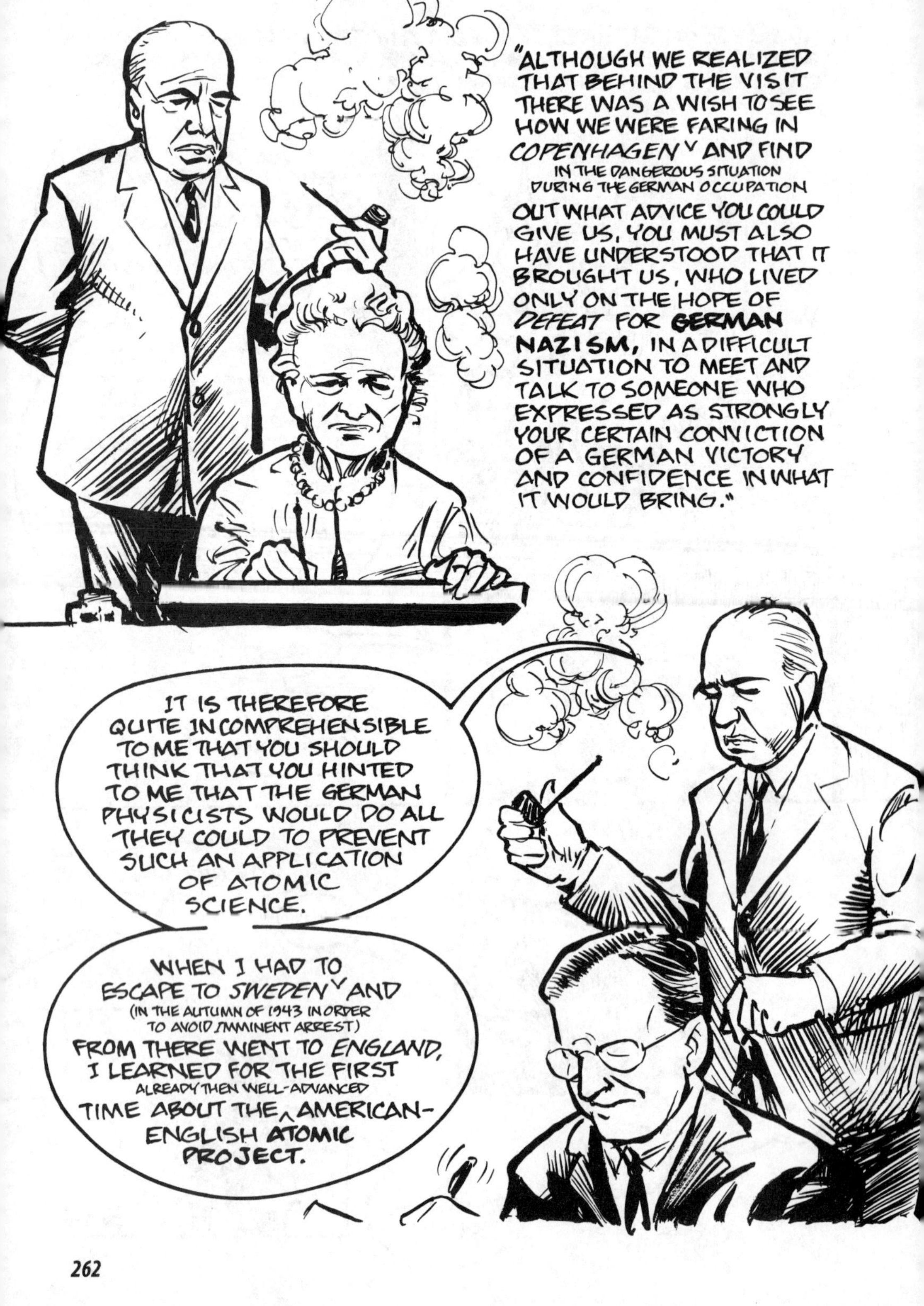
"ALTHOUGH WE REALIZED THAT BEHIND THE VISIT THERE WAS A WISH TO SEE HOW WE WERE FARING IN COPENHAGEN ˇ AND FIND
IN THE DANGEROUS SITUATION DURING THE GERMAN OCCUPATION
OUT WHAT ADVICE YOU COULD GIVE US, YOU MUST ALSO HAVE UNDERSTOOD THAT IT BROUGHT US, WHO LIVED ONLY ON THE HOPE OF DEFEAT FOR GERMAN NAZISM, IN A DIFFICULT SITUATION TO MEET AND TALK TO SOMEONE WHO EXPRESSED AS STRONGLY YOUR CERTAIN CONVICTION OF A GERMAN VICTORY AND CONFIDENCE IN WHAT IT WOULD BRING."
IT IS THEREFORE QUITE INCOMPREHENSIBLE TO ME THAT YOU SHOULD THINK THAT YOU HINTED TO ME THAT THE GERMAN PHYSICISTS WOULD DO ALL THEY COULD TO PREVENT SUCH AN APPLICATION OF ATOMIC SCIENCE.
WHEN I HAD TO ESCAPE TO SWEDEN ˇ AND
(IN THE AUTUMN OF 1943 IN ORDER TO AVOID IMMINENT ARREST)
FROM THERE WENT TO ENGLAND, I LEARNED FOR THE FIRST
ALREADY THEN WELL-ADVANCED
TIME ABOUT THE ^ AMERICAN-ENGLISH ATOMIC PROJECT.

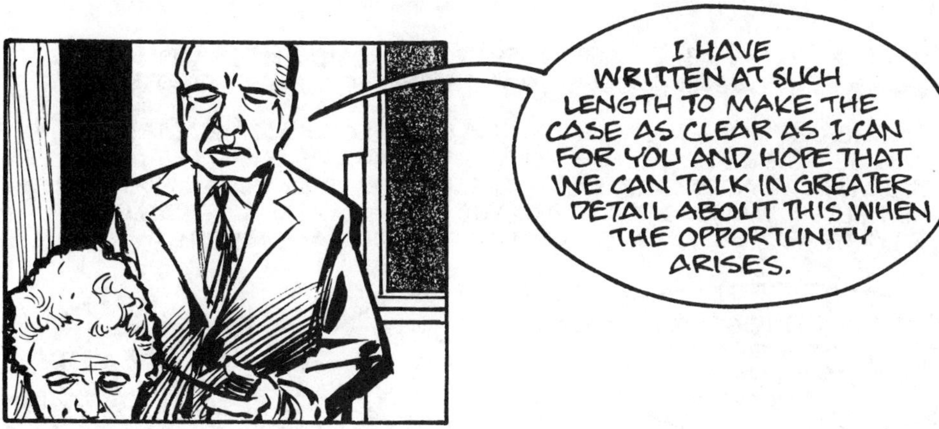
I HAVE WRITTEN AT SUCH LENGTH TO MAKE THE CASE AS CLEAR AS I CAN FOR YOU AND HOPE THAT WE CAN TALK IN GREATER DETAIL ABOUT THIS WHEN THE OPPORTUNITY ARISES.

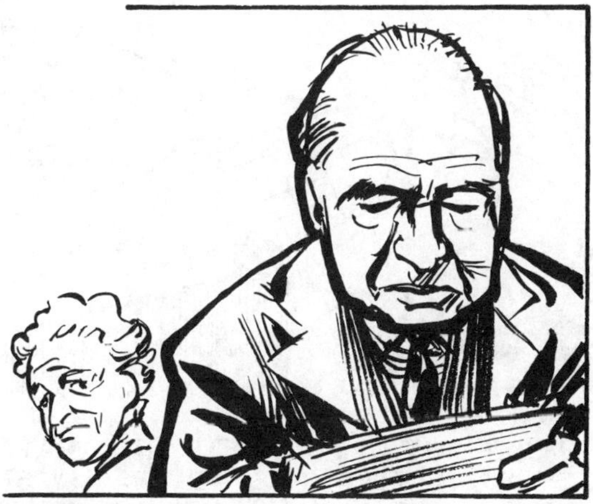

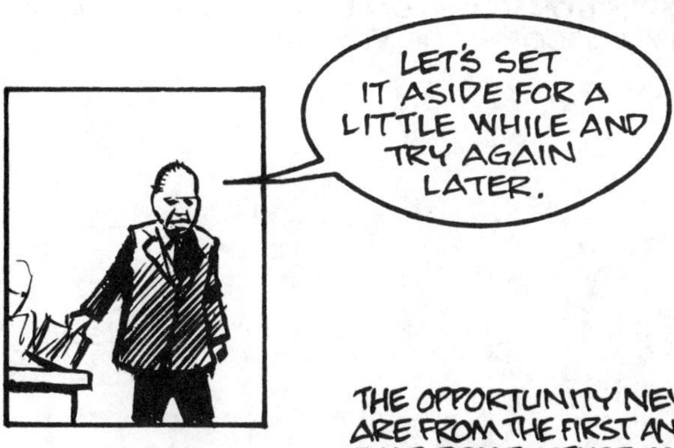
LET'S SET IT ASIDE FOR A LITTLE WHILE AND TRY AGAIN LATER.

THE OPPORTUNITY NEVER AROSE. THESE PASSAGES ARE FROM THE FIRST AND LAST DRAFTS OF LETTERS THAT **BOHR** NEVER COMPLETED AND NEVER SENT.

SO, THOUGH **BOHR** AND **HEISENBERG** WERE CORDIAL TO EACH OTHER, EXCHANGING LETTERS ON BIRTHDAYS AND OCCASIONS OF HONOR AND EVEN SOME VISITS, THE SPECIAL BOND BETWEEN THESE TWO FRIENDS—WHO THROUGH *COMPLEMENTARITY* AND THE *UNCERTAINTY PRINCIPLE* HAD BOUND HUMANITY TO **PHYSICS** WITH **MATHEMATICAL** CERTAINTY—REMAINED BROKEN.

THAT HE WASN'T ABLE TO SEND *THE* LETTER, MUCH LESS FINISH IT, AND BRING **HEISENBERG** AROUND TO HIS POINT OF VIEW IS SURPRISING.

ON THE ONE HAND, WE'VE SEEN THAT THE LARGER THE AUDIENCE, THE WORSE **BOHR** DID. (SO HIS PUBLISHED PAPERS, WITH THE LARGEST POSSIBLE READERSHIP, WERE OFTEN IMPENETRABLE.) AND HE WAS NOT FULLY AWARE OF THIS—TO THE VERY END HE HAD TROUBLE SAYING *NO* TO SPEAKING AND WRITING ENGAGEMENTS:

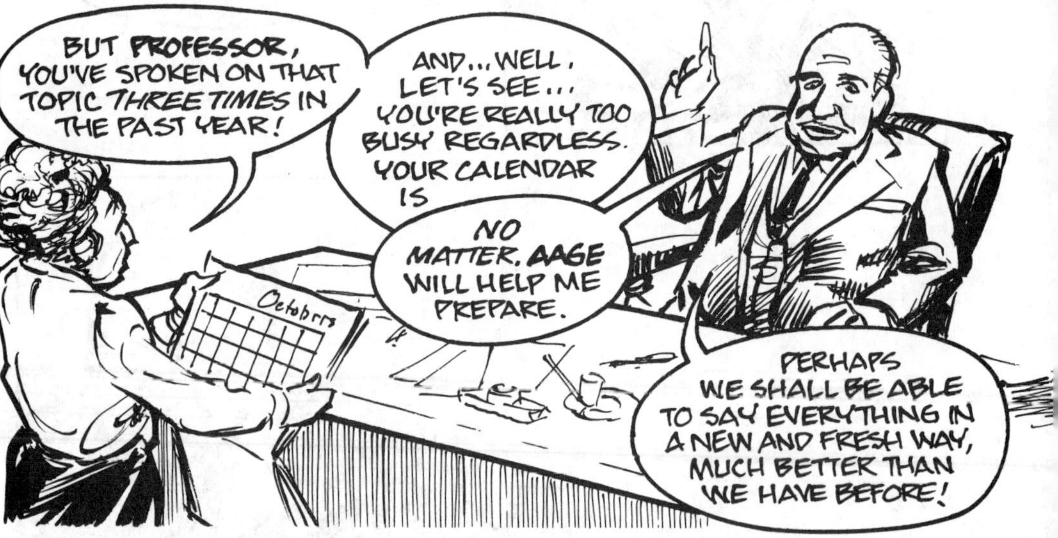
BUT **PROFESSOR**, YOU'VE SPOKEN ON THAT TOPIC *THREE TIMES* IN THE PAST YEAR!
AND... WELL. LET'S SEE... YOU'RE REALLY TOO BUSY REGARDLESS. YOUR CALENDAR IS
NO MATTER. **AAGE** WILL HELP ME PREPARE.
PERHAPS WE SHALL BE ABLE TO SAY EVERYTHING IN A NEW AND FRESH WAY, MUCH BETTER THAN WE HAVE BEFORE!

ON THE OTHER HAND, WE'VE SEEN THAT ONE-ON-ONE **BOHR** COULD WOO, SWAY AND FINALLY CONQUER ALMOST ANYONE, BE IT A *PRESIDENT* OR PHILANTHROPIST, SCIENTIST OR **KING**, ON POLITICAL AND SOCIAL MATTERS AS WELL AS ON PHILOSOPHY OR PHYSICS.

ALL BUT ONE SCIENTIST, ANYWAY...

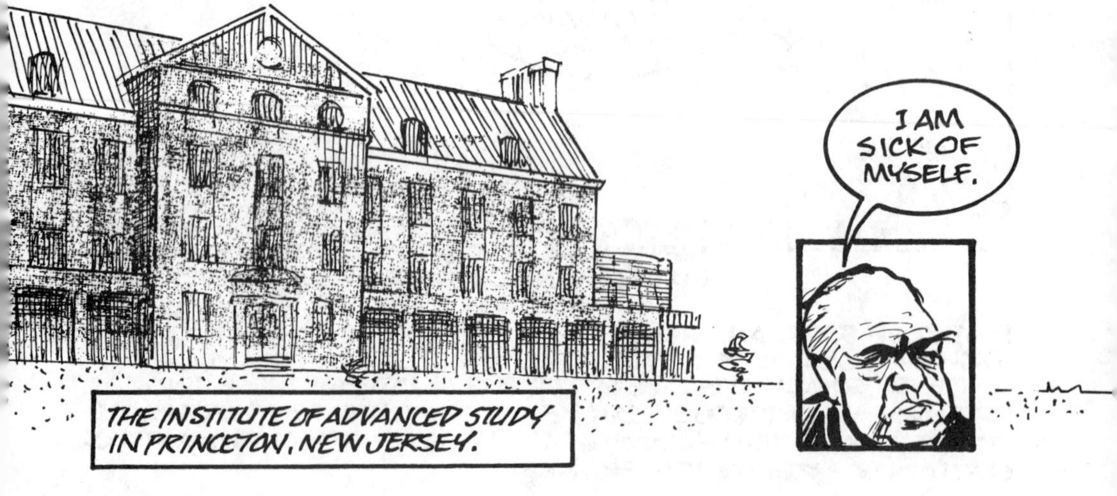
THE INSTITUTE OF ADVANCED STUDY IN PRINCETON, NEW JERSEY.
I AM SICK OF MYSELF.

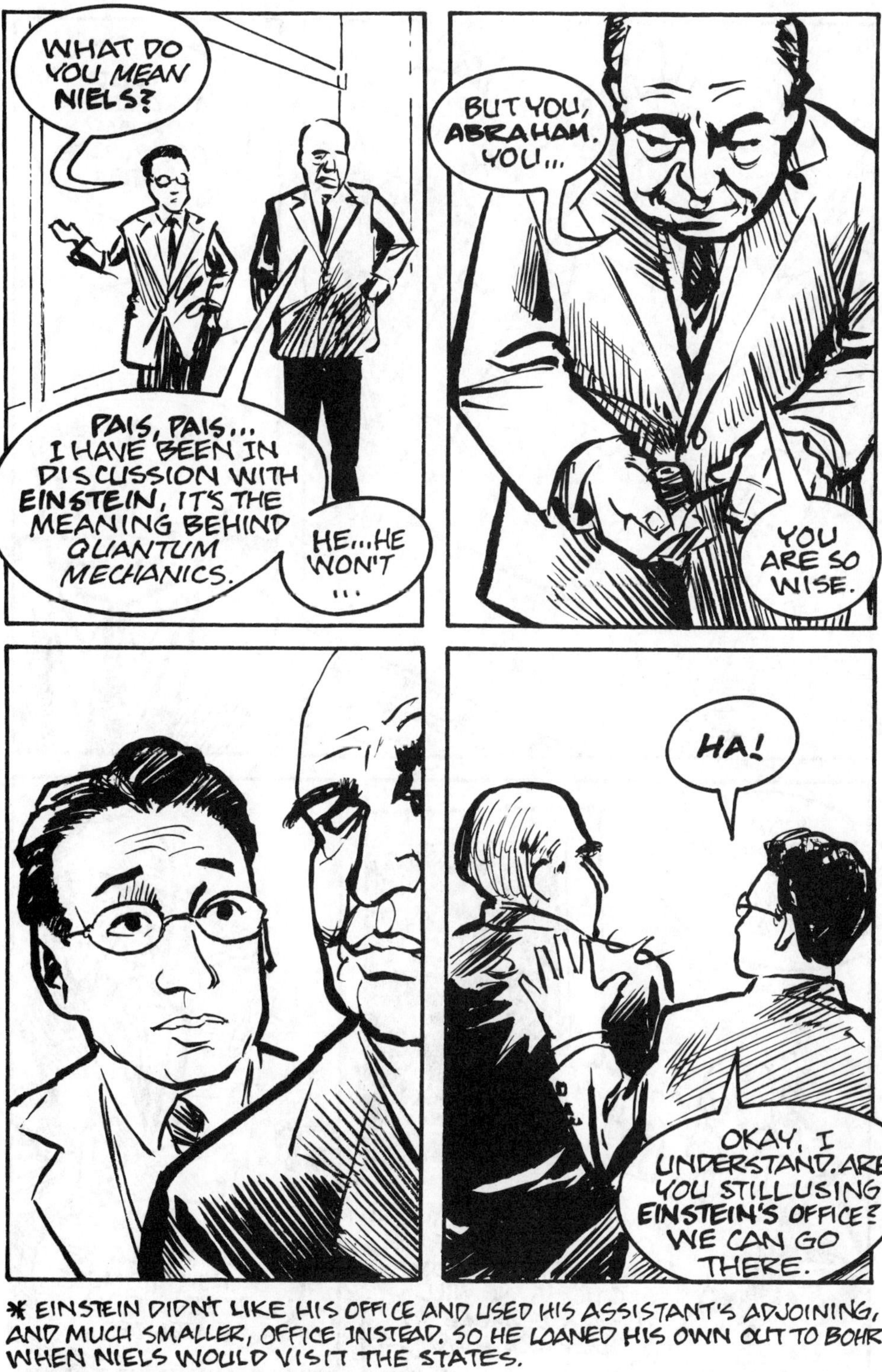
WHAT DO YOU MEAN NIELS?
PAIS, PAIS... I HAVE BEEN IN DISCUSSION WITH EINSTEIN, IT'S THE MEANING BEHIND QUANTUM MECHANICS.
HE...HE WON'T ...
BUT YOU, ABRAHAM, YOU...
YOU ARE SO WISE.
HA!
OKAY, I UNDERSTAND. ARE YOU STILL USING EINSTEIN'S OFFICE? WE CAN GO THERE.

* EINSTEIN DIDN'T LIKE HIS OFFICE AND USED HIS ASSISTANT'S ADJOINING, AND MUCH SMALLER, OFFICE INSTEAD. SO HE LOANED HIS OWN OUT TO BOHR WHEN NIELS WOULD VISIT THE STATES.

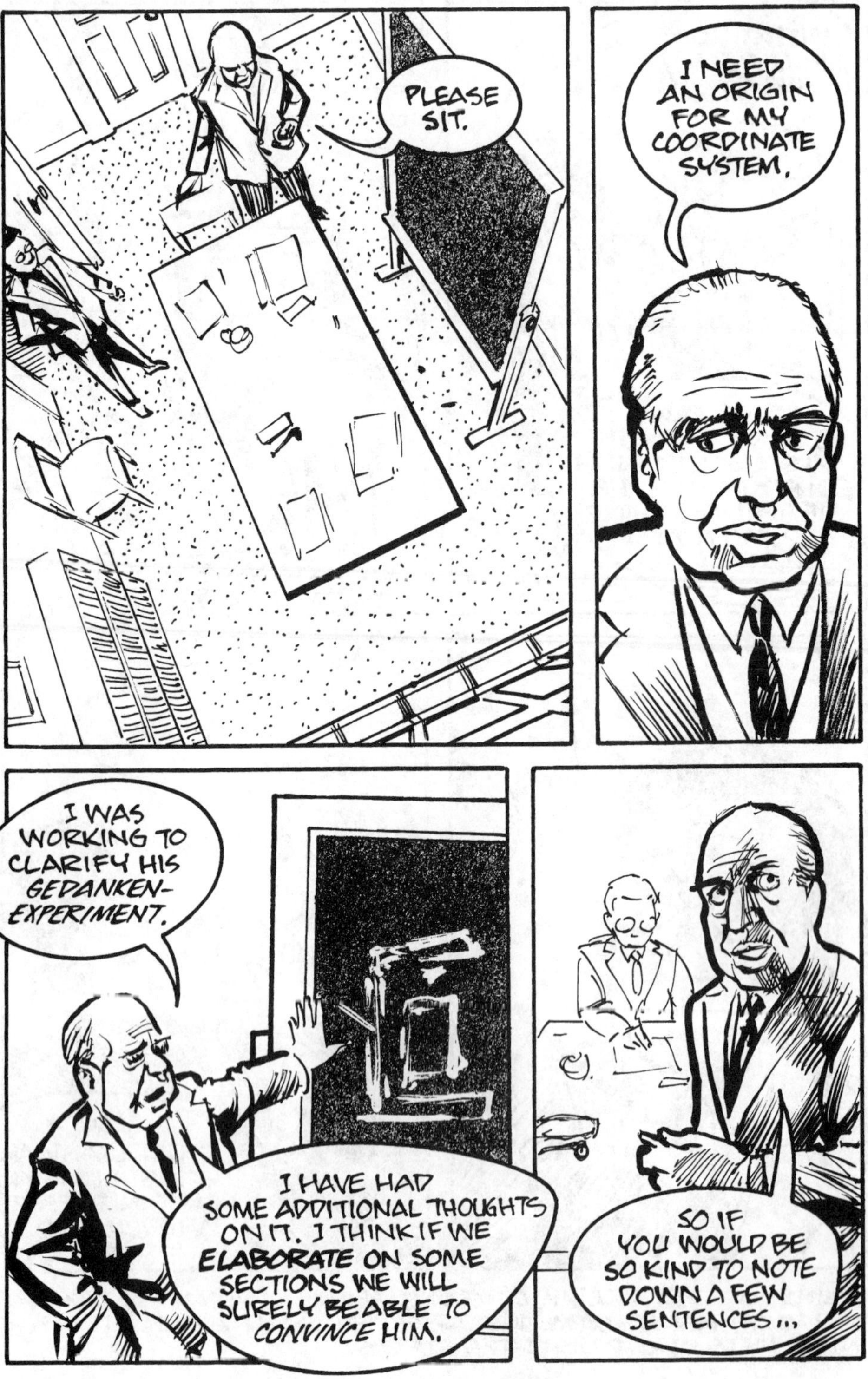
PLEASE SIT.
I NEED AN ORIGIN FOR MY COORDINATE SYSTEM.
I WAS WORKING TO CLARIFY HIS *GEDANKEN-EXPERIMENT.*
I HAVE HAD SOME ADDITIONAL THOUGHTS ON IT. I THINK IF WE **ELABORATE** ON SOME SECTIONS WE WILL SURELY BE ABLE TO *CONVINCE* HIM.
SO IF YOU WOULD BE SO KIND TO NOTE DOWN A FEW SENTENCES...

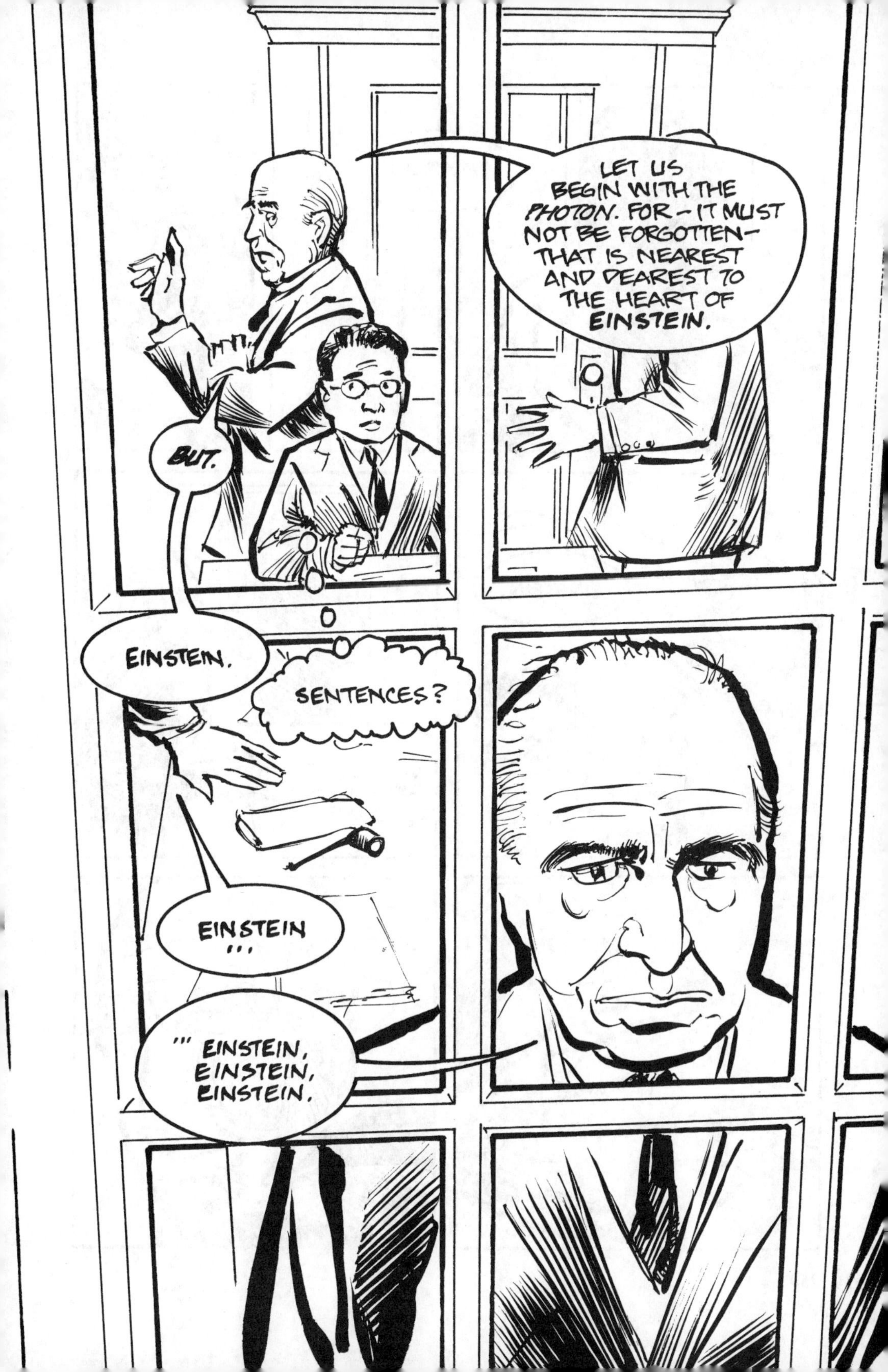
LET US BEGIN WITH THE *PHOTON*. FOR – IT MUST NOT BE FORGOTTEN – THAT IS NEAREST AND DEAREST TO THE HEART OF **EINSTEIN**.
BUT.
EINSTEIN.
SENTENCES?
EINSTEIN ...
... EINSTEIN, EINSTEIN, EINSTEIN.

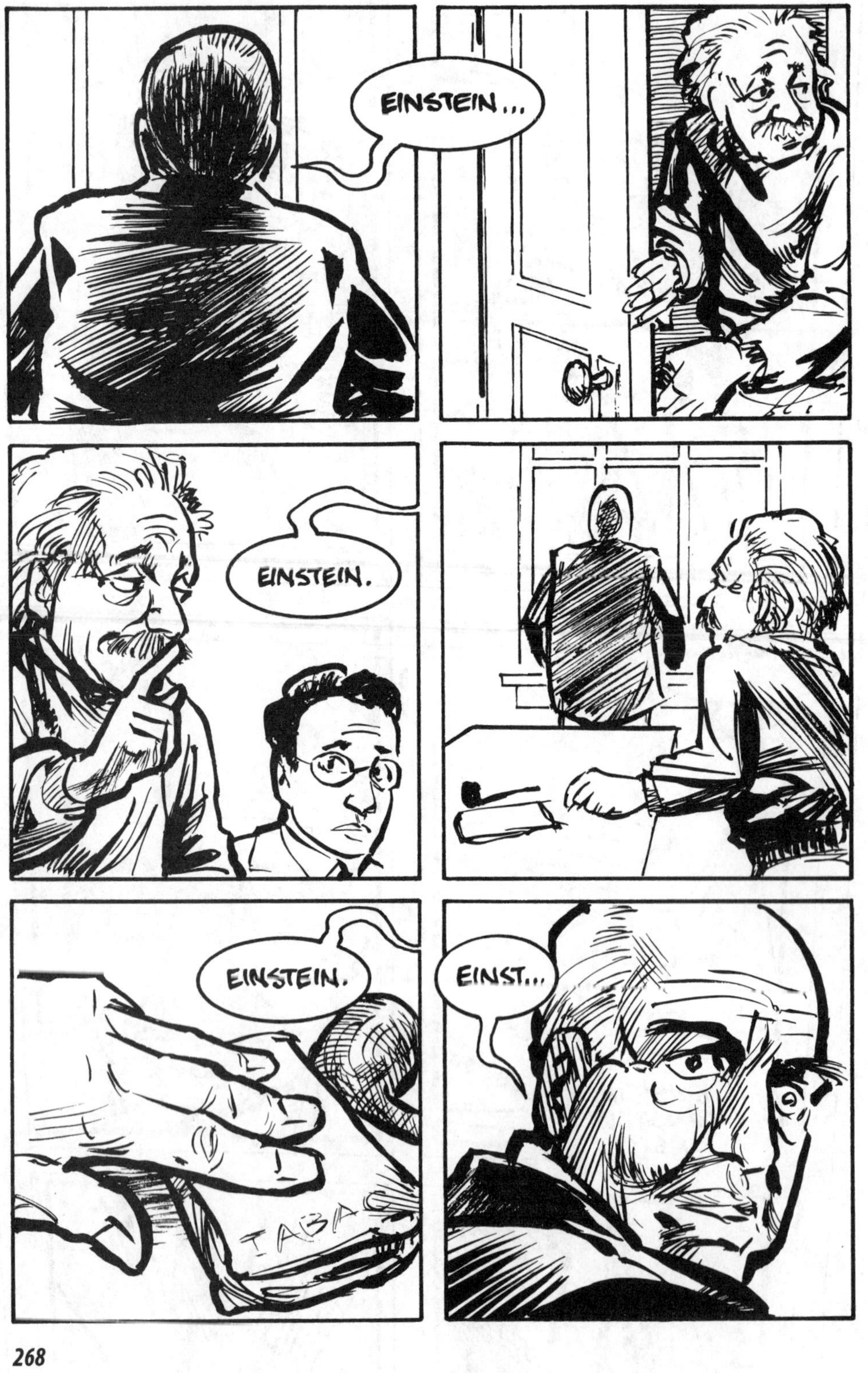
EINSTEIN...
EINSTEIN.
EINSTEIN.
TABAC
EINST...

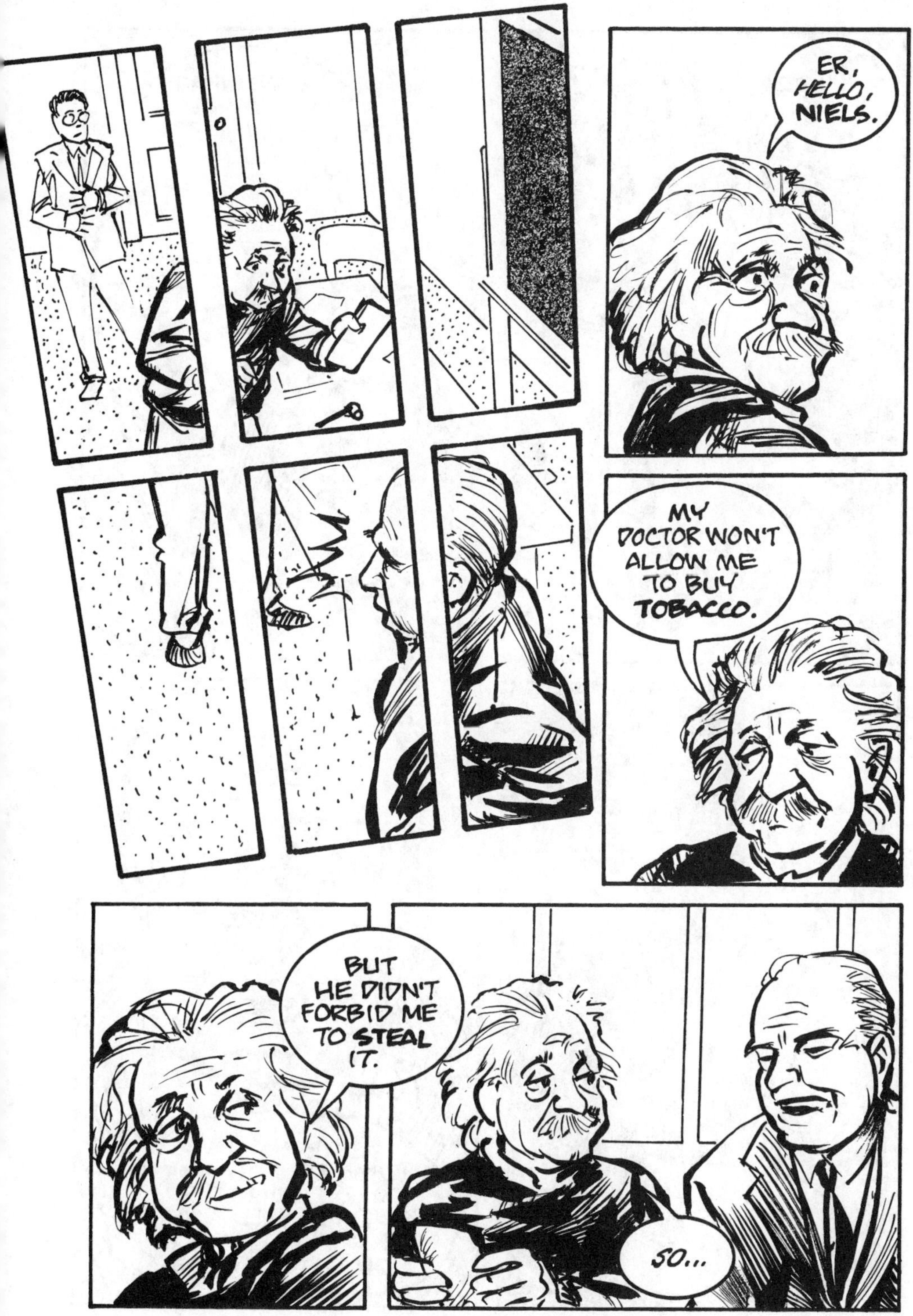

ER, HELLO, NIELS.
MY DOCTOR WON'T ALLOW ME TO BUY TOBACCO.
BUT HE DIDN'T FORBID ME TO STEAL IT.
SO...

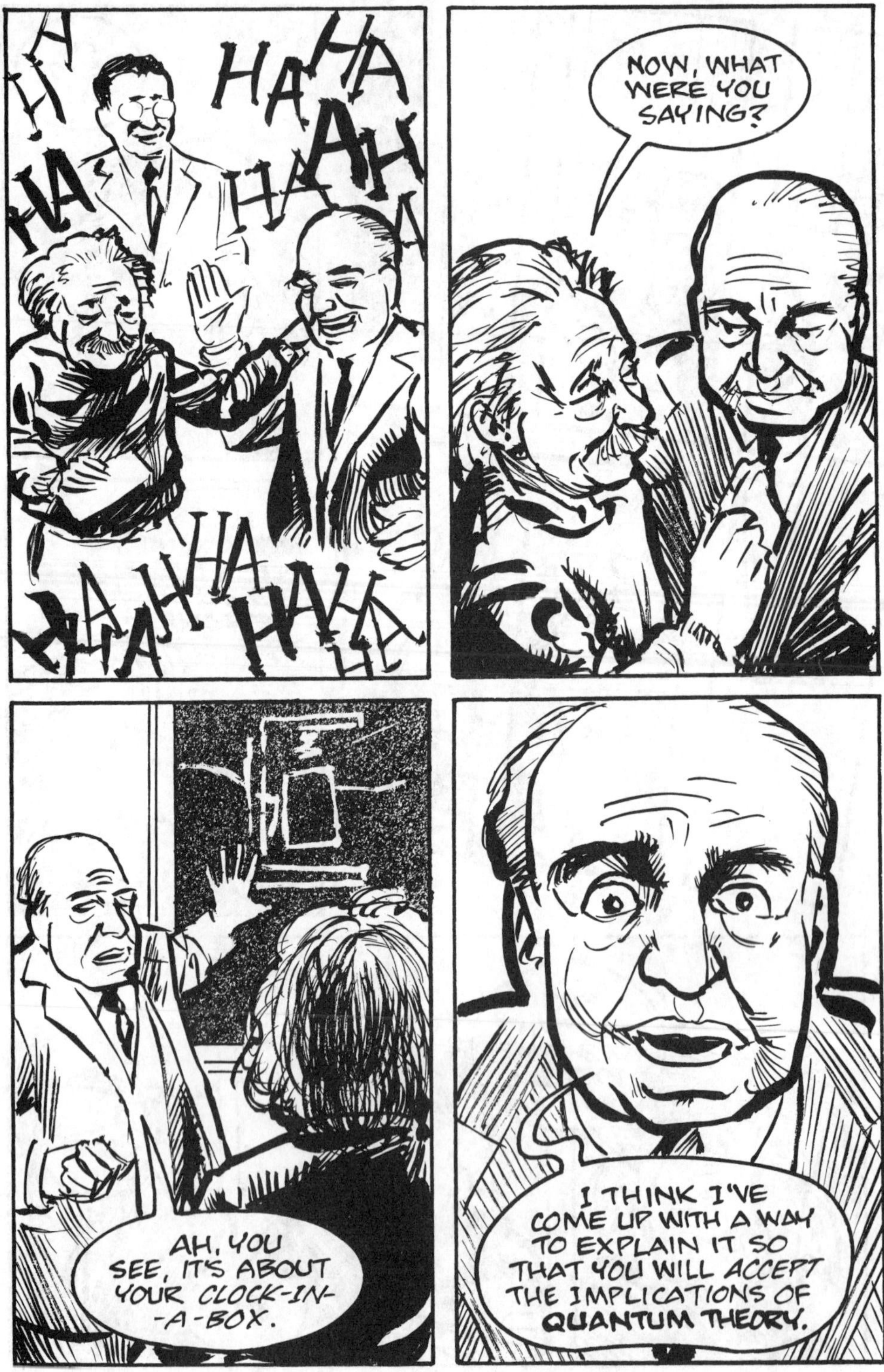
HA HA HA HA HA HA HA HA
NOW, WHAT WERE YOU SAYING?
AH, YOU SEE, IT'S ABOUT YOUR *CLOCK-IN--A-BOX*.
I THINK I'VE COME UP WITH A WAY TO EXPLAIN IT SO THAT YOU WILL *ACCEPT* THE IMPLICATIONS OF **QUANTUM THEORY**.

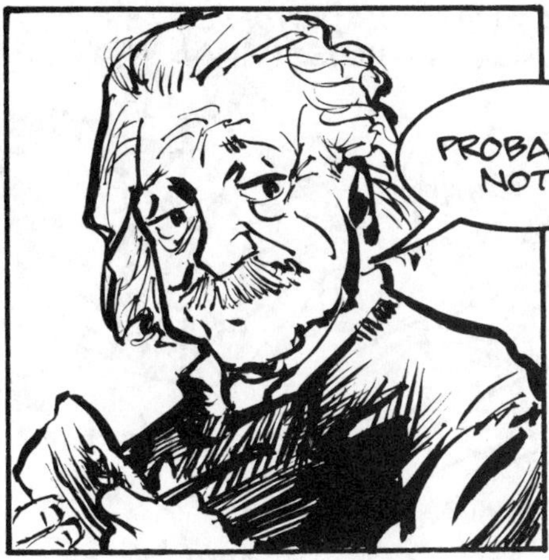
PROBABLY NOT.

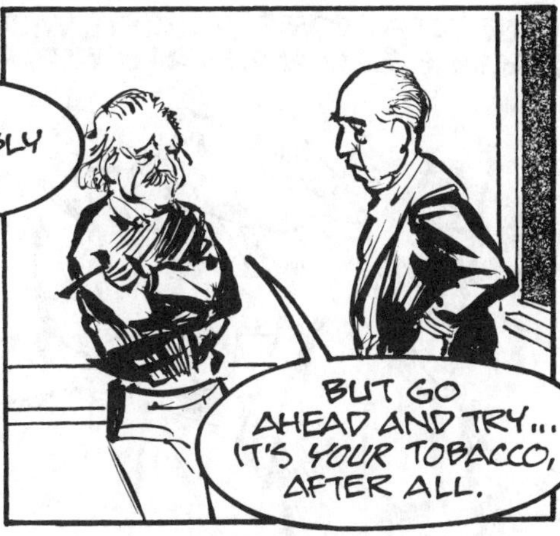
BUT GO AHEAD AND TRY... IT'S *YOUR* TOBACCO, AFTER ALL.

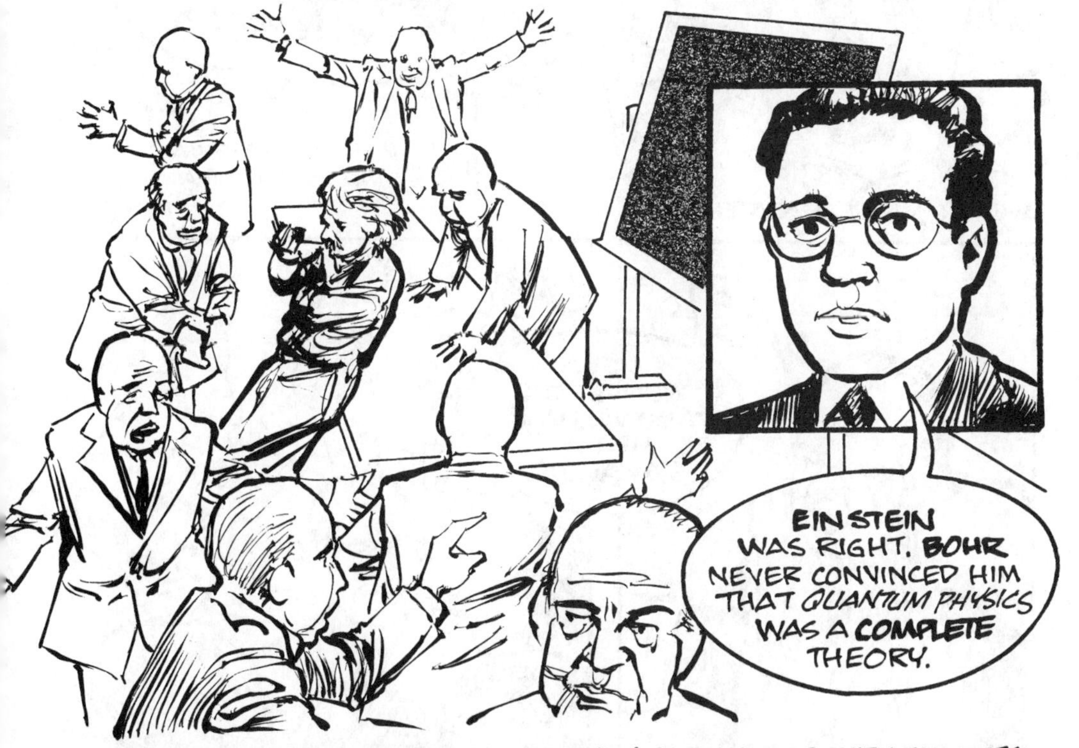
EINSTEIN WAS RIGHT. **BOHR** NEVER CONVINCED HIM THAT *QUANTUM PHYSICS* WAS A **COMPLETE** THEORY.

AND SO, PERHAPS YOU'RE THINKING IT FUNNY TO CONCLUDE WITH FAILURES. **BOHR** NEVER FULLY RECONCILED WITH **HEISENBERG**, AND NEVER PERSUADED **EINSTEIN** ABOUT *QUANTUM THEORY.*

(AND THERE WAS HIS *NOBEL PRIZE* WINNING **ATOMIC MODEL**. THE ONE YOU MAY REMEMBER FROM SCHOOL. THE ONE THAT'S **WRONG**.)

(AND THEN THERE WERE HIS IDEAS FOR AN *OPEN WORLD*... THE ONES REJECTED BY **CHURCHILL**, WHOSE PERSUASIVE POWERS PROVED GREATER THAN **BOHR'S**, AT LEAST WHEN IT CAME TO **ROOSEVELT**. THE EXPERIMENT WE'LL NEVER GET TO TRY.)

(AND TODAY FEW PHYSICISTS WORK IN THE TRADITION OF *DER KOPENHAGENER GEIST* AND EVEN FEWER READ HIS PHILOSOPHICAL WRITINGS.)

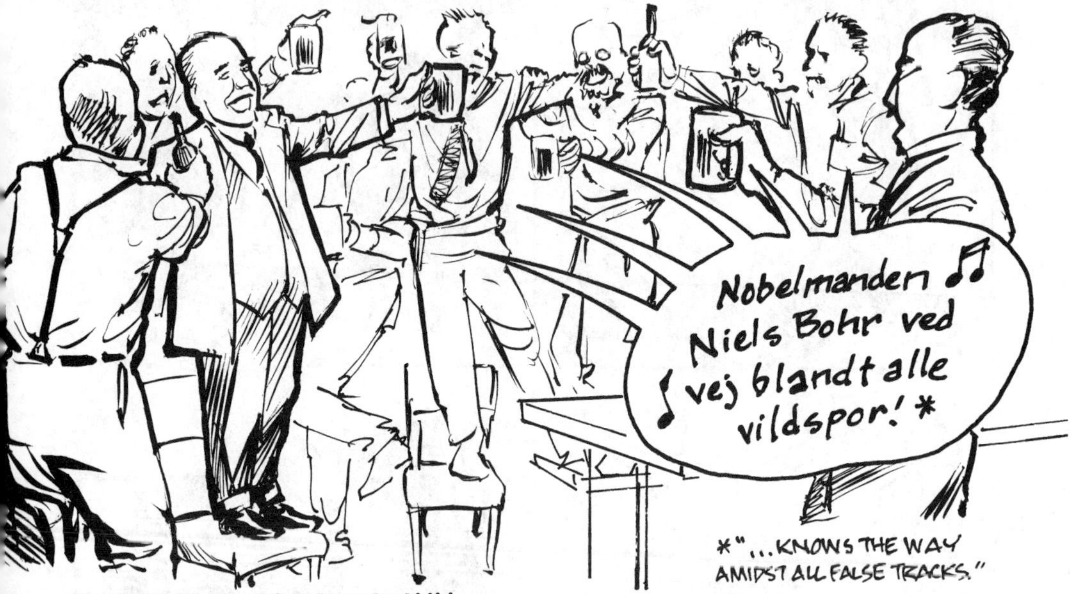
Nobelmanden Niels Bohr ved vej blandt alle vildspor! *
*"...KNOWS THE WAY AMIDST ALL FALSE TRACKS."

AND YET, WE CELEBRATE HIM.

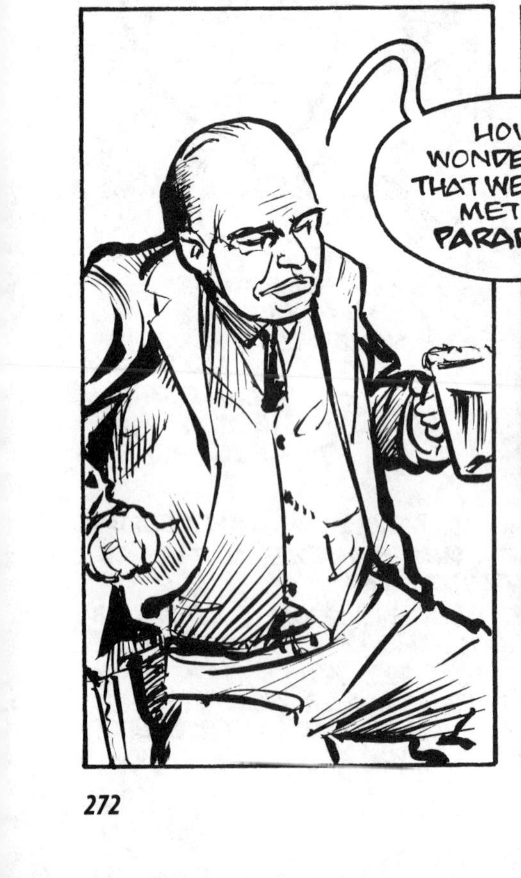
HOW WONDERFUL THAT WE HAVE MET A PARADOX.

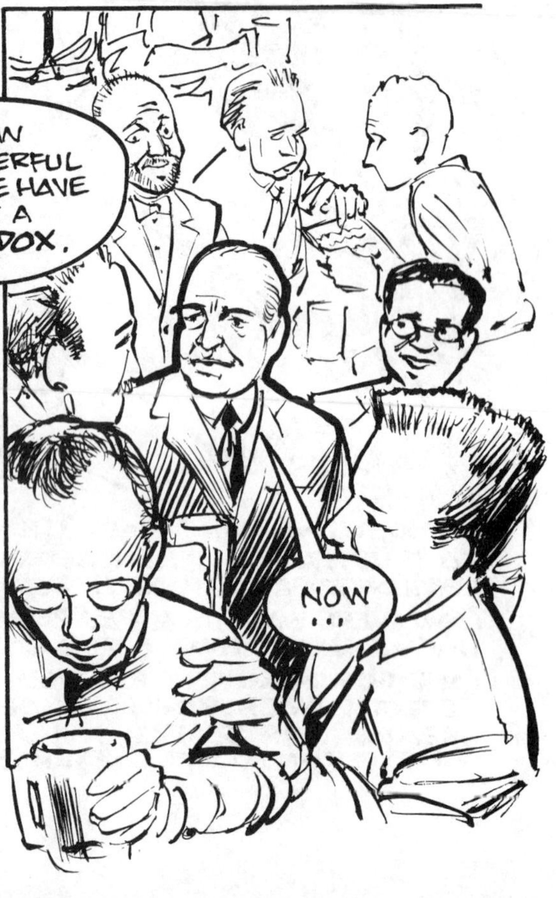
NOW ...

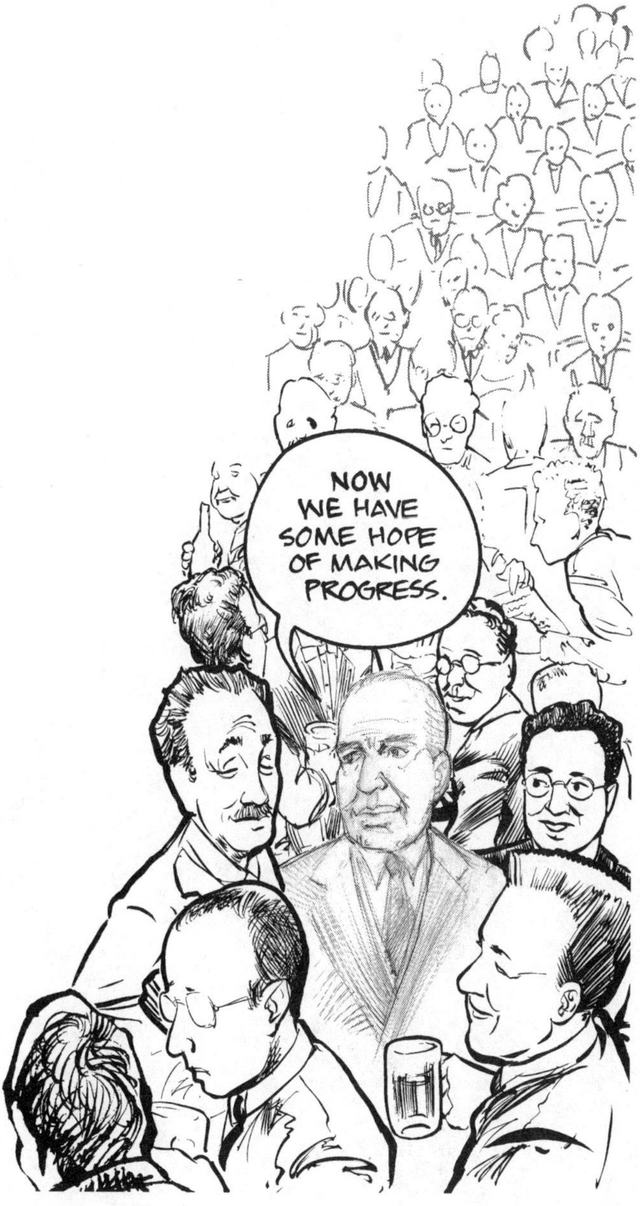
NOW WE HAVE SOME HOPE OF MAKING PROGRESS.

Endnotes*

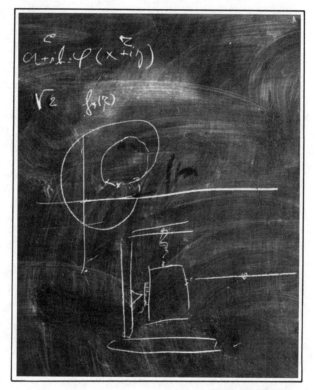

* see page 304

Apocrypha: An oft told ("Knowest thou?" "Well I know.") folk tale about young Niels.

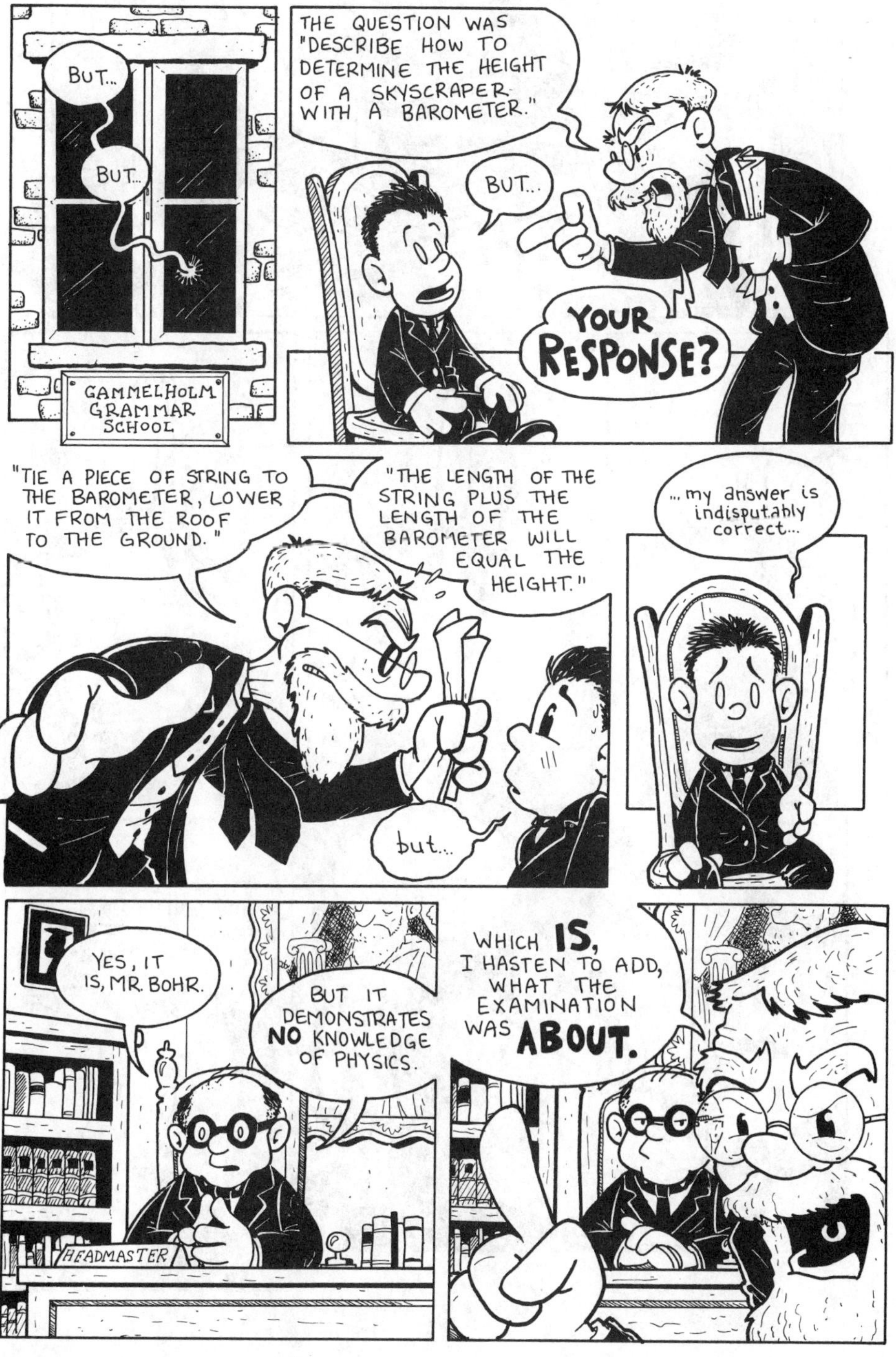
BUT...
BUT...
GAMMELHOLM GRAMMAR SCHOOL
THE QUESTION WAS "DESCRIBE HOW TO DETERMINE THE HEIGHT OF A SKYSCRAPER WITH A BAROMETER."
BUT...
YOUR RESPONSE?
"TIE A PIECE OF STRING TO THE BAROMETER, LOWER IT FROM THE ROOF TO THE GROUND."
"THE LENGTH OF THE STRING PLUS THE LENGTH OF THE BAROMETER WILL EQUAL THE HEIGHT."
but...
... my answer is indisputably correct...
YES, IT IS, MR. BOHR.
BUT IT DEMONSTRATES NO KNOWLEDGE OF PHYSICS.
HEADMASTER
WHICH IS, I HASTEN TO ADD, WHAT THE EXAMINATION WAS ABOUT.

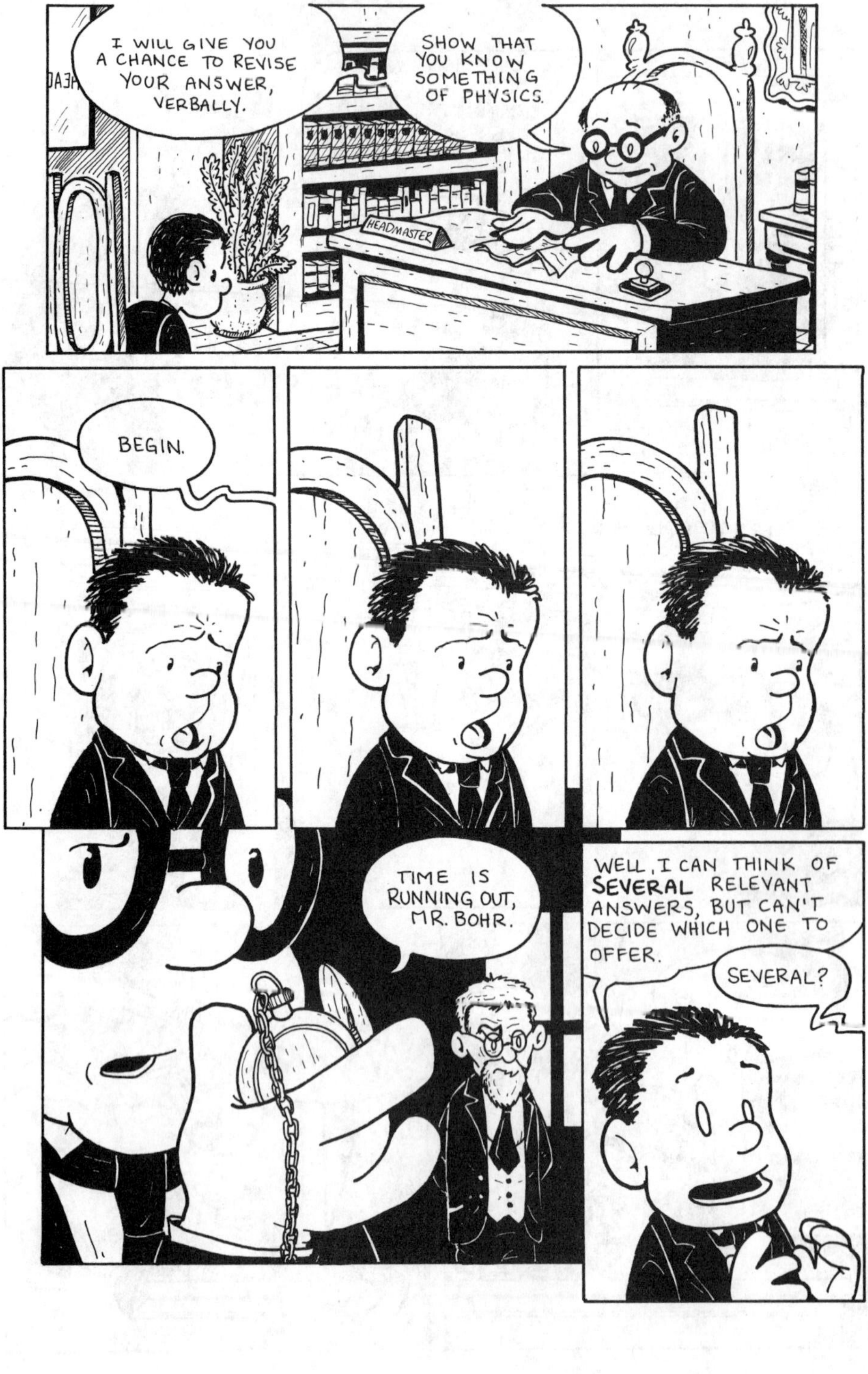
I WILL GIVE YOU A CHANCE TO REVISE YOUR ANSWER, VERBALLY.
SHOW THAT YOU KNOW SOMETHING OF PHYSICS.
HEADMASTER
BEGIN.
TIME IS RUNNING OUT, MR. BOHR.
WELL, I CAN THINK OF SEVERAL RELEVANT ANSWERS, BUT CAN'T DECIDE WHICH ONE TO OFFER.
SEVERAL?

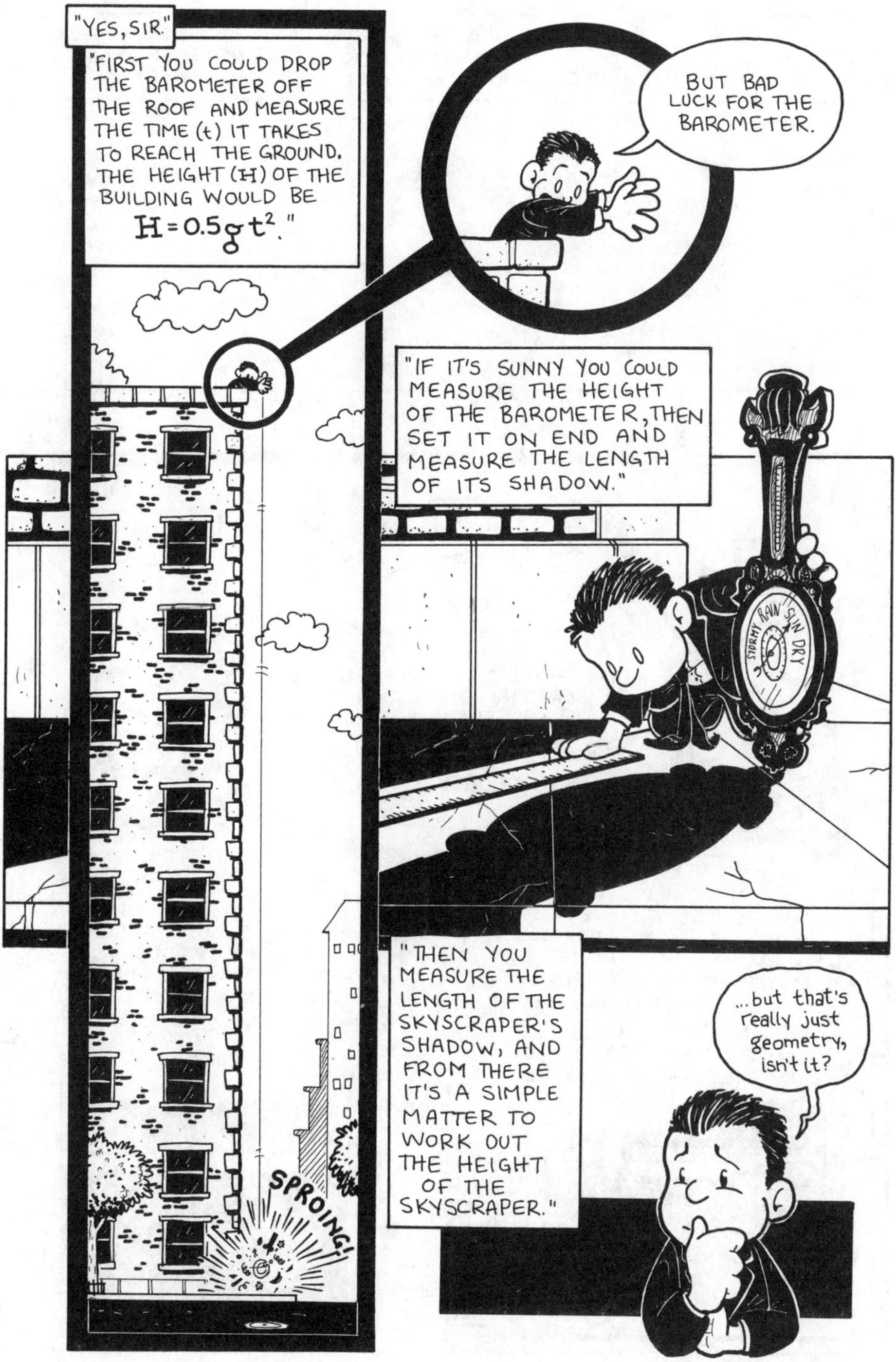
"YES, SIR."
"FIRST YOU COULD DROP THE BAROMETER OFF THE ROOF AND MEASURE THE TIME (t) IT TAKES TO REACH THE GROUND. THE HEIGHT (H) OF THE BUILDING WOULD BE $H = 0.5gt^2$."
BUT BAD LUCK FOR THE BAROMETER.
SPROING!
"IF IT'S SUNNY YOU COULD MEASURE THE HEIGHT OF THE BAROMETER, THEN SET IT ON END AND MEASURE THE LENGTH OF ITS SHADOW."
STORMY RAIN SUN DRY
"THEN YOU MEASURE THE LENGTH OF THE SKYSCRAPER'S SHADOW, AND FROM THERE IT'S A SIMPLE MATTER TO WORK OUT THE HEIGHT OF THE SKYSCRAPER."
...but that's really just geometry, isn't it?

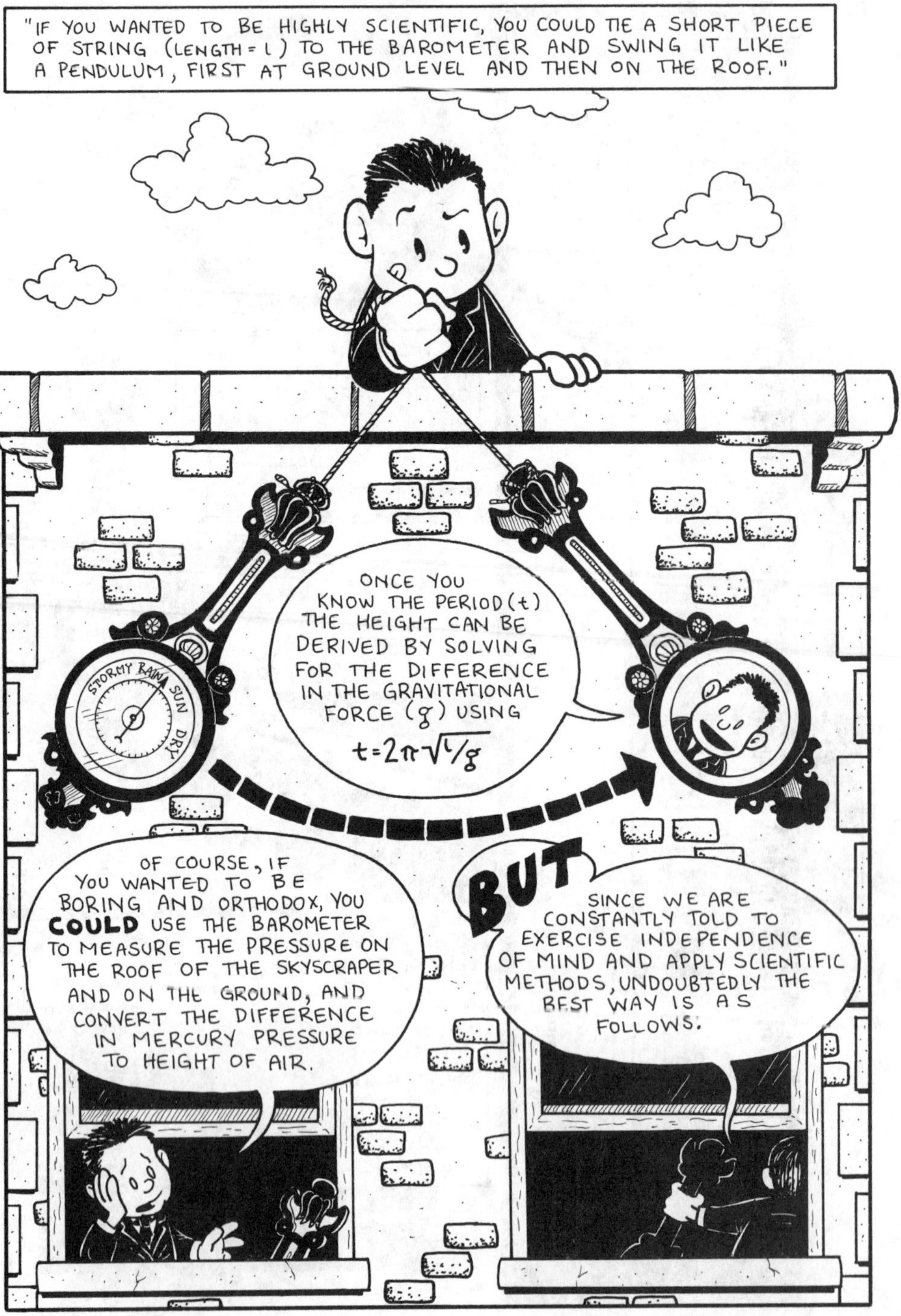
"IF YOU WANTED TO BE HIGHLY SCIENTIFIC, YOU COULD TIE A SHORT PIECE OF STRING (LENGTH = l) TO THE BAROMETER AND SWING IT LIKE A PENDULUM, FIRST AT GROUND LEVEL AND THEN ON THE ROOF."
STORMY RAIN SUN DRY
ONCE YOU KNOW THE PERIOD (t) THE HEIGHT CAN BE DERIVED BY SOLVING FOR THE DIFFERENCE IN THE GRAVITATIONAL FORCE (g) USING $t = 2\pi\sqrt{l/g}$
OF COURSE, IF YOU WANTED TO BE BORING AND ORTHODOX, YOU **COULD** USE THE BAROMETER TO MEASURE THE PRESSURE ON THE ROOF OF THE SKYSCRAPER AND ON THE GROUND, AND CONVERT THE DIFFERENCE IN MERCURY PRESSURE TO HEIGHT OF AIR.
BUT
SINCE WE ARE CONSTANTLY TOLD TO EXERCISE INDEPENDENCE OF MIND AND APPLY SCIENTIFIC METHODS, UNDOUBTEDLY THE BEST WAY IS AS FOLLOWS:

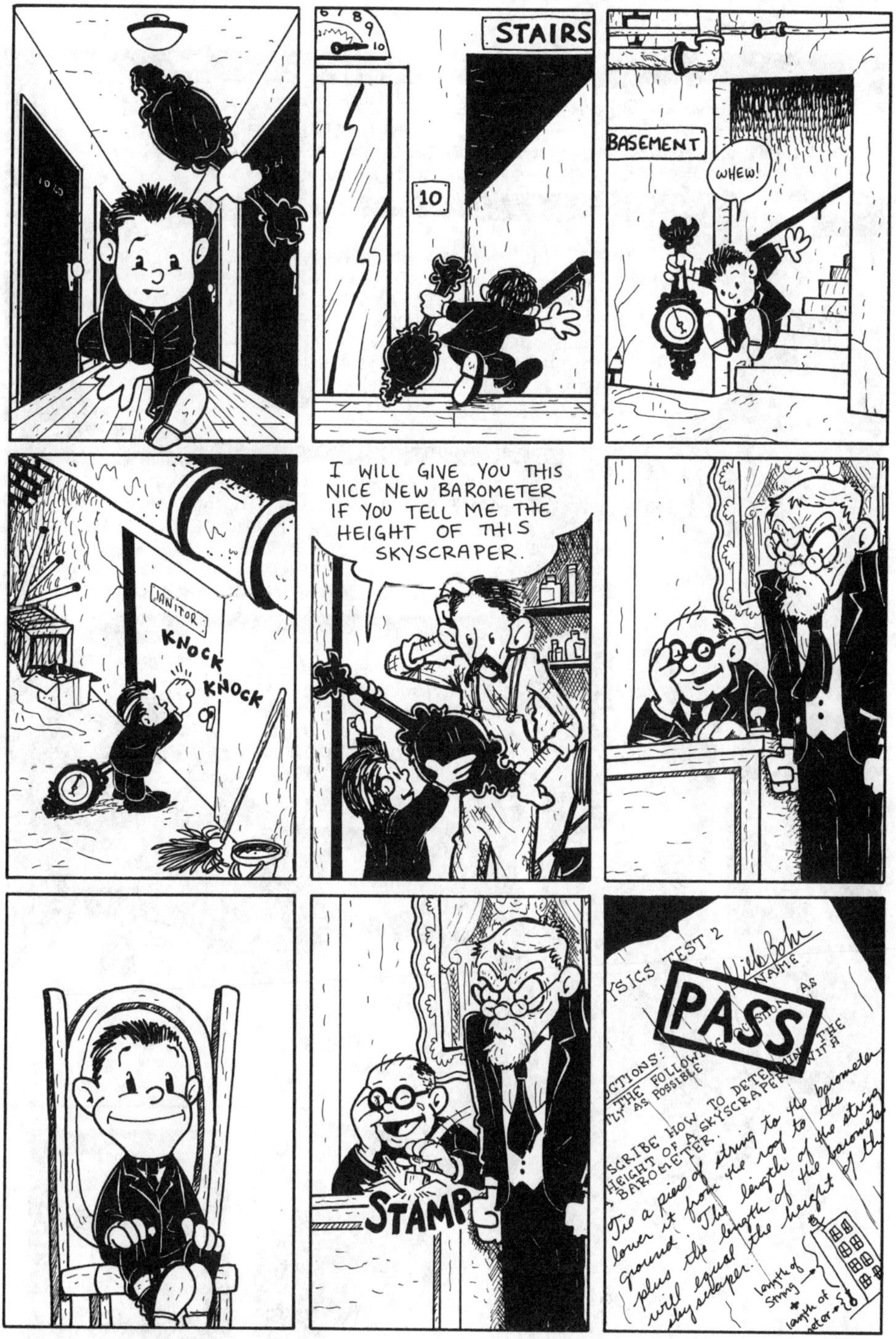
STAIRS
10
BASEMENT
WHEW!
JANITOR
KNOCK
KNOCK
I WILL GIVE YOU THIS NICE NEW BAROMETER IF YOU TELL ME THE HEIGHT OF THIS SKYSCRAPER.
STAMP
YSICS TEST 2
Niels Bohr
NAME
PASS
CTIONS:
THE FOLLOW
SCRIBE HOW TO DETE
HEIGHT OF A SKYSCRAPER
BAROMETER.
Tie a piece of string to the barometer lower it from the roof to the ground. The length of the string plus the length of the barometer will equal the height of the skyscraper.

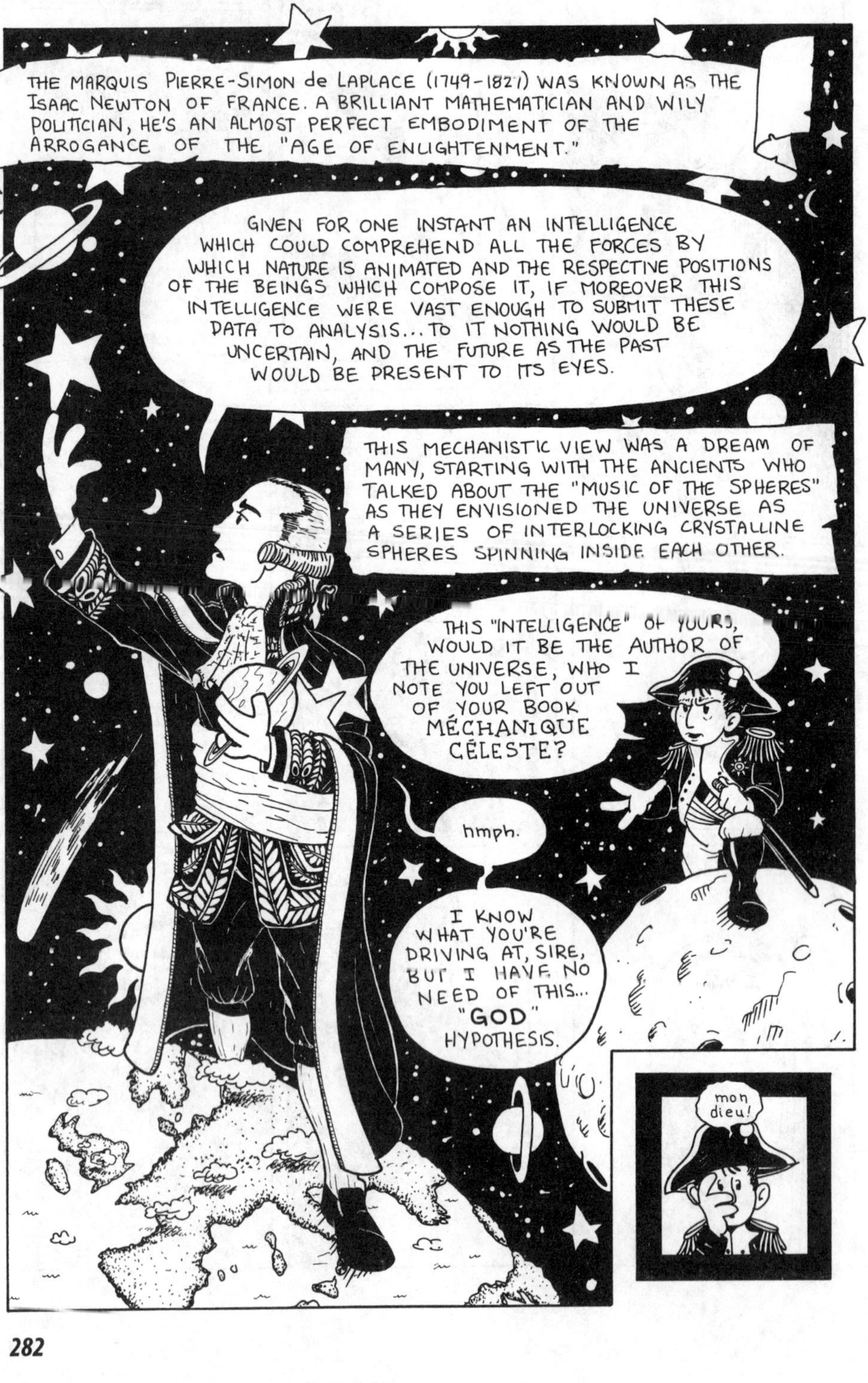
THE MARQUIS PIERRE-SIMON de LAPLACE (1749-1827) WAS KNOWN AS THE ISAAC NEWTON OF FRANCE. A BRILLIANT MATHEMATICIAN AND WILY POLITICIAN, HE'S AN ALMOST PERFECT EMBODIMENT OF THE ARROGANCE OF THE "AGE OF ENLIGHTENMENT."
GIVEN FOR ONE INSTANT AN INTELLIGENCE WHICH COULD COMPREHEND ALL THE FORCES BY WHICH NATURE IS ANIMATED AND THE RESPECTIVE POSITIONS OF THE BEINGS WHICH COMPOSE IT, IF MOREOVER THIS INTELLIGENCE WERE VAST ENOUGH TO SUBMIT THESE DATA TO ANALYSIS... TO IT NOTHING WOULD BE UNCERTAIN, AND THE FUTURE AS THE PAST WOULD BE PRESENT TO ITS EYES.
THIS MECHANISTIC VIEW WAS A DREAM OF MANY, STARTING WITH THE ANCIENTS WHO TALKED ABOUT THE "MUSIC OF THE SPHERES" AS THEY ENVISIONED THE UNIVERSE AS A SERIES OF INTERLOCKING CRYSTALLINE SPHERES SPINNING INSIDE EACH OTHER.
THIS "INTELLIGENCE" OF YOURS, WOULD IT BE THE AUTHOR OF THE UNIVERSE, WHO I NOTE YOU LEFT OUT OF YOUR BOOK MÉCHANIQUE CÉLESTE?
hmph.
I KNOW WHAT YOU'RE DRIVING AT, SIRE, BUT I HAVE NO NEED OF THIS... "GOD" HYPOTHESIS.
mon dieu!

Atoms and Void, Poetry and Madness

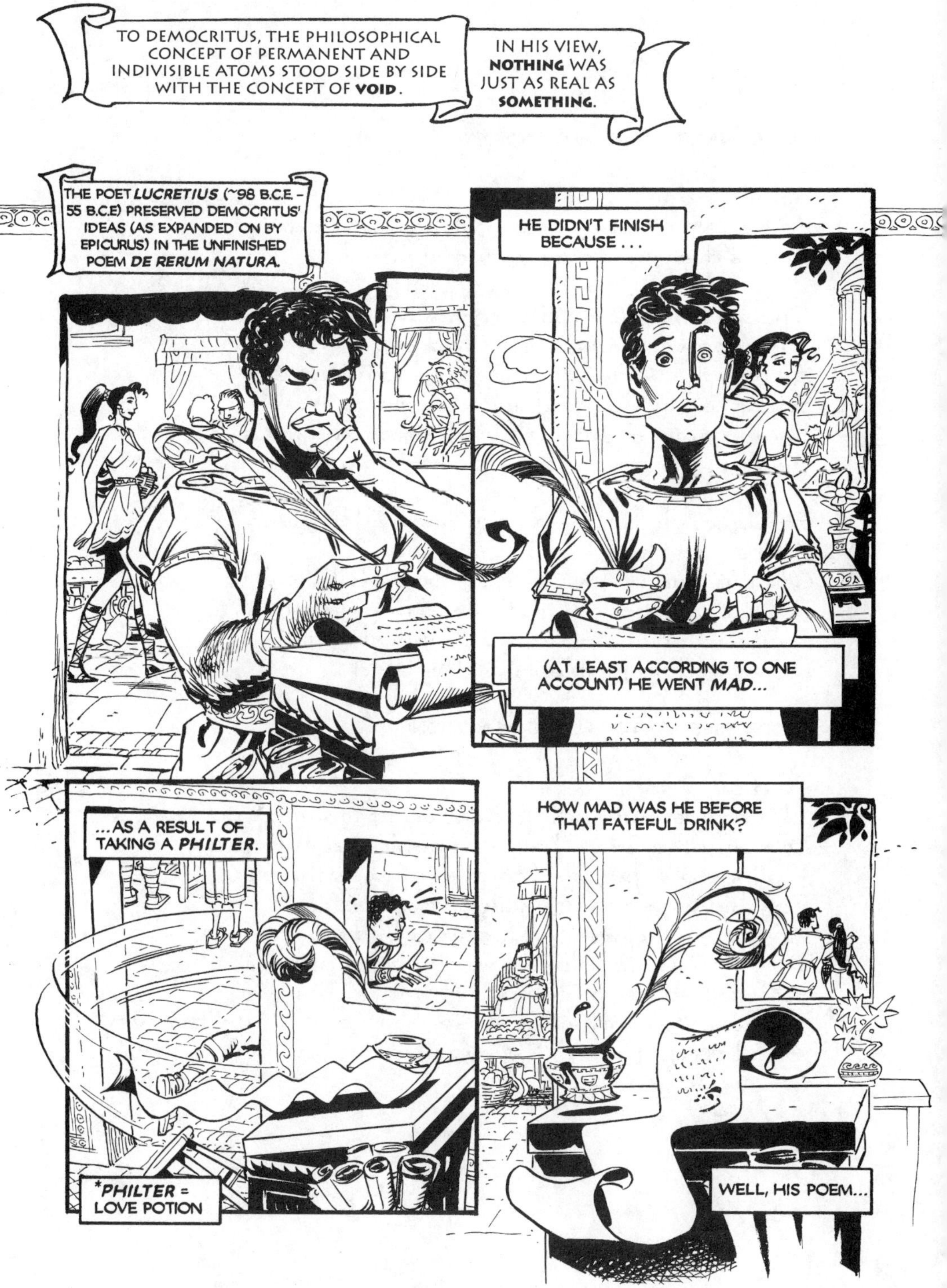
TO DEMOCRITUS, THE PHILOSOPHICAL CONCEPT OF PERMANENT AND INDIVISIBLE ATOMS STOOD SIDE BY SIDE WITH THE CONCEPT OF **VOID**.
IN HIS VIEW, **NOTHING** WAS JUST AS REAL AS **SOMETHING**.
THE POET *LUCRETIUS* (~98 B.C.E. - 55 B.C.E) PRESERVED DEMOCRITUS' IDEAS (AS EXPANDED ON BY EPICURUS) IN THE UNFINISHED POEM *DE RERUM NATURA*.
HE DIDN'T FINISH BECAUSE . . .
(AT LEAST ACCORDING TO ONE ACCOUNT) HE WENT *MAD*...
...AS A RESULT OF TAKING A *PHILTER*.
*PHILTER = LOVE POTION
HOW MAD WAS HE BEFORE THAT FATEFUL DRINK?
WELL, HIS POEM...

...TALKS ABOUT ATOMS AND ENTROPY:

Bodies, again,
Are partly primal germs of things, and partly
Unions deriving from the primal germs.

Once more, if nature had given a scope for things
To be forever broken more and more,
By now the bodies of matter would have been
So far reduced by breakings in old days
That from them nothing could, at season fixed,
Be born, and arrive at its prime and top of life.

For, lo, each thing is quicker marred than made;
And so whate'er the long Infinitude
Of days and all fore-passed time would now
By this have broken and ruined and dissolved,
That same could ne'er in all remaining time
Be builded up for plenishing the world.

...ADDRESSES NEWTON'S LAWS OF MOTION:

And so J say,
The atoms must a little swerve at times-
But only the least, lest we should seem to feign
Motions oblique, and fact refutes us there.
For this we see forthwith is manifest:
Whatever the weight, it can't obliquely go,
Down on its headlong journey from above,
At least so far as thou canst mark; but who
Js there can mark by sense that naught can swerve
At all aside from off its road's straight line?

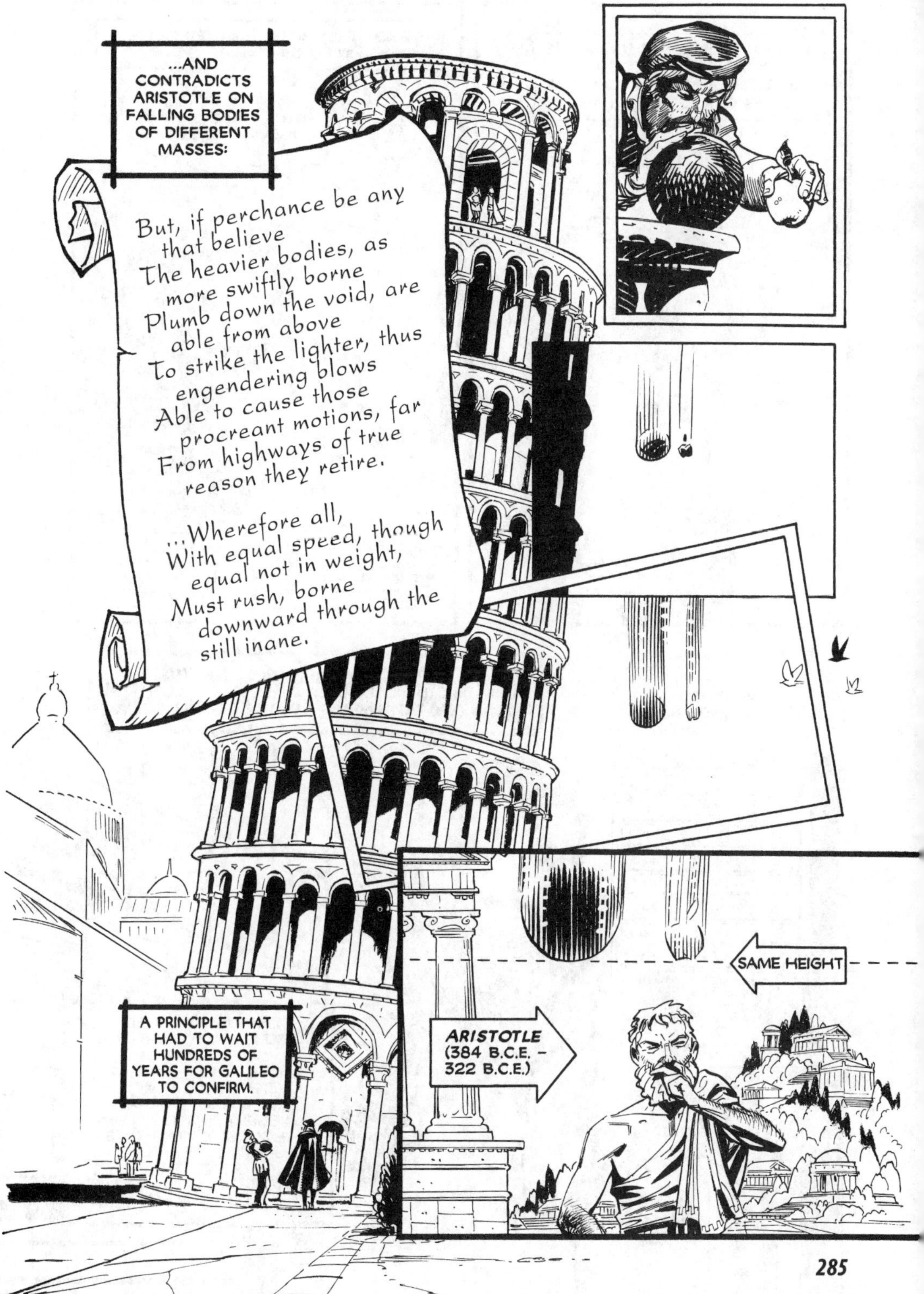
...AND CONTRADICTS ARISTOTLE ON FALLING BODIES OF DIFFERENT MASSES:
But, if perchance be any that believe
The heavier bodies, as more swiftly borne
Plumb down the void, are able from above
To strike the lighter, thus engendering blows
Able to cause those procreant motions, far
From highways of true reason they retire.
...Wherefore all,
With equal speed, though equal not in weight,
Must rush, borne downward through the still inane.
SAME HEIGHT
A PRINCIPLE THAT HAD TO WAIT HUNDREDS OF YEARS FOR GALILEO TO CONFIRM.
ARISTOTLE (384 B.C.E. – 322 B.C.E.)

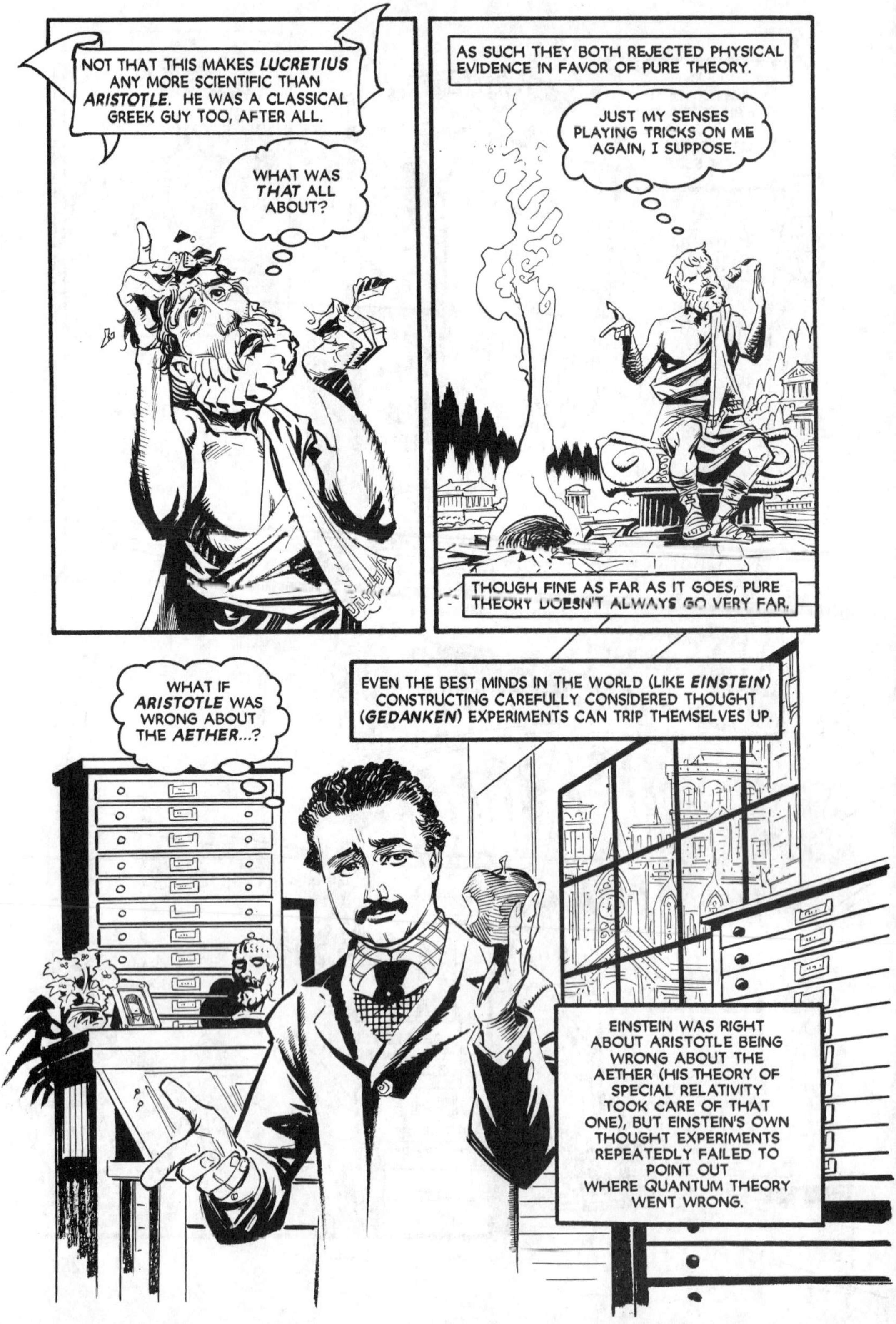
NOT THAT THIS MAKES LUCRETIUS ANY MORE SCIENTIFIC THAN ARISTOTLE. HE WAS A CLASSICAL GREEK GUY TOO, AFTER ALL.
WHAT WAS THAT ALL ABOUT?
AS SUCH THEY BOTH REJECTED PHYSICAL EVIDENCE IN FAVOR OF PURE THEORY.
JUST MY SENSES PLAYING TRICKS ON ME AGAIN, I SUPPOSE.
THOUGH FINE AS FAR AS IT GOES, PURE THEORY DOESN'T ALWAYS GO VERY FAR.
EVEN THE BEST MINDS IN THE WORLD (LIKE EINSTEIN) CONSTRUCTING CAREFULLY CONSIDERED THOUGHT (GEDANKEN) EXPERIMENTS CAN TRIP THEMSELVES UP.
WHAT IF ARISTOTLE WAS WRONG ABOUT THE AETHER...?
EINSTEIN WAS RIGHT ABOUT ARISTOTLE BEING WRONG ABOUT THE AETHER (HIS THEORY OF SPECIAL RELATIVITY TOOK CARE OF THAT ONE), BUT EINSTEIN'S OWN THOUGHT EXPERIMENTS REPEATEDLY FAILED TO POINT OUT WHERE QUANTUM THEORY WENT WRONG.

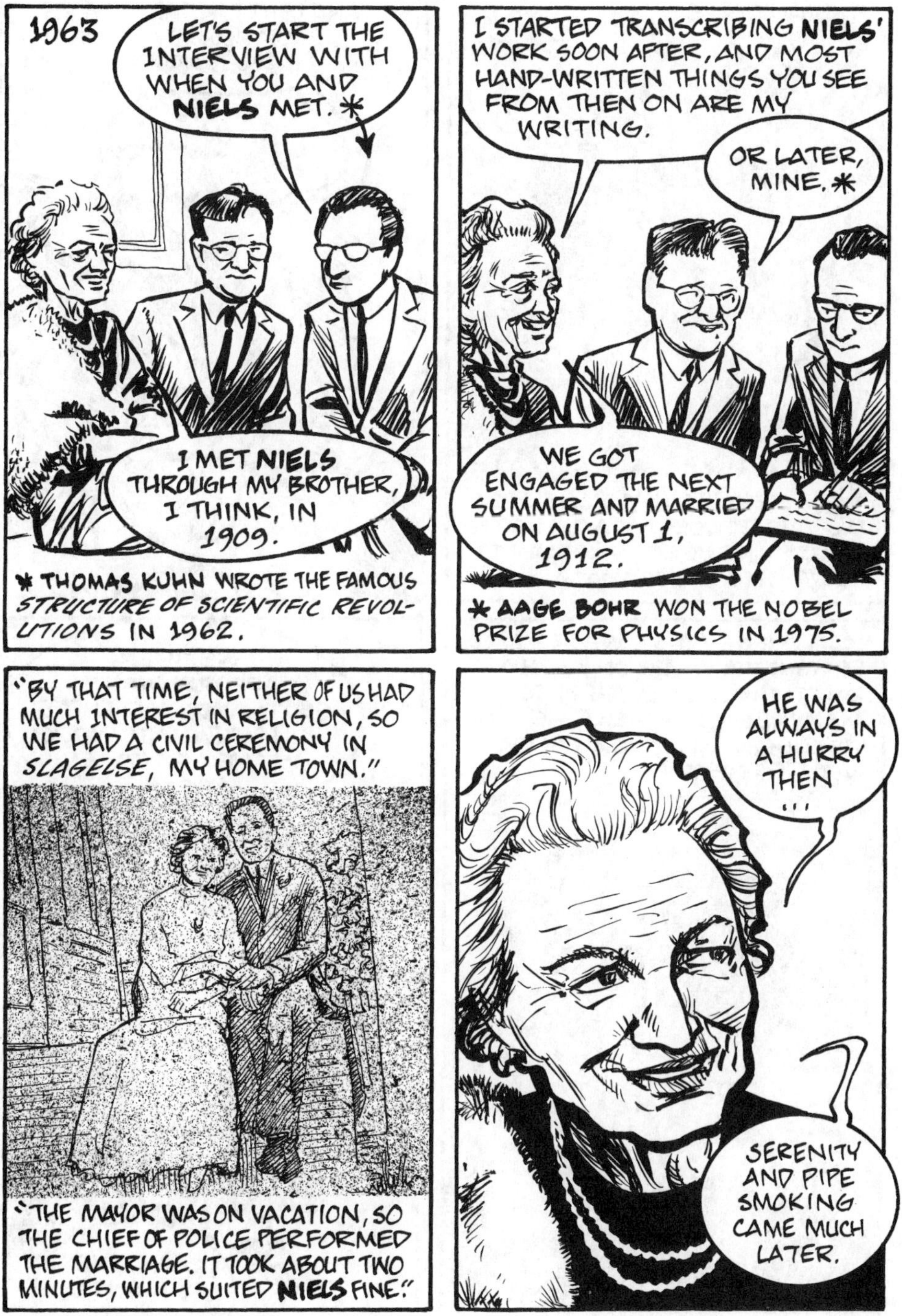
1963
LET'S START THE INTERVIEW WITH WHEN YOU AND NIELS MET. *
I MET NIELS THROUGH MY BROTHER, I THINK, IN 1909.
* THOMAS KUHN WROTE THE FAMOUS STRUCTURE OF SCIENTIFIC REVOLUTIONS IN 1962.
I STARTED TRANSCRIBING NIELS' WORK SOON AFTER, AND MOST HAND-WRITTEN THINGS YOU SEE FROM THEN ON ARE MY WRITING.
OR LATER, MINE. *
WE GOT ENGAGED THE NEXT SUMMER AND MARRIED ON AUGUST 1, 1912.
* AAGE BOHR WON THE NOBEL PRIZE FOR PHYSICS IN 1975.
"BY THAT TIME, NEITHER OF US HAD MUCH INTEREST IN RELIGION, SO WE HAD A CIVIL CEREMONY IN SLAGELSE, MY HOME TOWN."
"THE MAYOR WAS ON VACATION, SO THE CHIEF OF POLICE PERFORMED THE MARRIAGE. IT TOOK ABOUT TWO MINUTES, WHICH SUITED NIELS FINE."
HE WAS ALWAYS IN A HURRY THEN ...
SERENITY AND PIPE SMOKING CAME MUCH LATER.

"SO WE **DIDN'T** WANT TO LINGER IN TOWN AFTERWARDS, THOUGH MY MOTHER WANTED US TO HOST A FORMAL DINNER."

"**NIELS** ASKED, 'HOW IS IT POSSIBLE TO TAKE THREE HOURS FOR A DINNER? WE SHOULD THINK ABOUT WHAT TRAIN TO TAKE TO GET AWAY FROM IT ALL.'"

WE GOT ON A FERRY THAT EVENING AND LEFT FOR THE FIRST STOP OF OUR HONEYMOON IN **ENGLAND.**

"**CAMBRIDGE** FIRST, WHERE **NIELS** FINISHED A PAPER ON ALPHA PARTICLES, AND THEN TO **MANCHESTER** WHERE HE DISCUSSED ANOTHER PAPER WITH **ERNEST.**"

WE THEN MADE OUR WAY TO **SCOTLAND,** AND ENDED UP IN **NORWAY** TO WORK ON THE *HYDROGEN ATOM.*

AH, THE ROMANCE OF *YOUTH.*

Imitating Art

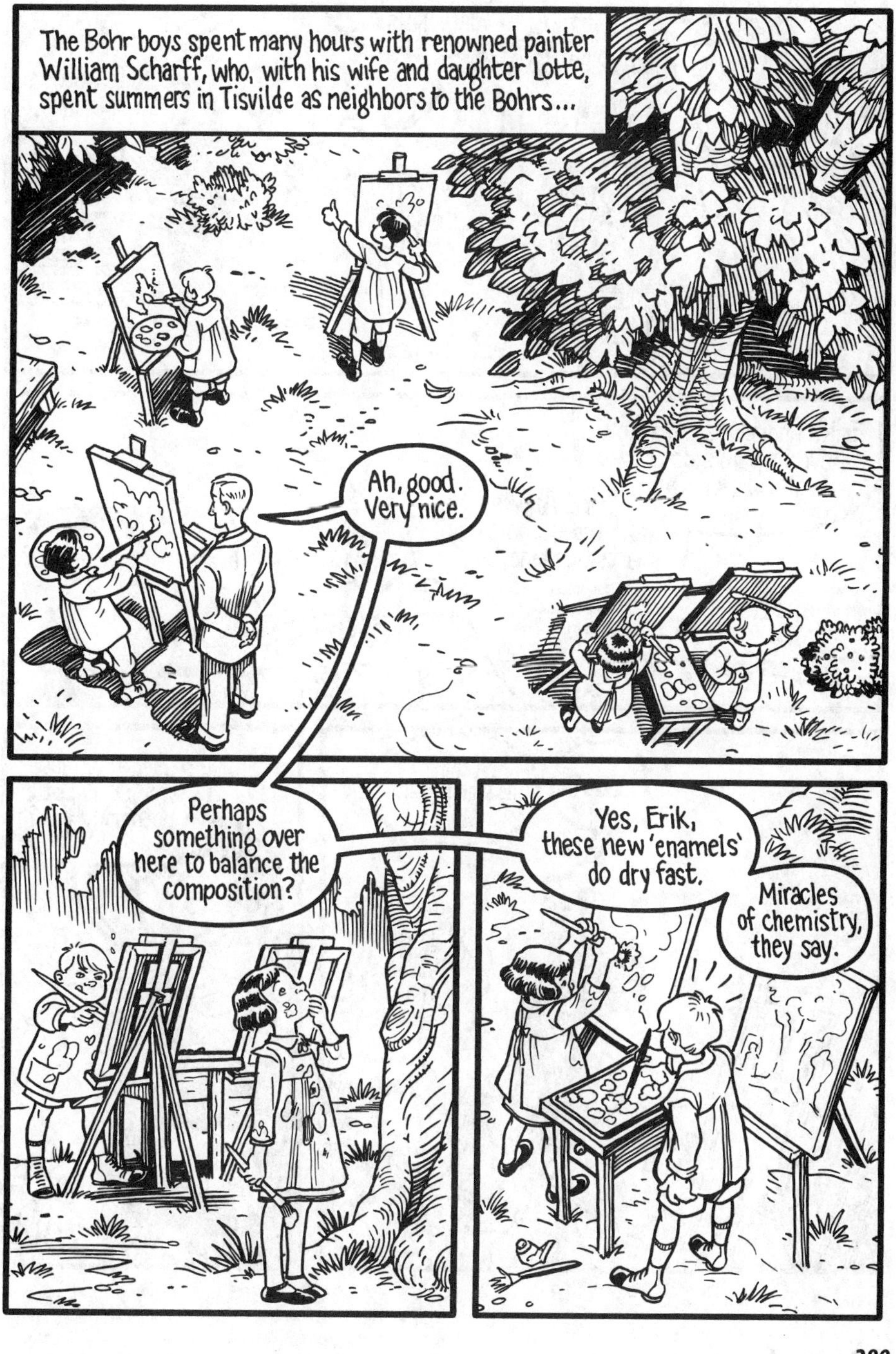

The Bohr boys spent many hours with renowned painter William Scharff, who, with his wife and daughter Lotte, spent summers in Tisvilde as neighbors to the Bohrs...
Ah, good. Very nice.
Perhaps something over here to balance the composition?
Yes, Erik, these new 'enamels' do dry fast.
Miracles of chemistry, they say.

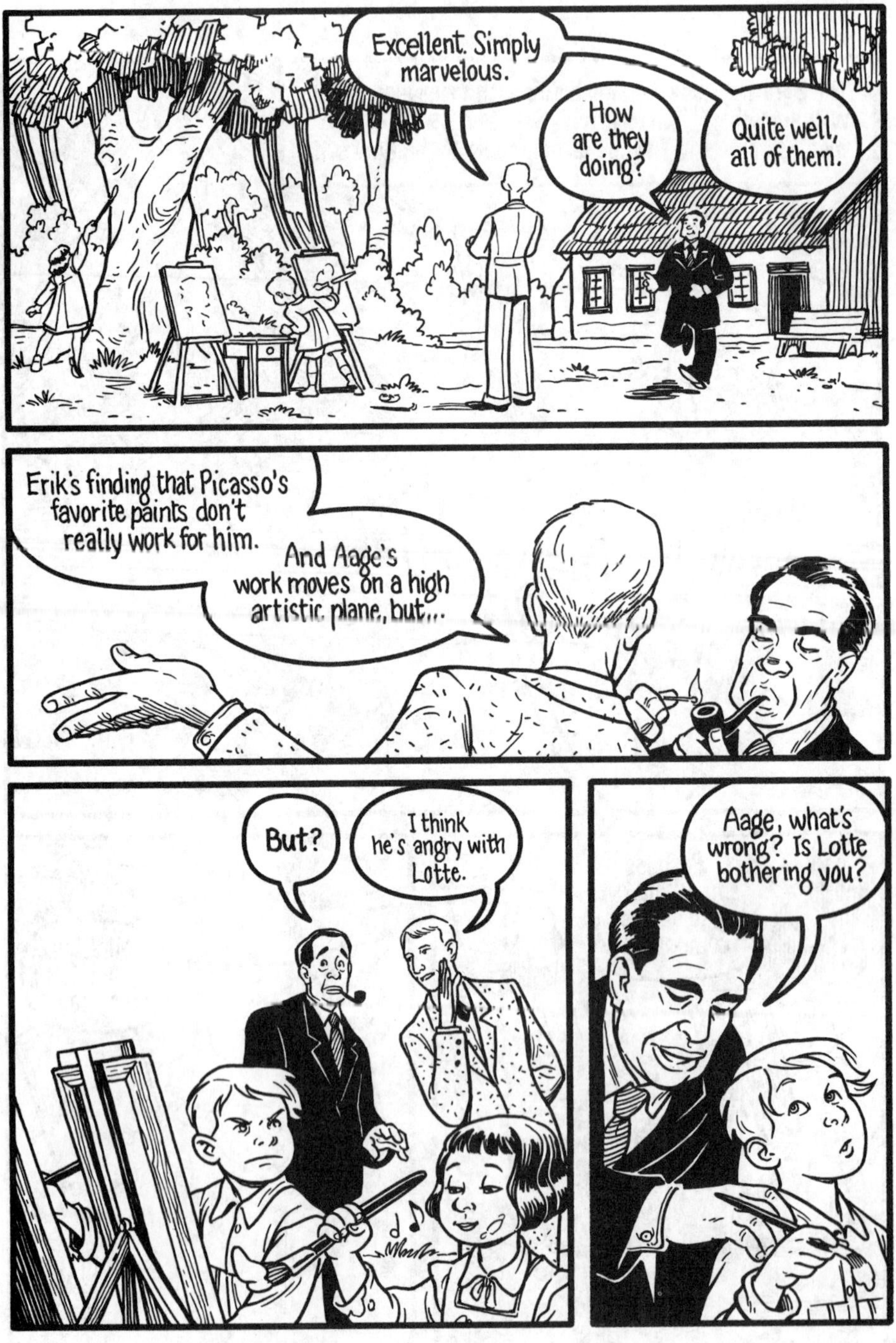
Excellent. Simply marvelous.
How are they doing?
Quite well, all of them.
Erik's finding that Picasso's favorite paints don't really work for him.
And Aage's work moves on a high artistic plane, but...
But?
I think he's angry with Lotte.
Aage, what's wrong? Is Lotte bothering you?

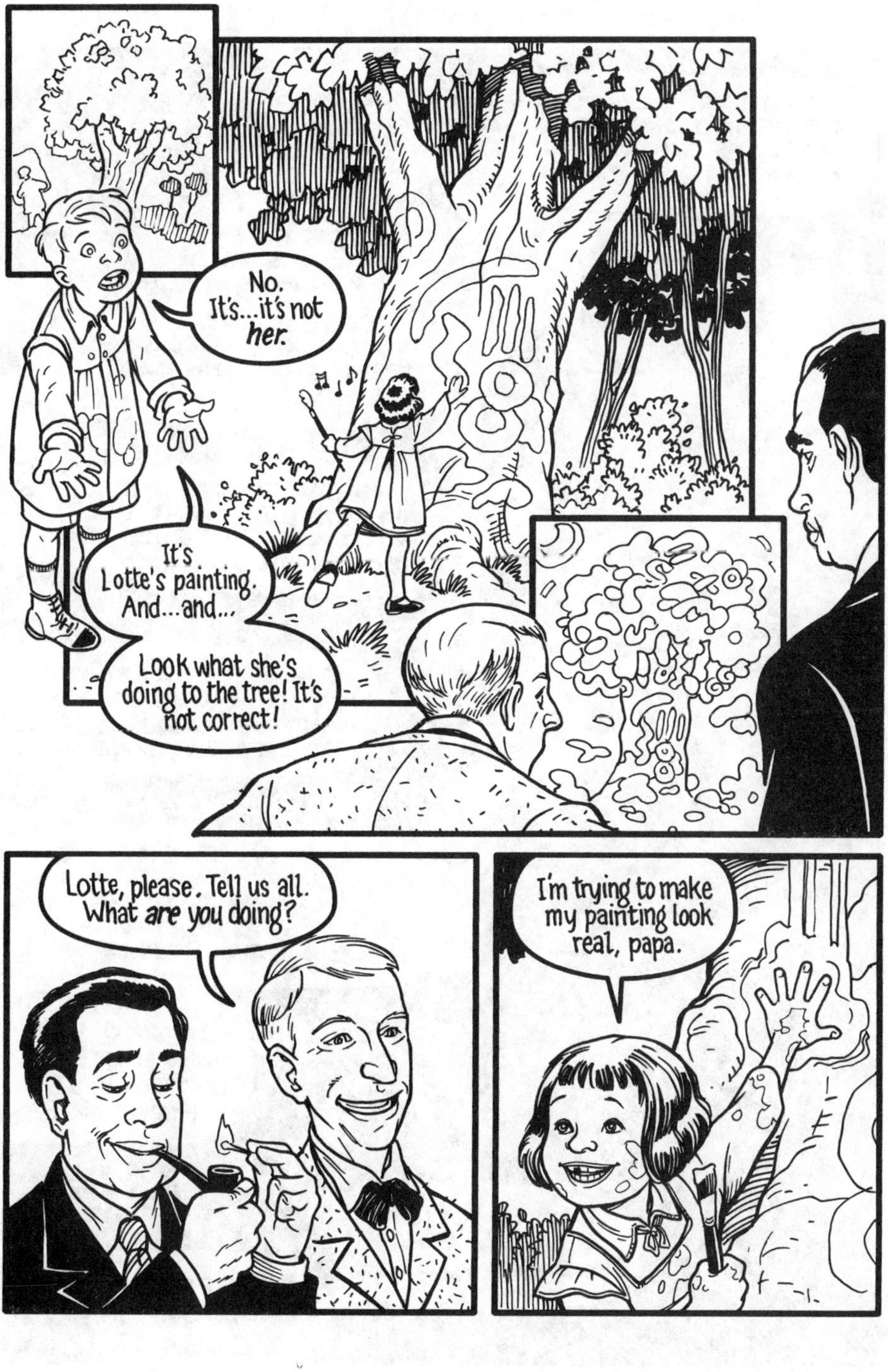
No. It's...it's not *her*.
It's Lotte's painting. And...and...
Look what she's doing to the tree! It's not correct!
Lotte, please. Tell us all. What *are you* doing?
I'm trying to make my painting look real, papa.

START WITH A COUPLE OF DEFINITIONS AND A COUPLE OF EQUATIONS WE KNOW TO BE *TRUE*.

THE FIRST EQUATION IS EINSTEIN'S $E=mc^2$ or —

$$E = m \times c \times c$$

AND THE FIRST DEFINITION IS *NEWTON'S* FOR *MOMENTUM*...

$$P = \text{mass} \times \text{velocity}$$

SO FOR A PHOTON, WHICH, BECAUSE ITS LIGHT, TRAVELS AT THE SPEED OF — WELL, LIGHT:

$$p = m \times c$$

WE CAN SUBSTITUTE MOMENTUM *P* FOR THE $M \times C$ PART IN EINSTEIN'S EQUATION AND GET...

$$E = p \times c$$

THE SECOND DEFINITION IS FOR A WAVE'S VELOCITY AND IT'S BEEN AROUND SINCE NEWTON AS WELL.

$$c = v \times \lambda$$

WHERE v = FREQUENCY OF A LIGHT WAVE (WAVES PER SECOND) AND λ = WAVELENGTH. PLANCK GAVE US OUR LAST PIECE OF THE PUZZLE WITH

$$E = h \times v$$

SO, IF WE TAKE $E = p \times c$ AND SUBSTITUTE $h \times v$ for E AND $v \times \lambda$ FOR C, WE GET —

$$h \times v = p \times v \times \lambda$$

DOING A LITTLE REARRANGING, WE GET $\lambda = h/p$

AS THE PRINCE WOULD SAY, VOILÁ!

Slater: The exception that tests the rule.

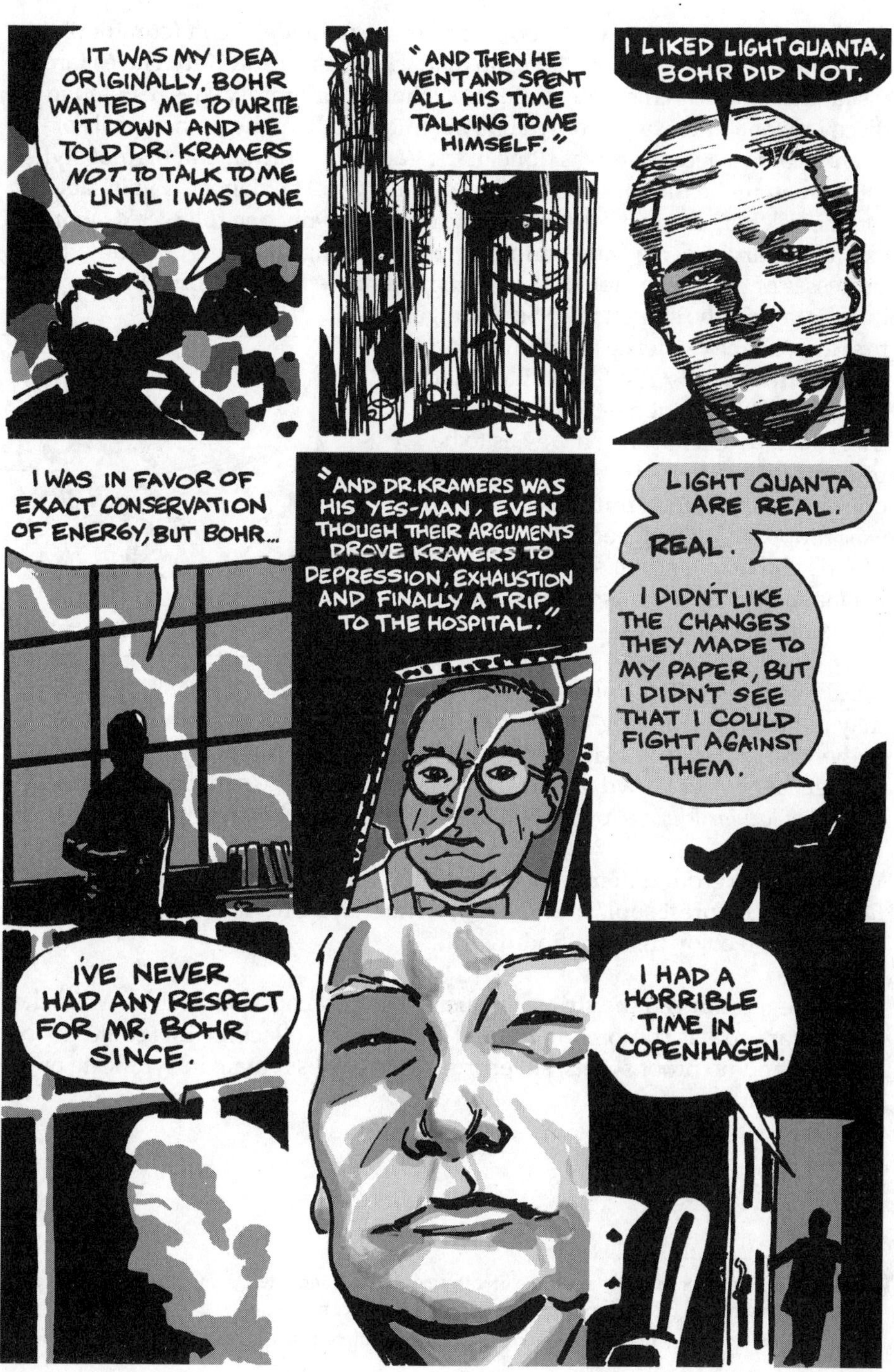
IT WAS MY IDEA ORIGINALLY. BOHR WANTED ME TO WRITE IT DOWN AND HE TOLD DR. KRAMERS NOT TO TALK TO ME UNTIL I WAS DONE
"AND THEN HE WENT AND SPENT ALL HIS TIME TALKING TO ME HIMSELF."
I LIKED LIGHT QUANTA, BOHR DID NOT.
I WAS IN FAVOR OF EXACT CONSERVATION OF ENERGY, BUT BOHR...
"AND DR. KRAMERS WAS HIS YES-MAN, EVEN THOUGH THEIR ARGUMENTS DROVE KRAMERS TO DEPRESSION, EXHAUSTION AND FINALLY A TRIP TO THE HOSPITAL."
LIGHT QUANTA ARE REAL.
REAL.
I DIDN'T LIKE THE CHANGES THEY MADE TO MY PAPER, BUT I DIDN'T SEE THAT I COULD FIGHT AGAINST THEM.
I'VE NEVER HAD ANY RESPECT FOR MR. BOHR SINCE.
I HAD A HORRIBLE TIME IN COPENHAGEN.

"Oh, That Dirac!"

An unusual but fortuitous collaboration between Randall Scott (curator of the Russell B. Nye collection at Michigan State University) and Katy Hayes (archivist at the American Institute of Physics' Niels Bohr Library) has resulted in the discovery of a hitherto unknown daily comic strip. Unique in the annals of science comics because it was done in the gag-a-day format and bigfoot style rather than in the Raymond / Foster tradition, "Oh, That Dirac!" ran in laboratory newsletters throughout the 1920s and 1930s. Only one full week's worth of examples survives, focusing on the rhetorical stylings and singular thought processes of the title character Paul Adrien Maurice Dirac[1] : Nobel Prize winner in 1933 (a prize he shared with Schrödinger), first to posit the existence of antimatter, and a man of few words[2] . So few, in fact, that his most famous quotation—"In science one tries to tell people, in such a way as to be understood by everyone, something that no one ever knew before. But in poetry, it's the exact opposite"—achieved notoriety among friends and fellow scientists not only for its resonance, but also for its unusual length of two complete sentences.

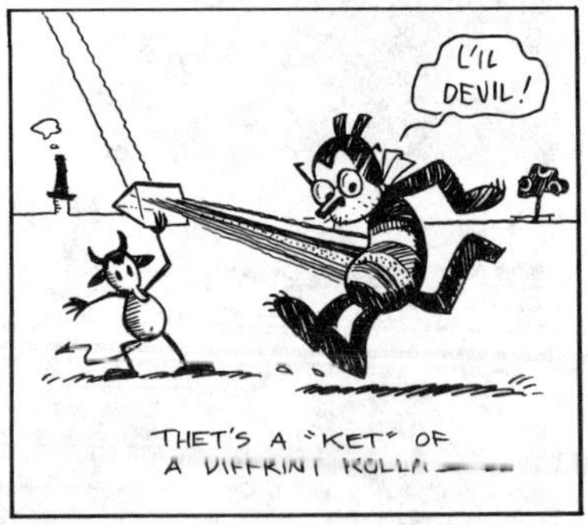
L'IL DEVIL!
THET'S A "KET" OF

Maxwell and Erwin (fragment ca. 1928)

Speaking of resonance, while the humor may not play well among modern and lay audiences, research by Hayes and Scott indicates that it was a big hit with the theoretical physics crowd, and received favorable reviews in the influential *Journal of Jocular Physics*, published at Bohr's Institute beginning in 1935.

With this background in mind, and knowing that Bohr said "Of all physicists, Dirac has the purest soul" and "Dirac did not have a trivial bone in his body," we hope you enjoy this rare find.

(We have reproduced the strips here using the best copies available. While the original artwork is rumored to be held in a private collection, this could not be verified, and no proof sheets, silverprints, or veloxes remain in syndicate or institutional archives.)

[1] Supporting characters alluded to in the literature of the day include a demon named Maxwell, a cat named Erwin, and an unnamed deity fond of shooting craps.

[2] Wags would have it that his vocabulary consisted, in its entirety, of "Yes," "No," and "I don't know."

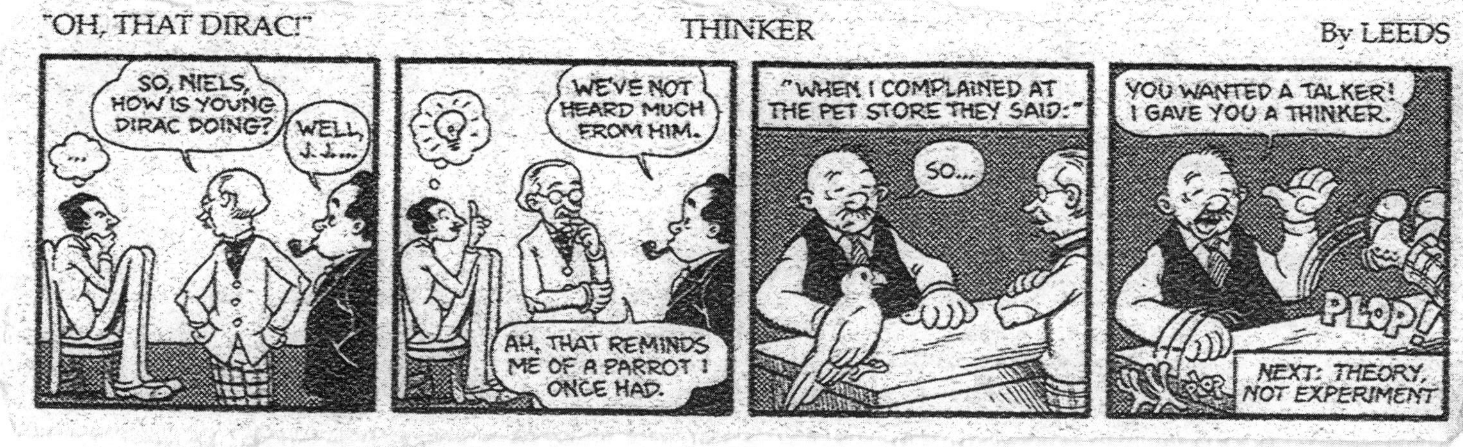
"OH, THAT DIRAC!"
THINKER
By LEEDS
SO, NIELS, HOW IS YOUNG DIRAC DOING?
WELL, I, I....
WE'VE NOT HEARD MUCH FROM HIM.
AH, THAT REMINDS ME OF A PARROT I ONCE HAD.
"WHEN I COMPLAINED AT THE PET STORE THEY SAID:"
SO...
YOU WANTED A TALKER! I GAVE YOU A THINKER.
PLOP!
NEXT: THEORY, NOT EXPERIMENT

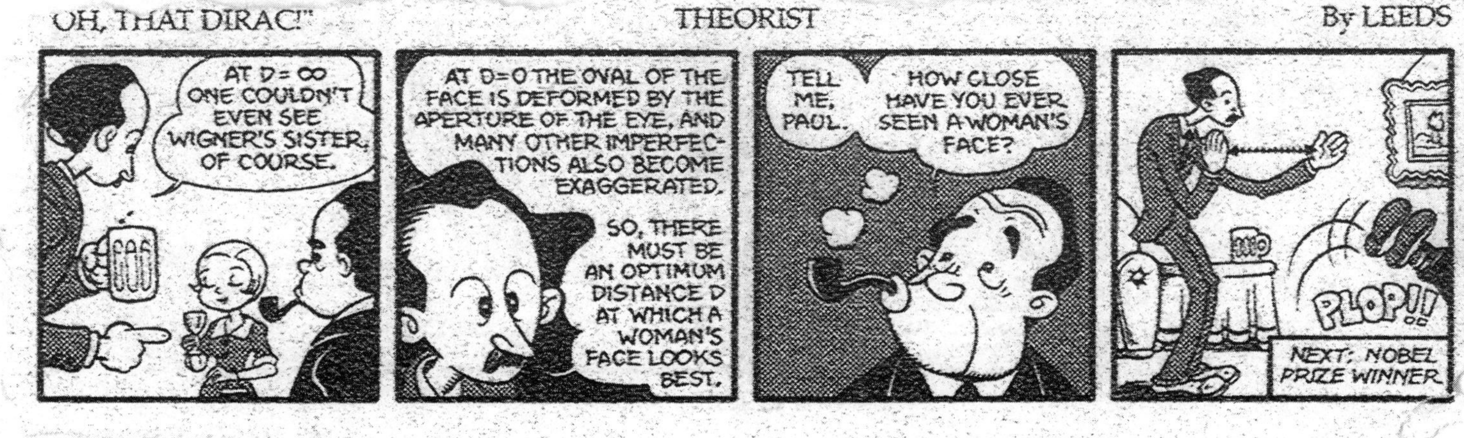
"OH, THAT DIRAC!"
THEORIST
By LEEDS
AT D = ∞ ONE COULDN'T EVEN SEE WIGNER'S SISTER, OF COURSE.
AT D=0 THE OVAL OF THE FACE IS DEFORMED BY THE APERTURE OF THE EYE, AND MANY OTHER IMPERFECTIONS ALSO BECOME EXAGGERATED.
SO, THERE MUST BE AN OPTIMUM DISTANCE D AT WHICH A WOMAN'S FACE LOOKS BEST.
TELL ME, PAUL.
HOW CLOSE HAVE YOU EVER SEEN A WOMAN'S FACE?
PLOP!!
NEXT: NOBEL PRIZE WINNER

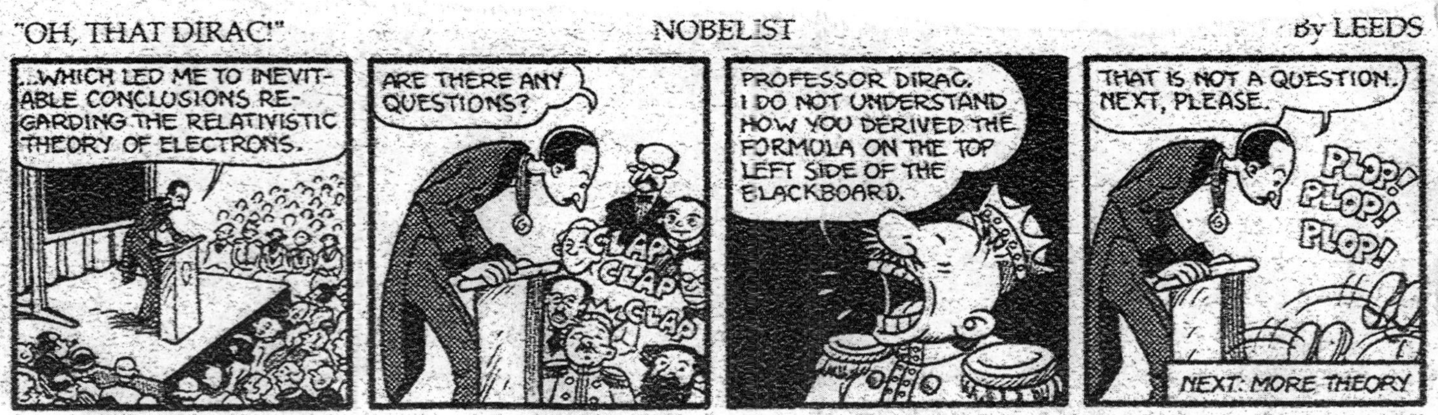
"OH, THAT DIRAC!"
NOBELIST
By LEEDS
...WHICH LED ME TO INEVITABLE CONCLUSIONS REGARDING THE RELATIVISTIC THEORY OF ELECTRONS.
ARE THERE ANY QUESTIONS?
CLAP CLAP CLAP
PROFESSOR DIRAC. I DO NOT UNDERSTAND HOW YOU DERIVED THE FORMULA ON THE TOP LEFT SIDE OF THE BLACKBOARD.
THAT IS NOT A QUESTION. NEXT, PLEASE.
PLOP! PLOP! PLOP!
NEXT: MORE THEORY

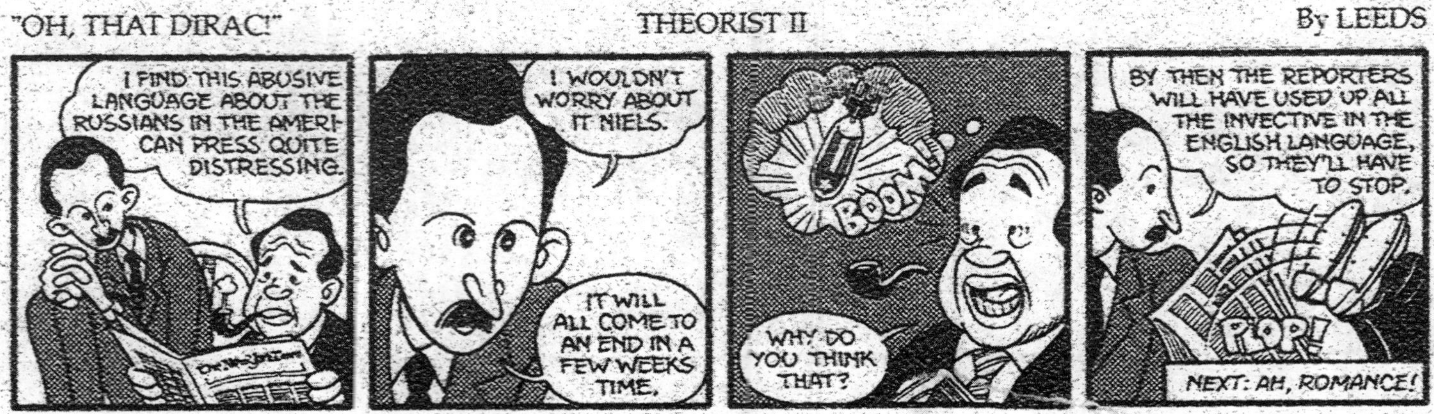
"OH, THAT DIRAC!"
THEORIST II
By LEEDS
I FIND THIS ABUSIVE LANGUAGE ABOUT THE RUSSIANS IN THE AMERICAN PRESS QUITE DISTRESSING.
I WOULDN'T WORRY ABOUT IT NIELS.
IT WILL ALL COME TO AN END IN A FEW WEEKS TIME.
BOOM!
WHY DO YOU THINK THAT?
BY THEN THE REPORTERS WILL HAVE USED UP ALL THE INVECTIVE IN THE ENGLISH LANGUAGE, SO THEY'LL HAVE TO STOP.
PLOP!
NEXT: AH, ROMANCE!

"OH, THAT DIRAC!" NEWLYWED By LEEDS

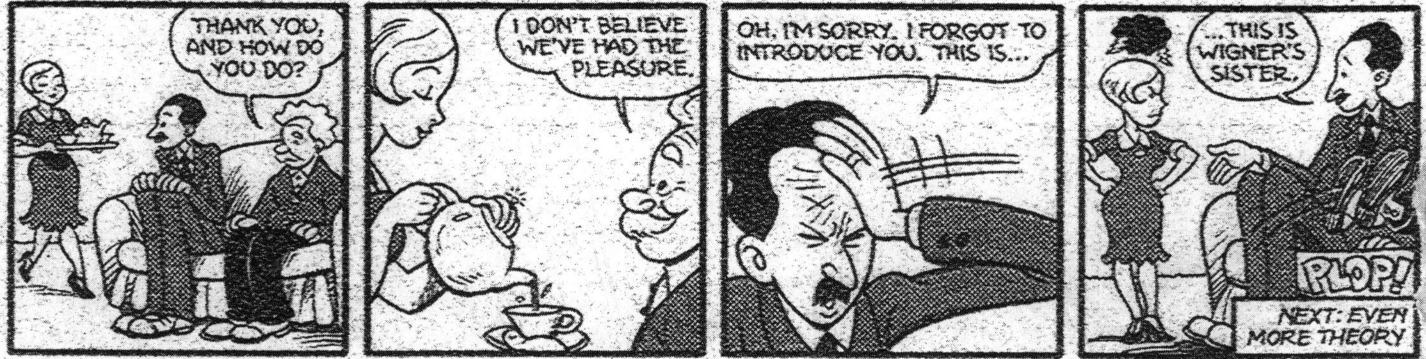

THANK YOU, AND HOW DO YOU DO?
I DON'T BELIEVE WE'VE HAD THE PLEASURE.
OH, I'M SORRY. I FORGOT TO INTRODUCE YOU. THIS IS...
...THIS IS WIGNER'S SISTER.
PLOP!
NEXT: EVEN MORE THEORY

"OH, THAT DIRAC!" THEORIST III By LEEDS

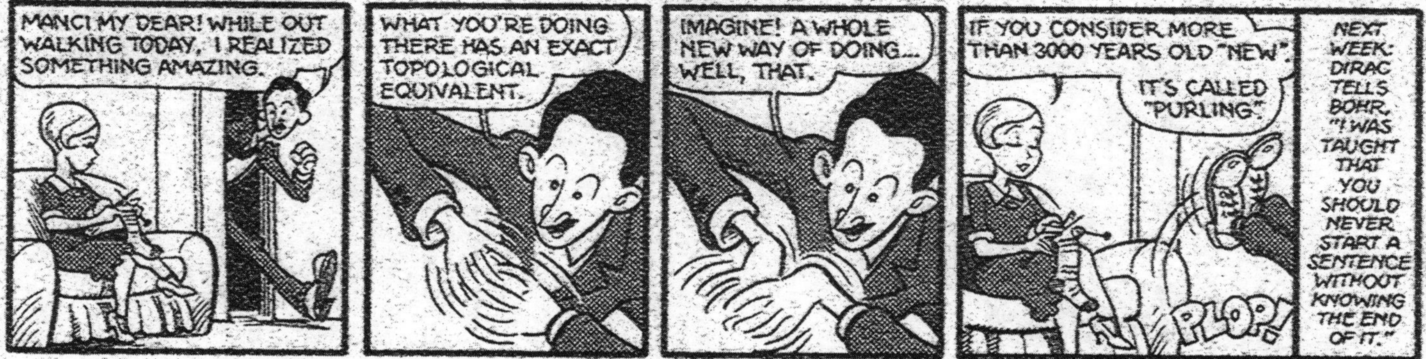

MANCI MY DEAR! WHILE OUT WALKING TODAY, I REALIZED SOMETHING AMAZING.
WHAT YOU'RE DOING THERE HAS AN EXACT TOPOLOGICAL EQUIVALENT.
IMAGINE! A WHOLE NEW WAY OF DOING... WELL, THAT.
IF YOU CONSIDER MORE THAN 3000 YEARS OLD "NEW".
IT'S CALLED "PURLING".
PLOP!
NEXT WEEK: DIRAC TELLS BOHR, "I WAS TAUGHT THAT YOU SHOULD NEVER START A SENTENCE WITHOUT KNOWING THE END OF IT."

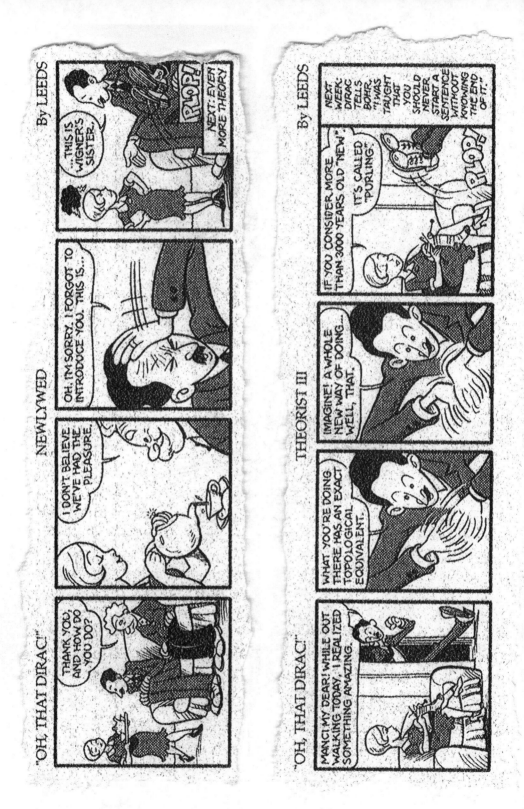

Kisa Gotami

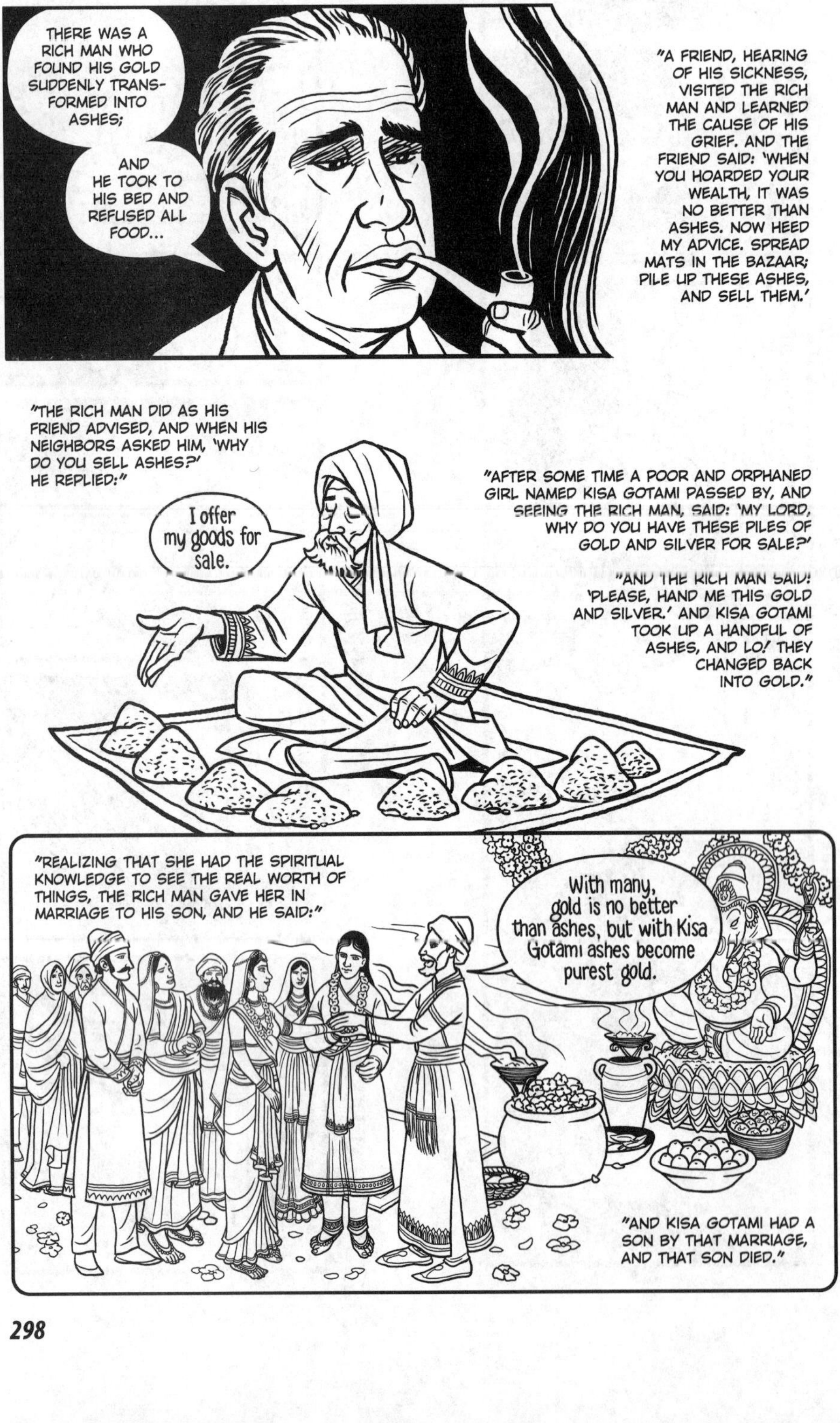
THERE WAS A RICH MAN WHO FOUND HIS GOLD SUDDENLY TRANS-FORMED INTO ASHES;
AND HE TOOK TO HIS BED AND REFUSED ALL FOOD...
"A FRIEND, HEARING OF HIS SICKNESS, VISITED THE RICH MAN AND LEARNED THE CAUSE OF HIS GRIEF. AND THE FRIEND SAID: 'WHEN YOU HOARDED YOUR WEALTH, IT WAS NO BETTER THAN ASHES. NOW HEED MY ADVICE. SPREAD MATS IN THE BAZAAR; PILE UP THESE ASHES, AND SELL THEM.'
"THE RICH MAN DID AS HIS FRIEND ADVISED, AND WHEN HIS NEIGHBORS ASKED HIM, 'WHY DO YOU SELL ASHES?' HE REPLIED:"
I offer my goods for sale.
"AFTER SOME TIME A POOR AND ORPHANED GIRL NAMED KISA GOTAMI PASSED BY, AND SEEING THE RICH MAN, SAID: 'MY LORD, WHY DO YOU HAVE THESE PILES OF GOLD AND SILVER FOR SALE?'
"AND THE RICH MAN SAID: 'PLEASE, HAND ME THIS GOLD AND SILVER.' AND KISA GOTAMI TOOK UP A HANDFUL OF ASHES, AND LO! THEY CHANGED BACK INTO GOLD."
"REALIZING THAT SHE HAD THE SPIRITUAL KNOWLEDGE TO SEE THE REAL WORTH OF THINGS, THE RICH MAN GAVE HER IN MARRIAGE TO HIS SON, AND HE SAID:"
With many, gold is no better than ashes, but with Kisa Gotami ashes become purest gold.
"AND KISA GOTAMI HAD A SON BY THAT MARRIAGE, AND THAT SON DIED."

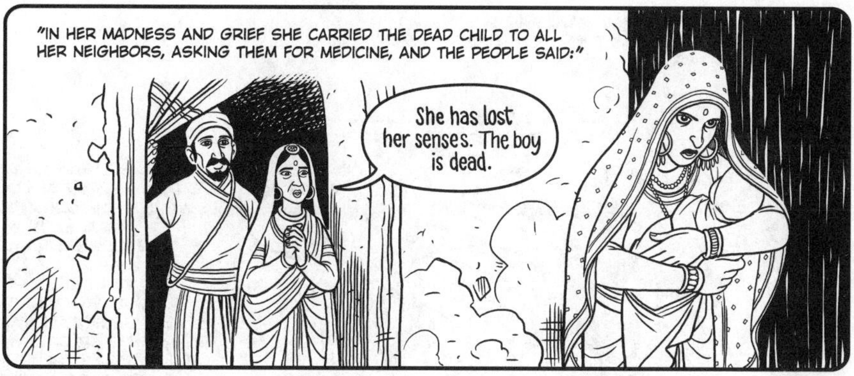
"IN HER MADNESS AND GRIEF SHE CARRIED THE DEAD CHILD TO ALL HER NEIGHBORS, ASKING THEM FOR MEDICINE, AND THE PEOPLE SAID:"
She has lost her senses. The boy is dead.

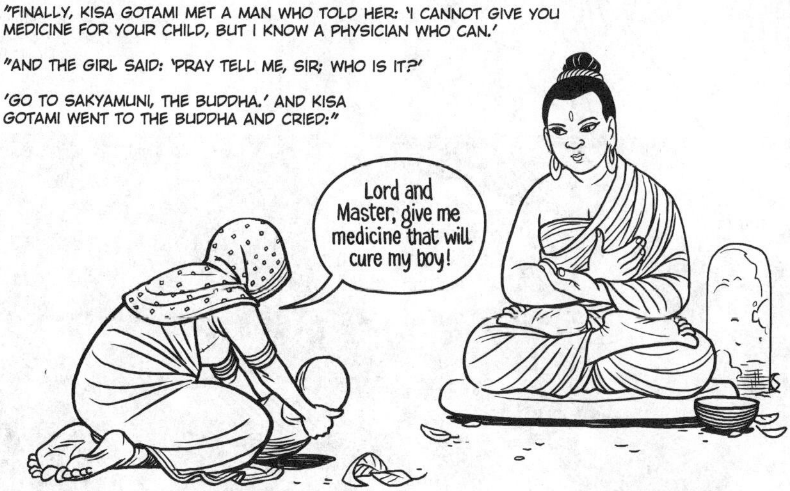
"FINALLY, KISA GOTAMI MET A MAN WHO TOLD HER: 'I CANNOT GIVE YOU MEDICINE FOR YOUR CHILD, BUT I KNOW A PHYSICIAN WHO CAN.'
"AND THE GIRL SAID: 'PRAY TELL ME, SIR; WHO IS IT?'
'GO TO SAKYAMUNI, THE BUDDHA.' AND KISA GOTAMI WENT TO THE BUDDHA AND CRIED:"
Lord and Master, give me medicine that will cure my boy!

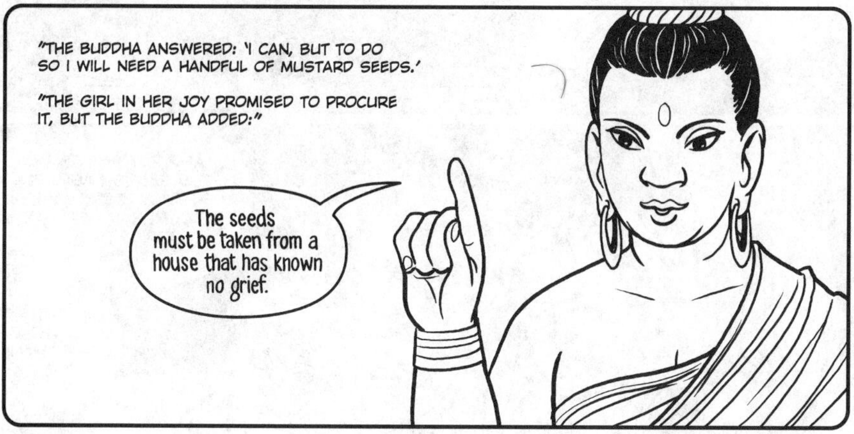
"THE BUDDHA ANSWERED: 'I CAN, BUT TO DO SO I WILL NEED A HANDFUL OF MUSTARD SEEDS.'
"THE GIRL IN HER JOY PROMISED TO PROCURE IT, BUT THE BUDDHA ADDED:"
The seeds must be taken from a house that has known no grief.

"KISA GOTAMI NOW WENT FROM HOUSE TO HOUSE, AND BECAUSE THE PEOPLE PITIED HER, AND BECAUSE MUSTARD SEED IS THE MOST COMMON OF SPICES, THEY SAID: 'GLADLY! TAKE AS MUCH AS YOU NEED.'

"BUT WHEN SHE ASKED, 'HAVE YOU HAD A SON OR DAUGHTER, A FATHER OR MOTHER, DIE IN YOUR FAMILY?' THEY ANSWERED HER:"

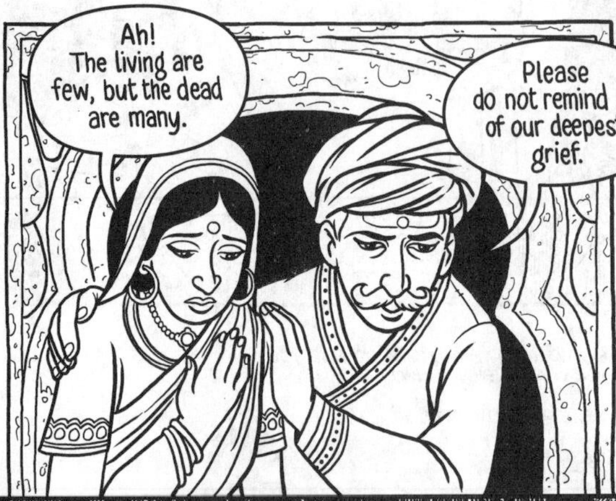
Ah! The living are few, but the dead are many.
Please do not remind us of our deepest grief.

"AND THOUGH SHE TRAVELED FOR YEARS, AND ALL OVER THE WORLD, SHE COULD NOT FIND A HOUSE IN WHICH NO BELOVED ONE HAD DIED.

"AND AT THE END OF HER TRAVELS, WHEN SHE NEARED HOME, KISA GOTAMI PAUSED TO SIT ABOVE HER CITY, WATCHING THE LIGHTS AS THEY FLICKERED UP AND WERE EXTINGUISHED AGAIN. AND SHE CONSIDERED HER FATE, AND THE FATE OF ALL FATHERS, MOTHERS, SONS, AND DAUGHTERS:"

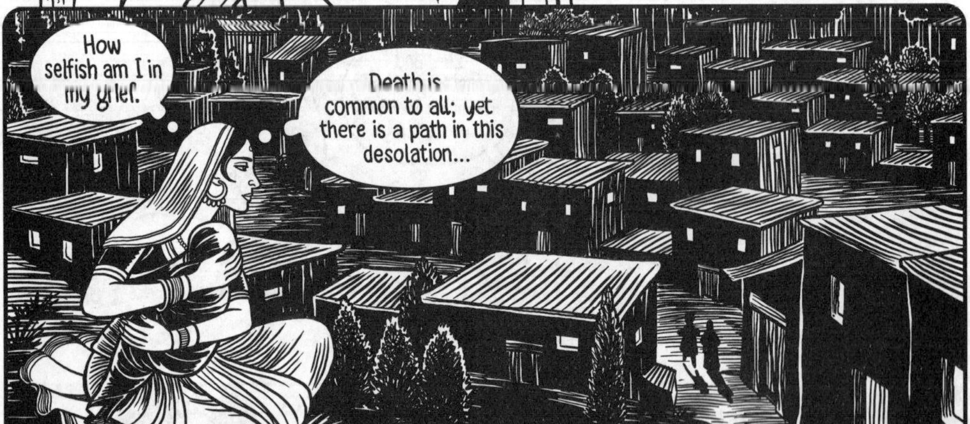
How selfish am I in my grief.
Death is common to all; yet there is a path in this desolation...

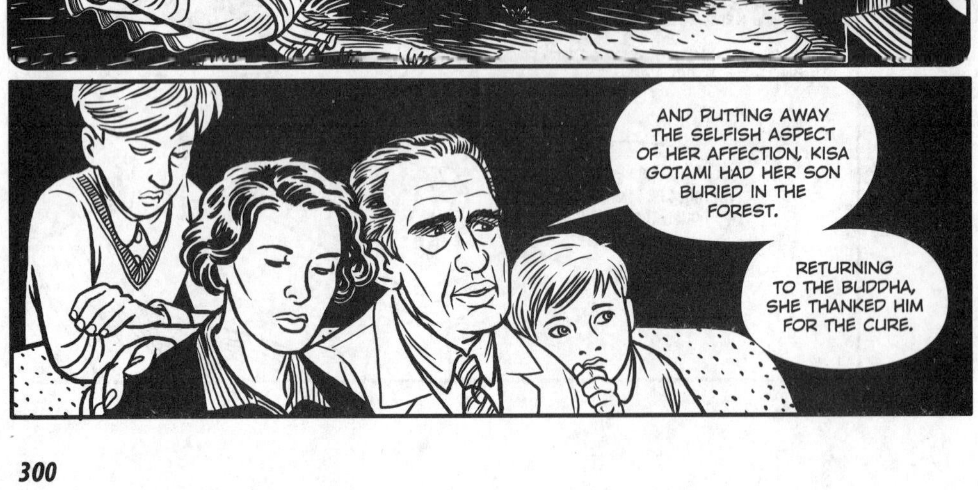
AND PUTTING AWAY THE SELFISH ASPECT OF HER AFFECTION, KISA GOTAMI HAD HER SON BURIED IN THE FOREST.
RETURNING TO THE BUDDHA, SHE THANKED HIM FOR THE CURE.

Armbands

THE APOCRYPHAL PART OF THE STORY GOES LIKE THIS: WHEN THE NAZIS FINALLY MADE CLEAR THEIR INTENT TO ROUND UP ALL DANISH JEWS, ALL THE CITIZENS OF DENMARK, STARTING WITH THE KING, DONNED THE TELLTALE YELLOW ARMBAND TO CONFUSE THE GESTAPO.

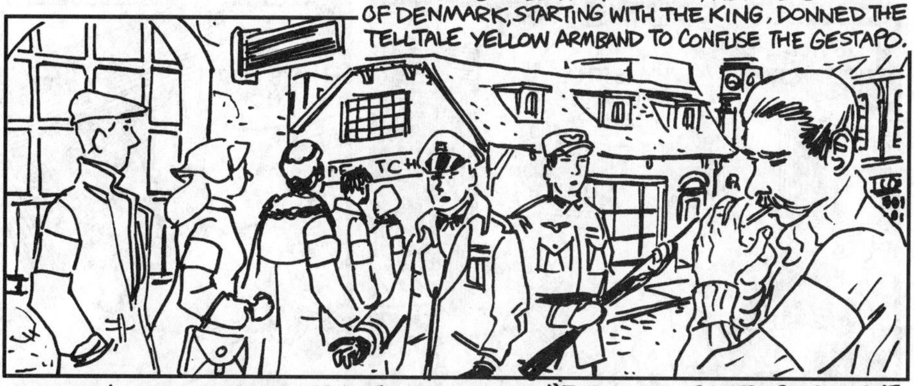

THIS ISN'T TRUE, AS BETTY SCHULTZ SAID LATER: "THE WINDOWS WERE BLACKED OUT, ALL THE WINDOWS, ALL THE PEOPLE AND THE STREETCARS AS WELL. THERE WERE TINY BLUE LAMPS, AND IT WAS NOT A GOOD THING TO GO OUT IN THE EVENING."

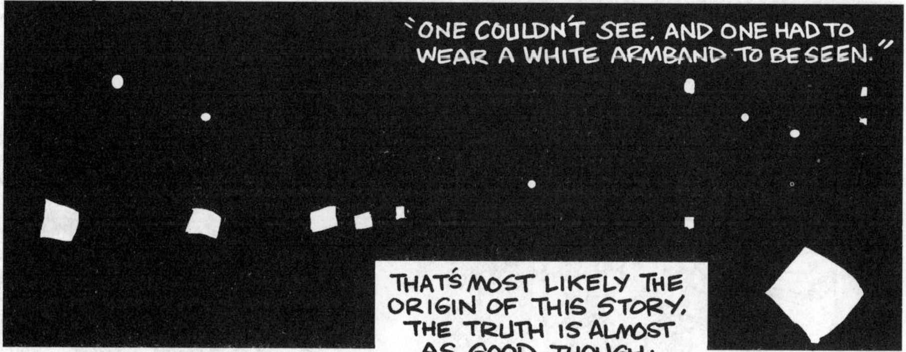
"ONE COULDN'T SEE, AND ONE HAD TO WEAR A WHITE ARMBAND TO BE SEEN."
THAT'S MOST LIKELY THE ORIGIN OF THIS STORY. THE TRUTH IS ALMOST AS GOOD, THOUGH:

GEORG FERDINAND DUCKWITZ, A HIGH GERMAN OFFICIAL, WARNED TWO DANISH POLITICAL LEADERS THAT THE JEWS WOULD BE ROUNDED UP STARTING AT 9 IN THE EVENING OF OCTOBER 1ST.

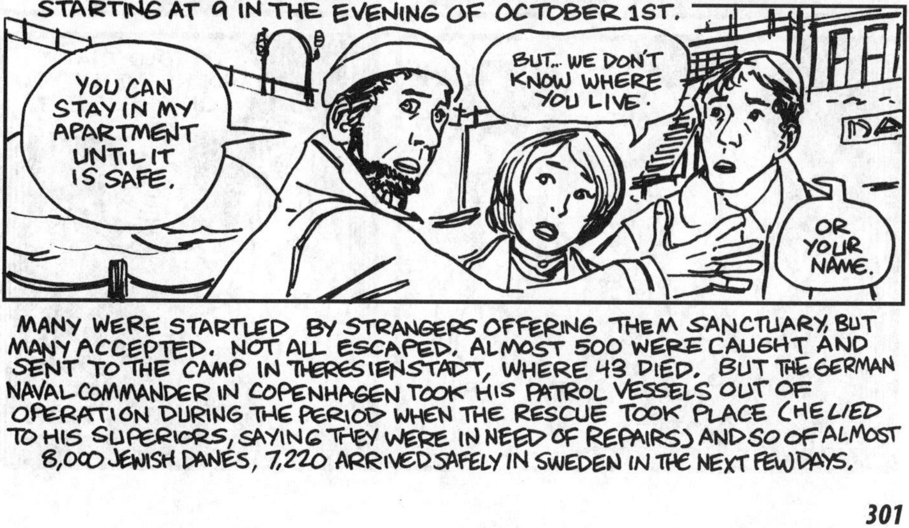
YOU CAN STAY IN MY APARTMENT UNTIL IT IS SAFE.
BUT... WE DON'T KNOW WHERE YOU LIVE.
OR YOUR NAME.

MANY WERE STARTLED BY STRANGERS OFFERING THEM SANCTUARY, BUT MANY ACCEPTED. NOT ALL ESCAPED. ALMOST 500 WERE CAUGHT AND SENT TO THE CAMP IN THERESIENSTADT, WHERE 43 DIED. BUT THE GERMAN NAVAL COMMANDER IN COPENHAGEN TOOK HIS PATROL VESSELS OUT OF OPERATION DURING THE PERIOD WHEN THE RESCUE TOOK PLACE (HE LIED TO HIS SUPERIORS, SAYING THEY WERE IN NEED OF REPAIRS) AND SO OF ALMOST 8,000 JEWISH DANES, 7,220 ARRIVED SAFELY IN SWEDEN IN THE NEXT FEW DAYS.

Horseshoes

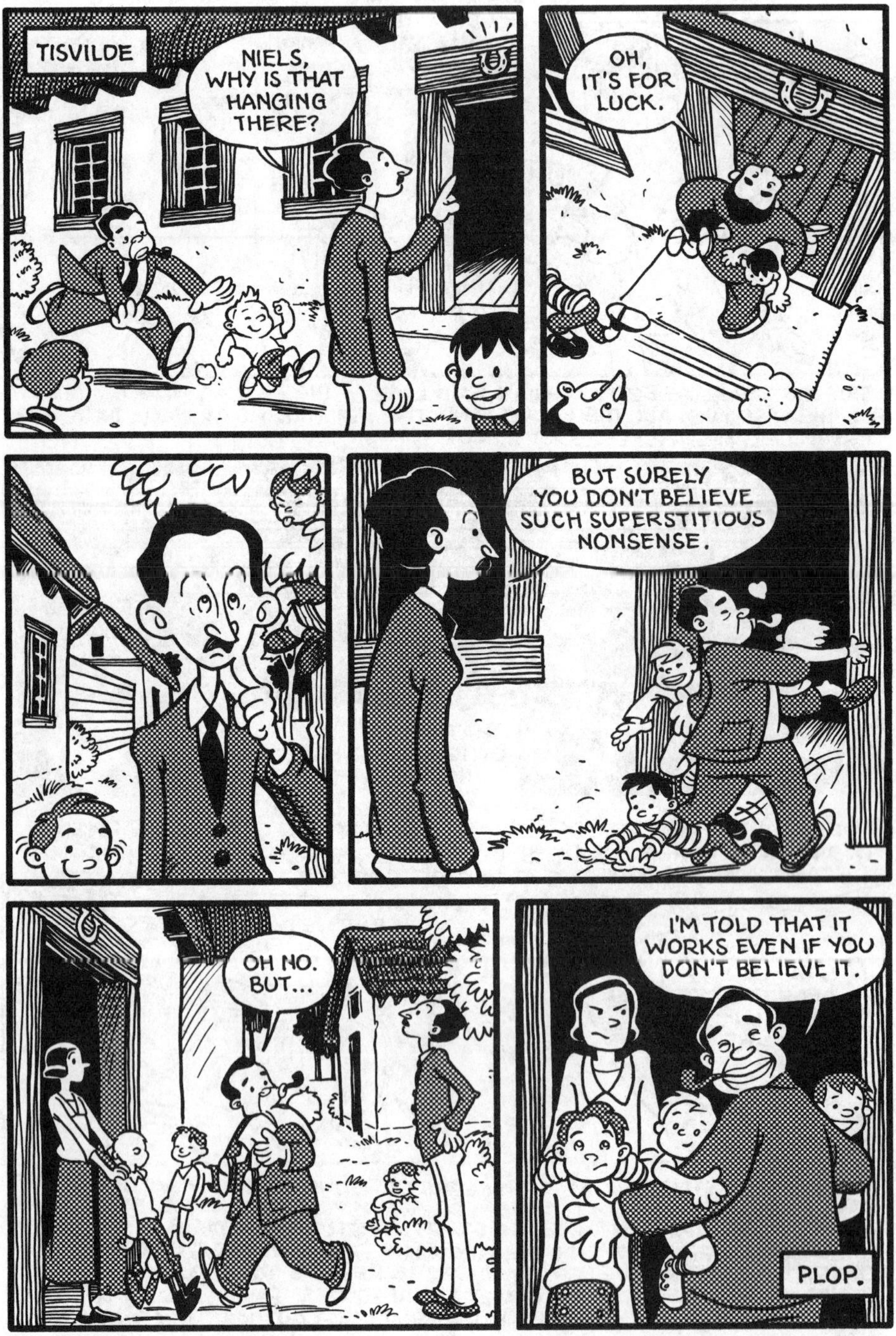
TISVILDE
NIELS, WHY IS THAT HANGING THERE?
OH, IT'S FOR LUCK.
BUT SURELY YOU DON'T BELIEVE SUCH SUPERSTITIOUS NONSENSE.
OH NO. BUT...
I'M TOLD THAT IT WORKS EVEN IF YOU DON'T BELIEVE IT.
PLOP.

Heisenberg's Memory

Under a dictatorship active resistance can only be practiced by those who pretend to collaborate with the regime. Anyone speaking out openly against the system thereby indubitably deprives himself of any chance of active resistance. For if he only utters his criticism from time to time in a politically harmless way, his political influence can easily be blocked. ...

If, on the other hand, he really tries to start a political movement, among students for instance, he will naturally finish up a few days later in a concentration camp. Even if he is put to death his martyrdom will in practice never be known, since it will be forbidden to mention his name. ...

I have always... been very much ashamed when I think of the people, some of them friends of my own, who sacrificed their lives on July 20 and thereby put up a real resistance to the regime.

But even their example shows that effective resistance can only come from those who pretend to collaborate.

Endnotes

BOHR'S LAST *RECORDED* WORDS, ON NOVEMBER 17, 1962, WERE ABOUT HIS FRIEND AND PHILOSOPHY TEACHER **HARALD HØFFDING.** THE TAPE ENDS WITH A TIRED **BOHR** SAYING TO **THOMAS KUHN:**

I THINK I MUST STOP.

BUT... I CAN TELL YOU A LITTLE BIT OF A STORY ABOUT HIM...

THE NEXT MORNING, LIKE EVERY OTHER MORNING, **BOHR** WENT BACK TO WORK.

HE ONCE AGAIN TACKLED THE AMBIGUITY OF LANGUAGE, ILLUSTRATING THE PROBLEM BY DRAWING THE TWO INTERWEAVING PLANES OF *RIEMANN GEOMETRY* WHICH LED HIM TO TALK ABOUT **THE BOX.** THOUGH HIS FRIEND HAD DIED MANY YEARS BEFORE, THE PROBLEM OF PERSUADING **EINSTEIN** REMAINED FRESH FOR HIM.

BUT AFTER LUNCH *THAT* AFTERNOON, UNLIKE EVERY OTHER AFTERNOON, **BOHR** DID NOT MAKE IT BACK TO THE BOX, BACK TO THE BLACKBOARD, BACK TO WORK.

References (etc.)

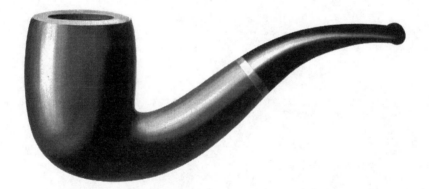

Ceci n'est pas Niels Bohr.

Primary Sources

Most of what you just read is true. But when we had to choose between a 100% accurate representation that didn't work visually or didn't serve the needs of the story well and something not as true to the facts or chronology but which packed more graphic or narrative punch, well, I wouldn't write this if we hadn't sometimes picked the latter.

Regarding the dialogue, Felicity Pors of the Niels Bohr Institute has assured me that Bohr's awkward prose style reads much better—elegantly, even—in the original Danish, although she acknowledges that his work is still tough going. So while much of what you saw (heard?) him say is as accurate as possible, even those lengthy sentences were the result of a great deal of editing.

Any fictionalizing, though, is not for lack of published references (which you'll see on the following pages) or original source material, which you can't get as easily. For the latter, special thanks to the American Institute of Physics (AIP) and the Niels Bohr Institute for making them available to researchers.

The AIP Niels Bohr Library provided the following:
Oral History Interview with Niels Bohr, 1962 October 31 to 17 November.
Oral History Interview with Margrethe Bohr, 1971 August 11.
Oral History Interview with Werner Heisenberg, 1962 November 30 to 12 July 1963 and 1970 June 16.
Oral History Interview with Betty Schultz, 1971 March 25 and 26.
Faust and Journal of Jocular Physics, volumes I-III (Reprinted on the Occasion of Niels Bohr's Centenary, October 7, 1985).

The Niels Bohr Institute in Copenhagen has made the Bohr-Heisenberg letters, in all their glorious ambiguity, available at *http://www.nbi.dk/NBA/papers/ introduction.htm* many years earlier than planned. They have also made the "Niels Bohr Collected Works" possible. These volumes (ten to date with one more anticipated at the time of this writing, all published by North-Holland) provide all Bohr's published papers, many facsimiles of original documents, and rare photographs. Finally, they published *The Niels Bohr Institute: October 7, 1965*, a pamphlet commemorating the Institute's official name change. It's the most helpful short course on the history of the Institute imaginable.

The University of New Hampshire provides excerpts from Werner Heisenberg's diaries, letters, and reminiscences from his sons at *http://werner-heisenberg.unh.edu* . Of particular interest is a letter he wrote in 1941 to his wife Elisabeth from Copenhagen. It doesn't clear anything up about the famous meeting with Bohr either. If only we could hear him "...tell you everything that happened to me" as he promised to do at the end of this note.

Books

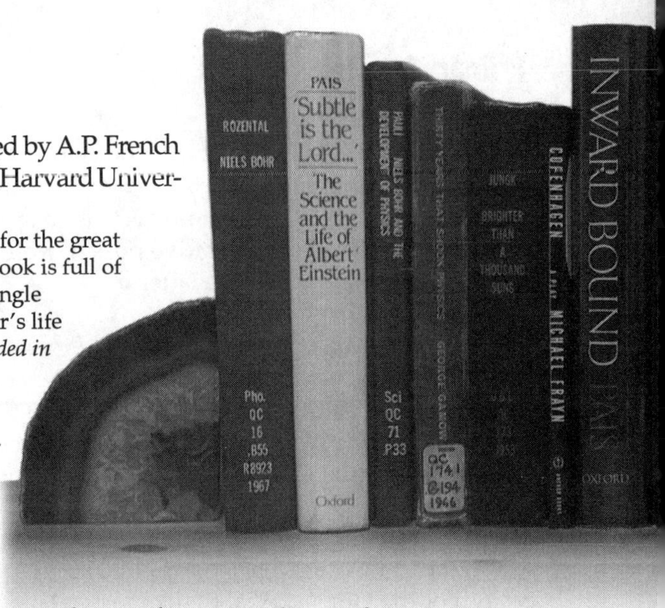
ROZENTAL
NIELS BOHR
Pho. QC 16 .B55 R8923 1967
PAIS
'Subtle is the Lord...'
The Science and the Life of Albert Einstein
Oxford
PAULI NIELS BOHR AND THE DEVELOPMENT OF PHYSICS
Sci QC 71 P33
THIRTY YEARS THAT SHOOK PHYSICS
GEORGE GAMOW
QC 174.1 G194 1966
JUNGK
BRIGHTER THAN A THOUSAND SUNS
COPENHAGEN
MICHAEL FRAYN
INWARD BOUND PAIS
OXFORD

Niels Bohr: A Centenary Volume edited by A.P. French and P.J. Kennedy (Cambridge, MA: Harvard University Press, 1985).

I admit it: years ago I bought this for the great pictures. But beyond the photos, this book is full of anecdotes, sidebars, and science. No single volume gives a better overview of Bohr's life and work, so if you've enjoyed *Suspended in Language* please seek it out.

Niels Bohr's Times in Physics, Philosophy, and Polity by Abraham Pais (Oxford: Clarendon Press, 1991).

The most comprehensive book about Bohr I know of. Pais was a first-rate physicist, and a friend and confidant of both Einstein and Bohr. His insights into their personalities and science are singular…as is the structure of his narrative. If you can get past that, between this and French & Kennedy's volume you'll get a complete and compelling picture of Niels Bohr as scientist and *mensch.*

Niels Bohr: His Life and Work as Seen by His Friends and Colleagues edited by Stefan Rozental (Amsterdam: North-Holland Publishing Co., 1967).

If you ranked the books I relied on by the number of passages I marked, this comes in at a close third to the two above. It falls somewhere in between them in terms of accessibility, but it's the most consistently personal of the three.

Niels Bohr: The Man, His Science, and the World They Changed by Ruth Moore (New York: Alfred A. Knopf, 1966).

An accessible biography of Bohr, written in a somewhat breathless style that may not satisfy serious historians but makes it worth seeking out for the rest of us.

In Search of Schrödinger's Cat: Quantum Physics and Reality by John Gribbin (New York: Bantam Books, 1984).

You can tell by the broken spine and smudged pages of my copy that this is still one of the best introductions to the unlikely ideas of quantum physics I've read. Recommended without reservation.

Thirty Years that Shook Physics: The Story of Quantum Theory by George Gamow (Garden City, NY: Doubleday & Company, 1966).

A great source of anecdotes about the superstar physicists of the early 20th century. Gamow was one of them, but lives on mostly via his cartoons and humorous writing—he was a frequent contributor to the *Journal of Jocular Physics*.

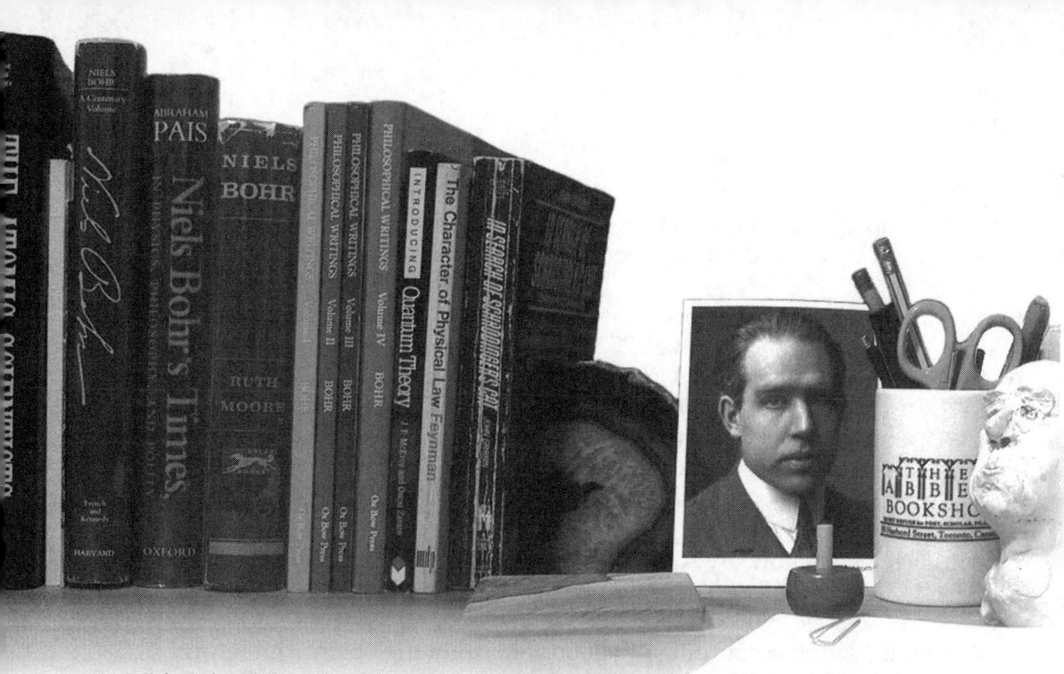
NIELS BOHR
ABRAHAM PAIS
Niels Bohr's Times
NIELS BOHR
RUTH MOORE
PHILOSOPHICAL WRITINGS Volume III BOHR
PHILOSOPHICAL WRITINGS Volume IV BOHR
INTRODUCING Quantum Theory
The Character of Physical Law Feynman
BOOKSHO

Niels Bohr Philosophical Writings, volumes I-IV by Niels Bohr (Woodbridge, CT: Ox Bow Press, 1987-1998).

The subtitles (e.g., "Essays on atomic physics and human knowledge," and "Causality and complementarity") indicate the breadth of Bohr's published work outside of physics journals. These are not page-turners, but dipping into them will give you a feel for Bohr's writing style without all that messy math stuff you'd probably want to skip over anyway.

Niels Bohr and the Development of Physics edited by Wolfgang Pauli (New York: McGraw-Hill Book Co., 1955).

An unusual *Festschrift*, in that its contributors actually made it a tribute to Bohr rather than using it as just another opportunity to add a line to their list of technical publications. For me, the most important article in it is Heisenberg's, which is simultaneously straightforward, difficult, and eloquent.

Copenhagen by Michael Frayn (New York: Anchor Books, 1998).

See this play, then read the script. It's wonderful. (There's also an excellent PBS adaptation of it for television, available on DVD.)

The nice thing about most non-fiction books is that the titles make their contents obvious. (Quick: If you only had *To Kill a Mockingbird* or *Ulysses*—by Joyce!—to go on, what would you say they're about?) So the following titles come recommended without further comment: *The Atomic Scientists* by Boorse, Motz, & Weaver; *The Character of Physical Law* by Feynman; *Introducing Quantum Theory* by McEvoy & Zarate; *Uncertainty* by Cassidy, *Mr. Tompkins in Wonderland* (OK, maybe some titles aren't obvious!) by Gamow; *Schrödinger* by Moore; any book by Abraham Pais; *Heisenberg's War* by Powers; *The Making of the Atomic Bomb* by Rhodes (yes, I recommend it every time); *Lise Meitner* by Sime, and; *The World of Physics*, edited by Weaver.

Articles

"The Philosophy of Niels Bohr" by Aage Petersen, *Bulletin of the Atomic Scientists*, vol. 19, no. 7, September 1963, 8-14.
  The first source I read the "suspended in language" quote in.

"Did Bohr Share Nuclear Secrets?" by Hans A. Bethe, Kurt Gottfried, and Roald Z. Sagdeev, *Scientific American*, vol. 272, no. 5, May 1995, 84-90; "The Scientist and the Statesmen: Niels Bohr's Political Crusade during World War II" by Finn Aaserud, *Historical Studies in the Physical and Biological Sciences*, vol. 30, no. 1, 1999, 1-47; and "What Did Heisenberg Tell Bohr about the Bomb?" by Jeremy Bernstein, *Scientific American*, vol. 272, no. 5, May 1995, 92-97.
  These are great pieces on the wartime intrigues Bohr found himself involved in.

"Quantum Teleportation" by Anton Zeilinger, *Scientific American*, vol. 282, no. 4, April 2000, 50-59 and "Trillions Entwined" by Graham P. Collins, *Scientific American*, vol. 285, no. 6, December 2001, 26.
  A more thorough accounting of teleportation, entanglement, qubits and other spookiness. The first article even has a one-page comic strip—the mark of quality in writing about science.

The following lectures/papers were presented at the "Copenhagen Symposium" held in Washington D.C. on March 2, 2002, sponsored by The Graduate Center of the City University of New York: "Notes on Comparing the Documents of Heisenberg and Bohr Concerning their Encounter in 1941" by Gerald Holton; "Frayn's 'Heisenberg': Fact or Fiction" by Jochen H. Heisenberg; "The Drawing or Why History is Not Mathematics" by Jeremy Bernstein; "'A Great and Deep Difficulty': Niels Bohr and the Atomic Bomb" by Richard Rhodes; "The Bohr-Heisenberg Meeting from a Distance" by Finn Aaserud; "On the Copenhagen Interpretation of Quantum Mechanics" by John Marburger.
  All are available at *http://web.gc.cuny.edu/ashp/nml/artsci/symposium.html* and provide accounts of Bohr and Heisenberg's meeting, their troubled relationship with each other, and the history they made. Jochen Heisenberg's memories of his father are particularly affecting.

Sites

Visit the terrific "Visual Quantum Mechanics" at *http://phys.educ.ksu.edu/* to see electron waves in action!

For something in a more classical mode, you can see a tippe-top simulation at *http://www.physik.uni-augsburg.de/~wobsta/tippetop/* , but you really should try and get ahold of one yourself. And you can (while supplies last) by visiting *http://www.gt-labs.com/* , where you'll also find an even more complete list of references.

The Writer and Artists

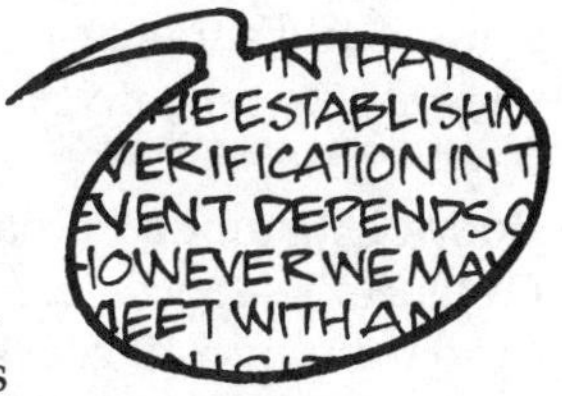

JIM OTTAVIANI [The Story, Endnotes, and References (etc.)] first learned about Niels Bohr when studying to become a nuclear engineer. He doesn't do engineering anymore; he now works as a university librarian. Other books he stayed up far past his bedtime to write include *Two-Fisted Science: Stories about scientists; Dignifying Science: Stories about women scientists;* and *Fallout: J. Robert Oppenheimer, Leo Szilard, and the political science of the atomic bomb.* He's currently at work on a (mostly) true tale of dinosaurs, cowboys, and scientists (the scientists are the "bad guys"). As for this book, first and foremost thanks to the artists who brought the script to life—Lee above all. Special thanks also go to Felicity Pors and Finn Aaseruud of the Niels Bohr Institute, Katy Hayes of the AIP Niels Bohr Archive, Dave Moran and Kris Olsson for checking my physics, Susan Skarsgard and Wesley Tanner for their typographic and design help, Linda Medley for checking my storytelling, Anders Bárány for his support and encouragement from the start, and to Kat for all of the above.

LELAND PURVIS [The Story, "The Honeymoon That Revolutionized Physics," and "Endnotes"] earned a B.A. in History from Portland State University in 1991. Self-taught as a visual artist and storyteller, he began self-publishing his comics short story anthology *Vóx* in 2000 and was awarded a Xeric Grant that same year. Comics of his character *Pubo* were recently re-published as a trade paperback collection by Dark Horse Comics. Thanks should go firstly to Jim for the opportunity to be a part of this project and his patience as it came to fruition, to Steve Lieber for his valuable input and support, to Mercury Studios in Portland for the occasional open drawing table, and thanks always to Rae for helping to keep heart and mind in a state that made it possible.

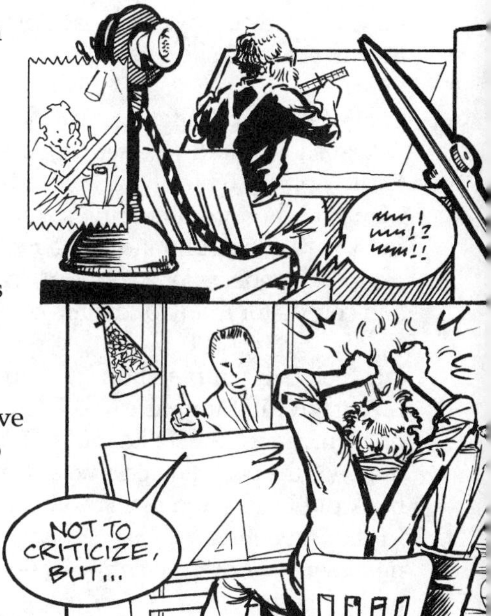
NOT TO CRITICIZE, BUT...

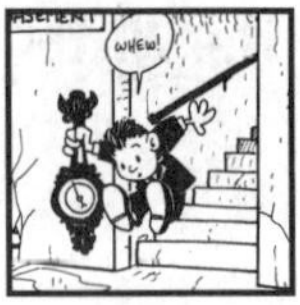
WHEW!

Jay Hosler ["Apocrypha" and "The Clockwork (Classical) Universe"] is an Assistant Professor of Biology at Juniata College, where he teaches Neurobiology and Invertebrate Biology. His first graphic novel, *Clan Apis,* is the biography of a honey bee and has been awarded a Xeric Grant, nominated for 5 Eisner and 3 Ignatz Awards and named to the Young Adult Library Services Association 25 Best Graphic Novels for 2002. In his second book, *The Sandwalk Adventures,* Charles Darwin and a follicle mite living in his left eyebrow talk about evolution, natural selection, myth-making and storytelling.

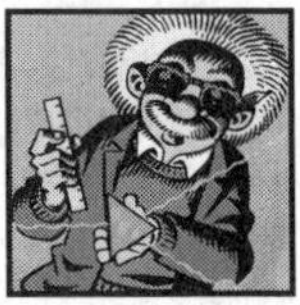

Roger Langridge ["Quantum Entanglement, Spooky Action at a Distance, Teleportation, and You"] has been a professional cartoonist since 1988. He has done work for most major comics publishers in the English-speaking world, including Marvel, DC, Dark Horse, Fleetway / 2000AD, Heavy Metal, Deadline, and Fantagraphics. His illustration credits include work for Penguin, Heinemann and Hodder, and a national advertising campaign by the Swiss Post Office. Most recently he has self-published *Fred the Clown,* which has been nominated for two Eisner and an Ignatz Award. The web version of *Fred the Clown* won a UK National Comic Award in 2003 for Best Online Strip.

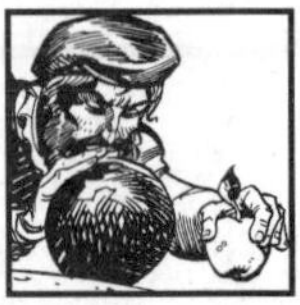

Steve Leialoha ["Atoms and Void, Poetry and Madness"] has been a comics artist since the early seventies and has worked for all the major comics companies and many of the minor ones as well on such comics as X-Men, Spider-man, Star Wars, Superman, Batman, Howard the Duck, and Dr. Strange. While currently best known for his ink-work, most prominently on the award-winning *Fables,* he's also an accomplished penciller and graphic designer.

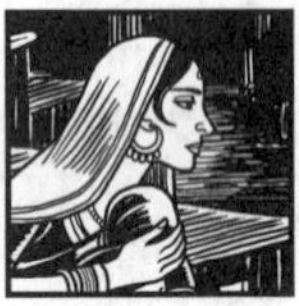

Linda Medley ["Imitating Art," "Oh, That Dirac!," "Kisa Gotami," "Horseshoes," and "Heisenberg's Memory"] is the author of *Castle Waiting,* which has garnered critical acclaim and won numerous honors, including several Eisner Awards and a grant from the Xeric Foundation. She received her BFA in Illustration from the Academy of Art in San Francisco, and has illustrated children's books and comics for many of the major publishers in those fields.

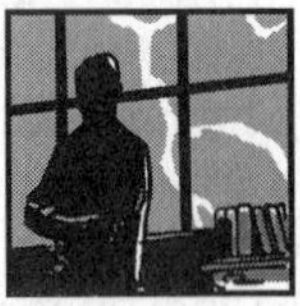

Jeff Parker ["Simple Math," "Slater," and "Armbands"] holds a B.A. degree in Literature and Communications from East Carolina University, where he taught English before entering illustration. For the past ten years he's worked for all the major comic book publishers and as a storyboard artist for Sony Animation. In 2003 he published *The Interman,* a critically acclaimed adventure graphic novel with a strong scientific undercurrent. It is currently in production for film at Paramount.

Timeline

~400 B.C.E	Democritus proposes the philosophical concept of permanent and indivisible atoms — "beings" that stand side by side with the void. Epicurus expanded on this, and the poet Lucretius (~98 B.C.E. - 55 B.C.E) preserved it in his unfinished poem *De Rerum Natura*.
1690	Christian Huyghens suggests light is composed of waves propagating through "ether."
1704	Isaac Newton suggests that light consists of very (very) small particles.
1853	Jonas Ångstrom makes the first observation of the hydrogen spectrum.
1869	Mendeléev introduces his first version of the periodic table.
1871	Ernest Rutherford is born (August 30).
1879	Albert Einstein is born (March 14).
1881	J.J. Thomson introduces the idea that an electrical charge has mass. Christian Bohr and Ellen Adler marry (December 14).
1883	Jenny Bohr is born (March 9).
1885	Balmer introduces his formula for the hydrogen spectrum. Niels Henrik David Bohr is born (October 7).
1887	Harald August Bohr is born (October 7).
1890	Margrethe Nørlund is born (March 7).
1897	J.J. Thomson discovers the electron.
1900	Wolfgang Pauli is born (April 25). Planck's discovery of the law of blackbody radiation kicks off the quantum revolution.
1901	Werner Heisenberg is born (December 5).
1903	Niels graduates from the Gammelholm school and enters Copenhagen University.
1905	A big year for Einstein: He postulates the light quantum (March), writes his first paper on special relativity (June), and his second featuring $E=mc^2$ (September).
1906	Rutherford discovers alpha particle scattering.
1907	Niels wins a gold medal for an essay on the surface tension of liquids. Christian Bohr is proposed for a Nobel Prize in physiology or medicine. (He gets nominated again in 1908.)
1909	Niels meets Margrethe. Niels gets his masters degree (December 2).
1910	Niels and Margrethe get engaged. Harald receives his Ph.D. in mathematics.
1911	Christian Bohr dies (February 3). Rutherford proposes a nuclear model of the atom (March 7). Niels receives a Ph.D. for his thesis on electron theory of metals (May 13), leaves for England to do post-doctoral research with J.J. Thomson (September), and then transfers over to Rutherford's lab in Manchester (December 8).

1912	While on a return visit to Manchester (March), Niels applies for a vacant professorship in physics in Copenhagen. He doesn't get the job (March-April). Niels and Margrethe get married in Slagelse (August 1). Niels becomes a Privatdocent, with his office in the Polytekniske Læreanstalt (September).
1913	Niels completes his paper on the quantum theory of hydrogen (April, published in July), proves beta decay is a nuclear process (August), and presents the first inklings of his correspondence principle (December).
1914	Niels petitions the Danish Government to create a professorship of theoretical physics for him (March 13). The Franck-Hertz experiment confirms Niels' idea of quantum jumps (April). Niels returns from a second visit to Manchester to take his job as an associate professor (October).
1916	Epstein & Schwarzschild propose a theory for the Stark effect, another success for Niels' theory (March). Kramers comes to Copenhagen (Fall). Christian is born (November 25).
1917	Niels petitions the physics faculty to establish an institute for theoretical physics (April 18).
1918	Niels creates a more detailed correspondence principle (April). Hans is born (April 7).
1919	Betty Schultz become Niels' secretary (January 2). Rutherford observes artificial transmutation of elements.
1920	Niels meets Planck and Einstein on a visit to Berlin (April). Erik is born (June 23). Einstein and Rutherford visit Copenhagen (August - September).
1921	The Institute for Theoretical Physics in Copenhagen opens (March 3).
1922	Niels lectures in Göttingen and meets Heisenberg and Pauli (June). Aage is born (June 19). Niels receives the Nobel Prize "for his investigations of the structure of atoms and of the radiation emanating from them." Pauli visits the Institute beginning in the fall, and stays through to the fall of 1923.
1923	Einstein visits Copenhagen (July). Niels visits the U.S. and makes contact with Rockefeller philanthropic institutes. Louis de Broglie (the Prince) describes wave-particle duality for matter (September).
1924	Bohr, Kramers, and Slater propose the radical notion that atomic processes only conserve energy statistically (February). The Bohr-Kramers-Slater theory is refuted experimentally (April-May). Ernest is born (March 7). Heisenberg visits Copenhagen (Easter), and starts working at the Institute (September - April 1925). Niels is permanently relieved of his teaching obligations, and the student body's sigh of relief is heard throughout Denmark. The Bohrs buy *Lynghuset* in Tisvilde.
1925	Pauli announces his exclusion principle (January). Heisenberg's first paper on quantum mechanics appears (July 25).

1926   Schrödinger's first paper on wave mechanics appears (January 26).
Heisenberg stays in Copenhagen a second time (May - June 1927).
Dirac writes his first paper on Q.E.D. in Copenhagen and sets everyone
straight (December).

1927   Davisson and Germer are the first to detect electron diffraction (March 3).
Heisenberg's paper on the uncertainty relation, written in Copenhagen,
appears (March 23).
Niels talks about complementarity in Como, Italy (September 16).
Einstein raises his first public objections to quantum mechanics at the
5th Solvay Conference (October 24-29).

1928   Harald is born (March 12).

1929   Bohr's Institute hosts its first international physics conference (April).

1930   Einstein's "clock-in-the-box" and Bohr's refutation of it are the highlight
of the 6th Solvay Conference (June 20).
Ellen Bohr dies (November 30).

1931   George Gamow finishes his first textbook on theoretical nuclear physics
and draws lots of cartoons while in Copenhagen (May).

1932   James Chadwick discovers the neutron (February).
Niels lectures on "Light and Life" (August).
The Bohr family moves into the Æresbolig (Residence of Honor).

1933   Beamtengesetz authorizes German universities to fire staff on grounds of
race or politics (April 7)—Niels and Harald become board members of
the Danish committee for support of refugee intellectuals.
Jenny dies (May 5).

1934   Induced radioactivity discovered (January).
The Mathematics Institute, under Harald, opens next door to Niels'
Institute (February 8).
Christian drowns in a sailing accident (July 2).
Franck and Hevesy, refugee scientists, join Bohr's Institute (April and
October).

1935   Einstein, Podalsky, and Rosen (E-P-R) write their paper and state their
paradox. Niels replies.

1936   Niels creates his theory of the compound nucleus.

1937   Niels takes a trip around the world, lecturing in the U.S., Japan, China,
and the Soviet Union.
Rutherford dies (October 19).
Niels lectures at Elsinore.

1938   The Institute formally inaugurates its accelerator section (April 5).
Niels writes on complementarity and human culture.

1939   Hahn and Strassman publish their discovery that barium shows up when
neutrons irradiate uranium (January 6) and Meitner and Frisch interpret the
results as fission (January 16).
Niels (and Fermi) report on fission while lecturing in the U.S. (January 26).
Niels proposes that fission or U-235 occurs because of slow neutrons,
and the Bohr-Wheeler theory of fission soon follows (February 7).
World War II begins (September 1).

1940   Niels donates his Nobel medal to Finnish relief (January).
Frisch and Peierls report on feasibility of atomic weapons (February-March).
Germany occupies Denmark (April 9).

1941	Heisenberg visits Denmark (October). Franklin D. Roosevelt OKs the Manhattan Project (October 9).
1943	James Chadwick invites Niels to England—he declines (February). Niels and Margrethe escape to Stockholm (September 29). Niels arrives in London and Aage soon follows (October 6). Kapitza invites Niels to Moscow (October 28). Niels and Aage leave for the U.S. (November 28). Niels meets with General Leslie Groves, Einstein, and Ambassadors Kaufmann and Halifax to express his concern about creating an open world (December).
1944	Niels meets with Justice Frankfurter in February, Churchill in London on May 16, and FDR in Washington, D.C. on August 26. Churchill and FDR reject Bohr's proposals (September 18).
1945	The Germans flee Denmark (May 4). VE day (May 8). Trinity (July 16). Hiroshima (August 6). Nagasaki (August 9). "Science and Civilization"—Niels' first public plea for an open world—appears in the *London Times* (August 11). VJ day (August 14). The Bohrs return to Denmark (August 25). The Soviets seek out Niels in Copenhagen (November).
1947	Niels receives the Order of the Elephant (October 7).
1950	Niels presents his open letter to the United Nations (June 9).
1951	Niels' brother Harald dies (January 22).
1952	Niels becomes the first director of CERN's Theoretical Division (Fall).
1955	Niels retires from his professorship (April 1). Einstein dies (April 18).
1956	Niels sends his second letter to the U.N. (November 9).
1957	Niels receives the first Atoms for Peace award (October 1).
1958	Niels opens the Risø research center (June 6). Pauli dies (December 15).
1962	Niels dies (November 18).
1965	The Institute for Theoretical Physics in Copenhagen is renamed the Niels Bohr Institute.
1975	Aage wins the Nobel Prize for the collective structure model of the atomic nucleus.
1976	Heisenberg dies (February 1).
1984	Margrethe dies (December 21).

Index